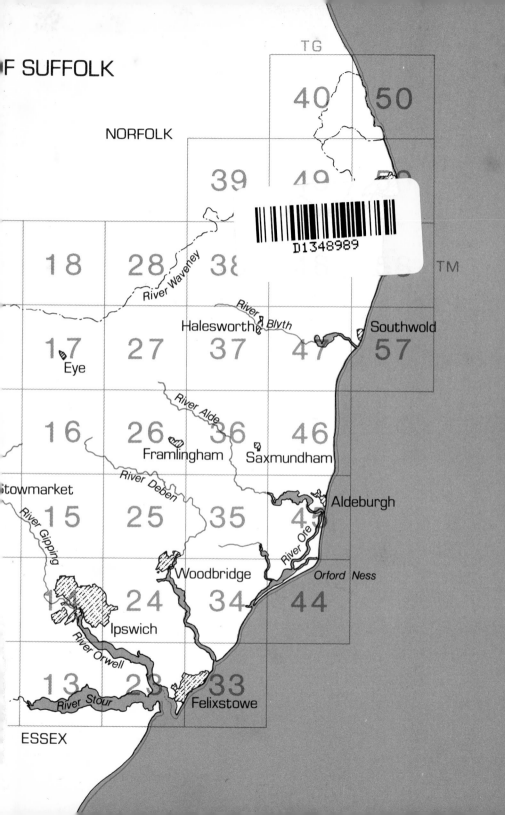

SIMPSON'S FLORA OF SUFFOLK

SIMPSON'S
FLORA OF SUFFOLK

Francis W. Simpson

PUBLISHED BY

SUFFOLK NATURALISTS' SOCIETY

1982

First published 1982

© Francis W. Simpson 1982

ISBN 0 9508154 0 3

Typesetting in Compugraphic Times by Monarch Origination, Ipswich
Printed at the Ancient House Press, Ipswich, Suffolk

Contents

CONTENTS

Illustrations

All photography in this publication is by Francis W. Simpson

Foreword

NEARLY a century has passed since the Rev. W. M. Hind's *Flora of Suffolk* appeared in print, embodying plant records based on early collections in herbaria and the communications of local and visiting botanists up to that time. Since then, botanical research in Britain has gathered impetus in many fields, not least in ecology, with its emphasis on defining the conditions which are essential for the well-being and survival of plants in our varied and ever changing countryside, while innumerable helpers have been engaged in mapping the distribution of this country's flora in recent years. Up-dated assessments of the botanical situation, county by county, continue to be presented by those who have been diligent in amassing and analysing data over a length of time and each local Flora tends to reflect the author's personal approach to his task, each in his own way striving to follow the fortunes of a wealth of species, occupying a variety of crannies, whose fate is governed by environmental factors which can change dramatically over the years. Francis Simpson has amassed a wealth of personal knowledge of Suffolk plants during the past fifty years. In his leisure time he has scanned the hedgerows, dunes, meadows, saltings, fens, heaths and woods in great detail on countless expeditions at all seasons. At the same time, he has enjoyed the special advantage of shouldering responsibility for the herbaria and current plant recording at the Ipswich Museum, besides serving the Suffolk Naturalists' Society as its Botanical Recorder. His dedication to what has been almost a lifelong task has come to fruition in this book. The early chapters will be found extremely valuable for the parts they play in setting the scene and recounting the history of change. Overall there is considerable emphasis on the loss of important habitats which has been witnessed increasingly over the years, emphasising the need for increasing effort in the field of conservation. I hope and believe that the fast-growing community of nature-lovers in Suffolk will rejoice in the publication of this *Flora* and make the utmost use of it in pursuing every possible means of ensuring that the rich and wonderful plant life of this county shall continue to delight and interest generations to come.

November 1981   Dr E. A. Ellis

Acknowledgements

DURING the many years in which this Flora has been in preparation, numerous organizations and individuals have rendered assistance in various ways, supplying records, checking identifications and contributing to the substantial cost of printing and publication. A list of those who have contributed records is appended to the catalogue of species. The author hopes that no name has inadvertently been omitted from this list or from the catalogue.

We, the author and the Suffolk Naturalists' Society, as sponsoring publishers, take this opportunity to acknowledge the generous financial support which has made the publication of the Flora possible.

Subscriptions towards publication had accumulated slowly over some years. In 1981 a generous donation of £1,000 from the Moncrieff Charity in Lowestoft encouraged our Society to make an effort to publish the Flora. With the co-operation of the Ipswich & District Natural History Society and the assistance of the Suffolk Trust for Nature Conservation, an appeal was launched for donations, loans and pre-publication sales at a reduced price. At the same time appeals were made to a wide range of local firms, organizations and individuals for donations or interest-free loans. The results were gratifying.

We record with thanks the very generous donations from
> R. C. Notcutt Ltd of Woodbridge
> Pauls & Whites Ltd of Ipswich
> The Guardian Royal Exchange Assurance
> A. Charles Phillips Ltd of Felixstowe
> Messrs Willis, Faber & Dumas of Ipswich.

We are indebted to
> Greene, King & Sons Ltd of Bury St Edmunds for an interest-free loan of £1,000.

Appended is a list of the firms, organizations and individuals contributing to the Suffolk Flora Fund.

In addition the author would like to thank the following: The Ipswich Borough Department of Recreation and Amenities, for the facilities afforded, enabling work on the Flora to be centred at the Museum from 1968-78. This was arranged by the late Earl of Cranbrook and Miss P. M. Butler, Curator of the Museum.

ACKNOWLEDGEMENTS

The Ipswich & District Natural History Society for their financial and other assistance.

Mr Colin Ranson for his chapter on the Geology of the County.

Mr Mark Hyde for records, especially of aliens, and also for reading the proofs.

Dr F. H. Perring for much advice and the supply of records from the Monks Wood Biological Centre.

Mrs G. Crompton for records of uncommon Breckland species.

Mr Norman Kerr for arranging substantial donations and loans and Mr H. E. Chipperfield for collection and banking of funds.

Mrs V. A. Heming for typing the original manuscript and other office work.

Mrs N. Hunt for typing later revisions to the Flora.

Misses B. and R. Copinger Hill for their continuous support.

The printers for their co-operation, especially Mr M. Castle.

Finally, the author would like to thank Mr Neville Hunt for his dedication, energy and perseverance — without his efforts the Flora would not have been published, and Mrs Enid Hyde for helping with a thorough revision of the manuscript, checking the proofs and also making available her records.

April 1982

Francis Simpson
and
the Suffolk Naturalists' Society

Suffolk Flora Fund

Donations and Loans

Mr B. Andrews
Ashbocking, Swilland & Witnesham WI
Mrs N. Barker
Mr F. V. Basham
Mr M. E. O. Benjamin
Miss E. H. B. Bernard
Mr A. G. Bishop
Mrs M. V. Boon
Mr and Mrs Bowden-Smith
Bury St Edmunds Naturalists' Society
Mrs V. N. Butcher
Mr T. R. Caddell
Mr J. H. Campion
Mr K. M. Carlisle
Mr E. S. Cheney
Miss E. P. Cockburn
Copdock and Washbrook Garden Club
Dr R. E. C. Copithorne
Miss E. Coppard
Mrs J. L. Craig
Mr M. F. Crick
Mr P. C. Crick
Miss D. Crow
Mrs B. A. Curtis
Mr and Mrs C. Curtis
Mr G. E. Curtis
Miss M. E. Day
Miss E. M. Debenham
Delta Materials Research Limited
Mrs G. E. Dickinson
Mr J. W. Dickson
Mr J. Dorling
Mrs P. Earwaker
Mr and Mrs B. Edwards

Miss R. K. Fincham
Miss C. Forrest
Mr J. A. Foster
Wing Commander F. J. French
Mr and Mrs Garrod
Miss Fay Gibson
Mr C. Gilbert
Mrs P. Gondris
Dr R. U. H. Goulder
Mrs Barbara Grant
Mr M. J. Graves
Mrs M. Gray
Greene, King & Sons Limited
Mr Harry Grimes
Guardian Royal Exchange Assurance
Hadleigh Naturalists' Society
Mr S. Harding
Mrs J. Harris
Miss J. Hartwell
Misses B. and R. Copinger Hill
Mr and Mrs Alan Hubbard
Mr Neville Hunt
Miss P. M. R. Hunt
Dr J. G. Hunter
Mr J. R. Hunter
Mrs E. M. Hyde
Mr M. A. Hyde
Ipswich Borough, Department of Recrea-
    tion & Amenities
Ipswich & District Natural History
    Society
Ipswich Numismatics Society
Miss D. E. Jay
Miss J. A. Kerry

Mrs M. E. Lawson
Dr J. W. Litchfield
Mrs A. M. Little
Lloyds Bank Limited
Mrs Lovick
Miss M. L. Lynn-Allen
Miss P. A. Lyon
Mrs F. M. Manning
Miss R. B. Manning
Mrs V. Mardell
Mr H. F. Meade
Midland Bank Limited
Mr D. H. Miller
Mr and Mrs P. Mills
Moncrieff Charitable Trust
Mr and Mrs Stanley Moore
Dr and Mrs J. Morgan
R. C. Notcutt Limited
Mr and Mrs H. Page
Mrs J. O. Paternoster
Pauls and Whites Limited
A. Charles Phillips Limited
Miss H. Pilgrim
Mr G. W. Pipe
Miss M. B. Powell
Mr B. R. Reynolds

Miss L. Riches
Mr Ian C. Rose
Mr John Russell
Dr D. W. Ryder-Richardson
Mrs R. Shuttleworth
Mr Francis W. Simpson
Mr A. C. Smith
Mrs Mary Stephenson
Mrs J. E. Stevenson
Mrs P. Stewart
Mr and Mrs R. Stewart
Stowmarket Naturalists' Society
Suffolk College, Natural History Society
Mrs M. Sykes
Mr B. O. Tickner
Mr P. J. Toshach
Miss J. N. Tusting
Mrs I. M. Vaughan
Mrs M. Ward
Mr and Mrs R. Warren
Miss A. Wattson
Mr and Mrs E. Westren
Willis, Faber and Dumas Limited
Mrs A. Wolfe
Six anonymous donations

The author has personally financed forty-eight pages of the colour plates and a number of other costs necessary for the production of this Flora.

CHAPTER ONE

Topography

SUFFOLK has frequently been described as one of the flat or low counties of England, with no apparent hills, and its landscape compared with that of Holland. This is true only for limited areas of North-east Suffolk bordering the R. Waveney from Beccles to Breydon Water, known as Lothingland, and also the area of fenland in the extreme North-west of the County about Mildenhall, West Row and Lakenheath, into Cambridgeshire.

Otherwise most of the County is pleasantly undulating, with many small valleys and rivers flowing into long estuaries, bordered by salt marshes and low cliffs. The highest parts of the County are in West and South-west Suffolk. Here, the 'East Anglian Ridge' has a maximum height of 420 ft, near Four Elms Farm, Depden. Much of West Suffolk, covered by the Boulder Clay drift, is between 200 ft and 300 ft, and only small areas between 300 ft and 400 ft. The land usually rises gently from the coast and there are few steep hills. From the estuary of the R. Orwell at Ipswich, the ground rises westward for a distance of about 12 miles to just over 300 ft at Nedging Tye, near Bildeston.

Attractive small hummocky hills, mainly composed of glacial sand and gravel, can be seen, especially in the valleys of the R. Stour and of its tributary the Box, near Stoke-by-Nayland, Polstead and Shelley, and also east of the main railway line between Bentley and Brantham in East Suffolk. There are some attractive heathery hills of Westleton Pebble Beds near Westleton village in East Suffolk, known as the 'Mumble Hills'. These have been much spoilt in recent years by gravel excavation. Close by are the Westleton Walks, which are just north of the Minsmere Bird Reserve, and form part of Dunwich Cliffs.

The Creeting Hills, near Needham Market, used to be a favourite beauty-spot, but they have now been spoilt by excavations and a by-pass.

At Ipswich the area of Stoke Hills, behind the main railway station was much frequented in early Victorian times before the railway came to Ipswich, and the tunnel and present station were constructed.

There is a large area of East Suffolk situated north of a line between Woodbridge and Stowmarket, almost to the R. Waveney, known as 'High Suffolk'. Many people wrongly consider this area to contain the highest land in the County. Most of it, however, is quite low compared with West Suffolk, and has a height of between only 150 ft and 180 ft.

Although Suffolk is described as one of the rural counties of England, and to newcomers it appears comparatively unspoilt, those who have lived in the County for many years know that there are few, if any, areas which have not been changed or spoilt in some way, especially in the years since the Second World War. These changes have, of course, had a very marked effect on the old flora.

When the Reverend Hind compiled his 'Flora of Suffolk' in 1889, the County was still exceedingly rural, and in remote parts undeveloped, with almost medieval practices carried out in agriculture, forestry and drainage. The network of railways had practically been completed and this, of course, brought changes, but the Rivers Stour, Gipping, Alde, Blyth and Waveney were still being used by the barges of the pre-railway era, and this continued in some areas even into the first quarter of the 20th century. The roads were mainly rough, narrow and winding, flanked by trees, tall hedges and flowering verges. The motor vehicle had only just arrived, and horse-drawn vehicles were everywhere. Flocks of sheep were numerous and there were cattle on every farm. Fields were small and towns, villages and hamlets more confined and not sprawling into the countryside as seen today. Thatched and tiled cottages were numerous and there was a working windmill in almost every parish. Estates were larger then, some with woods, plantations and coverts, which were more extensive than today.

In the eastern coastal belt, known as the 'Sandlings', was open heathland or sheepwalks, and in the west were the sandy wastes of Breckland with their scattered belts of trees and plantations, a scene which began to disappear in the 1920's, when the Forestry Commission commenced its operations. Breckland was exceedingly wild, as I well remember as a boy, with great flocks of Stone Curlew and other birds, and thousands of rabbits.

There were long stretches of clean beaches and cliffs, which were almost deserted for most of the year, without the swarms of visitors which we get today. Natural fens, marshes, bogs and other wetlands existed at that time in many areas. These have now been largely drained, although most of the fens around Mildenhall and Lakenheath had been re-claimed and cultivated in much earlier times.

2

Major Habitats of Suffolk

The Estuaries and Saltings

EXTENSIVE salt marshes with muddy creeks are a feature of the estuaries of Suffolk rivers. In summer they are bright with flowering plants including, Scurvy Grass, Sea Pinks, Common Sea Lavender and Sea Aster. There are several forms of Glasswort and Annual Seablite, which turn areas bright red in autumn. A feature of these muddy estuaries is the rapid growth of Cord Grass (*Spartina*). On the banks of the Stour estuary at Shotley and Erwarton, and on both shores of the R. Orwell, the saltings are being much eroded by the wash created by large boats now using the rivers.

The best areas for study are to be found bordering the north banks of the R. Deben between Ramsholt and Bawdsey, north of Shingle Street by the Ore, and by the Alde adjoining Snape Warren, where Marsh Mallow is still abundant. The south side of the Blyth estuary from Blythburgh to Walberswick is also good.

The verges of the saltings have their special flora, including Sea Milkwort, Slender Trefoil, Sea Arrow-grass, Sea Plantain, Club Rushes, Mud Rush and various sedges and grasses.

The Beaches

Before the very rapid increase of motor traffic and other developments since the end of the Second World War, much of the Suffolk coast and its estuaries had remained quiet and unspoilt. The natural flora flourished without interference from trampling and the general wear and tear which so often results in erosion and the destruction of natural vegetation.

The Suffolk beaches are mainly of sand and shingle, which are derived from the erosion of cliffs, which are sometimes situated several miles from the pebble beaches, the material having been carried by the North Sea Drift.

The cliffs at Bawdsey, Dunwich, Easton Bavents and Covehithe have been the source of much of the material.

Several of the rivers are associated with brackish meres or broads, which are really small estuaries enclosed by shingle and sand bars, as, for example, at Easton Broad, Covehithe and Benacre, north of Southwold.

Landguard Common, just south of Felixstowe Town (more correctly Langer Common, 'langer' = German and Dutch for 'long') is an extensive area of sand

and shingle at the mouth of the R. Orwell; it was mainly formed in medieval or earlier times and is really the silted-up bed of the river. Old maps show a river channel just north of the Common. This Common was well-known to early Suffolk botanists. It was formerly very open and a first-class habitat, with many rarities. In recent years, since approximately 1967, more and more of the Common has become enclosed and is now part of the Felixstowe Docks complex. In the future, only a very small area is likely to remain undeveloped.

At Felixstowe Ferry, north of the town, the golf links were formerly sand dunes at the mouth of the R. Deben. During the Second World War, when the links were not used for golf, they rapidly reverted to their original appearance and several species reappeared, perhaps derived from buried seeds, which had remained dormant for many years. To the east of the links is another area of shingle with a little sand, similar to, but smaller than, Landguard.

From Bawdsey Haven to East Lane there are cliffs of Pleistocene glacial sands and shelly Red Crag with an interesting basement bed of coprolites and other fossil material derived from earlier strata. These sandy beds rest on the Eocene London Clay; at low tide the sea bed is seen to be mainly of London Clay and there are often quantities of pyritised wood and occasionally fish teeth.

Before the Second World War, just south of Bawdsey Manor House, there was an area of sand and shingle with a flora very similar to that of Landguard Common. At that time the cliffs were being rapidly eroded, and nearly every high tide would reach them. Breakwaters and other defences to protect the cliffs have been constructed and a beach composed mainly of shingle has now built up. This shingle has been derived from erosion of the beaches between Aldeburgh and Shingle Street.

From Bawdsey East Lane to Shingle Street there is an extensive pebble beach with some brackish pools and relics of a once extensive salt marsh. Some of the area of the old sea beaches has been enclosed in recent years and used for grazing; quantities of the ancient shingle were removed, especially a little to the north of Shingle Street, during the War. This was used in the construction of the runways of local airfields. The area between the beach and the rising ground was, until quite recently, mainly grazing pasture, intersected by brackish dykes. It is now nearly all arable land and many of the dykes have been filled in. It is very probable that years ago the area was a salt marsh. On the original beach, the Sea Pea is abundant, also Yellow Horned Poppy and sometimes Yellow Vetch.

The cliffs in front of the Manor House are now much covered with naturalised garden plants, shrubs and other vegetation, especially Silver Ragwort and Tamarisk, which have spread in recent years.

At Shingle Street, although there is often an enormous invasion of visitors with their cars, an interesting flora still survives, including several of the rare Trefoils. The shingle beach is now dangerously narrow in front of the houses. It was formerly broad, showing several lines of old beaches enclosing lagoons, with a margin of salt marsh flora.

From the mouth of the R. Ore northwards to Orford Ness and Aldeburgh there is a most important shingle beach. This beach was formed by the diversion of the River Alde, which, in Roman times, it is said, entered the North Sea just south of Aldeburgh at Slaughden. The pebbles of this beach have been mainly derived from the erosion of the Westleton Pebble Beds of Dunwich Cliffs some seven miles north of Aldeburgh and perhaps partly from the cliffs of Easton Bavents. These cliffs were formerly the most easterly point in Britain.

Orford Ness Beach, south of the lighthouse, consists of a series of old shingle ridges. North of the lighthouse only one ridge remains and this has now become very narrow indeed and at Slaughden there is a danger of the sea breaking through again into the river. Formerly there were extensive grassy salt pastures between the beach and the river wall, and a track led from Slaughden to the lighthouse and to Lantern Marshes, but now the shingle beach has been pushed very close to the river. In early summer there are still several acres of Sea Pinks, Sea Campion, Sea Pea, Yellow Horned Poppy and the shingle form of Herb Robert. Much was changed by building and other development during the Second World War and in more recent times, and the former beauty and wildness of this part of the coast has been spoilt.

From Aldeburgh to Thorpeness is a shingle and sand beach, but it is rather overrun by visitors, and its flora is somewhat worn by trampling and the parking of motor vehicles. Sea Spurge is the chief plant of interest. A small stream, known as the Hundred River, which drains the ornamental mere, is now piped under the road and pleasure beach to the sea. At one time Thorpe Mere extended over one thousand acres and the little river flowed naturally across the beach.

North of Thorpeness, as far as Sizewell, runs a wide strip of old sand and shingle similar to the Denes of Lowestoft, and parts of Landguard Common, but the area is much overrun today. A little to the north of Sizewell is a nuclear power station; this rather ugly building and the supply lines dominate the area. The power station was built on an area of great botanical interest and importance and a number of very rare and attractive species have been lost. This part of the coast between Sizewell, Minsmere and the Dunwich Cliffs possesses the only really extensive sand dunes with Marram Grass to be seen in Suffolk. The flora also includes Sea Bindweed, Sheep's Bit, Sea Holly and English Stonecrop. Unfortunately the power station and the Minsmere Bird Reserve now attract a great many visitors and the beach is much frequented and some of the natural vegetation has been destroyed by trampling.

There was a mere in this area in the 18th century, but not on the site of the present Bird Reserve. It was south of this and of the knoll of land by Leiston Lower Abbey and there must have been extensive marshy ground surrounding the mere in those days. This has been revealed by excavation and peat deposits in the area. The pastures just north of Sizewell Belts, still rich with flora, are relics of this marshy area and mere. Before the War there was a cottage at Minsmere Sluice and a number of garden plants have survived, including Greater Periwinkle and Tree Lupin, which has increased.

5

We now come to Dunwich Cliffs. These are composed of sand and pebble beds and are much eroded by winter tides. An attractive area of heathland known as Westleton Walks stretches from the coast for a few miles inland, and is now partly a nature reserve.

From Dunwich Gap to Walberswick the beach is mainly of shingle with a now rather unstable ridge, which is constantly being eroded and needing repair after high tides. The sea frequently breaks gaps in the ridge or flows through the loose shingle to flood the adjoining marshes, now a bird reserve. This shingle beach was formerly quite wide over much of its length, and was composed of a number of ridges representing old beach formations. The majority of the interesting plants which were known there have been destroyed either by erosion, human interference or, more especially, by the bulldozers used to pile up the shingle. The area is now very popular with visitors.

From Southwold north to Covehithe there are low cliffs consisting of light clays, Norwich Crag sands and Pebble Beds. There are two small brackish broads, one at Easton Bavents and the other at Covehithe. These are formed by the shingle and sand beaches blocking the mouths of small rivers. The water from Easton Broad is now piped to the sea. In Easton Broad interesting Stoneworts have been found. At the back of Easton Broad is Easton Wood.

About a mile from Covehithe is Benacre Ness, which is an interesting old sand and shingle beach with adjacent heathland and Benacre Broad. During the Second World War a large quantity of shingle was removed from this site, creating pits which are sometimes flooded. The most interesting plant to be seen at Benacre Ness is the Grey Hair-grass. This grass was formerly very abundant, but is now much reduced, due to human interference and erosion. Sea Kale also occurs.

North of Benacre are Kessingland and the cliffs of Pakefield, which are now protected from erosion by a concrete wall. The area is much developed, with caravans, holiday camps and chalets, so that very few good habitats remain.

At Lowestoft there are sandy areas of beach known as the North and South Denes. These were formerly open, sandy, grassy beaches between the low cliffs and the sea, with just a few fishermen's huts and boats. Much development has taken place since 1945 and very little of the original Denes remains.

At Gunton, a little to the North of Lowestoft, are cliffs with Bracken and Heather. Beyond Gunton the coast at Hopton, Corton, Gorleston and South Town, Yarmouth, has been quite ruined by sprawling holiday camps and similar developments. There are low cliffs composed of Lowestoft Till and of basement beds of Forest Bed age with interesting remains. There are no stable beaches, except the remains of a small area adjacent to the Gorleston Golf Links.

The Rivers
The chief rivers of the County rise in the higher parts of the Boulder Clay regions and at one time their sources were in the extensive forests and woodlands which covered the entire area. There are few natural springs at their original

sources. Today some of the sources can be traced to the farm ponds and drainage ditches serving the area, which is now extensively farmed. Many of the rivers have become little more than dykes of rather polluted water, which are subject to seasonal rainfall, so that many are almost dry in the summer and overflowing in winter or during periods of heavy rainfall and storms.

Several of the main rivers and their tributaries have their sources quite close together, although the rivers themselves may flow in opposite directions, as in the case of the Waveney and the Little Ouse at Redgrave Fen. These rivers form the northern boundary of the County with Norfolk, the Waveney flowing eastward and the Little Ouse westward. To the south of the County, the R. Stour acts as the southern boundary with Essex for much of its length, except for the diversion of the boundary in the vicinity of Haverhill and Sudbury. The sources of the R. Stour are just over the border; they can be traced to farmland ditches and an area of woodland west of Sipsey Bridge, Great Bradley.

The main Suffolk tributaries of the Stour are the Rivers Glem, Box and Brett, and the Chad Brook. The R. Glem drains an area of high ground at Stradishall and Wickhambrook; some of its sources can be traced to old woodland or the sites of former woodland; it joins the Stour east of the old Glemsford railway station. About a mile further on, at Long Melford, the Stour receives the waters of the Chad Brook, which has its source at Rede, where there is some of the highest ground in Suffolk, at over 400ft. The R. Box is only a small river and its sources are near Great Waldingfield. It flows through Boxford, Polstead and Stoke-by-Nayland to Langham Mill. The R. Brett joins the Stour at Higham. This is the river that flows through Hadleigh. Its source can be traced to a pond at Brettenham and it flows through some very attractive countryside, through Chelsworth, Shelley and Layham. The main tributary of the Brett is the Lavenham Stream, which rises in high ground at Cockfield. The flora of the R. Brett at Hadleigh is quite rich, at least when it has not been cleaned out for some time.

The Stour Valley from Stratford St Mary eastward, through Dedham and East Bergholt, is famous for its association with the landscape painter, John Constable, who lived at one time at Flatford Mill. This is now a Field Centre. At Cattawade the R. Stour broadens out into an estuary, which becomes about 1½ miles wide at Holbrook, then narrows at Harwich Harbour and Shotley, where it is joined by the Orwell, before entering the North Sea at Landguard Point. The Orwell is the estuarine section of the R. Gipping and is tidal as far as the weir near the Seven Arches Bridge on the London Road in Ipswich.

The vegetation of the R. Stour can be observed at various points, such as between East Bergholt and Stratford St Mary, by following the valley footpaths. At Nayland there is a good representative flora of both aquatic and marginal plants.

The R. Gipping has its source at Mendlesham Green. At Combs Ford the Gipping receives the waters of the R. Rat, which rises at Felsham. The Gipping flowed direct into the Ipswich Dock before the New Cut was made. There are several small streams which feed the Gipping, but many of them have only a seasonal flow of water; for example, the Hemingstone and Coddenham streams, where most of the rainfall rapidly disappears through into the Chalk. The same applies to the chalk stream from Great Bricett, through Offton, Somersham, Little Blakenham and Bramford, which is dry for most of the year, with water flowing only when the Chalk becomes saturated or after heavy rainstorms. The road which serves these parishes follows the stream bed for much of its length.

Both the Stour and the Gipping were converted in the early 19th century for use as canals, and barges were taken as far as Sudbury on the Stour and Stowmarket on the Gipping. Barge trade continued on these rivers until late in the 1920's. The Gipping can be followed from Ipswich to Stowmarket on foot for much of the distance by means of the old tow path.

The aquatic and marginal vegetation of the R. Gipping can be studied from this old tow path, especially between Ipswich and Bramford. In spite of much pollution, many flowers can still be found; some attractive species, have, however, almost disappeared, or are very rarely seen. Water Violet was once common in ditches near Boss Hall and even in the river at Handford Bridge, and the Flowering Rush was formerly quite frequent from Ipswich to Bramford. We still can see the Arrowhead and the Yellow Water Lily and a newcomer, Fringed Water Lily. The land adjoining the river at Ipswich, Bramford, Claydon, Needham Market and Combs has now been much developed for industrial use and is often used as a dumping ground for rubbish — in some cases even the ditches have been filled in. I can recall attractive water-meadows with their ponds and little streams, which existed all the way between Ipswich and Stowmarket, with their varied, and often very rich flora. This was observed and collected by botanists from the early 19th century onwards and remained the pattern until the 1960's, when rapid changes took place in land use and large areas of pasture were drained and ploughed up between Needham Market and the Creetings.

Belstead Brook is a small tributary of the Orwell and enters that river at Bourne Bridge, Ipswich. This brook used to be a good trout stream. It has its source near Flowton, where it is known as Flowton Brook, and another tributary rises some distance inland, at Naughton.

The R. Deben drains a large area of High Suffolk. The estuary from Woodbridge to its mouth at Bawdsey (or Woodbridge Haven) is very attractive, but the river mouth is narrow and partly blocked by sand bars. The source of the Deben is at Brook Lane, Wetheringsett, and the ditch here drains Mendlesham Aerodrome. Near Debenham, at Derrybrook, the river bed also serves as a road leading to some farms and is situated between steep banks, forming a 'gully'. At one time the Deben was navigable as far as Debenham. An anchor found there in the river is in the Ipswich Museum.

The R. Finn is a small tributary of the Deben, which it enters at Martlesham Creek. Its source can be traced to ditches at Henley. Between Melton and Ufford the Deben has quite a rich flora. The valley of the Finn has been spoilt in recent

8

years through the cutting down of many trees, removal of hedges, drainage and ploughing up of old meadows and marshes. There were formerly good areas between Rushmere and Little Bealings; some Alder carr still remains.

The Mill River, another tributary of the Deben, which it enters at Kirton Creek, is a small but interesting river, as most of its water is derived from Red Crag springs and its flow and temperature are fairly constant, even in summer during dry periods. It is rarely in flood, as the area it drains is light, sandy soil. One source of the Mill River is the pond on Rushmere Common, which is supplied by underground springs. Several years ago, however, the river could be traced as far as a small pond in Sidegate Lane, Ipswich, near the present Northgate Schools. A small stream flowed from that pond, beside Humber Doucy Lane, and connected with a number of ponds, which have now been filled in.

The other source of the Mill River lies in springs in the valley near St Augustine's Church in Bucklesham Road, Ipswich. Formerly there were ponds and marshy ground near Derby Road Station, Ipswich, the site now occupied by factories. This river valley is very old and it is evident from the brickearth and other deposits that there was a large lake stretching from the Woodbridge Road to the Derby Road, which was then obviously the main source of the river.

The Mill River valley, through Purdis, Foxhall and Brightwell is, in places, still very wild and in a semi-aboriginal condition, in spite of being so near to Ipswich. This situation may not last for long as the pressure on land for new houses and other developments continues to grow. Extensive housing estates already cover former heathland right up to the boundaries of the Purdis Heath Golf Course and if this land had not been acquired by the Golf Club several years ago, there is no doubt that it would now have been completely spoiled by urban development.

There are some very ancient oaks obviously of natural origin on the edge of this valley. At Foxhall a few very large elms remain, although several have died or have been removed. A feature of this valley is the richness of its ferns, which were known to many early botanists. The Broad Buckler Fern is still abundant and the Great Panicled or Tussock Sedge can be seen in a number of habitats and is often associated with the Lady Fern.

The R. Alde has a number of small tributaries draining farmland and valleys west and north of Dennington. The Ore, which rises near Saxtead Green and flows through Framlingham, joins it near Snape, where both rivers widen into an estuary flowing east towards the North Sea just south of Aldeburgh at Slaughden. This estuary can either be called the Alde or the Ore. In Roman and earlier times, it is thought, the mouth of the river was at Slaughden, but it has since been diverted southward by the accumulation of shingle forming a bar known as Orford Ness. The mouth of the river is now about ten miles from Aldeburgh at Hollesley Bay, near Shingle Street.

The Butley River is a small tributary of the estuarine section of the Ore and enters that river near Havergate Island, which is situated in the estuary and is the only true island of the Suffolk coast. The Butley River has its source in some good springs just east of Eyke, near Friday Street. These springs are probably near the site of Staverton Manor, which was burnt down during the Peasants' Revolt in 1381.

Along the Suffolk Coast there are a number of small rivers, the mouths of which are blocked by sand and shingle, so that areas have become flooded and formed marshes or small broads, as is the case of the Hundred River, which supplies the mere at Thorpeness. There is also another Hundred River in North Suffolk, which enters the sea at Kessingland by means of a sluice. Former extensive marshland has been drained by a canal known as the Latymere Dam.

Other Suffolk rivers include the Minsmere River which enters the sea near the Bird Sanctuary via a sluice (before this was constructed a lake existed in this vicinity), the Dunwich River which is only very small, and the R. Blyth, which has its source at Laxfield and flows past Halesworth to Blythburgh and Walberswick. It was at one time used by barges as far as Halesworth.

The R. Waveney, which has its source at Redgrave Fen, flows eastward to the North Sea and joins the Norfolk R. Yare in Breydon Water. One of its Suffolk tributaries is the R. Dove, which can be traced south-west to its source at Mendlesham not far from the sources of the Gipping and Deben. It passes through Eye and joins the R. Waveney at Hoxne. A large number of very small streams feed the Waveney on its long course to Breydon Water, past Bungay and Beccles. There are extensive low-lying areas of marsh, water-meadows and carrs divided by ditches or dykes, which support a rich and interesting flora. Oulton Dyke connects the river with Oulton Broad and Lake Lothing and the sea at Lowestoft. The New Cut at Herringfleet and Haddiscoe connects the Waveney with the Yare. In the area of Herringfleet, St Olave's and Burgh Castle, the Marsh Sow-thistle is still common.

The Little Ouse flows westward from Redgrave and Lopham Fens to Thetford and is joined at Barnham, near Euston, by the Black Bourn or Upper Ouse. The Black Bourn can be traced to a source at Maypole Green, Bradfield St George, not far from Monks' Park Wood. There is also another source at Pakenham Fen, which is now much drained and of very little botanical interest. The Little Ouse was once navigable as far as Thetford. From Lakenheath to the Cambridgeshire boundary the surrounding fenland is protected from flooding by embankments. One of the main tributaries of the Little Ouse is the R. Lark, which flows through Bury St Edmunds and has sources in woods and fields at Whepstead not far from that of the Chad Brook, a tributary of the Stour. The very small R. Linnet rises in ponds in Ickworth Park and joins the Lark at Southgate Bridge, Bury St Edmunds. The Cavenham Stream, another tributary of the Lark, has sources at Hargrave and passes through some chalky Breckland areas at Risby and Cavenham. The stream has a dry bed for much of this section for most of the year, but re-appears from chalk springs at Cavenham and joins the Lark at Icklingham.

The R. Kennett can be traced to sources at Lidgate and flows through

Dalham and Moulton. The bed of the river is often dry, except in spring and after summer storms. This river crosses the western boundary of Suffolk into Cambridgeshire at Kennett and then re-enters the County at Freckenham, where its name changes to the Lee Brook, which joins the Lark.

The Broads

The Norfolk Broads are mainly fresh water. Recent research by Dr J. M. Lambert and others has shown that they are the result of peat-digging in the Middle Ages, the peat having been laid down in post-glacial times. They are therefore man-made.

In Suffolk we have two kinds of broads, those which are of similar origin to the Norfolk Broads and others which are brackish dammed-up estuaries of small rivers. In the North of the County in Lothingland we have Barnby Broad, Fritton Lake and Flixton Decoy. The first two are of similar origin to the Norfolk Broads, although Fritton Lake is said to be very old and there is geological evidence to suggest that a shallow lake or mere may have existed there in ancient times. Flixton Decoy may be partly man-made. Oulton Broad was, until 1830, tidal and connected with Lake Lothing, Lowestoft and the sea. Oulton Broad is, therefore, part of an estuary. Easton and Covehithe Broads, north of Southwold, are brackish and separated from the sea by bars of sand and shingle; however, the sea breaks in from time to time.

Benacre Broad, just south of Kessingland, is a shallow, swampy area with reeds; it is protected from the sea by the spit of sand and shingle called Benacre Ness. At one time there were small broads or meres at Dunwich, Minsmere and Thorpeness. The Minsmere Broad has been partly re-created on the Bird Reserve and there are extensive areas of flooded reed beds and swamps between Dunwich and Walberswick, now also a Bird Reserve. The Dunwich Marshes were flooded during the Second World War, but were formerly grazing pastures drained by dykes and wind-pumps.

Botanically, Fritton Lake or Decoy is the most interesting, with its verge of heath, its dykes and its fringe of woodland. However, a number of interesting plants have been found from time to time at Easton Broad.

A study of valley and plateau deposits of peats, alluvium and silts in the County points to the existence in interglacial and post-glacial times of extensive fresh water lakes or meres. Although the majority were filled in during the last Ice Age by drift and other material, some have managed to survive, although much reduced in size, in the form of small ponds, meres or swampy ground.

Framlingham Mere is very ancient, but the area of standing water is very small today compared with what it was even fifty years ago. Prehistoric elephant remains have been found in the deposits of this mere. Cornard Mere, near Sudbury, is also very ancient and is all that is left of a once huge lake, which occupied the Stour Valley during interglacial times. The small pond or mere on Rushmere Heath on the outskirts of Ipswich, which gives the village its name, is prehistoric and nearby was a Bronze Age settlement. The Decoy Ponds near

Bixley Heath, which are very old and known to have been in existence before 1732, are really relics of an ancient lake, once several miles in length, occupying the valley between the Woodbridge Road and Foxhall.

The Breckland Meres lie chiefly in Norfolk. The level of the water in them is controlled by the rise and fall of the water in the Chalk. Livermere at Ampton, near Bury St Edmunds, is partly ancient and is about two miles long and extends over seventy-five acres. It is similar to the Breckland meres, the level being partly controlled by the level of the water in the Chalk. Barton Mere, similar to the Breckland meres, near Pakenham, once extended over twelve acres. Sicklesmere at Little Whelnetham, a few miles south of Bury, was drained many years ago and was really a broadening of the R. Lark, and supplied by chalk springs. Mickle Mere is part of Pakenham Fen. Bosmere, near Needham Market, was part of the bed of the R. Gipping before it was canalized. Playford Mere is very small and now planted with trees.

Bogs, Fens and Marshes

Drainage, followed by cultivation has, in recent years, considerably reduced the number of first-class wetland habitats which had survived the changes of the 19th century. The neglected habitats have, in many instances, developed into alder carr or reed swamps with Willows and scrub.

Wet, acid heaths and bogs, where peat may still be developing, are now very small in extent and are sometimes associated with, or are on the borders of, the Fens. Plants noted on wet heaths are: Cotton Grass, Cross-leaved Heath, Petty Whin, Heath Lousewort, Heath Spotted Orchid, Round-leaved Sundew, Heath Rush, Tufted Sedge and Dwarf Willow. Ancient habitats still exist on heaths in East Suffolk, between Sizewell and Dunwich, at Walberswick, Blythburgh, Friston, Snape, Ashby and Barnby. Former habitats at Butley, Wantisden and Iken have been drained. Much of the former heath, bog and swamp near Ipswich has been filled in and built over.

In West Suffolk, small areas can be observed at Cavenham and Tuddenham and at Lakenheath and Wangford. Parts of Redgrave and Hinderclay Fens can also be descibed as acid bogs.

Fens developed in the river valleys of North Suffolk through peat cutting and lack of drainage. Those remaining are of considerable interest to the botanist because of their rich flora. Unfortunately the large Redgrave and Lopham (Norfolk) Fens are drying out and are being invaded by Birch, Willow and other trees and shrubs. Many of the species which once grew there have now disappeared. Great Fen Sedge usually denotes fen conditions. Parts of some fens are very calcareous with a rich association of grasses, sedges and frequently various orchids. In some fens are deep pools where Stonewort, Pondweed and Bladderwort grow.

Extensive valley fens at Redgrave are preserved by the Suffolk Trust. Redgrave Fen is part of a much larger area, which includes North and South

Lopham Fens on the Norfolk side of the Waveney. Smaller areas of fen still exist at Hinderclay and Thelnetham, but some drainage has taken place in recent years and a number of interesting plants have now gone. There are also fens, or fen-type marshes and bogs, at Hopton, Market Weston, Pakenham and Tuddenham. Relics of a once very extensive and rich fen occur at Lakenheath and Wangford, although these are becoming overgrown and are drying out. Very little of Mildenhall Fen remains. Mildenhall is the largest parish in the County and was once mainly undrained fen, but now, along with much of Lakenheath parish, is rich farmland.

Sites of former ditches and dykes often have a number of species which may be survivals of the original fen-type flora. In spite of the many drainage schemes carried out since 1950, there are still areas of wet pasture, marshes and swamps of various types, from basic to acid. Swamps usually develop after grazing and other management, such as clearing of ditches, ceases. At one time, hydraulic rams were a feature of many Suffolk valleys, but very few are now in working order; this apparatus, usually located near springs, was quite efficient in the drainage of wet pastures.

Some good examples of wet pastures and water-meadows exist in the Waveney Valley, especially east of Beccles, where the river flows through the area known as Lothingland. There are also some very wet undrained pastures north of Tostock in the Black Bourn valley, as well as some on the coast between Sizewell and Minsmere. In the valley of the Mill River between Purdis Farm and Brightwell there are some swampy, overgrown pastures, which formerly had quite a rich flora, with an abundance of Marsh and Spotted Orchids.

The Gulls or Gulleys and Channels

Little mention has been made in the past of the small, often wooded gulleys or channels, usually associated with the upper reaches of rivers or their tributaries. They were formed during the last Ice Age by the action of ice and vast quantities of melt and flood water leaving the huge ice fields covering the higher clay areas. This action gouged out the deep little valleys. These are short, usually not more than half to three-quarters of a mile long. They can be compared with the wooded gills or rills of some northern counties of England or Scotland, although of course they are much smaller. Suffolk gulls, with their steep sides, have of course never been cultivated and have, in some cases, retained their original vegetation. Some are very attractive; little reserves of much beauty with their endemic Elms and various flowering herbs and frequently ferns growing to perfection. One can visualise their former importance, as some of the streams or riverbeds have deep pools, which are never dry. In much earlier times they were the upper reaches of the main rivers where salmon, trout and other fish would have spawned, as still occurs in similar areas of the British Isles. It is a great pity that often farm, and other rubbish, especially pesticide drums, is dumped in these gulleys.

13

In East Suffolk, gulleys can be observed at Otley, Dallinghoo, Swefling, Peasenhall, Coddenham and Debenham. The Debenham one is called Derrybrook. Other examples are at Flowton, where it is called the 'Grindle', and at Offton, where it is called the 'Channel'. The streams cut deep into the Chalk.

In West Suffolk, examples can be found at Hawstead, Whepstead, Hargrave, Cavenham and between Lidgate, Dalham and Moulton.

There are a number of small gulls in the valley of the Stour, the R. Glem and Chad Brook, but these are not marked on Ordnance Survey maps.

East Suffolk Commons, and Heaths and Warrens of the Sandlings

Until about 1920 very extensive, open areas of heathland, common and marginal light arable land still existed on the light gravelly and stony soils of East Suffolk. There was an almost unbroken band from the fringes of Ipswich northward to the Lowestoft area. The soil is mainly very poor and acid. Reference to a geological map of the County will show this coastal area to be covered by the post-glacial sands and gravels of the Pebble Beds and the Coralline and Red Crags. Archaeological evidence suggests that the open forest and scrub, which covered the region, was cleared in quite early times by Neolithic man. Traces of this ancient forest can still be observed at Staverton, Butley and Sudbourne and along several of the valley slopes, where there are still many very old oaks. Many of the heaths still have their sandy tracks dating back to prehistoric times, and these support several interesting species: Mossy Stonecrop, Trefoils and Red Spurrey.

There are frequently ancient banks and ditches bordering the tracks, which marked the former fields and enclosures. Hedges in the Sandlings usually contain only a few species of trees and shrubs. During the First and Second World Wars some areas were cultivated, but this was mainly temporary; however, considerable areas have been brought back into cultivation, as at Sutton Walks and Iken Common in the late 1920's and early 30's, and elsewhere since the Second World War.

Open commons and greens of various sizes are to be found in a large number of parishes. Some are managed as recreation grounds and are, therefore, mainly of no interest botanically. Constant cutting and mowing, usually at the wrong times, reduces their interest and attraction; an example is Saxtead Green, where the former flora has been much reduced by the present management. Mellis and Bungay Commons are partly grazed. Wortham Green has not been grazed for a number of years and is becoming overgrown with coarse grasses and a certain amount of scrub. There is little left of its former flora of the ancient Boulder Clay grassland type.

Rushmere Common, near Ipswich, is a golf course on former heathland, but there are still small areas left of heather and grass. Newton Green, near Sudbury, is another golf course, and is all that remains of a formerly extensive open area. Several heathland types of plants have survived there, including Petty Whin and Ling. There is also a good pond at Newton Green.

14

Names of former heaths still occur on maps, although the areas are now cultivated, such as Levington Heath, Trimley Heath and Castlings Heath, Groton. In the 1930's some of these, such as Castlings Heath, were still quite extensive areas of semi-heathland, which were used for sheep grazing and where Sneezewort, Eyebright, Ling and a number of other heathland species occurred.

The former South-west Suffolk heaths occurred on local deposits of high-level gravels. These gravels contain brickearth deposits, where there must formerly have been lakes.

Wenhaston Common, near Halesworth, maintains a good heathland flora, although there appears to be more Bracken and grass than formerly and it is becoming increasingly surrounded by new housing developments. The soil is mainly sand and gravel, with pebbles of the Westleton Beds and Norwich Crag series, as it is also at Blythburgh.

Large housing estates now cover former heathland to the East of Ipswich at Bixley, and the once extensive Ipswich Race Course, near Nacton. Extensive heathland at Martlesham, which was formerly open and wild before being used as an airfield, is now developed for industry and housing.

The Sandlings at one time supported large flocks of sheep and goats. These animals kept the area open and prevented the growth of scrub and trees. It is probable that some deliberate burning may have been another factor which assisted the growth of Heather and some Gorse and controlled the spread of Bracken. The rabbit has also played a part in preventing the growth of trees. Some areas where there has been no grazing or burning for many years have reverted to scrub and woodland, with Birch, Hawthorn, Alder and Oak as the chief species. Blackthorn and Elm have spread from ancient boundary hedges and in some damp areas there are Aspen, Willows and other species. On Foxhall Heath, Birch woods have developed since the 1920's. Parts of Hollesley and Dunwich Heaths have some areas where Birch is spreading and one can observe the natural regeneration of woodland, especially where there are a number of seedling Oaks in various stages of development. Many are very stunted and small, although they may be at least fifty years old. One can visualise that, if these trees were allowed to remain for a few centuries, these areas might look like the Oak forest of the Sandlings before they were cleared. There are very few species of trees, except Birch and Oaks, but near the Forestry Plantations young conifers are beginning to colonise areas.

In East Suffolk the best areas of extensive heathland or common with a covering of Ling and Bell Heather can be seen at Blythburgh, Walberswick, Dunwich, Westleton, Tunstall Common, Bromeswell Heath (golf course) and Hollesley Common. Very little is left on Sutton Walks, which was formerly a very open area of heathland. Smaller areas still exist on Purdis Heath (mainly a golf course), Snape Warren, Ashby, Fritton, Covehithe, Benacre and Gunton. Westleton Walks is remarkable for its abundance of Cross-leaved Heath, although the habitat is mainly a dry, stony heath with only a thin covering of peat. South of Ipswich, there are very small relic heaths at Wherstead, Belstead and Bentley; probably at one time these were much larger. Ling can be seen on the banks of the railway cutting at Wherstead Woods and at one time there were some tall, ancient bushes in Holly Wood, Bentley, which was then a more open scrub-oak wood, with Birch and Chestnut.

Breckland Heaths

At one time four hundred square miles of North-west Suffolk and South-west Norfolk were a vast, wild, sandy heath. This area is known as Breckland. Thetford and Brandon are the main towns. The name was given to the region in 1925 by W. G. Clarke, author of 'In Breckland Wilds'. In Norfolk, the word 'breck' means stony field, or poor marginal land, which is cultivated only occasionally and then allowed to revert to grassland and heath. Before the Enclosure, Breckland was grazed by enormous flocks of sheep. The soil was frequently unstable and subject to much erosion and often there were sand storms, which almost engulfed villages and hamlets. Today, the only areas of loose sand or sand dunes are at Wangford Warren. The sand was derived from the disintegration of glacial drift. The climate of the area is of the Continental type with little rainfall and considerable variation in temperature. Forests were frequent. The soil is very porous and often much disturbed by large numbers of rabbits, which could, in the past, be seen in their thousands. Sand Sedge, Bracken, various grasses and Ling help to stabilise the light soils.

Today much of Breckland has been planted with conifers by the Forestry Commission and other areas have been brought into cultivation by improved methods. During the Second World War, Breckland was used extensively by the Armed Forces and several large camps and aerodromes were established, some of which are still in use. There are, however, still quite a few extensive areas left for the botanist and naturalist, which enable a study to be made of the flora and fauna of this unique area. There are a number of special Breck species of common wild plants, which are mainly restricted in Britain to this area, but which have a wider range in Europe. The flora, which resembles that of some open areas of Eastern Europe, is often described as the 'Steppe element' of the East Anglian flora. Some botanists suggest that it is a relic flora of the former Rhine Valley, before the North Sea came into existence. However, it is more than likely that this interesting flora is due solely to the special conditions which prevail. (I have seen a very similar flora on heaths in Jutland and southern Sweden.)

The best remaining areas of Breckland are in Suffolk. They are to be seen on Cavenham and Tuddenham Heaths, which are Nature Reserves, and also at Lakenheath and Wangford Warrens and Barnham Cross Common, near Thetford. These sites are in addition to those mentioned under 'Chalk Grassland'. There are also numerous grassy, roadside verges, tracks and private enclosures, where much of the Breckland flora persists.

Some Breckland species are now very rare or extinct; this is mainly due to loss of habitat. However, there have been a number of new arrivals to the area in recent years, mainly aliens of the waysides, marginal land and disturbed soil, such as that ploughed for fire-strips. There are also a few species which have found the shade of the conifer plantations to their liking.

Chalk Grassland

Chalk is the main rock formation of Suffolk, but over most of the County it is covered by glacial drift, Boulder Clay, sands, gravels and outwash of varied thickness, age and composition. In the East of the County it is the Upper Chalk and in the West, the Middle and Lower Chalks. There are several outcrops of the Upper Chalk in river valleys in the South-east, but the exposures are usually very limited in extent. Only in the extreme West, around Newmarket, do we find any expanse of Chalk at the surface. Here, as on Newmarket Heath, there is a wide expanse of very ancient downland-type of dry chalk grassland, with a rich flora of ancient and rare species. However, only about half of Newmarket Heath is in Suffolk; the rest, including the Devil's Ditch or Dyke, is in Cambridgeshire. Much of the chalk area around Newmarket was, before the Enclosure Acts, very open sheepwalk.

In Breckland the Chalk lies very near to the surface and is covered by only a thin layer of sandy soil. Here and there are chalk pits, and chalk debris has often been brought to the surface by ploughing, excavation for flint, and the action of moles and rabbits. The flora of Breckland is, therefore, often similar to that of chalk heaths and downs. A number of rare and interesting species occur.

North of Newmarket there are chalky pastures and similar small areas around Mildenhall, Lakenheath and Brandon. At one time, a few miles west of Bury, there were extensive chalk heaths at Risby, Cavenham, Icklingham and West Stow.

The downland type of open chalk pasture must have once existed in parishes closer to Bury, such as Westley, Great and Little Saxham, Ickworth, Sicklesmere and Chevington. All these parishes are recorded as sites for the now extinct Early Spider Orchid.

In East Suffolk the chief Chalk outcrops occur in the valleys of the R. Gipping and its tributaries, with exposures at Akenham, Bramford, Claydon, Barham, Needham Market, Great and Little Blakenham, Coddenham, Nettlestead, Somersham and Offton. Here, unfortunately, the chalkland is mainly either cultivated or used for houses or factories. Only very small patches of the original chalk grassland have survived. Several years ago large areas of Shrubland Park could be classed as downland, but the park has now been mainly planted with trees. Before 1940 there were a number of interesting roadside verges and ancient grassy quarries. The Coddenham pits have been used as a rubbish dump. In the Stour Valley at Great Cornard, Sudbury, Melford and elsewhere there are exposures and several old quarries, but these are now practically worthless botanically and are either overgrown or used by industry, or as rubbish dumps.

Woodlands and Parks

There is historical evidence that the County was very well forested from early Norman to Tudor times. Many of the wooded areas in Medieval Suffolk had open spaces of rough pasturage used for livestock and the numerous deer. Until fairly recently this pattern persisted in several wooded areas, with many small pastures or areas of cultivation interspersed with the woods and copses.

At the time of the Domesday Survey, much of the western portion of the County, stretching from Cosford to Bury St Edmunds, was woodland belonging to the Liberty of St Edmund. At Mendham Manor in the North of the County there was woodland of some 2,000 acres, and Melford Manor had about 500 acres of woodland and park. Some of the woods mentioned then still exist. For instance, Lemynge Wood of 90 acres, now called Lineage Wood, Le Speltue of 80 acres, now called Spelthorn Wood, and the Great Wood or Park of Elmsett, which once extended over 260 acres, but now covers only a very small area.

In Medieval and Tudor Suffolk there are records of woodland manors and their extensive parks. The largest then appears to have been at Westwood (Blythburgh and Walberswick), Henham with 1,000 acres, Framlingham with 600 acres, Huntingfield with Heveningham with 1,000 acres, and Staverton. A few of the ancient Oaks from these parks still exist. The 'Queen's Oak' at Huntingfield dates back to the visit of Queen Elizabeth I at the beginning of her reign.

In the 18th and 19th centuries, woods were linked by copses, groves, wooded bridle-ways and lanes. Some of the most thickly wooded areas of the County appear to have been in South-west Suffolk overlooking the Stour Valley between Nayland, Bures and Cornard; this is no doubt part of the Great Forest of Essex existing in Roman times. The parishes of Assington, Nayland, Bures and Leavenheath were largely wooded. Assington Thicks was then at least 3-4 times its present size. This wooded area was linked to another district of forest known as Milden Thicks, a few miles to the North-east. In the 19th century Milden Thicks consisted of a large number of very ancient woods and copses interspersed with small wooded pastures. Some of these woods still exist.

Another large area of forest in the South of the County existed on high ground in the Brett Valley at Shelley and Polstead (formerly a very heavily timbered parish). This area was connected with Raydon Woods, at one time far more extensive than today. Spurs of this forest can be traced to the Bentley, Belstead, Copdock and Wherstead complex of woods, and were also linked by way of Brimlin Wood, and other small groves, to the larger Hintlesham Woods and then northwards to Elmsett, Willisham and Barking. The Bramford and Burstall Woods are a spur of this great forest.

In the Bury St Edmunds region we can trace other extensive areas of forest on the high ground from Melford and Lavenham to Cockfield, Thorpe Morieux, Felsham, Bradfield St George, Bradfield St Clare, Gedding, Hessett and Beyton, with a spur to Woolpit, Shelland, Haughley, Elmswell and Gipping. West of Bury, good aboriginal woodland still exists around Saxham,

Barrow, Dalham and Ousden. However, the woods around Ickworth Park are not ancient and only date from the 18th or 19th centuries, the time of the layout of the Park and its surroundings.

There is another area of interesting and very ancient woodland in the extreme South-west of the County at Thurlow and Great Bradley, crossing the Cambridgeshire border to Ditton Park.

On the Boulder Clay in Central, Eastern and North-east Suffolk little remains of the ancient forest. The few woods that do exist have been drastically reduced, or changed, by clear felling and replanted with conifers. Bruisyard Wood is obviously ancient, as is also Dodd's Wood in Benhall and Rendham parishes. There are a few small woods or copses remaining which are partly aboriginal. Some woods are of uncertain age, for instance, Big Wood and Haw's Wood, near Thorington and Hinton, which are said to be part of the ancient Dunwich Forest. However, the majority of woods in North and North-east Suffolk are only plantations on former arable land, pasture, commons or heathland. Many were created specially for the preservation of game birds in the 18th and 19th centuries and are still called coverts.

There are a number of woods which have never been planted, but have developed naturally from scrub, which has grown up on neglected fields, waste or marginal land. The development of this type of woodland takes around 100-150 years, and the woods can usually be distinguished by their poor ground flora with some of the plants of the former arable land still persisting. There are often ancient thorns and other shrubs and it is also frequently possible to trace the ditches and overgrown field hedges in the complex of the wood from the ancient Oaks, which were once pollarded, and Elms and Hornbeams. Coe Wood, Peasenhall, is an example of such a wood, and the woods at Hicket Heath, Hessett, developed in this way, but now carry good timber and have been brought under management.

Between 1920 and 1939 many farms in Suffolk, involving hundreds or even thousands of acres, began to go out of cultivation, and scrub developed rapidly and here we saw examples of this natural regeneration . The last War brought this to an end and the areas concerned have practically all been re-claimed.

For economic and other reasons, very many parks have now been ploughed up and their trees removed. Helmingham Park of some 300 acres is probably the finest now surviving in Suffolk, with many fine old Oaks of known age. Scattered ancient trees, although many are now hollow, stag-headed and dying, may be seen on the sites of former manors, their gardens, parks and woodland. At The Slade, Barham, is a row of ancient Oaks, and at Erwarton Walk ('walk' means a passage through woods) and Park are some of the largest and oldest Spanish Chestnuts in the County. Unfortunately, all are now decaying and some have been removed.

The banks and verges of the main estuaries of the County, the Stour, Orwell, Deben and Alde, were only comparatively recently more wooded than is the case today. Fragments of what is obviously aboriginal wood and scrub still exist. A large number of ancient trees have either been felled, or have fallen, due to the erosion of cliffs. Relics of these trees can be observed littering the foreshore. Ancient woods still existing are Bridge Wood, near Alnesbourne Priory on the north bank of the R. Orwell, and part of the woodland on the grounds of Broke Hall, between Nacton and Levington. There is also a strip of ancient woodland on the south side of the Orwell at Chelmondiston, between Pin Mill and the Clamp House. Formerly Freston and Woolverstone Parks were more wooded than today with some very old Oaks. The ground flora of these parks suggests an ancient association, with Wood Anemones and, formerly, carpets of Primroses.

Iken Wood on the south bank of the R. Alde, opposite Snape Warren, is a probable relic. Some Elms, many of them centuries old, formed an attractive wooded fringe along the north bank of the R. Stour, between Brantham and Shotley, until fairly recent times. The majority have now been destroyed. There was a particularly attractive belt east of Stutton Ness towards Holbrook Creek. Although the Elms may have originally been mainly planted, it is suggested that some may be part of the native or aboriginal vegetation, as some of the woodland, herbaceous and bulbous flora still survives, where banks have been less eroded and cliffs are of hard glacial gravel.

Butcher's Broom is still fairly frequent. Bluebells, Primroses, Spurge Laurel, Wood Spurge, Wild Cherry and Spindle are relics of the Suffolk Forest, which once covered the whole area and extended right to the water's edge. One often sees clumps of Butcher's Broom which have existed for centuries, just managing to survive on the edge of low cliffs, which have been undermined by erosion. This, in turn, has been partly accelerated through the removal of trees. Sometimes the last clump of Bluebells or Primroses can be seen around the base of a tree or bush, which is about to fall on to the beach. On the Essex side of the R. Stour there are still large ancient woods, as at Wrabness and Ramsey, which are good examples of the types of wood which formerly existed on the Suffolk side of the river.

In the Oxlip and other Boulder Clay areas of the County it is fairly easy to recognise the majority of ancient habitats with their characteristic flora. On the light and gravelly soils in the East of the County there are a number of small semi-relic habitats, which at first sight do not appear to be very old; however, when looked at more closely, it is obvious that their flora contains the remnants of the vegetation of the area of early times, before the region became mainly light arable. For example, in the Shotley Peninsula there are many small woods and copses, which are now mainly composed of Sweet Chestnuts, Sycamore and conifers; however, once the vegetation consisted mainly of Oaks, Birch, Field Maple and Hazels and these trees still exist in limited numbers. There are still a number of old Oaks, although the majority of them are now past their best and are merely hollow stumps with only a few living branches. Many have been badly burned in recent times by stubble and hedge fires. It is likely that some of the trees were saplings in Medieval and even earlier times; one tree cut down at

Woolverstone was shown to be at least 900 years old and many others in the area obviously existed before the present park was enclosed in the 18th century. In the hedges of Berners Lane on the edge of the Park one can see several relic specimens and some dead stumps and on the banks of the Orwell and Stour there are still a few aboriginal trees, but these are rapidly disappearing due to erosion and felling.

Although Preservation Orders cover many trees, insufficient effort is being made to replace dying specimens or to conserve the natural saplings as they appear. Trees and shrubs and other vegetation greatly assist in preventing or reducing the erosion of the river banks and it is therefore most important to maintain a good natural verge of vegetation between high water mark and arable land. This was understood by the landowners of the past.

Hedgerows and Wayside Verges

In the past, and still to a limited extent, hedgerows with their banks and ditches have provided important habitats for the survival of many species in areas where woods and copses are absent. Hedges are unfortunately being destroyed at an alarming rate, and ancient roadside verges being reduced by road widening and by ploughing the fields right up to the road's edge. Although very many hedges, especially those of Hawthorn and Elm, were planted during the Enclosure Acts in the late 18th and early 19th centuries, there are others which are undoubtedly very much older and of considerable interest.

Ancient hedges and ditches often follow parish boundaries or old tracks and some may date back to Anglo-Saxon times. The number of native trees and shrubs found growing in a section of hedge 30 yards long, will often give an indication of its age. A hedge with ten or more species may be up to 1,000 years old. However, hedges on good, mixed or clay soils will usually have a better variety of species than those on poor, dry, sandy or gravelly soils. Some hedges on the Sandlings and in the Breckland, which are obviously ancient, have perhaps only a few species of very limited variety, such as Oak, Elm, Hawthorn, Blackthorn and Elder. Many of the very old hedges, especially on the clay soils, are relics of woodland boundaries and this can often be proved by reference to old maps and by the survival of some typical woodland species of flowering plants, such as Wood Anemone, Oxlip, Goldilocks, Woodruff, Wood Spurge, Betony, Woodrushes, Spurge Laurel and Butcher's Broom. Some hedges were formerly very wide indeed, having the appearance of a grove or even a copse, and contained many woodland trees and shrubs in addition to the ground flora. Such hedgebanks usually have a somewhat different herbaceous flora from those narrower hedges which normally divide fields. Plants like Cow Parsley and Garlic Mustard are often abundant. Banks, especially those on sandy soils, usually have a number of annual or biennial weeds. Crop spraying has had a very marked influence and has often reduced or exterminated many wild flowers of hedgerow and verge.

Roadside verges have changed considerably during the past fifty years and they are no longer such interesting or attractive habitats. Formerly many were rich grassland or semi-woodland habitats, and one can recall waysides which in spring were abundant with Primroses, Violets, Cowslips and other flowers.

On calcareous soils one could see flowers which are now scarce or very local, such as Felwort, Stemless Thistle, Carline Thistle, Rock-rose and various species of Orchids.

These changes have been brought about by a combination of factors. The verges of most secondary roads and minor roads were not cut or mown as is the practice today and there was less motor traffic. Passing animals, even the dust they raised, assisted plant growth. Cattle and flocks of sheep would frequently pause to graze and played a major part in controlling the growth of the vegetation. Bridle-paths and green lanes formed a characteristic feature of the countryside. They are often traceable for miles, linking villages, hamlets and isolated dwellings and were the only means of access; many green lanes still do link farms and farm buildings to more distant fields and pastures. Some of the tracks and bridle-paths are very ancient and were used by early travellers for the transport of goods by pack animals. These lanes were very muddy indeed in winter, but grassy in summer. A few of those that exist today have become overgrown with scrub and trees and can hardly be used. There are others which are still open, wide and grassy, with the characteristic flora of the area they pass through. They are usually too narrow for modern farm machinery and other vehicles and have, therefore, frequently lost one or both of their hedges and have become mere tracks. Some of the green lanes may be very early Saxon or Medieval and are relics of the 'balks' or strips which divided the open fields before the Enclosure Acts. An example is the Greenway at Gosbeck.

Meadows and Pastures

Meadows and pastures which are not treated with sprays or artificial fertilisers, or have not been ploughed up, have almost ceased to exist. At one time such habitats were features of the countryside, every farm had its horse or cattle pastures and the valley bottoms were rich with lush water meadows, which were used for grazing or hay cropping. These meadows and pastures were bright with Buttercups, Marsh Marigolds, Cowslips and Ox-eye Daisies. Various orchids, which are now rare, were very frequent and so were numerous species of grasses, rushes, sedges, umbellates, composites, clovers and vetches, as well as Restharrow, Ragged Robin, Fritillary, Bistort and Adder's Tongue fern. Associated with the meadows and pastures were hundreds of small ponds, which have now disappeared. These had, as their particular feature, a varied aquatic and marginal flora. The losses have been very great, and only very small areas remain where one can still see this rich flora and be reminded of the past beauty of the countryside. Protection is given to sites at Monewden, Otley, Framsden and Cransford. In Lothingland, and around Minsmere and Leiston, there are still large areas of grazing pastures bordered by dykes, some of which have retained their original flora, but the majority have been 'improved' or more effectively drained in recent years. Some small uneconomic areas have been totally neglected and have become overgrown with Willowherbs, Meadow Sweet, Willow, Alder, Hawthorn, Elms and other vegetation.

The flora of some country churchyards is similar to that of the old pastures; indeed, these are often as good as nature reserves, protected by walls and fences. Unfortunately, changes are now taking place and already several have had the tombstones removed, so that the churchyard can be machine-cut. No longer will Cowslips, Quaking Grass, Bee and Pyramidal Orchids, be allowed to flower where they were formerly frequent. In one churchyard the Man Orchid occurred, sometimes with as many as 30 flowering spikes. It was first seen in 1929 and no doubt it had been there for many years previously. The Old Cemetery at Ipswich has always been a good wild flower habitat, especially because of the great abundance of Meadow Saxifrage.

Railway Banks

Many of the railway banks have now become important habitats and reserves for local flora, which has totally or partially disappeared from the surrounding farmland. Railway tracks which are still in operation usually afford the best conditions for maintaining a fairly stable pattern. Those tracks which have been abandoned have, in many instances, become overgrown with scrub and have changed from grassland habitats to woodland.

The management of the banks is important, but this has changed in various ways since the passing of steam trains, before which frequent fires controlled the growth of brambles and scrub and kept down grass herbage. Banks are not cut so regularly now and often growth is checked only by occasional deliberate burning, or by the spreading of uncontrolled stubble fires.

Possibly the best colonies in the County of Golden Rod occur on the embankments at Ipswich and at Wherstead. Meadow Saxifrage is quite frequent on railway banks and can be seen flowering in profusion at several places, especially between Westerfield and Farnham and between Barham and Needham Market. Just north of Haughley junction there is an interesting cutting whose banks have a number of chalk-loving species: Dwarf Thistle, Yellowwort, Marjoram, Purging Flax, Bee and Pyramidal Orchids and Quaking Grass. Other good banks are located between Bury St. Edmunds and Higham with cuttings through the Chalk, and between Saxmundham and Darsham. The abandoned railway lines at Lavenham and Hadleigh are rich habitats. Both are now public footpaths.

Pits and Quarries

A large number of sand, gravel, chalk, clay and brickearth pits and quarries are scattered over the County. Some are very old and have not been worked for many years, while others are of more recent origin or are extensions of older workings. Abandoned pits have become habitats for the survival of local and rare flora; in one instance a chalk pit is now the most important site in Britain of the Military Orchid. Unfortunately, many are being used for refuse disposal, destroying in some instances centuries of colonisation by attractive plant communities, especially in the case of some of the Chalk and Coralline Crag pits.

The most ancient pits are some of those found in Breckland, where prehistoric man dug out flint for making tools. Flint has always been much used in the construction of buildings, especially churches, in the County. Chalk was burnt to make quicklime and cement, and in more recent times extensively quarried as a dressing for poor or acid soils. Modern methods of quarrying have tended to upset the plant pattern of the old quarries; in bygone days work was done mainly by hand with the assistance of horse-drawn vehicles and there was less disturbance of the old turf floors and the areas where work had ceased. Now the big machines and earth-movers rarely allow important old habitats to remain untouched. Grazing by sheep also prevented the growth of bushes.

Some of the clay and brickearth pits are quite old; almost every village seems to have had a brickyard at some period. Loam and marl pits were dug to obtain materials for dressing poor soils, especially in East Suffolk; most of these pits are only small. The Red Crag pits provided shelly or calcareous sand for dressing, but a large number of these pits were dug in the 19th century for their coprolites, which are rich in phosphates and which were made into fertiliser at the Bramford works.

The Boulder Clay and Chalk pits of the cement works at Claydon and Great Blakenham are still important habitats. Some of the pits in the Gipping and Stour valleys have become flooded, as at Barham, and near Long Melford; they are now useful as nature reserves. The hard Coralline Crag pits of the Orford, Sudbourne, Gedgrave and Ramsholt areas were dug mainly for building material. The use of this stone can be observed in churches at Chillesford, Orford, Ramsholt and also in Orford Castle.

Enormous quantities of sand and gravels have been, and are still being, extracted wherever possible for various uses. In Roman times the Septarian limestone, sometimes called Roman cement stone and found in seams in the London Clay of South-east Suffolk, was extracted, crushed and burnt. It was also collected from the foreshore of the Rivers Stour and Orwell, where it outcrops in the cliff. It can be seen in several churches in the area, and in other old buildings and walls: there are examples at Old Felixstowe, Erwarton and Harkstead.

CHAPTER THREE

The Changing Flora

CHANGES in land use, especially the loss of habitats, are a threat to the existence of a number of rare and local species. Some species have not been recorded since the 18th and 19th centuries and several have disappeared in recent times. It is possible that further intensive search might be rewarded and plants which are thought to be extinct may be refound. Several weeds of cultivation have almost disappeared, due to cleaner seeds and general changes in farming practice and the use of crop sprays.

Since the end of the Second World War I have observed some very marked changed in the flora of the County. In springtime there are now very few meadows and pastures that are yellow with Cowslips, Buttercups and Kingcups, pink with Lady's Smock and Ragged Robin, or white with Ox-eye Daisies. The flowers of spring and summer now beautify the waste places in our towns and disused railway tracks. The Oxford Ragwort, almost unknown in Suffolk before the War, is now abundant, and, flowering from spring till autumn, gives a brilliant yellow colour to the drab surroundings of the towns. It persists on most sites, even when constantly pulled up or sprayed.

Beaked Hawksbeard and Evening Primrose are common. In some places Wall Rocket, Hoary Cress, White Comfrey, Spring Beauty and Greater Celandine have increased. Buddleia appears in many waste places, even on walls and roofs. Rosebay Willow-herb (or Fireweed), although still common, has decreased since 1960.

Amongst the garden weeds, Gallant Soldier is often abundant, and Pink Oxalis is a really troublesome weed. Alexanders has become very abundant; its green, glossy leaves and tall flowering stems are most attractive. Dittander has spread to waste places; however, many of its former Ipswich sites have been developed. On walls, Yellow Corydalis and Ivy-leaved Toadflax are now common.

Extinct or probably extinct species, with date of last record

Adonis annua c. 1960.
Anagallis minima 1955.
Antennaria dioica c. 1935.
Arnoseris minima 1955.

Barbarea stricta 1889.
Blysmus rufus 1832.
Cardamine impatiens c. 1860.
Carex dioica c. 1958.

Extinct or probably extinct species — *continued*

C. elongata 1958.
C. lasiocarpa ?1860.
C. limosa 1834.
Cerastium pumilum before 1930.
Chara aculeolata c. 1885.
C. canescens 1957.
C. connivens 1911.
C. contraria 1885.
Coeloglossum viride 1960.
Crepis foetida c. 1880.
Crocus biflorus c. 1975.
C. purpureus c. 1972.
Damasonium alisma 1958.
Dianthus armeria c. 1950.
Drosera anglica c. 1960.
D. intermedia c. 1952.
Eleocharis acicularis c. 1950.
E. multicaulis c. 1950.
E. quinqueflora c. 1860.
Equisetum hyemale c. 1906.
E. sylvaticum 1775.
Eriophorum latifolium 1952.
Eryngium campestre 1902.
Filago pyramidata 1955.
Galeopsis segetum 1862.
Galium tricornutum c. 1960.
Genista pilosa c. 1830.
Gentiana pneumonanthe 1860.
Gentianella campestris c. 1850.
Gnaphalium luteo-album 1956.
Gymnocarpium dryopteris 1941.
Halimione pedunculata 1923.
Hammarbya paludosa c. 1880.
Herminium monorchis c. 1936.
Holosteum umbellatum c. 1880.
Lactuca saligna 1958.
Lathraea squamaria 1968.
Lathyrus montanus 1835.

Limosella aquatica c. 1860.
Liparis loeselii 1974.
Littorella uniflora c. 1950.
Lycopodium clavatum 1941.
L. inundatum c. 1860.
Lythrum hyssopifolia 1933.
Melampyrum arvense 1860.
Mentha pulegium 1946.
Myriophyllum alterniflorum 1930.
Nitella flexilis 1932.
N. opaca c. 1935.
N. translucens 1812.
Oenanthe silaifolia 1974.
Ophrys sphegodes 1793.
Orchis ustulata 1961.
Orobanche caryophyllacea c. 1940.
O. purpurea 1933.
Otanthus maritimus c. 1880.
Polygonum mite c. 1934.
P. oxyspermum ssp. raii 1909.
Potamogeton praelongus 1931.
Potentilla tabernaemontani c. 1889.
Pulicaria vulgaris 1963.
Pulsatilla vulgaris 1939.
Pyrola rotundifolia 1906.
Radiola linoides 1906.
Rhynchospora alba c. 1840.
Scirpus cernuus 1934.
Scutellaria minor 1905.
Senecio integrifolius 1876.
S. paludosus c. 1850.
S. palustris c. 1850.
Serratula tinctoria 1972.
Tolypella glomerata 1883.
T. nidifica 1957.
Vaccinium oxycoccos c. 1810.
Valerianella rimosa 1901.
Viola stagnina c. 1968.

Rare or local species with few records

Aceras anthropophorum
Aconitum napellus
Acorus calamus

Agrostemma githago
Ajuga chamaepitys
Alchemilla filicaulis ssp. vestita

Rare or local species with few records — *continued*

Alisma lanceolatum
Allium oleraceum
A. roseum ssp. bulbiferum
Alopecurus aequalis
A. bulbosus
Alyssum alyssoides
Anagallis tenella
Anchusa officinalis
Apium inundatum
Aristolochia clematitis
Artemisia campestris
Atropa belladonna
Baldellia ranunculoides
Blechnum spicant
Blysmus compressus
Botrychium lunaria
Brachypodium pinnatum
Butomus umbellatus
Calamagrostis stricta
Callitriche obtusangula
Campanula glomerata
C. latifolia
Carex acuta
C. appropinquata
C. binervis
C. curta
C. demissa
C. diandra
C. echinata
C. ericetorum
C. hostiana
C. laevigata
C. lepidocarpa ssp. lepidocarpa
C. x pseudoaxillaris
C. pulicaris
C. rostrata
C. strigosa
C. vesicaria
Centaurea cyanus
Centaurium pulchellum
Ceterach officinarum
Chamaemelum nobile
Chara aspera

C. globularis
C. hispida
Chenopodium botryodes
C. vulvaria
Cicuta virosa
Cirsium dissectum
C. eriophorum
Colchicum autumnale
Crithmum maritimum
Cuscuta europaea
Cystopteris fragilis
Dactylorhiza incarnata
D. traunsteineri
Daphne mezereum
Drosera rotundifolia
Dryopteris cristata
D. pseudo-mas
Eleocharis uniglumis
Epipactis palustris
E. purpurata
Festuca juncifolia
Frankenia laevis
Fumaria densiflora
F. parviflora
Gagea lutea
Galeopsis angustifolia
Galium parisiense ssp. anglicum
Genista anglica
Gentianella amarella
Geranium columbinum
G. sanguineum
Gymnadenia conopsea
Gymnocarpium robertianum
Herniaria glabra
Himantoglossum hircinum
Hippocrepis comosa
Hordelymus europaeus
Hypericum androsaemum
H. elodes
H. maculatum
Hypochoeris maculata
Inula crithmoides
Juncus bulbosus

Rare or local species with few records — *continued*

J. compressus
Juniperus communis
Lathyrus palustris
L. tuberosus
Leonurus cardiaca
Limonium binervosum
Linum bienne
L. perenne ssp. anglicum
Luzula forsteri
L. sylvatica
Lythrum portula
Marrubium vulgare
Melampyrum cristatum
Menyanthes trifoliata
Moenchia erecta
Monotropa hypopitys
Mycelis muralis
Myosurus minimus
Myrica gale
Nepeta cataria
Nymphoides peltata
Oenanthe aquatica
O. crocata
O. pimpinelloides
Orchis militaris
Orobanche hederae
O. loricata
O. rapum-genistae
Osmunda regalis
Papaver argemone
P. hybridum
Parnassia palustris
Pedicularis palustris
P. sylvatica
Petroselinum segetum
Peucedanum palustre
Pilularia globulifera
Pimpinella major
Pinguicula vulgaris
Polygonatum multiflorum
Polygonum minus
Potamogeton alpinus
P. coloratus

P. compressus
P. friesii
P. gramineus
P. obtusifolius
P. perfoliatus
P. polygonifolius
P. trichoides
P. x zizii
Prunus padus
Puccinellia rupestris
Pulmonaria officinalis
Ranunculus arvensis
R. omiophyllus
R. lingua
Rosa mollis
R. scabriuscula
R. stylosa
R. tomentosa
Rumex maritimus
R. palustris
Ruppia cirrhosa
Sagina maritima
Sambucus ebulus
Sanguisorba officinalis
Scandix pecten-veneris
Schoenus nigricans
Scirpus caespitosus
S. fluitans
S. setaceus
S. sylvaticus
Scleranthus perennis ssp. prostratus
Scrophularia umbrosa
Sparganium minimum
Spiranthes spiralis
Suaeda vera
Teucrium scordium
Thelypteris limbosperma
Thesium humifusum
Tolypella intricata
Torilis arvensis
Trientalis europaea
Tulipa sylvestris
Urtica pilulifera

28

Rare or local species with few records — *continued*

Utricularia minor
Valerianella carinata
Verbascum lychnitis
Veronica praecox
V. spicata ssp. spicata

V. triphyllos
Vicia tenuissima
Viola palustris ssp. palustris
Vulpia fasciculata

Doubtful Species and Unsubstantiated Records

There are records of a number of species which are not supported by authenticated specimens or other valid evidence. We all know how unusual plants do, from time to time, turn up in odd places, so we must be careful not to rule out the possibility of finding some species in this list.

Hind, in his Flora, doubted the occurrence of a few species which have subsequently been found, and he also lists others which were incorrectly determined.

It has proved impossible to obtain some of the information required even concerning a number of records made in comparatively recent years.

Doubtful Species

Allium scorodoprasum	No specimen.
Bilderdykia dumetorum	No specimen.
Bufonia tenuifolia	Davy herbarium specimen, no locality.
Carex flava	Confusion following renaming of the group.
C. punctata	No specimen.
C. serotina	Confusion following renaming of the group.
Centaurium littorale	No authentic specimen.
Cephalanthera damasonium	No specimen.
C. longifolia	No specimen, very early record.
Dryopteris aemula	No authentic specimen.
Eriophorum gracile	No authentic specimen.
Juncus acutus	No specimen.
Lamium molucellifolium	No specimen.
Leocojum vernum	No specimen.
Limonium bellidifolium	No authentic specimen.
Melampyrum sylvaticum	No authentic specimen.
Melica nutans	No authentic specimen.
Myosotis secunda	No specimen.
Ophrys fuciflora	Original record doubted by Hind.
Orobanche alba	Specimen not checked.
Platanthera bifolia	No authentic specimen.
Polygonum maritimum	No authentic specimen.
Potamogeton acutifolius	No specimen.
Sagina subulata	No specimen.
Salvia pratensis	Original records doubted by Hind.

Doubtful Species and Unsubstantiated Records — *continued*

Spergularia bocconii	No specimen.
Stellaria nemorum	No specimen.
Utricularia australis	No authentic specimen.
U. intermedia	No specimen.
Vaccinium uliginosum	No specimen.
Vicia orobus	No specimen.

Increasing species

Only those marked 'N' are natives.
Several of the species listed here are not recorded in Hind's Flora of 1889.

Acer pseudoplatanus	Mahonia aquifolium
Allium paradoxum	Melilotus alba
Amsinckia intermedia	Montia perfoliata
Bromus diandrus	Oenothera erythrosepala
Buddleja davidii	Oxalis corymbosa
Campanula rapunculoides	Papaver somniferum
Cardaria draba ssp. draba	Pentaglottis sempervirens
Centranthus ruber	Petasites fragrans
Cerastium tomentosum	Reynoutria japonica
Chamomilla suaveolens	Rhododendron ponticum
Conyza canadensis	Rosa rugosa
Corydalis lutea	Sedum album
Crepis vesicaria ssp. taraxacifolia	S. reflexum
Cymbalaria muralis	Senecio squalidus
Descurainia sophia	S. viscosus
N? Diplotaxis tenuifolia	Sisymbrium altissimum
N Dryopteris dilatata	Smyrnium olusatrum
Epilobium adenocaulon	Sonchus palustris
N E. angustifolium	Spartina anglica
Erysimum cheiranthoides	Symphoricarpos rivalis
Galinsoga parviflora	Symphytum orientale
Heracleum mantegazzianum	Veronica filiformis
Impatiens glandulifera	V. persica
Lupinus arboreus	

CHAPTER FOUR

Geology of Suffolk

by C. E. Ranson

IN THIS account of the geology of Suffolk I shall briefly describe the rocks and the evolution of landforms in the County, emphasising their effects on the distribution of soils and plants.

The rocks at the surface in Suffolk are young, geologically speaking. Table 1 summarises them, and for general information on these and older rocks, readers should consult Chatwin (1961). Other accounts, notably of the crags amd glacial deposits, have been published by Spender (1967 and 1972), Baden Powell (1948), Bristow and Cox (1973) and West and Donner (1956).

After the end of the Cretaceous period there were slight earth movements and a brief break in deposition. The Lower Cainozoic sediments accumulated in the gentle depressions and they were later folded more intensively to form the London Basin as we know it today. Suffolk lies on the edge of the northern limb of the Basin. The Chalk was raised in the west and now slopes gently from about 350 ft OD (106 m) to ground level in the Gipping Valley and to -70 ft OD (-21 m) on the coast. This sloping surface was the western shoreline for the sea in which the later Cainozoic sediments — the Crags — formed. The shoreline lay roughly from Sudbury to Stowmarket and Diss.

During the Pleistocene there were fluctuations in the climate. After the warm phase in the Cromerian, the next cold phase was so intense that glaciers formed in the uplands of Britain and Northern Europe. They spread into Eastern England bringing with them clay, chalk and rock fragments, and stones, principally from the West and North. On reaching Norfolk and Suffolk, the ice sheets also picked up the sands and gravels of the Crags. In South-eastern Suffolk and Essex they began to melt as fast as the ice sheets were moving forward, and the meltwater washed great quantities of muds, sands and gravels from the bed of the glaciers. The finer materials were carried far to the south east into what is now the North Sea, but the sands and gravels remained close by and in Suffolk contribute to the great heaths between the A12 and the coast.

While this was going on, the bed load of the glacier was accumulating behind the ice-front, and the stiff chalky clays (Boulder Clays) of mid-East Anglia were laid down.

Within the general pattern there are many local variations. the more notable of these are the frequent patches of sand and gravel at the surface in mid-Suffolk

Table 1. Geological Succession in Suffolk
(After West 1968, Mitchell, Penny, Shotton and West, 1973)

Quaternary	Upper	Beaches, saltmarshes and parts of the coast. Terrace gravels of R. Gipping. Late glacial deposits of Redgrave and Lopham Fen. Interglacial deposits of Bobbitshole, Ipswich and Wortwell. Terrace gravels of R. Waveney at Broome and Homersfield. Peats, clays and gravels at High Lodge, Mildenhall.
	Middle	Interglacial deposits at Hoxne, S. Elmham and Sicklesmere. Boulder Clays/tills and associated flint-rich gravels; seen in pits and cliffs throughout Suffolk. These with a small admixture of silt (of loëssic origin?) form the soils of most of the County. Sands, silts and peats at base of Corton cliffs (so-called 'Cromer Forest Bed' of early literature). White ballast of Stour Valley, Stowmarket and Halesworth areas: quartz/quartzite-rich pebble gravels and sands: probably widespread. Silts seen at foot of Pakefield cliffs. Flint pebble gravels of N.E. Suffolk — the Westleton Beds. Silt and clays of the Chillesford/Aldeburgh area — the Chillesford Beds and the 'Norwich Crag' of Aldeburgh and Sizewell, but not Easton Bavents.
	Lower	Sands, silts and clays of Easton Bavents — Covehithe cliffs, including the 'Norwich Crag' lithology here. The Red Crag (sands and pebbly gravels, some shelly) of East and Mid Suffolk.

Cainozoic	Coralline Crag	Shelly sand and soft limestone at Orford and Aldeburgh.
	London Clay	The basal grey/brown clays exposed beneath Crag in the Orwell and Deben estuaries, Felixstowe and at Bawdsey.
	Reading Beds	Silty clays of the Sudbury area and the Gipping Valley.
	Thanet Beds	Clays, often silty with flint pebble bed immediately on the chalk surface in the Sudbury area and Gipping Valley.

Mesozoic (Upper Cretaceous only)	Upper Chalk	Soft white chalk with flints of Mid and East Suffolk seen around Bury St Edmunds, Sudbury, and in the Gipping Valley.
	Middle Chalk	Soft and hard white chalk with flints of West Suffolk — the Mildenhall and Brandon chalk.
	Lower Chalk	Hard grey, pink or whitish chalk with no flints of extreme West Suffolk — seen at West Row, Mildenhall.

Figure 1. Typical cross-section of plateau and of valley sides in Mid and East Suffolk (West of A12 Ipswich-Lowestoft Road)

Soils	Dry, thin, poor	Deep, fertile loams with an admixture of fine silt (loëss). The Loëss thickens to 2-3 ft (60-90cm) in places	Dry, thin poor often strong. Wet — boggy in flushes.	Deep clays or loams, poorly drained.	Rich alluvial silt, sometimes gravels. Often flooded in winter. Occasional fen.
Semi-natural vegetation	Remnants of former heaths e.g. Babergh Heath and Hadleigh Heath.	Many small remnants of ancient woodland e.g.: Bradfield Woods (near Bury), Groton Wood. Some converted to conifer plantations, e.g. Link Wood, Rushbrooke, Bruisyard Wood, Saxmundham. Few, isolated remains of ancient pastures on farmland (e.g. Mickfield Meadow) of roadside verges, greens and commons e.g. Long Melford and Mellis.	Remnants of former extensive heaths e.g.: Leavenheath, Nayland. Little woodland except on steep slopes and on flushes, e.g. Arger Fen, Bures. Acid flushes carry Golden Saxifrage and Great Horsetail.	Remnant ancient grassland, often gone rank through neglect. Streams and ditches near valley bottom often rich in waterside and aquatic plants.	Remnant, ancient grassland, e.g. Shalford Meadows, Little Cornard, Raydon Common, Hopton (Diss), fens at Redgrave, Hopton, Pakenham (latter four not associated with London Clay)

Patches of sand and gravel

Chalky Boulder Clay

Sand and Gravel, including White Ballast

water seepage

London Clay, Reading Beds, Thanet Clays and Silts

Chalk

flush

valley silt and gravel

(e.g. Leavenheath and Woolpit), and the fact that the Boulder Clay is very variable in composition: exposures often show small pockets of sands, chalk or pure clay.

In bringing all this debris into Mid and East Suffolk, the ice sheets dug into the rocks near and on the Chalk ridge in the west of the County. The great peat-and-silt-filled basin of the Fens, and the virtually soil-less chalk of Breckland and Barton Mills bear testimony to this denudation.

Successive cold phases after the active glaciation of East Anglia led to dry conditions and the spread of dust (silt and fine sand) over the whole area by strong persistent winds.

Between these cold phases there were mild to warm phases whose existence we know of through the study of lake deposits formed on the Boulder Clay surface. Research by West (1956, 1957, 1968) gives us a good idea of the vegetation of the times.

The most recent warm phase, from c. 8000 B.C. to the present day, is well represented in the clays, silts and peats of Broadland (Lambert 1960) and the Fens (Godwin 1956) and the valley fens of Suffolk (Tallentire 1953, Heathcote, 1975). The tidal flats, saltmarshes and beaches of the coast, and, of course, the soils now developed on the underlying strata, also belong to the current warm phase. It is these soils and the parent materials underlying them which form the substrates for all the terrestrial flora of Suffolk.

Geology and Plants
The published geological maps of the Institute of Geological Sciences cover the whole of Suffolk at the 1:63360 scale, though only the Saffron Walden, Sudbury, Ipswich and Woodbridge, and Felixstowe sheets are in print. These and the others can be consulted at the Geological Museum in London and probably at local museums. During the last five years the IGS has mapped parts of the Ipswich and Woodbridge and Felixstowe areas at 1:25000 scale as part of an investigation into the sand and gravel resources of this part of East Anglia. IGS Reports 72/9 (Woodbridge) and 73/13 (Shotley and Felixstowe) are available. These are helpful, but often only detailed local knowledge of the geological variations can guide botanists in looking for particular plant associations. Indeed, plant associations are often the geologist's best guide to soils and their parent rocks! The close relationship between soils and plants has been elegantly developed and demonstrated in the Breckland by Watt over the past fifty years or more, and his many papers describe the work in great detail (see for example, Watt (1947 and 1971) and Tansley (1938). Rackham (1975) refers to this relationship in East Anglian woodland and Simpson (1965) described the flora associated with outcrops of the Coralline Crag.

The geological variation occurs on two scales: the broad variation described on the published geological maps which leads botanists to look for acid heathland species in the Sandlings of East Suffolk and calcareous clay grassland floras in the meadows and verges of central Suffolk, and the subtler, but ecologically very important, small-scale variations over a few tens of yards at a time within the broad variations.

The larger-scale variation arises from the major geological events described earlier, and local variation is due to three factors. First, variation arises from streams and rivers cutting down through the more or less horizontal strata and exposing narrow bands of rocks which would otherwise not be available to plants. The second factor, often closely related, is the way this downcutting can produces spring lines along a valley-side and at the botton (see Figure 1 on page 33). The third is the variation caused by gradual or abrupt small-scale changes in the sub-soil. This phenomenon is frequent on the Boulder Clay and although it is present in farmland, it is best seen in the variation of the floras of ancient woodland. Rackham (1975) has shown that factors such as degrees of acidity and wetness varying independently with particle size and slope control the composition of the flora. Since plants are greatly influenced by the physical and chemical qualities of the top 6 - 8″ (15 — 20 cm) of the soil and by its water status, extremes as great as any experienced in the whole of Great Britain can be found over a 50 yard (c. 45m) range in a single wood.

Another factor which botanists should bear in mind is the strong biological continuity over the past 10,000 years — just as strong as the geological continuity. This is manifest in primary woodland — those woods which have carried trees and shrubs continuously since the last cold phase of the Ice Age. Although modified by management, the flora is directly derived from the prehistoric forest. This continuity also applies to the fauna, but particularly to the land surface and soils in these woods. Thus such sites are almost living fossils from the recent geological past.

BIBLIOGRAPHY OF REFERENCES

General

Chatwin, C. P.   1961   East Anglia and Adjoining Areas. British Regional Geology, 4th edition. HMSO.

Funnell, B. M.   1971   The History of the North Sea.
Bull. Geol. Soc. Norfolk 20 2-16

Funnell, B. M.   1972   The History of the North Sea.
Bull. Geol. Soc. Norfolk 21 2-10

Greensmith, J. T.   1973   The Estuarine Region of Suffolk and Essex. Geological
R. G. Blezard   Assn. Guides. No. 12
C. R. Bristow
R. Markham and
E. V. Tucker

Ranson, C. E. (ed.) 1970   The Geology of Norfolk. Updated reprinted edition of the 1961, version published as part of Vol. 19 of the Transaction of the Norfolk and Norwich Naturalists' Society

Spencer, H. E. P.	1966- 1972	A Contribution to the Geological History of Suffolk *Trans. Suffolk Nat. Soc.* 13 (4) 197-209 Summary of the Geological Sequence (5) 290-313 The Geological History of the Orwell-Gipping System (6) 366-389 The Glacial Epochs *Trans. Suffolk Nat. Soc.* 15. (2) 148-194 The Interglacial Epochs (4) 279-356 The Early Pleistocene (6) 517-519

Cretaceous

Peake, N. R. & J. M. Hancock	1970	The Upper Cretaceous of Norfolk in The Geology of Norfolk ed. G. P. Larwood and B. M. Funnell. Reprinted ed. C. E. Ranson 1970.

Quaternary

Beck, R. B., B. M. Funnell & A. R. Lord	1972	Correlation of Lower Pleistocene Crag at depth in Suffolk. *Geol. Mag.* 109 (2) 137-139
Funnell, B. M. & R. G. West	1961	The Early Pleistocene of Easton Bavents, Suffolk. *Q. Jl. Geol. Soc. London* 118, 125-141
Hey, R. W.	1967	The Westleton Beds Reconsidered *Proc. Geol. Assoc. Lond.* 78 427-445
Lord, A. R.	1969	A Preliminary Account of Research Boreholes at Stradbroke and Hoxne, Suffolk. *Bull. Geol. Soc. Norfolk* 18, 13-
Mitchell, G. F. L. F. Penny F. W. Shotton R. G. West	1973	A Correlation of Quaternary deposits in the British Isles. *Geol. Soc. Lond.* Special Report No. 4 99pp.

Flora

Godwin, H.	1956	History of the British Flora. London University Press.
Watts, A. S.	1947	Patterns and Process in the Plant Community. *J. Ecol.* 35, 1-22
Rackham, O.	1971	Historical studies and woodland conservation in The Scientific Management of Animal and Plant Communities for Conservation. Blackwell, Oxford.
Rackham, O.	1975	Hayley Wood. Cambridge University Press.
Simpson, F. W.	1965	Flora of the Coralline and Red Crags of East Suffolk. *Trans. Suffolk Nat. Soc.* 13 7-10
Tansley, A. G.	1938	The Vegetation of the British Isles. Cambridge University Press.

CHAPTER FIVE

Climate

DURING much of the year the Suffolk climate is more continental than oceanic and very similar to that of Holland and Denmark. It is generally a few degrees warmer in winter, due to the winds blowing over the North Sea, or to a westerly air stream. Every year there are certain periods, especially during late winter and early spring, when persistent and sometimes bitterly cold and dry north or north-east winds blow, often reaching gale force and retarding spring growth. The dry winds also occur at intervals during the summer months, usually when pressure is high over the Continent. Then, over coastal areas, temperatures are much lower than inland. The north-easterly winds are often associated with sea cloud, mist or fog, which sometimes last for periods of a week or even longer; then the sky finally clears and the weather remains dry and sunny for several days.

Rainfall
The coastal belt of East Suffolk extends a few miles inland, following the main line of the estuaries and river valleys and is visibly drier than the rest of the County, except perhaps the West Suffolk Brecklands. This coastal area enjoys a sunny climate, but with smaller variatiations in temperature. During the summer months one can sometimes observe a distinct weather pattern with clouds inland and bright sunny weather with an almost cloudless sky towards the coast; not infrequently the rest of the County may be experiencing showers or even severe thunder-storms, due to conditions created by the sea breezes. The coastal belt often remains dry for as much as a month longer than inland areas and has a total annual rainfall of some two to three inches less than that recorded for West Suffolk.

Summer Rain-storms
Thunder-storms with heavy rain and hail often affect areas of the County during the summer and autumn. The beginning and build-up of local storms have been observed to follow a certain pattern; they often have their origins at the heads of the main river valleys. The Gipping valley storms commence a few miles west of Stowmarket over Finborough and travel east as far as Claydon before breaking up and travelling in a northerly direction. The Deben and Alde valley storms are

sometimes very severe locally and extend over a large area of High Suffolk. These storms are frequently accompanied by hail. In the hail belt, north and east of Stowmarket, special insurance is taken out by farmers against damage to crops.

Another area which is sometimes prone to severe storms is the Blyth valley, west of Halesworth. These storms may either travel due east and pass over the coast between Walberswick and Dunwich or travel in a northerly or north-easterly direction to the Waveney valley and pass out to sea north of Yarmouth.

More general storms, which originate over the Continent, come up from the South or South-east and may affect the whole County, including the coastal belt. These storms are sometimes severe with rainfall of between one and three inches.

Snowfall

Snowfalls in the county are very irregular; however, the north-eastern area between Lowestoft and Yarmouth (Norfolk) often has heavy falls or showers, which do not affect the rest of the County. This is caused by the extreme easterly position of that part of Suffolk, which resembles much more the climate of the coastal area of Norfolk.

Sunshine

Comparatively few records have been kept over a long period at any inland Suffolk site, but it is generally noticed that the coastal and Breckland areas enjoy more hours of bright sunshine than the rest of the County. The amount of clear, bright and warm sunshine which now reaches the earth is steadily being reduced by pollution, caused by the increase of vapour trails from the numerous jets which continually pass over the County. Under certain atmospheric conditions these vapour trails spread out and cause almost total high haze, which results in a very noticeable change in temperature. Very cool north and north-west winds usually prevent, or rapidly disperse, these trails, but it is very rare nowadays that we have completely cloudless spring and summer days, as in days gone by.

From observations kept over many years in Ipswich, the maximum number of consecutive completely cloudless days was ten, recorded in March, 1933.

Temperature

A study of the records of temperature in the County during the past 100 years shows that there has been really very little change in a generally established pattern — there have been a number of very cold winters and very hot summers.

A few summers have recorded temperature exceeding 90°F (32°C); however, in some cool summers the highest maximum temperatures have failed to reach 80°F (26°C). Readings are often taken in places near to buildings affording some shelter and they do not therefore give a correct idea of what temperatures and conditions may have been in various habitats subjected to local conditions, such as marshes with lower winter temperatures, frost hollows and sheltered woodland.

The cutting down of trees and the removal of woods, scrub and hedgerows have changed local weather conditions, destroying important micro-climates with their extra precipitation, such as dew and mist, differences in temperature and protection from winds.

Temperatures on sunny days are often very much higher in woods, copses and near hedgerows. In damp open glades during summer, almost tropical conditions of heat and humidity often arise. Local conditions play a major part in the survival of several rare species and colonies have been exterminated simply by the removal of a particular line of trees or an ancient hedge. These changes are more apparent to older naturalists, who can remember the freshness and sweetness of dewy spring and summer mornings, full of the scents of herbs and the foliage of trees and hedges.

Extremes of climatic conditions affect the growth, flowering and seeding of plants and play a far more important role in their survival and distribution than is indicated by mere records. Spring and early summers have frequent long periods of drought with dry, easterly winds, sunshine and rapid evaporation, combined with severe night frosts. This is a critical time for some species, especially Orchids, which rely on a satisfactory rainfall to produce their flowering spikes. In some seasons entire colonies fail and the spikes wither away prematurely.

A very hot, dry period during the summer will cause many marshes and other watery habitats to dry up completely. Such conditions also affect woodland flora. Some annual and biennial species may not appear because of this. Cold winters, with severe ground frost and no protective covering of snow, kill off tender species. However, dry autumns do not seem to be so harmful.

Summer thunder-storms often bring rain at the right period, but the amount varies greatly. Some areas may have quite heavy falls, while others remain perfectly dry, especially the sandy areas of the coastal belt. Rainfall may be too heavy, and the water drains away rapidly to the lower slopes.

Crocus biflorus   Silvery Crocus   Grundisburgh 1938

CHAPTER SIX

Comparison with the European Flora

THERE are a number of botanists who still tend to treat the British flora as isolated from the rest of the Continent of Europe; this was general practice by authors of Floras until quite recently and probably arose because few botanists travelled as much as is the case today. Now they are more easily able to study the marked similarity of certain areas of the Continent close to Britain. The similarities are not surprising when one remembers that Britain was joined to the rest of Europe only a few thousand years ago, even after the end of the last Ice Age, and the Suffolk rivers were tributaries of the Thames, which joined the Rhine near the Wash. Hind in his Flora of Suffolk, 1889, does, however, devote a section to comparing the flora of Holland with that of Suffolk.

I have been able to make a number of visits to Western Europe and study the strong relationship which exists between our East Anglian flora and areas of Holland, Denmark, North Germany and Southern Sweden. In Holland there are still a few fens and reserves in which the flora today is almost identical to that of our East Anglian fens, as they were in the 1930's. Species seen include several which are now rare or almost extinct in East Anglia, especially in Suffolk, such as Sundews (*Drosera* spp.), Common Butterwort (*Pinguicula vulgaris*), Fen Orchid (*Liparis loeselii*), Red Rattle (*Pedicularis palustris*), Heath Lousewort (*P. sylvatica*), Petty Whin (*Genista anglica*), Grass of Parnassus (*Parnassia palustris*), still abundant in several habitats in Holland, and Great Fen Ragwort *(Senecio paludosus),* but this is not a frequent plant. Flowering Rush *(Butomus umbellatus*) can often be seen flowering in quantity during July beside dykes in Holland between Alkmaar and Haarlem. On the coast near the Hoek, Field Eryngo (*Eryngium campestre*) also occurs. This species is now thought to be extinct in Suffolk. Field Wormwood (*Artemisia campestris*) is common on coastal dunes and heathland in Holland northwards to Jutland and across into Southern Sweden.

Rare Breckland and Sandlings type flora can be observed, especially in Northern Jutland and the coastal areas of Southern Sweden around the Kattegat, with such species as Perennial Knawel (*Scleranthus perennis*), though this is a different subspecies from the East Anglian plant. Some very rare or extinct Breckland and chalk-loving species have now also become rare in continental Europe, where the flora is suffering similar pressures as in Britain.

Some of the more attractive species are, however, protected by law. The beautiful Pasque Flower (*Pulsatilla vulgaris*) is one of the special plants preserved in Sweden, but I have only seen it on one small heathy pasture at Simlangsdalen, near Halmstad. Spiked Speedwell (*Veronica spicata* ssp. *spicata*) associated with Bloody Cranesbill (*Geranium sanguineum*), Maiden Pink (*Dianthus deltoides*) and others of our Breckland species, have been observed in small quantities on the Island of Laesio in the Kattegat, only surviving because the habitat was adjacent to a church in an area hardly worth re-claiming. On old Breckland-type heathland, which has so far escaped afforestation, Juniper (*Juniperus communis*) occurs, a shrub which has long been extinct in the Suffolk Breckland. Grey Hair-grass (*Corynephorus canescens*) was found in some quantity on bare, open heathland in a similar type of habitat to that in which it has been recorded at Wangford Warren and Lakenheath.

Marsh Gentian (*Gentiana pneumonanthe*), now extinct in Suffolk but still to be found in Norfolk, was also observed on the same Island of Laesio flowering on the edge of a marsh among the low bushes of Bog Myrtle (*Myrica gale*). This was very similar habitat to an area at Barnby, near Lowestoft, where Bog Myrtle once flourished. Common Clubmoss (*Lycopodium clavatum*) and Sundews (*Drosera* spp.) were also found on damp heathland. These plants are now considered to be extinct in Suffolk, or almost so.

Although the Oxlip (*Primula elatior*) is widespread in continental Europe, I have so far been unable to find a wood or forest area as rich as some of our Suffolk woods with this species and its associated flora. Our East Anglian Oxlip woods appear to be almost unique, and it is important that we have preserved such woods in the County for posterity, Felshamhall Wood and Monks' Park Wood (the Bradfield Woods). The Common Primrose (*Primula vulgaris*), the Wood Anemone (*Anemone nemorosa*), and other spring flowers, which carpet many of our Suffolk woods and copses, often give a finer display than can be observed anywhere else in North-west Europe. One has to travel a long distance, east of the Alps, to the small Alder carr-type woods of the great plain of the Danube to see carpets of Primroses comparable with those of many of our Boulder Clay woods after coppicing.

Some of the remaining Bluebell woods in East Suffolk, especially in the Ipswich area, cannot be matched anywhere else in Europe. These woods are extremely attractive and are an important feature of our heritage, which should be preserved. Unfortunately they are very vulnerable indeed as the pressures continue for new roads and other developments. Some of the ancient woods and copses have already (1981) suffered through the construction of the Ipswich Southern By-Pass.

It is not generally known that on the shingle beaches of Suffolk grow the finest colonies of the Sea Pea (*Lathyrus japonicus*) to be found anywhere in Western Europe, where one can travel for many miles finding only quite small colonies. The salt marsh and estuarine flora of North-west Europe is very similar indeed to that of Suffolk and East Anglia.

CHAPTER SEVEN

The History of Botanical Studies in Suffolk

A NUMBER of famous British botanists have contributed to our knowledge of the flora of the County. Their work has spread over several centuries, dating from the 16th century herbalists.

The distribution of the plants in the County, past and present, has been compiled from many sources — published works, diaries, manuscript lists, herbaria, correspondence and sometimes only word of mouth.

The late N. P. Simpson of Bournemouth spent many years extracting published records relating to the British flora. These were published in 1960, in 'A Bibliographical Index of the British Flora'. There are very many references in this to Suffolk plants, some of which are not generally known and the publications in which they appear are not readily available to botanists.

The Sea Pea (*Lathyrus japonicus*) was, in 1555, the first species to be recorded in the County, when it was discovered on the shingle between Orford and Aldeburgh during a famine.

JOHN CAIUS (or KEY) (1510-1573) the founder of Caius College, Cambridge, may have been the first writer to record this occurrence. Dr BULLEN, Rector of Blaxhall from 1550 to 1554, also recorded it in his Herbal, published in 1662.

Dr WILLIAM TURNER of Morpeth, Northumberland (c. 1510-1568), who was educated at Pembroke College, Cambridge, has been described as the Founder or Father of English Botany. He published herbals, giving names of plants in Greek, Latin, Dutch and French. He also gave various county records, though only two for Suffolk, Broad-leaved Helleborine (*Epipactis helleborine*) and Wood Spurge (*Euphorbia amygdaloides*), the latter at Nettlestead.

JOHN GERARD (1545-1612), a herbalist and barber-surgeon, issued in 1597 his famous Herball. Thirteen Suffolk plants are listed. In 1633 a second and enlarged edition added only one plant, Sea Spurge (*Euphorbia paralias*), found at Landguard Point.

JOHN PARKINSON (1567-1650) the King's (James I) herbalist, and apothecary of London, recorded only seven Suffolk plants in his 'Theatrum Botanicum', published in 1640; two of the records were taken from Gerard's Herball.

REV. JOHN RAY (1627-1705) was born at Black Notley, Essex, the village where he also died. John Ray was certainly the most distinguished British naturalist of the period. His work and influence on the Natural System of Classification is still recognised. He made several botanical excursions, on horseback, visiting various parts of England, Wales and southern Scotland, listing the plants he saw. In 1663 he commenced a continental journey, which lasted three years. His published works assisted Linnaeus with his classification. Ray added nineteen new plants to the Suffolk list.

REV. ADAM BUDDLE (1660-1715) resided at Henley, Suffolk, for a short period. His herbarium and manuscript provided the first record for five species in the County.

J. J. DILLENIUS (1687-1747), the German botanist, and Professor of Botany at Oxford, edited John Ray's Synopsis, published in 1724, adding thirteen new records for Suffolk.

A number of other botanists of the 17th and 18th centuries, who made contributions to our knowledge of Suffolk plants, include WILLIAM HOW (1619-1656), JAMES SHERARD (1666-1737) and THOMAS MARTYN (1735-1825), Professor of Botany at Cambridge. In 1763, Martyn published his 'Plantae Cantabrigienses', including lists of some of the rarer plants growing in England and Wales. Later, in 1797, he issued the first part of P. M. Miller's 'Botanical Dictionary'. The original work was first published in 1724. Martyn completed the revision in 1807.

JOSEPH ANDREWS was an apothecary of Sudbury and collected between 1710 and 1762. His herbarium is in the British Museum and has given us a number of interesting first records.

REV. SIR JOHN CULLUM (1732-1785) of Hawstead, contributed about 500 new species of flowering plants to the Suffolk list. He was a well-versed naturalist and competent observer. His 'Naturalist's Journal' (1772-1785) of daily observations is in some ways as interesting and important as Gilbert White's 'Natural History of Selborne'. Unfortunately it has never been published. In 1774 he published his 'History of Hawstead', which contains a list of the wild plants of the parish. His various records are frequently accompanied by habitat notes, which give a picture of the country around Bury St Edmunds in the late 18th century. Sir John also recorded the flora of the Suffolk coast and other parts of the County. Several of the plants he found are now extinct or very rare.

SIR THOMAS GERY CULLUM (1741-1831) was born at Hardwick, the brother of Sir John. He became a surgeon, practising in Bury St Edmunds, and was also an excellent botanist. His work was recognised by Sir J. E. Smith, author of 'The English Flora', who dedicated this work to him. Sir T. G. Cullum also added a large number of new plant records to the flora. These are given in Gillingwater's 'History of Bury', 1804, and the 'Botanist's Guide', 1805.

REV. GEORGE CRABBE (1754-1832) the poet, was born at Aldeburgh. He resided in Suffolk for a number of years, holding curacies at Aldeburgh, Great Yarmouth and Framlingham. He compiled lists of plants which he observed in the various parishes and added a number of species. Loder's 'History of Framlingham', 1798, gives a list of 226 flowering plants, compiled by Crabbe.

THOMAS JENKINSON WOODWARD (c. 1745-1820) was a native of Bungay and a lawyer. He added a number of plants to the County list and was also a contributor to the Second Edition of Withering's 'Botanical Arrangement of British Plants' and to 'English Botany'. With Dr Goodenough, he wrote 'British Fuci' in 1793. Some of his specimens are in the Ipswich Museum Herbarium.

LILLY WIGG (1749--1828) was born at Smallburgh in Norfolk and died at Great Yarmouth. He had a number of occupations, including schoolmaster, and bank clerk in Dawson Turner's bank at Great Yarmouth. He contributed several Suffolk records to the 'Botanist's Guide', to Withering's 'Botanical Arrangement of British Plants', 1787-93, and also to 'English Botany'.

REV. CHARLES SUTTON (1756-1846) was a Norfolk man, born in Norwich. He married a sister of the Rev. William Kirby of Barham. On a botanical excursion to the sea coast at Orford, in August, 1787, Sutton and Kirby recorded many interesting plants, some of which are the first records for the County. These records were unknown to Hind. Many species mentioned in their account either still exist in the same locality or have only recently become extinct, due to land reclamation, as at Wantisden Bogs, and marshes at Bromeswell. There are a few sheets of Sutton's specimens in the Ipswich Museum Herbarium.

REV. WILLIAM KIRBY (1759-1851), the famous entomologist, and Rector of Barham, near Ipswich, was born at Witnesham. His grandfather was John Kirby, who published in 1735 a topographical work on Suffolk. Although generally known for his work on entomology, he was also a good botanist. Unfortunately, few of his finds seem to have been recorded. In the Ipswich Museum there is an old collection of mainly Suffolk plants of the late 18th and early 19th centuries, which was known as the 'Kirby Herbarium'. This incomplete collection of many rare and early Suffolk specimens is probably the herbarium which was purchased by Kirby from the Ipswich Literary Institute and presented to the Ipswich Museum in 1851. It contains no specimens which I consider to have been collected by Kirby.

DAWSON TURNER (1775-1858) of Great Yarmouth, a banker, was a very keen botanist and, in conjunction with Dillwyn, published the 'Botanist's Guide' in 1805. This contained early references to a number of interesting Suffolk plants. Some of his specimens are preserved in a collection at the Ipswich Museum. He also wrote 'British Fuci' in 1802. A large number of Norfolk specimens, which he probably collected, are also in Ipswich Museum Herbarium.

SIR WILLIAM JACKSON HOOKER (1785-1865) was born at Norwich. He became interested in flowering plants at a very early age and took a keen interest in growing them, becoming Director of Kew Gardens in 1841, where he remained until 1865. He made many expeditions in search of plants. Some of his Scottish and early finds are preserved in the herbarium at Ipswich Museum. In 1813 he came to live at Quay Street, Halesworth, but his house and garden have now been destroyed. 'The British Flora' was published in 1842. Dawson Turner encouraged Hooker, giving him financial support, to set up a brewery at Halesworth. Hooker married Turner's eldest daughter in 1815.

SIR JOSEPH DALTON HOOKER (1817-1911) was the second son of Sir William Hooker. He was born at Halesworth, succeeded his father as Director of Kew in 1865 and held the position for twenty years.

DAVID ELISHA DAVY (1769-1851) lived at Ufford and Yoxford. He was Reviewer-general of Transferred Duties and travelled widely in England and Ireland. He contributed to the 'Botanist's Guide', and several first records can be attributed to him. Some of these specimens are preserved in the Ipswich Museum Herbarium, dating from c. 1790-1815.

CHARLES JOHN PAGET (1811-1844), and his brother, SIR JAMES PAGET (1814-1899), born at Great Yarmouth, were general naturalists. They wrote the 'Sketch of Natural History of Yarmouth', published in 1834, which included a list of local plants.

REV. PROF. JOHN STEVENS HENSLOW (1796-1861), was for many years Rector of Hitcham, and was author with Edmund Skepper of 'Flora of Suffolk', 1860. He was Professor of Mineralogy and then Botany at Cambridge. He was President of the Ipswich Museum and was also interested in geology. While Rector of Hitcham he educated the local children in botany. His herbarium of Hitcham plants is preserved at the Ipswich Museum.

EDMUND SKEPPER (1825-1867) was born at Oulton. He was a dispenser at Bury and joint author, with the Rev. J. S. Henslow, of the 'Flora of Suffolk', 1860.

REV. EDWIN NEWSON BLOOMFIELD (1827-1914), was born at Wrentham. He lived at Great Glemham for a number of years. He contributed to Henslow and Skepper's 'Flora of Suffolk' and added a few new plant records to the County. He was also an excellent lepidopterist and published his 'Lepidoptera of Suffolk' in 1890.

REV. FRANCIS WILLIAM GALPIN (1858-1945) was Rector of Harleston, Norfolk, in the Waveney Valley. In 1888 he published an account of the 'Flowering Plants, Ferns and Allies of Harleston', including a sketch of the geology, climate and natural characteristics of the neighbourhood. His catalogue contains records of many finds made on the Suffolk side of the Waveney, as well as those from Norfolk. His book is dedicated to: 'My friends and fellow workers, the members of the Harleston Botanical Club'.

REV. WILLIAM MARSDEN HIND (1815-1894), was born in Ireland and educated at Trinity College, Dublin. He was Rector of Honington from 1875 until his sudden death in 1894. Before he came to Suffolk, Hind had formed a large herbarium of British plants. This he presented to Trinity College, Dublin, in 1870. In the preparation of the 'Flora of Suffolk' he was assisted by the Rev. Churchill Babington, Rector of Cockfield. Dr Babington died before the publication of the Flora in 1889. During the preparation of the Flora, Dr Hind made a large collection of Suffolk specimens, which he presented to Ipswich Museum. In fact, he formed two separate collections at the same time. They were divided and housed in different storage areas of Ipswich Museum. Part of the collection was not discovered until some storage drawers were cleared in 1952. Hind's 'Flora of Suffolk' was considered to be a very good and useful guide. It was sold to subscribers at five shillings per copy. The Ipswich Museum also has Hind's manuscript of the 'Flora', as well as correspondence and other related material used in its preparation.

SIR CHARLES JAMES FOX BUNBURY (1809-1886), of Mildenhall and Great Barton, was a botanist of considerable knowledge and experience, who studied plants in various parts of the world. He presented his herbarium to the University of Cambridge. However, many of his duplicates of Suffolk specimens are in Lady Blake's Herbarium in the Ipswich Museum.

Various Suffolk and Local Guides of the late 18th and 19th centuries give lists of some of the more interesting plants. The 19th century lists were generally extracted from published books, chiefly the 'Botanist's Guide' of 1805 and the 'New Botanist's Guide', published 1835-7, compiled by H. C. Watson, famous for his 'Topographical Botany'. In 1887, Dr J. E. Taylor, curator of the Ipswich Museum from 1872 to 1894, published a 'Tourist's Guide to the County of Suffolk', which gives some of the more interesting plants.

For the two decades after the publication of Hind's 'Flora of Suffolk', there appears to have been a period of comparative inactivity, when little further real progress was made. A number of outside, but well-known, botanists of the period visited the County to add to their herbaria. As Cambridge is so close to Breckland, many botanists and students have always been attracted to this area and some of their finds are preserved in the extensive collections at Cambridge.

CHARLES EDGAR SALMON (1872-1930), author of the 'Flora of Surrey', examined Hind's collection, and found a number of incorrect and doubtful determinations, which were published in the 'Journal of Botany' under 'Notes upon Hind's Flora of Suffolk', 1907.

WILLIAM A. DUTT (1870-1939), was a native of Norfolk. He was a naturalist and author of books on East Anglia. He lived at Lowestoft and Carlton Colville and recorded, with Mrs Baker, a large number of new aliens for the County, mainly in that area.

In 1911 an account of the Botany of Suffolk was published in the 'Victoria County History', Vol. II. This account was prepared in 1906 by A. Bennett, Rev. E. N. Bloomfield, W. A. Dutt, Rev. J. D. Gray, Rev. W. M. Rogers and Rev. G. R. Bullock-Webster. A list of Suffolk plants was given with descriptions of botanical regions and the more interesting species to be found. Very few new species or records were added which had not already been published in Hind's Flora.

Some Ipswich naturalists, not satisfied with the Natural History side of the Ipswich Scientific Society, formed in 1907 a separate Society, known as the Ipswich and District Field Club.

ARTHUR MAYFIELD (1869-1956), was born in Norwich. He was a schoolmaster at Mendlesham, Suffolk, and his work on the botany of the County extended from about 1890 until a few years before his death. He made a special study of the Flora of his own parish and was an expert on the mosses, lichens, hepatics and fungi of the County. Many of his records were published in the journals of the Ipswich and District Field Club and the Ipswich and District Natural History Society and the Transactions of the Suffolk Naturalists' Society and other Societies. Arthur Mayfield was also a conchologist and his collection of land and freshwater shells is preserved in Ipswich Museum. His fine collection of lichens was given to the Norwich Museum. His thorough and accurate work added much to our knowledge of the County's flora.

STEPHEN J. BATCHELDER (1870-1949), was born at Yarmouth. He was a teacher in Ipswich and a keen botanist. A founder member of the Ipswich and District Field Club, he worked closely with Arthur Mayfield.

JAMES ATKINS (died 1911). Born at Beccles, Atkins lived for many years at Bromley in Kent, afterwards retiring to Bungay, and finally to Ipswich. He first studied ferns and later took up flowering plants and formed a good general herbarium of those found in the Ipswich district (1907-1910). This is now in the Ipswich Museum. The collection contains several interesting specimens, many now extinct or very rare in the area. A list was published in the 'Journal of the Ipswich and District Field Club', Vol. II, 1909. Unfortunately, like so many amateur botanists, James Atkins did not collect specimens of some of the more difficult orders, includes the rushes, sedges and grasses, so that his herbarium is far from as complete as would be liked and leaves a gap in our knowledge of these important orders.

During the First World War very little botanical activity was possible. The REV. JULIAN TUCK of Tostock and the REV. J. E. SAWBRIDGE of Thelnetham continued to collect local rarities and sent them for display at Ipswich Museum. After the War it was some time before any really enthusiastic botanist emerged in the County. The Botanical Society and Exchange Club of the British Isles (now the Botanical Society of the British Isles) was active in various ways and held a few field meetings in the County, although there were less than half-a-dozen Suffolk members. This club was at that time dominated by the figure of DR GEORGE CLARIDGE DRUCE (1850-1932), who exerted a great deal of influence on the study of the British Flora for a number of years.

In 1931 RONALD BURN appeared on the scene. Formerly a lecturer in Classics at Glasgow University, he came to Suffolk to live with his father, who was Rector, first at Hundon and then at Whatfield. Burn had absolutely no knowledge of botany, but with nothing to do, he decided to take up a study of wild flowers. He pursued this subject with the utmost vigour on foot, cycle and other forms of transport. With a copy of Hayward's 'Botanist's Pocket Guide', revised by G. C. Druce, an old Bentham and Hooker and various library books and visits to Ipswich Museum with specimens for identification, he was soon able to strike out on his own. Unfortunately Burn could never really adjust himself to the requirements of a field botanist; every specimen had to fit exactly to every detail of a description, otherwise it must be a new variety or some micro-species. He became a follower of Druce and would always be speaking of 'bowing to Druce'. He later turned his attention to lichens. During his stay in Suffolk, until just after his father's death in 1939, Burn claimed a number of interesting finds, but many have never really been substantiated. To those who did not know him, Burn appeared a strange and rather unusual character wandering round the Suffolk countryside. He died in 1974.

In 1932 MISS EDITH RAWLINS came to Suffolk to be a governess to Lady Rowley's children at Holbecks, Hadleigh. Miss Rawlins was a keen member of the Wild Flower Society and soon made the acquaintance of Burn and together they explored the County. During her stay in Suffolk, Miss Rawlins twice won the annual prize given by the Wild Flower Society for the largest number of flowers recorded in a year in the Society's diary. She left Suffolk at the outbreak of the Second World War and went to Ireland.

In 1929, CLAUDE MORLEY of Monk Soham, dissatisfied with the progress of Natural History in the County, helped to found the Suffolk Naturalists' Society. This was a real step forward, bringing the botanists together. Ronald Burn became the first recorder for the County, but resigned after a few years.

In the 1930's, E. R. LONG (1870-1948), of Lowestoft was very active, recording plants, mainly around Lowestoft and in Lothingland, in a well-kept diary.

DAVID J. CARPENTER (died 1966). A native of South Wales, he taught in Belfast and retired to Felixstowe. He was a good botanist and general natural historian. While at Felixstowe he recorded the plants of the district.

Other workers were H. K. AIRY SHAW of Woodbridge and Kew, MISS N. CRACKNELL of Marlesford, MRS C. BULL of Levington and MISS E. JAUNCEY of Ipswich.

Shortly after I returned to the Ipswich Museum from war service in 1946, the curator, Guy Maynard, suggested that I should publish a new Flora of Suffolk. However, I was not really ready and my knowledge of the distribution of certain species was limited, so I commenced work on a card index and intended to have a check list published in the Transactions of the Suffolk Naturalists' Society, to enable botanists to send me further records. Claude Morley, Hon. Secretary and Editor, had agreed that something on these lines should be done, but that it should be published over a period of years, as it would be too long for one part of the annual Transactions. Claude Morley died in 1951.

MISS JANET C. N. WILLIS (1882-1976), was appointed Honorary Secretary of the Suffolk Naturalists' Society in 1951 after the death of its founder, Claude Morley. She was an MA of Manchester University, and held a teaching post at West Kirby, Cheshire, before retiring and coming to live in Ipswich. Her grandfather was the Rev. Henry Marcus Willis, a former Rector of Trimley St Mary, near Felixstowe. During her eighteen years of office, Miss Willis helped in organising the recorders of the County, who took part in the map recording of the Botanical Society. Her work, and that of various helpers, has in part formed a sound basis in compiling the Flora.

Very many helpers were required to assist in this project, by marking specially prepared cards or by submitting lists of all the species which occurred in a 10km square or part of a square. The final results were published in the 'Atlas of the British Flora', 1962.

During this map recording in the 1950's, a Flora Committee was set up to organise the publication of a new Suffolk Flora. The first meeting was held on December 6th, 1955. Miss Willis, with the assistance of a few members of the Society, began to transfer records on to index cards. The index cards and the B.S.B.I. record cards were handed over to me in 1968, when Miss Willis, owing partly to age, felt unable to carry on with this project.

In the 1960's and early 1970's a more detailed and accurate survey of the Breckland was carried out by several botanists. Surprisingly, only a small number of new records were added to our knowledge of that area. In addition Dr F. H. Perring supplied me with a set of master cards of the Suffolk Flora, based on the records made during the B.S.B.I. Map Distribution Scheme.

Since I took over the work of completing the Suffolk Flora, several botanists, especially visitors, have supplied me with lists and other information, which have served also as a check on older or doubtful sites.

CHAPTER EIGHT

Other Sources of Information

OLD MAPS and herbaria often supply information on the habitats of now extinct, rare and interesting flora. Joseph Hodskinson's Map of Suffolk in 1783 shows many commons, greens, heaths and large woods, which have disappeared or exist today in name only. The first more accurate Ordnance Survey maps of 1838-40 are very good; however, even by that time many of the features shown on Hodskinson's map had gone, especially some of the extensive heaths and common land. Several of these habitats were the collecting areas of the botanists of the late 18th and early 19th centuries and supplied several of our first Suffolk records. The old herbaria reveal the wealth of the Suffolk flora of bygone days. In several instances the collectors have added very interesting descriptions of the habitats.

The Ipswich Museum Herbarium comprises an extensive collection of Suffolk specimens. The number of individual sheets is probably 15,000. It is not possible to give an accurate figure of the number of specimens, as usually more than one specimen is on each sheet or on each page of the bound volumes. I have examined all the collections and have found a few specimens to be incorrectly named.

The Museum has several very important early collections, with specimens dated as early as 1790. It is likely that one collection contains the actual specimens confirming several records in the 'Botanist's Guide' by Dawson Turner and Lewis Dillwyn, published in 1805. This collection comprises specimens which were sent to Davy of Yoxford by Dawson Turner, Lilly Wigg, Thomas Woodward, W. J. Hooker, Rev. G. R. Leathes and other important Suffolk and Norfolk botanists. Unfortunately, about half of this collection is missing. Apparently Hind did not examine the various Ipswich Museum herbaria when compiling his Flora. They were certainly in the possession of the Museum at the time when Dr J. E. Taylor became the curator in 1872.

There are two small, but very interesting, anonymous collections of specimens made in the Ipswich area between 1810 and 1835. The earlier of these two collections is now attributed to John Notcutt, of St Peter's, Ipswich. They have supplied several first records of an earlier date than those given in Hind's Flora. The majority of species are now extinct. From these collections one can visualise the richness and beauty of the countryside around the town in the early 19th century.

A Hortus Siccus of eight volumes of dried specimens, compiled between 1840 and 1860, contains several rarities collected in Suffolk and elsewhere by various botanists, possibly on behalf of Ipswich Museum or a local Society.

The Museum also possesses a herbarium compiled by Lady Blake between 1840 and 1850, another compiled by the Rev. Prof. J. S. Henslow, c. 1860, containing Hitcham plants and one by the Rev. Prof. Edward Cowell of Ashbocking. In addition there is a small collection of local plants by Miss Manning of East Bergholt and a folio of specimens from the Needham Market area by Miss Jefferies.

CHAPTER NINE

The Magic of the Suffolk Flora

IT MAY be difficult for younger readers to visualise the beauty of the Suffolk countryside and its many wild flowers that still existed in the period between the two World Wars. Changes were taking place, but not on such a large scale as we have seen in recent times. These changes appear to be accelerating unfortunately. Villages and small towns had hardly expanded and had remained almost static for many years. Right into the early 1930's the motor car was still comparatively uncommon. There were no tractors. The horse was used as it had been for centuries. The real countryside seemed everywhere, just beyond the towns. The lanes, bridleways, and footpaths had their banks of Primroses and Violets and were lined by thick, tall hedges, many trees and small fields. Even the main roads were often no more than lanes. One thinks of the road from Hadleigh to Sudbury as an example and a section between Boxford and Newton is still known as Boxford Lane.

It was no problem finding many of the wild flowers which are rare or local today. The flowers were there each season and there seemed no fear of their disappearing. Woods and copses were still managed in the old way with their standard trees and coppice. Every year during winter and early spring the woodman would be cutting a section of coppice as woodmen had done for centuries. In the following April, May and June for two or three subsequent years, a profusion of flowers would appear.

In springtime a magic existed in the woods with their carpets of flowers. They seemed lit up, beautiful and enchanting and there was a chorus of birdsong such as is never heard today. There were carpets of Archangel, Anemones, Violets, Primroses, Oxlips and Water Avens, followed by Bluebells, Foxgloves, Herb Paris and Orchids.

Many of the old woods have now changed beyond recognition or gone forever. I can still recall visits to some especially lovely woods during this period, like the woods of Belstead and Bentley with their glades of Anemones, followed by a sea of Bluebells. The woods around Alnesbourne Priory leading down to the Orwell Shore at Mansell's Grove were also very beautiful with Archangel, Bluebells and Primroses; the Orwell shore and the saltings beyond, a mass of Sea Pinks. Other favourite bluebell woods were those at Sudbourne — Sudbourne Great Wood, an aboriginal oak wood now reduced to a thin strip, which in earlier days was much more extensive and, when viewed from Iken, looked full of mystery.

There were the Primrose and Oxlip woods of the clay soils with their great variety of flowers and wonderful scents. In many woods the Primroses, Oxlips, Anemones and Violets grew in such profusion that in some cases it was almost impossible to walk in some of the clearings without treading upon this carpet of flowers. Later the Early Purple Orchid would come up, sometimes in hundreds, and in June the Wood Spotted Orchids and Greater Butterfly Orchids would flower in thousands. Some of these woods exist today, but are very much changed. They still have their rides and many of the old flowers survive, in spite of the coniferous trees which have been planted, replacing the ancient deciduous trees and shrubs. One thinks of Lineage Wood, Stanstead Great Wood, Raydon Wood, Bruisyard Wood, Muckinger Wood, Culpho Wood and Park Wood, Chevington. Fortunately a few woods, or parts of woods, remain unchanged, such as the Bradfield Woods (Monks' Park and Felshamhall Wood) and Bull's Wood, Cockfield, to remind us of the glory of our heritage. However, some of the best Suffolk woods have gone, for example Lucy Wood, Elmsett, which, although small, was a real gem.

In the early 1920's before afforestation commenced in East Suffolk, the heaths, commons and warrens of the Sandlings were very extensive and stretched from the R. Orwell along the entire coastal stretch almost to Yarmouth. They were on the doorstep of Ipswich and one could walk mile after mile along the ancient track-ways used during Neolithic times and the Bronze Age. Everywhere there were the heathland flowers, the Bell Heather, Ling, Harebells, Carline Thistles and Honeysuckle. There were the sounds of the heathland birds and thousands of bees, both hive and wild species. Some of the areas were very wild and deserted; beautiful stretches of countryside, and it was indeed an experience to walk from Bromeswell to Butley and Wantisden or across Sutton Walks and Hollesley Heath to Shingle Street. In North-west Suffolk the Breckland was still very open and it seemed one vast semi-desert, stretching as far as the eye could see, to the Fens and Ely Cathedral on the horizon. There were belts of pines and a few mixed plantations, but these did not appear to spoil the open nature of the country. Not only was there the special Breck flora, but also countless numbers of the birds of open spaces, such as great flocks of Stone Curlew. Rabbits often reached plague proportions.

The river valleys still had their old pastures, water-meadows and marshes, which were so rich and colourful in spring and summer, yellow with Buttercups, Cowslips and, in some areas, Oxlips. There were tall Marguerites, Clovers, Meadow Saxifrage, Green-winged Orchid, Spotted Orchid and, in the wetter places, Kingcups and sometimes thousands of spikes of various Marsh Orchids. Suffolk rivers, streams, ponds and ditches were fringed with a great variety of most attractive flowers and many of the aquatic species were more abundant than they are today. During summer, a botanical ramble following the R.

Gipping from Ipswich to Claydon would be very rewarding. Water Violet was frequent, even right up to the Handford Bridge, Ipswich. Yellow Water Lily and Arrowhead grew in the deeper parts of the river. Flowering Rush grew every few yards and Marsh Cinquefoil in a number of habitats. The Gipping and its banks between Ipswich and Sproughton now convey a very sorry picture and little remains of its former beauty.

The Chalk flora of the Gipping valley especially was very good. The Man Orchid occurred in a number of sites, such as wayside verges, grassy banks, and the edges of quarries, and it was possible to find as many as two hundred flower spikes in a favourable season. This orchid is now very rare and local, needing very special protection. Felwort or Autumn Gentian grew on some wayside verges and Wild Thyme was seen in many old quarries, especially growing on and around ant-hills.

The vegetation of public parks has changed considerably during the passing of the years. In the 1920's it was still possible to find Cowslips in Christchurch Park, Ipswich, and other flowers and relics of the 19th century, when the park was privately owned and used for grazing. In Alexandra Park, Ipswich, the Pignut was common and managed to survive until about 1970. Holywells Park, also in Ipswich, was a sanctuary for its flora and bird life, with its Bluebells, Primroses, Sweet Violets and Wild Garlic, until it was opened to the public. Among its birds, the nightingale was very common.

The Suffolk Fens were a paradise for the botanist, with the richness and variety of their flora. The insectivorous plants, the three species of Sundew and the Common Butterwort, were abundant at Redgrave and other nearby fens, along with various Orchids, including the Fragrant Orchid, which occurred in immense numbers during July. Some of the spikes were especially well developed. There were many colour variations in the Early Marsh Orchids. The Marsh Helleborine was still common. In some out-of-the-way Fens the now extinct Fen Orchid could still be found in quite considerable numbers. The lovely Grass of Parnassus was abundant at Redgrave, where it is now very scarce indeed.

Between 1920 and 1940 a great deal of poor, arable farmland and rough grazing pasture, especially on the poorly drained Boulder Clay, went out of cultivation and soon became colonised by a rich and interesting flora and some species flourished to an almost unbelievable extent. Bee Orchids often appeared in their thousands around Grundisburgh, Wattisham, Barking, Ringshall and elsewhere. Other species of orchids, such as the Green-winged Orchid, the Early Purple Orchid, the Wood Spotted Orchid, the Pyramidal Orchid and the Greater Butterfly Orchid were often observed in large numbers.

Much of the Suffolk coast was still undiscovered and one could often wander all day along deserted beaches. Transport was limited and the holiday season then only extended for a few weeks of each year, from the last week in July until the first week in September. For the rest of the year, few people visited the coast, unlike today when easy travel and access enables them to invade the coast practically every week-end, even during the winter and early spring months. Wear and tear, and trampling, destroys or restricts the flora. One can recall the quiet beauty of Shingle Street and the great beaches stretching from East Lane, Bawdsey to Aldeburgh.

CHAPTER TEN

Conservation

NATURE conservation is not fully understood by the majority of ordinary people. To most people it means the preservation of an open space with some grass, trees and water, with ample facilities for various forms of recreation, plus a car park and picnic area. However, conservation has now become such an important subject, as the pressures of development continue to threaten and destroy much of our natural environment, that it should be taught in every school as part of the curriculum. It should also be thoroughly understood by every developer and planner.

The survival of habitats must not be left to chance. In recent years very many people have become aware of the great danger ahead, as they see the quality of life, especially the natural things, being rapidly eroded and replaced by ugly uniformity. Often something may happen quite suddenly, affecting their lives. Perhaps a wood, copse, hedge or a bit of heathland may be completely destroyed. One day machines move in and one is quite powerless to prevent destruction. The general situation is becoming very serious in some areas and one can only become pessimistic about the future. Almost daily one sees or hears about some important or interesting habitat being destroyed or damaged. The large excavators, dredgers, power-saws and other machinery are with us and have already completely devastated some of our Suffolk scenery.

In earlier times much of the wild life was preserved by reason of the very large private estates. Heavy taxation, death duty and inflation has meant the rapid splitting up and disintegration of many of these estates. A large number of new owners have completely changed the former pattern of estate management.

Until quite recently many botanists collected and preserved many of our rare flowers in herbaria, rather than allowing them to remain growing. Certain species were virtually robbed of every specimen by collectors. Many attractive species were dug up and removed to gardens. Woolpit Lilies and Suffolk Fritillaries were sold in London streets. During the 19th century there was a fern craze and the Rev. Zincke in his 'History of Wherstead' relates how a local site was robbed of its beautiful ferns and afterwards looked as though it had been blown up by dynamite. In the 1920's and 1930's the gypsies of Bramford Road, Ipswich, used to dig up Primroses, Cowslips, Early Purple Orchids and Ferns from local sites and hawk them round the streets of the town. People continue to remove Primroses to their gardens and in some places these have now been completely exterminated. Snowdrop bulbs are also frequently dug or pulled up, as well as various wild orchids, which stand little chance of survival in the conditions of an ordinary garden.

In the past the distribution of several species was reduced or threatened by the digging up of roots for herbal and other purposes. The tubers of the Early Purple Orchid were used in the preparation of a drink known as 'salep' and the roots of the Sea Holly were candied. Fortunately, the majority of these practices have died out in this century and medicinal herbs and other plants are now specially cultivated in gardens and nurseries.

New roads are constantly threatening and destroying habitats. We have seen, for instance, how a section of the Stowmarket By-pass has virtually destroyed the once attractive Creeting Hills, just north of Needham Market. The Ipswich Southern By-pass will destroy or damage a number of valuable woodlands and other types of habitat. Industry, houses and water development will continue to expand. It is unfortunate that many sites which were constructed as wartime aerodromes have been allowed to develop into industrial areas like, for example, the large-scale development at Martlesham Heath, a once extensive tract of beautiful ancient heathland.

It is very unfortunate that the lovely narrow valley between Tattingstone and Holbrook should have to be used as the site of a new reservoir known as Alton Water. This small valley was undoubtedly one of the best unspoilt remaining ones in East Suffolk and contained a number of important, although small, sites with a great wealth of interesting flora. Alton Covert was especially good, with its Red Crag springs and an abundance of such species as both the Alternate and Opposite-leaved Golden Saxifrages.

The Royal Society for Nature Conservation was the first national society in Britain to be concerned with the conservation of botanical and other habitats. It has acquired a few reserves in different parts of the country. Perhaps the most important is the Suffolk Bradfield Woods.

The Suffolk Preservation Society was founded in 1929, but has until recently been mainly concerned with buildings. The Society has, however, helped in saving trees from being felled, for example, a line of roadside Oaks at Assington. More recently the Society has co-operated with other preservation societies and with the Planning Authorities over conservation in general, especially of landscapes.

Agriculture and forestry have done more to change and destroy our flora than any other factors. Between the two World Wars farms were going out of production and large areas in the County were becoming very interesting habitats, as they reverted back to nature. Almost every farmer kept horses and a few cattle or sheep, and required grassland for their upkeep. This grassland was sometimes very ancient and had not been ploughed for centuries. About 1937 there were signs that there could be another war. There was a great revolution in farming; the tractor had been invented and was replacing the horse; woodland

and other land was being ploughed up and the danger to habitats was becoming apparent. In 1938 a chain of ancient Fritillary meadows, west of Debenham, from Derrybrook to the source of the R. Deben, was ploughed up. This was an area where the Fritillary was probably indigenous. There was little time left to save even one site, but, with the help of a few local naturalists and a small grant from the Royal Society for Nature Conservation, I was able to save a site of approximately 4½ acres at Mickfield. This was the first Suffolk nature reserve.

Towards the end of the Second World War, the Royal Society for Nature Conservation urged the Government to set up an organisation to look into the whole question of conservation in Britain. Various naturalists' societies were approached for information concerning suitable areas in need of protection and I was asked to submit a list of some of the more important sites in the County. The late Lord Ullswater, a prominent conservationist at the time, presided at a meeting in Ipswich to discuss the matter. In addition, the Government set up a board known as the Nature Conservancy, (now the Nature Conservancy Council) with limited funds, to acquire sites for national nature reserves and to schedule other sites for protection, to be known as 'Sites of Special Scientific Interest'. These sites are protected only by agreement with the owners or occupiers. This practice has continued. However, scheduling a site only gives limited protection.

In the 1950's and early 1960's the Royal Society for Nature Conservation organised the setting up of various County Naturalist Trusts, including one in Suffolk. The Suffolk Trust is now well established and acts as the major organisation in the County for the conservation of wild life habitats. Although the Trust does not actually own many reserves, it makes certain arrangements with owners to preserve interesting areas from changes which might threaten them. Greater support for the Trust is essential, to safeguard more of our threatened and vanishing heritage. The Trust also has agreements to protect a number of roadside verges from cutting, but unfortunately this does not always safeguard flora from the effects of crop spraying on adjacent fields. The sprays are often blown across a road to opposite verges.

The conservation of many woods, copses and hedges, which have played such an important part in the preservation of our landscape and wild life, has not always received sufficient support. As a result, several large areas of the County have now become very bare, as in Cambridgeshire and Lincolnshire. Very few people really realise the extent of the tree and hedgerow losses over the past twenty years. Although no actual figures are available, it is estimated that several million trees, mainly native species, have been destroyed, along with thousands of miles of hedgerow. This process continues. As we look across the countryside, we can see that the majority of the remaining trees, especially the Oaks, are past their best and are rapidly dying back. The Elms, which were such a feature of the landscape, are dying from Dutch Elm disease. In some areas practically every remaining old hedgerow tree shows signs of damage by burning, resulting from stubble fires. We should like to see the retention of more of our native trees and hedges, especially those bordering roads, ancient parish boundaries and the once important green lanes. Unfortunately, many of the original lanes have now been made hedgeless and have been ploughed up, although they are still rights of way. There are, however, Tree Preservation Orders in the County, covering limited areas of woodland, a few amenity belts of trees and some individual specimens.

Hedgecutting machines, besides making hedges look very unsightly, do not allow for the growth and development of the natural saplings. In the past these would be left by the hedge trimmers. The natural saplings and strong basal growths form the real basis for the replacement of trees. They are indigenous specimens and grow more rapidly and will succeed where planted trees fail. They cost nothing to buy and there are no labour charges for planting and staking. Every year I see seedling trees, especially Oaks, coming up from acorns. Many could be left to develop and perhaps be marked in some way to ensure their conservation. This work could be carried out by preservation societies and schools. This idea appears to be the most satisfactory way of making sure of the survival of many of our native trees and replacing the millions we have lost in the past two decades.

When property changes hands, it is usually the trees that suffer most. Even trees with Preservation Orders on them are not always immune from damage. Quite a number of people consider that trees, to be trees, must be lopped and trimmed to stumps, only allowing for annual growth of small branches. Trees must be allowed to grow naturally to be beautiful. Local authorities, to whom lovely grounds and parks have been donated, usually fell large numbers of trees and remove shrubs and other natural vegetation, so that grass-cutting machines can operate without hindrance, turning once attractive areas into mere recreation grounds.

The draining and ploughing-up of marshes and old river valley meadows and pastures has accelerated during recent years, as has the filling in of thousands of ponds and many old ditches. This has, of course, meant the almost complete disappearance of several habitats of interesting species. Formerly in Suffolk, more especially on the clay areas, almost every field had ditches, which drained into ponds and these helped to maintain many small springs and streams. Farms and cottages also had their ponds, which supplied their domestic requirements and there were many roadside ponds. These have also disappeared with the coming of piped water supplies.

The wetlands are important catchment areas for maintaining our underground water supplies and the continual loss of such areas will, in the long run, result in the drying up of many springs and the lowering of the water level in the chalk.

The upper reaches of many of our rivers have been destroyed or changed. Trees and other vegetation have been removed and the river beds are now little more than drainage channels. Bends and other obstructions have been removed to hasten the flow of water to the sea, and marginal vegetation has continually been cut back. More recently there has been a restoration of several village ponds. These, however, are usually quite unsuitable as habitats for many forms of wild life and are merely ornamental duck ponds.

The demand for water increases, yet we continue to destroy or damage the resources. Extraction of underground water from bore holes at Redgrave has seriously affected Redgrave and Lopham Fens, causing them to become too dry, with the consequent loss of many interesting and rare species. Some plant communities are very delicately balanced and the removal of surrounding vegetation and their water supply can cause their complete disappearance. There is little doubt that the retention of the natural vegetation assists in increasing the annual rainfall and humidity of the district.

There appears to be far too much indiscriminate cutting of many wayside verges and hedgebanks. The wild flower lover complains that as soon as the countryside is decked with its spring display, the machines come out. This process goes on throughout the summer. Cowslips are cut off before their seeds can ripen, the stems of Orchids likewise suffer. Orchids send up only one annual flowering stem and these are often cut off before, or during, flowering in May, June or July.

The increasing demands for recreational facilities on the sea coast and its estuaries place additional strains on various habitats, especially the beaches. In Suffolk we have designated areas of the coast and estuaries for special protection. However, this does not prevent some developments, such as new power stations, radio sites, car parks, caravan sites and marinas. Some sea-shore plants are very vulnerable to human disturbance through trampling and wearing away of the dunes and shingle ridges. The vegetation of parts of the Minsmere Cliffs and nearby beaches has been worn away by an excess of visitors, as have other areas at Felixstowe Ferry, Bawdsey and Benacre.

The commons, heaths and warrens fringing the estuaries are frequently burned and many of those in private hands have been ploughed up in recent years, such as Iken Warren, Sutton Walks and Snape Warren.

The ancient fringes of trees bordering the estuaries are disappearing through erosion, as after the high tides of January, 1953, and also through felling and burning. Thousands of old trees have vanished and unfortunately have not been replaced. This tree fringe represents, in some instances, relics of the forest which once came down to the shores.

The protection from picking and uprooting of certain attractive flowers growing in vulnerable positions, such as near paths and waysides, cannot always be carried out. Individuals can sometimes protect colonies, for example, by concealing them with old bracken and brambles and other dried vegetation. At other times it may be possible to give some protection at weekends, when usually the greatest danger arises, by acting as a warden at that site. For instance, I successfully guarded a fine flowering colony of Sea Holly, growing close to a path near Dunwich, by sitting near the plants for several weekends. I can usually identify vandals, even at a distance!

Eriophorum latifolium Broad-leaved Cotton-grass Brent Eleigh 1939

CHAPTER ELEVEN

Some Suffolk Habitats to Visit

BEGINNERS, students and more especially visiting botanists, frequently request information concerning the areas of the County where some of the typical or local flora may be observed. The following list covers a wide range and variety of habitats. It must be stressed that many sites are not fully accessible; permission must be obtained where necessary. However, public roads or footpaths border or cross the majority, and from these the flora may be studied. Specimens of uncommon species should never be collected.

The Suffolk Trust for Nature Conservation owns, leases, manages or has certain agreements with owners of a number of sites. Only a few of the sites are mentioned in this list, because of the difficulty of access or the safe-guarding of rare species. More details should be obtained from the Secretary of the Trust. Maps which show public roads, bridleways and footpaths should always be consulted.

West Suffolk
Clare Country Park.
(Suffolk County Council).
Old railway station and castle remains. Railway cutting and water habitats.
A number of interesting species have been observed in the area. The soil is mainly Chalky Boulder Clay.

Monks' Park and Felshamhall Wood.
(Royal Society for Nature Conservation).
Primary and secondary woodland. Relic flora on Boulder Clay.
Footpath.

Groton Wood.
(Suffolk Trust for Nature Conservation).
Primary and medieval woodland. Interesting flora. Small-leaved Lime.
No public footpath.

Cavenham and Tuddenham Heaths.
(Nature Conservancy Council).
Dry heath and Breck to wet marsh and fens, bordering the R. Lark.
Public tracks.

West Stow Heath and Icklingham Plains.
>   (Private and Forestry Commission).
>   Good flora with several Breckland species.
>   Access by public tracks.

Cornard Mere, near Sudbury.
>   (Common land).
>   Marsh flora: very little open water remains.

Lakenheath Poor's Fen.
>   (Suffolk Trust for Nature Conservation).
>   Fen and heath vegetation.
>   Access by application to warden.

East Suffolk

Saxtead Green, near Framlingham.
>   Typical High Suffolk green on Boulder Clay, with ditches and a pond.

Hadleigh, old railway track.
>   Mainly through Boulder Clay. Good flora with a few local species.
>   Footpath to Raydon.

Staverton Park and The Thicks.
>   (Private).
>   Very ancient deer park with many pollarded oaks and large hollies.
>   Dry woodland.
>   View from road or footpath.

Wolves Wood, near Hadleigh.
>   (Royal Society for the Protection of Birds).
>   Typical woodland on Boulder Clay with a variety of trees, shrubs and herbs.
>   This wood is probably very old. Its more correct name is Wool's Wood after Wool's Hall, which was nearby.
>   No public footpaths, but adjacent to road.

Westleton Heath (Nature Conservancy Council) and Dunwich Common.
>   Acid heathland species.
>   Limited access.

Rushmere Common, near Ipswich.
>   (Golf Course).
>   Dry, sandy and gravelly habitats, close to town. A number of typical heathland species have survived.
>   Public footpaths.

Piper's Vale, Gainsborough Lane, Ipswich.
>   (Borough of Ipswich).
>   Ancient former heath and woodland sloping down to the R. Orwell.

Wenhaston Common.
>   Sandy and gravelly common with general typical flora and some marginal species from adjacent arable.
>   Public footpaths and tracks.

Redgrave Fen.
>(Suffolk Trust for Nature Conservation).
>Old valley fen. Many interesting species have been recorded from this fen. Much drier than formerly.
>One public footpath.

River Gipping, especially between Ipswich and Bramford, and at Needham Market.
>Aquatic and marginal vegetation.
>Access by old towing path.

River Waveney at Bungay and Beccles.
>Aquatic and marginal flora.
>Access by public paths.

Finn Valley.
>(Private).
>Alder Carr between Rushmere and Playford. Small area with mixed flora bordering the R. Finn.
>Access by footpath only.

Burgh Castle and Breydon Water and Marshes.
>(Private and Nature Conservancy Council).
>Estuarine, salt marsh and other habitats.
>Limited access by public footpaths.

Blyth Estuary.
>(Private and Nature Conservancy Council).
>Interesting area with variety of habitats, estuarine, marshes and heathland.
>Access by public footpaths and by track of old Southwold Railway, Blythburgh to Walberswick.

Snape Marshes, River Alde.
>(Mainly private).
>Brackish marshes. Good flora.
>Access by footpaths only.

Aldeburgh, south to Slaughden, and Rivers Alde and Ore.
>Coastal, shingle beaches and salt marshes.
>Limited access by footpaths only.

Orford, R. Ore.
>Saltings, dykes and general habitats.
>Public footpath on embankment to Gedgrave.

Woodbridge, banks of the R. Deben and saltings between Martlesham Creek, Kyson and Melton.
>Mainly salt marsh flora, dykes and pastures.
>Access by public footpaths.

Chelmondiston, Pin Mill, R. Orwell estuary.
>Salt marshes and general adjacent habitats.
>Public footpaths.

Benacre to Kessingland.
    Coastal flora, several interesting species survive.
Walberswick to Dunwich.
    (Partly Nature Conservancy Council).
    Heaths, marshes, brackish and coastal flora. Extensive reed beds.
    Access by public paths.
Sizewell to Thorpeness.
    Shingle and sandy beach. Varied flora.
Hollesley and Shingle Street.
    Maritime habitats, shingle beach and salt marsh flora.

East and West Suffolk
River Stour near East Bergholt, at Bures, Nayland and Sudbury.
    Access by footpaths and old towing paths.

State forests
Mainly coniferous. These have usually been planted by the Forestry Com-
    mission on heaths, Breckland and poor agricultural land. They are situated
    in various districts and often extend over considerable areas.
Forests to visit:
    Rendlesham; Tunstall; Dunwich; The King's Forest, in Breckland.
    In the glades and more open spaces, some of the flora of the former habitats
    survives.
    Access is usually by public roads, tracks and paths.

For information on other sites the Suffolk Trust for Nature Conservation
can be contacted.

CHAPTER TWELVE

Arrangement and Classification of the Flora

Nomenclature

AS FAR AS possible the arrangement and nomenclature is based on J. E. Dandy's 'List of British Vascular Plants', published in 1958, and his corrections given in 'Watsonia 7 — Journal and Proceedings of the Botanical Society of the British Isles', and also the already published parts of 'Flora Europaea' (Vols. I, II, III and IV). This arrangement is very similar to that of Clapham, Tutin and Warburg's 'Flora of the British Isles', Second Edition, 1962. Synonyms have been given, where appropriate, to enable those botanists who do not possess these works to identify the majority of plants concerned, and it is hoped that readers possessing only some of the popular older books on wild flowers will be able to trace most species. A large number of the popular books on wild flowers give only a selection of the more attractive flowers. Many species in this Flora will not be found in these books.

Many changes in nomenclature have been made since Hind's 'Flora of Suffolk', 1889, and there have been several problems in correlating some of his records with present-day classification.

For the Charophyta, the arrangement used is, with certain revisions, that of G. O. Allen's 'British Stoneworts', 1950.

English Names

English names, including a large number of old local names, are given, unless the plant concerned is a critical species or subspecies, or an alien or casual, where there is so far no recognised English name. Names we have used include the official ones suggested by the Botanical Society of the British Isles. It is probable, however, that a number of old or local Suffolk names have been omitted. Various wild flowers have the same name; for instance, the name 'Cuckoo Flower' can refer to several species flowering during April and May with the arrival of the cuckoo, e.g. Lady's Smock (*Cardamine pratensis*), Early Purple Orchid (*Orchis mascula*), Wood Anemone (*Anemone nemorosa*), Ragged Robin (*Lychnis flos-cuculi*). Another example is Shirt Buttons or Billy Buttons, which can refer either to Greater Stitchwort (*Stellaria holostea*) or to White Campion (*Silene alba*).

Liparis loeselii   Fen Orchid   Thelnetham 1939

CHAPTER THIRTEEN

Recording

RECORDS in the Flora are based on the 10-kilometre grid squares of the Ordnance Survey Maps. The Flora covers the pre-1974 boundaries, but includes also two small areas south of the Rivers Waveney and Little Ouse, now in Norfolk. One of these areas, part of Lothingland, comprises the parishes of Burgh Castle, Belton, Bradwell, Gorleston and Southtown. The second area, south of the Little Ouse at Thetford, comprises Barnham Cross Common and Thetford Warren. It was agreed with the Editors of the Norfolk Flora that we should treat both these areas botanically as belonging to Suffolk. Newmarket, in the extreme West of the County, is in Suffolk, but only a small area of Newmarket Heath. The rest of the Heath and also the Devil's Ditch are in Cambridgeshire.

In 1852 H. C. Watson had the idea of dividing Britain into 112 'vice-counties' for the recording of its flora. He divided Suffolk into two vice-counties, East Suffolk (v.c. 25) and West Suffolk (v.c. 26), the division of the County being the one degree line of longitude. Records in this Flora are not based on the Watsonian vice-county system. All 10 km. squares in 100 km. square 52 (TL) are taken to be West Suffolk and all those in 100 km. squares 62 (TM) and 63 (TG) are taken to be East Suffolk. We include a map to enable readers to refer to the squares where the species have been recorded. For the uncommon species, which have only been recorded in a few squares, details of parishes or actual habitats have been included. In the case of a few very rare species, which might be in danger from collectors and other hazards, no exact site is mentioned. However, keen botanists should still be able to find the majority of rarities, if still in existence, by studying maps and geological formations and by understanding the requirements of a particular species.

Some of the squares have not been fully recorded, while others have been covered very well by more than one botanist. Some species may therefore be more frequent than the records show, especially critical species and those which many botanists have tended to avoid, such as grasses, sedges, rushes and ferns. While some contributors supplied more than one complete card covering several parishes, others only marked a few of the common or well-known flowers.

However good the records in a flora appear to be, certain errors do occur, which, for a number of reasons, are not always eliminated by the editor. The botanist supplying the records may be considered first-class and therefore it is thought unnecessary to verify them. Sometimes a map has not been used, and so a particular habitat, perhaps a wood, heath or common, even one bearing a parish name, may actually be in more than one parish. Sometimes a recorder has supplied list of plants thought to have been found in his or her home parish, but which have in fact been found in a number of adjacent parishes. Hind's Flora obviously has a number of such errors; for instance, some of the parish records for uncommon Breckland plants are thought to be incorrect. Where the parishes of Icklingham, Cavenham, Risby and Tuddenham have been mentioned for some species, it is considered that the species only occurred on one site, and the recorder, without a map, may have looked for a landmark, probably a church, to site the find. A few old herbarium sheets which I have examined have given more precise information.

In compiling this Flora it has proved quite impossible to be absolutely certain that every 10 km square number quoted is correct or to include every record. The number of errors is, however, I feel, relatively small, and some readers may be able to rectify the mistakes for themselves.

However long one may take to compile a Flora it can never be complete, as the countryside and its habitats are changing all the time. New plants are appearing and spreading and the natives retreating. I have brought the Flora up to date by including recent records and existing sites for some of the more interesting species. Most of these sites are on public rights of way.

CHAPTER FOURTEEN

The Catalogue

EACH entry in the catalogue consists of:

(1) Scientific name, plus synonyms, where necessary.
(2) English name, plus local name, if in common use.
(3) Date of first record, with name of recorder.
(4) Status of the species in Suffolk.
(5) Notes on habitat and relative frequency.
(6) Detailed distribution in (a) West and (b) East Suffolk on the basis of the 10 km squares, or of individual parishes.
(7) Interesting recent records or sites, such as public footpaths or reserves, where the species may still be seen.

Unless otherwise stated, all records are post-1950. The majority of the recent records have been made by F. W. Simpson, M. A. Hyde and Mrs E. M. Hyde.

Of the squares shared with other counties, all but two have been treated as complete Suffolk squares. In the case of 08 and 56, of which only very small areas are in Suffolk, only uncommon plants have been included. These squares have been ignored when a species is said to be in 'All squares except . . .' or 'All squares'.

The term *'alien'* is frequently applied to any plant that does not appear to be native in its particular habitat. There are a number of classes of aliens: *casuals*, which appear from time to time and are not established; these include those found on waste ground around docks, timber yards, tanneries, etc. and those which derive from discarded bird seed and imported seed, such as, for example, Canary Grass; *established aliens*, which are able to maintain their stations and even increase their range, such as Pineapple Weed; *naturalised introductions*, such as Winter Heliotrope and Buddleia; *colonists*, which include some of the long-established weeds of arable land, cornfields and waysides. A familiar example is the Common Poppy. It must be remembered that the artificially created waysides have been colonised by both natives and aliens.

The term *'denizen'* is often used to describe a number of species which are regarded as natives of the British Flora, but which do not always occur in their natural habitats and are dependent on man-made habitats, such as walls and buildings.

CATALOGUE
OF
SPECIES

CHARACEAE

STONEWORT FAMILY

Stoneworts have been rather neglected by botanists, owing to the difficulty of identification. There is, however, an excellent book by the late G. O. Allen, "British Stoneworts".
Stoneworts favour clean, clear water, such as undisturbed ponds, ditches, dykes, calcareous wet fens and slow-flowing rivers. They prefer alkaline habitats, which are rich in lime. They are often found in an encrusted condition.

Nitella opaca (Bruz.) Agardh   Opaque Nitella   Dawson Turner 1799

In ponds, pools and ditches. Very rare. Last recorded by R. Burn from a pond near Camp's Wood, Brent Eleigh. Date unknown, but probably in the mid-1930's. Recorded in Hind's Flora from Lakenheath in 1883 by Dr G. C. Druce, and from Hopton in 1799. (Hb. Dawson Turner).

Nitella flexilis (L.) Agardh   Flexile Nitella   Buddle 1724

In ponds and ditches. Very rare or overlooked. Only recorded for East Suffolk. The last time I saw this species was in a pond at Elmsett (sq. 04) in 1932. Habitat now destroyed. Recorded in Hind's Flora from Hopton Common, Fritton Decoy and in ponds about Henley.

Nitella translucens (Pers.) Agardh   Translucent Nitella   Sir W. J. Hooker 1812

In ponds and lakes. Very rare or extinct. The only record dates back to 1812, when found by Sir W. J. Hooker at Browston in a turf pit (sq. 40).

Nitella mucronata (A. Braun) Miquel var. **mucronata** Canon G. R. Bullock-Webster 1897

In ponds and rivers. Found in the Little Ouse in 1897. Although claimed for Norfolk, it could very well also belong to Suffolk, as the Little Ouse is the County boundary.

Nitella tenuissima (Desv.) Kütz.

In fen pools. Very rare. Recorded for Lopham Fen in Norfolk in 1897. This species could also occur in the pools of Redgrave Fen, as the two fens adjoin, and are only divided by a ditch, the R. Waveney.

Tolypella intricata (Trent. ex Roth) Leonh.   Intricate Tolypella
(*T. polysperma* Ziz)   C. C. Babington 1860

Native. In pools and ditches. Very rare and sporadic in its appearance. Last recorded by F. W. Simpson from a ditch at Mickfield (sq. 16) between 1963 and 1965, but has not been seen since. Recorded in Hind's Flora from Bury St Edmunds in 1860.

Tolypella glomerata (Desv.) Leonh.   Glomerate Tolypella   Dr G. C. Druce 1883

Native. In ditches and dykes. Sometimes in brackish conditions. Very rare or overlooked. Recorded from Lakenheath in 1883.

Tolypella nidifica (O. Müll.) Leonh.   G. H. Rocke 1957

Native. Found in brackish water. Very rare. Collected at Easton Broad (sq. 57) in 1957, and determined by G. O. Allen.

Chara canescens Desv. & Lois.   Finder not recorded c. 1890
(C. crinita Wallr.)

In brackish broads, pools and ditches. Rare, possibly extinct.
E: 57, Easton Broad, c. 1920 and in 1957 (G. H. Rocke), detd. G. O. Allen; 58, Benacre Broad, c. 1890.

Chara vulgaris L. var. **vulgaris**   Common Stonewort   Sir J. Cullum 1773
                                     Common Chara

In ponds, ditches, streams and rivers. More frequent on the Chalky Boulder Clay. Formerly common with a widespread distribution in both East and West Suffolk, now much reduced.
W: 67, Mildenhall; Freckenham, 1977 (F.W.S.).
E: 24, Brightwell, 1980 (F.W.S.).
There are two other recorded varieties, namely:
var. **papillata** Wallr. Very rare. Recorded by Hind from Thelnetham in 1883. Mildenhall, 1977. Detd. Mrs J. A. Moore.
var. **longibracteata** (Kütz.) Groves and Bullock-Webster. Not uncommon and possibly overlooked. Recorded from Aldham, Lt. Blakenham and Mildenhall, 1977.

Chara hispida L.   Hispid Chara   Sir J. Cullum 1774

In fen pools and ditches. Local and decreasing. Still occurs, but is now extinct in some former localities recorded by Hind.
W: 95, Cockfield Rectory Moat, 1939; 97, Hopton Fen, 1981 (F.W.S.). Detd. Mrs J. A. Moore.
E: 07, Redgrave Fen; Thelnetham Fen, c. 1950.

Chara contraria A. Braun ex Kütz.   Opposite Chara   Hind 1883

In ponds and ditches. Very rare or extinct. It is similar to *C. vulgaris*, but a smaller and more variable species. There are no recent records. Recorded in Hind's Flora from Livermere, 1885.

Chara aculeolata Kütz.   Prickly Chara   Hind 1883
(*C. polyacantha* A. Braun)

In fen pools. Very rare or extinct. Recorded in Hind's Flora from Thelnetham, Market Weston, Sapiston and Barton Mere. Last seen in Thelnetham in 1940 (F. W. Simpson).

Chara aspera Deth. ex Willd.   Rough Chara   Hind 1876

In fen pools and lakes. Rare and local. A very brittle species, heavily encrusted. Hind records it from Coney and Market Weston, Hopton and Redgrave Fens, and also from Benacre Broad. Recorded by F. W. Simpson from Redgrave Fen (sq. 07) c. 1952.

Chara connivens Salzm. ex A. Braun

Recorded in 1911 in the Victoria County History of Suffolk, but no parishes mentioned.

Chara globularis Thuill.   Brittle Chara   Hind 1876
(*C. fragilis* Desv.   Hedwig's Chara
var. *hedwigii* (Bruz.) Kütz.)

In ditches and sandy pools, both fresh and brackish. Rare or overlooked. A very variable species with extreme forms linked by intermediates. Much confused in the past.
W: 86, Hengrave Hall Park, 1932 (F.W.S.); 95, Felshamhall Wood, 1972 (F.W.S.).

PTERIDOPHYTA

Nomenclature has undergone several changes in recent years and both the Latin and English names used for some species are very numerous and confusing to many amateur botanists. Earlier names are often omitted from recent British Floras. However, we have given the synonyms where possible.

LYCOPODIACEAE

CLUBMOSS FAMILY

Lycopodium inundatum L.   Marsh Clubmoss   Davy 1795

Native. On wet heaths. Now extinct. Recorded in Hind's Flora from Tuddenham, Herringfleet, Lound and Belton Commons, Bungay and Westleton, but there are no records during the present century. Last record, c. 1860.
Davy's specimen from Westleton Heath, 1795, is in Hb. Ipswich Museum.

Lycopodium clavatum L.   Common Clubmoss   Sir J. Cullum 1773
                          Stagshorn Clubmoss

Native. Found on heaths. Probably extinct. The only record in Hind's Flora is from Tuddenham Heath (sq. 77) and the only known record for Suffolk during the present century is from Snape (sq. 35) by Mrs J. Gray in 1941.

EQUISETACEAE

HORSETAIL FAMILY

Equisetum hyemale L.   Rough Horsetail   Sir J. Cullum 1775
                          Dutch Rush

Native. Banks of streams and moist places in woods. Probably extinct in Suffolk. This interesting species formerly occurred in at least six parishes in West Suffolk, and is recorded in Hind's Flora from the Bradfields, Hawstead, Drinkstone, Woolpit, Hardwick and Hitcham. All these parishes lie within the four map squares 85, 86, 95 and 96. The habitats were no doubt ancient and the plant endemic to this area. There is a later record for Lothingland in Victoria County History. We can assume that these habitats have long been destroyed or greatly changed, as nothing has been seen of this species since c. 1906. All the old records were made by good botanists. The plant is now very rare in E. and S. England. The stems have a 'flinty' exterior coating, and were formerly used by Dutch cabinet makers for polishing furniture.

EQUISETACEAE

Equisetum fluviatile L. Water Horsetail J. Andrews 1746
(*E. limosum* L.) Smooth Naked Horsetail

Native. In ponds, ditches and marshes. Common.
W: All squares except 64; 65; 66; 68; 75; 78; 84; 95.
77, Tuddenham Heath, 1979.
E: All squares except 05; 16; 17; 27; 28; 38; 44; 47.
35, Snape, 1981; 39, Bungay, 1981.

Equisetum fluviatile × telmateia F. W. Simpson 1928

This interesting hybrid extends over an area of marshy ground and on the banks of the R.
Deben near Glevering Mill, Wickham Market. The area was formerly a shallow lake in the
Deben watercourse. Observed in this habitat in 1928 but not then identified. Detd. E. L.
Swann, 1972.

Equisetum palustre L. Marsh Horsetail J. Andrews 1743

Native. In wet pastures, marshes, and beside ponds and rivers. Common.
W: All squares except 64; 65; 66; 74; 75; 85.
76, Gazeley, 1979.
E: All squares except 26; 36; 48.
24, Playford, 1981; 25, Bromeswell Green, 1980.

Equisetum sylvaticum L. Wood Horsetail Sir J. Cullum 1775

Native. Damp woods and shady banks. Very rare or extinct. Recorded in Hind's Flora
1889, but no locality mentioned. This is one of the species I have not found in the County,
although there are many suitable habitats. The recent records are very doubtful. A rather
beautiful Horsetail, which has disappeared in recent years from a number of localities and
decreased in others in Gt Britain and Ireland. Last authentic record 1775.
E: 04, Hadleigh, 1960; 37, Halesworth (E. R. Long).

Equisetum arvense L. Common Horsetail Sir J. Cullum 1773
Corn Horsetail

Native. A weed of cultivated fields, hedge banks, quarries and rough places. Very
common. Prostrate plants are frequent.
All squares.

Equisetum arvense × fluviatile Mrs J. Gray 1941
(*E.* × *litorale* Kühlew. ex Rupr.)

A rare hybrid found in damp old pastures and wayside ditches.
E: 04, Hintlesham, 1978; 07; 13, Stutton; 36, Benhall.

Equisetum arvense × telmateia F. W. Simpson 1974
(*E.* × *dubium* Dostál)

E: 24, edge of a shady marsh at Foxhall, an old-established colony; 40, Belton, 1977.

Equisetum telmateia Ehrh.　　　Great Horsetail　　　　　　Woodward 1805
(*E. maximum* auct.)

Native. Damp woods, banks, cliffs and wet pastures, especially where there are springs. More frequent in the South-east on the London Clay and Red Crag. Locally abundant.
W: 74; 83, Lt. Cornard; 93, Polstead; Bures; Stoke-by-Nayland; 94, Brent Eleigh, 1981; 97, Ixworth Thorpe.
E: 03, East Bergholt; Capel St Mary; 04, Hadleigh; 13, Bentley; Tattingstone; Woolverstone; Freston; Wherstead; Stutton; 14, Bourne, Chantry and Holywells Parks, Ipswich; Washbrook; Sproughton; 23, Levington; Shotley; Pin Mill; Falkenham; 24, Playford; Gt and Lt. Bealings; 25, Melton; Bromeswell; 33, Bawdsey; 34, Sutton; Ramsholt; 37, Cookley, 1979; 38, Spexhall, 1976; 46, Leiston; 48, Ellough; Barnby; 49, Ilketshall St Lawrence. Still there, 1981, in the majority of these sites.

Illustrated page 466

OPHIOGLOSSACEAE

ADDER'S TONGUE FAMILY

Ophioglossum vulgatum L.　　　Adder's Tongue　　　　　　J. Andrews 1746

Native. Old pastures, pits, scrub and damp clay woods. Widespread and fairly frequent, but has disappeared from many habitats in recent years, due to land reclamation.
W: All squares except 65; 66; 67; 75; 83; 86; 88; 98.
94, Chelsworth, 1981.
E: All squares except 03; 17; 23; 26; 27; 28; 33; 38; 44; 45; 48; 58; 50.
04, Hintlesham, 1981; 05, Barking, 1981; 16, Framsden, Fritillary Meadow, 1981; 25, a large colony in old pasture, Rookery Farm, Monewden, 1981; 46, Minsmere, 1981.

Illustrated page 466

Botrychium lunaria (L.) Sw.　　　Moonwort　　　　　　Sir J. Cullum 1773

Native. Heaths and old pastures. Very local and possibly extinct in some former habitats.
W: 77, Mildenhall, 1980; Black Hill, Icklingham, 1967 (J. M. Schofield) and Deadman's Grave, 1973; 78, Lakenheath Warren, 1974; Wangford Warren; 88, Thetford Warren.
E: 59, Lowestoft; 40, Belton Heath (reported extinct, 1947).

OSMUNDACEAE

ROYAL FERN FAMILY

Osmunda regalis L.　　　Royal Fern　　　　　　Sir J. Cullum 1776
　　　　　　　　　　　　Flowering Fern

Native. Wet, boggy heaths and carrs, dune-slacks. Very scarce. Formerly more frequent, but now extinct in many old habitats.
E: 13, Woolverstone (planted, recorded in Hind's Flora and still there in 1981); 46, Sizewell, site destroyed by the construction of the Power Station; 47, Dingle Marshes; 40, near Fritton Lake.
Hind also recorded it from Aldeburgh, Iken, Herringfleet, Benacre, Lound, Flixton, Hopton, but it is probably now extinct at these sites.

ADIANTACEAE

MAIDENHAIR FAMILY

Adiantum capillus-veneris L.   Maidenhair Fern   F. W. Simpson 1977

Denizen on walls. Native in S.W. England, Wales and Ireland.
W: 93, Nayland, well-established colony, 1980 (J. C. Williams).
E: 14, small colony on a sheltered brick wall near the centre of Ipswich, 1977-1981; also in
grating, Arcade St, Ipswich, 1977 (M. A. Hyde).   *Illustrated page 465*

PTERIDACEAE

RIBBON FERN FAMILY

Pteris cretica L.   Ribbon Fern   F. W. Simpson 1962
                         Cretan Brake

Native of S. Europe. Found in the old brickwork of a street drain at the junction of Rope
Walk and Milner Street, Ipswich. Detd. A. C. Jermy.

DENNSTAEDTIACEAE

BRACKEN FAMILY

Pteridium aquilinum (L.) Kuhn   Bracken   Sir J. Cullum 1773
(*Pteris aquilina* L.)   Common Brake

Native. Heaths, commons, woods, banks, chiefly on sand or gravel. Often dominant and
smothering other flora . Very common. Also found in towns on walls. Reproduction by
spores is not very frequent and is more frequently observed on buildings. The young
plants with their rounded pinnules can easily be mistaken for other species of ferns.
All squares.

THELYPTERIDACEAE

MARSH FERN FAMILY

Thelypteris limbosperma (All.) H. P. Fuchs   Mountain Fern   Paget 1834
(*Dryopteris oreopteris* (Ehrh.) Maxon   Lemon-scented Fern
Aspidium oreopteris (Ehrh.) Sw.)

Native. On old heaths and in woods. Very rare.
W: 95, Felshamhall and Monks' Park Woods.
E: 49; 40, Fritton Decoy; Ashby Warren.

Thelypteris palustris Schott   Marsh Fern   J. Andrews 1754
(*Dryopteris thelypteris* (L.) A. Gray)

Native. On wet heaths and in woods. Rare and decreasing.
W: 77; 78; 98.
77, Cavenham, Ash Plantation, 1979.
E: 07; 24; 49; 40.
24, Bixley Decoy, 1979; 40, Belton, 1978.

ASPLENIACEAE

SPLEENWORT FAMILY

Asplenium trichomanes L.   Maidenhair Spleenwort   Rev. G. Crabbe 1798

A denizen on walls, churches, ruins and old buildings. Rather scarce.
W: All squares except 64; 65; 67; 68; 93; 97; 98.
74, Clare Country Park on Station wall, in quantity, 1976; 76, Moulton, 1981; 88, Santon Downham, 1981.
E: All squares except 15; 17; 33; 35; 40; 44; 46; 50.
14, Ipswich, 1981; 16, Thorndon Church, 1975; 24, Woodbridge Station, 1981; 26, Framlingham Castle; 39, Bungay, 1981; 49, Carlton Colville, 1973.

Asplenium adiantum-nigrum L.   Black Spleenwort   Sir J. Cullum 1773

Native on old hedge-banks and a denizen of walls. Fairly widespread.
W: 66; 74; 76; 77; 83; 85; 87; 88; 93; 94; 95; 96.
87, West Stow, 1980; 96, Beyton, Churchyard wall, 1979.
E: 03; 05; 06; 07; 13; 14; 16; 17; 23; 25; 26; 35; 38; 39; 46; 47; 48; 58; 59; 40; 50.
13, Woolverstone School, 1981; 14, Washbrook, 1977; Wherstead, 1980; 23, Trimley, railway bridge, 1980; 23, Landguard Fort, 1979; 39, Bungay, 1981.
Hb. Ipswich Museum: 'At Wherstead between Mr Vernon's and Stalls Valley Farm, west side of the road with *Polypodium vulgare*', c. 1820 (John Notcutt).

Asplenium ruta-muraria L.   Wall-rue   Parkinson 1640

A denizen on walls, bridges and old buildings. Widespread and fairly frequent.
W: All squares except 65; 67; 68; 75; 83; 93; 95; 98.
66, Moulton Churchyard wall, 1978; 74, wall, Clare Country Park, 1976.
E: All squares except 06; 14; 15; 16; 28; 33; 34; 36; 37; 44.
23, Trimley Station, 1981; 39, Bungay, 1981; 57, Southwold Churchyard wall, 1979.
Rev. G. R. Leathes gathered a specimen from Aldeburgh Church walls in 1795 and it could still be found there in 1975.   *Illustrated page 464*

Ceterach officinarum DC.   Rusty-back Fern   Parkinson 1640
(*Asplenium ceterach* L.)

Native. On old walls and buildings. Very rare.
W: 86, Bury St Edmunds, 1955.
E: 28, Church wall, Mendham (destroyed during restoration, 1970/71); 36, Benhall, 1941; 59, brick wall by Lake Lothing, 1977 (R. S. Briggs). Still there, 1981.
Recorded by Hind only from Bury St Edmunds, Lavenham, Mendham Church wall and Framlingham.

ASPLENIACEAE

Phyllitis scolopendrium (L.) Newm.   Hart's-tongue Fern   Rev. G. Crabbe 1798
(*Scolopendrium vulgare* Sm.
Asplenium scolopendrium L.)

Native. Shady banks, sides of ditches, old walls, wells, churches and ruins. Widespread, but not usually in any quantity. A number of varieties have been reported, usually in gardens.
W: All squares except 67; 68; 76; 77; 87.
E: All squares except 44; 40; 50.
A very fine colony on both banks of a deep ditch in sq. 33, with fronds approaching 2 ft growing with Male and Shield Ferns, 1981. (F. W. Simpson).   *Illustrated page 465*

ATHYRIACEAE

LADY FERN FAMILY

Athyrium filix-femina (L.) Roth   Lady Fern   Sir J. Cullum 1773
(*Asplenium filix-femina* (L.) Bernh.)

Native. In damp woods, carrs, beside streams and ditches. Frequent. A variable species.
W: 77; 78; 87; 88; 93; 95; 96; 97; 98.
77, Cavenham, 1977; 95, Monks' Park Wood, 1980.
E: 03; 04; 13; 14; 16; 23; 24; 25; 34; 35; 36; 39; 45; 46; 47; 49; 57; 58; 40.
14, Ipswich, 1981; 24, Playford, 1981; Foxhall, 1981; 35, Campsey Ash, 1980.
A very fine colony of this and other species of Ferns were destroyed during the construction of the Ipswich Southern By-pass, 1981, at Brazier's Wood, Ipswich.

Cystopteris fragilis (L.) Bernh.   Brittle Bladder Fern   Moore 1859

Native. On shady and damp brick walls, in wells and drains. Very rare. It could occur in several suitable habitats. Several species of young ferns could be mistaken for this species. There is a record from Southwold in 1934, where it was noted that moisture seeping from the cliff by a longshoreman's shelter had given rise to a strong growth of Brittle Ferns and Liverworts. Hind's Flora has two doubtful records, from Bungay and Yoxford.
W: 74, Clare, one plant on wall, 1976 (F. W. Simpson).

Matteuccia struthiopteris (L.) Tod.   Ostrich Fern   F. W. Simpson 1950

An introduced alien, this fern has long been naturalised in a wood at Woolverstone (sq. 13) and is probably to be found elsewhere. It is very surprising that it is not known as a British plant, as it is a native of continental Europe, growing in boggy woods and glades by streams. There are many suitable habitats, especially in N. Britain and Scotland.

ASPIDIACEAE

MALE FERN FAMILY

Polystichum aculeatum (L.) Roth   Hard Shield Fern   Sir J. Cullum 1776
(*P. lobatum* (Huds.) Chevall.)

Native. In hedge-banks, woods, ditches and copses. Frequent.

ASPIDIACEAE

W: 83; 85; 86, Rushbrooke; 87, Gt Fakenham; 93, Polstead; Wiston; 94, Kersey; 95, Thorpe Morieux; Rattlesden; Bradfield St George; 96, Hessett; Beyton.
E: 03, East Bergholt; 04; 06, Wetherden; 13, Bentley; Woolverstone; 14, Bramford; 16, Kenton; Mendlesham; Wetheringsett; 17, Stoke Ash; 24, Playford; 25; 33, Felixstowe, 1981; 34, Boyton; 36, Peasenhall; 37, Wissett; 48, Mutford.
Hb. Ipswich Museum, 'At Belstead, in the hedges on both sides of the road between the Buck's-horns and the Windmill, and at Wherstead, in the hedges on the west side of a wood by Stalls Valley,' 1819 (John Notcutt).

Polystichum setiferum (Forsk.) Woynar   Soft Shield Fern   John Notcutt 1818
(*P. angulare* (Willd.) C. Presl)

Native. In shady hedge-banks, ditches and woods, more especially in the South-east on clay and loamy soils. Not very common.
W: 84; 85; 88; 93; 94; 95; 96.
93, Polstead.
E: 04; 06; 07; 13; 14; 23; 25; 26; 33; 36; 47; 48.
13, Bentley; Stutton, 1974; 23, Chelmondiston; Erwarton, 1980; Harkstead, 1980; 33, Felixstowe, 1981; 48, Weston, 1973.
Hb. Ipswich Museum, 'Ipswich. In the lane branching out of the London Road to Stone Lodge, 1818' (John Notcutt).

Dryopteris filix-mas (L.) Schott   Male Fern   Sir J. Cullum 1772
(*Lastrea filix-mas* (L.) C. Presl)

Native. Very variable, in woods, hedge-banks, copses, on walls and buildings. Common. All squares except 65; 68; 98.

Dryopteris filix-mas × pseudomas   F. W. Simpson 1969
(*D.* × *tavelii* Rothm.)

A rare or overlooked hybrid, sometimes found in old woods.
E: 04, Hintlesham, 1981; 13, Bentley, 1980; Freston, 1980; 24, Playford, 1981.

Dryopteris pseudomas (Woll.) Holub & Pouzar   Golden-scaled Male Fern
(*D. borreri* Newm.)   Rev. F. Barham Zincke 1893

Native. In woods. Rare. May be recognised in Spring by its light green fronds and abundant golden scales. In the Rev. F. Barham Zincke's 'History of Wherstead' (1893), it is suggested that the spread of this fern, known then as *Lastrea filix-mas* var. *paleacea*, in the Wherstead/Freston area, was attributed to spores from plants growing in the Vicarage garden. These were brought from Devon in 1861. One is not able to confirm or deny this. However, no specimens have been seen in any early 19th century herbaria of ferns from this area.
W: 87, Livermere, 1969 (A. J. Worland); 93, Bures; Assington.
E: 04, Hintlesham, 1981; 05, Barking, 1981; 13, Stalls Valley and Cutler's Wood, Freston, 1981; Dodnash Wood, 1981; Bentley Long Wood; Harkstead, 1981; 14, Ipswich, Fishpond Covert, 1980; 24, Playford, colony of twenty specimens, 1981 (F. W. Simpson).

Illustrated page 465

Dryopteris cristata (L.) A. Gray   Crested Fern   Davy 1799
(*Lastrea cristata* (L.) C. Presl)

Native. Aboriginal in bogs on acid heaths. Very rare and extinct in some former localities.
E: 13, Bentley (doubtful record); 24, Bixley Decoy, Ipswich; 47, Walberswick Heath; 40, Ashby Warren (1956, immature plants).
Recorded in Hind's Flora from Fritton Decoy, Westleton Heath, Bixley Decoy and Barnby.
Davy's specimen from Westleton, Old Decoy, is in Hb. Ipswich Museum.

THE CRESTED FERN AT BIXLEY DECOY

Although the Crested Fern was first recorded at Bixley Decoy early in the 19th century, there is little doubt that it had been growing there for a considerable time, possibly thousands of years. A decoy existed before 1732. The main area where the fern occurred was on the swampy heathland near the first decoy pond. It grew among the reeds and the tussocks of *Carex paniculata*, a few small Birches and some Willows. This was a rather special type of habitat, formerly remote, open and undisturbed. When I first observed this fern about 1925, there was a flourishing colony of about thirty fine healthy specimens. This colony remained fairly stable until about 1950, when it rapidly commenced to decline. A careful search of the whole area in 1975 revealed that only three very small specimens remained, and these appeared to be dying. The decline and disappearance of this very rare fern from this habitat can be attributed to the following causes:—
(1) Collectors.
(2) Pollution from a nearby engineering factory. Often a pall of poisonous yellow and black sulphurous fumes lies over this valley. Even reeds and tussocks of sedge have died, and the swamp water is now much polluted also from road drainage and a new housing estate.
(3) A causeway constructed across the swamp in the fern's main area.
(4) At least two fine specimens were destroyed by trampling by anglers.
(5) Some overgrown Willows and Birches.
Soon all that will be left of this fern will be a few herbarium specimens and a photograph taken in 1936.

BUCKLER FERNS

Dryopteris dilatata is a very frequent fern in Suffolk, occurring in a large number of habitats both wet and dry, marshes, shady hedge-banks, and on wet heaths. It is now a very common, and often abundant, fern in the older parts of the coniferous plantations which cover such large areas of the County. It is certainly more frequent today than it was in Hind's time.
    D. carthusiana is, however, a local or even rare fern which is decreasing. It is found in shady woods and on some heaths among Birches. This fern can also be found growing in the drier parts of the Boulder Clay woods associated with primroses, anemones, and herbs. The true *D. carthusiana* is a far more delicate and refined fern than *D. dilatata*. The scales on its stem are much lighter and its fronds are a lighter green. Young specimens of *D. dilatata* are frequently mistaken for this species. However, I believe that the hybrid between the species is far more frequent than is commonly supposed, as many intermediate forms can be observed in most of the habitats where *D. dilatata* is abundant.

Dryopteris carthusiana (Vill.) H. P. Fuchs   Narrow Buckler Fern   John Notcutt 1819
(*D. lanceolatocristata* (Hoffm.) Alston
D. spinulosa Watt)

Native. In shady woods, wet heaths and marshes. Frequent. Young specimens of *D. dilatata* are mistaken for this species.
W: 67; 77; 78; 85; 87; 93; 94; 95; 96; 98.
77, Mildenhall, 1980; Cavenham Heath, 1980; 95, Monks' Park Wood, 1980.
E: 04; 05; 07; 13; 14; 23; 24; 25; 35; 45; 46; 47; 49; 58; 59; 40.
13, Bentley, Holbrook and Wherstead, 1981; 25, Bromeswell Common, 1980.
Hb. Ipswich Museum: 'On the Hassock-like tufts in the Morass between the Bucklesham Road and the Decoy Ponds', Novr. 1819 (John Notcutt). The 'Hassock-like tufts' refer to *Carex paniculata* which still grows in this area with specimens of this fern.

Dryopteris carthusiana × **cristata**   Lloyd's Fern   Hind 1887
(*D.* × *uliginosa* (Newm.) O. Kuntze ex Druce
Lastrea uliginosa Newm.)

Recorded in Hind from a boggy wood at Barnby and near Ipswich. Also recorded for Wherstead by the Rev. F. Barham Zincke in the 'History of Wherstead', 1893.

Dryopteris dilatata (Hoffm.) A. Gray   Broad Buckler Fern   Henslow and Skepper 1860
(*D. austriaca* auct.)   Roth's Fern

Native. Woods, shady banks, damp heaths. Very frequent. Now abundant in the new Suffolk forests.
W: All squares except 64; 65; 66; 68; 74; 75; 83; 97.
87, West Stow, King's Forest, abundant, 1981; 95, Monks' Park Wood, 1976.
E: All squares except 06; 16; 17; 26; 27; 28; 37; 38; 44; 48.
35, Tunstall and Rendlesham Forests, 1981.

Dryopteris carthusiana × **dilatata**   F. W. Simpson 1957
(*D. lanceolatocristata* × *dilatata*
D. × *deweveri* (Jansen) Jansen & Wachter)

This hybrid is not uncommon where the two species grow together. Overlooked.
W: 67, Mildenhall; 77, Cavenham, 1977; 95, Monks' Park Wood, 1980.
E: 07, Redgrave Fen, 1980; 13, Bentley; Holbrook; Freston; Wherstead; 24, Purdis Farm, 1980; 35, Eyke; Butley; Chillesford; 40, Ashby; Fritton.

Dryopteris aemula (Ait.) O. Kuntze   Hay-Scented Buckler Fern   Hind 1883
(*Lastrea aemula* (Ait.) Brackenr.)

Native. In old woods and hedge-banks. Hind's Flora has one record of the species from a copse at Lound in 1883, but the specimen in his herbarium is more likely to be *D. dilatata*.

Gymnocarpium dryopteris (L.) Newm.   Oak Fern   Dr E. F. Warburg 1941
(*Thelypteris dryopteris* (L.) Slosson)

Native. In damp, shady woods. Recorded by Dr E. F. Warburg from Ash Plantation on Cavenham Heath (sq. 77). Probably extinct.

Gymnocarpium robertianum (Hoffm.) Newm.   Limestone Fern   A. W. Punter 1965
(*Thelypteris robertiana* (Hoffm.) Slosson)

Native. Usually found in limestone areas.
W: 78, south of Brandon, under young pine plantation, on chalk, 1966.
E: 14, Ipswich, on a late 18th century tomb, St Lawrence's Churchyard (A. W. Punter);
also a young specimen on a sheltered wall about a quarter of a mile from the original site,
1981 (F. W. Simpson).   *Illustrated page 464*

BLECHNACEAE

HARD FERN FAMILY

Blechnum spicant (L.) Roth   Hard Fern   Sir J. Cullum 1773
(*B. boreale* Sw.)   Herringbone Fern
Native. Woods, heaths, banks and sides of ditches on acid soils. Scarce and decreasing.
W: 77, Bombay Fen on west bank of Eriswell Lode; 93, Stack Wood, Polstead, c. 1960.
E: 13, Bentley, 1980; 14, Belstead; 34; 35, Campsey Ash; 46, Sizewell; 47, Walberswick;
Hinton, 1980; 49, Herringfleet; 58; 59, Lound; 40, Fritton Decoy; 50, Hopton.
                                                              Illustrated page 463

POLYPODIACEAE

POLYPODY FAMILY

Polypodium vulgare agg.   Common Polypody   Hb. Ipswich Museum 1828

Native. On old hedge-banks, tree stumps, walls, roofs and coastal dunes. Frequent, but
less common than formerly, due to the destruction of habitats.
All squares except 64; 65; 67; 68; 83; 97.
Specimen in Hb. Ipswich Museum, 'Road near the Barracks, Ipswich, 1828'. Collector
not recorded.

Polypodium vulgare L.   Polypody

This species is apparently uncommon in the County. Until all the findings of *P. vulgare*
agg. can be correctly identified, we are unable to give a more accurate picture of its
distribution. There is one post-1950 record for sq. 46 and also one pre-1950 for sq. 95.

Polypodium interjectum Shivas   Intermediate Polypody   F. W. Simpson 1946

This species has been derived from the hybridization of *P. vulgare* L. and *P. australe* Fée
a species found in the Mediterranean and south Atlantic region. It prefers shadier and
damper sites than *P. vulgare* and is also found on sand-dunes.
W: 77.
E: 06; 36; 37; 46; 47; 48; 58.
46, Sizewell, 1979; Minsmere, 1981; 47, Blythburgh, 1946; still there 1981; 58, Benacre
and Kessingland, 1980.
There is a pre-1950 record for sq. 95.   *Illustrated page 465*

MARSILEACEAE

PILLWORT FAMILY

Pilularia globulifera L.   Pillwort   Stone 1805

Native. Edges of ponds and lakes. Very rare. Recorded by Hind from Hopton Common and Bungay and also found by W. A. Dutt at Flixton in 1898. Dr E. A. Ellis records that he has found it flourishing along the shores of the Hopton Ponds (TG 50) as recently as 1980. It is interesting that it has survived in the parish where it was first discovered in 1805.

AZOLLACEAE

WATER FERN FAMILY

Azolla filiculoides Lam.   Water Fern   A. Mayfield 1935
                                 Azolla

Introduced. Native of N. and S. America. Naturalised in dykes and ponds.

Recorded only from East Suffolk, where it is sometimes abundant, though its appearance is uncertain from year to year, especially after severe winters.

E: 05, Stowmarket, pond in old brickyards, 1979; 13, Stutton; 24, Bucklesham; 37, Ubbeston; 39, Bungay, 1977, (P. Stearn); 44, Orford; Gedgrave, 1976; 45, Sudbourne; 47, Southwold, 1980; 49, Somerleyton, 1974; 59, Flixton, 1972, (P. G. Lawson).

SPERMATOPHYTA

GYMNOSPERMAE

PINACEAE

PINE FAMILY

Pseudotsuga menziesii (Mirb.) Franco   Douglas Fir
(*P. douglasii* (Lindl.) Carr.)

Introduced from Western N. America and planted, especially in Breckland. Natural regeneration can occur.

Picea abies (L.) Karst.   Norway Spruce
(*P. excelsa* Link)

Originally introduced from N. and C. Europe. The traditional 'Christmas Tree'. Much planted. Natural regeneration occurs.

Larix decidua Mill.   European Larch
(*L. europaea* DC.)

Introduced. A frequently planted tree, especially on light soils. Rarely naturalised.

PINACEAE

Pinus nigra Arnold ssp. **nigra**   Austrian Pine

Introduced from S.E. Europe and planted, but not so extensively as ssp. *laricio*. Occasionally naturalised. The timber of this tree is of poor quality, and it is usually planted for shelter rather than for timber.

Ssp. **laricio** (Poir.) Palibin   Corsican Pine

Introduced and much planted in Breckland and other areas in East Suffolk, for example Rendlesham Forest. Natural regeneration is frequent, and this pine colonises heaths.

Pinus sylvestris L.   Scots Pine   Sir J. Cullum 1773

Possibly native in a few habitats, but mainly planted and naturalised, colonising heathland. Very frequent on sandy soils. A few of the trees which have been felled in recent years have been over 200 years old and may in some instances be relics of former native mixed pine-woods, as around Fritton Decoy and near Butley.

CUPRESSACEAE

CYPRESS FAMILY

Chamaecyparis lawsoniana (A. Murray) Parl.   Lawson's Cypress

Introduced. Native of W. United States. Frequently planted. Sometimes seeding.

Juniperus communis L. ssp. **communis**   Juniper   Sir J. Cullum 1773

Native or introduced. On dry, chalky heaths and in grassy places. Rare.
W: 76, Dalham, 1981 (probably native); 86, Ickworth Park.

TAXACEAE

YEW FAMILY

Taxus baccata L.   Yew   Sir J. Cullum 1773
                        Ife (Suffolk)

Planted and semi-naturalised. Very frequent in churchyards. Bird-sown specimens not uncommon.
Probably in all squares.

ANGIOSPERMAE

DICOTYLEDONES

SALICACEAE

WILLOW FAMILY

SALIX   WILLOWS AND SALLOWS

The distribution of some of the species found in the County is not at present accurately known. The identification of some of the willows is a challenge to any amateur botanist, the reasons being the ease with which the species can hybridise and the extreme variation of the hybrids. The fact that the male and female catkins are on separate trees or bushes adds to the difficulties.

The first year growth from pollarded examples can be misleading when compared with that from mature ones. No attempt has been made to give any of the tertiary hybrids which no doubt occur. It is considered that generally speaking some species are now less frequent than their hybrids.

Salix pentandra L.   Bay Willow   Woodward 1805

Probably introduced, perhaps native in a few habitats. Swampy woods near rivers and ditches. Rare.

W: 67, Mildenhall; 68, Lakenheath; 77, Barton Mills; Icklingham; 78, Brandon; 87, West Stow; 93, Polstead.

E: 38, near R. Waveney at Bungay.

Hind recorded this from Worlingham, Bungay and Kelsale.

Salix fragilis L.   Crack Willow   Sir T. G. Cullum 1804

Probably native, and also introduced. Riversides, marshes, hedges and plantations. Frequent. Much work remains to be done on this species. There appear to be a number of varieties or subspecies. These may have been selected and propagated in bygone times, being grown for various uses, with others introduced from the continent. Hybridisation has no doubt complicated their true identity. The female tree is much more common than the male, as it will pollard much better and has therefore been planted in preference. Some of the Suffolk trees appear to be very old and have been sadly neglected for many years. All squares.

Salix fragilis × pentandra   E. J. Clement 1966

(*S. × meyerana* Rostk. ex Willd.)

A rare hybrid willow found in damp places.

W: 78; 88, near Thetford Golf Club House and R. Ouse.

E: 14, Tuddenham St Martin; 15, Swilland, detd. by E. L. Swann; 35, Hacheston.

WEEPING WILLOWS

The true Weeping Willow, *Salix babylonica* L. which is probably a native of China, is a small tree and is not grown in this country. A number of hybrids or varieties of willows have been raised, which have 'weeping' branches. These are frequently planted for ornament in parks, gardens, by roadsides, ponds and rivers. The most frequently planted is probably S. *alba* var. *vitellina* × *babylonica*. There is also another variety, S. *alba* var. *pendula,* which is also called a Weeping Willow, but this has green, not golden, stems. Another hybrid is S. *babylonica* × *fragilis*. This is a smaller tree.

Salix alba L.   White Willow   Sir J. Cullum 1775

Native and also extensively planted. Wet woods, marshes, beside streams and rivers. Frequent.

All squares.

Var. **coerulea** (Sm.) Sm. (Cricket-bat Willow). Introduced into wet plantations, etc. Probably frequent, but distribution not recorded.
Var. **vitellina** (L.) Stokes (Golden Osier). Mainly planted for ornamental use. Frequent.
Var. **pendula,** including hybrids and forms of Weeping Willow.

Salix triandra L.　　Almond Willow　　　　　　　　　　Sir J. Cullum 1773

Native, and also frequently planted, in carrs, by rivers and streams. Grown as an osier. A variable species.
W: 64; 67; 77; 78; 84; 88; 94; 95; 98.
77, Cavenham and Icklingham.
E: 03; 04; 35; 38; 46; 47; 49; 40.
49, Beccles; North Cove, 1974.

Salix triandra × viminalis
(*S.* × *mollissima* Ehrh.)

Found in wet places with the parents. Probably occurs, but overlooked.

Salix nigricans Sm.　　Dark-leaved Willow　　　　　　E. J. Clement 1966

Native or introduced. In swamps and flooded gravel pits. Rare and normally confined to the northern part of the British Isles. A colony of some 14 bushes, male and female, in a mixed *Salix* swamp in an old gravel pit at Red Lodge Warren, Freckenham (sq. 67) was found by E. J. Clement in 1966 and confirmed by R. D. Meikle. Still there, 1980 (D. R. Donald).

Salix cinerea L.　　Common Sallow　　　　　　　　　　Paget 1834
　　　　　　　　　　　Grey Sallow
(Including *S. cinerea* L. ssp. *cinerea* and ssp. *oleifolia* Macreight. Records for ssp. *oleifolia* are given separately).

Native. Wet woods, marshes, fens, ponds and waste ground. Very frequent. Many records may, however, refer to hybrids.
All squares.

Salix cinerea L. ssp. **oleifolia** Macreight
(*S. cinerea* L. ssp. *atrocinerea* (Brot.) Silva & Sobr.)

Native. It is doubtful whether this subspecies occurs in Suffolk, and, though there are records, it is possible that these may belong to other forms of *S. cinerea* or the hybrid *S. aurita* × *cinerea.*
W: 93.
E: 03, Flatford; East Bergholt; 14, Tuddenham St Martin; 24, Purdis Farm; 25, Melton; 35, Campsey Ash; 45, Aldeburgh; 40, Fritton.

Salix cinerea × purpurea　　　　　　　　　　　F. W. Simpson c. 1950
(*S.* × *sordida* A. Kerner)

Recorded from Mickfield and Bradfield St George, in the 1950's.

Salix cinerea × repens　　　　　　　　　　　　F. W. Simpson 1977
(S. × *subsericea* (Döll)

E: 07, Redgrave Fen, 1977, conf. E. L. Swann; 39, Bungay Common, 1980.

Salix cinerea × viminalis   F. W. Simpson c. 1948
(*S.* × *smithiana* Willd.)

In wet places, especially on old, neglected osier beds and their margins, flooded gravel workings and quarries. I believe this is a common hybrid, but overlooked. It has been seen at Onehouse, Old Newton, Glemsford and Freckenham.

Salix aurita L.   Eared Sallow   Davy 1799
                         Round-eared Sallow
Native. Damp woods, marshes and wet heaths. Many specimens appear to be hybrids and the species is not very common. *S. aurita* is never a large tree, usually only a bush.
W: 64; 75; 77; 83; 93; 95; 96; 98.
93, Arger Fen, 1970; 95, Monks' Park Wood, 1972; 98, Knettishall Heath.
E: 04; 05; 07; 15; 16; 17; 25; 45; 47; 48; 49; 40; 50.

Salix aurita × caprea
(*S.* × *capreola* A. Kerner ex Anderss.)

Occurs in damp woods, carrs and marshes. Probably a not uncommon hybrid, but overlooked.

Salix aurita × cinerea
(*S.* × *multinervis* Döll)

Found in woods, marshes and wet places. It is probably common, but overlooked.

Salix aurita × repens   Borrer 1804
(*S.* × *ambigua* Ehrh.)

Recorded in Hind from Hopton.

Salix caprea L.   Great Sallow   Sir J. Cullum 1773
                         Goat Willow
                         Pussy Willow

Native. The true *S. caprea* is not very common. Much of what appears to be *S. caprea* is of hybrid origin. This is the first of the willows to flower. It is mainly restricted to primary woodland and old secondary woodland, copses and ancient hedges, mostly on clay soil. During March and April the male of the species is easily identified even from a distance, by the large bright yellow catkins and strong growth. *Salix cinerea* and its hybrids flower slightly later (the flowering period may extend into May). The catkins are smaller, on spreading bush-like trees with slender branches.
All squares except 28; 44.
Some of the records may refer to other species and hybrids.   *Illustrated page 456*

Salix caprea × cinerea   F. W. Simpson 1957
(*S.* × *reichardtii* A. Kerner)

This hybrid is variable, but the majority examined are similar to smaller forms of *S. caprea*. It is frequent in clay woods, scrub and old quarries. Very much under-recorded.
W: Park Wood, Chevington (sq. 75), 1957; Felshamhall Wood and Monks' Park Wood

(sq. 95), 1969; also from Freckenham (sq. 67), 1977.
E: 15, Barham Pits, 1980; 23, Chelmondiston, 1981; 40, Belton, 1977.

Salix caprea × viminalis F. W. Simpson c. 1948
(*S. × sericans* Tausch ex A. Kerner)

In wet woods, old neglected osier beds and flooded gravel pits. Probably frequent and overlooked. It occurs at Onehouse, Glemsford, Hacheston and Undley Delph.

Salix repens L. ssp. **repens** Creeping Willow J. Andrews 1721
Dwarf Willow

Native. Wet heaths and fens. Rare and decreasing. Now extinct in several habitats. There are several described forms, but the size and growth of this shrub seems to depend entirely on the type of habitat.
W: 68; 77; 78; 86; 87; 88; 98.
78, Lakenheath Poor's Fen, 1979.
E: 05; 07; 45; 40; 50.
07, Redgrave Fen, 1977; 40, Belton, 1977.

Salix viminalis L. Common Osier J. Andrews 1745

Native and planted. Marshes and flooded gravel pits. Frequent. There are many plantations in various parts of the County and some are still managed, while others have been neglected and are now overgrown.
W: All squares except 64; 65.
67, Freckenham, 1980; 78, Lakenheath and Wangford.
E: All squares except 07; 13; 26; 27; 28; 35; 36; 37; 38; 44; 46; 47; 59; 50.
05, Creeting St Mary, 1981; 06, Haughley, 1981; 15, Barham, 1981.

Salix × calodendron Wimm. Grey Willow Rev. E. F. Linton 1883
(*S. acuminata* Sm., non Mill.)

Introduced, but origin doubtful, possibly N. Europe. In marshes and fens and beside rivers and streams. Recorded in Hind's Flora from Hopton and Worlingham, but there are no known records during the present century. Possibly overlooked.
Some authorities regard this species as being a hybrid between *S. caprea, S. cinerea* and *S. viminalis.*

Salix purpurea L. Purple Willow Sir J. Cullum 1775

Native. In fens, wet, old woods, in valley bottoms and beside streams. Sometimes planted as a hedge in open fenland. Locally common or overlooked, but appears to be more frequent in West Suffolk.
W: 68; 77; 78; 86; 87; 88; 93; 95; 97.
68/78, Lakenheath, 1980; 68, Mildenhall, 1980.
E: 03; 07; 24; 39; 49.
07, Wortham Ling, 1980; 24, Bixley Decoy, 1981; 39, Bungay, 1980; 49, Beccles, 1974.

Salix purpurea × viminalis Green-leaved Willow F. W. Simpson c. 1950
(*S. × rubra* Huds.)

A rare hybrid, which has not been seen in Suffolk since c. 1950, at Onehouse.

Populus alba L.   White Poplar   Paget 1834
                        Abele

Native. Also frequently planted and naturalised in damp plantations and wet pastures.
W: 65; 66; 67; 74; 76; 77; 84; 86; 87; 88; 97; 98.
77, Mildenhall, 1980.
E: 04; 05; 07; 14; 15; 16; 23; 25; 27; 28; 33; 35; 36; 39; 44; 45; 46; 47; 48; 57; 58; 59.
23, Levington, 1981; 33, Bawdsey, 1980; 39, Bungay Common, 1981, planted with *P. canescens*.

Populus canescens (Ait.) Sm.   Grey Poplar   Paget 1834

Native or introduced. In plantations, copses and hedges, especially near the coast. This species spreads easily by means of root suckers. Frequent. Sometimes recorded in error for *P. tremula* or *P. alba*.
W: 66; 74; 76; 77; 78; 83; 86; 87; 88; 94; 95; 96; 97.
77, Icklingham, 1981; 96, Beyton, 1981; 97, Sapiston, 1980.
E: 03; 13; 23; 25; 26; 33; 34; 35; 46; 47.
23, Chelmondiston, 1981; 34, Hollesley, 1981.
It is considered that *P. canescens* probably originated as a hybrid between *P. alba* and *P. tremula*.

Populus tremula L.   Aspen   Sir J. Cullum 1773

Native. In woods and copses and on moist heaths and fens. Common in the old, damp Boulder Clay woods; well distributed over most of the County.
W: All squares except 65; 66; 67; 98.
E: All squares except 06; 26; 27; 28; 44; 59; 40; 50.

Populus gileadensis Rouleau   Western Balsam Poplar   F. W. Simpson 1950
(including *P. trichocarpa* Hook.) Balm of Gilead

Introduced from Western N. America. Planted in woods and beside streams. Not frequent. The tree grows rapidly and produces numerous suckers. It can be detected from a distance when growth commences in late April, by the very strong balsam-like scent of the buds and young leaves.
W: 65, Lt. Bradley, 1975; 86, Culford, 1979; 93, Polstead, 1950; still there, 1980.
E: 13, Holbrook, 1981; 14, Lt. Blakenham, 1981; 25, Ufford, 1981.

Populus tacamahacca Mill.   Eastern Balsam Poplar   F. W. Simpson 1960

Introduced from Eastern N. America. Planted in parks and beside rivers.
W: 86, Bury St Edmunds, by the R. Lark.
E: 04, Hadleigh.

Populus nigra L.   Black Poplar   Sir J. Cullum 1773

Native. Wet pastures, damp valley woods and beside streams, ponds and rivers.
Generally rare with a scattered distribution, often only single trees. Formerly more frequent. Hybrid poplars, especially the Black Italian Poplar, may be mistaken for this species. The Black Poplar, with its attractive outline and the red catkins of the male trees in spring, used to be a feature of several of our Suffolk valleys. The female tree is very rare.

W: 66; 68; 74; 76; 77; 78; 84; 85; 86; 87; 88; 93; 95; 96; 98.
66, Exning, 1977; 77, Icklingham and Cavenham, 1981; 78, Wangford, 1980; 86, Bury St Edmunds; 95, beside pond, Felshamhall Wood, an old tree (F. W. S.); 96, Thurston, 1980 (Mrs E. M. Hyde).
E: 03; 04; 05; 06; 07; 14; 15; 16; 24; 25; 34; 35; 36; 38; 45; 46; 47; 48; 58; 59; 40.
04, Hadleigh, 1981; 06, Old Newton; Stowmarket; 07, Finningham, 1977; 15, Barham, 1981; Stonham Aspal, 1981 (J. A. Foster); 24, Grundisburgh, four trees, 1981; 35, Blaxhall; Snape, 1981; Marlesford, 1980; 36, Farnham, 1981; 47, Blythburgh, 1980 (P. G. Lawson); 48, Henstead, 1980 (P. G. Lawson); 59, Oulton, 1976.   *Illustrated page 460*

cv. **Italica**   Lombardy Poplar

Introduced and planted in parks and ornamental gardens. There is an avenue at Nacton, near Amberfield School and the Decoy.

Populus × **euramericana** (Dode) Guinier   Hybrid Black Poplar
(*P.* × *canadensis* Moench)

A number of hybrid Poplars have been raised in Europe since about 1790 and introduced into Britain. These hybrids are crossings between *P. nigra* and two American species *P. deltoides* Marshall and *P. angulata* Ait. Planted in the right habitats, they are of rapid growth. They have therefore been used to much advantage by roadsides, in parks, as screens and shelter belts, and plantations on damp uncultivated land, in carrs and river valleys. It is doubtful whether any can be classed as really naturalised. Some do spread by suckers.
The chief cultivars are:—

cv. **Serotina**   Black Italian Poplar   F. W. Simpson c. 1936

A very frequent tree in Suffolk and often mistaken for *P. nigra*, especially when observed in river valleys. Probably introduced early in the 19th century. Male trees only. Found in all districts.

cv. **Aurea**   Golden Poplar

Said to be a form of cv. *Serotina* with golden-coloured leaves. Planted in parks and gardens.

cv. **Regenerata**   Railway Poplar

This variety is planted chiefly in towns, waste places and on railway embankments. It is fairly frequent in Suffolk. Female trees only, with pale green catkins, dropping at the end of July with an abundance of white 'wool' or 'fluff'.

cv. **Robusta**
(*P. angulata* × *P. nigra* cv. *Plantierensis*)

This is the variety of Poplar which has been extensively planted commercially in the County since the end of the Second World War, especially in marshes, clear-felled damp woodland and also as roadside trees.
Young trees are very vigorous and mature in about thirty years. Male trees only.

MYRICACEAE

BOG MYRTLE FAMILY

Myrica gale L.   Bog Myrtle   Rev. G. Crabbe 1810
                     Sweet Gale

Native. In bogs and on wet heaths. Very rare.
W: 78, Lakenheath, Pashford Poor's Fen, 1981.
E: 07; 47, Walberswick, 1975; 49, Barnby Broad, probably now extinct; North Cove. The colony at Walberswick appeared to be dead in 1977, due to flooding of the area by the high tide in January, 1976.
Hind recorded the species from Lakenheath, Ampton, Lound, North Cove, marshes South of Oulton Broad, Barnby Broad and Worlingham. There is a specimen in Hb. Atkins from Worlingham, 1905.

JUGLANDACEAE

WALNUT FAMILY

Juglans regia L.   Walnut

Introduced. Rarely naturalised. Native of S.E. Europe and Asia. Sometimes found in hedges, old pastures and on the sites of former gardens, and orchards. Supposed to have been introduced by the Romans. When the R. Gipping was dredged some years ago at Sproughton, large numbers of walnuts were found in the mud. C. A. Watchman has found seedlings in the quarries at Gt Blakenham. The nuts are placed in crevices by rooks.

BETULACEAE

BIRCH FAMILY

Betula pendula Roth   Silver Birch   Sir J. Cullum 1773
(*B. verrucosa* Ehrh.   White Birch
B. alba auct.)

Native. Heaths and woods. More frequent on light soils. Common and sometimes becoming dominant on heathland.
All squares.

Betula pendula × **pubescens**   Dr O. Rackham 1970
(*B.* × *aurata* Borkh.)

This hybrid has probably been overlooked.
W: 95, Felshamhall Wood.
E: 50, locality not recorded.

Betula pubescens Ehrh.   Downy Birch   Hind 1876

Native. Wet woods, heaths and carrs. Frequent.
(a) ssp. **odorata** (Bechst.) E. F. Warb. Some forms are very fragrant, especially in spring and early summer after rain.

(b) ssp. **pubescens** has pubescent twigs and is not scented, or less so. The subspecies have not been determined in the records below.
W: All squares except 65; 66; 67; 74; 84; 85; 86.
E: All squares except 05; 15; 16; 17; 26; 27; 28; 33; 36; 37; 38; 39; 44.

Alnus glutinosa (L.) Gaertn.   Alder   Sir J. Cullum 1773

Native. Wet woods, fens, carrs, and beside streams and rivers. Very frequent and widespread.
All squares.

CORYLACEAE

HAZEL FAMILY

Carpinus betulus L.   Hornbeam   Sir J. Cullum 1773
Harbour (Suffolk)

Native. In all the old woods, copses and ancient hedges, especially on clay soils. Frequent. Although indigenous, there are signs that it was formerly planted for coppice. Usually a small tree. Well-developed examples are often to be seen in parks and other habitats. Seedlings are uncommon.
W: All squares except 68; 78; 88.
94, Bull's Cross Wood, 1979; 95, Bradfield Woods, 1980; 96, Pakenham Wood, 1979.
E: All squares except 33; 34; 35; 44; 49; 59; 40; 50.
04, Wolves Wood, 1981; Hintlesham, 1981; 13, Holbrook, 1981; 24, Alder Carr, Playford, 1981; 37, Linstead Magna, 1981.   *Illustrated page 447*

Corylus avellana L.   Hazel   Sir J. Cullum 1773

Native. Woods, copses, hedges and scrub, especially on the Boulder Clay. Widespread and common.
All squares.

Corylus maxima Mill.   Filbert
Cob Nut

Introduced and grown in gardens, shrubberies and orchards. Native of the Balkans. The nuts are much larger than those of the Hazel and the involucre is about twice as long as the nuts. Except for its fruit, it is not always easy to distinguish from the Wild Hazel. Seedlings are sometimes observed in the vicinity of old or semi-derelict gardens and orchards. The Filbert usually has longer and straighter stems before branching.

Corylus avellana × maxima   Hazel/Filbert Cross   F. W. Simpson 1974

Although this hybrid is not mentioned in Floras, it may possibly not be uncommon, but passed by, as it is not easy to recognise. The fruits are intermediate in size and shape between the two species and the bracts longer and larger than in the Hazel. Stems and general habit of growth are also intermediate.
E: 24, one specimen at the edge of a marsh at Foxhall. First recognised in 1974, although quite an old bush, c. 70/80 years. Growing among Hazels. The nearest cultivated Filberts are about one mile from this habitat. 47, Westleton, 1980 (F. W. Simpson).

FAGACEAE

BEECH FAMILY

Fagus sylvatica L.   Beech   Sir J. Cullum 1773

Native or planted. Woods, plantations, hedges and parks. Probably native, although also planted in the South-west of the County on the Chalk. Reproduction takes place from seed in all areas. Copper Beeches are common in parks and there is a fine avenue at Freston Park.

All squares.

Castanea sativa Mill.   Sweet Chestnut   J. Andrews 1745
(*C. vulgaris* Lam.)

Native of S. Europe. Extensively introduced into parks, plantations and old woods on light soils, replacing *Quercus robur* L. and other native trees and shrubs. Reproduces naturally from the nuts, which vary considerably in size and shape. Widespread.

Illustrated page 462

Quercus ilex L.   Holm Oak   Loudon 1838
Evergreen Oak
Ilex

Introduced. Native of the Mediterranean region. Planted and sometimes almost naturalised. Self-sown specimens occur. Frequent near the sea coast. The Holm Oak may have been introduced during the Roman occupation and first planted in Suffolk at Felixstowe and Walton, where there was an extensive occupation site and a Fort. It is very frequent in the area.
W: 86.
E: 03; 05; 06; 13; 14; 15; 23; 24; 27; 33; 35; 46; 47; 58; 59.
Seedlings at Harkstead, Woolverstone, Ipswich (old brickfields, Dales Road), Orwell Park and Bawdsey Cliffs, all 1981.

Quercus cerris L.   Turkey Oak   F. W. Simpson 1925

Introduced. Frequently planted, also self-sown and bird-sown. In woods, parks, hedges and old scrub. Under-recorded.
W: 77; 83; 84; 86; 94; 95; 96.
E: 04; 06; 13; 14; 15; 16; 17; 23; 24; 25; 33; 34; 35; 36; 37; 46; 48; 58; 40.

Quercus petraea (Mattuschka) Liebl.   Durmast Oak   Sir J. Cullum 1773
(*Q. sessiliflora* Salisb.)   Sessile Oak

Native or introduced. In woods and plantations. Very rare in Suffolk. It is probable that some of the trees are hybrids with *Q. robur* (Hind records the species as a subspecies of *Q. robur* L. with records from Pakenham, Dalham Wood and Gt Bealings).
W: 83; 86; 95; 96.
E: 03; 13, Woolverstone, 1981 (two trees, one near the church); 15; 46; 47; 49, Fritton Decoy.

Quercus petraea × robur   Hybrid Oak   F. W. Simpson 1952
(*Q. × rosacea* Bechst.)

This hybrid may be not infrequent, and has possibly been overlooked.
E: 13, in hedge at Harkstead, 1980; 49, wood near Fritton Lake.

Quercus robur L.   Common Oak   Sir J. Cullum 1773
(*Q. pedunculata* Ehrh.)   Pedunculate Oak

Native. Woods, plantations, hedgerows, scrub and cliffs. Very common, sometimes dominant, especially on clay soils. However, the Oak trees of Suffolk are disappearing from the landscape, as the ancient woods are clear felled and hedges removed. A few Oaks exist which are very old indeed, and are said to date from Domesday times. It is very likely that the majority of the Oaks in Staverton Park and the Thicks at Eyke and Butley were in existence in medieval times during the Peasants' Revolt in 1381, when the Manor House of Staverton (situated in Office Piece) was destroyed by the rebels. Some of the Oaks in Helmingham Park are also ancient. Many Oaks in Suffolk are slowly dying; this seems to be due to a number of causes, — probably too much drainage resulting in the lowering of the water table, the removal of much natural vegetation, producing a drier atmosphere, and pollution by sulphur-dioxide and other poisonous gases. The oldest specimens have usually been pollarded. A few Suffolk specimens are estimated to be at least 1,000 years old, as at Staverton, Purdis Heath and Barham.

The Common or Pedunculate Oak is far more variable than is generally believed, especially in the shape of the leaves and acorns. The leaves can be deeply pinnately lobed, or have only small rounded lobes; they can be flat or curved at the edges. Acorns from different trees vary considerably; some may be ellipsoid, much longer than broad, while others are squat and oblong; the stalks or peduncles may be long and thin or short and thick. A large proportion of the wild Oaks of river banks and Breckland have small squat acorns and it is therefore thought that these Oaks are of aboriginal stock. They are of much slower growth and longer life and do not develop such fine trunks as the varieties with long acorns.

All squares.

ULMACEAE

ELM FAMILY

ELMS

A very large number of Elms have been felled in recent years, mainly as a result of Dutch Elm Disease or the removal of hedgerows and other habitats. The Elm is native in the British Isles, but many have been planted in the past to form hedgerows and coverts, and in woodlands and plantations, where they have become naturalised and have spread by means of suckers. They have also been planted as ornamental trees in parks. Some of the large Elms which have been felled have been shown to be at least two or three hundred years old. It is likely that some of the Elms in primary woodlands, especially in valleys and near streams in the Suffolk Gulls and the edges of the cliffs of our estuaries, especially the Stour, Orwell and Deben, are relics of former forests.

Elm remains are found in inter-glacial and post-glacial deposits and are the same species as found in the County today. Some of the species of Elms are very difficult to identify, as their appearance changes according to age; that is, the leaves and shoots of suckers or young trees are different from those of the branches and leaves on mature specimens. It is now supposed that there are three native species found in Suffolk: *Ulmus glabra* Huds., Wych Elm, *U. procera* Salisb., English Elm, and *U. minor* Mill., Smooth-leaved or Small-leaved Elm, and a large number of varieties and several hybrids. Mature trees are usually the easiest to identify, even from a distance. *U. minor* is the most variable of the Suffolk Elms and a number of local forms or races occur. Three distinctive forms have been described as species: *U. angustifolia* (Weston) Weston, Cornish Elm, *U. plotii* Druce, Plot's Elm, and *U. coritana* Melville, Coritanian Elm. Intermediates, probably hybrids, occur. *U.* × *hollandica* Mill., Dutch Elm, is probably not native and is the Elm frequently planted in parks in recent years.

Seedling Elms are not frequent. They can be found on marginal land, scrub and in abandoned quarries. The fertility of the seeds is said to be in the region of 1:10,000. One has to be certain that they are actually seedlings and not the suckers or relics of old hedges or trees.

Ulmus glabra Huds. ssp. **glabra**   Wych Elm   E. Skepper 1860
(*U. montana* With.   Large-leaved Elm
U. scabra Mill.)   Hop Elm

Native. In woods, hedges and copses. A tree with few suckers. Seeds of this Elm are more fertile than those of other species, and hybrids are not uncommon.
All squares except 98; 37; 38; 58; 40.
There is a 'weeping' form of this tree (f. *pendula* (Loud.) Rehd.) near Bentley Station and also at Stutton.

Ulmus × **hollandica** Mill. var. **hollandica**   Dutch Elm
(*U. glabra* × *minor*)   B.S.B.I. Mapping Scheme c. 1960

Planted in parks and gardens. This tree is said to be immune to Dutch Elm Disease.
W: 67; 77; 87; 88.
E: 06, Onehouse.

Ulmus × **hollandica** Mill. var. **vegeta** (Loud.) Rehd.   Huntingdon Elm
(*U. glabra* × *minor*)   H. D. Wiard 1968

In woods and copses. Rare.
E: 88, Thetford; Barnham; 95, Felshamhall Wood.

Ulmus procera Salisb.   English Elm   Sir J. Cullum 1773
(*U. campestris* Mill.)

Native and often planted. In hedges, thickets and the margins of woods. Common. Reproduces by suckers. Although recorded for all squares, this species may well have not been correctly identified.

Ulmus minor Mill.   Smooth Elm   Hind's Flora 1889
(*U. carpinifolia* G. Suckow
U. stricta (Ait.) Lindl.)

Probably native in a few habitats, also planted. Old woods, copses and hedgerows. Frequent. A variable species, but it is usually possible to identify fully developed trees by the outline and rather pendulous, slender branches. There are several forms, some of which may be hybrids.

W: 65; 66; 76; 83; 86; 87; 88; 93; 94; 95; 97.
95, Monks' Park Wood, 1980.
E: 03; 04; 05; 06; 07; 14; 17; 24; 34; 47; 59.
14, Piper's Vale, Ipswich, 1981, detd. Dr R. Melville; 24, Playford, 1981.

Ulmus minor × plotii   F. W. Simpson 1961
(*U.* × *viminalis* Lodd.)
A rare hybrid found at Otley Gull (sq. 15/25).

Ulmus angustifolia (Weston) Weston   Cornish Elm
Native or planted. In hedges or thickets, usually near the coast. Uncommon.

Ulmus plotii Druce   Plot's Elm   F. W. Simpson 1957
Native. In hedgerows and thickets, usually in moist valleys. Rare or overlooked.
E: 33, Felixstowe; 35, Wantisden, 1957.

Ulmus coritana Melville   Coritanian Elm   F. W. Simpson 1956
Native. In old hedgerows, valley woods and copses. Not uncommon, but overlooked.
W: 76; 97.
E: 03; 05; 06; 14.

Ulmus coritana × glabra   F. W. Simpson 1957
In old hedgerows and woods. A rare hybrid.
W: 64, Thurlow.
E: 04, Hintlesham and Ramsey Woods; 23, Nacton.

Ulmus coritana × plotii   East Anglian Elm   Dr R. Melville c. 1939
                                Small-leaved Elm
Native. In hedges, thickets and woods. Variable, probably frequent and mistaken for
other Elms. Dr Melville described it as 'common along the coastal plain from Ipswich and
Felixstowe to Lowestoft and Beccles, extending inland at least as far as Diss and
Debenham' (The Journal of Botany, 138-145, May, 1939.)

MORACEAE

MULBERRY FAMILY

Ficus carica L.   Fig   G. Maynard 1920
Introduced. Much cultivated in the Mediterranean region. Self-sown specimens occur. For
many years there was a fine specimen growing in Ipswich Museum gardens. This was a
seedling which appeared about 1920, according to G. Maynard, who was curator at the
time. The tree was destroyed c. 1960. Today in 1981 there is a tree in Vernon Street,
Ipswich, which is about 70 years old. Another tree was discovered by the R. Gipping near
West End Road, Ipswich in 1980. Three seedlings were seen below a cellar grating of a
house at Freston in 1974; they have been there since about 1947 (F. W. Simpson). Still
there, 1981.

CANNABACEAE

HEMP FAMILY

Humulus lupulus L.   Hop   Sir J. Cullum 1773

Doubtfully native. Probably introduced and naturalised. Often a relic of earlier cultivation. Found in hedges, thickets and overgrown old gardens. Very frequent.
All squares.
The male plant is less frequent. It has been recorded from:
W: 66, Exning, 1977; 67, Freckenham, 1977; 76, Barrow, 1976; 96, Tostock, 1980.
E: 04, Hadleigh, 1981; 13, Harkstead, 1981; Chelmondiston, 1976; Tattingstone, 1981; 14, Foxhall Road, Ipswich, 1981; 23, Erwarton, 1980; Falkenham, 1979; 35, Snape, 1981; 37, Halesworth; Walpole, 1979; 47, Holton, 1976; 48, Westhall, 1979.

Cannabis sativa L.   Indian Hemp   Prof. Henslow 1858
                         Pot

Casual. Introduced from Asia. Found in waste places, rubbish tips and gardens, probably originating from imported birdseed.
E: 14, Ipswich (garden); 23, Chelmondiston Tip (one specimen 1974 and 1975); 36, Yoxford (garden), 1970 (Mrs M. Stephenson); 59, Lowestoft Denes.

URTICACEAE

NETTLE FAMILY

Urtica dioica L.   Common Nettle   Sir J. Cullum 1773
                       Stinging Nettle

Native. Waysides, waste places and woods, especially on light soils. Abundant.
All squares.

Urtica urens L.   Small Nettle   Sir J. Cullum 1773

Native. A weed of cultivated ground, waste places and sandy heaths. Very frequent, especially in cabbage fields and farmyards.
All squares.

Urtica pilulifera L.   Roman Nettle   Dillenius 1724

An alien, probably introduced in Roman times. It is common as a weed in S. Europe. At one time it was frequent in the Yarmouth, Gorleston and Lowestoft areas of Norfolk and North Suffolk. The late E. R. Long records having seen a dried specimen collected at Lowestoft by the late Miss Cleveland, but failed to find it himself over a period of 40 years.
There is only one post-1950 record:
E: 45, Iken, by churchyard wall, 1955.
Hind recorded it for Clare, Gorleston, Lowestoft, Bungay, Beccles, Thorpe, Aldeburgh and Felixstowe.

Parietaria diffusa Mert. & Koch   Pellitory-of-the-Wall   Sir J. Cullum 1772
(*P. officinalis* auct., non L.)

Native, colonising old walls, and buildings, especially churches. Rarely on stony ground, shingle beaches and hedge-banks. Frequent.
W: All squares except 65; 67; 68.
E: All squares except 05; 06; 07; 16; 35; 36; 37; 48; 40.
Hedge-banks at Orford, 1976 and Newbourn, 1981.

Soleirolia soleirolii (Req.) Dandy   Mind-your-own-Business   F. W. Simpson 1950
(*Helxine soleirolii* Req.)

Introduced. Native of the Balearic Islands, Corsica and Sardinia. May be found colonising old damp walls, wells and other brickwork, garden paths and outside and inside greenhouses.
W: 94, Lt. Waldingfield.
E: 14, Ipswich, several sites, 1981; 15, Coddenham; 23, Nacton; 25, Ufford, 1976; 33, Felixstowe; 36; 47, Blythburgh.

SANTALACEAE

SANDALWOOD FAMILY

Thesium humifusum DC.   Bastard Toadflax   Dillenius 1724

Native. Dry, chalky banks, heaths and quarries. Very scarce, almost extinct.
W: 76, Risby, 1971; Dalham; 77, Barton Mills; Cavenham.
E: 14, Claydon (Miss E. S. Rowling, before 1956).
Hind recorded it from Newmarket Heath, Risby Heath, Bury St Edmunds and Brandon.

LORANTHACEAE

MISTLETOE FAMILY

Viscum album L.   Mistletoe   Sir J. Cullum 1773

Native. A parasite on various trees and shrubs. Frequent, but not so common as formerly. The host species on which it has been recorded include Apple, Hawthorn, Poplar, Elm, Hazel, Maple, Medlar, Lime and Ash.
W: 64; 75; 76; 77; 83; 85; 86; 93; 94; 95; 96.
76, Kentford, 1977; 86, Westley, on Hawthorn, 1970; Horringer, also on Hawthorn.
E: 03; 04; 05; 06; 13; 14; 15; 16; 17; 24; 25; 35; 36; 46; 47; 40.
06, Haughley Park on Lime, 1981; 14, Ipswich on Ornamental Crabs, 1981; also on Poplar, 1981; 17, Thornham Magna on Poplar and Lime, 1981; 25, Easton, 1976.

Illustrated page 516

ARISTOLOCHIACEAE

BIRTHWORT FAMILY

Asarum europaeum L.   Asarabacca   Mrs Dunlap 1847

Doubtfully native, and probably always a relic of cultivation. A medicinal plant, grown for its roots, which provide a strong irritant. ('The Ginger Plant'). Rare. The only recent record is from sq. 36, where it was reported as being naturalised in gardens at Rose Hill, Farnham in 1970. Recorded in Hind's Flora from Rougham and Wortham.

Aristolochia bodamae Dingler   H. D. Wiard 1969

Introduced. Native of Greece and Turkey.
88, Elveden, Marmansgrave Wood, 1969-77.

Aristolochia clematitis L.   Birthwort   Woodward 1796

Alien, introduced from C. and S. Europe. Rare, or extinct. It was formerly cultivated as a medicinal plant.
E: 24, Martlesham Rectory (now extinct); 28, Weybread, by porch of St Andrew's Church, 1971.
Hind recorded this for Livermere, Rougham, Hessett, Stuston and the Abbey Grounds at Bury St Edmunds.

POLYGONACEAE

DOCK FAMILY

Polygonum maritimum L.   Sea Knotgrass   Miss M. M. Whiting 1957

Native. On sandy sea-shores, above high water mark. Recorded from the Southwold-Walberswick area. No authentic specimen seen.

Polygonum patulum Bieb.   F. W. Adams 1954

A casual, native in C. and E. Europe. Collected by F. W. Adams at Lakenheath.

Polygonum oxyspermum Meyer & Bunge ex Ledeb. ssp. **raii** (Bab.) D. A. Webb & Chater
(*P. raii* Bab.)   Ray's Knotgrass   J. Atkins 1909

Native. On sea-shores, usually beyond high water mark. Possibly extinct in Suffolk.
E: 23, Landguard Common, 1909 (Hb. Atkins); 47, Southwold (recorder unknown, possibly an error.)
Recorded in Hind's Flora for Landguard Fort, Felixstowe. However, his herbarium specimen is actually a variety of *P. aviculare.*

Polygonum aviculare agg.   Common Knotgrass   Sir J. Cullum 1773
                                   Stoneweed or Wireweed (Suffolk)

Native and introduced. A weed of fields, waste places and paths. Very common. A most variable aggregate. Some forms may be only variants, resulting from habitat conditions. The principle species comprising the aggregate are given below.
All squares.

Polygonum aviculare L.   Knotgrass   Sir J. Cullum 1773
(*P. heterophyllum* Lindm.)

Tracks, waysides, waste places, and the sea-shore. The most frequent species everywhere.

Polygonum rurivagum Jord. ex Bor. Hind's Flora 1889

A weed of cultivated fields, especially on chalky soils. Probably frequent but overlooked. In corn fields it often grows rapidly after the corn is cut.

Polygonum arenastrum Bor. Small-leaved Knotgrass Hind's Flora 1889
(*P. aequale* Lindm.)

Native or colonist. A weed of waste places, arable land, roadsides and tracks, where it frequently forms a mat-like growth. Probably common, but not as frequent as *P. aviculare*, for which it has been mistaken. Although we have few records, it is likely that it occurs in all squares.
W: 67, Mildenhall; 75, Stansfield; 77; 87, Shelterhouse Corner; 94; 95; 97, Knettishall Heath.
E: 23, Felixstowe; Landguard Common; 25; 33, Felixstowe Ferry; 35; 46, Thorpeness; Sizewell; 47, Walberswick.
Maritime forms of *P. aviculare* L. and *P. arenastrum* Bor.
Various forms of both species are frequently found on sandy and shingle beaches, sea cliffs and embankments. These are sometimes mistaken for *P. oxyspermum* ssp. *raii.* However, the plants are usually much stronger with thicker, shorter branches. There are fewer leaves and these are often shed early, before the seeds are ripe.
These coastal forms have been named by some authorities as *P. littorale* Link (*P. littorale* auct., pro parte), which is a variety of *P. arenastrum.*
This variety has been seen at Landguard Common, Felixstowe Ferry, Thorpeness and Sizewell. Hind recorded it from Sutton.

Polygonum microspermum Jord. ex Bor.

Recorded in Hind's Flora from Honington, Nayland and Stoke-by-Nayland. Now included under *P. arenastrum.*

Polygonum calcatum Lindm.

In dry places. Rare. Recorded by R. Burn from Stansfield in 1934. Possibly only a small form of *P. arenastrum.*

Polygonum minus Huds. Small Water Pepper Henslow & Skepper 1860

Native. Wet pastures and the margins of ponds. Very rare or overlooked.
W: Not recorded recently. Hind records it for the edge of a pool in Fakenham Wood.
E: 48, Beccles, 1971; 58, Gisleham.

Polygonum mite Schrank Tasteless Water Pepper Wilson 1831
Mild Persicaria

Native. Margins of ponds and ditches. Very rare or extinct. Only one known record for Suffolk during the present century, from Martlesham Creek (sq. 24), c. 1934, by R. Burn. Small forms of *P. persicaria* may be confused with this species. Recorded by Hind from Honington, Fakenham, Troston, Bury St. Edmunds, Lound and Beccles.

Polygonum hydropiper L. Common Water Pepper Rev G. Crabbe 1798

Native. Wet places, margins of ponds and damp heaths. Common.
W: All squares except 64; 66; 67; 68; 76; 85; 95; 96.
65, Lt. Thurlow, 1977; 77, Cavenham, 1979.

E: All squares except 16; 44; 59; 50.
04, Hadleigh, 1980; 13, Holbrook Mill Stream, 1981; 25, Bromeswell Common, 1980.

Polygonum persicaria L.   Redshank   Sir J. Cullum 1773
                               Persicaria

Native. A weed of cultivated and waste, damp places, especially farmyards, riverbanks and ponds, and in cattle pastures. Very frequent, and variable.
All squares.   *Illustrated page 512*

Polygonum lapathifolium L.   Pale Persicaria   J. Andrews 1755

Native. Found on cultivated ground and in waste places. Common.
W: All squares except 75.
E: All squares except 26; 28; 35; 38; 44; 48; 58; 59; 40.
Pink flowers at Erwarton, Harkstead and Bucklesham in 1976.

Polygonum nodosum Pers.   J. Andrews 1738

This species has now been shown to be merely a variety of *P. lapathifolium*.

Polygonum amphibium L.   Amphibious Bistort   J. Andrews 1739

Native. In wet pastures, marshes, ponds, lakes and beside rivers, but frequently found in drier habitats, and then rarely flowering.
W: All squares except 65; 95; 98.
67, Mildenhall, 1980; 68, Lakenheath, 1980; 83, Cornard Mere; 93, by the R. Stour at Nayland.
E: All squares except 05; 06; 16; 26; 35; 37; 44; 46; 47.
13, Holbrook Mill Stream, 1981; Alton Reservoir, 1980; 14, by the R. Gipping at Ipswich, 1981; 39, Bungay, 1981; 58, Benacre, 1981.

Polygonum bistorta L.   Common Bistort   J. Andrews 1747
                              Snake-root

Native. In old wet meadows, damp woods and marshes. Formerly not uncommon. Due to drainage and ploughing up of sites, it is now extinct in some of the localities listed below.
W: 77, Herringswell; Eriswell; 86; 94, Monks Eleigh; Chelsworth.
E: 04, Hadleigh, 1981; Nedging; 05, Combs; Abbot's Hall, Stowmarket, 1974; Gt. Finborough; 25, Grundisburgh; 28, St. Cross, South Elmham; 34, Butley; Chillesford; Capel St. Andrew; 35, Marlesford; 37, Wenhaston; Halesworth; 38; 46, Minsmere; 47, Wenhaston.   *Illustrated page 480*

Polygonum amplexicaule D. Don   M. A. Hyde 1974

Introduced. Native of the Himalayas. Frequently grown in gardens.
E: 23, Chelmondiston Tip, 1974.

Polygonum viviparum L.   Viviparous Bistort   Finder unknown, 1957

Native of mountain areas. Recorded from Ipswich (sq. 14) in 1957. Possibly a garden escape. No specimen seen.

Polygonum polystachyum Wall. ex Meissner   Mrs E. M. Hyde & P. G. Lawson 1977

Alien. Native of Assam and Sikkim. Waste places, sometimes established. A garden relic.
E: 45, Friston.

Bilderdykia convolvulus (L.) Dum.   Black Bindweed   Sir J. Cullum 1773
(*Polygonum convolvulus* L.)

Native or colonist. A weed of arable ground and waste places, also clearings in woods.
Very frequent.
All squares.
Polygonum convolvulus var. *subalatum* Lej. & Court recorded from Martlesham Creek,
c. 1935 (R. Burn).

Bilderdykia dumetorum (L.) Dum.   Copse Bindweed   R. Burn c. 1935
(*Polygonum dumetorum* L.)   Copse Buckwheat

Native. In woods, thickets and hedges. Uncommon. There is some doubt that this species
has, in fact, been found in the County. It is similar to large specimens of *B. convolvulus,*
which can also frequently be found in clearings in woods and on wood margins. R. Burn
felt very certain that he had found it in Lineage Wood, near Long Melford. This wood is
very old and dates back to the Domesday Survey. Formerly mainly a deciduous oak wood,
it has now been felled and replanted with conifers.

Bilderdykia aubertii (L. Henry) Moldenke   Russian Vine   Miss J. C. N. Willis 1964
(*Polygonum aubertii* L. Henry
P. baldschuanicum auct., non Regel)

Introduced. Native of W. China and Tibet. Cultivated and occasionally escaping, or
found on the sites of former gardens.
W: 66, Moulton, 1981; 88, Thetford.
E: 14, Wherstead, 1981; 23, Felixstowe; 24, Hemley, 1980; 33, Bawdsey, 1978; 46,
Westleton, 1980; 47, Dunwich, 1975; 48, Weston; 57, Southwold.

Reynoutria japonica Houtt.   Japanese Knotweed   F. W. Simpson 1924
(*Polygonum cuspidatum* Sieb. & Zucc.)

Alien. Native of Japan. Cultivated and naturalised in the South of Britain. Found in
derelict gardens, waste places, shrubberies and on railway embankments. Frequent and
increasing.
W: 77; 78; 83; 86; 87; 93; 94; 96.
77, Mildenhall, 1980; 86, Bury St Edmunds, 1981; 96, Elmswell, 1981.
E: 03; 05: 06; 07; 13; 14; 23; 24; 33; 34; 36; 37; 45; 46; 47; 48; 49; 59.
14, Ipswich, many sites, 1981; 24, Hasketon, 1979; Newbourn, 1980.

Reynoutria sachalinensis (F. Schmidt Petrop.) Nakai in Mori   Giant Knotweed
(*Polygonum sachalinense* F. Schmidt Petrop.)   Miss J. C. N. Willis 1957

An alien, introduced from Sakhalin Island. Sometimes cultivated and escaping.
W: 75; 88.
88, Thetford.
E: 13; 14; 47; 48.
13, Woolverstone, 1981; Bentley, 1980 (originally planted); Harkstead, 1974; 14,
Holywells Park, Ipswich, 1981; 47, Dunwich, 1976; 48, Weston.

Fagopyrum esculentum Moench   Buckwheat   Sir J. Cullum 1773
(*F. sagittatum* Gilib.)   Brank (Suffolk)

A native of Asia, where it is cultivated as a cereal or fodder crop. Introduced into Britain. Sown as a crop, or scattered, for pheasant food. A constituent of bird food. Occasional.
W: 77; 84, Spelthorn Wood; 87, Wordwell; Culford; North Stow Farm; 93, Assington; 95, Brettenham.
E: 04, Hadleigh; 13, Woolverstone; 14, Ipswich; 16, Mendlesham; 24, Brightwell; Newbourn; 46, Dunwich; 47, Reydon, 1974; 48, Ellough.

Fagopyrum tataricum (L.) Gaertner   G. Mead 1960

Casual. Cultivated in Europe. Known in Suffolk only from a single record at Brantham.

Rheum rhabarbarum L.   Rhubarb   Mrs. E. M. Hyde 1974

Native of Asia. Found on rubbish tips and as a relic of cultivation.
E: 13, Woolverstone on waste ground, 1974; 17, Thorndon, 1974; 23, Chelmondiston Tip, 1974.

RUMEX   DOCKS

A rather difficult and somewhat neglected group of plants. Further research is needed.

Rumex acetosella L.   Sheep's Sorrel   Sir J. Cullum 1773

Native. Poor grassland, heaths, coastal dunes and shingle, arable fields, woodland glades and plantations. Very frequent. A variable species, depending very much on soil and habitat. The brightest flowering specimens are found in open situations on the sea coast.
All squares.   *Illustrated page 504*

Rumex tenuifolius (Wallr.) Löve   Narrow-leaved Sheep's Sorrel   J. E. Lousley 1948

Native. Dry places, heaths, fixed dunes, waysides. Local.
W: 76; 77; 78; 87; 88; 93; 97; 98.
Frequent in Breckland, 1981.
E: 03; 04; 13; 14; 23; 28; 34; 45; 46; 50.
14, Piper's Vale, Ipswich, 1981; 46, between Sizewell and Dunwich, 1981.

Rumex acetosa L.   Common Sorrel   J. Andrews 1747

Native. In meadows, pastures and damp waysides. Common. All squares.

Rumex frutescens Thouars   H. Boreham and N. S. P. Mitchell 1956
(*R. cuneifolius* Campd.)

Introduced. Native of S. America. Naturalised in a number of coastal places in Britain, usually on dune-slacks and near harbours.
E: Aldeburgh (N. S. P. Mitchell); Thorpeness (H. Boreham). The records may possibly refer to the same site.

Rumex hydrolapathum Huds.   Great Water Dock   Sutton & Kirby 1787

Native. Beside rivers and streams and in ditches and ponds. Also estuaries. Frequent.
W: All squares except 65; 66; 75; 85; 94; 95.
67, Mildenhall, 1980; 83, Cornard Mere.
E: All squares except 06; 17; 26; 27; 37; 38; 48.
14, Ipswich, by the R. Gipping, 1981; 34, Sutton, 1981; 35, Eyke, 1979; 45, Snape, 1981; 46, East Bridge, 1980.

Rumex hydrolapathum × obtusifolius   Hybrid Water Dock   F. W. Simpson c. 1950
(*R. × weberi* Fisch.-Benz.)

This hybrid is thought to be fairly frequent in the County. Examples may be observed in several habitats by rivers, dykes and streams. It is usually a much smaller plant than *R. hydrolapathum*. In East Suffolk I have seen it by the Rivers Gipping, Deben and Waveney, and also bordering dykes, even brackish ones, between Bawdsey and Orford.

Rumex patientia L.   Mrs E. M. Hyde 1980

Alien. Native of S. Europe. Waste places.
E: 14, Ipswich, on waste ground beside the R. Gipping. Conf. E. J. Clement.

Rumex crispus L.   Curled Dock   Sir J. Cullum 1773

Native. Waste places, fields and shingle beaches. Very frequent. All squares.

Rumex conglomeratus Murr.   Sharp Dock   Sir J. Cullum 1773
                                  Clustered Dock

Native. In wet pastures, ditches and fens. Common.
W: All squares except 65.
E: All squares except 05; 06; 07; 17; 28; 37; 38; 39; 44; 58; 59; 40.

Rumex sanguineus L.   Wood Dock   J. Andrews 1744
                           Red-veined Dock
                           Blood Dock

Native. Pastures, woods, waysides and waste shady places. Frequent.
All squares except 65; 78; 07; 24; 37; 58.

Rumex pulcher L. ssp. **pulcher**   Fiddle Dock   Davy 1794

Native. Old pastures, waysides and waste places. Formerly locally frequent. Now decreasing.
W: 66; 67; 76; 77; 86; 87; 88; 93.
67, Freckenham, 1979; 77, Mildenhall, 1980; Icklingham, 1980.
E: 03; 04; 05; 07; 14; 23; 24; 25; 35; 36; 39; 44; 45; 46; 47; 48.
23, Felixstowe, 1980; 39, Bungay, 1981.

Rumex obtusifolius L. ssp. **obtusifolius**   Broad-leaved Dock   Rev. G. Crabbe 1798

Native. On waste ground and roadsides. A weed of cultivation, especially near farm buildings and stack yards. Common. A very variable species, whose forms have not been fully worked out yet. It is possible that some may be hybrids.
All squares.

Rumex palustris Sm.   Marsh Dock   Davy 1802

Native. In marshes, beside streams and rivers. Uncommon.
W: 77; 78; 87; 88; 97.
77, Mildenhall; 78, Lakenheath; Brandon; 88, Euston; 97, Hopton.
E: 04; 07; 17; 23; 48; 58.
48, Beccles, 1971.
Specimens in Hb. Davy: 'Marsh below Burgh Castle, 1802'.

Rumex maritimus L.   Golden Dock   J. Andrews 1751

Native. Broads, marshes, fens and muddy places, inland and near the sea. Rare, and apt to be confused with *R. palustris*, which grows in similar habitats. *R. maritimus* is a variable species.
W: 68; 78; 88; 97.
68, Lakenheath, 1980.
E: 14; 23; 25; 33; 46; 48; 49; 57; 58.
14, Ipswich, 1979 (M. A. Hyde); 49, Beccles, 1976; 57, South Cove, 1974; Easton Bavents.
Specimen in Hb. Davy from Dunwich, 1795.

Muehlenbeckia complexa (Cunn.) Meisn.   Wire Plant   F. W. Simpson 1975

Introduced. Native of New Zealand. A small shrub which can become established and naturalised in suitable coastal habitats. (It has been established on Herm in the Channel Islands since 1911 and is now locally abundant and smothering other vegetation on the Isles of Scilly).
E: 33, Bawdsey Cliffs.

CHENOPODIACEAE

GOOSEFOOT FAMILY

Beta vulgaris L. ssp. **vulgaris**   Sugar Beet

Cultivated. Discarded roots found on tips, waysides and waste ground. Often persisting. Frequent.

Ssp. **maritima** (L.) Arcangeli   Sea Beet   Sutton and Kirby 1787
(*B. maritima* L.)

Native. On the sea coast, especially edges of cliffs and embankments. Very frequent.
E: All coastal and estuarine squares.   *Illustrated page 500*

Ssp. **vulgaris** × ssp. **maritima**   F. W. Simpson c. 1960

This hybrid, for which these are the only records, occurs on the coast.
E: 23, Erwarton; Harkstead; 34, Sutton.

Chenopodium multifidum L.   Mrs R. Paul 1948
(*Roubieva multifida* (L.) Moq.)

Casual. Found in S. Europe, probably native of S. America. Probably imported with animal feeding stuffs. Its occurrence in Suffolk is limited to one record from Wherstead (sq. 13), where it has been reported as naturalised around the stables of a farm.

Chenopodium bonus-henricus L.   Good King Henry   Sir J. Cullum 1773

Established alien. Formerly cultivated. Waysides and waste places, usually near dwellings. Not very frequent and decreasing. Said to be rich in vitamins and a valuable vegetable.
W: All squares except 65; 66; 68; 83; 84; 85.
87, Flempton, 1979; 88, Barnham, 1980.
E: All squares except 05; 26; 33; 34; 38; 44; 48.
14, Blacksmith's Corner, Belstead, 1980; 39, Bungay, former Station, and Outney Common, 1980.   *Illustrated page 509*

Chenopodium foliosum Aschers.   Hb. Wilson 1831
(*Blitum virgatum* L.)

Casual. Native of the Alps and mountains of Spain and Portugal. Recorded in Hind's Flora from waste ground, Bury St Edmunds.

Chenopodium capitatum (L.) Aschers.   Strawberry Goosefoot
Miss I. Sherwood 1965

A rare casual of unknown origin, probably introduced from the continent of Europe. Sometimes found naturalised in fields and on rubbish dumps. The only known records for Suffolk are from Rushmere in 1965 (sq. 24), and Kesgrave in 1967.

Chenopodium glaucum L.   Glaucous Goosefoot   Miss E. Jauncey 1938
Oak-leaved Goosefoot

A rare casual of waste places. Native of continental Europe.
E: 23, Hare's Creek, Shotley; 59, Lowestoft.

Chenopodium rubrum L.   Red Goosefoot   Sir J. Cullum 1774

Native and colonist. Waste places, especially about farms, manure heaps, rubbish dumps and edges of shallow, muddy ponds. Frequent. It is probably only native near the sea, beside pools and on damp shingle. Very variable, according to habitat.
All squares except 64; 74; 83; 96; 98; 26; 27; 28.

Chenopodium botryodes Sm.   Small Red Goosefoot   Sir J. E. Smith 1828
Bunchy Goosefoot

Native. Margins of ditches and brackish pools near the sea. Very rare.
E: 48, Frostenden, 1974 (M. A. Hyde); 57, Easton Bavents, 1946 (F. W. Simpson).

Chenopodium hybridum L.   Sowbane   Sir T. G. Cullum and Davy 1804
Maple-leaved Goosefoot

Doubtfully native. A rare casual of waste places, arable land and gardens.
W: 67, West Row, 1977; 76, Cavenham, 1978; 77, Cavenham Heath; Eriswell; 78; 86, Bury St. Edmunds Abbey gardens; 93, Nayland, 1974.
E: 03, Layham; 15, Coddenham Pit, 1974.
Hb. Davy specimen from Sibton Abbey, 1804.

Chenopodium polyspermum L.   Many-seeded Goosefoot   J. Andrews 1743

Colonist. A weed of cultivated and waste ground. Frequent.
W: 68; 76; 77; 86; 87; 88; 93; 94; 95; 97.
68, Mildenhall, 1977; 86, Fornham All Saints; 87, Elveden.
E: 03; 04; 05; 06; 13; 14; 16; 23; 24; 25; 26; 27; 36; 37; 38; 47; 48; 49; 59.
13, Brantham, in quantity, 1975; 16, Wetheringsett, 1979; 23, Trimley, 1980; 47, Bramfield, 1976, former woodland.

Chenopodium vulvaria L.   Stinking Goosefoot   Davy 1797

Possibly native near the coast. A colonist or rare casual elsewhere. Always scarce or rare, and now extinct in some former habitats.
W: 64, Chalkdon Hill, Haverhill; 75, Chevington.
E: 15, Coddenham; 23, Landguard Common; 33, Felixstowe Ferry; 34, Alderton; 37, Halesworth; 59, Lowestoft.
Specimen in Hb. Davy from 'beach at Aldborough 1797'.
Also Hb. Ipswich Museum: 'Ipswich occasionally and very sparingly on the hedge-bank of the London Road between the Town and Handford Bridge.' August, 1827 (John Notcutt).

Chenopodium urbicum L.   Upright Goosefoot   Davy 1802

Possibly native. A rare casual or weed of cultivation.
W: 67, Mildenhall; 77; 86, Ickworth Park.
E: 06, Onehouse Hall Farm; 14, Lt. Blakenham; 15, Shrubland Park, Barham; 33; 58, Benacre Broad; 59, Lowestoft.
Davy's specimen from 'near Burgh Castle, 1802' is in Hb. Ipswich Museum.

Chenopodium murale L.   Nettle-leaved Goosefoot   Davy 1802

Native. An uncommon casual of fields and waste places.
W: 77, gravel pit, south of Barton Mills; 86, Rushbrook Hall, Lt. Welnetham.
E: 13, Woolverstone, 1976 (M. A. Hyde); 33, Felixstowe; 49.
Hb. Davy specimen from near Yarmouth, 1802.

Chenopodium ficifolium Sm.   Fig-leaved Goosefoot   Paget 1834

A colonist. A weed of rubbish tips, waste places, arable land and manure heaps. Uncommon, but probably overlooked.
W: 65; 67; 76; 78; 86; 87; 88; 94; 95; 97.
67, Worlington, 1977; 78, Maidscross Hill; 94, Brent Eleigh, 1981; 95, Thorpe Morieux, 1977.
E: 05; 13; 14; 38; 48; 49; 58.
14, Bramford, 1980 (E. Milne-Redhead); 48, Beccles, 1974.

Chenopodium opulifolium Schrad. ex Koch & Ziz   Grey Goosefoot
F. W. Simpson 1938

A casual from S. Europe. Known in Suffolk only from Landguard Common, Felixstowe (sq. 23). Detd. at Kew.

Chenopodium album L.　　White Goosefoot　　　　　Sir J. Cullum 1773
(incl. *C. reticulatum* Aell.)　Fat Hen
　　　　　　　　　　　　　Muckweed (Suffolk)

Native or colonist. Cultivated and waste ground. Frequent, often abundant, especially in sugar beet fields. A variable species.
All squares.

Spinacia oleracea L.　　Spinach　　　　　　　Miss J. C. N. Willis 1960
(*S. inermis* Moench)

Probably a native of W. Asia. Cultivated as a vegetable. Occasionally found as a garden escape. Recorded from a roadside near Hadleigh in 1960.

Atriplex halimus L.　　Shrubby Orache　　　　　　　R. Burn 1929

An introduced shrub, native of S. Europe, planted near the sea. Uncommon. The large colony formerly at Minsmere was destroyed after the 1953 floods during the building of a new embankment.
E: 13, Brantham, 1929, still there, 1980; 14, Handford Hall, Ipswich; 23, Nacton, 1979; 33, Felixstowe and Bawdsey; 46, Minsmere, now extinct.

Atriplex hortensis L.　　Garden Orache　　　　　　　E. R. Long c. 1935

A rare alien known in Suffolk from a record at Lowestoft by E. R. Long, and, in 1971, from a rubbish tip at Beccles (P. Lawson and A. Copping).

Atriplex laciniata L.　　Frosted Orache　　　　　　　Stone c. 1790
(*A. sabulosa* Rouy)　　Mealy Orache

Native. On sandy beaches above normal high tide mark. Scarce. First recorded in the County at Pakefield.
E: 23, Landguard Common; Nacton Shore; Erwarton, 1973; Shotley, 1977; 33, Bawdsey; Felixstowe Ferry; 34, Ramsholt; 46, Thorpeness; Minsmere; 47, Walberswick.

Atriplex littoralis L.　　Grass-leaved Orache　　　　　　Davy 1796
　　　　　　　　　　　　Shore Orache

Native. Sea coast and estuaries. Often abundant above high-water level, especially on embankments and the edges of salt marshes. There is a specimen from Aldeburgh in Hb. Davy, 1796.
All coastal and estuarine squares.

Atriplex patula L.　　Common Orache　　　　　　　J. Andrews 1744

Native near the sea. Also occurs as a weed of arable land and waste places. Common.
All squares.

Atriplex hastata L.　　Spear-leaved Orache　　　　　　Davy 1794
(*A. deltoidea* Bab.)　　Hastate Orache

Native. Very variable. A species of the foreshore, where it colonises areas above high water, especially where there is flood debris from salt marshes and other drift material.

Frequent, sometimes abundant. Occurs inland occasionally, but could be mistaken for *A. patula*.
W: All squares except 65; 67; 68; 75; 76; 78; 85; 93.
E: All squares except 06; 15; 26; 27; 28; 36.

Atriplex glabriuscula Edmondst.   Babington's Orache   W. L. Notcutt 1850
(*A. babingtonii* Woods)

Native. On the sea coast, usually on shingle beaches or mixed sand and shingle. Probably frequent, but overlooked.
E: 13; 23; 33; 34; 45; 46; 47; 57; 58; 59.
23, Shotley, 1979; Trimley St Mary, 1981; 45/46, Aldeburgh to Thorpeness, 1979.

Halimione portulacoides (L.) Aell.   Common Sea Purslane   Sutton & Kirby 1787
(*Atriplex portulacoides* L.
Obione portulacoides (L.) Moq.)

Native. Salt marshes and sides of muddy estuaries. Very frequent, sometimes dominant, along the coast and estuaries.
E: 03; 13; 14; 23; 24; 25; 33; 34; 35; 44; 45; 46; 47; 57; 59; 40; 50.

Halimione pedunculata (L.) Aell.   Stalked Sea Purslane   Rev. H. Bryant 1764
(*Atriplex pedunculata* L.
Obione pedunculata (L.) Moq.)

Native. In salt marshes. Extinct. The last known Suffolk record is from Walberswick in July, 1923. (H. S. Redgrove). It formerly occurred about Yarmouth in Norfolk, and Gorleston, Breydon Water, Shingle Street and Aldeburgh. As there are very many suitable habitats on the Suffolk coast, it may be re-found.
There is a specimen in Hb. Ipswich Museum 'gathered by the Ferry at Southwold, Sept. 1798' by Rev. G. R. Leathes.

Kochia scoparia (L.) Schrad.   Burning Bush   M. A. Hyde 1974
Alien, native of continental Europe. Grown in gardens and often appearing on rubbish tips and in waste places.
E: 14, Ipswich, waste ground near the R. Gipping, 1974; 23, Chelmondiston Tip, 1974.

Arthrocnemum perenne (Mill.) Moss   Perennial Glasswort   Mrs Casborne 1830
(*Salicornia perennis* Mill.
S. radicans Sm.)

Native. On the edges of salt marshes, usually where there is some sand and shingle. Locally frequent, mainly in the South-east of the County.
E: 13, Stutton; Harkstead, 1981; 23, Erwarton, 1974; Trimley, 1981; Shotley; 33, Felixstowe Ferry, 1977; 34, Hollesley; Shingle Street, 1979; Ramsholt, 1976; 44, Orford; Havergate Island, 1979; 45, Aldeburgh; Iken; 47, Walberswick, 1975.

Illustrated page 498

SALICORNIA   GLASSWORT or SAMPHIRE

The annual species are difficult to determine and the botanist must be prepared to study them over a number of seasons in all their habitats and throughout their period of growth right up to the autumn when the frost or cold weather sets in, because this gives them their characteristic colours. In the autumn it is possible to identify species by their colour at some distance, when they are growing in quantity.

It seems clear that some species prefer certain habitats. Some prefer the drier parts of salt marshes, which are rarely flooded at high tide, while others grow in very soft mud, usually submerged by high water. One often has to collect a number of specimens of each species for comparison. This plant is still gathered for pickling and for use as a vegetable.

The perennial species of Glasswort *(Arthrocnemum perenne)* is distinctive, with its woody prostrate stems, and can hardly be confused with the annual Glassworts, unless of course, the plants are seedlings in their first year of growth. The fleshy stems of the perennial species are a different shade of green from those of the annual species and even during the growing season, before the autumn, they are usually shaded with orange or yellowish tints.

Salicornia agg.   Marsh Samphire

Annual species of Salicornia are very common, sometimes abundant, in all suitable coastal and estuarine habits. The actual species have, in most cases, not been determined.

Salicornia europaea L.   Marsh Samphire   Dawson Turner 1805
(including *S. stricta* Dum.   Common Glasswort
S. herbacea (L.) L.)

A native annual. In salt marshes, usually near the high tide mark. Common. A variable species. In autumn the plant becomes a yellow colour or, less commonly, pink.
E: 13, Stutton; Cattawade; 23, Trimley Marshes; 24, Martlesham; Waldringfield; 33, Felixstowe; 34, Butley; 44, River Ore; Havergate Island, 1973; 45, Alde Estuary; 46, Sizewell; 47, Walberswick Beach; Blythburgh Marshes; 58, Benacre; 59, Lowestoft.

Illustrated page 502

Salicornia obscura P. W. Ball & Tutin   F. W. Simpson 1950
(? a variant of *S. europaea*)

A native annual. On open mud at the sides of channels and pans in salt marshes. Dull green in colour. Distribution not yet accurately known, but is unlikely to be common.
E: 13, Woolverstone; 34, Shingle Street, Hollesley; 47, Dunwich; Walberswick.

Salicornia ramosissima Woods   Branched Glasswort
(including *S. gracillima* (Towns.) Moss   Victoria County History of Suffolk 1911
S. appressa Dum.
S. smithiana Moss)

Native. An annual plant of salt marshes, usually in the drier areas on wet sand or sandy mud. Frequent. A very variable plant; every form can be found from single to branched specimens. This *Salicornia* becomes red or purplish red in the autumn.
E: 13, Brantham; 34, Boyton marshes; 44, estuary of the River Ore; Havergate Island, 1973; 45, River Alde; 47, Walberswick; Blythburgh Marshes; 58, Covehithe.

Salicornia pusilla Woods   Fragmenting Glasswort   B.S.B.I. Mapping Scheme c. 1955
(including *S. disarticulata* Moss)

An annual, native on the drier areas of salt marshes. Frequent. A branched and usually bushy plant. Light green, becoming brown or yellow in the autumn, with red or pink tips to the branches.

E: 14, Orwell Estuary; 24 and 33, Deben Estuary; 34, Butley River; 44, River Ore; Havergate Island, 1973; 45, River Alde.

Salicornia nitens P. W. Ball & Tutin   F. W. Simpson 1950

A native annual on salt marshes. Usually associated with warm, damp mud and in pans in the higher zones. Probably common, but distribution not yet ascertained. The plants are an attractive shape and appear partly translucent, especially when wet. In the autumn they become brown, purple and orange.
E: 34, Shingle Street, Hollesley.

Salicornia fragilis P. W. Ball & Tutin   Fragile Glasswort

A native annual. On soft, wet mud in the lower zones of salt marshes and creeks. Plants usually with only primary branches. Dull green, becoming dull yellowish green. Probably common and sometimes dominant. Distribution not yet fully recorded, but it occurs in the estuaries of the Ore, Alde and Deben rivers.

Salicornia lutescens P. W. Ball & Tutin

A native annual. Similar to *S. dolichostachya* and may probably be only a variety of this species. On firm and dry mud, or muddy sand. Distribution unknown in Suffolk.

Salicornia dolichostachya Moss   Bushy Glasswort   R. Burn 1933

Native. Usually on bare mud or muddy sand, colonising the lowest zones of salt marshes and muddy creeks. Common.
E: 13, Cattawade; Stutton; 24, Martlesham Creek; 33, Bawdsey; 34, Butley River; 44, Havergate Island, 1973; 47, Walberswick.
It is probable that a number of hybrids, as yet unrecorded, occur. Some of the above species may possibly be intermediate or variable fertile hybrids. Much work remains to be done on this difficult group.

Suaeda vera J. F. Gmel.   Shrubby Sea Blite   Rev. G. R. Leathes 1797
(*S. fruticosa* auct.)

Native. Salt marshes, where there is some sand or shingle. Very rare.
E: 23, Trimley, marshes near Walton Fort, one bush, first seen in 1932 and still there in 1980 (F. W. Simpson); 24, Martlesham (L. W. Howard). Also Mrs I. M. Vaughan, 1981. One bush only.
Recorded by Leathes as 'gathered at Southwold, July 1797' and by Hind from Southwold, Walberswick and Aldeburgh. Hb. Atkins notes 'banks of the Orwell 1908'. (Could this have possibly been gathered from the Trimley specimen!)   *Illustrated page 501*

Suaeda maritima (L.) Dum.   Annual Sea Blite   Davy 1795

Native. In salt marshes and muddy creeks. Abundant.
All coastal and estuarine squares.

Salsola kali L. ssp. **kali**   Prickly Saltwort   Sutton and Kirby 1787

Native. On sandy beaches, above high water mark. Scarce and not so frequent as formerly.

E: 33, Bawdsey, near the Ferry; 34, Shingle Street; 46, between Sizewell and Dunwich; 47, Walberswick; 57, Easton Bavents, 1980; Southwold; 58, Covehithe; 59, Lowestoft; Pakefield; 50, Hopton. *Illustrated page 498*

Ssp. **ruthenica** (Iljin) Soó   Spineless Saltwort   Lowestoft Field Club 1951
(incl. *S. pestifer* A. Nels.)   Russian Thistle

A casual of waste ground. Recorded in Suffolk, from North Quay, Lowestoft in 1951 and from Lakenheath in 1956, and 1975 (M. G. Rutterford and P. J. O. Trist).

AMARANTHACEAE

PIGWEED FAMILY

Amaranthus hybridus L.   Green Pigweed   F. W. Simpson 1957
(*A. chlorostachys* Willd.)   Green Amaranthus

Casual. Native of tropical and subtropical America.
W: 77, Barton Mills Tip, 1977 (M. A. Hyde). Detd. E. J. Clement.
E: 05, Combs, waste heap at the Tannery, 1957 (F. W. Simpson), detd. at Kew; 23, Pin Mill, chicken-run, 1964 (M. A. Hyde), detd. by J. P. M. Brenan.

Amaranthus bouchonii Thell.   J. Keeble & N. Kerr 1959

An introduced alien, origin uncertain.
E: 13, Brantham, sugar beet field, 1959-60, detd. at Kew; Woolverstone, in field of newly-sown rye-grass, 1976 (M. A. Hyde), detd. by J. P. M. Brenan.

Amaranthus retroflexus L.   Common Amaranthus   F. K. Eagle 1852
    Pigweed

Introduced from N. America. A weed or casual of cultivated ground and waste places. Very variable. Not very frequent. (In Hind's Flora as *A. blitum* L.)
W: 66, Exning, new By-pass, 1975; 68, Mildenhall, 1977; 77, Eriswell; 96, Pakenham; also recorded for Risby, Barrow and Brandon.
E: 04, Hadleigh; Whatfield; 05, waste heap at the Tannery, Combs; 13, Brantham; 14, Ipswich, 1974-5; 23, Chelmondiston; 24, Brightwell; 35, Snape; 37, Wenhaston; Oulton Broad c. 1898 (Mrs F. Baker).

Amaranthus blitoides S. Watson   J. E. Lousley, R. Graham, D. McClintock 1949

Casual. Native of C. and N. America. In a carrot field, Capel St Andrew. Detd. by J. P. M. Brenan.

Amaranthus albus L.   Tumble Weed   Rev. G. R. Leathes 1815
    White Pigweed

Alien. Native in N. America, sometimes found as a casual of cultivated fields, gardens and waste places.
E: 14, garden in Constitution Hill, Ipswich; 23, Felixstowe Docks; 47, Blythburgh.

Amaranthus thunbergii Moq.   F. W. Simpson 1958

Casual. The only known record for Suffolk is from a waste heap at the Tannery, Combs, (sq. 05) in 1958. Specimen determined at Kew.

Amaranthus viridis L.   F. W. Simpson 1958

Casual. The only known record for Suffolk is from a waste heap at the Tannery, Combs, (sq. 05) in 1958. Specimen determined at Kew.

PHYTOLACCACEAE
POKEWEED FAMILY

Phytolacca americana L.   Indian Poke   Mrs H. Munro-Cautley c. 1948
(*P. decandra* L.)   American Poke Weed
                                 Inkberry

Usually a casual. Native of N. America. Cultivated in the south of France.
E: 06, on waste ground at the I.C.I. Factory, Stowmarket 1953 (Mrs L. Linnch); 14, one specimen appeared in the garden of 'Drumbeg', Dale Hall Lane, Ipswich, c. 1948; 35, garden at Wickham Market, 1960 (R. W. J. Kefford).

Phytolacca latbenia (Moquin) Maxim.   Mrs E. M. Hyde 1962

Alien. Native of Nepal. Plantations, shrubberies, field margins.
E: 13, Woolverstone, 1962-77, probably birdsown. Detd. at Kew.

Phytolacca acinosa Roxb.   S. J. Batchelder 1927

Alien. Native of China and Japan, cultivated in India. Known in Suffolk by a single record from an Ipswich garden in 1927. Specimen identified at Kew.

AIZOACEAE
MESEMBRYANTHEMUM FAMILY

Carpobrotus chilensis (Mol.) N. E. Brown   Ice Plant   F. W. Simpson 1925

Introduced. Probably a native of S. Africa, although first described from the coast of California, where it was probably an early introduction.
Naturalised on cliffs at Bawdsey (sq. 33) and the Rock Gardens near the Spa Pavilion, Felixstowe (sq. 33). Also seen elsewhere in gardens at Felixstowe, but cultivated.
The date of introduction to the Felixstowe Spa Gardens is unknown, but it was definitely growing there in the early 1930's.
It was probably planted on the cliffs in front of Bawdsey Manor early in the present century, when the gardens were laid out. The face of the sand and Crag cliffs were partly consolidated with cement to protect them from erosion and to form the rock gardens, and this, and other plants, flourished. It was quite abundant in the mid-20's and I took specimens and tried to grow them in my Ipswich garden without success. However, after the R.A.F. took over the grounds in 1939, the garden became neglected and overgrown, but the plant has managed to survive in reduced quantities and has been steadily decreasing ever since. A little still remained in 1979.
It is very surprising that, as it is only half-hardy, it should have survived some very cold

winters, especially that of 1963, exposed to the bitter winds off the North Sea.
We are very much obliged to the late J. E. Lousley for the identification of this specimen.
For a long time this plant was thought by all local botanists to be *C. edulis* (L.) N. R. Br.,
Hottentot's Fig. However, this species has much larger, usually yellow, flowers and it was
due to a visit to the Isles of Scilly and Mr Lousley's Flora on these Isles that I realised the
Suffolk plant was certainly not *C. edulis*.

TETRAGONIACEAE

NEW ZEALAND SPINACH FAMILY

Tetragonia tetragonoides (Pallas) O. Kuntze   New Zealand Spinach
(*T. expansa* Murr.)   F. W. Simpson 1946

Native of Australasia. Introduced and cultivated, sometimes escaping, and may be found
on rubbish tips and waste places. Recorded in Ipswich (sq. 14).

PORTULACACEAE

PURSLANE FAMILY

Portulaca oleracea L.   Purslane   Dowager Countess of Cranbrook c. 1950

Casual, probably native of continental Europe. Uncommon. Occurring on cultivated
ground and in waste places. Annual.
E: 35, Snape (Priory Gardens); 46, Aldringham, in a kitchen garden, 1973/4 (Mrs J.
Hughes).

Montia fontana L., agg.   Blinks   Sir J. Cullum 1774
(*M. verna* Necker   Water Blinks
M. minor Gmel.)

Native. In damp sandy places on heaths and commons. Sometimes also in dry habitats,
such as lawns and paths. Occasional. A very variable species.
The Suffolk plants recorded are:—
(a) ssp. **fontana** (*M. lamprosperma* Cham.)
(b) ssp. **chondrosperma** (Fenzl) Walters (*M. verna* auct.) probably the most frequent
form. There is a record in Hind's Flora for this subspecies from Barnham.
The records below have not been divided into subspecies.
W: 77, Tuddenham St Mary; 84, Boxted; 95, Rattlesden.
E: 03, East Bergholt; 13, Harkstead and Woolverstone, 1980; 14, Chantry Park, Ipswich;
23, Levington; Erwarton; Chelmondiston; 27, Fressingfield, 1981; 34, Butley, 1980; 35,
Chillesford; 36, Bruisyard; 47, Blythburgh; Walberswick; 49, Herringfleet; Beccles; 40,
Fritton; Ashby, 1974.

Montia perfoliata (Willd.) Howell   Spring Beauty   H. G. Glasspoole 1859
(*Claytonia perfoliata* Donn ex Willd.) Perfoliate Claytonia

Alien. Introduced from N. America. It has become established and is spreading. Found in
sandy hedge-banks, open plantations and thickets, especially with Elm.
W: Recorded from squares 64; 67; 76; 77; 78; 83; 86; 87; 88; 93; 94; 96; 97.

Abundant in Breckland, 1981.
E: All squares except 06; 07; 16; 27; 28; 38.
Very frequent on the Sandlings, 1981.   *Illustrated page 510*

Montia sibirica (L.) Howell   Pink Purslane   Finder not recorded c. 1900
(*Claytonia alsinoides* Sims
C. sibirica L.)

Introduced. Native of Western N. America. Recorded from Lowestoft and Snape, at various times from 1900 to 1956. Also from Westleton in a coppice, 1981 (Dr A. T. Pagan).

CARYOPHYLLACEAE

PINK FAMILY

Arenaria balearica L.   Balearic Pearlwort   P. G. Lawson 1978

Introduced. Native of the W. Mediterranean islands. Frequently grown in gardens and sometimes escaping.
E: 46, Westleton.

Arenaria serpyllifolia L.   Thyme-leaved Sandwort   Sir J. Cullum 1773

Native. Dry, sandy places and on walls. Frequent.
All squares.

Var. **macrocarpa** Lloyd   F. W. Simpson 1948

Native. A coastal form of *A. serpyllifolia* on shingle and sandy beaches. Local.
E: 33, Bawdsey; 45, Thorpeness; Aldeburgh; 46, Dunwich; 47, Walberswick.

Arenaria leptoclados (Reichb.) Guss.   Lesser Thyme-leaved Sandwort
                                        Slender Sandwort   Lady Blake c. 1830

Native. In dry, sandy places, especially tracks on heaths and on walls. Probably frequent. This plant may, however, be only a variety of *A. serpyllifolia*. Both grow in similar habitats.
W: 66; 68; 74; 75; 76; 77; 78; 84; 86; 87; 88; 93; 94; 96; 98.
E: 03; 04; 05; 07; 13; 14; 15; 16; 17; 23; 25; 27; 34; 39; 44; 47.

Moehringia trinervia (L.) Clairv.   Three-nerved Sandwort   Sir J. Cullum 1774
(*Arenaria trinervia* L.)   Three-veined Sandwort

Native. In woods and on shady banks. Frequent, but overlooked.
W: All squares except 65; 66; 67; 68.
77, Cavenham, 1980; 97, Stanton, 1980.
E: All squares except 17; 33; 37; 44; 50.
13, Woolverstone, 1981; 15, Barham, 1980.

Minuartia hybrida (Vill.) Schischk.   Fine-leaved Sandwort   J. Andrews 1721
(*Arenaria tenuifolia* L.)

Native. In dry, sandy, fallow arable fields, especially in Breckland and on old walls and embankments. Local or rare. Probably less frequent than in Hind's day.
W: 64; 67; 76; 77; 78; 86; 87; 88; 97; 98.
77, Icklingham, 1979; 78, Lakenheath, 1974.
E: 04; 14; 39; 46; 48; 40.
46, Dunwich, 1966; 40, walls of Burgh Castle, 1963.

Honkenya peploides (L.) Ehrhart   Sea Sandwort   T. Martyn 1763
(*Arenaria peploides* L.)

Native. On sandy and shingly beaches. Formerly frequent, now much reduced, due to erosion and trampling by visitors.
E: 13, Harkstead, 1981; 23, Landguard Common; Trimley, 1981; 33, Bawdsey; Felixstowe Ferry, 1980; 34, Shingle Street, 1981; 45, Aldeburgh; Thorpeness, 1980; Sudbourne, 1976; 46, Sizewell, 1979; Dunwich; Minsmere; 47, Dunwich to Walberswick; 57, Southwold; Easton Bavents, 1980; 58, Kessingland, 1980; Benacre, 1981; Covehithe; 59, Lowestoft, 1980; 50, Corton, 1975.   *Illustrated page 501*

Bufonia tenuifolia L.   Bastard Chickweed

Noted by Hind as recorded from marshes near Yarmouth in 1828 by Davy, but considered by him to be probably an error. Davy's specimens, with no locality given, are in Hb. Ipswich Museum.

Stellaria nemorum L.   Wood Stitchwort
                     Wood Chickweed

Native. Found in damp, shady woods. It is very doubtful whether *S. nemorum* occurs naturally in Suffolk. Although there are many suitable habitats, I have never found a specimen. This not unattractive plant can be seen in old woods and glens, particularly in the Border Counties. It is sometimes very prominent. Once seen it cannot be mistaken for *Myosoton aquaticum* or other species, such as large forms of *S. media*.
Records for Sternfield and Thorpeness in 1941 must be regarded as open to question, in the absence of voucher specimens. There is also a record for Onehouse.

Stellaria media (L.) Vill.   Common Chickweed   Sir J. Cullum 1773

Native. An abundant weed of cultivated ground and waste places. A very variable species.
All squares.

Stellaria neglecta Weihe   Greater Chickweed   Sir J. Cullum 1773
(*S. umbrosa* Opiz & Rufr.)

Native. Shady lanes, banks, copses and woods, chiefly on sandy soils. Locally frequent and probably overlooked.
W: 77; 83; 93.
77, Eriswell; 93, Lt. Cornard, 1965.
E: 04; 05; 07; 13; 14; 16; 24; 25; 27; 37; 39; 47; 58.
05, Bosmere, 1975; 13, Freston, 1979; 27, Syleham, 1980.

Stellaria pallida (Dum.) Piré   Lesser Chickweed   Sir J. Cullum 1773
(*S. apetala* auct.)

Native. On dry sandy soils, chiefly in Breckland and the Sandlings of the coastal areas; also on sand dunes and commons. Locally frequent. This plant is often mistaken for forms of *S. media*. *S. pallida* occurs in Breckland, sometimes in shady habitats, under pines and along tracks and clearings in the plantations. Under-recorded.
W: 75; 76; 77; 78; 87; 88.
E: 23; 34; 35; 39; 47; 49; 58.

Stellaria holostea L.   Greater Stitchwort   Sir J. Cullum 1773
                  Balaam's Smite (Suffolk)
                  Shirt Buttons

Native. Hedgerows, glades and open places in woods, especially on light soils. Common except in Breckland, where it is rare.
All squares.   *Illustrated page 453*

Stellaria alsine Grimm   Bog Stitchwort   Sir J. Cullum 1773

Native. Sides of streams and ditches and muddy places. Frequent, particularly in East Suffolk.
W: 77; 78; 83; 86; 87; 88; 93; 94; 95; 96; 97; 98.
77, Tuddenham Heath, 1978.
E: 03; 04; 05; 13; 14; 15; 23; 24; 25; 27; 28; 35; 36; 38; 39; 45; 46; 47; 59; 40; 50.
13, Freston, 1981; 25, Bromeswell, 1980; 39, Bungay, 1981. Also frequent in the Gipping Valley, 1981.

Stellaria palustris Retz.   Marsh Stitchwort   Sir J. Cullum 1776
(*S. glauca* With.)

Native. In old turfy, damp pastures, grassy fens and marshes. Rare and decreasing due to change or loss of habitats. It is probable that this species has been recorded in error for the frequent *S. graminea,* which looks similar in many aspects and is often found in damp, old grassland, as well as on heaths. *S. palustris* now appears to be restricted to a few sites in the north-west of the County and in Lothingland.
W: 67; 76; 77; 78; 83; 86; 87; 88; 93; 97; 98.
78, Lakenheath, 1975.
E: 03; 04; 07; 15; 24; 25; 35; 37; 46; 47; 49; 57; 59; 40.
46, East Bridge; 59, Carlton Colville, 1978 (P. G. Lawson); 40, Belton, 1978.
Hb. Ipswich Museum: 'In the meadows between the Bramford Road and the River', June 1819 (John Notcutt).

Stellaria graminea L.   Lesser Stitchwort   Sir J. Cullum 1773

Native. Old pastures, grassy waysides and heaths. Frequent.
W: All squares except 65; 67; 68; 74; 84; 85.
E: All squares except 06; 37; 57.

Holosteum umbellatum L.   Umbellate Chickweed   Sir J. Cullum 1773
                    Jagged Chickweed

Native. Formerly found on old walls and Breckland heaths, but now extinct. The species is recorded in Hind's Flora from Bury St Edmunds 'on a wall leading from Maywater Lane to Southgate Street. Formerly it grew on thatched roofs just beyond the railway station, Northgate, Bury. Plentiful on walls at Eye, and sparingly on the ruins at Hoxne Abbey.' This species was probably once frequent in Breckland; its fruits have been found to be common in the deposits of the ancient Breckland meres. Last record c. 1880.

Cerastium biebersteinii DC.

An alien, native in the Caucasus. The species has been recorded twice since 1950, in squares 44 and 46, but exact localities are unknown. Perhaps recorded in error for *C. tomentosum*.

Cerastium tomentosum L.   Dusty Miller   J. L. Gilbert 1941
Snow-in-Summer

An established alien. Native in S.E. Europe and the Caucasus. Usually a garden escape or outcast on roadsides and railway embankments. More frequent than formerly, and increasing. Not recorded in Hind's Flora.
W: 66, Moulton and Newmarket, 1974; 77, Mildenhall; Icklingham, 1980; 78, Lakenheath, 1980; Wangford; 84, Sudbury; 86, Bury St Edmunds; Westley, 1980; Fornham St Martin; 87, West Stow; 94.
E: 03; 04, Hadleigh; 05, Needham Market, 1981; 06, Wetherden, 1977; 13, Bentley; Brantham, 1974; 14, Ipswich, railway embankment, 1981; Bramford; 23, Landguard Common, 1979; 24, Martlesham, 1980; Rushmere, 1981; 25; 33, railway embankment, Felixstowe; Felixstowe Ferry, 1979; Bawdsey; 35, Campsey Ash, near Station, 1981; 37, Halesworth, 1981; 45, Aldeburgh, 1978; 47; 48, Shadingfield, 1976; 57, Southwold, 1980; 59, Lowestoft, 1980; 40, Belton, 1977.

Cerastium decalvans Schlosser & Vuk.   F. W. Simpson 1976

Introduced. Native of Europe. Very similar to *C. tomentosum,* but without the dense white woolly appearance of that species. The flowers resemble those of *C. arvense*.
E: 24, on a hedgebank at Gt Bealings, 1981. Detd. P. D. Sell.

MOUSE-EAR CHICKWEEDS

The identification of some species presents difficulties to many botanists. This is due to great variation in size and growth, usually depending on habitat. In the dry and poor conditions of Breckland and the Sandlings, plants are frequently small and mat-like, scarcely rising above ground-level.

Cerastium arvense L.   Field Mouse-ear Chickweed   Sir J. Cullum 1773

Native. Sandy and chalky fallow fields, waysides and heaths. Very frequent in the Breckland. Now extinct in many of its former East Suffolk habitats.
W: 66; 67; 68; 75; 76; 77; 78; 83; 86; 87; 88; 93; 95; 97; 98.
77, Mildenhall, Cavenham, Tuddenham, Icklingham, all in 1981; 78, Wangford, Lakenheath, Brandon, all 1981.
E: 03; 14; 15; 16; 23; 24; 34; 35; 38; 39; 45; 46; 47; 58; 59; 40; 50.
24, Purdis Heath, 1981; 47, Westleton, 1979.   *Illustrated page 468*

Cerastium fontanum Baumg. ssp. **triviale** (Link) Jalas   Common Mouse-ear Chickweed
(*C. holosteoides* Fr.   J. Andrews 1745
C. vulgatum L.)

Native. Found in cultivated and waste places, waysides and coastal areas. Very common, especially in Breckland.
All squares.

Cerastium glomeratum Thuill.   Sticky Mouse-ear Chickweed   J. Andrews 1745
(*C. viscosum* auct.)

Native. A weed of poor pastures and banks. Also found on sandy and gravelly tracks, heaths, dunes, old walls and maritime shingle. Frequent, especially in Breckland and near the coast.
W: All squares except 65; 67; 68; 85.
E: All squares except 06; 15; 24; 26; 36; 37; 44; 46; 47; 48; 49; 58; 59; 40; 50.

Cerastium semidecandrum L.   Little Mouse-ear Chickweed   J. Andrews 1744

Native. Heaths, dry places, sand dunes and sea cliffs. Frequent in the Breckland. Common.
W: 66; 68; 76; 77; 78; 86; 87; 88; 97; 98.
E: 03; 05; 07; 13; 15; 17; 24; 25; 28; 33; 34; 35; 39; 44; 45; 46; 47; 50.

Cerastium pumilum Curt.   Dwarf Mouse-ear Chickweed   Dr G. C. Druce 1913
                                Curtis's Mouse-ear Chickweed

Native. On dry, chalky grassland and heaths. Rare and local. Stated in Clapham, Tutin and Warburg's Flora of the British Isles to occur in Suffolk. The only known record is from Lowestoft.

Cerastium diffusum Pers.   Sea Mouse-ear Chickweed   Rev. G. Crabbe 1805
(*C. atrovirens* Bab.   Dark Green Mouse-ear Chickweed
C. tetrandrum Curt.)

Native. A coastal species, found on old shingle and sand. Occasionally inland. Local.
W: 78, 88, Thetford Warren.
E: 13, Harkstead, 1978; 23, Landguard Common, 1977; 33/34, Felixstowe to Shingle Street; 46, Minsmere; 47, Southwold.

Moenchia erecta (L.) Gaertn., Mey. & Scherb.   Upright Chickweed   Sir J. Cullum 1773
(*Cerastium erectum* (L.) Coss. & Germ.)

Native. On dry, sandy heaths and commons. Now very rare. Extinct in some former habitats.
W: 77, Cavenham; 88, Thetford.
E: 33, Felixstowe; 35, Eyke; Blaxhall; Wantisden; Tunstall; 38, Bungay; 47, Blythburgh; Buss Creek, near Reydon; Walberswick, 1980; Southwold, 1981; 49, Beccles, 1980 (P. G. Lawson); 40, Fritton.
There is a specimen in Hb. Atkins from Nacton Heath, 1908.

Myosoton aquaticum (L.) Moench   Water Chickweed   Sir J. Cullum 1772
(*Cerastium aquaticum* L.
Stellaria aquatica (L.) Scop.)

Native. In old marshes, beside streams and rivers, in damp, peaty woods and alder carrs. Frequent.
W: All squares except 64; 65; 75; 76; 85.
83, Cornard Mere, 1975; 93, by the R. Stour at Nayland; 96, Pakenham Fen; 97, Hopton, 1981.
E: All squares except 06; 16; 23; 28; 33; 44; 48; 58; 59; 50.
07, Redgrave Fen; 14, by the R. Gipping, Ipswich to Bramford, 1980; 24, Playford, 1981; 35, Gromford, 1981; 39, Bungay, 1981.

Sagina nodosa (L.) Fenzl   Knotted Pearlwort   J. Andrews 1746
Native. On the edge of fens and ditches. Also on moist heaths, expecially in areas flooded during the winter. Local and becoming scarcer.
W: 64; 67; 68; 76; 77; 78; 83; 87; 88; 93; 95; 97; 98.
67, Mildenhall, 1977; 77, Tuddenham Fen, 1978; 78, Lakenheath, 1974.
E: 07; 45; 46; 47; 58; 59; 40.
07, edge of Redgrave Fen, 1972.

Sagina subulata (Sw.) C. Presl   Heath Pearlwort   Mrs R. Clark 1965
                                       Awl-leaved Pearlwort
Native. On dry, sandy and gravelly heaths. Its occurrence in Suffolk is supported by only one record, from North Stow Farm (sq. 87) in 1965. The distribution of the species is normally mainly confined to the North and West of the British Isles, and the record must therefore be considered as doubtful in the absence of vouching material. It could have been in error for *S. ciliata*.

Sagina procumbens L.   Procumbent Pearlwort   Sir J. Cullum 1773
Native. On paths, old walls, lawns, pastures and the sides of streams. Common.
All squares.

Sagina apetala Ard.   Annual Pearlwort   Rev. G. Crabbe 1798
                            Common Pearlwort
Native. Dry, sandy places and walls. A variable species. Common.
W: All squares except 64; 65; 67; 68; 83; 95.
E: All squares except 26; 27; 28; 35; 48.
Some of these records may refer to *S. ciliata*.

Sagina ciliata Fr.   Ciliate Pearlwort   Newbould 1847
(including *S. filicaulis* Jord.)
Native. Dry, bare sandy ground, heaths, tracks, sandpits, and walls. Occasional.
W: 67; 76; 77; 86; 87.
E: 03; 04; 13; 17; 28; 34; 35; 44; 45; 47; 58; 50.

Sagina maritima Don   Sea Pearlwort   J. Backhouse 1810
Native. On old dunes and edges of salt marshes. Scarce or overlooked.
E: 23, Orwell Shore, Nacton; 33, Bawdsey; Felixstowe Ferry; 34, Hollesley; Boyton; Shingle Street; 45, Sudbourne Beach; Iken; 46, Westleton; 47, Southwold; 58, Kessingland.

Scleranthus perennis L. ssp. **prostratus** P. D. Sell   Perennial Knawel   Ray 1696

Native. Dry, sandy Breckland heaths. Very rare. Now extinct in some former sites. This subspecies is only known in the Norfolk and Suffolk Breckland.

W: 77, Barton Mills; Eriswell; Mildenhall; Icklingham; 78, Lakenheath; Eriswell; 88, Barnham Cross Common; Thetford Heath. Known (1980) in only three sites.

Illustrated page 467

Scleranthus annuus L. ssp. **annuus**   Annual Knawel   Sir J. Cullum 1773

Native or colonist. On dry sandy soils, heaths, commons, arable and waste places. Common.

W: All squares except 65; 66; 68; 74; 75; 84; 85.
E: All squares except 05; 16; 26; 27; 36; 37; 38; 48; 49; 59; 50.

Ssp. **polycarpos** (L.) Thell.   Annual Knawel   E. L. Swann 1973

Native. Heaths of Breckland and East Suffolk. Probably frequent, but overlooked.
W: 67, Mildenhall, 1979; 77, Icklingham, 1973; Cavenham; 78, Eriswell.
E: 35, Tunstall Common; 47, Wenhaston.

Herniaria glabra L.   Glabrous Rupture-wort   Sir T. G. Cullum 1804
                            Smooth Rupture-wort

Native. On chalky and sandy heaths. Rare. This species does not occur in Suffolk outside Breckland. Sometimes introduced into gardens as a ground-cover plant.

W: 66, Herringswell, 1980; 67, Worlington; 76, Risby; Kentford; Herringswell; Higham, 1980; Gazeley, 1980; 77, Tuddenham.

Also recorded from Barton Mills, Mildenhall, Freckenham, Icklingham and Cavenham, but not seen recently.

Spergula arvensis L.   Corn Spurrey   Sir J. Cullum 1773
                            Field Spurrey
                            Cowquake (Suffolk)

Native, or an early introduction. Dry, sandy, arable fields on poor acid soils. Common, often abundant.

W: All squares except 65; 66; 68; 74; 75; 84; 85.
E: All squares except 26; 50.
Var. **arvensis** recorded from Belstead, Wherstead and Aldham.
Var. **sativa** (Boenn.) Mert. & Koch recorded from Southwold, 1951.

Spergularia media (L.) C. Presl   Greater Sea Spurrey   Sutton & Kirby 1787
(*S. marginata* Kittel)

Native. In the drier parts of salt marshes. Also on sea embankments. Frequent. A perennial species.

E: 03; 13; 14; 23; 24; 25; 33; 34; 35; 44; 45; 46; 47; 58; 59; 40; 50.
13, Holbrook and Harkstead, 1981; 45, Snape, 1981.
A fully double-flowered variety occurred for a number of years at Bawdsey on the edge of the sea embankment. This was destroyed in 1972 by the burning of the grass bank and adjacent salt pastures.

Spergularia marina (L.) Griseb.　　Lesser Sea Spurrey　　　Sutton and Kirby 1787
(*S. salina* J. & C. Presl)

Native. In dry and wet areas of salt marshes. Often abundant in suitable habitats. A much smaller plant than *S. media* and more widespread. An annual species.
E: 03; 13; 14; 23; 24; 25; 33; 34; 44; 45; 46; 47; 59; 40; 50.
Frequent in all estuarine squares, 1981.

Spergularia rubra (L.) J. & C. Presl　　Common Sand Spurrey　　Sir J. Cullum 1773
(*Arenaria rubra* L.)　　　　　　　　　　Red Sand Spurrey

Native. Dry sandy and gravelly heaths, quarries and tracks. Locally frequent.
W: Recorded from squares 66; 67; 76; 77; 78; 86; 87; 93; 97; 98.
77, Cavenham Heath, 1980; 98, Knettishall Heath, 1981.
E: All squares except 06; 07; 16; 27; 28; 36; 37; 38; 44.
24, Brightwell and Newbourn, 1981; 39, Bungay, 1981; 45, Snape, 1981; 47, Blythburgh and Walberswick, 1981.

Spergularia bocconii (Scheele) Aschers. & Graebn.　　Boccone's Sand Spurrey
　　　　　　　　　　　　　　　　　　　　　　　　　J. L. Gilbert 1942

Probably introduced. Native of S.W. Europe and the Mediterranean region. Dry, sandy localities. Recorded from a cornfield near Orwell Park in 1942. Probably a casual. No specimen seen.

Lychnis coronaria (L.) Desr.　　Rose Campion　　　　　F. W. Simpson 1947

Introduced. Native in S.E. Europe. Frequently grown as a garden plant and persists for a number of years when discarded.
W: 76, Herringswell, edge of woodland, 1980 (Mrs E. M. Hyde).
E: 13, Brantham and Holbrook, 1974; Stutton, 1976; 14, Ipswich, Wherstead Road, 1974; 24, Rushmere, 1976; 33, Felixstowe Ferry, 1979; Bawdsey, 1947-1972; 35, Snape, 1980 (F. W. Simpson).

Lychnis flos-cuculi L.　　Ragged Robin　　　　　　　Sir J. Cullum 1773

Native. Marshes, wet pastures and glades in woods on the clay soils. Frequent, but not so common as formerly and decreasing rapidly. A white-flowered form has been recorded from Foxhall, and Dagworth, near Haughley, and a pale pink form from Badley. A double-flowered form recorded from Capel St Andrew.
All squares.　　　　　　　　　　　　　　　　　　*Illustrated page 478*

Agrostemma githago L.　　Corn Cockle　　　　　　　Sir J. Cullum 1773
(*Lychnis githago* (L.) Scop.)

A colonist, probably introduced from the Mediterranean area. Formerly an attractive and common weed of cornfields. Now very scarce and only appearing occasionally, probably from deeply buried seeds brought to the surface during cultivation or drainage.
W: 75, Hawkedon, 1970; 78; 87, Elveden and Icklingham, 1979 (J. L. Raincock); 96, Woolpit.
E: 14, Ipswich, 1978 (Mrs H. S. Thompson); 16, Mendlesham; 25, Charsfield, Debach and Burgh area, 1957; 33, Walton; 34, Hollesley; Sutton; 35, Snape; 36, Benhall Green;

37, Wissett; 45, Iken; 47, Dunwich, 1978; 58, Gisleham.
Some of these records date from the early 1950's.

Silene nutans L.   Nottingham Catchfly   Hind 1885

A colonist, probably introduced into the County, though native in other parts of Britain.
Waste places and fields. Rare.
W: 77, Eriswell.
E: 23, Felixstowe Docks, 1936; 36, Sternfield.

Silene catholica (L.) Ait. fil.   G. Wolsey 1857

Introduced. A native of Italy. Recorded by Hind as having been found at Gt Livermere,
near Bury St Edmunds, and also in a shrubbery at Southgate Green, Bury St Edmunds.

Silene otites (L.) Wibel   Spanish Catchfly   Sare 1650

Native. Wayside verges, banks and heaths in Breckland. This species is one of the
Breckland specialities. Locally frequent, although it has disappeared from a number of
sites, due to afforestation and ploughing.
W: 67, Mildenhall; Freckenham; 68, Lakenheath; 77, Tuddenham Heath; Cavenham;
Eriswell, 1981; Icklingham, 1981; Barton Mills, 1981; 78, Lakenheath, 1980; Eriswell,
1980; Wangford, 1980; 88, Barnham Cross Common; Santon Downham.

Illustrated page 468

Silene vulgaris (Moench) Garcke ssp. **vulgaris**   Bladder Campion   Sir J. Cullum 1774
(S. inflata Sm.)   Whitebottle

Native. Waysides, quarries, embankments. More frequent on chalky soils.
All squares.   *Illustrated page 474*

Ssp. **maritima** (With.) A. & D. Löve   Sea Campion   Sir J. Cullum 1771

Native. Sea coast, chiefly on shingle beaches. Frequent, sometimes abundant. The colour
of the calyx varies from pale green to purplish-brown.
E: 13, Harkstead; 23, Landguard Common; 33, Felixstowe; Bawdsey; 34, Shingle Street;
Hollesley; Boyton; 44, Orford; 45, Sudbourne; Aldeburgh; 46, Dunwich; 47,
Walberswick; 57, Southwold; Easton Bavents; 58, Benacre.   *Illustrated page 503*
A form with pale flowers and pale green calyx was recorded from Shingle Street and
Landguard Common.

Silene armeria L.   Sweet William Catchfly   J. S. Wilkinson and J. Atkins 1908

Introduced from S. and C. Europe and widely cultivated in gardens, whence it may
escape and become naturalised. Known in Suffolk from Ipswich (J. S. Wilkinson) and
'banks of the Orwell' in Hb. Atkins, both 1908.

Silene noctiflora L.   Night-flowering Campion   Sir J. Cullum 1773
(Melandrium noctiflorum (L.) Fr.)   Night-scented Catchfly

Native or colonist. A weed of cultivation in arable fields and field edges. Less frequent
than formerly. Seldom in large numbers.
W: All squares except 65; 68; 84; 88; 98.
66, Exning, 1977; 67, Mildenhall, 1977; 94, Brent Eleigh, 1981.

E: Recorded from squares 04; 06; 14; 15; 16; 23; 25; 26; 33; 34; 38; 39; 59.
04, Bramford, 1981; 14, Thurleston, Ipswich, 1977; 34, Hollesley, 1976.
Hb. Ipswich Museum: 'From a turnip-field by Stone Lodge, Ipswich. Occasionally found in corn and turnip fields about Ipswich, south and south-west of the Town', c. 1820 (John Notcutt).

RED AND WHITE CAMPION

Although the White Campion is described as native of the British Isles, there appears to be some doubt and it is more likely that it is a long established colonist. Its usual habitat is waste places, hedge-banks and cultivated ground. This seems to point to its status as an introduction, probably in Neolithic times with the advent of cultivation. When found near the sea or on estuarine cliffs, it could perhaps be regarded as native.
Hybrids between the Red and White Campions are very frequent on light, rich soils, especially in hedge-banks and on margins of woods. The hybrids, which are fertile, are very variable and many intermediates can be found. The colour of the flowers is usually a pink shade.
White-flowered forms of the Red Campion occur occasionally and can be easily mistaken for hybrids.

Silene alba (Mill.) E. H. L. Krause   White Campion   Sir J. Cullum 1773
(*Melandrium album* (Mill.) Garcke   Billy Buttons
Lychnis alba Mill.)   Plum Puddings (Suffolk)

Native. In woods and copses on light sandy soils, waysides, waste places and fallow fields. Very common in suitable habitats.
All squares.

Silene alba × dioica   Hybrid Campion   C. C. Babington 1840
(*Lychnis × intermedia* (Schur) Druce)

A not uncommon hybrid where both parent species occur. Variable in growth and in the colour of its flowers. It is very frequent in the Ipswich and Shotley areas and is more frequent than records suggest in other parts of the County.
W: 74; 76; 77; 85; 86; 87; 94.
E: 03; 04; 05; 06; 13; 14; 17; 23; 24; 25; 33; 35.

Silene dioica (L.) Clairv.   Red Campion   Sir J. Cullum 1773
(*Melandrium rubrum* (Weigel) Garcke)

Native. Open woodland, copses, clearings in plantations, waysides. Very frequent. Usually on light, sandy soil. Often associated with bluebell woods, flowering before the bracken comes up.
All squares.   *Illustrated page 454*
White-flowered forms at Freston, Stoke-by-Nayland, Bentley, Purdis Heath.

Silene muscipula L.   Mrs M. Southwell 1950

A casual from the Mediterranean region. First recorded for Suffolk on a derelict poultry run at Lakenheath in 1950, and again in 1962 by M. G. Rutterford.

Silene dichotoma Ehrh.   Forked Catchfly   Mrs F. Baker c. 1900

A casual. Native in E. Europe and W. Asia. Single record from Oulton Broad.

Silene gallica L.   English Catchfly   J. Andrews 1738
(*S. anglica* L.)   Small-flowered Catchfly

Native or colonist. A weed of light cultivated fields. Local and decreasing.
W: 77; 78; 86; 87; 94; 95.
86, Hengrave 1965.
E: 13; 16; 23; 24, Woodbridge (Notcutt's Nurseries), 1974; 35; 36; 46; 47; 57; 58; 40; 50.
40, Lound, 1977.
Hb. Ipswich Museum: 'By the side of the footpath in the cornfields between Spring-head
Lane St Helens and Rushmere Heath,' c. 1820 (John Notcutt).
Var. **quinquevulnera** (L.) Koch: 58, Benacre, 1978.

Silene conica L. ssp. **conica**   Sand Catchfly   Sir J. E. Smith 1800
                                         Striated Catchfly

Native. Sandy fields, sand-pits and sandy ground near the sea. Generally scarce, but still
not uncommon in Breckland.
W: 67, Mildenhall; Freckenham; Worlington; 76, Risby; 77, Icklingham; Barton Mills,
1981; 78, Lakenheath, 1980; Wangford; Eriswell; 86, West Stow; 88, Brandon.
E: 05, Combs Ford beside the A45, from seed sown by Mr and Mrs Mitchell in 1956,
about 550 plants; 23, Landguard Common; Felixstowe, 1980; 24, Lt. Bealings; 34, Red
Crag pit, near Butley Mill; 45, Aldeburgh, 1978; 46; 58, Kessingland; 59, Oulton Broad.
Illustrated page 469

Silene conoidea L.   Mrs F. Baker c. 1900

A casual from the W. Mediterranean region. Recorded by Mrs Baker from Oulton Broad.

Gypsophila pilosa Huds.   Mrs F. Baker c. 1890
(*G. porrigens* (L.) Boiss.)

A casual, native of W. Asia. Known in Suffolk only from a single record from Oulton
Broad.

Saponaria officinalis L.   Soapwort   Sir J. Cullum 1773
                                 Bouncing Bett

Introduced and established. Waysides, waste places and sites of former gardens.
Common. Double-flowered forms are frequent.
W: All squares except 64; 65; 66; 68; 74; 83; 85; 95.
78, Maidscross Hill, Lakenheath, 1980; 86, Fornham All Saints, 1980; 87, Elveden, 1980;
98, Knettishall, 1979.
E: All squares except 06; 07; 16; 17; 26; 27; 36.
14, Ipswich, several sites, 1981; 35, roadside, A12, between Wickham Market and
Marlesford, 1980; 38, Bungay, 1981. Variety with white double flowers at Snape, 1976 (N.
Kerr).   *Illustrated page 508*

Vaccaria pyramidata Medic.   Cowherb   Mrs McAubrey c. 1889
(*Saponaria vaccaria* L.)   Cow Basil

Casual. Introduced from Europe or Asia, where it is a weed of cultivated fields. In waste

places and gardens, usually from waste cage-bird seed. First recorded from Beccles in Hind's Flora. Also found by Mrs F. Baker at Lowestoft and Oulton Broad in 1899.
E: 14, Ipswich, garden in Ascot Drive, 1969 (Miss L. Riches); 23, Felixstowe Docks, c. 1936; 35, Snape, 1980 (F. W. Simpson).

Petrorhagia saxifraga (L.) Link   Tunic Flower   P. G. Lawson 1976
(*Tunica saxifraga* (L.) Scop.)

Introduced. Native of continental Europe.
E: 45, Thorpeness, escape from cultivation. (Detd. E. L. Swann).

Petrorhagia prolifera (L.) P. W. Ball & Heywood   Proliferous Pink   E. F. Long 1935
(*Kohlrauschia prolifera* (L.) Kunth
Dianthus prolifer L.)

Native, in dry, sandy places in S. England. Rare. The only Suffolk record is from Felixstowe Docks in 1935 and was probably a casual from the Continent.

Dianthus barbatus L.   Sweet William   Mrs E. M. Hyde 1973

Naturalised garden escape. Native of continental Europe.
E: 13, Bentley, 1975; 14, Wherstead Churchyard, 1973; 23, Chelmondiston Tip, 1974.

Dianthus caryophyllus L.   Clove Pink   J. Andrews 1745

Introduced from S. Europe and N. Africa, and naturalised on old walls. Hind's Flora has a single record from the walls of Crowe Hall at Debenham in 1879. Also recorded from Debenham by S. J. Batchelder in the 1930's.

Dianthus plumarius L.   Wild Pink   First recorded 1834
                             Common Pink

Introduced from S.E. Europe. Naturalised on old walls and dry sunny banks, usually near or outside gardens.
W: 86, Westley Road, Bury St Edmunds.
E: 16, Mendlesham; 23, edge of Landguard Common, probably from garden rubbish.

Dianthus deltoides L.   Maiden Pink   Sir J. Cullum 1773

Native. Sandy heaths, chiefly confined to Breckland. Less frequent than formerly, due to afforestation.
W: 67, Mildenhall; 76; 77, Icklingham, c. 1950; Cavenham Heath; 86, Bury St Edmunds; 87, West Stow Heath, 1980; 88, Thetford.
E: 13, Stutton; 14, Whitton; Rushmere Common, c. 1950; 36, Benhall Green, pre-1950.
                                                          Illustrated page 468
Dianthus armeria L.   Deptford Pink   Davy 1828

Native. On dry sandy waysides, pastures and commons. Not seen recently. Probably extinct. Last record c. 1950.
E: 15, Coddenham, c. 1950.
Recorded in Hind's Flora from Barton, Sudbury, Bungay, Oulton, Mendham, Wetheringsett, Coddenham and Needham Market. Specimens in Hb. Ipswich Museum: roadside, Kersey, 1850, and Bungay, 1907. There is also an old record for Creeting in 1879.

NYMPHAEACEAE

WATER LILY FAMILY

Nymphaea alba L.   White Water Lily   J. Andrews 1745
(*Castalia alba* (L.) W. Wood)

Probably introduced. Mainly found in ornamental ponds, lakes and rivers, where it is often planted.
W: 64; 77; 78; 85; 86; 87; 88; 93; 95; 96.
E: 03; 04; 13; 14; 27; 28; 34; 38; 39; 48; 49; 40.

Nuphar lutea (L.) Sibth. & Sm.   Yellow Water Lily   Sir J. Cullum 1775
(*Nymphaea lutea* L.)   Brandy-bottle
Native. In rivers, ponds and dykes. Frequent in our major rivers, although not always flowering.
All squares except 65; 66; 67; 75; 76; 06; 07; 57.   *Illustrated page 487*

CERATOPHYLLACEAE

HORNWORT FAMILY

Ceratophyllum demersum L.   Spined Hornwort   J. Andrews 1745
Dark Hornwort

Native. In ditches, rivers, lakes and ponds. Also in brackish ditches. Not uncommon, but not as frequent as formerly.
W: 68; 75; 84; 86; 87; 88; 93; 96; 97.
68, Lakenheath; 88, Euston.
E: 03; 13; 14; 15; 16; 26; 34; 37; 39; 44; 45; 46; 47; 48; 49; 57; 58.
13, Cattawade, 1975; 14, in the R. Gipping between Ipswich and Bramford, 1981; 39, Mettingham, 1980; 44, Gedgrave; 46, Thorpeness Mere, 1973.

Ceratophyllum submersum L.   Spineless Hornwort   J. Andrews 1745
Pale Green Hornwort
Native. In rivers, dykes and ponds. Also in brackish ditches. Not very frequent or possibly overlooked and confused with *C. demersum*.
W: 83, Lt. Cornard; 84, Sudbury.
E: 23, Shotley, 1981; 33, Felixstowe Ferry; 34, Alderton; Boyton; Shingle Street; 45, Sudbourne; 46, Dunwich; Leiston; 47, Walberswick; Darsham; 58, Benacre.

RANUNCULACEAE

BUTTERCUP FAMILY

Helleborus foetidus L.   Stinking Hellebore   J. Sherrard 1724
Setterwort (Suffolk)
Native or introduced. In hedges and thickets, usually on Chalk or Chalky Boulder Clay.

Formerly frequent, now rare. Sometimes a garden escape, and on the sites of old cottages. It was once grown for its medicinal properties.

W: 66; 86; 93; 94; 95; 96.

66, Moulton, 1978 (Mrs E. M. Hyde); 94, Monks Eleigh, 1975 (J. A. Foster).

E: 05; 07; 15; 16; 24; 26; 27; 36; 38; 59.

07, roadside, Thelnetham, 1975; 24, Playford, 1976; 38, Flixton, 1976 (P. G. Lawson). There is a specimen in Hb. Davy from 'the lane, top of Banier's Green, Laxfield, 1796.'

Illustrated page 451

Helleborus viridis L. ssp. **occidentalis** (Reut.) Schiffn. Woodward 1805

Green Hellebore
Bear's Foot

Native. In woods and copses, usually on loamy or chalky soils. Local or rare. Extinct in several of its earlier habitats, due to removal to gardens.

W: 64, Haverhill; 93, Newton, 1977; 96, Beyton; Pakenham.

E: 04, Kersey; Flowton; Hintlesham, 1981; 36, Bruisyard Wood.

This species is recorded in Hind's Flora from Beyton, Bury St Edmunds, Felsham, Hitcham, Kettlebaston, Bungay, Benhall, Hoxne, and Blunt's Wood. There is a specimen in Hb. Atkins from Nettlestead, 1909. *Illustrated page 449*

Eranthis hyemalis (L.) Salisb. Winter Aconite Hind 1876

Introduced from S. Europe. naturalised in plantations, parks and churchyards. Frequent, sometimes abundant.

W: 76: 77; 85; 86; 87; 93; 96.

77, Icklingham; Barton Mills, 1980.

E: 03; 13; 14; 15; 17; 23; 24; 26; 27; 35; 36; 37; 38; 46; 48; 49; 40.

03, Capel St Mary, 1981; 23, Nacton, 1981; 24, Playford, 1981. *Illustrated page 457*

Nigella arvensis L. J. S. Wilkinson 1908

Casual. Native of most of Europe. Waste places. Only one record, from Ipswich.

Nigella damascena L. Love-in-a-Mist L. J. Hyde 1981

Casual. Native of S. Europe. Waste places and former gardens. This is the commonly cultivated species.

39, Bungay, waste ground.

Caltha palustris L. Kingcup Rev. G. Crabbe 1798

Marsh Marigold
May Blobs

Native. Marshes, wet meadows, woods and copses, besides streams, ditches and ponds. Frequent, but decreasing. A variable species; the usual form has bright orange-yellow flowers with ovate or rounded sepals. There is, however, a frequent form, usually taller, with fewer flowers and much paler sepals which are almost lemon-yellow, more oblong and narrowed to a point. Kingcups used to be abundant in many wet pastures and river valleys throughout the County, but they have become less frequent, and almost exterminated in several areas, through the use of sprays, draining and ploughing. They persist in wet woods, especially of the Alder carr type.

All squares except 65; 66; 67; 76; 50   *Illustrated page 482*

A semi-double form reported from Capel Green, near Butley.

Aconitum napellus L. sensu lato   Monkshood   Rev. E. A. Holmes 1840
(*A. anglicum* Stapf)   Wolfbane

Introduced from continental Europe and naturalised. Damp woodland, sites of former gardens. Formerly cultivated for the very poisonous properties of the roots, which were once used as a bait for wolves, hence its old name of 'Wolfbane'! Rare.

W: 75, Chevington; 76, Saxham; 86; 87, Barnham, 1980.

E: 04, Hadleigh, 1981; 13, Stutton; 14, Ipswich; 24, Foxhall; 36, Benhall. Only two recent records.   *Illustrated page 451*

Consolida orientalis (Gay) Schroedinger ssp. **orientalis**   Eastern Larkspur
(*Delphinium orientale* Gay)   Mrs M. Southwell 1955

Casual or garden escape, introduced from S.E. Europe and W. Asia. Field margins, waste places and rubbish tips. There is some doubt about the status of this species in the County and some records may refer to *C. ambigua*.

W: 67, Mildenhall; 77, Tuddenham (E. L. Swann).

E: 05, Badley; 14, Westerfield; 47, Walberswick.

Consolida ambigua (L.) P. W. Ball & Heywood   Common Annual Larkspur
(*Delphinium ajacis* auct.)   Rev. H. Bryant 1764

Casual and introduced. Native in the Mediterranean region. Often a garden escape. Formerly a scarce or local weed of cornfields; now found in waste places and on rubbish tips, especially near docks. Frequent about towns. Flowers are usually dark blue, although sometimes they are a paler blue, pink or white.

W: 66, Exning, 1977; 67, Mildenhall, 1980; 77, Barton Mills Tip, 1977; 86, Westley Road, Bury St Edmunds; 87, Fakenham Magna; 88, Thetford; 93, Stoke-by-Nayland; 94, Semer; 96, Woolpit; Elmswell; Thurston, 1981.

E: 04. Nedging; Naughton; 05, Needham Market, 1981; 06, Bacton; 13, Brantham, 1979; Woolverstone; 14, Wherstead; Sproughton; Tuddenham Pit; Ipswich, waste ground, 1981; 15, Creeting St Mary; 17, Eye; 23, Felixstowe Docks; Chelmondiston Tip; Shotley; 24, Rushmere, 1976; 33, Felixstowe Ferry, 1979; 57, Southwold; 59, Lowestoft; 40, Burgh Castle.

Consolida regalis S. F. Gray   Forking Larkspur   E. R. Long 1929
(*Delphinium consolida* L.)

A rare casual of waste places, introduced from Europe and W. Asia. Known in Suffolk by a single record from Lowestoft.

Anemone nemorosa L.   Wood Anemone   Rev. G. Crabbe 1798
   Wind Flower

Native. In old woods, copses and hedges which were formerly woodland, old pastures and parkland. Found chiefly on the Boulder Clay, where it is often abundant. Absent from Breckland. The colour of the flowers varies from white to pink and mauve.

W: All squares except 66; 67; 68; 77; 78; 87; 88; 98.
Monks' Park and Felshamhall Woods, 1981.
E: All squares except 17; 33; 38; 44; 47; 49; 58; 40; 50.
Woods at Freston, Wherstead and Bentley, 1981.   *Illustrated page 445*
Double-flowered forms recorded from Polstead, Hintlesham, Wherstead and
Saxmundham (naturalised in the garden of the old Chantry, 1981).
Hb. Ipswich Museum, 'Waller's Grove, plentifully', c. 1820. Also a specimen with a two-
flowered scape and double involucre, from same site, 28th April, 1820.

Anemone ranunculoides L.   Yellow Wood Anemone   Turner 1834

An introduction, native in Europe and W. Asia. Naturalised in plantations and on former
garden sites. Uncommon. The only recent records are from North Wood, Culford (sq. 87)
by Mrs Harrison, and from Southgate, Bury (sq. 86), both in 1960, and from Pakenham
(sq. 96), 1980, by Mr & Mrs P. Sheppy.

Anemone apennina L.   Blue Anemone   Rev. E. J. Moore c. 1840

Introduced. Native of S. Europe. Frequently grown in gardens, from which it may escape
and become naturalised. Hind records it growing wild in a meadow adjoining the garden
at Helmingham Hall. A small colony naturalised on a verge near Christchurch Mansion,
Ipswich, 1962-79, probably dates from the time when the Mansion and Park were
privately owned.

Pulsatilla vulgaris Mill.   Pasque Flower   Sir J. Cullum 1771
(*Anemone pulsatilla* L.)   Dane's Blood

Native. On old chalky heaths and ancient earthworks. Probably now extinct in Suffolk. It
still occurs just outside the County in Cambridgeshire. At one time it was probably
frequent around Bury St Edmunds, when large areas were uncultivated and used only for
sheep and rough grazing.
Hind records the plants as rare and becoming extinct as long ago as 1889, though still to be
found on Newmarket Heath and Cavenham Heath and at Saxham and Bury.
Like *Sambucus ebulus, P. vulgaris* is known as Dane's Blood, as it is another species
which is thought to grow where blood has flowed. Many of its habitats are certainly on
ancient British earthworks and such places possess much of their aboriginal flora. The
last place where it was seen in Suffolk, in 1939, was in such a habitat, the remains of a
once extensive ditch and embankment, which crossed Cavenham Heath to Icklingham
(sq. 77). This earthwork must not be confused with the one between Risby and
Cavenham, which I have searched many times in vain for this attractive flower.

Clematis vitalba L.   Traveller's Joy   Sir J. Cullum 1773
                          Old Man's Beard

Native. In hedges, woods, copses, old chalk pits and on Red Crag. Frequent, especially on
Chalk or Boulder Clay. Uncommon in some areas of the East Suffolk Sandlings.
All squares.

Adonis annua L.   Pheasant's Eye   Sir J. Cullum 1775
(*A. autumnalis* L.)

An alien from S.W. Europe and S.W. Asia. Occurs as a casual. Now very rare. Dry fields,
waste places and on rubbish heaps. Last record c. 1960.

W: 78, Lakenheath, c. 1960.
E: 14, Cliff Lane, near Ipswich Docks, c. 1939; 23, Walton Ferry and Felixstowe, pre-1950.

Ranunculus repens L.   Creeping Buttercup   Sir J. Cullum 1774

Native. Damp pastures, ditches, shallow ponds, open glades in woods, cultivated ground. Very frequent.
All squares.

Ranunculus acris L. ssp. **acris**   Meadow Buttercup   Sir J. Cullum 1773
                                      King's Cob (Suffolk)

Native. Pastures, marshes and waysides. Common, but less abundant than formerly.
All squares.

Ranunculus bulbosus L. ssp. **bulbosus**   Bulbous Buttercup   Rev. G. Crabbe 1798
                                            Early Buttercup

Native. A weed of old meadows and pastures, grassy waysides, commons, greens and churchyards. Still frequent, but has certainly decreased in recent years, as the meadows and pastures have been ploughed up. In Suffolk, this species has always been associated with bright, flowery meadows, rich with Cowslip, Common Daisy, Meadow Saxifrage, Earthnut, Good Friday Grass, Sweet Vernal Grass and many other species.
All squares.

Ranunculus sardous Crantz   Hairy Buttercup   Rev. G. Crabbe 1798
(*R. hirsutus* Curt.)

Native. In moist pastures, especially near the coast, where it is sometimes common. A casual weed of waste places and damp arable fields. Particularly frequent on the coast of Lothingland.
W: 86; 93; 94; 95; 96.
E: 03; 04; 13; 14; 23; 33; 34; 36; 37; 44; 45; 46; 47; 49; 57; 59; 40; 50.
13, Cattawade marshes, 1978; 23, Falkenham, 1978; 33, Felixstowe Ferry, 1979; 57, Southwold, 1979; 40, Belton, 1977.
A double-flowered variety recorded from Whatfield and Aldeburgh.

Ranunculus arvensis L.   Corn Buttercup   Davy 1794
                          Corn Crowfoot
                          Hedgehogs

Probably introduced. A weed in cornfields, chiefly on the Boulder Clay. Formerly frequent, but now rare, due to improved grain sifting methods, stubble burning and spraying. Now very difficult to find. The number of squares indicated below does not reflect the present (1981) distribution.
W: All squares except 65; 66; 67; 68; 76; 84; 86; 87; 97.
E: All squares except 07; 13; 17; 26; 28; 34; 35; 44; 59; 40; 50.
Known as 'Jie' at Wingfield.

Ranunculus parviflorus L.   Small-flowered Buttercup   J. Andrews 1742

Native. An annual species, found on dry banks, sandy commons and tracks. Very rare.

E: 03, East Bergholt, 1958 (F. J. Bingley); 23, Landguard Common, 1981 (A. Copping); 46, Westleton, 1957.
Hind's Flora gives nine sites, including Bergholt and Landguard Fort.

Ranunculus auricomus L. Goldilocks Sir J. Cullum 1774
Wood Buttercup

Native. In woods and copses and beside old lanes on clay soils. Frequent, but overlooked. Common in churchyards.
W: All squares except 65; 67; 68; 77; 88; 98.
Recent records: churchyards at Barrow, Chevington, Hargrave, Kedington, Stradishall.
E: All squares except 26; 33; 34; 35; 49; 58; 40; 50.
Recent records: Bramford, Hintlesham, Holbrook, Chelmondiston, Harkstead, Little Wenham, Botesdale, Barking, Mickfield.
Hb. Ipswich Museum: 'In Waller's Grove plentiful', c. 1820 (John Notcutt).

Illustrated page 461

Ranunculus sceleratus L. ssp. **sceleratus** Celery-leaved Crowfoot Sir J. Cullum 1774

Native. On mud, beside streams, ditches and ponds, or in shallow water. Frequent. A fasciated specimen recorded at Covehithe (sq. 58) in 1952.
All squares except 65; 67; 68; 75; 78.
Plants are often seen in spring with floating leaves and can easily be mistaken for one of the Water Crowfoots.

Ranunculus ficaria L. Lesser Celandine Wilson 1831
Pilewort

Native. Woods, hedge-banks, old pastures and banks of streams. Abundant.
Ssp. **ficaria** All squares.
Ssp. **bulbifer** Lawalrée in Robyns Leaves with axillary bulbils. Less frequent than ssp. *ficaria*. Usually found in shady habitats. Recorded from squares 65; 66; 67; 75; 86; 94; 03; 16; 27; 28; 36; 38; 59.
36, Saxmundham, 1981 (F. W. Simpson).
Ssp. **ficariiformis** Rouy & Fouc. Plants larger, with yellowish-white sepals. Native of S. Europe. Introduced and occasionally grown in gardens. 36, Saxmundham, c. 1965 (Misses B. and R. Copinger Hill).
A large tetraploid form of *R. ficaria* occurs in a garden at Walberswick, where it was probably introduced.

Ranunculus flammula L. ssp. **flammula** Lesser Spearwort Sir J. Cullum 1773

Native. In marshes, beside ponds and rivers, in damp open glades and rides, especially of the Boulder Clay woods. Locally frequent, but decreasing.
W: All squares except 64; 65; 66; 67; 74; 75; 83; 85; 87.
76, Kentford; 77, Cavenham, 1979; Tuddenham, 1979; 78, Pashford Poor's Fen, 1979.
E: Recorded from squares 04; 05; 06; 13; 14; 16; 17; 25; 26; 28; 33; 35; 36; 37; 39; 44; 45; 40.
05, Barking, 1981; 13, Bentley, 1979; 17, Redlingfield, 1977; 25, Bromeswell Common, 1980; 35, Gromford, 1975; 39, Bungay, 1981; 40, Belton, 1977.

Ranunculus lingua L.   Greater Spearwort   Rev. G. Crabbe 1798

Native. In fens and marshes and beside dykes and rivers. Local or rare. Decreasing and now extinct in some former habitats.

W: 68; 77; 78, Brandon; Lakenheath; 83, Cornard Mere.

E: 07, Redgrave Fen; 14, banks of the R. Gipping, Ipswich; 36, Parham, 1980; Gt Glemham; 39, Outney Common, Bungay, 1981; 49, Herringfleet; Carlton Colville, 1980; 59, Carlton Colville, 1976.   *Illustrated page 481*

BATRACHIUM SECTION   WATER CROWFOOTS

This group consists of a number of species and subspecies which are not always easy to identify, because they appear to vary considerably according to habitat and other conditions affecting growth. Much depends on the depth of water in which they are found and the amount of sunlight they receive. Those growing in very shallow water produce floating leaves more readily than those growing in deep water in shady situations. Flowers are more readily produced when plants are growing in more open habitats in shallow water and even on wet mud.

Submerged leaves are not always a basis for the correct identification of species, that is to say, whether or not they collapse when removed from the water. The leaves of *R. circinatus* remain rigid when in or out of the water. If one can examine the mature achenes, so much the better.

Ranunculus hederaceus L.   Ivy-leaved Water Crowfoot   John Notcutt c. 1820

Native. Edges of muddy ponds and semi-dry ditches. Scarce.

W: 77; 86; 98.

77, Icklingham.

E: 03; 13; 24; 33; 34; 36; 45; 47; 49; 58; 59; 40.

13, Harkstead, 1981; Woolverstone, 1977; 47, Walberswick, 1975; 58, Benacre, 1974; 40, Belton, 1977.

Hb. Ipswich Museum specimen: 'In the Dikes in a meadow in the 2nd Dale between Bolton Mill and Dale Hall', c. 1820 (John Notcutt).

Ranunculus omiophyllus Ten.   Round-leaved Crowfoot   E. Skepper 1862
(*R. lenormandii* F. W. Schultz)   Lenormand's Water Crowfoot

Native. In shallow ponds and on mud. Rare. I believe some of the Suffolk records may be mistakes and that the species observed was *R. hederaceus*.

W: 77, Icklingham; 83, Cornard Marsh.

E: 05, Baylham; 13, Bentley; 15, Baylham; 23, Kirton; Falkenham Marsh; 33, Felixstowe; 34, Butley.

Ranunculus baudotii Godr.   Brackish Water Crowfoot   Hind 1883
(*R. confusus* Godr.)

Native. In brackish ditches and shallow ponds near the sea. Rare or uncertain in its appearance from year to year.

E: 13; 23; 33; 34; 45; 46; 47; 57.

13, Brantham; Holbrook, 1974; 23, Shotley, 1978; Walton, 1979; 33, Felixstowe Ferry, 1973; 34, marsh ditch at Alderton, 1972; Sutton, 1978; 45, Sudbourne; 46, Minsmere Marsh; 47, Southwold, 1979 (P. G. Lawson); 57, Easton Broad.

RANUNCULACEAE

Ranunculus peltatus Schrank   Water Crowfoot   Hind 1883
(*R. floribundus* Bab.
R. aquatilis L. ssp. *peltatus* (Schrank) Syme)

Native. In ponds and dykes. Not very common. This Water Crowfoot is very attractive when flowering. The flowers are large and often carpet a pond in late April and May.
W: 84, Sudbury; 85, Lawshall; 88, Brandon; 93, Newton Green Pond; 94, Brent Eleigh.
E: 03, East Bergholt village pond; 04, Nettlestead; 05, Barking; 13, Harkstead, 1981; 14, Copdock; 39, Bungay, 1981; 48, Sotterley.   *Illustrated page 487*

Ranunculus penicillatus (Dum.) Bab.   Water Crowfoot   Miss Lathbury 1835
(*R. pseudofluitans* (Syme) Newbould ex Baker & Foggit
R. aquatilis L. ssp. *pseudofluitans* (Syme) Clapham)

Native. In streams and rivers flowing through, or from, the Chalk. Rare, and probably overlooked. I have observed this Water Crowfoot in the R. Lark at Icklingham and Barton Mills, and in the Cavenham chalk stream, c. 1950 (F. W. S.). Also in the R. Lark at Worlington and the R. Kennett at Freckenham in 1977.

Ranunculus aquatilis L.   Common Water Crowfoot   John Nottcutt c. 1820
                    Pickerel Weed (Suffolk)

Native. In ponds, ditches and slow-moving rivers. Fairly frequent. May be confused with other species when found growing on mud of dried-up ponds or ditches.
W: All squares except 66; 67; 68; 74; 76.
77, Tuddenham, 1978.
E: All squares except 15; 35; 48; 49; 58; 50.
23, Chelmondiston, 1977; 27, Fressingfield, 1981.
Hb. Ipswich Museum: 'In a stagnant ditch on the north side of the Foxhall Road, opposite the Mill', c. 1820 (John Notcutt).

Ranunculus trichophyllus Chaix in Villars ssp. **trichophyllus**   John Notcutt c. 1820
            Thread-leaved Water Crowfoot
            Water Fennel

Native. In ponds and ditches. Common. This is the most frequent Water Crowfoot in the County, although not recorded from a number of squares, or possibly mistaken for *R. aquatilis*.
In ssp. **drouetii** (F. W. Schultz) Clapham the leaf segments are finer and collapse when taken from the water. However, I consider that the two subspecies merge, and it is often difficult to make a decision. The amount of lime encrustation on the leaf segments is an important factor.
W: All squares except 65; 66; 68; 74; 78; 83; 84; 88.
67, Mildenhall, 1977; 76, Kentford, 1980; 94, Brent Eleigh, 1981.
E: All squares except 25; 27; 28; 33; 35; 37; 47; 49; 58; 59; 40; 50.
13, Wherstead, 1978; 23, Shotley, 1981; 36, Cransford, 1971; 39, Bungay, 1978.
Hb. Ipswich Museum: 'Stagnant ditches to the N.E. and N.W. of Boss Hall', c. 1820 (John Notcutt).

Ranunculus circinatus Sibth.   Fan-leaved Water Crowfoot   Sir J. Cullum 1774

Native. In ponds, ditches and rivers. Formerly very frequent, now scarce due to the filling up of farm ponds. More common in ponds on the Chalky Boulder Clay, where the plant gets heavily encrusted with lime.

W: 84, R. Stour at Sudbury; 93, R. Stour at Nayland, 1980; 95.

E: 03; 04, Naughton; 05; 14, R. Gipping, Ipswich, 1980; 36; 39, Bungay and Mettingham, 1980; 45, Aldeburgh; 46, East Bridge; 49, Carlton Colville; 59, Oulton, 1977; 40; 50.

Ranunculus fluitans Lam.   River Water Crowfoot   Sir C. J. F. Bunbury 1858

Native. In rivers and streams with strong currents. Limited distribution only. Most frequent in the R. Stour and the Little Ouse.

W: 67, Freckenham and Worlington, 1977; 77, in the R. Lark at Cavenham, Mildenhall and Icklingham; 88, Santon Downham, in the Little Ouse, 1977; 93, in the Mill Race at Nayland; 97, Sapiston; 98.

E: 04, Hadleigh, in the R. Brett; 24, R. Finn at Martlesham, 1981; 28, Homersfield; 38, Bungay; 39.

Myosurus minimus L.   Mousetail   J. Andrews 1745

Probably native. On the borders of damp fields and also as a garden weed. Generally rare or overlooked, formerly more frequent.

W: 83, Gt Cornard.

E: 03, Layham; 04; 13, Woolverstone; Holbrook, 1974 (Mrs G. Williams); 14, Washbrook, 1979 (Miss A. Seward); 15, Stonham Aspal, 1981, introduced with soil on plants from Kesgrave (J. A. Foster): 23, Falkenham; 24, Playford; Kesgrave; 25, Wickham Market; 47, South Cove; 49, Herringfleet; 59, Blundeston.

Hb. Ipswich Museum: 'In a gate-way in a meadow above Handford Bridge, between the Bramford Road and the River', 1819 and 1827.

Aquilegia vulgaris L.   Columbine   Sir J. Cullum 1773
                              Dollycaps

Native or introduced. Waysides, fens, woods and sites of former gardens. In the majority of its habitats it is probably a relic of cultivation; however, at Lakenheath and Hopton it appears to be native. The colour of the flowers varies, but is usually a shade of blue, mauve, pink or reddish purple. It is probable that in some instances the plants observed are not this species, but are hybrids of garden origin.

W: 66, Moulton, 1974; 67, Freckenham, 1977; 78, Lakenheath; 86, Bury St Edmunds; 93; 94, Lavenham, 1979; 97, Hopton Fen (extinct 1980); Troston.

E: 03, Raydon Wood; 04, Hintlesham, 1980; 07, Burgate, 1975; 14, Washbrook; Bramford; 15, Stonham Aspal, 1981; 16; 36; 44; 47, railway embankment at Darsham, 1979 (now destroyed by spraying).

Thalictrum minus L.   Lesser Meadow Rue   Dillenius 1724

Ssp. **minus** Native. On dry, chalky banks and heaths in Breckland. Rare or local, perhaps often overlooked.

W: 66, Newmarket; 76, Cavenham; Dalham, 1980; 77, Eriswell; Icklingham, 1980; 78, Lakenheath; 86, Bury St Edmunds, Shaker's Lane, site endangered by By-pass, 1980; 87, West Calthorpe Heath; West Stow, 1979; 88, Thetford.

Ssp. **arenarium** (Butcher) Clapham (*T. dunense* Dum.; *T. Maritimum* Syme) Native. On sand dunes and cliffs near the sea. Recorded in Hind's Flora for Corton and Gorleston. Now extinct.
There are also 1980 records from Harkstead and Woolverstone (Mrs E. M. Hyde), both relics of cultivation, and a similar record from Elmswell.

Thalictrum flavum L. ssp. **flavum**   Common Meadow Rue   J. Andrews 1740

Native. In marshes and beside rivers. Not very common and decreasing.
W: Recorded from squares 67; 68; 77; 78; 83; 88; 93; 96; 98.
77, Cavenham, 1977; 83, Cornard Mere, 1981; 98, Euston, 1981.
E: All squares except 04; 15; 23; 33; 34; 37; 44; 45; 58; 40; 50.
07, Wortham Ling, 1980; 14, by the R. Gipping, Ipswich, 1981; 25, Bromeswell Common, 1981; 39, Mettingham, 1980; Bungay, 1981.

BERBERIDACEAE

BARBERRY FAMILY

Epimedium alpinum L.   Barren-wort   J. Atkins 1910

Introduced. Native of C. Europe. Cultivated and occasionally naturalised in old gardens and shrubberies.
E: 04, Overbury Hall, Layham (Hb. Atkins); 14, in the wild part of an old garden at Crane Hill, Ipswich, c. 1956.

Berberis vulgaris L.   Barberry   J. Andrews 1745
                           Pipperidge (Suffolk)

Native and introduced. In hedges, shrubberies, plantations and woodlands. Not very common. This shrub is sometimes infested with the aecidia of the Black Rust or blight of wheat.
W: 66; 76; 77; 78; 86; 87; 88; 94; 95; 96.
76, hedges at Moulton, 1980; 86, Shaker's Lane, Bury St Edmunds, 1979.
E: 03; 04; 13; 15; 16; 24; 27; 36; 37; 45; 40; 50.
45, hedge at Sudbourne, Snape to Orford road opposite 'Fazeboons', 1975, (Misses B. & R. Copinger Hill).

Berberis darwinii Hook.   Mrs E. M. Hyde 1980

Introduced. Native of Chile. First discovered by Charles Darwin in 1835 on the famous voyage of the 'Beagle'.
W: 78, Brandon. Conf. E. J. Clement. Naturalised in light woodland, with *Hypericum calycinum* L., Rose of Sharon.

Berberis darwinii × empetrifolia   F. W. Simpson c. 1935
(*B. × stenophylla* Lindl.)

Introduced. Planted on banks of the A12 at Martlesham and Woodbridge (sq. 24), and almost naturalised. Originated from Notcutt's Nurseries Limited, Woodbridge. Still there, 1981. Also Marlesford (sq. 35), beside the A12, originally planted, but now well-established, 1981.

Mahonia aquifolium (Pursh) Nutt.   Oregon Grape   Hind 1887
(*Berberis aquifolium* Pursh)   Holly-leaved Barberry

Introduced from N. America. Planted in shrubberies, woods, game reserves. Often bird-sown. Frequently naturalised. Increasing.
W: All squares except 65; 68; 83; 84; 85.
76, Herringswell, 1981; 78, Brandon, very frequent, 1981.
E: Recorded from squares 03; 04; 06; 07; 13; 14; 16; 23; 24; 25; 28; 35; 39; 45; 46.
13, Harkstead, 1981; 23, Chelmondiston, plantation, 1981; 24, Martlesham, 1980; 45, Chillesford, 1980.

PAPAVERACEAE

POPPY FAMILY

Papaver somniferum L.   Opium Poppy   Paget 1834

Alien, from S. Europe. A casual or garden escape. On rubbish tips and waste places. Very frequent. Formerly also a cornfield weed, known as the White Poppy, the flowers of which were always white, with a purple blotch at the base of the petals.
W: 64; 66; 67; 74; 76; 77; 78; 86; 87; 88; 93; 96.
E: 03; 05; 06; 13; 14; 15; 16; 17; 23; 24; 25; 33; 34; 35; 44; 45; 46; 47; 49; 40.
Double and semi-double forms are not uncommon and have been found at Brantham in 1979, Walberswick, 1974, Lt. Blakenham, 1981 and Barton Mills, 1977.
A colony of the White Poppy appeared on sand and silt dredged from the R. Waveney at Bungay in 1980 (F. W. Simpson).

Papaver rhoeas L.   Common Poppy   Sir J. Cullum 1773
                         Field Poppy
                         Corn Poppy

Colonist. Probably introduced. Cornfields, waste places, roadsides. Very common, but not as abundant as formerly. A very variable species.
All squares.
A fairly frequent but by no means common, form has a black patch at the base of the petals. It is not known for certain whether this is really a subspecies or even a separate variety. The flowers are usually a darker shade of red, often with larger blooms on larger plants. In this County it is possible that it may have arisen as a result of the cultivation of ornamental Shirley Poppies. These usually have the same dark blotches at the base of the petals. In the Mediterranean region and other parts of Europe, the blotched form is more frequent. Plants with lilac and orange-coloured flowers also occur. *Illustrated page 513*

Papaver dubium L.   Long-headed Poppy   Sutton & Kirby 1787
                         Long-headed Corn Poppy

Introduced. Arable fields, waysides and waste places. Frequent, but decreasing. Far less common than *P. rhoeas,* though still frequent in the coastal squares.
W: All squares except 65; 68; 75; 83; 93.
E: All squares except 06; 07; 15; 17; 26; 27; 28; 36; 44.

Papaver dubium × rhoeas   H. Wiard 1968

In fields and waste places. A very rare or overlooked hybrid.
Recorded only from sq. 78 in the Breckland Survey in 1968.

Papaver lecoqii Lamotte   Yellow-juiced Poppy   E. Skepper 1860
                                  Babington's Poppy
                                  Lecoq's Poppy

A colonist of field margins and waysides. Rare. Sap turning yellow on exposure to air.
Some botanical authorities consider this species to be merely a variety of *P. dubium*.
W: 95, Hitcham, 1980 (A. L. Bull).
E: 25, Sycamore Farm, Swilland (J. Digby); 34, Hollesley; 47, Blythburgh Bridge.

Papaver argemone L.   Prickly Poppy   Sir J. Cullum 1774
                             Long Prickly-headed Poppy
                             Small Corn Poppy

Colonist. On the edges of cornfields, disturbed waysides and waste places. Not very
frequent and usually only in small numbers.
W: 75; 76; 77; 78; 86; 88; 93; 94; 95; 96; 97.
86, Bury St Edmunds, 1978; 96, Beyton and Thurston, 1979.
E: 03; 04; 14; 23; 24; 33; 35; 45; 46; 47; 48; 59; 50.
14, Tuddenham, 1975; 23, Chelmondiston, 1981; 45, Friston, 1981; 47, Westleton, 1975.

Illustrated page 515

Papaver hybridum L.   Rough Poppy   Sir T. G. Cullum 1804
                             Round Prickly-headed Poppy

A colonist. On the borders of arable fields and waste places, usually on chalky soils and
the Red Crag sands. Rare. Uncertain in its appearance. Usually only a few specimens.
W: 56, Exning, 1974; 76, Kentford; Gazeley, 1981 (Mrs E. M. Hyde); 77, Mildenhall; 78,
Lakenheath; Wangford; 97, Lt. Fakenham.
E: 16, Mendlesham; 23, near Maltings, Felixstowe Dock; 24, Kirton; Newbourn; 34,
Buckanays Farm, Alderton, on Red Crag sand.

Papaver atlanticum (Ball) Cosson   Mrs E. M. Hyde and M. A. Hyde 1978

Introduced. Native of Morocco. A garden throw-out, readily seeding and increasing in
waste places.
W: 77, Chalk Hill Quarry, Barton Mills, 1980 (F. W. Simpson).
E: 03, Capel St Mary, roadside bank, 1981; 23, Trimley Station, 1978-81; 45, by coast
road, Aldeburgh (Mrs E. M. Hyde and M. A. Hyde), detd. E. J. Clement; 46, roadside
verge, Westleton, 1978-81 (P. G. Lawson); 47, Dunwich Forest, dry open sandy ride, 1980
(F. W. Simpson).

Meconopsis cambrica (L.) Vig.   Welsh Poppy   J. Atkins 1908

Native in Wales and S.W. England. Introduced and naturalised in a few places in Suffolk.
W: 74, Hundon Churchyard, 1974; 96, Pakenham. Also recorded from Ampton, 1933
(H. D. Hewitt).
E: 13, Woolverstone Churchyard, 1976. Specimen in Hb. Atkins: Overby Hall, Layham,
1908.

Roemeria hybrida (L.) DC. Violet Horned Poppy Mrs F. Baker c. 1900

An alien from C. and S. Europe. Formerly occurred in East Anglia as a cornfield weed. Now rare. Recorded from Oulton Broad about the beginning of the century and from Felixstowe Docks in May, 1938. The only recent record for Suffolk is by M. G. Rutterford, who identified a specimen growing in a chicken run at Lakenheath in 1956 (sq. 78). (Mr Rutterford has a painting of this specimen.)

Glaucium flavum Crantz Yellow Horned Poppy T. Martyn 1763

Native. Sea coast, on sand and shingle beaches. Frequent. Casual inland.
W: 93, Boxford (casual).
E: 04, Offton (casual); 23 Landguard Common; 33, Felixstowe Ferry; Bawdsey; 34, Shingle Street; 44, Orford; 45, Aldeburgh; Sudbourne; 46, Dunwich to Sizewell; Thorpeness; 47, Walberswick; 57, Easton Bavents; Southwold; 58, Kessingland; Benacre; Covehithe; 59, Lowestoft. Seen in all these coastal parishes between 1979 and 1981.

Illustrated page 494

Glaucium corniculatum (L.) Rudolph Red Horned Poppy Mrs F. Baker 1890
Scarlet Horned Poppy

Introduced from S. Europe and the Mediterranean. Usually a casual of waste places near ports. Recorded from Oulton Broad by Mrs F. Baker in 1890, from Ipswich by J. S. Wilkinson in 1908, and from Lakenheath in 1954 by M. G. Rutterford.

Chelidonium majus L. Greater Celandine Sir J. Cullum 1773
Wartweed
Wretweed (Suffolk)

An established colonist in towns and villages, especially near old walls. Frequent. This species was probably introduced in early times and cultivated, its yellow sap being used as a cure for corns and warts. A double-flowered form has been recorded from Dale Hall Lane and St Nicholas Churchyard, Ipswich (sq. 14), from Crowfield (sq. 15) and from Aldeburgh (sq. 45).
All squares except 68.
There is a specimen of var. **laciniatum** (Mill.) Syme in Hb. Ipswich Museum, dated 1843, from Ipswich.

Eschscholzia californica Cham. Californian Poppy F. W. Simpson c. 1950

An alien, native in California and Oregon. Sometimes found as a garden escape on rubbish tips and waste places. It may persist on dry, sandy soils in grassy places. It has been observed flowering in the same place at Felixstowe for several years.
W: 67, Mildenhall, roadside, 1977.
E: 05, Stowmarket; 13, Freston Hill, 1966-1980; 14, Rushmere St Andrew; 15, Coddenham Tip, 1974; 23, Chelmondiston Tip, 1974; 33, Felixstowe Station, 1976; 45, Aldeburgh.

Hypecoum procumbens L. J. S. Wilkinson 1908

A casual, native of S. Europe. Only one record from Ipswich.

FUMARIACEAE

FUMITORY FAMILY

Corydalis claviculata (L.) DC.   White Climbing Fumitory   J. Andrews 1745
Climbing Corydalis

Native. Old woods, copses and heaths on sandy or gravelly soils. Frequent in the South-east near the coast.
W: 77; 93.
E: 03; 04; 13; 14; 23; 24; 25; 33; 34; 35; 44; 45; 46; 47; 48; 57; 58. Common in woods at Freston, Holbrook, Bentley, Benacre and Dunwich. Also on heaths at Rushmere, Snape, Aldringham and Westleton.
Hb. Ipswich Museum: 'On the north east side of the woods by Downham Reach'. The date of the water mark on the mounting paper is 1809. The species still occurs in this locality. 'The flowers of this plant change in drying from pale straw-colour to a full yellow'. They had retained this colour when examined in 1975.   *Illustrated page 510*

Corydalis lutea (L.) DC.   Yellow Fumitory   Rev. E. J. Moore 1840
Yellow Corydalis

An introduction from S. Europe. Naturalised on walls. Frequent.
W: All squares except 68; 85; 95; 98.
74, Clare Country Park, 1976; 87, walls at West Stow, 1980; 96, Pakenham, 1980.
E: All squares except 07; 34; 58; 59.
04, Kersey, common, 1980; 14, Ipswich, common on walls in many places, 1981; 39, Bungay, 1981.

Corydalis bulbosa (L.) DC.   Tuberous Corydalis   Mrs E. Reid 1975

Introduced. Native of continental Europe.
E: 23, Chelmondiston, naturalised in hedgebank. Detd. at Kew. Both white and purplish-pink flowers growing together. Still there, 1981.   *Illustrated page 510*

Corydalis solida (L.) Sw.   Purple Fumitory   Rev. J. D. Gray 1880
(*C. bulbosa* auct., non (L.) DC.
C. halleri Willd.)

Introduced from S. and E. Europe and N.W. Asia. Grown in gardens and occasionally escaping or becoming naturalised on the sites of former gardens. Uncommon. Recorded in Hind's Flora from Nayland and Oulton Broad, but the only record in recent times is from Bucklesham in 1953 (Miss J. C. N. Willis).

Fumaria capreolata L. ssp. **babingtonii** (Pugsl.) P. D. Sell   White Rampant Fumitory
(*F. pallidiflora* Jord.)   Davy c. 1828

Native. Hedges, borders of fields and waste places. Locally common.
W: Not recorded.
E: 13, Woolverstone; Wherstead; Freston, 1977; 14, Lt. Blakenham; Ipswich, 1981; 23, Kirton; Levington; Trimley St Mary, 1981; Erwarton, 1979, Chelmondiston, 1981; Shotley; Landguard Common; 24, Melton; Hemley Churchyard, 1980 (also recorded at

this site by Davy, 1828); 25; 33, Felixstowe Ferry, on dumped soil, near Martello Tower; Maybush Lane and other sites in Old Felixstowe, 1980.
Hb. Ipswich Museum, specimen from Walton, 1832. Collector unknown.

Fumaria bastardii Bor.　　Bastard's Rampant Fumitory　　　　　　Hind 1882
(*F. confusa* Jord.)
A colonist. Widespread in continental Europe. May be found on the edges of cultivated fields. Very rare or overlooked. There are no known records for the present century. Hind recorded it for Honington, Bradwell, Hopton and Gorleston, but the Bradwell and Hopton records are *F. officinalis*.

Fumaria muralis Sond. ex Koch ssp. **boraei** (Jord.) Pugsl.　　　　Hind 1875
　　　　Ramping Fumitory
　　　　Wall Fumitory
Native. Hedge-banks, walls, cultivated and waste places. Rare or overlooked.
E: 04, Semer; 13, Freston; Glebe Lane, Woolverstone; Holbrook, 1981; 33, Felixstowe Ferry; 49, Somerleyton; 50.

Fumaria densiflora DC.　　Dense-flowered Fumitory　　　　　　Hind 1887
(*F. micrantha* Lag.)
Native. In cultivated fields and waste places. Very rare.
W: 94, Kersey; Monks Eleigh; 97.
E: 04, Hadleigh; 33, Felixstowe Ferry, 1966 (R. D. English).

Fumaria officinalis L. ssp. **officinalis**　　Common Fumitory　　Sir J. Cullum 1775
Native. Cultivated ground, waste places and quarries. Common.
All squares except 84; 07; 17; 26; 37; 44.
A variety recognised by some authorities as ssp. **wirtgenii** (Koch) Arcangeli was recorded from Sapiston (sq. 97) in 1962.

Fumaria vaillantii Lois.　　Vaillant's Fumitory　　Sir C. J. F. Bunbury 1873
A colonist. Widespread in Europe. Arable fields, on calcareous soils. Very rare or overlooked.
W: 66, Exning, 1977 (F. W. Simpson).
E: 48, Wrentham, 1979; 49, Beccles Tip, 1975 (P. G. Lawson). Conf. E. L. Swann.

Fumaria parviflora Lam.　　Small-flowered Fumitory　　Rev. J. Dalton 1805
Native or colonist. Arable fields on light, chalky soils, disturbed chalky banks and quarries. This species appears after chalk grassland has been disturbed, especially in Breckland. It is probable that the seeds remain dormant for a very long period and germinate when the surface is broken up. Rare or overlooked.
Hind considered it rare, though he recorded it for a number of localities including 'several places near Ipswich'.
W: 76; 77; 78; 97.
76, Barrow Bottom; 97, Knettishall.
There is a specimen in Hb. Atkins from Wherstead, 1907.

144

Hb. Ipswich Museum: specimens collected by Rev. G. R. Leathes from Westley, and also three sheets 'collected by Mr Hooker from near Bury'. No dates, but all probably early 19th century.

CRUCIFERAE

CRUCIFER OR CABBAGE FAMILY

Sisymbrium irio L.   London Rocket   Sir J. Cullum 1773

Possibly once native, but now only a casual of fields and waste places. Rare.
W: 77; 86, Bury St Edmunds.
E: 04, Hadleigh; 14, Ipswich, Tower Churchyard, 1974 (F. W. Simpson); Freston, on waste heap, 1977 (M. A. Hyde). Detd. by E. J. Clement.

Sisymbrium volgense Bieb. ex E. Fourn.   M. A. Hyde 1980

Alien. Native of E. Russia. Waste places.
E: 04, Hadleigh, several extensive patches on the disused railway line, near former station. Conf. E. J. Clement. Noted, but not recognised, by other local naturalists before 1980. Date of introduction unknown.

Sisymbrium altissimum L.   Tall Rocket   E. Skepper 1861
                                  Tumbling Mustard

A naturalised alien. Native in C. Europe. Found in waste places, especially on the light soils of Breckland. Frequent and increasing. There is only one record in Hind's Flora, for Lowestoft in 1861.
W: 66; 67; 68; 76; 77; 78; 85; 86; 87; 88; 96; 97.
66, Herringswell, 1980; 76, Gazeley, 1980; 77, Barton Mills, 1981; 78, Lakenheath, 1980; 86, Bury St Edmunds, 1980; 87, Barnham, 1980.
E: 04; 13; 14; 15; 23; 24; 25; 28; 34; 35; 45; 46; 47; 48; 59; 50.
04, Hadleigh, 1980; 14, Ipswich, 1981; 25, Melton, 1980; 35, Wantisden, 1980.

Sisymbrium orientale L.   Eastern Rocket   Mrs F. Baker 1900
(*S. columnae* Jacq.)

An established alien. Native in S. Europe, N. Africa and the Near East. Found in waste places, especially near docks and railway sidings. More frequent than formerly.
W: 74; 76; 77; 78; 86; 88; 96; 97.
78, Lakenheath, 1980; 86, Bury St Edmunds Station, 1980.
E: 04; 13; 14; 15; 17; 23; 24; 33; 38; 45; 47; 49; 57; 59.
14, Ipswich, various sites, 1981; Lt. Blakenham, 1976; 23, Landguard Common, 1973; 57, Southwold, 1974.

Sisymbrium polyceratium L.   Many-podded Hedge Mustard   Sir T. G. Cullum 1785

Casual. Native of S. Europe.
W: 86. There is an interesting note in Hind's Flora. This small annual was believed to have been introduced by Dr Goodenough and grew in School Lane, Northgate Street, and

145

other parts of Bury. The Botanist's Guide, 1805, relates that 'This plant was about 20 years ago thrown out of the garden of the late Rev. Mr Laurent, but now grows in great quantity about Bury, and is perfectly naturalised.' Last recorded, 1860.

Sisymbrium officinale (L.) Scop.   Hedge Mustard   Sir J. Cullum 1773

Native. Hedge-banks, waysides and waste places. Very frequent.
All squares.
Var. **leiocarpum** DC. recorded from sq. 45 in 1950, from sq. 14, Ipswich, in 1976 and sq. 23, Harkstead, 1976. Probably elsewhere and overlooked.
This glabrous variety may possibly be only a form associated with the damper conditions of some late summers and autumns, following heavy rain.

Descurainia sophia (L.) Webb ex Prantl   Flixweed   Sir J. Cullum 1773
(*Sisymbrium sophia* L.)

A colonist, doubtfully native. On waste and cultivated ground, especially edges of fields and farmyards on the light soils of East Suffolk and in Breckland. Very frequent.
W: All squares except 64; 65; 74; 75; 83; 85; 93; 95.
E: All squares except 03; 05; 06; 17; 26; 27; 28; 38; 39; 50.

Alliaria petiolata (Bieb.) Cavara & Grande   Garlic Mustard   Rev. G. Crabbe 1798
(*A. officinalis* Andrz. ex Bieb.)   Jack-by-the-Hedge
      Sauce Alone

Probably native. Hedgerows and borders of woods. Frequent, but now decreasing, due to crop spraying and removal of hedges.
All squares.

Arabidopsis thaliana (L.) Heynh.   Thale Cress   Sir J. Cullum 1774
(*Sisymbrium thalianum* (L.) Gay   Common Wall Cress
Arabis thaliana L.)   Turkey Pod

Native. Dry sunny banks, sandy waysides, fallow fields, margins of heaths, walls and old tracks. Common.
All squares except 64; 65; 68; 85; 95.

Myagrum perfoliatum L.   Mitre Cress   Mrs F. Baker c. 1900

A casual from the Mediterranean region and S.E. Europe. Known in Suffolk from Oulton Broad, about 1900. Also from Honey Hill, Lt. Saxham (sq. 86) in 1963 (Miss P. Jackson).

Isatis tinctoria L.   Woad   Winch 1835

Introduced from C. and S. Europe. Found as a rare casual or garden weed. Formerly cultivated in East Anglia as a dye. Recorded from Woodbridge (sq. 24) in 1937.

Bunias orientalis L.   Warty Cabbage   Hind 1882

A casual from E. Europe and W. Asia. Hind recorded it only from Elveden in 1882. The only Suffolk record during the present century is from Bushy Green, Hadleigh, between 1933 and 1935, made by R. Burn and Miss E. Rawlins.

146

CRUCIFERAE

Erysimum durum J. & C. Presl　　　　　　　　　　W. C. Barton 1913
(*E. hieracifolium* L. ssp. *durum* (J. & C. Presl) Hegi)
Casual. Native of E. and C. Europe. Waste places.
W: Mildenhall, 1913, Hb. Kew, collected by W. C. Barton.

Erysimum repandum L.　　　　　　　　　　　　Mrs F. Baker c. 1890
A casual from S. Europe. Known in Suffolk from a single record from Oulton Broad.

Erysimum cheiranthoides L.　　Treacle Mustard　　　　　Newton 1724
Colonist. Cultivated and disturbed waste ground. Common and well distributed. More
frequent than formerly, especially on roadsides and edges of fields.
All squares except 84; 85; 93; 94; 17; 57; 58.

Hesperis matronalis L.　　Dame's Violet　　　　　J. Andrews 1744
　　　　　　　　　　　　　Sweet Rocket
Introduced from continental Europe, W. and C. Asia. A naturalised garden escape.
Found on sites of former gardens, banks of rivers and waste places.
W: 68; 74; 75; 76; 77; 78; 86; 87; 94; 95; 96; 98.
74, Kedington, near Mill, 1976; 87, West Stow, 1980.
E: 04; 05; 13; 14; 15; 16; 17; 23; 24; 36; 46; 48; 58; 59.
04, Hadleigh by the R. Brett, 1974; 05, Needham Market by the R. Gipping, 1980; 14,
Sproughton; 16, near Bedingfield, 1973; 23, Chelmondiston Tip, 1974; 24, Woodbridge,
1981; 48, Barsham, 1974.

Malcolmia africana (L.) R. Br.　　African Stock　　　Mrs F. Baker c. 1900
A casual, probably a native of S. Europe. Recorded from Oulton Broad.

Malcolmia maritima (L.) R. Br.　　Virginia Stock　　　　R. Burn 1930
Cultivated in gardens. Native in the Mediterranean region and occasionally found on
waste ground.
E: 13, Brantham, 1930; 23, Chelmondiston Tip, 1975 (Mrs E. M. Hyde).

Cheiranthus cheiri L.　　Wallflower　　　　　　Sir J. Cullum 1773
　　　　　　　　　　　　Gilliflower
Introduced. A naturalised garden escape on old walls, railway banks and waste ground.
Native in the E. Mediterranean. The plants growing on the old walls of the Abbey ruins at
Bury St Edmunds are probably of early origin and are almost identical with the true wild
species. Frequent.
W: 67; 77; 78; 86; 88; 93; 96.
86, railway cutting, Ipswich side of Bury Station, 1979; 96, Thurston Station, under
platform, 1980.
E: 05; 14; 16; 23; 26; 27; 33; 36; 37; 38; 39; 44; 46; 47; 49; 58; 59; 50.
14, Ipswich, old wall, 1981; 23, Landguard Fort, 1977; 26, Framlingham Castle, 1979; 39,
Bungay Castle and Church ruins, 1980.

Cheiranthus × allionii hort.   Siberian Wallflower   Mrs E. M. Hyde 1975

Casual, of garden origin. Found on tips and waste places.
W: 77, Barton Mills, 1977.
E: 03, East Bergholt, 1977; Holton St Mary, 1975; 04, Hintlesham.

Matthiola incana (L.) R. Br.   Stock   E. C. Norman 1957

Introduced, native of the Mediterranean region. Grown in gardens, and sometimes found on waste ground and rubbish tips.
E: In a wood at Chediston.

Matthiola longipetala (Vent.) DC.   Night-scented Stock   Mrs F. Baker c. 1900
ssp. **bicornis** (Sibth. & Sm.) P. W. Ball

A casual, native of Greece and Asia Minor. Known in Suffolk only from the record from Oulton Broad.

Chorispora tenella (Pall.) DC.   D. Dupree 1953

Casual, native in S.E. Europe. Known from a single record from waste ground at Lakenheath.

Euclidium syriacum (L.) R. Br.   Mrs F. Baker c. 1890

A casual of waste places, native of E. Europe and W. Asia. Known only from Oulton Broad.

Barbarea vulgaris R. Br.   Common Winter Cress   Sir J. Cullum 1774
                    Yellow Rocket

Native. Sides of streams, rivers, ditches, wet pastures. Frequent.
W: All squares except 67; 83; 98.
93, Polstead by the R. Box; 76, between Dalham and Moulton, 1981.
E: All squares except 33; 37; 45; 58; 50.
13, Holbrook, by the Mill Stream, 1981; 35, by the R. Deben at Ufford, 1981.

Barbarea stricta Andrz.   Small-flowered Winter Cress   Lady Blake 1840
                    Small-flowered Yellow Rocket

Native or introduced. Stream banks and waste places in scattered localities. Recorded in Hind's Flora from Thurston, Fornham, Wixoe and Stoke-by-Nayland, but there are no subsequent records.

Barbarea verna (Mill.) Aschers.   Early-flowering Yellow Rocket.   J. Andrews 1745
(*B. praecox* (Sm.) R. Br.)

Casual. Native of S.W. Europe. Found in waste places and occasionally on cultivated ground, where it may perhaps be a relic of former cultivation as a salad plant.
W: 87.
E: 45, Aldeburgh, 1978 (M. A. Hyde). Detd. E. J. Clement.

Barbarea intermedia Bor.   Medium-flowered Winter Cress   Rev. J. D. Gray 1885
                    Intermediate Yellow Rocket

An established alien or casual, native in W. Europe and the W. Mediterranean region. Waysides, edges of fields and waste places. Rare or overlooked.

W: 93, Stoke-by-Nayland.
E: 14, near Stoke Bridge, Ipswich, 1981 (F. W. Simpson), detd. E. J. Clement; 46, Thorpeness; 38, Mettingham.

Rorippa amphibia (L.)   Besser   Great Yellow Cress   Sir J. Cullum 1773
(*Nasturtium amphibium* (L.) R. Br.)   Great Water Rocket

Native. In ponds, ditches, beside rivers and old wet gravel pits. Not very frequent, but sometimes occurring in quantity.
W: 68; 75; 77; 78; 86; 88; 93; 96; 97; 98.
68, Lakenheath, 1980.
E: 06; 07; 14; 15; 16; 27; 35; 39.
14, Ipswich by R. Gipping, 1981; 15, Baylham Fishponds, 1977; Barking, 1981; 39, Bungay, 1981.
Hb. Ipswich Museum; 'In the boggy part of a piece of arable land between the Bramford Road and the River, north of Handford Bridge and by the side of Delphs in the meadows adjoining', c. 1810.

Rorippa sylvestris (L.) Besser   Creeping Yellow Cress   Davy 1796
(*Nasturtium sylvestre* (L.) R. Br.)   Water Rocket

Native. On the sides of streams, damp pastures, and occasionally a weed of wet arable land. Uncommon or local.
W: 75; 77; 78; 83; 86; 87; 88; 96; 97.
97, Fakenham.
E: 03; 13; 14; 23; 25; 36; 38; 39; 45; 46; 49; 58.
13, Brantham, 1979; 14, Bramford Chalk-pit, 1979.
Hb. Davy: specimen from Bungay Common, 1796.

Rorippa islandica (Oeder) Borbás   Marsh Yellow Cress   Woodward 1796
(*Nasturtium palustre* (L.) DC., non Crantz)

Native. On the margins of ponds, ditches and dykes, and the edges of wet pastures. Now rather local or scarce.
W: 67; 68; 77; 83; 84; 86; 87; 88; 96; 97; 98.
68, Lakenheath, 1980.
E: 03; 04; 05; 07; 14; 16; 23; 36; 38; 45; 48; 49; 50.
03, Stratford St Mary, 1979; 14, Bramford, 1979.

Armoracia rusticana Gaertn., Mey. & Scherb.   Horse Radish   Sir J. Cullum 1775
(*Cochlearia armoracia* L.)

Introduced from S.E. Europe and W. Asia. A naturalised garden escape in waste places, on railway embankments, and riversides. Frequent, sometimes spreading extensively, forming large colonies.
All squares.

Nasturtium officinale R. Br.   Watercress   J. Andrews 1745
(*Rorippa nasturtium-aquaticum* (L.) Hayek)

Native. In wet places and streams, especially on the Chalk and Crag. Common. This plant remains green all the year.
All squares.

Nasturtium microphyllum (Boenn.) Reichenb.   Miss J. C. N. Willis c. 1950
(*Rorippa microphylla* (Boenn.) Hyl.)   Brown-leaved Watercress
                                           One-rowed Watercress

Native. In streams and wet places. Frequent. This plant has purplish-brown leaves in autumn and winter in habitats subject to frost.
W: 75; 76; 77; 85; 95; 96; 97.
E: 03; 16; 23; 26; 38; 47; 48.

Nasturtium microphyllum × officinale   Finder not recorded 1957
(*Rorippa microphylla × nasturtium-aquaticum*
R. × sterilis Airy-Shaw)

Wet places and streams. Probably frequent, but overlooked.
E: 04, Hadleigh, 1957.

Cardamine amara L.   Large Bitter Cress   Gerarde 1597

Native. In streams, marshes and wet woods, especially where there are springs. Often grows with Watercress. Frequent in the South-east of the County. Less frequent or scarce elsewhere.
W: Recorded from squares 67; 77; 83; 84; 86; 87; 88; 93; 94.
77, Mildenhall, 1980; 93, Leavenheath, 1977.
E: All squares except 15; 16; 17; 33; 34; 44; 45; 46; 59; 40; 50.
04, Hadleigh, 1981; 14, Ipswich by the R. Gipping, 1981.   *Illustrated page 488*

Cardamine pratensis L.   Lady's Smock   Gerarde 1597
                                Cuckoo Flower

Native. Damp pastures, fens and woodland glades. Frequent.
All squares except 65; 66; 67; 33.
A double-flowered form has been recorded from Theberton, Burstall and Freston Park.
Subsp. **hayneana** (Welw.) O. E. Schulz = *C. matthiolii* Moretti has been recorded from Hadleigh (R. Burn).

Cardamine impatiens L.   Narrow-leaved Bitter Cress   E. Skepper 1860

Probably introduced. A rare species of very local distribution in shady woods or on damp rocks or walls. There is one record of the species in Hind's Flora from a shady damp corner of the Botanic Gardens at Bury St Edmunds, but there have been no further records.

Cardamine flexuosa With.   Wavy Bitter Cress   John Notcutt c. 1820
                                  Wood Bitter Cress
                                  Zig-zag Lady's Smock

Native. Damp woods on sandy or alluvial soils, shady banks and sides of streams and ditches. Locally frequent.
W: 77; 84; 86; 87; 88; 93; 94; 95; 97.
77, Cavenham, 1978; 94, Brent Eleigh, 1974.
E: 03; 04; 07; 13; 14; 15; 23; 24; 25; 28; 33; 35; 36; 37; 39; 46; 47; 49; 58; 40.
14, Washbrook, 1980; Freston, 1980; 25, Bromeswell, 1980.

Specimens Hb. Ipswich Museum from: 'Spring-head Lane, St Helen's. Towards the top of Dairy Lane and at the lower corner of Bolton adjoining', c. 1820 (John Notcutt).

Cardamine hirsuta L.   Hairy Bitter Cress   Gerarde 1597

Native. Banks, margins of sandy heaths, tracks, waste places and gardens. Common, sometimes abundant.
W: All squares except 65; 66; 67; 68; 75; 84; 85; 93.
E: All squares except 05; 17; 27; 40.

Cardaminopsis arenosa (L.) Hayek   F. W. Simpson 1959
(*Arabis arenosa* (L.) Scop.)

Casual. Native of continental Europe. Known in Suffolk only from waste heaps at the gas works at Bury St Edmunds (sq. 86). Detd. at the British Museum.

Arabis glabra (L.) Bernh.   Tower Mustard   J. Andrews 1746
(*Turritis glabra* L.   Smooth Rock Cress
A. perfoliata Lam.)   Perfoliate Rock Cress

Native. On dry banks and heaths. Rare, formerly locally frequent.
W: 78, Lakenheath; 88, Barnham Cross Common; 93, Stoke-by-Nayland; 97, Gt Fakenham.
E: 23, Nacton; 24, Brightwell; Foxhall Heath, 1980; Purdis Heath; Rushmere Common; Waldringfield; 46, Westleton; 47, Thorington.

Arabis hirsuta (L.) Scop.   Hairy Rock Cress   Sir J. Cullum 1774

Native. On dry, chalky banks and in old quarries, occasionally on walls. Scarce, except in the Breckland, where it is locally frequent.
W: 67; 68; 76; 77; 78; 86; 87; 96; 97; 98.
77, Icklingham, 1980; 78, Lakenheath, 1980; Brandon, 1980.
E: 06; 07; 14; 16; 33; 36.
07, Wortham Ling, 1980; 14, Lt. Blakenham, 1972.

Arabis turrita L.   Tower Rock Cress   J. Atkins 1910

Introduced. Native of C. and S. Europe. Naturalised on old walls. Hb. Atkins, specimen from Lt. Blakenham.

Arabis caucasica Schlecht.   Garden Arabis   F. W. Simpson 1948

Introduced. A native of S. Europe, commonly cultivated and escaping, or thrown out with garden waste.
W: 66, Moulton, 1976; 86, Bury St Edmunds.
E: 14, Ipswich; 23, Landguard Common; 45, Slaughden End, Aldeburgh.

Lunaria annua L.   Honesty   F. W. Simpson 1948
(*L. biennis* Moench)

Introduced. Native in S.E. Europe. A common garden plant, often escaping and found on wayside banks, sides of ditches, waste ground and in churchyards. The dried shiny septa are frequently used for decoration in churches and on graves.

151

W: 66; 67; 77; 83; 86; 87; 88.
67, Worlington, 1980; 87, Culford, 1981.
E: 03; 04; 13; 14; 15; 23; 24; 27; 33; 44; 45; 46; 47; 59.
13, Woolverstone Churchyard, 1975; 24, Foxhall and Playford, 1981; Kyson, near Woodbridge, 1981; 33, Felixstowe, near the Grove, 1980.

Alyssum saxatile L.　　Yellow Alyssum　　　　　Mrs E. M. Hyde and M. A. Hyde 1978

Introduced. Native of E. Europe.
W: 66, Exning, 1978, naturalised on a wall (F. W. Simpson); 76, Kentford, on a wall.

Alyssum alyssoides (L.) L.　　Small Alison　　　　　　　　　Mrs French c. 1850

A naturalised alien or casual from Europe and W. Asia. There is a possibility that it could be a native of Breckland and the Sandlings. Sandy heaths, sand pits and light arable soils.
W: 77, Eriswell, 1980; Icklingham.
E: 05, Needham Market, 1973 (Mrs M. Kershaw); 34, Sutton, 1967 (Miss R. Barker); 45, Aldeburgh; 58, Covehithe. The small colony in Sutton still existed in 1980.
The only record in Hind's Flora is from a clover field at Woolpit. There are further old records from a railway bank at Carlton Colville, 1898, and Easton Bavents, 1896.

Alyssum hirsutum Bieb.　　Hairy Alison　　　　　　　　　Mrs F. Baker c. 1890

An alien from S.E. Europe. This is a single record of the species from Oulton Broad.

Berteroa incana (L.) DC.　　Hoary Alison　　　　　　　Rev. J. D. Gray 1878
(*Alyssum incanum* L.)

An alien from S.E. Europe. There is a single record of the species from Oulton Broad. usually only a casual. Not frequent.
W: 66, Newmarket, 1980 (G. M. S. Easy); 77, Eriswell; 78, Brandon, 1973.
E: 14, Ipswich.
Hind's Flora records it as a stray, accidentally introduced, found at Culford Heath and Nayland.

Lobularia maritima (L.) Desv.　　Sweet Alison　　　　　　　　Paget 1834
(*Alyssum maritimum* (L.) Lam.)　　White Alyssum

Introduced. Native in the Mediterranean region. Sometimes almost naturalised on coastal sands. Extensively grown in gardens. Seeds itself from throw-outs. Frequent.
W: 66; 75; 76; 77; 88.
66, Exning, 1977.
E: 13; 14; 23; 24; 33; 34; 35; 36; 45; 46; 47; 49; 57.
14, New Cut, Ipswich, 1981; 33, Felixstowe Ferry, 1980; 45, Thorpeness, 1980.

Erophila verna (L.) Chevall. ssp. **verna**　　Common Whitlow Grass　　Sir J. Cullum 1773
(*E. vulgaris* DC.
Draba obconica (De Bary) Hayek)

Native. Dry, open places, old walls and roofs. Common. A very variable species.
W: All squares except 64; 65; 68; 85; 93.
E: All squares except 27; 33; 37; 48; 49; 58.
A colony with rich pink flowers seen by a track to Warren Lodge, Lakenheath, 1973.

Ssp. **praecox** (Stev.) Walters   Early Whitlow Grass   Victoria County History of
(*E. praecox* (Stev.) DC.   Suffolk 1911
Draba praecox Stev.)

Native. Dry, open places, walls and paths. No localities recorded. Not recorded in Hind's
Flora, but appears in the list of Suffolk Plants in the Victoria County History of Suffolk,
published in 1911.

Ssp. **spathulata** (A. F. Láng) Walters.   Round-podded Whitlow Grass
(*E. boerhaavii* (Van Hall) Dum.   F. W. Simpson 1951
Draba spathulata (A. F. Láng) Sadler)

Native. Dry heaths, tracks and walls. Rare or overlooked. Much work remains to be done
on the distribution of the Whitlow Grasses.
E: 34, Shingle Street.
Not recorded in Hind's Flora.

Cochlearia danica L.   Danish Scurvy Grass   Sir J. Cullum 1773
                               Early Scurvy Grass

Native. Sea coast and estuaries. Occasionally inland. Very small forms of this species can
be found flowering among the dry grasses of sea embankments, and on the edges of sandy
salt marshes, in March and early April. Sometimes there are large patches and I have
found the flowers to be pleasantly scented. Not very frequent.
E: 13, Harkstead, 1981; 23, Landguard Common, 1977 (Hb. Atkins, 1909); 33, Bawdsey;
Felixstowe Ferry, 1978; 34, Shingle Street, 1980; 44, Orford; Orford Ness, 1973;
Havergate Island, 1979; 45, Sudbourne; 46, Dunwich; Thorpeness, 1980; 47,
Walberswick; 58, Covehithe.
Inland sites: 77, Barton Mills, 1980. Alongside the A11 for about 350 yards. 24,
Martlesham, 1981. Alongside the A12 over a similar distance. Both records by Mrs E. M.
Hyde.

Cochlearia officinalis L. ssp. **officinalis**   Common Scurvy Grass   Sir J. Cullum 1773

Native. Drier areas of salt marshes and banks of tidal rivers. Formerly not uncommon.
Now appears to be extinct, as there are no recent records. Some of the records below may
refer to *C. anglica*.
E: 03; 14; 23; 24; 25; 33; 35; 44; 45; 46; 47; 49; 59; 40; 50.

Cochlearia anglica L.   Long-leaved Scurvy Grass   Sir J. Cullum 1773
                               English Scurvy Grass

Native. In muddy salt marshes and estuaries. Frequent.
E: 03; 13; 14; 23; 24; 25; 33; 34; 35; 44; 47; 49; 57; 59; 40; 50.
Frequent in salt marshes between the Stour Estuary and Aldeburgh, 1981.
Hb. Ipswich Museum: 'Spoon-wort. Side of the River between Stoke Bridge and the
Locks, about high water mark, plentiful. On the shore by the Ostrich', c. 1810 (John
Notcutt). This species was always very common on the muddy banks of the river on the
northern side from near Stoke Bridge to beyond the Princes Street Bridge, until the banks
were paved in 1973. In some seasons the banks were white with flowers.

Illustrated page 503

Cochlearia anglica × officinalis   F. W. Simpson 1948
(*C.* × *hollandica* Henrard)
Saltings. Rare.
E: 23, Harkstead, 1976; 34, Hollesley and Boyton.

Camelina sativa (L.) Crantz   Gold-of-Pleasure   J. Andrews 1745
A casual. Native in E. Europe and W. Asia. Formerly introduced into flax fields with
seed. Also in imported cage-bird seeds. Found in waste places and on cultivated ground.
Cultivated in Europe and Asia for its oil-yielding seeds.
W: 78, Lakenheath; 86, Timworth.
E: 03, East Bergholt; 14, Ipswich; Whitton; Rushmere Heath; 23, Felixstowe Docks; 24,
Woodbridge; 33, Felixstowe.

Capsella bursa-pastoris (L.) Medic.   Shepherd's Purse   Davy 1793
Native or colonist. A weed of cultivated fields, waysides and waste places. Very common
and variable. There are a number of micro-species; no attempt has been made to separate
them for this Flora.
All squares.

Teesdalia nudicaulis (L.) R. Br.   Shepherd's Cress   J. Andrews 1745
Native. Sandy heaths and dry banks, especially in Breckland. Formerly frequent on the
Sandlings of East Suffolk, but now scarce, mainly due to afforestation. Extinct in several
areas.
W: 67; 76; 77; 78; 86; 87; 88; 96; 98.
77, Icklingham, 1981; 87, Barnham, 1980.
E: 07; 13; 14; 24; 33; 34; 35; 39; 44; 45; 46; 47; 58; 59; 40.
14, Belstead, 1979; 24, Martlesham, roadside bank, 1980 (J. R. Palmer); 44, Orford Ness,
1973; 47, Blythburgh and Walberswick, 1978.
Hb. Ipswich Museum: 'On the bank on the south side of the Walton road adjoining the
Race Ground and on the Sheep Walks by the Decoy Ponds between a Barn and the
Ponds', May 3rd, 1819 (John Notcutt).

Thlaspi arvense L.   Field Penny Cress   Ray 1690
Colonist. Cultivated fields, and disturbed waste ground, especially around farms.
Common.
All squares.

Thlaspi perfoliatum L.   Perfoliate Penny Cress   W. R. Roberts 1921
Casual in Suffolk. Usually found in limestone areas. The only record is from Woodbridge.

Iberis sempervirens L.   Evergreen Candytuft   F. W. Simpson 1977
Introduced. Native of high mountains in the Mediterranean region. Frequently cultivated
in gardens and sometimes naturalised.
E: 14, small colony on bank at Derby Road Station, Ipswich; still there, 1981.

Iberis amara L.   Wild Candytuft   Mrs Dunlap 1847

Formerly found in chalky fields in Breckland. Now extinct. Recorded in Hind's Flora as a casual or stray from cultivation, from Honington, Barton, Walsham, Cavenham and Gt Thurlow.

Iberis umbellata L.   Candytuft   W. A. Dutt 1899

An annual or biennial species of Candytuft, cultivated in gardens. Waste places. The first Suffolk record was from Oulton Broad.
E: 23, Chelmondiston Tip, 1971-74.

Lepidium campestre (L.) R. Br.   Pepperwort   Lawson 1696
                                        Field Pepperwort

A colonist. Waysides, borders of fields, waste places and on beaches. Locally frequent.
W: 64; 76; 86; 94; 96.
76, Herringswell, Gazeley and Kentford, all 1980.
E: 03; 04; 06; 07; 13; 14; 16; 23; 24; 33; 34; 35; 36; 37; 38; 39; 45; 47; 57; 58; 59; 50.
14, Ipswich, 1981; 33, Felixstowe Ferry, 1975; 34, Shingle Street, 1981; 58, Benacre, 1980.

Lepidium heterophyllum Benth.   Smith's Cress   Rev. G. R. Leathes 1834
(*L. smithii* Hook.)   Smith's Pepperwort

A colonist. On roadsides, field verges, railway sidings. Rare and decreasing.
W: 86, Bury St Edmunds.
E: 13, Bentley Woods (Hb. Atkins, 1910); 24; 36, Yoxford; 47, Thorington; 49; 59, Gunton; Oulton; 50, Hopton (E. Milne-Redhead).

Lepidium sativum L.   Garden Cress   Wilson 1833

Introduced and cultivated. Found in waste places and on rubbish dumps.
W: 74; 77.
E: 13; 23; 35; 44; 45; 49; 59.
23, Felixstowe, 1977.

Lepidium ruderale L.   Narrow-leaved Pepperwort   Dillenius 1724

Native. Chiefly on sea embankments. Also in waste places. Not very common.
E: 13; 17; 23; 25; 26; 33; 35; 39; 44; 45; 46; 47; 48; 49; 57; 58; 59; 40; 50.
23, Chelmondiston, 1981; Shotley, 1980; 33, Felixstowe Ferry, 1978; 47, Reydon, 1978; Blythburgh, 1980 (both records, P. G. Lawson); 40, Belton, on embankment, 1977.
Hb. Ipswich Museum: 'Side of the river between Stoke Bridge and the Locks, nearest the Bridge. North-west end of the Marsh Wall between Peter's Dock and Nova Scotia', 1818 (John Notcutt).

Lepidium perfoliatum L.   Perfoliate Pepperwort   W. A. Dutt 1899
A casual from E. Europe and W. Asia. Recorded from Oulton Broad in 1899.
E: 15, Stonham Aspal, one specimen in garden probably introduced with grass seed, 1974 (J. A. Foster); 23, Felixstowe Dock Maltings, 1939 (F. W. Simpson). Detd. at Kew.

Lepidium latifolium L. Dittander Culpeper 1650
Broad-leaved Pepperwort

Native. This plant, which is characteristic of salt marshes and coastal areas, has certainly increased since Hind's time. It can be seen, often growing in great abundance and forming dense colonies, along the coastal strip between Southwold and the R. Stour. Not only does it favour salt marshes, but also waste ground. In Ipswich it has colonised a number of sites away from the R. Orwell. It will sometimes survive even when roads and paths are constructed, with plants appearing between the cracks or forcing their way up through the tarmac. It still occurs at Blythburgh and Snape Bridge, as recorded in the 18th century. It is steadily spreading inland, along the railways and roads and near tips.

W: 77, east of Icklingham; 86, Bury St Edmunds by R. Lark and near Fornham Priory, 1981; Bury Station, 1981.

E: 04, Hadleigh; 05, Stowmarket, 1981; 06, Haughley, 1981; 13, Freston, Wherstead, Woolverstone, Harkstead, Holbrook and Brantham, all 1981; 14, Rushmere Heath; Sproughton; Ipswich, very common, 1981; Bramford, Bullen Lane, 1981; 15, Barham Pits, 1979; 17, Eye, 1980; 23, Chelmondiston, Levington, Nacton, Trimley, Felixstowe, Shotley and Erwarton, all 1981; 24, Waldringfield; Foxhall Tip, 1981; Brightwell, 1980; Woodbridge, 1981; 33, Bawdsey; Felixstowe Ferry; 34, Boyton; Sutton; 25, Snape, 1981; 44, Orford; 45, Aldeburgh; Thorpeness; 47, Blythburgh and Walberswick, 1981; 57, Southwold.

Hb. Ipswich Museum: 'On the banks of the Salt River, between Stoke Bridge and the Locks, plentiful', c. 1809 (John Notcutt). *Illustrated page 486*

Cardaria draba (L.) Desv. ssp. **draba** Hoary Cress E. Skepper 1859
(*Lepidium draba* L.) Hoary Pepperwort

An established alien, native in the Mediterranean region and W. Asia. Said to have been introduced into England by the Military after an expedition to Walcheren in 1809. Formerly rare, now a frequent and troublesome weed of field borders, commons, waysides and sea embankments.

W: All squares except 65; 85; 87; 93; 97.
86, Bury St Edmunds, 1981.
E: All squares except 15; 26; 38; 46; 48.
23, Landguard Common, 1981; 34, Boyton, 1981.

Its former comparative rarity is evidenced by the fact that Hind's Flora records it only from Fornham St Martin, Bury St Edmunds, Cockfield, Landguard Fort and Coddenham.

Coronopus squamatus (Forsk.) Aschers. Swine Cress Sir J. Cullum 1773
(*C. procumbens* Gilib. Wart Cress
Senebiera coronopus (L.) Poir.)

Probably a colonist. Waste places, especially farm tracks on clay soils. Common.
All squares.

Coronopus didymus (L.) Sm. Lesser Swine Cress Hind's Flora 1889
(*Senebiera didyma* (L.) Pers.)

A colonist, introduced from S. America. Bare waste places, tracks, sometimes in lawns. Uncommon, but increasing.

W: 76; 83; 86.

E: 03; 04; 07; 13; 14; 23; 25; 35; 36; 39; 45; 46; 47; 58; 59; 50.

13, Woolverstone, 1980; 14, Belstead Road, Ipswich, 1981; 23, Pin Mill, 1979; 45, Sudbourne, 1975, (increasing, M. Keer).

This species is mentioned in Hind's Flora with the comment 'Most unlikely to occur in Suffolk'. Hind has one doubtful record from Rede.

First authentic record: E. R. Long 1926, waste ground near Lowestoft Harbour (sq. 59).

Conringia orientalis (L.) Dum.   Hare's Ear Mustard   Dillenius 1724
(*Erysimum orientale* (L.) Crantz, non Mill.)

Casual. Native in the E. Mediterranean region. Cultivated land and waste places.
W: 88; 94.
E: 04; 05; 14; 58; 59.

Conringia austriaca (Jacq.) Sweet   P. G. Lawson & A. Copping 1970
(*Erysimum austriacum* (Jacq.) Roth)

A casual. Native in C. and S.E. Europe. Rubbish tips and waste places. Rare. Similar to *C. orientalis* but taller, and the flowers are smaller and lemon-yellow. The fruit is eight-angled.
E: 49, Beccles.

Diplotaxis tenuifolia (L.) DC.   Wall Rocket   John Notcutt 1818

A colonist. Old walls, waste places and roadsides. Formerly scarce, now frequent.
W: 66; 76; 77; 78; 86; 87; 88; 97.
66, Newmarket, 1981; 86, Bury St Edmunds, 1981; Rougham, 1981; 87, Ampton; 88, Euston; 97, Hopton; Honington.
E: 04, Hadleigh; 05, Stowmarket; 13, Woolverstone; 14, Ipswich, many sites, 1981; Rushmere; Wherstead; Freston; 15, Barham; Pettaugh; 23, Chelmondiston; Shotley; Felixstowe Docks; 24, Foxhall, on waste soil brought from Ipswich; Woodbridge Railway Station; 25, Melton; 34, Sutton, 1973; 35, Marlesford, 1977; 35, Benhall; Lt. Glemham; 45, Aldeburgh; 46, Dunwich (since 1842); 47 Walberswick; 49, Beccles; 59, Lowestoft, 1980; 40, Belton, 1977; 50, South Town.
Ipswich specimen in Hb. Ipswich Museum: 'On the Garden Wall, west side of the road by St Nicholas Church', 1818 (John Notcutt).

Diplotaxis muralis (L.) DC.   Annual Wall Rocket   Sutton and Kirby 1787
(*Brassica muralis* (L.) Huds.)   Stinkweed

An established alien. Waste places, gardens, arable fields, railway tracks and paths. Locally frequent in the South-east of the County.
W: Recorded from squares 66; 67; 68; 74; 76; 77; 78; 86; 87; 88; 96; 98.
78, Lakenheath, 1980; 86, Bury St Edmunds, 1979.
E: All squares except 03; 05; 06; 07; 16; 26; 27; 40.
A frequent weed of gardens and waste places on the east side of Ipswich and in Felixstowe, 1981.
Var. **caulescens** Kittel (formerly var. *babingtonii* Syme) recorded from Ipswich, Felixstowe, Alderton, Oulton Broad.

Brassica elongata Ehrh.   Mrs F. Baker c. 1890

A casual. Introduced from S. E. Europe. Sometimes found in cornfields and in the neighbourhood of ports. Recorded only from Oulton Broad.

Brassica oleracea L.   Wild Cabbage   Prof. Cowell 1870

Probably native in S. and S. W. England. Recorded in Hind's Flora from Pakefield and Felixstowe, 'usually on sea cliffs, especially chalk; very rare in Suffolk'. There are no known records of the species since Hind's Flora and it is not known whether that record is for the genuine native. Relics of cultivated varieties are frequent.

Brassica napus L.   Rape   Sir J. Cullum 1773

Introduced and cultivated as a crop. Occurs as a casual or weed of waysides, waste places and tips.

Brassica juncea (L.) Czern.   Chinese Mustard   F. W. Simpson 1952
(*Sinapis juncea* L.)

A casual. Native in Asia. The only known record of the species for Suffolk is from Felixstowe Docks (sq. 23). Specimen determined at Kew.

Brassica nigra (L.) Koch   Black Mustard   Mrs Casborne 1831
(*Sinapis nigra* L.)

Native. By the sea, on cliffs and embankments. Very common, frequently abundant. Inland it is a colonist of waste places, and the banks of rivers.
W: Recorded from squares 76; 83; 86; 87; 88; 96; 97.
E: All squares except 05; 07; 16; 17; 39; 48; 49.
13, Holbrook, 1981; 23, Shotley, on embankment, 1981; 33, Felixstowe and Bawdsey, 1981; 45, Aldeburgh, 1981.

Sinapis arvensis L.   Charlock   Sir J. Cullum 1773
(*Brassica sinapis* Vis.)   Wild Mustard

Native or colonist. A very frequent weed of arable fields and waste places. Often very abundant on recently disturbed chalky soil.
All squares.

Sinapis alba L.   White Mustard   Mrs Casborne 1832
(*Brassica hirta* Moench
B. alba (L.) Rabenh.)

Introduced. Native in the Mediterranean region. A relic of cultivation. Fields and waste places. Much less frequent than formerly.
W: All squares except 64; 65; 67; 68; 84; 85; 98.
E: All squares except 05; 06; 07; 15; 17; 26; 27; 28; 33; 34; 36; 39; 47; 48; 49; 58; 59; 40; 50.
14, Ipswich market, 1981; 16, Stonham Aspal, abundant across a field where gas pipes had been laid, 1979 (both records, Mrs E. M. Hyde).

Eruca vesicaria (L.) Cav.   S. J. Batchelder 1935

Native of the Mediterranean region. Occasionally found as a casual on waste ground. The only record for Suffolk is from Landguard Common (sq. 23).

Eruca sativa Mill.   Mrs F. Baker c. 1890
(*Brassica eruca* L.)

A casual from the Mediterranean region and E. Asia. Formerly cultivated for a medicinal oil extracted from its seeds. Recorded from Oulton Broad about 1890 and from Ipswich by J. S. Wilkinson in 1908.

Erucastrum gallicum (Willd.) O. E. Schulz   Hairy Rocket   Hind 1885
(*Brassica gallica* (Willd.) Druce)

Established alien. Native in W. and C. Europe. Waste places, roadsides and rubbish tips. Rare.
W: 67; 68, Mildenhall, 1977; Lakenheath, 1980; 76, Herringswell; 77, Mildenhall, 1976; 78, Undley Common and near Pashford Poor's Fen, Lakenheath, 1976; 87, Rushford; Euston.
E: 14, Wherstead; 23, Landguard Common and Felixstowe Docks; 35, Snape.

Rhynchosinapis cheiranthos (Vill.) Dandy   Wallflower Cabbage
                                                Mrs E. M. Hyde 1975

Alien. Waste places. Native of continental Europe.
E: 45, Aldringham and Aldeburgh. Established on track near disused railway. Still there, 1980.

Hirschfeldia incana (L.) Lagr. -Foss.   Hoary Mustard   Hind 1884
(*Brassica adpressa* Boiss.
Sinapis incana L.)

Alien. A native of the Mediterranean region, where it is a weed of cultivation. Docks and waste places.
W: 68, Sedge Fen, near Mildenhall, 1964, now arable land.
E: 06, Haughley Green (Mrs J. Harris), detd. E. J. Clement; 23, Felixstowe Docks, 1936; Landguard Common, c. 1950; 37, Halesworth; 59, Corton.
Hind records it only from Euston and Bardwell.

Erucaria hispanica (L.) Druce   F. W. Simpson 1936
(*E. aleppica* Gaertn.)

A casual, native of S. Greece and the Aegean. Rare. The only record is from Felixstowe Docks (sq. 23) in 1936. Detd. at Kew.

Cakile maritima Scop. ssp. **maritima**   Sea Rocket   T. Martyn 1763

Native. On sandy beaches in scattered colonies. Locally frequent in some seasons.
E: 23; 33; 34; 45; 46; 47; 57; 58; 59; 40; 50.
Recorded from the following parishes: Bawdsey, Benacre, Corton, Erwarton, Felixstowe, Gunton, Kessingland, Lowestoft, Minsmere, Ramsholt, Shotley, Southwold, Trimley St Martin and Walberswick.

Rapistrum perenne (L.) All.   P. J. O. Trist 1968
Casual. Native of C. Europe.
W: 77, Icklingham.

Rapistrum rugosum (L.) All.   Bastard Cabbage   J. S. Wilkinson 1908
A casual of waste and arable land. Native of S. Europe. Three subspecies have been
recorded in the County, but not all recorders have made the distinction. Such records are
listed after those for the three subspecies, and include J. S. Wilkinson's first record for
Ipswich.

Ssp. **rugosum**   Mrs E. M. Hyde 1976
E: 14, Ipswich, former site of Stoke Green Chapel, 1976; Sproughton rubbish tip, 1977;
45, Thorpeness, 1978 (P. G. Lawson).

Ssp. **orientale** (L.) Arcangeli   P. F. Sheppy 1975
E: 06, Stowupland, 1975; 14, Ipswich, former site of Stoke Green Chapel, 1976;
Wherstead, 1975 (Mrs E. M. Hyde); Sproughton, 1977; 25, Easton, 1980 (E. Milne-
Redhead).

Ssp. **linnaeanum** Rouy & Fouc.   F. W. Simpson 1935
E: 23, Landguard Common, 1935.

Other records:
W: 64; 94.
E: 13, Holbrook, roadside, 1980; 14, Ipswich, 1908; Freston; Washbrook, 1980; 23,
Landguard Common; Felixstowe, abundant near Coastguard Station, 1980; 40, Belton,
1977. Abundant in Ipswich, beside the R. Gipping, near Riverside Rd., 1981.

Crambe maritima L.   Sea Kale   Davy 1805
Native. On shingle beaches. Usually small colonies or single specimens. Sites often subject
to erosion.
E: 23, Landguard Common, 1981; Shotley, one plant, 1975; Trimley St Mary, 1981; 33,
Bawdsey, 1981; Felixstowe Ferry, 1979; 34, Shingle Street, 1981; North Weir Point, fine
colony, 1981; 44, Havergate Island; Orford Ness; 45, Sudbourne; 46, Dunwich;
Minsmere; Thorpeness, 1974; 47, Walberswick; Dunwich, 1979; 58, Benacre; Covehithe;
Kessingland, 1980; 59, Lowestoft.   *Illustrated page 500*

Raphanus sativus L.   Garden Radish   F. W. Simpson 1935
Introduced. Origin doubtful. The cultivated Radish occasionally occurs as a garden escape
and on rubbish tips and waste places.
W: 83.
E: 14, Ipswich; 23, Felixstowe Docks and Landguard Common; 46, Dunwich.

CRUCIFERAE

Raphanus raphanistrum L. Wild Radish Sir J. Cullum 1773
White Charlock
Runch

A colonist and a weed of cultivation, especially on light soils, disturbed waysides and waste places. The flowers vary in colour, especially near the coast. The chief forms are (a) forma **alba** F. Gér. White flowers with lilac veins. Common. (b) forma **ochrocyanea** F. Gér. Pale yellow flowers with lilac veins. Frequent.
All squares except 65; 68; 75; 85.
Proportionately those with white flowers are twice as frequent as those with yellow.

Raphanus maritimus Sm. Sea Radish Henslow & Skepper 1860

Native. On the sea coast. Rare. I believe that some of the Suffolk records are incorrect and refer to either *R. sativus* or *R. raphanistrum*.
E: 33; 34; 47; 57; 58; 59.
58, Kessingland, 1980 (F.W.S.); 59, Lowestoft, 1980 (Mrs E. M. Hyde).

RESEDACEAE

MIGNONETTE FAMILY

Reseda luteola L. Dyer's Rocket Sir J. Cullum 1773
Dyer's Weld

Native. A colonist of quarries, especially on Chalk and gravel, also on waste ground and cliffs. Formerly cultivated for its dye. Frequent.
All squares except 65; 75; 17; 26; 27; 38; 48.

Reseda alba L. Upright Mignonette Dr Trimen 1859
White Mignonette

Introduced from the Mediterranean region. A casual of waste ground, especially near the sea. Rare.
W: 86, Bury St Edmunds, 1946.
E: 14, Ipswich, 1979; 33, Bawdsey Ferry; 59, Park Estate, Oulton.
Recorded in Hind's Flora only from Lowestoft and Kirkley.

Reseda lutea L. Wild Mignonette Sir T. Browne 1668

Native. Quarries, waysides and disturbed soils, especially on the Chalk. Very frequent.
W: All squares except 65; 74; 83; 84; 85; 95.
Very common in Breckland, 1981.
E: All squares except 13; 16; 17; 26; 28; 37; 38; 48; 49.
14, Bramford, 1981; 15, Coddenham, 1981; 45, Knodishall, 1980.
W. G. Clarke in 'In Breckland Wilds' reports that in 1668 Sir Thomas Browne said 'this groweth not far from Thetford and Brandon, and plentiful in neighbour places'.

Illustrated page 470

DROSERACEAE

SUNDEW FAMILY

Drosera rotundifolia L.   Common Sundew   Sutton and Kirby 1787
                                 Round-leaved Sundew

Native. Wet heaths, bogs and fens. Almost extinct. Has almost disappeared during the period of recording.

W: 77, Tuddenham St Mary; 78, Lakenheath; 97, Weston Fen.

E: 07, Redgrave, Thelnetham and Hinderclay Fens; 17, Syleham; 27, Wingfield; 35, Wantisden Heath; 46, Westleton, 1978; 47, Walberswick Common; 49, Somerleyton; 40, Belton.

Recorded in Hind's Flora in addition from Eriswell Lode, Mildenhall, Cavenham, Fritton, Lowestoft, Benacre, Dunwich, Snape.

The first record by Sutton and Kirby was from Wantisden Heath, where it survived until c. 1950, when the heath was drained and ploughed up.

Drosera anglica Huds.   Great Sundew   Wilson 1830
                               English Sundew

Native. In fens and bogs. Always very rare. Now extinct, due to drainage and collectors.

E: 07, Thelnetham and Redgrave Fens. Last record c. 1960.

Hind records it also for Tuddenham, Mildenhall and Lakenheath.

Drosera anglica × rotundifolia   Hind 1882
(*D. × obovata* Mert. & Koch)

E: Redgrave Fen. Specimen in Hind's Herbarium identified by C. E. Salmon. Both parents were to be found in the Fen at that period.

Drosera intermedia Hayne   Long-leaved Sundew   Davy 1805
(*D. longifolia* auct.)

Native. In fens and bogs. Very rare, now probably extinct, due to drainage and collectors.

W: No recent records.

E: 07, Thelnetham, Redgrave and Hinderclay Fens; 27, Wingfield.

Last record, c. 1952.

There is a herbarium specimen from Tuddenham, collected by the Rev. G. R. Leathes, early 19th century and Hind records it for Tuddenham, Lakenheath, Lound, Beccles, Belton, Fritton and Westleton.

CRASSULACEAE

STONECROP FAMILY

Crassula tillaea L.-Garland   Mossy Stonecrop   Sir J. Cullum 1773
(*Tillaea muscosa* L.)   Mossy Tillaea

Native. Bare heaths and sandy tracks. Frequent, especially in Breckland and on the Sandlings of East Suffolk.

W: 76; 77; 78; 87; 88; 98.

77, Tuddenham and Cavenham, 1980; 78, Lakenheath, 1980; 87, West Stow, 1979.

E: 24; 25; 34; 35; 36; 45; 47; 49; 58; 40.
24, Foxhall, 1975; 34, Bromeswell, 1981; Sutton, 1981; 35, Butley, 1981; 47, Westleton, 1980; 58, Benacre, 1974.

Crassula helmsii (T. Kirk) Cockayne   Mrs E. M. Hyde 1979
An Australasian waterweed, sold commercially as an oxygenator and now found in a number of natural habitats in Gt Britain.
E: 15, Barham, flooded gravel pit, in great abundance, 1980 (M. A. Hyde); 33, Felixstowe Spa Gardens, 1979. Detd. E. J. Clement.

Umbilicus rupestris (Salisb.) Dandy   Navelwort   Hind's Flora 1889
(Cotyledon umbilicus-veneris auct.)   Pennywort
Denizen. Old walls. Very rare in Suffolk.
E: Sibton Abbey c. 1960. Conf. M. Bendix and J. E. Lousley. Name of finder not recorded. 46, Westleton, 1978 (P. G. Lawson).
Hind gives Honington, Bildeston and Thorpe, near Aldeburgh.

Sempervivum tectorum L.   Houseleek   Sir J. Cullum 1779
                               Welcome-home-husband-however-drunk-you-be
Introduced from continental Europe. Found on old walls and roofs. Usually planted. Formerly frequent, now becoming scarce. At one time it was to be seen in most cottage gardens and on old buildings. It was cultivated for its medicinal properties, especially for the curing of warts.
W: 65; 66; 78; 94; 95.
E: 04; 14; 16; 34; 36; 38; 45; 47; 59; 40.
14, Bramford, 1980, too inaccessible to have been planted (F. W. Simpson).

Sedum telephium L. ssp. **telephium**   Orpine   Sir J. Cullum 1773
(S. purpurascens Koch)   Livelong
Native. Old clay woods and hedge-banks. Well distributed, but scarcer than formerly.
W: 83; 86; 93; 94; 96; 97.
93, Polstead, 1977; 94, Brent Eleigh, 1981.
E: 03; 04; 05; 07; 13; 24; 25; 28; 34; 35; 36; 39; 47; 48; 49; 58; 40; 50.
13, Woolverstone, 1981; Holbrook, 1980; 35, Campsey Ash, 1978; 47, Blythburgh, 1980; 48, Frostenden Churchyard, 1980 (P. G. Lawson); 58, Covehithe, 1980; 40, Belton, 1978.
Hb. Ipswich Museum: 'On a hedge bank in a field to the north of the King's Barracks and in Waller's Grove', c. 1810 (John Notcutt).   *Illustrated page 462*

Sedum spurium M. Bieb.   F. W. Simpson 1971
An introduced species, native of the Caucasus. Frequently planted in rockery gardens and on banks. Escaping and becoming naturalised, especially on shingle.
E: 33, Felixstowe Ferry, 1979; 34, Shingle Street, 1981; 46, Thorpeness.

Sedum reflexum L.   Large Yellow Stonecrop   Sir J. Cullum 1773
Introduced from continental Europe. Frequently found as a garden escape on banks, waysides and waste places. Widespread and increasing, but more common in East Suffolk.

W: 74; 78; 86; 93.
74, Barnardiston Church bank, 1976; 93, Polstead, 1977.
E: 03; 04; 05; 13; 14; 23; 24; 25; 33; 34; 35; 36; 39; 44; 45; 46; 47; 48; 49.
33, Felixstowe Town Station, 1981; 35, roadsides at Marlesford and Snape, 1981;
Campsey Ash station, beside track, 1981; 39, Bungay, 1981.

Sedum forsteranum Sm.   Rock Stonecrop   F. W. Simpson 1930
(*S. rupestre* auct.)

Introduced, occasionally naturalised. Found on hedge-banks and old walls. Very local.
E: 04, Hadleigh; 13, Brantham; 34, Shingle Street, Hollesley; 44, Orford; Gedgrave; 45;
49, Oulton.

Sedum acre L.   Wall-pepper   Sir J. Cullum 1773
Biting Stonecrop

Native. Dry, sandy and stony places, shingle beaches, walls and roofs. Frequent.
All squares except 68; 83; 85; 96; 48.
Abundant, 1981, on old roofs at Hadleigh and on old runways, Debach Airfield.

Illustrated page 470

Sedum album L.   White Stonecrop   Sir J. E. Smith 1800

A naturalised alien, found on dry, sunny hedge-banks, cliffs and old walls. An increasing
garden escape.
W: 66, Moulton, 1981; Newmarket, 1980; 67, Worlington Cemetery, 1977; 77,
Cavenham, 1980; 85; 86, Bury St Edmunds, 1980; 93; 94.
E: 04; 07; 13, Brantham, 1974; 14, by the Gipping, Ipswich, 1979; 23, Felixstowe, 1980;
25; 33, Bawdsey Cliffs, 1976; 34, Shingle Street, 1981; 38; 45; 46; 47, Walberswick, 1974;
49; 57, Southwold Cliffs, 1974; 58.
Abundant on old runways, Debach Airfield, 1981. Also common in many parishes in the
Saxmundham region, 1981.

Sedum anglicum Huds.   English Stonecrop   Dillenius 1724

Native. Sea coast and sandy places. Rather scarce. Inland, a colonist or escape from
cultivation.
W: 86, Bury St Edmunds (Corpn. Works Yard).
E: 05, Needham Market; 16; 23, Landguard Common, 1977; 34, Shingle Street, 1981; 35,
Snape; 44, Orford Ness; Havergate Island (introduced from Orford Ness in 1973); 45,
Aldeburgh; 46, Dunwich; Sizewell; Minsmere; 47, Walberswick, Blythburgh, 1980; 57,
Easton Bavents; 58, Covehithe; Benacre Denes; Kessingland, 1980; 59, Gunton.
Hb. Ipswich Museum: specimen collected by Davy at Blythburgh, 1796.

Sedum dasyphyllum L.   Thick-leaved Stonecrop   Mrs Casborne 1837

Introduced from S. Europe. Found on old roofs and walls. Rare.
E: 04, Holbecks, near Hadleigh; 23, Nacton. Both records pre-1950.
Hind listed Rickinghall Inferior, Troston Hall, Abbey walls at Bury St Edmunds and
Drinkstone.

SAXIFRAGACEAE

SAXIFRAGE FAMILY

Saxifraga × urbium D. A. Webb　　　London Pride　　　　　　Atkins 1908
(*S. spathularis × umbrosa*)
The origin of this plant is unknown and it does not normally occur in a wild state. It is a common garden plant, which can withstand adverse town conditions.
There is a specimen in Hb. Atkins from Bramford in 1908, probably from a garden. There was a small colony established on the edge of a wood at Hasketon, first seen in 1969 (F. W. Simpson), but this obviously originated from garden rubbish, which is frequently dumped in this area.

Saxifraga tridactylites L.　　　Rue-leaved Saxifrage　　　　　Sir J. Cullum 1773

Native. Old walls, roofs, churchyards, dry fallow fields, sandy heaths and commons, especially in the Breckland. Frequent, but much less common than formerly. Extinct in some areas, due to the destruction of old buildings and to afforestation.
W: 65; 67; 68; 76; 77; 78; 84; 86; 87; 88; 93; 94; 95; 96; 97.
76/77, Cavenham; Icklingham; Tuddenham, all 1981; 93, Nayland, 1977 (E. Milne-Redhead).
E: 04; 07; 13; 14; 23; 26; 33; 34; 35; 36; 45; 49; 40.
13, roof of the old Forge, Stutton, now destroyed; 14, Bramford, 1979; 23, Landguard Common, 1977.
Hb. Ipswich Museum: 'Walls and roofs in Ipswich, frequent', c. 1820 (John Notcutt). Five sites are listed. No specimens have been observed in Ipswich for several years.

Saxifraga granulata L.　　　Meadow Saxifrage　　　　　　J. Andrews 1745

Native. Grassy places, old pastures, railway banks, churchyards and open rides in woods. Frequent, sometimes abundant. However, it has decreased or vanished from some areas, due to the ploughing up of old pastures.
W: All squares except 65; 68; 75; 83; 85; 95.
87, West Stow, 1981; 88, Santon Downham, 1981; 96, Pakenham Churchyard, 1980.
E: All squares except 03; 26; 33; 44; 46; 58; 59; 40.
14, Ipswich Cemetery; Rushmere, railway embankment; 15, Baylham, railway embankment; Coddenham; 24, near Gt Bealings Church; Hemley; Playford, railway embankment; 35, Campsey Ash and Farnham. All records 1981.
For a number of years this species has been observed growing beside the railway line between Rushmere and Farnham, actually on the ballast near the verges and usually only on the east side of the tracks. In some seasons it is quite abundant and plants can also be seen flowering between the sleepers, but again only on the east side. Apparently the plants manage to overcome the annual spraying of the tracks (F.W.S.).　　　*Illustrated page 470*

Bergenia crassifolia (L.) Fritsch　　　Elephant's Ears　　　　F. W. Simpson 1975

Introduced. Native of N. and C. Asia. Commonly cultivated; sometimes almost naturalised.
W: 66, Exning, waste ground, 1977.
E: 24, Playford, one plant in a copse, probably derived from garden waste, 1976.

165

Tellima grandiflora (Pursh) Dougl. ex Lindl.   Fringe Cups   Mrs E. M. Hyde 1959
Introduced. Native of N. America. Grown in gardens, sometimes naturalised.
E: 13, Woolverstone, 1959-1980.

Tolmiea menziesii (Pursh) Torr. & Gray   P. F. Sheppey 1975
Introduced. Native of Western N. America.
E: 05, Bosmere, in wooded area, 1975.

Chrysosplenium alternifolium L.   Alternate-leaved Golden Saxifrage
James Turner 1805

Native. Sides of small streams and ditches and in boggy woods, especially where there are fresh springs. Not very common. This species favours an area in the South-east of the County where there are numerous Red Crag springs and is usually found growing with *C. oppositifolium.*
W: 83, Lt. Cornard; 93, Polstead, 1981; Assington; Bures; 94, Brent Eleigh.
E: 03, Layham; 13, Wherstead; Stutton; Freston, 1981; Bentley, 1980; 14, Nacton; 24, Playford, 1981; 25, near Wickham Market; 34, Capel St Andrew; 49, Carlton Marshes; 59, Lowestoft.
Hb. Ipswich Museum: 'In a small boggy plantation at the foot of Freston Tower with *C. oppositifolium* and *Adoxa moschatellina* plentiful'. 'By the side of the small Brook in Freston Wood, close to the footpath', c. 1820 (John Notcutt). Both species of *Chrysosplenium* survive in these habitats, 1981.

Chrysosplenium oppositifolium L.   Opposite-leaved Golden Saxifrage
Sir J. Cullum 1774

Native. In similar habitats to *C. alternifolium,* but much more frequent. Occasionally abundant. Rare on or absent from much of the Boulder Clay.
W: 83; 84; 85; 93; 94; 95.
93, Polstead, 1981; 94, Brent Eleigh, 1978.
E: 03; 04; 13; 14; 16; 23; 24; 25; 35; 36; 38; 39; 59.
04, Hintlesham, 1977; 13, Freston, Wherstead and Bentley, all 1981; 14, Brazier's Wood, Ipswich, 1981; 23, Chelmondiston, 1981; 24, Nacton, 1981; Alder Carr, Playford, 1981; 25, Bromeswell, 1981; Carlton Colville, 1978 (P. G. Lawson).
Hb. Ipswich Museum: 'At the top of Springhead Lane, St Helen's'. (Survived in this area until c. 1960). 'In a small Grove or Plantation, called Elm-tree-hill, at the back of Pond Hall', c. 1820 (John Notcutt). The Ipswich Southern By-pass has destroyed most of this habitat and the remaining Elm trees are now dead or dying. The Golden Saxifrage may just survive in a small remaining area. (F. W. Simpson, September 1981).

Illustrated page 483

PARNASSIACEAE

GRASS OF PARNASSUS FAMILY

Parnassia palustris L.   Grass of Parnassus   Gerarde 1597
Native. In alkaline fens, marshes and old, wet pastures. Rare and decreasing. Now extinct in most of the squares listed below.
W: 68; 77; 78; 83; 84; 97.

E: 07; 14; 35; 36; 46; 58; 59; 40.

07, Redgrave Fen, 1980; 35, Gromford Reserve, Snape, 1979.

There is a specimen in Hb. Atkins from Bixley Decoy, 1908. 'Abundant in marshes from Haddiscoe to Oulton', Henslow and Skepper, 1860.

ESCALLONIACEAE

ESCALLONIA FAMILY

Escallonia macrantha Hook. & Arn.   F. W. Simpson 1948

Native of Chile. Widely planted and occasionally naturalised.

E: 33, Bawdsey Cliffs, almost naturalised, still there, 1977.

GROSSULARIACEAE

GOOSEBERRY FAMILY

Ribes rubrum L.   Red Currant   Sir J. Cullum 1774

(*R. sylvestre* (Lam.) Mert. & Koch

R. vulgare Lam.)

Probably native and also introduced. In damp woods and carrs. Very frequent. The wild Red Currant occurring in Suffolk is constant and has very small fruit. It is very rare to find any bushes bearing large fruits, except in hedges near gardens, or on sites of former cultivation, although bird-sown seedlings must be frequent. The Red Currant has been cultivated for about 600 years, and the cultivated form is said to be a hybrid.

W: All squares except 65; 67; 68; 74; 83.

E: All squares except 15; 26; 27; 36; 37; 38; 45; 48; 58; 59; 50.

Ribes nigrum L.   Black Currant   Sir J. Cullum 1775

Native and introduced. In damp woods and carrs. Not very common.

W: 74; 76; 77; 78; 84; 86; 87; 88; 94; 95; 98.

77, Ash Plantation, Cavenham, 1977; 78, Pashford Poor's Fen, 1979.

E: 04; 07; 13; 16; 24; 25; 34; 35; 46; 40.

24, Bixley Decoy, 1981; Playford Mere, 1981; 35, ride near Friday Street, probably bird-sown from nearby cultivation, 1975.

Ribes aureum Pursh   Golden-flowered Currant   H. Dixon Hewitt 1908

Introduced. Native of N. America. Recorded in 1908 as 'apparently established at West Stow Schools and near Rampart Hill, Icklingham'.

Ribes sanguineum Pursh   Flowering Currant   Mrs D. Jay 1965

A native of Western N. America, often planted in gardens for ornamental purposes. May become naturalised. Also bird-sown.

W: 75, old garden site at Chevington; 77, Barton Mills, 1981; 96, Thurston, 1981.

E: 14, Witnesham, 1974 (Mrs E. M. Hyde); Ipswich, 1981; 24, Bixley Decoy and edge of Crag Pit, Foxhall, near Monument, 1977 (F. W. Simpson); 35, Rendlesham, 1976; 46, Dunwich, 1965 (Mrs D. Jay).

Ribes uva-crispa L.   Gooseberry   Sir J. Cullum 1773
(*R. grossularia* L.)

Native. Common in open woods, plantations, hedges and sites of former gardens. More frequent on light soils. Very variable. Many are not truly the native form, but are probably bird-sown from gardens.
W: All squares except 64; 65; 66; 67; 68; 74.
E: All squares except 06; 17; 27; 44; 48; 40; 50.

PLATANACEAE

PLANE TREE FAMILY

Platanus occidentalis × orientalis   London Plane
(*P.* × *hybrida* Brot.)

Introduced and planted in parks and towns. Common. This species is very suitable for town areas, as it can withstand atmospheric pollution better than the majority of trees. There is a fine large specimen with a girth of 23 feet at Woolverstone, 1977.

ROSACEAE

ROSE FAMILY

Spiraea salicifolia L.   Bridewort   Miss J. C. N. Willis 1960
                               Willow Spiraea

Introduced from E. Europe and Asia. Sometimes found naturalised in plantations and on the sites of former gardens.
W: 87, West Gouch Plantation, west of Elveden Park, 1968; 95, Brettenham, 1960.
E: 14, Ipswich; 46, Minsmere; 57, Easton Bavents, 1980.

Filipendula vulgaris Moench   Dropwort   Sir J. Cullum 1773
(*Spiraea filipendula* L.)

Native. Dry chalky heaths and pastures. Rare and decreasing. Extinct in many of its former habitats.
W: 65; 66, Newmarket; 76, Risby, 1979; Gazeley, 1980; 77, Icklingham, 1977; Elveden, 1979; Herringswell, 1980; Cavenham, 1979; Tuddenham, 1979; Barton Mills, 1981; Dalham, 1981; 86; 87; 88, Santon Downham; 96; 97; 98, Knettishall, 1981.
E: 07, Wortham, 1979 (A. Copping); 17, Stuston; 35, Snape, 1981 (L. J. Hyde).
There is a specimen in Hb. Ipswich Museum collected c. 1820. 'Under a clump of trees, four fields to the north of a cottage and barn, at the back of Mr Fonnereau's Wood' (John Notcutt). The Wood, since destroyed, was just to the north of Christchurch Park. Also specimen in Hb. Atkins from Sproughton, 1910.   *Illustrated page 477*

Filipendula ulmaria (L.) Maxim.   Meadow Sweet   Sir J. Cullum 1773
(*Spiraea ulmaria* L.)

Native. Marshes, fens, damp pastures, ditches and wet woods. Common. Often abundant and dominant.
All squares except 66; 44.   *Illustrated page 481 and page 484*

Kerria japonica (L.) DC.   Jew's Mallow   M. A. Hyde 1974

Introduced, native of China. This shrub is found in hedges and on sites of former gardens. It is nearly always double-flowered.

E: 23, near Pin Mill, Chelmondiston, several well-established bushes about half a mile from nearest dwellings. Still there, 1981.

RUBUS   BRAMBLE

The list of Suffolk *Rubi* in this Flora has been compiled from the records of A. L. Bull, E. S. Edees, J. R. Ironside-Wood and the late B. A. Miles. A. L. Bull has made a special study of this genus in both Norfolk and Suffolk since 1970.

W. M. Hind in his 1889 Flora published a long list. Several of his records were incorrect and specimens in his herbarium at the Ipswich Museum have been examined by A. L. Bull and re-named. Nomenclature has changed considerably since Hind. The majority of the names in this list are those used by W. C. R. Watson. Where different or where a more recent name is used, Watson's synonym is given.

The majority of *Rubi* prefer the gravelly, sandy and more acid soils of our heaths, commons, open woodlands, hedges and verges. However, the sandy Breckland is not very rich in Brambles. The coastal belt between the Stour Valley and Covehithe, especially the Shotley Peninsula, is very good. Old woods at Assington, Belstead, Bentley, Holbrook, Polstead and Sudbourne are still very rewarding. Areas at Dunwich, Foxhall and Martlesham are worth visiting. Uncommon species have been recorded from Spelthorn Wood, near Long Melford.

The average botanist gets to know various *Rubi* by sight, but unfortunately is unable to identify the species accurately without the guidance of an expert. The fruit picker also knows which kind bears the best berries and the ones with the sharpest thorns.

Herbarium specimens of Suffolk *Rubi* are housed at the Museums of Ipswich (Hind), Norwich (A. L. Bull) and South Kensington (J. R. Ironside-Wood *et al.*). There are also collections held by the University of Cambridge, Department of Botany (B. A. Miles, W. C. R. Watson *et al.*).

Rubus spectabilis Pursh   F. W. Simpson 1964

Introduced. A native of Western N. America. Planted and occasionally naturalised.

E: 13, Stalls Valley, Freston.

Rubus idaeus L.   Raspberry   Sir J. Cullum 1773

Native. In moist woods and fens, on damp heaths and waysides. Frequent and increasing. In Redgrave Fen a form with light yellow fruits.

W: All squares except 64; 65; 66; 68; 75.
E: All squares except 06; 15; 16; 26; 37.

Rubus caesius L.   Dewberry   Sir J. Cullum 1773

Native. Woods, heaths, waysides and other habitats, usually on clay soils. Frequent. 'Caesian hybrids' can be found throughout the County.

W: 64; 65; 74; 76; 84; 85; 86; 87; 94; 95.
E: 04; 05; 06; 07; 17; 25; 26; 36; 37; 48.

The above records refer only to the true plant. Probably under-recorded.

Rubus fruticosus sensu lato   Blackberry   Sir J. Cullum 1773
                                     Bramble

Native. Occurs in every type of habitat. Very variable, and includes the large number of species, forms and hybrids which follow.
All squares.

SECTION: SUBERECTI

Rubus plicatus Weihe & Nees   Dr C. Babington 1870

W: Not recorded recently. Hind gives Cockfield.
E: 45, Watling Wood, near Orford (B. A. Miles); Snape Warren (J. Ironside-Wood); 58, Covehithe (A. L. Bull).

Rubus arrheniiformis W. C. R. Wats.   A. L. Bull 1972

E: 40, Fritton Warren.

Rubus affinis Weihe & Nees   Hind 1882

E: 24, Bell Lane, Foxhall; 59, Corton Cliffs. Both records A. L. Bull.
Hind's specimen from Gorleston (sq. 50).

SECTION: TRIVIALES

Rubus conjungens (Bab.) Warren   Hind 1882

W: 66, Exning; 68, Undley; 77, Icklingham (A.L.B.); Mildenhall (E.S.E.); 78, Lakenheath; 87, Ampton; 96, Rougham; Rattlesden (J.R.I.-W.).
E: 03, Stratford St Mary (J.R.I.-W.); 14, Bramford; 17, Stuston; 25, Bromeswell; Melton (J.R.I.-W.); 34, Capel St Andrew (J.R.I.-W.); 39, Outney Common, Bungay; 44, Gedgrave; 45, Sudbourne (A.L.B. & B.A.M.); 46, Minsmere; 47, Walberswick; 59, Corton; Blundeston.

Rubus eboracensis W. C. R. Wats.   A. L. Bull 1975

E: 07, Mellis; Wortham; 24, Lt. Bealings; 36, Gt Glemham; 37, Walpole; 39, Outney Common, Bungay; 49. All records by A. L. Bull. Possibly under-recorded.

Rubus sublustris Ed. Lees   Hind 1881

More frequent near the coast. Often mistaken for robust *R. caesius.*
W: 64; 68; 76; 84; 85; 86; 93.
E: 04; 05; 06; 07; 13; 15; 17; 23; 24; 25; 27; 44; 45; 46; 47; 49; 57; 58.

Rubus balfourianus Bloxam ex Bab.   Hind 1881

Prefers damp situations. Rare or overlooked.
E: 23, Erwarton, 1972 (F. W. Simpson); 46, Minsmere Beach (A.L.B.); Dunwich (J.R.I.-W.).
A number of unnamed local species occur in this section, especially one with pink flowers and obovate leaflets which is widespread in woods on the clay. A densely glandular white-

flowered plant occurs in the Brecks, which E. S. Edees suggests is near *R. britannicus* Rogers.

SECTION: SYLVATICI

Rubus gratus Focke   Hb. Ipswich Museum 1858

W: 98, Knettishall Heath (E.S.E.).

E: 13, Holbrook Park (E.S.E.); Tattingstone (A.L.B.); 58, Covehithe (A.L.B.).

Specimen in Hb. Ipswich Museum from Belstead Wood. Collector unknown.

Rubus sciocharis Sudre   B. A. Miles 1966

E: 35, The Thicks, Rendlesham Forest (B.A.M. *et al.*); 45, Watling Wood, near Orford (B.A.M.).

Rubus nitidiformis Sudre   B. A. Miles 1966

(*R. nitidioides* W. C. R. Wats.)

W: 94, Polstead Heath (E.S.E.).

E: 13, Dodnash Wood (E.S.E.); Bentley Long Wood (A.L.B.); 45, west side of Sudbourne Great Wood (B.A.M. *et al.*).

The next two species were formerly united under *R. carpinifolius* Weihe & Nees. 90% of the British material is referable to the first named.

Rubus platyacanthus Muell. & Lefèv.   E. S. Edees 1973

E: 13, Dodnash Wood; Holbrook Park (E.S.E.).

Rubus adspersus Weihe ex H. E. Weber   A. L. Bull 1976

A plant of damp sandy commons.

E: 39, Outney Common, Bungay.

Rubus nemoralis P. J. Muell.   Hind 1882

(*R. selmeri* Lindeb.)

Locally plentiful on sandy heaths, especially near the coast.

W: 77, Tuddenham Heath; Barton Mills; 78, Maidscross Hill, Lakenheath; Brandon Park.

E: 03, East Bergholt (B.A.M.); 07, Wortham Ling (A.L.B.); 15, Coddenham (A.L.B.); 24, Brookhill Wood, Foxhall; Martlesham (J.R.I.-W.); Brightwell (A.L.B.); 34, Sutton; Hollesley (E.S.E. *et al.*); Butley (A.L.B.); 35, The Thicks, Rendlesham Forest (B.A.M. *et al.*); Bromeswell (J.R.I.-W.); 39, Outney Common, Bungay (A.L.B.); 45, Sudbourne Great Wood; Watling Wood (E.S.E.); 46, Westleton (E.S.E.); 47, Toby's Walks, Blythburgh (J.R.I.-W.); 49, Herringfleet Hills (A.L.B.); Fritton (E.S.E.); 57, coast, north of Southwold (E.S.E.); 58, Covehithe (A.L.B.); 59, Corton (A.L.B.); 40, Ashby Dell; Waveney Forest (A.L.B.).

Rubus laciniatus Willd.   Cut-leaved Bramble   F. W. Simpson 1958
American Blackberry

A naturalised garden escape, easily recognised by its deeply-divided leaves.
W: 75, locality and recorder unknown; 78, Brandon Waterworks; Brandon Park
(A.L.B.).
E: 14, Ipswich, several sites; 24, Bixley Decoy (F.W.S.); 39, Outney Common, Bungay, in
great abundance, 1973, (Dr E. A. Ellis), still there, 1981 (F.W.S.), 45, Snape (F.W.S.); 47,
Wenhaston (R. Mabey).

Rubus lindleianus Ed. Lees   Hind 1882

Frequent in hedgerows and woods. Does not shun clay.
W: 84; 87; 93; 94; 95; 96; 97.
E: 03; 04; 05; 06; 07; 13; 14; 15; 23; 24; 25; 26; 34; 35; 36; 39; 45; 46; 47; 48; 49; 58; 40.

Rubus macrophyllus Weihe & Nees   J. R. Ironside-Wood 1970

Local in woods in the South-east of the County. Frequent along the Stour valley.
W: 93, Assington Thicks (A.L.B.).
E: 03, Polstead; East Bergholt (A.L.B.); 13, Bentley; Tattingstone; Freston (A.L.B.);
Holbrook Park (J.R.I.-W.); 14, Belstead Wood (A.L.B.); 23, Shotley (A.L.B.); 34,
Butley; 35, edge of Rendlesham Forest, near Butley (J.R.I.-W.); 36, Bruisyard Wood
(A.L.B.).

Rubus subinermoides Druce   E. S. Edees 1973

W: 94. Stack Wood, Polstead (E.S.E.); Groton Wood (A.L.B.).
E: 23, roadside through wood, south of Chelmondiston (E.S.E.).

Rubus amplificatus Ed. Lees   E. S. Edees 1973

W: 93, Assington Thicks (A.L.B.).
E: 03, Highlands, East Bergholt (A.L.B.); 14, Brazier's Wood, Ipswich (A.L.B.); 24,
Levington; Brightwell (A.L.B.); 36, Bruisyard Wood (E.S.E.).

Rubus pyramidalis Kalt.   Hind 1881

Woods and thickets, uncommon.
W: 93, Assington Thicks (E.S.E.).
E: 07, Westhall Wood (A.L.B.); southern margin of Redgrave Fen (E.S.E.); 14, Belstead
Wood (A.L.B.); 15, Sandy Hill, south of Coddenham (E.S.E.); 23, Chelmondiston
(A.L.B.); 35, The Thicks, Rendlesham Forest (B.A.M. *et al.*); 45, Watling Wood, near
Orford (B.A.M.); 49, Fritton, side of road to Ashby Dell (E.S.E.); Herringfleet Hills
(A.L.B.); 40, Fritton Warren (A.L.B.).

Rubus poliodes W. C. R. Wats.   B, A. Miles 1966

Scattered throughout the County, though commonest near the coast.
W: 86, Great Fir Covert, Risby; 87, roadside belt between Barnham and Euston; 93, field
path to Birch Avery, Assington.
E: 14, Brazier's Wood, Ipswich; 15, Sandy Hill, south of Coddenham; 24, Brookhill
Wood, Foxhall (J.R.I.-W.); Waldringfield; Martlesham; 25/35, Bromeswell (E.S.E. *et*

172

al.); 34, Hollesley; 45, Church Walks, Sudbourne (E.S.E.); 46, Aldringham; Dunwich; 48, Mutford Wood; 49, Herringfleet Hills.

Rubus polyanthemus Lindeb.   Hind 1881

Frequent in woods and hedgerows and on heaths. The commonest species after *R. ulmifolius.*
W: 77; 78; 84; 86; 87; 88; 93; 94; 95; 96; 97; 98.
E: All squares except 16; 17; 23; 26; 33; 37; 44.

Rubus elegantispinosus (Schumach) Weber   E. S. Edees 1973

E: 17, Hoxne Wood; 27, The Grove, west of Stradbroke.
Hb. specimens detd. in 1976 by H. E. Weber. Also collected by A. L. Bull.

Rubus cardiophyllus Muell. & Lefèv.   B. A. Miles 1966

Rare in Suffolk, though may be abundant locally. This species has been much confused with the next, even by the experts.
E: 03, East Bergholt, Allen's End and the Highlands, where it is abundant; 07, south side, Redgrave Fen (E.S.E. *et al.*); 14, Brazier's Wood, Ipswich; 24, Foxhall; 46, Aldringham. The above records have all been seen by A. L. Bull.

Rubus boudiccae A. L. Bull & E. S. Edees   A. L. Bull 1977

Frequent, and often abundant on gravel and sand. Superficially like *R. cardiophyllus,* from which it may have been derived (E. S. Edees). Flowers large with non-contiguous flat, not cupped, petals. Leaves round or slightly obovate, base entire, not cordate, felted beneath. Some old records of *R. maassii* should probably be placed here, as it is sometimes very close to that species (E.S.E.).
Named after Queen Boadicea, who had the same overall range, from Norfolk to just over the Essex border, and proved a thorny problem to the Romans.
W: 87, Ampton Field; 88.
E: 24; 25; 27; 34; 36; 39; 45; 46; 47; 48; 49; 58.
Especially abundant at Dunwich and Covehithe.

Rubus errabundus W. C. R. Wats.   A. L. Bull 1978

E: 46, Dunwich Common. A single clump of this Scottish species.
It is assumed that the seed was sown by a migrating member of the Thrush tribe.

Rubus anglocandicans A. Newton   A. L. Bull 1980

E: 24, frequent on Foxhall Heath.

SECTION: DISCOLORES

Rubus ulmifolius Schott   Davy 1795

Native. This is the most abundant bramble in the County. It is very tolerant of adverse conditions and will grow on very poor, sandy and stony soils, as well as on clay and chalk, near the sea on cliffs and shingle beaches, and on commons exposed to salt spray. It can be recognised by its pink, purplish flowers, small leaflets which are white beneath, and stems of a reddish purple shade on the surface exposed to the sun, and armed with strong prickles.

It is one of the last brambles to ripen. Its fruits are usually harder and drier than other kinds, but they are very sweet when really ripe and may be produced in large quantities, and sometimes persist into late December, withstanding moderate frosts. This species hybridises freely with other species and the hybrids are fertile.

Occurs in all squares. *Illustrated page 477*

Rubus ulmifolius × caesius Hybrid Dewberry F. W. Simpson 1937

A very frequent hybrid in the East of the County, occurring on heaths, in hedges and along the sea coast. Much of what passes for true *R. caesius* is likely to be this hybrid.

W: 68, Mildenhall, 1977.

E: 23, Erwarton, 1972; 24, Foxhall, 1981; 33, Bawdsey, 1976; 34, Alderton; 46, Leiston; Sizewell; Dunwich Beach, 1980; 47, Blythburgh; Walberswick.

All above records by F. W. Simpson.

Rubus ulmifolius × vestitus A. L. Bull 1978

A sterile hybrid, usually not difficult to identify.

W: 95, south side of Pye Hatch Wood, Buxhall.

E: 35, Snape, 1981 (F.W.S.).

Rubus procerus P. J. Muell. Himalayan Giant J. R. Ironside-Wood 1971

A garden escape, rapidly spreading.

W: 66, Exning; 67, Freckenham; 76, Cavenham; Barrow; 84; 85, Alpheton. The above records made by A. L. Bull.

E: 05, Onehouse; 14, Bramford; 15, Coddenham; 24, Foxhall (E.S.E.); Levington; 25/35, Bromeswell; 36, Bruisyard (E.S.E. *et al.*); 37, Walpole; 46, Thorpe Heath (J.R.I.-W.); 47, Wenhaston (F.W.S., J.R.I.-W.).

SECTION: SPRENGELIANI

Rubus sprengelii Weihe A. L. Bull 1978

E: 13, Belstead Wood, in small quantity; Old Hall Wood, Bentley.

SECTION: APPENDICULATI

Rubus vestitus Weihe & Nees sensu stricto Hind 1883

Widely distributed and locally common.

This form with deep pink petals and filaments and red styles is less common.

W: 76, Gt Saxham; 95, Pye Hatch Wood, Buxhall.

E: 03, Polstead; 04, Raydon; 13, Belstead Wood; Bentley Long Wood; Freston; 35, Iken Wood.

Var. **albiflorus** Boul.

Petals pale pink or whitish, filaments white, styles green. A woodland bramble, commoner in the West than the East. Occasionally cultivated.

W: 64; 65; 76; 77; 78; 84; 85; 86; 87; 88; 93; 94; 95; 96; 97; 98.
E: 03; 04; 07; 13; 17; 23; 28; 38; 46; 47; 48; 49; 50; 40.

Rubus conspersus W. C. R. Wats.   E. S. Edees 1973
W: Arger Fen; Assington Thicks.
E. S. Edees and A. Newton now (1980) consider that this plant is more probably an
aberrant form of *R. criniger* (E. F. Linton) Rogers. A. Newton has suggested 'var.
trifolius'.

Rubus radula Weihe ex Boenn.   Hind's Flora 1889
A species of woods and hedgerows, commonest in the West.
W: 76, Gt Saxham; 77, Barton Mills; 84, Stanstead Great Wood; Lineage Wood; 86,
Great Fir Covert, Risby; 87, by Icknield Way, Icklingham; North Stow; Wordwell
(E.S.E.); 93, Birch Avery, Assington; 95, Bull's Wood, Cockfield; 98, Rushfordroad
Belts, Euston (E.S.E.).
E: 07, Mellis Common; 15, Sandy Hill, Coddenham (E.S.E. *et al.*); 17, Thornham Parva;
35, Campsey Ash.

Rubus echinatus Lindl.   Hind 1884
Scattered distribution, but most plentiful near the Essex border.
W: 77, Barton Mills (E.S.E.); 86, Rougham; 87, Sansom's Plantation (E.S.E.); 93, Birch
Avery (A.L.B.); Tiger Hill; Assington Thicks (E.S.E.).
E: 03, East Bergholt (J.R.I.-W.); 07, Redgrave Fen (E.S.E.); 13 Holbrook Park (E.S.E.);
Belstead Wood; Tattingstone; Freston; 14, Belstead Wood; 23, Chelmondiston (E.S.E. *et
al.*); 24, Purdis Heath (F.W.S.).

Rubus echinatoides (Rogers) Dallman   B. A. Miles 1966
W: 93, Assington Thicks (E.S.E.); 95, Monks' Park Wood, 1980 (A.L.B.).
E: 03, East Bergholt (B.A.M.); 13, Holbrook Park (E.S.E.); Bentley; Tattingstone;
Freston; 14, Brazier's Wood, Ipswich; 24, Brightwell; 45, west side of Sudbourne Great
Wood (B.A.M. *et al.*); 58, wood margins at Covehithe (E.S.E., A.L.B.).

Rubus infestus Weihe ex Boenn.   J. R. Ironside-Wood 1980
(*R. taeniarum* sensu Watson)
E: 24, Foxhall (J.R.I.-W. & A.L.B.); 25, Bromeswell (J.R.I.-W.).

Rubus rudis Weihe ap Bluff & Fingerh.   E. S. Edees 1973
Rare in East Anglia generally.
W: 93, Assington Thicks (E.S.E. *et al.*); 94, Bull's Cross Wood (E.S.E.).
E: 48, abundant in an orchard by Mutford Wood.

Rubus flexuosus Muell. & Lefèv.   Rev. J. D. Gray 1884
(*R. foliosus* Weihe)
Local in woods. More frequent near the Stour Valley. Very distinct with its leafy zigzag
stem and small pink flowers.

W: 93, Assington Thicks; Arger Fen (E.S.E.); 94, Groton Wood (A.L.B.); Stack Wood (E.S.E.).
E: 03, Polstead (A.L.B.); 04, Wolves Wood (E.S.E. *et al.*); Raydon (A.L.B.); 13, Holbrook Park (E.S.E.); Bentley; Tattingstone (A.L.B.).

Rubus fuscus agg.   E. S. Edees 1973
E. S. Edees writes:
'We are not sure what Weihe and Nees intended by this name and several related brambles have been grouped under it in this country and abroad. The Suffolk plant recorded below can be placed here for the time being.'
A. L. Bull has found another widespread species which he considers to be probably one of the *R. fuscus* agg., as yet unnamed.
W: 84, Spelthorn Wood; 97, west side of Park Grove. Both records E.S.E.

Rubus adamsii Sudre   W. C. R. Watson 1939
W: 64, Lawn Wood, Withersfield (W.C.R.W. *et al.*).

Rubus pallidus Weihe & Nees   E. S. Edees 1973
W: 93, Birch Avery, Assington (A.L.B.).
E: 13, Holbrook Park (E.S.E.).

Rubus euryanthemus W. C. R Wats.   E. S. Edees 1973
E: 27, The Grove, Hoxne (E.S.E. *et al.*).

Rubus insectifolius Muell. & Lefèv.   A. L. Bull 1977
W: 94, Groton Wood.

Rubus rufescens Muell. & Lefèv.   Hind 1881
Locally common, sometimes abundant in woods, even on clay.
W: 93, Arger Fen; 94, Stack Wood; 95, Bradfield Woods; 97, Park Grove; Great Grove; Fakenham Wood.
E: 03, wood near East Bergholt; 04, Wolves Wood; Middle Wood; 05; 06; 13, Holbrook Park; 23, wood south of Chelmondiston; 25, Old Park Wood (J. W. Digby); 35, Bromeswell Heath (J.R.I.-W.); 46, Westleton Walks (B.A.M.); 48.

Rubus raduloides (Rogers) Sudre   J. R. Ironside-Wood 1972
Rather scarce in woods.
W: 84, Stanstead Great Wood (A.L.B.).
E: 03, East Bergholt (J.R.I.-W. *et al.*); 13, Tattingstone; 17, Denham Wood; 35, field margin behind Iken Wood.

Rubus leightonii Lees ex Leighton
E: 49, Somerleyton. Specimen in Hb. Oxford University, collected by L.C., August 1899. Comm. A. Newton.

Rubus phaeocarpus W. C. R. Wats.   A. L. Bull 1980
E: 24, Brightwell.

Rubus diversus W. C. R. Wats.   B. A. Miles 1966
Frequent and locally dominant in parts of the South-east of the County.
E: 03, Highlands, East Bergholt; 13, Belstead Wood; 14, Belstead Wood; Brazier's
Wood; 24, Martlesham (B.A.M. *et al.*); Kesgrave Hall Wood (J.R.I.-W.).

SECTION: GLANDULOSI

Rubus murrayi Sudre   E. S. Edees 1973
W: 84, Spelthorn Wood. A. L. Bull considers it is not the true *R. murrayi* in this wood.

Rubus hylocharis W. C. R. Wats.   A. L. Bull 1978
E: 48, Mutford Wood.

Rubus dasyphyllus (Rogers) E. S. Marshall   B. A. Miles 1966
Woods and wood borders. The commonest woodland bramble in the County.
W: 77; 84; 86; 87; 93; 94; 95; 96; 97; 98.
E: 03; 04; 05; 06; 07; 13; 14; 15; 23; 24; 25; 27; 35; 36; 37; 45; 46; 47; 48; 49; 58; 59; 40.

Rubus bellardii Weihe and Nees   F. W. Simpson 1932
This is a low-growing bramble of moist woods, distinguished by its large ternate leaves.
Many brambles have a few ternate as well as quinate leaves on the same shoot, but in *R.
bellardii* all the leaves are ternate.
W: 84, Spelthorn Wood (F.W.S., E.S.E.); Stanstead Great Wood (A.L.B.); 94, Groton
Wood (A.L.B.).

Rubus leptadenes Sudre   A. L. Bull 1979
E: 13, roadside by woodland, Tattingstone.
E. S. Edees considers it is probably this species, which has also been found by A. L. Bull
at Hempstead, Norfolk, in 1977.

ROSA   WILD ROSES

Much work remains to be done on this genus in Suffolk. The subspecies, varieties and
hybrids, especially of *Rosa canina* and *R. arvensis,* have not been adequately recorded.
The rapid destruction of hedgerows and scrub in recent years has had a very adverse effect
on the former abundance of Wild Roses in many areas.

Rosa multiflora Thunb.   F. W. Simpson 1973
Introduced about 1800. Native of China and Japan.
In an old hedge on the site of a former garden at Martlesham (sq. 24) 1973 (F. W.
Simpson). A lovely specimen with creamy-white fragrant flowers.
Variety with double flowers.
Between Pin Mill, Chelmondiston and the Clamp House (sq. 23) 1974 (Mrs E. M. Hyde).

Appearing naturalised, although planted by the owner of a 'house-barge' formerly moored at this spot for several years. Also at West Stow (sq. 87), 1980 (F. W. Simpson).

Rosa arvensis Huds.   Field Rose   Sir J. Cullum 1773

Native. In hedges and woods, chiefly on the Chalky Boulder Clay. Common.
W: All squares except 66; 67; 68; 78.
76, Dalham, 1981; 95, Felshamhall Wood, 1980.
E: All squares except 34; 35; 44; 45; 48; 58; 59; 50.
05, Wattisham, 1980; 13, Harkstead, 1981; 25, Debach, 1981; 46, Knodishall, 1981.

Illustrated page 507

Rosa pimpinellifolia L.   Burnet Rose   Sir J. Cullum 1775
(*R. spinosissima* L.)

Native. Old heaths and scrub. Also planted and naturalised. Rare and decreasing.
W: 67, Worlington Cemetery, 1979.
E: 34, Shingle Street, 1967; 46, Dunwich and Minsmere Cliffs; Westleton, 1978; 58, Kessingland; 40, Fritton, 1950 (F. W. Simpson).
Variety with double flowers naturalised in St Mary's Churchyard, Bungay, 1980 (F.W.S.). The so-called 'Dunwich Rose' is usually considered to be the Burnet Rose, which is indigenous in this area. One 19th century writer suggested that it was the Field Rose (*R. arvensis*). This is most unlikely, as the Field Rose does not grow on the sandy soils of Dunwich, but further inland on the heavier clay soils. The legend that the Dunwich Rose was brought by monks from Normandy suggests that the Rose was probably a cultivated variety. The monks would hardly have planted a rose already growing wild, almost on the Monastery site. A rambler rose, with single purplish or violet coloured flowers used to grow on the edge of Dunwich Cliffs, near the Monastery. Although I consider that this rose was a relic of a former cottage garden, there is still the possibility that it was the variety introduced by the monks.

Rosa rugosa Thunb.   Japanese Briar Rose   F. W. Simpson c. 1934

Introduced and established. Native of N. China and Japan. Often planted on the light sandy soil of Breckland in game coverts. Also used for hedging, as at Sutton and elsewhere. Frequently occurs as a casual near the coast and on other suitable sites. It is likely to maintain its hold and appears to be slowly spreading.
W: 66; 93; 98.
E: 05; 23; 24; 25; 33; 34; 45; 46; 47; 59; 40.
24, Sutton, 1981; 33, Bawdsey Cliffs, 1979; 45, Aldeburgh, 1979.
Variety with white flowers: 59, Lowestoft, 1974-80 (Mrs E. M. Hyde). Double-flowered variety in St Nicholas Churchyard, Ipswich.

Rosa stylosa Desv.   Long-styled Rose   E. Skepper 1862
(*R. systyla* Bast.)

Native. Hedges, margins of woods and copses. Rare or overlooked.
W: 94, hedge near Groton Wood, 1975 (M. J. Wigginton). Conf. by G. G. Graham.
E: 25, Melton; 38, Spexhall.

Rosa canina agg.   Dog Rose   Sir J. Cullum 1773

Native. Hedges, woods, copses, heaths and scrub. Very frequent. There are numerous varieties and forms, some of which may be of hybrid origin. Hybrids can be extremely variable.

The aggregate is recorded for all squares.

Rosa canina × rubiginosa   F. W. Simpson 1967
(*R. × latens* W.-Dod)

Probably a not infrequent hybrid of hedges, scrub and waste places, but overlooked.
W: 78, Brandon, 1977.
E: 04, Hintlesham, 1981; 13, Stutton, 1967; 35, Blaxhall, 1981 (F. W. Simpson).

Rosa subcollina (Christ) Dalla Torre & Sarnth.   Mrs E. M. Hyde 1970

Possibly native.
E: 13, near the river at Woolverstone. Determined by Mrs I. M. Vaughan as being nearest to this species. No ripe fruits were, however, then available.

Rosa obtusifolia Desv.   Hind's Flora 1889

Native. Hedges, margins of woods, copses and scrub. Overlooked.
W: Not recorded recently. Hind gives Burgate.
E: 07, roadside hedge near Redgrave Fen, 1962 (E. L. Swann); 25; 35, Blaxhall, village hedge, 1980; 46, Theberton, 1980. (The last two records by Mrs I. M. Vaughan).

Rosa corymbifera Borkh.   Hairy-leaved Dog Rose   Hind's Flora 1889
(*R. dumetorum* Thuill.)

Probably frequent. In hedgerows, open scrub and old quarries. Its distribution has not been recorded. This rose is sometimes listed as one of the very many varieties of *R. canina* agg.

Rosa tomentosa Sm.   Soft-leaved Rose   Woodward & Dawson Turner 1802
(*R. mollissima* Willd.)

Native. In woods and hedges. Occasional, but probably overlooked. Hind lists it from a number of parishes and comments 'occurs in all the districts'.
W: 67; 74; 75; 85; 94; 95.
67, Mildenhall, 1977; 94, Polstead, 1980 (E. Milne-Redhead). Detd. by Mrs I. M. Vaughan.
E: 04, Wolves Wood, Hadleigh; 35, Blaxhall; 36, near Framlingham; 46, Theberton; (these records by Mrs I. M. Vaughan, 1980); 48, Barsham, 1976 (F. W. Simpson).

Rosa scabriuscula Sm.   Downy-leaved Rose   Woodward & Dawson Turner 1805

In woods, copses, hedges and scrub. Rare. No recent records.
W: 86, Bury St Edmunds, 1930.
Recorded in Hind's Flora from Ixworth Thorpe, Shelland, Hardwick, Bury St Edmunds, Little Thurlow and Westleton.

Rosa mollis Sm.   Downy Rose   B.S.B.I. Mapping Scheme c. 1952
(*R. villosa* L. ssp. *mollis* (Sm.) Crépin)

Native. In old hedges, copses, wood and scrub. Scarce and local.

W: 75; 85; 86; 93; 94; 95.
85, Lawshall, c. 1954; 95, Felshamhall Wood.
E: 04, Hintlesham, 1957; 38, Ilketshall St Lawrence, 1957.

Rosa rubiginosa L.   Sweet Briar   Sir J. Cullum 1773

Native. Hedges, chalky scrub and open woodland on the margins of heaths and commons. Sometimes planted for hedging. Still frequent, but decreasing.
W: All squares except 65; 66; 68; 74; 84; 85.
76, Dalham, 1981; 78, Brandon, 1980; 96, Gt Barton, 1980.
E: All squares except 03; 05; 06; 13; 17; 24; 26; 27; 38; 44; 58.
04, Hintlesham, 1981; 23, Landguard Common, 1977; 33, Bawdsey, 1979; 34, Hollesley, 1980; 46, Leiston Common, 1980.

Rosa micrantha Borrer ex Sm.   Small Sweet Briar   T. W. Gissing 1855

Native. Scrub, woodland, old hedges and quarries. Rare. Probably overlooked and sometimes confused with *R. rubiginosa* L. There are few known records of the species in Suffolk since the beginning of this century and its present distribution is unknown. Hind recorded it from Honington, Timworth, Troston, Market Weston, Barton, Nayland, Hartest, Polstead, Wiston, Hopton, Benacre, Worlingham, Wrentham and Badingham. Recorded from Coddenham, 1963, Iken and Theberton, 1981 (Mrs. I. M. Vaughan).

Agrimonia eupatoria L.   Common Agrimony   Sir J. Cullum 1773

Native. Grassy waysides, sunny open glades and the edges of woods, chiefly on light or mixed soils.
All squares.   *Illustrated page 473*

Agrimonia procera Wallr.   Fragrant Agrimony   Miss E. Rawlins 1932
(*A. odorata* auct., non Mill.)

Native. Open woodland, scrub and hedges. Perhaps not uncommon, but its distribution is not properly known.
W: 76; 86, Fornham St Genevieve; 87, Troston; 94, Edwardstone (Miss Rawlins); 95, Felshamhall Wood and Monks' Park Wood; 96; 97.
E: 14, Belstead, 1975-8 (Mrs E. M. Hyde).

Sanguisorba officinalis L.   Great Burnet   F. J. Eagle 1810
(*Poterium officinale* (L.) A. Gray)

Native. In grassy fens. Rare.
W: 78; 86; 87; 88; 96.
78, Pashford Poor's Fen and Drove, 1981; 86, Timworth.
E: 07; 17; 35; 47; 59; 40.
07, Thelnetham Fen, 1981.   *Illustrated page 483*

Sanguisorba minor Scop. ssp. **minor**   Salad Burnet   Sir J. Cullum 1773
(*Poterium sanguisorba* L.)   Lesser Burnet

Native. In dry, grassy places on chalky soils. More frequent in Breckland. Scarce and decreasing in the East of the County, where it is extinct in many former habitats.

W: All squares except 67; 83; 93; 94.

74, Clare Country Park, 1976; 76, Dalham, 1981; Herringswell, 1980; Risby and Cavenham, 1981; 77, Icklingham, 1981; Worlington, 1981; 87, Gt Livermere, abundant, roadside verge, 1980.

E: All squares except 03; 06; 13; 26; 28; 36; 37; 38; 39; 49; 57; 50.

14, Lt. Blakenham, 1976; 15, Coddenham, 1980.

Ssp. **muricata** Briq.   Fodder Burnet   Rev. J. D. Gray 1878
(*Poterium polygamum* Waldst. & Kit.)

An alien, native of the Mediterranean region. Introduced and formerly grown as a fodder crop. Very similar to ssp. *minor*. A relic of cultivation on the borders of fields, waysides and waste places. Once frequent, now rare.

E: 04, Aldham, 1976; 05, Needham Market; 34, Shingle Street, Hollesley, 1980; 45, Thorpeness, 1976; 49.

Recorded in Hind from Fakenham, Higham, Culford Heath and Mendham Hill.

Acaena novae-zelandiae Kirk   Pirri-pirri Bur   Lowestoft Field Club 1952
(*A. anserinifolia* auct.)

An alien, native in Australia and New Zealand, introduced into Britain with wool. First recorded in Suffolk in 1952 from the edge of Easton Wood at Easton Bavents (sq. 58). Still there, 1980. This area was occupied by the Army during the Second World War and it is thought that the plants or seeds were introduced with building material or by other means, during the period 1940-46; perhaps brought from the established colonies in North Norfolk (Kelling Heath or Sheringham).

Also recorded from Wangford Warren (sq. 78), 1964 by Dr O. Rackham.

Geum rivale L.   Water Avens   J. Andrews 1745

Native. In damp Boulder Clay woods, old wet meadows and rough pastures. Locally abundant in West Suffolk, but absent from a large part of East Suffolk. This species is associated with the Oxlip woods of the County, where it occurs over a wide area in the majority of the woods on the higher ground. It hybridises freely with *G. urbanum*.

W: All squares except 64; 66; 68; 74; 93; 94.

95, Monks' Park Wood, 1980; Bull's Wood, Cockfield, 1981; 96, Pakenham, 1978.

E: Recorded from squares 05; 06; 15; 38.

06, Shelland, 1976.   *Illustrated page 454*

Geum urbanum L.   Herb Bennet   Sir J. Cullum 1773
                        Wood Avens

Native. Shady waysides, woodland clearings and glades. Frequent.

All squares.   *Illustrated page 455*

Geum rivale × urbanum   Hybrid Avens   Mrs Carss 1860
(*G. × intermedium* Ehrh.)

A fertile and very variable hybrid. In Boulder Clay woods and copses, old wet pastures, ditches and carrs. Usually associated with one or, rarely, both parents. Sometimes frequent in coppiced woods with *G. rivale*. Where only *G. urbanum* occurs, hybrids are very rare. Some of the hybrids have most attractive flowers with orange petals.

W: 76, Denham; 85, Lawshall; 86, Fornham All Saints; 88, Santon Downham; 94, Lavenham; Newton; 95, Bradfield St Clare and Bradfield St George, 1980; Cockfield; Thorpe Morieux; Felsham Wood; Felshamhall Wood and Monks' Park Wood, 1980; 96, Woolpit; Hessett; 97, Sapiston, 1981 (Mrs E. M. Hyde); Fakenham Wood.
E: 05, Battisford; 06, Shelland, 1976 (F. W. Simpson).

Potentilla fruticosa L.   Shrubby Cinquefoil   L. W. Howard c. 1968

Introduced. The only Suffolk record comes from the south bank of Martlesham Creek, near where it joins the R. Deben. Probably a seedling derived from Notcutt's Nurseries, Woodbridge, who have grounds at Martlesham, not far from this site.

Potentilla palustris (L.) Scop.   Marsh Cinquefoil   Sir J. Cullum 1773
(*Comarum palustre* L.)

Native. In bogs and very wet meadows, ditches and fen pools. Not very frequent and becoming scarce.
W: 67; 76; 77; 78; 83; 84; 87; 96; 97; 98.
77, Icklingham; Hurst Fen, Holywell Row; 78, Pashford Poor's Fen; 83, Cornard Mere, 1975; 97, Stanton.
E: 04; 14; 24; 45; 46; 47; 48; 49; 59; 40; 50.
45, Snape, 1980; 59, Oulton, 1978 (P. G. Lawson); 40, Belton, 1977.

Illustrated page 488

Potentilla anserina L.   Silverweed   Sir J. Cullum 1773

Native. Waysides, damp pastures, heaths and the edges of salt marshes, often on drift. Common. The leaves may be silver on both sides, one side, or not at all.
All squares.

Potentilla argentea L.   Hoary Cinquefoil   Sir J. Cullum 1773

Native. Dry, sunny, open tracks, heaths, old ruins. Locally frequent.
W: 65; 66; 76; 77; 78; 86; 87; 88; 93; 96; 97; 98.
66, Herringswell, 1980; 76, Kentford, Gazeley, both 1981; 88, Barnham, 1980.
E: 03; 04; 05; 13; 14; 15; 17; 23; 24; 25; 28; 33; 34; 35; 36; 37; 39; 45; 46; 47; 49; 58; 59; 40.
04, Hadleigh, old railway track; 14, Wherstead, 1980; 15, Barham Pits, 1980; 24, Foxhall, 1981; 34, Shingle Street, 1981; 39, Bungay, 1981; 47, Blythburgh, 1981; 58, Benacre, 1980.
Hb. Ipswich Museum: 'South side of the Foxhall Road by the Mill on the hedgebank with *Hypericum pulchrum'*, c. 1810 (John Notcutt).
It was recorded by Paget on Burgh Castle Wall, c. 1830 and was still there when visited in 1970 (F. W. Simpson).

Potentilla norvegica L.   Norwegian Cinquefoil   Mrs F. Baker c. 1900

Introduced. A native of N. and C. Europe, found as a casual of waste places, but distribution is very limited in Suffolk. First record, Oulton Broad.
E: 14, Ipswich; 24, Woodbridge; 25, Grundisburgh; 47, Southwold Harbour; Walberswick. All records from the 1950's.

Potentilla intermedia L.   Mrs F. Baker 1901

Casual. Native of N. and C. Russia. In waste places. The first Suffolk record was from Oulton Broad. Recorded also in 1981 from Rampart Field (sq. 77) by Mrs J. Harris. Detd. by Dr S. M. Walters.

Potentilla recta L.   Sulphur Cinquefoil   P. T. Marsden 1954

Introduced. Native of C. and S. Europe. In meadows, waste places, on roadside verges and on heaths. Sometimes a garden escape. Rare.
W: 77, Mildenhall.
E: 13, Brantham, 1978; Bentley, 1979; 23, Harkstead, 1976; 24, Martlesham Heath; 25, Otley, 1973 (Mrs E. M. Hyde); 28, Weybread Gravel Pits; 47, roadside between Westleton and Blythburgh, 1973 (Mrs A. Hughes); 49, Somerleyton; 59.

Potentilla tabernaemontani Aschers.   Spring Cinquefoil   Sir J. Cullum 1774
(*P. verna* auct., non L.)

Native. Formerly occurring on chalky heaths west of Bury St Edmunds. Hind's Flora contains records from West Stow Heath, Icklingham, Culford, Lackford, Cavenham Severals and Risby Heath. There have been no records of the plant since Hind's record from West Stow, c. 1889. It is almost certainly extinct in Suffolk.

Potentilla erecta (L.) Räusch.   Common Tormentil   Sir J. Cullum 1773
(*P. tormentilla* Stokes)

Native. Acid heaths, pastures and open places in woods. Common, but decreasing.
W: All squares except 65; 66; 67; 74; 84; 85; 93.
77, Cavenham and Tuddenham Heaths, 1980; 95, Bradfield Woods, 1980.
E: All squares except 05; 15; 16; 23; 26; 27; 33; 44.
07, Redgrave Fen, 1980; 45, Snape and Tunstall, 1981; 46/47, Westleton, 1980.

Potentilla erecta × reptans   R. Burn 1930
(*P.* × *italica* Lehm.)

Probably overlooked.
W: 94, Groton.

Potentilla anglica Laicharding   Trailing Tormentil   Dawson Turner 1805
(*P. procumbens* Sibth.)

Native. On heaths and woodland rides. Rare. Many of the records are doubtful.
W: 87; 94;
E: 03; 13; 14; 23; 24; 28; 33; 45; 46; 47; 58; 40.

Potentilla anglica × erecta   F. W. Simpson c. 1935
(*P.* × *suberecta* Zimm.)

E: 47, Blythburgh and Walberswick Heaths, c. 1935. Specimens identified by R. Burn.

Potentilla reptans L.   Creeping Cinquefoil   Sir J. Cullum 1773

Native. Waysides, margins of heaths, and pastures. Common.
All squares.

Potentilla sterilis (L.) Garcke   Barren Strawberry   Sir J. Cullum 1773

Native. Old pastures, waysides and in woods, especially on the Boulder Clay. Common.
W: All squares except 65; 66; 67; 68; 78; 88; 98.
E: All squares except 17; 26; 37; 44; 57.

Fragaria vesca L. Wild Strawberry Rev. G. Crabbe 1798
Wood Strawberry

Native. Open places in woods on clay soils, rough pastures, waysides, railway banks and quarries. Frequent.
All squares except 68; 78; 34; 44; 49; 57; 50.

Fragaria moschata Duchesne Hautbois Strawberry Mrs French 1851
(*F. elatior* Ehrh.)

Introduced from C. Europe and naturalised. Very rare and seldom found flowering. The only records for Suffolk are from Park Wood, Barking, from Combs Wood near Stowmarket (both sq. 05), from an area of grassy heath near Langley Wood, Brent Eleigh (sq. 94) and from Haughley Thicks (sq. 06). Hind's Flora records the species from only two localities, namely Bury St Edmunds and from the woods at Great Bradley.

Fragaria chiloensis × virginiana Garden Strawberry F. W. Simpson c. 1928
(*F. × ananassa* Duchesne)

A garden introduction. Usually an escape or a relic of cultivation. Possibly bird-sown in quarries, on railway banks and in waste places. Very variable.
W: 66; 74; 77; 83; 94; 95.
66, Newmarket, 1974; 77, Barton Mills.
E: 05; 06; 17; 23; 24; 35; 36; 59.
06, Haughley, 1974; 17, Eye, disused railway line, 1981 (Mrs E. M. Hyde); 35, Campsey Ash, station yard, 1980 (F. W. Simpson).

Duchesnea indica (Andr.) Focke Indian Strawberry Dr N. B. Eastwood 1962

Alien. Introduced from Asia. There is a single record for Suffolk from Lowestoft.

Alchemilla filicaulis Buser ssp. **vestita** (Buser) M. E. Bradshaw Lady's Mantle
(*A. minor* auct.) Sir J. Cullum 1776

Native. Damp, grassy old pastures, lanes and woodland glades. Very rare. Recorded in 1932 in an old lane beside Bull's Wood at Cockfield (sq. 95) on a moist and clayey site with *Ophioglossum vulgatum*. Further recorded from Snape (sq. 35) by Major H. Buxton in 1933.
The Cockfield site was known from 1932. There was a small colony, but by 1953 it had disappeared. This may be the site known to Hind and Babington and recorded for Cockfield Parish. The Snape habitat was also an old grassy lane, although I never saw any specimens and am unable to confirm the actual species, though accept the identification from a reliable botanist.
A new habitat was found by J. Digby in 1972 in an old pasture at Cransford (sq. 36). Inspection of the site revealed that it was growing plentifully on one side of the pasture and a few plants also occurred on what was formerly another pasture adjacent to a felled wood. The wood was probably planted on the site of a much larger pasture. Some ancient oaks, about 200 years old, suggest that the *Alchemilla* could have existed here for many years, overlooked.

Aphanes arvensis L.   Parsley Piert   Sir J. Cullum 1774
(*Alchemilla arvensis* (L.) Scop.)

Native. Cultivated fields, poor grassland, banks, open woodland and bare places. Common. Much confused with *A. microcarpa*, which was not recognised as a British plant until about 1949.
W: All squares except 64; 67; 68; 93.
E: Recorded from squares 03; 04; 05; 13; 14; 17; 23; 24; 25; 34; 39; 44; 47; 58; 50.

Aphanes microcarpa (Boiss. & Reut.) Rothm.   Slender Parsley Piert
                                                                    H. D. Geldart 1838
Native. On heaths and sandy acid soils. Frequent in all suitable open habitats. This species is not easily distinguished from *A. arvensis*.
W: 67; 74; 75; 76; 77; 84; 86; 87; 88; 93; 97; 98.
E: 03; 13; 34; 35; 44; 45; 46; 47; 58; 59; 40.

Pyrus communis L.   Pear   Sir J. Cullum 1773
Possibly native in a few sites. Usually introduced. Hedges, woods, scrub, waste places and sites of former gardens and orchards. Seedlings found growing on waste ground, rubbish tips and in quarries have come up from pips of thrown-away cores. Compared with the frequency of apple seedlings, pear seedlings are rare.
W: 66, Exning, 1977; 75, Wickhambrook; 78; 87, West Stow; 93; 94, Lavenham, disused railway line, 1979; 95, Bradfield St George, 1980; 96, Norton Wood; Tostock.
E: 05; 07, Redgrave, 1980; 13, Harkstead, 1981; Woolverstone; Stutton Cliff; 14, Ipswich, near Derby Rd Station; Dales Rd old brickfield, 1978; 15, Gosbeck; 16, Mendlesham; 23, Levington; 25, Framsden; 26; 34, Sutton; 35, Chillesford; 36, Sibton; 38, Ilketshall St Lawrence; 48, Rushmere; Stoven; 40, Belton, 1979.

MALUS SYLVESTRIS AND M. DOMESTICA   WILD APPLE TREES

The majority of the so-called wild crab apples recorded for the County are in fact only semi-wild varieties of cultivated apples. One can observe seedlings coming up on waste ground, especially in towns near children's playgrounds, picnic areas, waysides and hedges, railway lines, even between paving stones and by walls, in fact, anywhere where apple cores are discarded and the pips can germinate and grow. Seedlings, if they are allowed to develop into trees, will generally fruit in about 10 years, producing apples which are usually hard and small, green, red or yellow. Trees with broad leaves generally bear the best apples. Those with narrow leaves, sometimes with a reddish tinge and thin stems, produce apples more like true crabs. Side shoots are frequently short and terminate in a sharp point.
The wild indigenous Crab Apple is an uncommon tree of old woods, ancient hedges and copses, and the cliff scrub of our estuaries. The trees are usually small and even thorny. The fruits are green, turning yellow, and are small with long thin stalks, similar to those of the Siberian Crab, which is commonly planted in gardens and along some road verges.
Apple trees which are relics of cultivation often persist on sites of former gardens and orchards. Sometimes they are in woods, usually near their margins, where once there were keepers' or woodmen's cottages. A few apple trees have also been planted on road verges.

Malus sylvestris Mill.   Crab Apple   Sir J. Cullum 1773

Native. In old hedgerows, woods and thickets. Not very frequent and decreasing. This is the true wild Crab Apple, thorny and with small leaves and fruit.

W: 76, Barrow; Kentford; Gt Saxham, 1977; 77, Cavenham, 1977; 84, Acton; 86, Risby, 1977; 94, Groton Wood; 95, Bradfield St George; Buxhall; Felshamhall Wood and Monks' Park Wood, 1980; 96, Beyton; Norton; Gt Barton; 97, Stanton.

E: 04, Offton; Somersham, 1980; Hintlesham, 1981; Wolves Wood, Hadleigh, 1980; 07, Botesdale; Redgrave; 13, Bentley; Wherstead; Stutton; 14, Belstead; Lt. Blakenham, 1979; 17, Eye; 24, Gt Bealings, 1981; Playford, 1980; Grundisburgh, 1979; 27, Syleham, 1980; 28, Weybread, 1980.

Malus domestica Borkh.   Apple
(*M. sylvestris* Mill. ssp. *mitis* (Wallr.) Mansf.)

Introduced. Usually seedlings from cultivated apples. Hedges, waste places, quarries, woods, commons and railway banks. Probably in all squares.

Sorbus aucuparia L.   Rowan   J. Andrews 1731
(*Pyrus aucuparia* (L.) Ehrh.)   Mountain Ash

Native and introduced. In old woods, on sandy or gravelly soils. Native specimens may be seen in woods at Wherstead, Belstead, Bentley, Holbrook, Iken and Staverton. Many bird-sown specimens in a variety of habitats.

W: All squares except 64; 65; 66; 67; 68; 74; 77; 83; 84; 95; 97.
87, West Stow, 1977.

E: All squares except 05; 06; 07; 15; 16; 26; 27; 36; 37; 39; 44; 48.
24, Martlesham Heath, 1980; Purdis Heath, 1981; 35, Tunstall Common, 1980; 46, Westleton, 1980; 47, Walberswick Heath, 1980. All bird-sown.

Sorbus torminalis (L.) Crantz   Wild Service Tree   J. Andrews 1744
(*Pyrus torminalis* (L.) Ehrh.)

Native. This tree is still quite frequent in an area of Suffolk south and south-west of Ipswich to the Stour Valley. It occurs in old woodland, copses and hedges. Some of these hedges, and even woodland margins, are ancient parish boundaries. Sizes of specimens vary from well-grown trees to coppice or small hedgerow examples, frequently with many suckers. It is known to occur, or did until recently, in the parishes of Bentley, Capel St Mary, Lt. Wenham, Hadleigh, Hintlesham and Stoke-by-Nayland. In one wood, five well-developed trees have been observed with a number of saplings. It is also to be found in N. Essex, south of the R. Stour. The habitats of this tree are probably relics of the ancient forest which once covered much of the area.

W: 75, Chevington; 83; 93, Stoke-by-Nayland; Polstead; 94, Kersey.
E: 03; 04; 05; 13; 34; 36; 37.
03, East Bergholt; Capel St. Mary; 04, Hintlesham, 1981; Lt. Wenham, 1976; Hadleigh, 1974; Bramford, 1976; 05, Barking; 13, hedges at Dodnash and Holly Woods, 1980; 34, Capel St Andrew; 36, Bruisyard; 37, Bramfield.
Hb. Davy, specimen from Darsham, 1797, in Ipswich Museum.

Sorbus aria (L.) Crantz   Common White Beam   Woodward 1805
(*Pyrus aria* (L.) Ehrh.)

Native and introduced. In woods, copses, old quarries, scrub and ancient hedges. On Chalk or very chalky Boulder Clay. A very rare native in Suffolk, but frequently planted in woods, parks and plantations. Several of our records may refer to *S. intermedia*.
W: 76, Barrow; 77, Mildenhall; 84, Acton; Sudbury; 94; 96.
E: 03; 05, Finborough; 07, Thelnetham Fen; 26, Brandeston; 38; 45; 47, beside a dyke near Wolsey's Bridge, Wangford, 1976, possibly planted (P. Stearn).

Sorbus intermedia (Ehrh.) Pers.   Swedish White Beam   J. D. Gray 1892
(*Pyrus intermedia* Ehrh.)

Introduced. Planted and bird-sown. Some of the records for *S. aria* may refer to this species.
W: 87, Livermere Park.
E: 13, Tattingstone; Holbrook; Woolverstone, 1974-1981, bird-sown (Mrs. E. M. Hyde). Conf. by E. J. Clement.

Amelanchier lamarckii F.-G. Schroeder   Snowy Mespil   M. A. Hyde 1975
Juneberry

Introduced. Native of Eastern N. America. Occasionally naturalised.
E: 13, Woolverstone. Still there, 1981.

Cotoneaster horizontalis Decaisne   Rock Cotoneaster   Mrs E. M. Hyde 1975

Introduced. Native of W. China. Frequently cultivated.
W: 67, Freckenham, 1977; 86, Bury St Edmunds, 1981.
E: 04, Hadleigh, by Church, 1981; 39, Bungay, 1981 (both records F. W. Simpson); 47, Walberswick. Walls of Church ruins, bird-sown, 1975 (Mrs E. M. Hyde).

Cotoneaster simonsii Bak.   Khasia Berry   Finder not recorded c. 1950

Introduced. Native in the Khasia Hills, India. Planted in shrubberies and sometimes naturalised. Seed may be distributed by birds.
W: 77; 78; 97.
78, Brandon, 1980.
E: 13, Tattingstone, in old woodland, 1980; 14, Ipswich, Derby Road Station, 1981 and Dales Road old brickyard, 1978; 34, Shingle Street, 1981; 46, Aldringham, in quantity, 1957.

Cotoneaster franchetii Bois   M. A. Hyde 1979

Introduced. Native of W. China and Tibet.
E: 14, on waste ground near Bramford Road, Ipswich. A single bush, perhaps bird-sown. Detd. E. J. Clement.

Mespilus germanica L.   Medlar   E. R. Long c. 1930

Introduced from S.E. Europe and S.W. Asia. Occasionally planted for its fruit and may become naturalised. The only records for Suffolk are from Blundeston and Lowestoft.

Crataegus laevigata (Poir.) DC.   Midland Hawthorn   Sir J. Cullum 1773
(*C. oxyacanthoides* Thuill.)

Native. In hedges, woods and scrub. Not very common and never as frequent as *C. monogyna*. Occasionally planted. Probably under-recorded.
W: 76, Gt Saxham, 1977; 94, Brent Eleigh, 1974; Groton Wood, 1977; Polstead, 1975; 95, Buxhall, 1978; Bull's Wood, Cockfield, 1979; 96, Gt Barton, 1976.
E: 04, Hintlesham, 1981; 16, Framsden, 1980.

Crataegus laevigata × monogyna   Hybrid Hawthorn   Breckland Survey 1968
(*C. × media* Bechst.)

An uncommon or overlooked hybrid of woods and hedges.
W: 76, Higham; Gazeley; 94; 95, Felshamhall Wood.

Crataegus monogyna Jacq.   May   Sir J. Cullum 1773
                                  Hawthorn

Native. In woods, copses, hedges, scrub, quarries and on commons. Very common. Often planted and rapidly colonising suitable habitats. A number of varieties occur. Forms with pink, rose or red flowers, single or double, are quite frequent.
All squares.
Var. **laciniata** Stev.   Cut-leaved Hawthorn
W: 93, Polstead, c. 1950 (F. W. Simpson).

PRUNUS (Subgenus **Prunus**)   SLOES, PLUMS AND DAMSONS

The identification of the various species, varieties and hybrids occurring in Suffolk presents a number of problems both to amateur and professional botanists. The first species to flower, usually in early March, is the Cherry Plum. This is an introduced species, much planted in the past as a hedge shrub surrounding orchards, especially on light soils. The flowers appear with the leaves and the species is generally not very prickly, bearing only a few thorns, or branches terminating in a spike. Some botanists mistakenly believe it to be the early Blackthorn, *P. spinosa* var. *macrocarpa*. Fruit is only produced in favourable seasons and is usually green. The ornamental garden variety, var. *atropurpurea*, which has bronze or reddish foliage, bears fruit which is reddish-purple when ripe. There is also a double-flowered form of this variety and, to complicate matters still further, in Suffolk the Cherry Plum is called the Greengage Plum.
The Blackthorn or Sloe is abundant. It is a very thorny shrub or small tree, whose flowers appear before the leaves. There are also forms with fewer spines and flowers, which are hybrids with cultivated Plums or Damsons. When produced, the fruits of these hybrids are few, usually shaped like Damsons, very bitter and much larger than Sloes. Occasionally one finds a small tree bearing green or yellow fruits, which is probably the Wild Greengage or perhaps is derived from the Golden Plum. These trees have very few thorns, but must not be confused with the Bullace, now a scarce hedgerow shrub or small tree, bearing clusters of green and yellow fruits and usually associated with hedges surrounding old gardens. Sometimes Plums and Damsons occur in hedges and wood margins, usually as suckers from trees of former gardens or orchards.

ROSACEAE

Prunus cerasifera Ehrh.   Cherry Plum   F. W. Simpson 1918
(*P. divaricata* Ledeb.)

Introduced. Native of E. Europe. Planted for hedging and shelter for young plantations
and orchards. Widespread. The flowers and leaves appear at the same time.
W: 66; 67; 76; 77; 78; 86; 87; 93; 96.
77, Barton Mills, 1981; 86, Bury St Edmunds, 1981; 93, Polstead, 1975.
E: 03; 04; 06; 13; 14; 15; 17; 23; 24; 25; 33; 34; 35; 36; 46; 47.
14, Bramford, Sproughton and Ipswich, Alexandra Park, 1981; 24, Gt Bealings,
Martlesham and Playford, 1981; 35, Bromeswell, Eyke and Rendlesham, 1980.

Prunus spinosa L.   Blackthorn   Sir J. Cullum 1773
                           Sloe

Native. Hedges, thickets and woods. Very common. This species is included under *P.
communis* in Hind's Flora.
All squares.

Prunus domestica × spinosa   F. W. Simpson 1940
(*P. × fruticans* Weihe)

This hybrid is more frequent than the records suggest.
W: 66, Exning, 1977; 77, Icklingham, 1981 (F. W. Simpson); Barton Mills, 1979; 94,
Brent Eleigh, 1976 (Mrs E. M. Hyde). Detd. at Kew.
E: 16, Mickfield; 23, Chelmondiston, 1981; 24, Playford, in a copse, 1981; Foxhall, 1981.

Prunus domestica L.   Plum   Sir J. Cullum 1773
(*P. communis* Huds.)

A very variable species, which has been divided into three subspecies. Intermediates occur.
(a) ssp. **domestica** (Wild Plum). Found in hedges, thickets, on sites of former gardens and
waste places. Many specimens derived from discarded plum-stones or bird-sown.
Recorded from Exning; Chelsworth; Thorpe Morieux; Foxhall, 1981; Playford; Hemley,
1980; Tattingstone; Alderton; Minsmere.
(b) ssp. **insititia** (L.) C. K. Schneid. (Bullace). Introduced and naturalised in hedges and
thickets. Usually near the sites of old cottages. Rarely cultivated.
Recorded from Nayland; Mendlesham; Earl Soham; Witnesham; Alderton; Chelmondiston; Foxhall; Harkstead (last three records all 1981).
(c) ssp. **italica** (Borkh.) Hegi (Greengage). Larger than ssp. *insititia* and more like ssp.
domestica. Fruit green, rarely produced. A rare tree in hedges and old garden sites.
Recorded from Rushmere, near Ipswich; Pakenham, 1975; Harkstead, 1981.

Prunus avium L.   Wild Cherry   T. Martyn 1797

Native. In woods, copses and hedges. Frequent. More common in the South-east of the
County, especially on soils covering the London Clay.
W: 66; 74; 75; 76; 77; 78; 83; 86; 87; 93; 94; 95; 96.
Frequent in woods and hedges at Polstead, 1981.
E: 03; 04; 05; 13; 14; 15; 23; 24; 25; 27; 33; 35; 36; 39; 46; 47.
Frequent on the Shotley Peninsula, 1981.

Prunus cerasus L.   Sour Cherry   Dale 1696
Dwarf Cherry

Introduced. Probably bird-sown from gardens. In hedges, woods and copses. Rare.
W: 76; 86, Bury St Edmunds; 93; 96, Beyton, 1952 (F. W. Simpson).
E: 16, Wetheringsett; 36, Benhall; Gt Glemham.

Prunus padus L.   Bird Cherry   Rev. G. Crabbe 1798

Native. In damp woods and copses. Sometimes bird-sown. Rare.
W: 75, Ousden; 77, Barton Mills; 87, Wordwell; 93, Newton.
E: 33, The Grove, Felixstowe, 1980 (F. W. Simpson); 34, Water Wood, Butley (F. W. Simpson); Sutton; 36, Bruisyard; 59, Gunton and Corton; 40, Fritton Lake.

Illustrated page 452

Prunus lusitanica L.   Portugal Laurel   F. W. Simpson c. 1930

Introduced. Native of Spain and Portugal. Frequently planted in woods and shrubberies. Self-sown seedlings have been observed at Freston, Woolverstone and Nacton, and probably occur elsewhere.

Prunus laurocerasus L.   Common Laurel

Introduced. Native in S.E. Europe and S.W. Asia. Planted in woods, copses and shrubberies. Frequent. Bird-sown specimens are not uncommon.

LEGUMINOSAE

PEA FAMILY

Laburnum anagyroides Medic.   Laburnum   Breckland Survey c. 1965
Golden Rain

Introduced. Native of C. and S. Europe. Frequently planted in gardens and plantations. Self-sown seedlings are not uncommon.
W: 66; 76 and 86, Breckland Survey. (Planted.)
E: 33, Felixstowe Town Station, seedlings, 1974.

Cytisus scoparius (L.) Link   Broom   Sir J. Cullum 1773
(*Sarothamnus scoparius* (L.) Wimmer ex Koch)

Native. On sandy or gravelly soils on heaths, commons and waste places. Frequent.
All squares except 64; 65; 68; 75; 26.
A form with white flowers occurred in Monks' Park Wood in 1946. Plants with yellow and brown flowers occur occasionally. The latter are probably hybrids with garden varieties.   *Illustrated page 470*

Teline monspessulana (L.) C. Koch   Montpelier Broom   M. A. Hyde 1979

Introduced. Native of Mediterranean region. Waste places. This shrub is frequently grown in gardens and readily produces seedlings.
E: 13, Brantham; Holbrook, 1980; 33, Felixstowe Ferry, 1980.

Genista tinctoria L.   Dyer's Greenweed   Sir J. Cullum 1773

Native. Rough pastures, commons and roadside verges. Formerly rather frequent, now becoming rare, as habitats rapidly disappear. The plant was formerly cultivated for its dye. It is probable that, in many of its sites, it is a relic of cultivation.

W: 75; 83; 86; 87; 95; 96.
E: 04; 05; 06; 07; 13; 15; 16; 17; 23; 25; 27; 28; 36; 37; 38; 45; 46; 48; 49.
16, Wetheringsett, 1974; 25, Monewden, 1980; 27, Fressingfield, 1981; 38, Ilketshall St Margaret, 1981; 48, Redisham; Sotterley, 1980 (P. G. Lawson).

Genista pilosa L.   Hairy Greenweed   Sir J. Cullum 1771
                         Hairy Broom

Native. On the dry, sandy heaths of Breckland. Now extinct. The last (unconfirmed) record was by Mrs R. Clarke from a plantation at Cavenham (sq. 77) in 1965. It was formerly to be found in several sites north-west of Bury, at Culford, Lackford, Icklingham, Risby, West Stow, Tuddenham and Livermere. The majority of suitable habitats have now been reclaimed for farming or afforestation, and the chance of re-finding this species is remote.
There is a specimen in Hb. Ipswich Museum: 'Gathered on Cavenham Heath, where it grows abundantly, but the stems are so closely pressed to the ground that it is difficult to find'. Probably collected by Rev. G. R. Leathes, c. 1800. Also another specimen collected by Lady Blake, c. 1830 from 'near the windmill at West Stow'.
'Heaths near Bury, which are perfectly yellow with it when in flower, but after flowering it is with difficulty found, the stems lying so close to the ground.' (Mr Woodward, c. 1793.)

Genista anglica L.   Petty Whin   J. Andrews 1754
                         Needle Furze

Native. Damp heaths and fens. Very local and decreasing. Extinct in several former habitats.
W: 76, Risby; 77, Tuddenham Fen, 1979; 84, Newton Green, 1974; 97; 98.
E: 07, Redgrave Fen, 1980; Hinderclay Fen; Thelnetham Fen, 1981; 14, Rushmere Common and Warren House Heath, Ipswich (now extinct); 24, Martlesham Heath; 36, Benhall Green.
Hb. Ipswich Museum: 'Between the Race Ground and the Warren House', c. 1820. A colony survived in the marsh near St Augustine's Church, Ipswich, until 1973, when the site was developed.

Spartium junceum L.   Spanish Broom   F. W. Simpson 1934

Introduced and naturalised. Native of the Mediterranean region and S.W. Europe. Dry places, old gardens and waysides.
E: 03, East Bergholt; 13, Brantham, 1980, now producing seedlings; 33, Felixstowe; 34, Shingle Street, Hollesley, 1976.

ULEX   GORSES

There are three species of gorse to be found in the County. Most botanists are able to identify the winter and spring flowering Common Gorse, *Ulex europaeus* L. which grows so abundantly on commons, heaths and other habitats, preferring sandy or gravelly poor soils. The other two species, *U. gallii* Planch. and *U. minor* Roth are often passed over, especially by amateurs, as small autumn flowering (July to October) forms of the Common Gorse. Their distribution in the County has been much confused; some of the old records of *U. minor* may have been identified in error for *U. gallii*. The descriptions

191

and illustrations in the majority of floras are very confusing, especially when describing the flowers. Perhaps the best and most accurate are the 'Drawings of British Plants', by Stella Ross-Craig. *U. gallii* is a much stronger and more upright shrub then *U. minor*, the prickles firmer, stems stouter, flowers larger and more the colour of *U. europaeus*. Indeed, it does often look like a small version of the Common Gorse, when the two are growing together. Some specimens may very well be hybrids, as seen at Rushmere Common and in the Purdis Heath area near Ipswich. *U. minor* is a weak shrub often more prostrate than upright, unless it has the support of surrounding vegetation, the thorns are soft and easily bent, stems thinner and covered with hairs which are clearly visible, almost felted or down-like in some specimens. The flowers are also smaller and of a more lemon-yellow shade (rarely orange); they appear to be more closed than open, fewer in number on each branch and mainly terminal, in loose clusters.

Ulex europaeus L. ssp. **europaeus**   Gorse   Sir J. Cullum 1773
                                             Furze
                                             Whin

Native. Heaths, commons, hedges and waste places on light or gravelly soils. Common, often abundant.
All squares except 64; 65; 68; 74; 26.

Ulex europaeus × **gallii**   Hybrid Gorse   F. W. Simpson 1973

This hybrid is probably not uncommon in Suffolk where the two species occur together. The bushes are variable in size and strength. Some are about as tall and large as the Common Gorse. The flowers appear in the autumn and can be seen at their best in late September, before the Common Gorse commences to flower in early January and February. The flowers of the hybrid are smaller, its thorns are firm and slightly curved, the new stems downy, but not so much as in the Dwarf Gorse (*U. minor*), and the pods are few and smaller. There appear to be many intermediates.
E: 24, Rushmere Common, 1981; Foxhall, 1980; Purdis Heath, 1980; 35, Tunstall, 1980; 40, Belton, 1977.

Ulex minor Roth   Dwarf Gorse   Henslow and Skepper 1860
(*U. nanus* Forst.)   Dwarf Furze

Native. On dry, sandy or gravelly heaths, mainly in East Suffolk. Occasional. Often confused with *U. gallii*.
W: 76, Higham, 1981 (Mrs E. M. Hyde). Detd. by P. M. Benoit; 77, Tuddenham St Mary.
E: 24, Bucklesham, 1980; 46, Sizewell; Dunwich Common; 47, Walberswick Common; 40, Belton.

Ulex gallii Planch.   Western Gorse   Rev. W. H. Purchas 1861
                            French Furze

Native. On the heaths of East Suffolk. Sometimes mistaken for *Ulex minor*.
E: 14; 24; 34; 35; 45; 46; 47; 40.
14, Nacton Heath, 1981; 24, Rushmere, 1981; 35, Tunstall, 1980; 45, Snape, 1981; 46/47, Dunwich, 1980; Westleton, 1980; 47, Blythburgh, 1981; 40, Fritton, 1973; Belton, 1977.

Illustrated page 472

Lupinus luteus L.   Annual Yellow Lupin

Introduced from the Mediterranean region. Formerly grown as a fodder crop or for improving light soils, especially in East Suffolk and in areas of Breckland.

Lupinus angustifolius L.   Sweet Blue Lupin   Mrs M. Southwell 1953

Introduced. Native in Spain. Recorded only twice in Suffolk, from Eriswell by Mrs Southwell in 1953 and from Brandon Waterworks by H. D. Wiard in 1965. Probably ssp. *angustifolius.*

Lupinus micranthus Guss.   Bitter Blue Lupin
(*L. hirsutus* sensu L.)

An introduction from S. Europe. Cultivated as a fodder crop or for soil improvement in Breckland and on the light, sandy soils of East Suffolk, though less frequently than formerly.

Lupinus polyphyllus Lindl.   Garden Lupin   N. S. P. Mitchell 1956

Native of N. America. Often cultivated in gardens and sometimes found as a garden escape or throw-out.
W: 66, Newmarket Station, 1974.
E: 05, Stowmarket, 1956; 06, Haughley, 1981; 13, Brantham, near the Decoy, 1974; 14, Ipswich, 1977; 23, Chelmondiston, 1973-4.

Lupinus arboreus Sims   Tree Lupin   G. Staunton c. 1900

Introduced. Native of N. America. Naturalised on heaths, dunes, railway banks and waste places. Frequent, sometimes plentiful, as between Aldeburgh and Dunwich.
W: 67, Freckenham, 1977; 76, Kentford; Higham, 1980; 77, Icklingham; Barton Mills; 87.
E: 04, Hadleigh, 1981; 05, Combs; Gt Finborough; 06, Wetherden; 13, Brantham; Bentley; 14, Ipswich, several sites; 23, Chelmondiston; Kirton, 1980; 24, Foxhall; Martlesham; Woodbridge (all 1981); 33, Bawdsey; 34, Shingle Street and Hollesley, 1981; 35, Eyke; Snape, 1981; 44, Orford; 45, Aldeburgh; Sudbourne; Thorpeness; 46, Aldringham, 1980; Leiston; Sizewell; Minsmere; 47, Walberswick; Reydon; Southwold; Wenhaston, 1980; 49, Beccles, 1980; 57, Southwold; Easton Bavents; 58, Benacre; Pakefield; Kessingland; 59, Lowestoft, 1980; 40, Belton, old railway track, 1977.
Kessingland has been called 'Lupin Land'. Introduced there by George Staunton, Lord of the Manor of Kessingland, of White House, formerly situated near the beach.

Illustrated page 502

Robinia pseudoacacia L.   False Acacia   F. W. Simpson 1978

A flowering tree, introduced from Eastern N. America and planted in woods, parks and plantations, where it may become almost naturalised and regeneration can occur.
W: 66, Moulton, 1978; 76, Herringswell, 1980; 77, Mildenhall and Barton Mills, 1980.

Galega officinalis L.   Goat's Rue   H. D. Wiard 1967
French Lilac

An alien, introduced from Europe and W. Asia. A garden escape or throw-out, becoming naturalised in waste places and on waysides. (In its native habitats it can sometimes be seen growing in profusion in damp pastures and besides rivers. I have seen it in parts of the Balkans, creating, when in flower, a very attractive sight.)

W: 88, Thetford.
E: 03, Capel St Mary, 1979 (N. Hunt); 13, Brantham, 1974 (D. Smee); 15, Barham, 1981 (N. Hunt); 17, Eye, 1974, white flowers (Mrs E. M. Hyde); 23, Felixstowe; 24, Hasketon (J. Digby); 37, Halesworth, 1980 (P. G. Lawson).

Colutea arborescens L.   Bladder Senna   P. J. O. Trist 1962

Introduced from the Mediterranean region. Found as a casual in waste places. Rare.
W: 66, Newmarket Station, 1977; 77, Tuddenham, in a chalk pit, 1962 (P. J. O. Trist).
E: 14, Wherstead, near the Strand, site destroyed in 1974 (Mrs E. M. Hyde); near Ipswich Railway Station, 1981; 24, Rushmere, 1977 (F. W. Simpson); Westerfield Railway Station, 1977-81 (F. W. Simpson).

Astragalus hamosus L.   Miss F. E. Crackles 1980

Alien. Native in the Mediterranean region. Waste places.
E: 14, Ipswich, many plants on waste ground alongside the R. Gipping. Conf. E. J. Clement.

Astragalus danicus Retz.   Purple Milk Vetch   Gerarde 1597

Native. Dry chalky and sandy banks, waysides and heaths. Confined to Breckland, where it is still locally frequent.
W: 66, Newmarket; 76, Risby Heath, 1980; 77, Icklingham, 1981; Eriswell; Worlington, 1976; 78, Lakenheath Warren, 1974; 86; 87, Elveden, 1979; Barnham; Icklingham; West Stow, 1977; 88; 97.   *Illustrated page 472*

Astragalus glycyphyllos L.   Milk Vetch   Gerarde 1597
                                  Wild Liquorice

Native. Hedges, waysides and edges of woods and thickets. Usually on Chalk or Chalky Boulder Clay. Generally uncommon, but locally frequent.
W: 84, Sudbury; 93, Stoke-by-Nayland; Bures; 94, Preston; 95, Hitcham; Cockfield; 97, Coney Weston, 1981 (L. J. Hyde).
E: 04, Whatfield, 1980; Aldham; 05, Baylham; Creeting St Mary, 1981; 06, Old Newton, 1975; Stowupland, 1980; 15, Hemingstone; Creeting St Mary, 1981; Barham; Coddenham, 1981; 17, Brome Airfield, near Eye; 23, Nacton.   *Illustrated page 472*

Cicer arietinum L.   Chick Pea   Mrs F. Baker c. 1890

An alien, cultivated in S. Europe for the edible seeds. Known in Suffolk only from a single record from Oulton Broad.

Vicia orobus DC.   Upright Vetch   F. A. Basham 1955

Native. Known in Suffolk only from a single record from Bury St Edmunds (sq. 86) in 1955.

Vicia cracca L.   Tufted Vetch   Sir J. Cullum 1773

Native. Damp old pastures, fens, cliffs, hedges and edges of woods. Frequent.
All squares.

Vicia tenuifolia Roth   Fine-leaved Vetch   Miss J. C. N. Willis 1960

Established alien. Native in S. Europe.
W: 77, roadside on the A11 near Barton Mills, 1970 (P. J. O. Trist), still there, 1980.
E: 04, Hadleigh, old railway bank 1960, still there, 1981.

Vicia sylvatica L.   Wood Vetch   H. J. Boreham 1953

Native in parts of Britain, though not in Suffolk. May be found in waste places or scrub.
The only known record is from Bury St Edmunds, possibly a garden escape.

Vicia villosa Roth ssp. **villosa**   M. A. Hyde 1979

Casual. Native of Europe. An annual species, easily confused with the perennial *Vicia cracca* L.
E: 14, on waste ground near Bramford Road, Ipswich. Conf. E. J. Clement.

Vicia monantha Retz.   One-flowered Lentil   Hind 1885

Casual. Native of S. Europe.
E: 14, Ipswich Docks on ballast.

Vicia hirsuta (L.) S. F. Gray   Hairy Tare   Sir J. Cullum 1773

Native. Waysides, grassy places, margins of woods, railway embankments. Frequent.
All squares except 65; 68; 75; 27.

Vicia tenuissima (Bieb.) Schinz & Thell.   Slender Tare   Mrs French 1840
(*V. gracilis* Lois.)

Native. On the margins of woods and copses and in bushy or grassy places. Very rare or
overlooked. May be mistaken for *V. tetrasperma*.
W: 83; 93, Arger Fen, Bures; 94, Camps Wood, Brent Eleigh and Kersey (pre-1950).
E: 04, Hintlesham; Aldham, near Rectory, 1972 (A. W. Punter); 25, Earl Stonham, 1975;
45, Sudbourne.

Vicia tetrasperma (L.) Schreb.   Smooth Tare   Sir J. Cullum 1773

Native. Clearings in old woods, chiefly on the Boulder Clay, grassy places, especially near
the coast and sea cliffs. Frequent and well distributed.
W: All squares except 65; 66; 67; 68; 76; 77; 78; 88; 98.
94, Brent Eleigh, 1981; 97, Coney Weston, 1981.
E: All squares except 15; 26; 28; 49; 40; 50.
04, Hadleigh, disused railway line, 1981; 13, Holbrook Creek, 1981; 33, Felixstowe Ferry,
1977.

Vicia sepium L.   Bush Vetch   J. Andrews 1744

Native. Hedges, waysides and open places, in woods and copses. Frequent, especially on
the Boulder Clay.
All squares except 65; 67; 68; 78; 98; 49; 57; 50.   *Illustrated page 447*
Variety with cream-coloured flowers near Chelsworth, 1938, and with pink flowers,
Harkstead, 1973.

Vicia sativa L. and **V. angustifolia** L.

Much confusion still exists regarding the status and identification of these two species, which are frequently incorrectly recorded.

V. sativa L. (*V. segetalis* Thuill.) is a very common plant of waysides, hedge-banks and grassy waste places. It is often quite hairy.

V. sativa ssp. **sativa** (Common Tare) is sometimes cultivated as a fodder plant, especially for sheep, or to improve the soil. It is a much larger hairy plant and occurs as a casual on field borders and waste places, but it rarely persists. It is considered to be an introduction.

V. angustifolia L. is a more slender, often hairless plant, which can readily be identified by its very pretty reddish-purple flowers. It occurs on rather acid, dry sandy or gravelly soils of heaths, cliffs and railway banks. *V. angustifolia* usually flowers a few weeks later than *V. sativa*. It is a much neater plant in all its stages of growth. However, one frequently sees examples which appear to be intermediates between the species; they may be hybrids. Some botanists treat the two species as an aggregate, *V. sativa* agg. (*V. sativa* ssp. *nigra* (L.) Ehrh.)

Vicia sativa L.　　Common Vetch　　　　　　　　　　Sir J. Cullum 1773
(*V. segetalis* Thuill.)

Native. Waysides, banks, grassy places, open woodland glades and waste places. Very frequent. The pods are brown and much larger than *V. angustifolia*.
All squares.
Ssp. **sativa** (Common Tare) Introduced. Native of W. Asia. Occasionally cultivated as a fodder crop. Occurs as a casual in waste places or a relic of cultivation on field borders. Flowers much larger, usually of two distinct shades, pale and dark purple.
No recent records.

Vicia angustifolia L.　　Narrow-leaved Vetch　　　　　Sir J. Cullum 1773
(*V. sativa* L. ssp. *angustifolia* (L.) Gaud.)

Native. On old grassland, heaths, waysides, railway embankments and sea cliffs. Frequent. A variable species, sometimes confused with *V. sativa* L. The pods of *V. angustifolia* are black.
W: All squares except 65; 85.
77, Barton Mills, 1981; 87, Icklingham, 1980.
E: All squares except 16; 25; 38; 48; 59.
04, Hadleigh and Raydon, 1981; 34, Sutton, 1981; 45, Snape, 1981.　　*Illustrated page 471*

Vicia lathyroides L.　　Spring Vetch　　　　　　　　　　J. Andrews 1750

Native. Dry heaths, sandy places, railway banks and near the coast. Frequent.
W: 66; 67; 76; 77; 78; 83; 86; 87; 88; 93; 96; 98.
Common in Breckland, 1981.
E: 03; 04; 05; 13; 14; 15; 16; 23; 24; 25; 28; 33; 34; 35; 39; 44; 45; 46; 47; 58; 59; 50.
24, Rushmere, 1981; Playford, 1981; Foxhall, 1980; 45, Iken, 1981; Snape, 1981; 47, Walberswick, 1980.

Vicia lutea L.　　Yellow Vetch　　　　　　　　　　　　Humphrey 1775

Native. On cliffs and shingle beaches, where it is sometimes abundant, more rarely on sandy beaches.

196

E: 23, Landguard Common, 1978; 33, Bawdsey, 1981; Felixstowe; 34, Shingle Street, 1981; Boyton; 44, Orford Ness; Havergate Island, 1979; 45, Sudbourne; Thorpeness; 46, Leiston; 59, Pakefield Cliffs. *Illustrated page 495*

Vicia hybrida L.   Hairy Yellow Vetch   W. J. Cross 1882

A casual, native of S. Europe. A weed of fields and waste places. Very similar to *V. lutea*. *V. hybrida* has larger yellow flowers of a deeper yellow colour, a hairy standard, emarginate leaflets, solitary flowers at each node and unequal calyx-teeth.

Hind's record for *V. lutea* 'Among Lucerne at Brandon' is incorrect. M. A. Hyde examined the herbarium specimen at Ipswich Museum and found it to be *V. hybrida*. It was collected from a sandy field on the 30th May 1882. The finder was W. J. Cross. The only other known record is from an arable field at Shelley (sq. 03) made by T. Dipnall in 1919.

Vicia bithynica (L.) L.   Bithynian Vetch   Rev. G. Crabbe c. 1798
                                 Rough-podded Purple Vetch

Native or casual. On sea cliffs and in hedges. Rare.
E: 04, Hadleigh; 13, Freston, 1978 (M. A. Hyde); 47, Blythburgh; 49, Carlton Colville; Beccles; 58, Kessingland, 1974; 59, Pakefield Cliffs.

Vicia narbonensis L.   Mrs F. Baker c. 1900

A casual, native in S. Europe. Known in Suffolk only from the record from Oulton Broad.

Vicia faba L.   Broad Bean
                      Horse Bean

Introduced from the Mediterranean region, it is a plant which has been frequently cultivated, both here and in continental Europe. May be found as an escape or relic of cultivation on roadsides, margins of fields and rubbish tips.

Lathyrus japonicus Willd. ssp. **maritimus** (L.) P. W. Ball   Sea Pea   Caius 1555
(*L. maritimus* Bigel.)

Native. On shingle and mixed sand and pebble beaches, above high water mark. Locally common and abundant. This attractive species can be found between Landguard Point, Felixstowe, and Kessingland in all suitable habitats. It has increased considerably in recent years, in some areas where it was rare or almost unknown. At one time it was uncommon north of Aldeburgh, but was abundant on Sudbourne and Orford beaches, south to Shingle Street and Bawdsey, as far as East Lane. The beach between East Lane, Bawdsey, and the mouth of the Deben was sandy, but after the erection of groins in front of the Manor House, shingle began to accumulate and the Sea Pea is now common in this area. South of Aldeburgh, from Slaughden to Orford Beach, the shingle beach has been much reduced and disturbed for the past 25 years by erosion and mechanical devices building up a shingle ridge, and very little of the plant now survives, where formerly there were extensive patches. The Sea Pea is one of the outstanding plants of our Suffolk flora and exists in greater quantity and profusion here at the limit of its range than can be observed anywhere else in Western Europe. Wear and erosion of the beaches, due to the influx of visitors and development, is continuously reducing the available habitats of our coastal flora. During the last war, when the popular beaches were closed to the public, plants soon appeared where they had not been observed for many years. On the beach at Felixstowe, between Cobbold Point and the Manor House, the Sea Pea was common. The Yellow Horned Poppy (*Glaucium flavum*) was especially plentiful, and even grew on the Promenade, finding places between the concrete slabs.

A rare form with white flowers was recorded from Shingle Street in 1969.

E: 23, Landguard Common, much decreased in recent years, due to trampling; Trimley St Mary, 1977; 33/34, Felixstowe Ferry to Shingle Street, common but decreasing in some areas, due to erosion and trampling; Boyton, a few colonies; shingle spit from North Weir Point (Nature Reserve), large colonies, abundant; 44, Havergate Island; Orford Beach; 45, Sudbourne Beach to Aldeburgh, decreased considerably since 1946, due to rapid erosion of the old shingle ridges, the use of bulldozers and various developments of the area; Aldeburgh to Thorpeness, a few colonies persisting, but may become extinct, due to the pressure of visitors; 46, Sizewell to Minsmere, several colonies; 47, Dunwich Beach to Walberswick, formerly abundant, now much reduced, since c. 1954, due to the considerable erosion of the former wide shingle beach and the increasing pressure of visitors wearing away the remaining shingle ridge; 57, Southwold; 58, Easton and Covehithe Beaches, a few colonies observed 1947-60, destroyed by erosion; Benacre Ness, several colonies, the beach has been considerably eroded in recent years; Kessingland; Pakefield, 1980. *Illustrated page 494*

Lathyrus montanus (L.) Bernh.   Bitter Vetch   Sir J. Cullum 1776
(*L. macrorrhizus* Wimm.)

Native. There has always been some doubt about its occurrence in Suffolk. It is recorded in Henslow & Skepper's Flora for Honington. Sir J. Cullum mentioned it in his journal for May 3rd, 1776, and there is also a record for Campsey Ash in 1835. Although so far I have been unable to find it in the County, I believe that it did occur very sparingly at one time, and may still survive. The plant prefers very old woods, copses and hedge banks on clay and loamy soils, more especially the London Clay. The best area to search is in the very South of the County, the Stour Valley, where the soil and other conditions are more favourable.

Lathyrus pratensis L.   Meadow Vetchling   J. Andrews 1757

Native. Hedges, damp pastures, grassy places. Common.
All squares.

Lathyrus palustris L.   Marsh Pea   Buddle 1698
                              Marsh Vetchling

Native. In old marshes, fens and bogs. Very local and decreasing. This species is now mainly restricted to a small area of Lothingland.
W: 78, Lakenheath Fen, 1980.
E: 49, Carlton Colville, 1975; Barnby; Worlingham; 59, Oulton, 1976; Blundeston; 40, Bradwell; Belton, 1979.

Lathyrus tuberosus L.   Tuberous Pea   J. Rasor 1907
                              Fyfield Pea
                              Earthnut Pea

An introduced colonist or casual, native in Europe and Western Asia. Rare. It is not recorded in Hind's Flora. This is the species which has been known since about 1800, naturalised in cornfields and hedges at Fyfield and other places in Essex. A specimen found at Whitton near Ipswich, was shown on the botanical table at Ipswich Museum in July, 1914. This plant produces edible tubers on its roots like those of *Bunium bulbocastanum*. 'These plants are sold in the markets of Holland', J. C. Loudon's 'Encyclopaedia of Plants', 1836. It was recommended in 'The Garden' of July, 1886, for planting at the foot of a hedge or fence 'this pretty little species scrambles over and about it in a pretty way'. It therefore may still survive as a relic of cultivation in a number of old gardens or sites of former gardens.

W: 78, Wangford, on site of former garden, 1974 (Z. Gathercole); 86, Bury St Edmunds; 88; 96, Woolpit, railway embankment (J. Rasor).
E: 14, Whitton, 1914.

Lathyrus grandiflorus Sibth. & Sm.   Everlasting Sweet Pea   F. W. Simpson 1970

Introduced. Native of the Balkan Peninsula, S. Italy and Sicily. On sites of former cottage gardens, banks and hedges. This species is often confused with both *L. latifolius* L. and *L. odoratus* L. (Sweet Pea). It flowers in May and early June and there are only one or two large sweet-scented flowers on each stem. Seed pods are rarely produced.

E: 14, Ipswich, St George's St, 1970 (site destroyed, July 1976); Myrtle Road, 1981; 16, Thorndon.

Lathyrus rotundifolius Willd.   Round-leaved Vetch   Finder not recorded c. 1957

Native of E. Russia and W. Asia. About 20 specimens were found in a sandpit at Blaxhall, c. 1957.

Lathyrus sylvestris L.   Narrow-leaved Everlasting Pea   J. Andrews 1745

Doubtfully native, or introduced. In hedges and scrub and on railway embankments. Uncommon. Some of the records below probably refer to *L. latifolius*.

W: 83, Lt. Cornard; 86, Bury St Edmunds; 88, Thetford Warren; 93, Stoke-by-Nayland; 97, Troston.
E: 07; 37.

Lathyrus latifolius L.   Broad-leaved Everlasting Pea   F. W. Simpson c. 1928

An introduced alien from S. Europe. Frequently grown in gardens and escaping. Flowers large, rich magenta, rarely white. In hedgerows, sites of former gardens, and waste places.

W: 78, Lakenheath; Brandon; 87, Gt Livermere, 1980.
E: 03; 04; 13; 14; 23; 33; 35; 57; 59.
03, East Bergholt; 04, Offton; 13, Brantham, 1980; 14, Ipswich, waste places, sites of former gardens; Westerfield Station, 1981; Tuddenham sand pit, 1976; 23, Landguard Common; Chelmondiston, 1974; 33, Bawdsey, 1975; 35, Campsey Ash, 1981; 57, Southwold, 1974.   *Illustrated page 515*
White-flowered form recorded from Westerfield Station and Campsey Ash, both in 1981.

Lathyrus sphaericus Retz.   Round-seeded Vetchling   Hind 1885

A casual with crimson flowers. Native of continental Europe. Sometimes found on ballast. Recorded by Hind from Ipswich Docks.

Lathyrus hirsutus L.   Hairy Vetchling   F. W. Simpson 1981
Possibly native. Dry grassy places. Rare.
W: 97, small colony, Coney Weston, July 1981. Conf. E. J. Clement.

Lathyrus nissolia L.   Grass Vetchling   J. Andrews 1743
Native. Grassy seaside banks, sides of dykes and the drier parts of salt marshes. Old
pastures and waysides. Frequent near the coast, but rare inland.
W: 64; 78; 83; 86; 87; 94; 97, Coney Weston, 1981 (Mrs E. M. Hyde).
E: 03; 04; 13; 15; 23; 24; 26; 33; 34; 37; 44; 45; 46; 48; 49; 59; 40.
23, Landguard Common, 1977; Shotley, 1980; 33, Felixstowe Ferry, 1977; 34, Shingle
Street, still frequent, 1981; 46, East Bridge, 1978 (P. G. Lawson).
Hb. Ipswich Museum: 'In the same field with the Brick Kiln to the north of Brook's Hall
with *Chironia centaurium* (Common Centaury), sparingly,' Aug. 1817 (John Notcutt).
Illustrated page 499

Lathyrus aphaca L.   Yellow Vetchling   Sir J. Cullum 1773
A native or casual weed of waysides, waste places and fields. Rare. Two forms occur in
the County. One, probably native, grows on old grassy wayside verges, the other occurs as
a casual.
W: 67; 78; 94, roadside at Monks Eleigh, one plant, 1974 (Mrs J. Willis); grassy verge,
Brent Eleigh, 1981.
E: 04, Aldham, roadside verge near Rectory, 1960-76 (A. W. Punter), still there, 1981; 15,
Earl Stonham, roadside, 1980 (E. Milne-Redhead).
Hind's Flora gives 16 sites for the County. There is a specimen in Hb. Atkins from 'banks
of the Orwell' in 1908. *Illustrated page 507*

Pisum sativum L.   Garden Pea
Probably a native of E. Europe. Cultivated. Sometimes found on rubbish tips, as at
Woolpit Tip (sq. 96) in 1974, and Barton Mills Tip (sq. 77) in 1977.
Var. **arvense** (L.) Poir. (*P. arvense* L.)   Field Pea
Formerly much cultivated as a fodder crop and for improving light soils. Flowers usually
lilac or purple.

Ononis spinosa L. ssp. **spinosa**   Spiny Restharrow   Sir J. Cullum 1773
Native. Old pastures, waysides and commons, chiefly on clay soils. Fairly frequent, but
less abundant than formerly.
W: All squares except 66; 67; 68; 78; 83; 84; 93.
75, Rede, 1977; 76, Gt Saxham, 1980.
E: All squares except 03; 13; 24; 33; 44; 49; 59; 40; 50.
07, Mellis Common; 23, Shotley, 1981; 25, Clopton, 1981; 34, Alderton.
Illustrated page 507

Ononis repens L.   Common Restharrow   Sir J. Cullum 1773
(*O. arvensis* auct.)   Creeping Restharrow
                         Rassals (Suffolk)
Native. In old pastures, on waysides and on the coast, especially on sand and shingle
beaches, and on cliffs. Common.
W: All squares except 68; 75; 93.
76, Risby and Cavenham, 1980; 97, Coney Weston, 1981.

E: All squares except 07; 17; 24; 26; 28; 38; 39.
04, Hadleigh, old railway track, 1981; 33, Bawdsey, 1980; 46, Sizewell, 1980.
The white-flowered form was found at Aldeburgh and Southwold in 1971.

Ononis repens × spinosa ssp. **spinosa**   F. W. Simpson c. 1950
Hybrids were found on the coast at Dunwich and Sizewell during the 1950's.

Melilotus altissima Thuill.   Tall Melilot   Gerarde 1597
(*M. officinalis* auct.)

Native or introduced. Waste places and the margins of fields and woods, especially on the
Boulder Clay. Over-recorded. Some of the records may refer to *M. officinalis* (L.) Pallas.
W: All squares except 65; 66; 67; 88; 93; 97; 98.
68, Lakenheath, 1980; 76, Dalham, 1981; 96, Woolpit, 1979.
E: All squares except 03; 07; 23; 28; 33; 35; 38; 39; 44; 46; 49; 58; 40.
13, Brantham, 1979; 15, Coddenham, 1978.

Melilotus alba Medic.   White Melilot   Henslow & Skepper 1860

An introduction from continental Europe and Asia, colonising waysides, waste places and
fallow fields. Frequent. Recorded in Hind's Flora only from Mildenhall and Cockfield.
W: All squares except 64; 65; 74; 83; 85; 93; 94.
Very frequent in Breckland, 1981.
E: All squares except 06; 07; 17; 26; 27; 28; 34; 35; 37; 44; 40; 50.
13, Holbrook Creek, 1981; 14, Ipswich, 1981; 23, Felixstowe, 1980.

Melilotus officinalis (L.) Pallas   Common Melilot   John Notcutt c. 1820
                                    Field Melilot

A colonist, introduced from continental Europe. Found on the borders of fields and waste
places. Frequent.
W: All squares except 67; 83; 85.
76, Gt Saxham, 1979; 86, Bury St Edmunds, 1981.
E: All squares except 17; 26; 27; 28; 34; 37; 44; 46; 48; 58.
14, Ipswich, 1981; 24, Gt Bealings, 1981.
Hb. Ipswich Museum: 'Melilot Trefoil. King's Clover. Hart's Clover. Cornfields. By the
side of the Towing Path, between the Locks and Handford Bridges' c. 1820 (John
Notcutt).

Melilotus indica (L.) All.   Small Melilot   Hind 1882
(*M. parviflora* Desf.)   Small-flowered Melilot

A casual, native from the Mediterranean region to India. Found in waste places, especially
near docks and railways. Rare.
W: 86, Bury St Edmunds.
E: 14, Ipswich, 1981; 23, Felixstowe, rail sidings and waste ground at the Docks; 45,
Snape Maltings, 1978.
This species was recorded by Hind only from a bare patch near Breydon Water in
October, 1882.

Trigonella caerulea DC.   Blue Fenugreek   Mrs F. Baker 1899
A casual from E. Europe. Only record from Oulton Broad.

Trigonella foenum-graecum L.   Fenugreek   J. S. Wilkinson 1908
A casual. Cultivated for fodder in C. and S. Europe. Recorded from Ipswich.

Trigonella hamosa L.   Mrs F. Baker 1899
A casual from the Mediterranean region. Only record from Oulton Broad.

Medicago lupulina L.   Black Medick   Sir J. Cullum 1773
                       Nonsuch
Native. Fields, waysides and waste places. Often grown as a fodder plant. Frequent.
All squares.

Medicago sativa L. ssp. **sativa**   Lucerne   Sir T. G. Cullum 1804
                       Alfalfa
                       Purple Medick
A fodder plant introduced from the Mediterranean and W. Asia, now established and naturalised in some districts, where it is very frequent.
All squares except 65; 85; 93; 07; 27.

Ssp. **falcata** (L.) Arcangeli   Sickle Medick   Buddle c. 1698
(*M. falcata* L.)   Yellow Medick
Native. On dry, chalky and sandy soils. Found frequently in Breckland, and more rarely near the coast.
W: 66; 67; 76; 77; 78; 86; 87; 88; 96; 97; 98.
78, Lakenheath, 1980; 86, Westley, 1981; 87, West Stow, 1980; 97, Fakenham Magna, 1981.
E: 23; 33; 44; 45; 58; 59; 50.
23, Felixstowe, 1980; 33, Felixstowe Ferry, 1980; 44, Orford, 1979.
Recorded by the Rev. G. Crabbe in his 'Catalogue of Plants', 1798, at Orford and Sudbourne.

Medicago sativa ssp. **falcata** × ssp. **sativa**   Hybrid Wild Medick
(*M. sylvestris* Fr.   Sir T. G. Cullum 1804
M. × *varia* Martyn)
Frequent in Breckland, where both parents occur. Rare near the coast.
W: 67; 76; 77; 78; 86; 87; 88; 97.
67, Worlington; Freckenham, 1979; 76, Higham; 77, Icklingham, 1981; 78, Lakenheath, 1980; 86, Westley, 1981; Fornham St Martin; Timworth; 87, Barnham; Elveden; 88, Thetford; 97, Fakenham Magna, 1981.
E: 14; 23; 33; 44; 45; 58; 59; 50.
14, banks of R. Orwell, on sand probably brought from Landguard Common, 1981 (M. A. Hyde); 23, Landguard Common; Felixstowe, 1980; 33, Felixstowe Ferry, 1979; 44, Gedgrave; Orford, 1973; 45, Sudbourne, 1979; 58, Kessingland; 59, Lowestoft; 50, Hopton.

Medicago arabica (L.) Huds.   Spotted Medick   J. Andrews 1745
(*M. maculata* Sibth.)   Calvary Clover

Native. Very frequent along the coast on grassy banks and in pastures and waste places. Inland it is not so common.
W: Recorded from squares 66; 77; 83; 84; 86; 87; 93; 94; 95; 96.
E: All squares except 06; 07; 16; 17; 27; 38; 44; 48; 49; 58.   *Illustrated page 470*

Medicago polymorpha L.   Hairy Medick   Ray 1690
(*M. hispida* Gaertn.   Toothed Medick
M. denticulata Willd.)

Native on sandy beaches and commons near the sea. A casual on ballast and in waste places and on rubbish tips. Very variable. A number of forms have been described.
W: 88; 93.
E: 05; 14; 23; 24; 28; 33; 34; 35; 44; 45; 46; 47; 49; 59.
14, Ipswich, by R. Gipping, 1978-81 (M. A. Hyde); 23, Landguard Common, 1975 (F. W. Simpson); Chelmondiston Tip, 1977 (M. A. Hyde); 35, Snape Maltings, 1978 (M. A. Hyde).

Medicago minima (L.) Bartal.   Bur Medick   Ray 1690
Native. Dry sandy heaths and old tracks, and on the sea coast. Frequent in the Breckland and on the Sandlings.
W: 66; 67; 68; 76; 77; 78; 87; 88; 97; 98.
66, Herringswell, 1980; 76, Kentford, 1980; 78, Lakenheath, 1980.
E: 05; 14; 23; 24; 33; 34; 35; 44; 46; 47; 49; 59.
23, Felixstowe, 1980; 34, Sutton, 1981; Shingle Street, 1981.

Trifolium ornithopodioides L.   Birdsfoot Fenugreek   J. Andrews 1727
(*Trigonella ornithopodioides* (L.) DC.)

Native. Tracks, usually on the edges of saltings. Probably fairly frequent, but overlooked. Mainly confined to the coastal area.
E: 13, Cattawade; Holbrook, 1980; 15, Barham, 1979 (Mrs E. M. Hyde); 23, Landguard Common, 1977; Trimley St Mary, 1979; 24; 33, Bawdsey; Felixstowe; 34, Hollesley; Boyton; 35, Snape; Chillesford; 44, Orford; Havergate Island; 45, Sudbourne Marshes; Iken Heath; 46, Sizewell; 47, Blythburgh and Walberswick Heaths; 57, Walberswick, 1975; 58, Covehithe, 1979 (P. G. Lawson); 59, Gunton.

Trifolium repens L.   White Clover   Sir J. Cullum 1773
                    Dutch Clover
                    Sucklings (Suffolk)

Native. Also introduced. Pastures, waysides, lawns and waste places. Common.
All squares.
Proliferous forms are not uncommon, and have been recorded from Whatfield, Semer, Leavenheath and Snape. Also, forms with foliaceous calyces have been observed.
Pink-flowered White Clover.
This is a fairly frequent colour variant and may be confused by some botanists with *T. hybridum* or *T. fragiferum*.

Trifolium hybridum L.   Alsike Clover   Mrs French 1850

Introduced or a colonist. Native of continental Europe. Occasionally grown as a crop. Waysides, borders of fields and pastures. Decreasing.
W: All squares except 65; 67; 68; 78; 83; 84; 95; 97; 98.
74, Clare, 1976; 87, Barnham, 1973; 96, Pakenham, 1978.
E: All squares except 17; 26; 27; 28; 33; 34; 39; 44; 45; 48; 49; 58; 59; 50.
13, Woolverstone, 1981; 23, Walton, 1980; 36, Saxmundham area, 1981.

Trifolium glomeratum L.   Clustered Clover   Ray 1690

Native. Dry, open sandy heaths, tracks, old sand dunes and commons. Locally frequent. Mainly confined to the coast. Very rare, or possibly overlooked, in the Breckland.
W: 76, Higham Heath, 1957; 77, Cavenham, 1949; Tuddenham, 1953; Icklingham, 1981, the last three records all made by Dr D. E. Coombe; 97, Coney Weston, 1981 (F. W. Simpson).
E: 13; 23; 24; 25; 33; 34; 35; 36; 39; 44; 45; 46; 47; 48; 49; 58; 59.
13, Holbrook Churchyard, 1980; 24, Brightwell, 1981; Sutton, 1981; 45/46, Aldeburgh and Aldringham, 1981.
In 1981 abundant in several parishes where it had not been recorded before — Bungay, Snape, Rushmere St Andrew, Shingle Street and Butley.

Trifolium suffocatum L.   Suffocated Clover   Rev. G. R. Leathes 1796
Throttled Clover

Native. On dry heaths, commons, sandy tracks and the sea coast. Scarce.
W: 77, Cavenham, 1979; Icklingham, 1981 (Dr D. E. Coombe); 78, Lakenheath, 1980.
E: 23; 24, Sutton, 1981; 25; 33; 34, Shingle Street, 1981; 35, Snape, 1981; 37; 39, Bungay, 1981; 44, Orford Ness and Havergate Island, 1971-3; 45, Aldeburgh, 1981; Iken; Thorpeness, 1980; 47; 58; 59; 40, Fritton, 1974.

Trifolium fragiferum L.   Strawberry Clover   J. Andrews 1740

Native. Chiefly in grassy places and marshes near the sea and estuaries, also waysides and fields on the Boulder Clay. Frequent.
W: All squares except 64; 65; 66; 67; 68; 76; 77; 83; 84; 88; 93; 98.
86, Gt Barton; 87, Euston.
E: All squares except 05; 06; 17; 28.
13, Freston, near the Tower; 23, Woolverstone, 1981; 26, Dennington, roadside near the church; 45, Sudbourne, 1975; 47, Blythburgh, 1980; 57, Southwold, 1975; 40, Bradwell; Breydon Water, south bank, 1973.   *Illustrated page 506*

Trifolium resupinatum L.   Reversed Clover   Dr Trimen 1859

A native of Asia and a casual of waste places and rubbish tips. Rare.
E: 05, the Tannery at Combs; 34, Boyton; 44, Orford; 46, Sizewell; 49, Herringfleet.
There is a specimen in Hb. Atkins from Lowestoft, 1906. Dr Trimen's record was also for Lowestoft.

Trifolium campestre Schreb.   Hop Trefoil   Sir J. Cullum 1773
(*T. procumbens* L., nom. ambig.)

Native. Pastures, waysides, railway embankments and cliffs. Not so frequent as formerly. Prefers clay soils.
All squares.

Trifolium dubium Sibth.   Lesser Yellow Trefoil   Sir J. Cullum 1773
(*T. minus* Sm.)

Native. Grassy waste places and pastures. Very frequent.
All squares.

Trifolium micranthum Viv.   Slender Trefoil   Sir J. Cullum 1774

Native. Old grassland, waysides and heaths. Not very common, or possibly overlooked and mistaken for *T. dubium* Sibth.
W: 67; 76; 77; 84; 86; 87; 88; 93; 94; 96.
67, Freckenham, 1977.
E: 03; 04; 13; 14; 16; 17; 23; 24; 26; 34; 37; 39; 45; 46; 47; 58; 59.
13, Woolverstone, garden weed, 1981; 23, Erwarton, 1978; 24, Sutton, 1981; 37, Halesworth, 1979; 47, Walberswick, 1974.

Trifolium striatum L.   Soft Knotted Trefoil   J. Andrews 1745

Native. Dry, sandy places, banks, tracks, cliffs and the coast. Frequent.
W: All squares except 64; 65; 68; 74; 75; 85; 88; 93; 94; 98.
66, Herringswell, 1980; 76, Kentford, 1980.
E: All squares except 05; 06; 16; 27; 49.
14, Belstead, 1975; Ipswich, 1981; 23, Landguard Common, 1977; 24, Sutton, 1981; 35, Rendlesham, 1980; 44, Orford Ness, 1973; 47, Southwold, old railway track, 1973.

Trifolium arvense L.   Hare's-foot Clover   Sir J. Cullum 1773

Native. Sandy places, heaths, the sea coast, cliffs, pits and waste ground. Very frequent, often abundant.
W: All squares except 64; 65; 68; 83; 84; 85; 93.
66, Herringswell, 1981; 97, Coney Weston, 1981.
E: All squares except 27.
04, Hadleigh Railway line; 14, Ipswich; 15, Creeting St Mary; 35, Campsey Ash. All 1981 records.   *Illustrated page 517*

Trifolium scabrum L.   Rough Trefoil   Ray 1696
                        Rough Clover

Native. On dry, sandy and gravelly heaths, commons, banks, tracks and sea cliffs. Locally frequent.
W: 66; 67; 76; 77; 78; 83; 86; 87; 88; 97; 98.
76, Gazeley, 1978; 77, Tuddenham, 1977; 87, West Stow, 1978.
E: 05; 14; 23; 24; 33; 34; 44; 45; 46; 47; 58; 59; 40; 50.
15, Coddenham, 1980; 23, Felixstowe, 1980; 33, Bawdsey, 1977; 34, Sutton, 1981; Shingle Street, 1981; 44, Orford Ness, 1981; 45, Thorpeness, 1974.

Trifolium stellatum L.   Starry Clover   Rev. E. A. Holmes 1840

Casual. Native in S. Europe. Usually near the coast, in waste places and on road verges. Recorded in Hind's Flora as occurring 'between Southwold and the Pier', though Hind regarded this record as doubtful.

Trifolium incarnatum L. ssp. **incarnatum**   Crimson Clover   E. Skepper 1862
                                                    Napoleon (Suffolk)

Introduced and formerly grown as a fodder crop. Native of the Mediterranean region. Now scarce, and only seen sparsely on waysides and the borders of fields, where it is usually a relic of cultivation. At one time fields of Crimson Clover presented a very attractive feature of the countryside, especially on chalky soils.
W: 75; 86; 94; 95; 96.
E: 03; 04; 13; 14; 16; 27; 35; 44; 45; 48.
13, Tattingstone By-pass, Bentley, 1975-78 (Mrs E. M. Hyde); 14, Ipswich on waste ground, 1980 (M. A. Hyde).

Ssp. **molinerii** (Balb. ex Hornem.) Syme   Long-headed Clover   E. F. Linton 1887

The only Suffolk record is from Brandon.

· **Trifolium pratense** L.   Red Clover   Sir J. Cullum 1773

Native, also introduced. Pastures and waysides. Cultivated, usually with grass, for hay and for improving soil. Very frequent or abundant.
Var. **parviflorum** Bab. The native plant is now rare. It is much smaller than the cultivated one, with darker rose, red or even white flowers. Formerly frequent in very old calcareous pastures and on grassy verges. It has crossed with various cultivated strains and these can usually be recognised.
W: 97, Coney Weston and Sapiston, 1981.
E: 24, Hemley, 1979; 39, Bungay, 1981.
White-flowered form at Brandon, 1980 and Sapiston, 1981.
Var. **sativum** Sturm. The cultivated plant is very common and variable. Many strains have been raised and become naturalised. The majority are strong-growing and have pale pink or light rose flowers.
All squares. This covers the distribution of both var. *parviflorum* and var. *sativum* taken together.

Trifolium lappaceum L.   Mrs F. Baker c. 1900

An alien species from the Mediterranean region. Recorded by Mrs Baker from Oulton.

Trifolium medium L.   Zigzag Clover   Sir T. G. Cullum 1804

Native. On old woody banks, waysides, in railway cuttings, quarries and rough pastures. Usually on Chalk, Boulder Clay and Coralline Crag. Well distributed, but usually restricted to small colonies. Decreasing.
W: 64; 74; 83; 85; 86; 93; 94; 95; 96.
Few recent records for West Suffolk.
E: 03; 04; 05; 06; 07; 14; 15; 16; 23; 25; 27; 33; 36; 37; 38; 39; 45; 46; 47; 48; 49; 59; 40.
04, Hadleigh, 1980; 37, Linstead Magna, 1981; 39, Mettingham, 1980; 46, Knodishall, 1980.   *Illustrated page 506*

Trifolium ochroleucon Huds.   Sulphur Clover   Sir. J. Cullum 1775

Native. Waysides, old pastures, railway embankments, chiefly on the Boulder Clay and Chalk. Frequent in some areas, but decreasing elsewhere.
W: 64; 67; 75; 76; 84; 85; 86; 94; 95; 96.
76, Hargrave, 1980; 94, Brent Eleigh, 1980; 97, Sapiston, 1981.
E: 04; 05; 06; 07; 15; 16; 25; 26; 27; 28; 36; 37; 38; 39; 46; 47; 48.
07, Botesdale, 1976; 15, Crowfield to Pettaugh; 16, Aspall; 38, Ilketshall St Andrew and South Elmham, 1980; 48, Ringsfield and Sotterley, 1980 (P. G. Lawson).
Common in the Wattisham and Semer areas, 1980.   *Illustrated page 506*

Trifolium squamosum L.   Sea Clover   Wigg 1804
(*T. maritimum* Huds.)

Native. In grassy and waste places near the sea. Very rare or possibly now extinct.
E: 23, Felixstowe, 1935 (Miss E. Jauncey); Walton Ferry, 1946. In 1978 a large colony was discovered (F. W. Simpson) near the Dooley Fort. Unfortunately this site has now been destroyed (1980), becoming part of the Felixstowe Dock complex.
Recorded by Hind from near Yarmouth and Shingle Street.   *Illustrated page 505*

Trifolium squarrosum L.   Squarrose Clover   Sir T. Gage 1813

A casual, native in Spain. Recorded in Hind's Flora only from Lawshall and Hengrave in the early 19th century.

Trifolium subterraneum L.   Subterranean Clover   J. Andrews 1745
                                  Burrowing Clover

Native. Dry, sandy, open places, heaths, trackways, especially near the coast. Formerly frequent, now much less common and decreasing.
W: 77; 86.
E: 03; 13; 14; 23; 24; 33; 34; 35; 37; 39; 44; 45; 46; 47; 49; 58; 59.
13, Woolverstone, 1981; 14, Bourne Park, Ipswich, 1976; 34, Sutton, 1981; 44, Orford Ness; Havergate Island, 1973; 46, Dunwich, 1974; Aldringham, 1981.

Lotus tenuis Waldst. & Kit. ex Willd.   Narrow-leaved Bird's-foot Trefoil
                                  Slender Bird's-foot Trefoil   Sir J. Cullum 1773

Native. Damp grassy places near the coast, where it is sometimes abundant on the edges of salt marshes. Rare elsewhere.
W: 78; 87; 88; 95.
78, Lakenheath.
E: 04; 13; 23; 24; 33; 34; 35; 44; 45; 46; 47; 57; 58; 59; 40.
23, Shotley, 1980; 33, Bawdsey; 34, Sutton; Hollesley, 1981; 45, Sudbourne, 1975; Snape, 1981; 40, Bradwell; pastures by Breydon Water.

Lotus corniculatus L.   Common Bird's-foot Trefoil   Sir J. Cullum 1773
                             Bacon-and-Eggs
                             Trotters

Native. In old pastures, on waysides, the sea coast, sand dunes and fixed shingle beaches. Very common. The colour of the flowers varies from pale yellow to reddish orange.
All squares.   *Illustrated page 505*

Lotus uliginosus Schkuhr   Greater Bird's-foot Trefoil   J. Andrews 1743
(*L. pedunculatus* auct., non Cav.)   Marsh Bird's-foot Trefoil

Native. In marshes, damp woodland glades, and banks of streams and rivers. Common.
All squares.

Anthyllis vulneraria L.   Kidney Vetch   J. Andrews 1743
Ladies' Fingers

Native. On heaths and old fallow fields, chiefly on chalky soils. Sometimes abundant in
Breckland. Scarce in East Suffolk, decreasing, and now extinct in former habitats.
Ssp. **vulneraria**
W: All squares except 65; 68; 74; 75; 84; 85; 93; 97.
Common in Breckland squares, 1981.
E: All squares except 03; 06; 16; 17; 23; 34; 37; 39; 44; 45; 48; 50.
15, Coddenham, c. 1970; Barham, 1979; 24, edge of Rushmere Common, 1975.
Ssp. **vulgaris** (Koch) Corb. var. **pseudovulneraria** Sag.
66, Newmarket; 77, Foxhole Heath; 78, Wangford; 96, Pakenham.

Ornithopus perpusillus L.   Bird's-foot   Sir J. Cullum 1773

Native. Dry, sandy heaths, commons and tracks. Frequent.
W: All squares except 64; 65; 68; 74; 75; 83; 84; 85; 95.
Frequent in the Breckland.
E: All squares except 26; 27; 38; 48; 50.
24, Rushmere Common, 1981; 35, Tunstall, 1980; 39, Bungay, 1981; 46, Aldringham,
1981.

Coronilla varia L.   Crown Vetch   Mrs F. Baker 1900

Introduced. Native of C. and S. Europe. Sometimes naturalised. May be found on waste
ground, usually near docks. The original record was from Oulton Broad in 1900, and it
has since been recorded from Lowestoft (sq. 59) and from Felixstowe Docks (sq. 23) in
1952, specimen determined at Kew.

Coronilla scorpioides (L.) Koch   W. A. Dutt 1899

A casual, native in the Mediterranean region. Known in Suffolk only from two records at
the end of the 19th century from a ballast heap at Lowestoft and from Oulton Broad.

Hippocrepis comosa L.   Horseshoe Vetch   Gerarde 1597

Native. On old, chalky heaths, banks, roadside verges and chalk-pits. Mainly found in
West Suffolk, where it is scarce and decreasing. Believed to be now extinct in East
Suffolk.
W: 66, Newmarket; 76, Risby; Dalham, 1981; 77, Icklingham; Barton Mills, 1981;
Cavenham, 1981; Worlington, 1981; 78, Lakenheath.
E: 14, Lt. Blakenham, 1939 (now extinct); 15, Coddenham (now extinct).
Recorded by Hind from Risby Heath, Newmarket Heath, Barton Mills, Dalham, Barrow
Bottom, Sudbury, Offton and Somersham.   *Illustrated page 475*

Scorpiurus muricatus L.   Mrs M. Daman 1974

Casual, from bird-seed. Native of S. Europe.
E: 25, Dallinghoo, 1974. Detd. by E. J. Clement.

Onobrychis viciifolia Scop.   Sainfoin   Sir J. Cullum 1773
(*O. sativa* Lam.)   Cock's Head

Native or a relic of cultivation. Sometimes cultivated as a fodder crop. Waysides, margins
of fields and chalk quarries. Formerly frequent, but now more local. Still fairly frequent
in Breckland.
W: All squares except 65; 68; 85; 93; 94.
76, Dalham, 1980; 77, Barton Mills, 1980; 86, Bury St Edmunds, 1980.
E: All squares except 13; 17; 27; 28; 33; 35; 37; 38; 44; 47; 49; 58; 59; 40; 50.
04, Hadleigh, disused railway line, 1980; 14, Claydon, 1980.

OXALIDACEAE
WOOD SORREL FAMILY

Oxalis corniculata L.   Procumbent Yellow Sorrel   Hb. Ipswich Museum 1834
                            Yellow Oxalis
                            Sleeping Beauty

Introduced. Origin uncertain. Found in gardens, especially on and near brick walls and
paths. Often a troublesome weed, difficult to eradicate. It has increased in recent years.
W: 86; 93; 94; 96.
E: 13; 14; 16; 23; 24; 25; 26; 27; 33; 35; 44; 49; 58; 59; 50.
04, Hadleigh Churchyard, 1981; 14, Ipswich, 1981.
Hb. Ipswich Museum, collector unknown: 'Goldrood 1834' (Name of a house in Belstead
Road, Ipswich.)

Oxalis exilis A. Cunn.   Least Yellow Sorrel   F. W. Simpson 1980
(*O. corniculata* L. var. *microphylla* Hook. f.)

Introduced. Native of Australasia. A yellow-flowered species like a very small *O.
corniculata*.
E: 14, Ipswich, Old Cemetery, on a grave, 1981 (M. A. Hyde). Conf. R. P. Libbey. Also
weed in pot, Ipswich, 1980 (F. W. Simpson).

Oxalis europaea Jord.   Upright Yellow Sorrel   Hind 1875
(*O. stricta* auct.)

Introduced from the European continent. A garden weed or casual.
W: 93, Boxford; 96, Ixworth.
It is recorded in Hind's Flora for Honington.

Oxalis articulata Savigny   Pink Oxalis   F. W. Simpson c. 1960
(*O. floribunda* Lehm.)

Introduced. Native of the Argentine. A common garden plant, especially in cottage
gardens. It may sometimes be seen on hedgebanks, usually near cottages, on sites of
former gardens and on rubbish tips. This species is quite hardy and its leaves remain green

during the winter. In sheltered sunny positions it may be observed commencing to flower in March. The colour of the flowers, which are borne in umbels, varies in shade from light to dark pink, or sometimes white. This plant does not produce bulbils around its thick woody root.

E: 14, Ipswich, 1981; 23, Shotley, 1976; 24, Gt Bealings, 1960-1977.

Oxalis acetosella L.   Wood Sorrel   Sir J. Cullum 1773

Native. In old woods, copses, and lanes. Frequent. This is probably the true St Patrick's Shamrock. A pale lilac-flowered variety has been found in Woolpit Wood (sq. 96).

W: All squares except 65; 66; 67; 77; 78; 87; 88; 97; 98.

95, Felshamhall Wood and Monks' Park Wood, 1980.

E: All squares except 17; 27; 28; 33; 37; 38; 44; 50.

04, Hintlesham, 1981; 13, Freston Woods, 1981; 35, Staverton, 1979; 58, Benacre, 1981.

Hb. Ipswich Museum: 'Cuckoo-bread. Sour Trefoil. Freston Wood,' c. 1820 (John Notcutt). Still there in 1981.   *Illustrated page 451*

Oxalis corymbosa DC.   Pink Bulbous Oxalis   F. W. Simpson c. 1950

Introduced. Native of S. America. A garden weed, rapidly increasing by numerous bulbils, produced around the bulbous roots. It is also to be found on rubbish tips and waste ground near houses. Once established it is almost impossible to eradicate, as cultivation only spreads the bulbils, which root very freely. The leaves of this species usually die down in the autumn after frosts and do not re-appear until late in March or April, flowering much later than *O. articulata.*

W: 68, Lakenheath; 76, Kentford; Moulton.

E: 13, Harkstead; Woolverstone, 1981; 14, Ipswich, 1981; 24, Woodbridge; 36, Gt Glemham; 45, Aldeburgh; 47, Southwold; 57, Reydon.

Oxalis latifolia Kunth   Mexican Oxalis   Mrs E. M. Hyde 1981

Introduced. Native of Tropical South America. A pink-flowered species, similar to *O. corymbosa,* spreading by underground bulbils. A pernicious weed.

E: 14, Ipswich, Bourne Park, weed in flower bed. Detd. M. A. Hyde. Conf. R. P. Libbey.

GERANIACEAE

GERANIUM FAMILY

Geranium sanguineum L.   Bloody Cranesbill   Sir J. Cullum 1773

Both native and introduced. Old grassy waysides, banks and earthworks on dry, chalky soils. Very rare as a native plant. Sometimes planted on banks and rockeries outside gardens and found on or near sites of former gardens.

W: 76, Dalham and Gazeley (native), 1981; 86, Bury St Edmunds.

E; 14, Claydon (introduced); 28; 35, Blaxhall, 1980; 36, Benhall (introduced); 39, Mettingham, 1980; 45, Aldeburgh, 1978; 49, Barnby; 59, Kirkley, near Lowestoft.

Illustrated page 492

Geranium pratense L.   Meadow Cranesbill   Sir J. Cullum 1775

Doubtfully native; probably a garden escape or alien. Waysides and sites of old gardens. Scarce. The many squares listed below probably refer to individual plants near gardens.

W: 75; 76; 78; 83; 86; 88; 93; 95; 96; 97.
76, Gt Saxham, 1980; Gazeley, 1981; 88, Santon Downham, 1977; 97, Barningham, 1981.
E: 03; 04; 05; 06; 07; 13; 14; 16; 17; 24; 26; 36; 37; 38; 39; 45; 46; 47; 48; 49; 57; 58; 59; 40.
05, Combs Ford, Stowmarket, site of a former cottage garden, 1981; 14, Bramford;
Rushmere, 1981; 38, South Elmham St James, 1974; 46, Darsham Station, 1977.

Illustrated page 493

Geranium sylvaticum L.   Wood Cranesbill   Mrs Bevan 1887
Probably introduced near gardens and plantations. Unlikely to be truly native unless
found on edges of old damp woods, fens and carrs. Very rare.
W: 97, Ixworth.
E: 14, Westerfield Road, Ipswich; 24, Waldringfield; 59, Lowestoft. All these records date
from the 1960's.
Hind's Flora has only one record of the species by Mrs Bevan from Whepstead. There are
specimens in Hb. Atkins from Ipswich, 1909, and Bungay, 1907.

Geranium endressii Gay   French Cranesbill   F. J. Bingley 1958
Introduced. Native of the W. Pyrenees. A garden escape. Known in Suffolk only from a
single record from sq. 03.

Geranium endressii × versicolor   P. G. Lawson 1977
Introduced. Waste places, tips and near gardens. A fertile hybrid.
E: 45, Knodishall.

Geranium versicolor L.   Pencilled Cranesbill   W. A. Dutt 1897
(*G. striatum* L.)

An established alien, native in S. Italy. Often a garden escape. Its usual habitat is shady
banks and waysides.
E: 05, Creeting St Mary; 15, Coddenham; 44; 48, Stoven; Sotterley, 1980; 59, Lound.

Geranium ibericum × platypetalum   Blue Garden Geranium   F. W. Simpson 1977
(*G. × magnificum* Hyl.)

A common garden plant. Sometimes a throw-out or on sites of former gardens. This plant
has larger flowers and leaves than *G. pratense*. Some of the records for *G. pratense* may
belong to this hybrid.
W: 66, Exning, 1977.

Geranium phaeum L.   Dusky Cranesbill   Mrs Cobbold 1800
An alien introduced from C. and S. Europe. Often an escape from cultivation. Found in
plantations, hedge-banks, lanes and grassy places near dwellings.
W: 76; 86; 88; 95.
E: 03; 04; 05; 07; 15; 24; 25; 36; 38; 39.
05, Barking, 1975; 07, Mellis, 1970.

Geranium pyrenaicum Burm. f.   Mountain Cranesbill   F. Turner 1805
Pyrenean Cranesbill
An established alien, introduced from Europe and found on waysides, railway banks and

waste ground. Very frequent. Has increased since Hind's Flora was published, although then described as 'tolerably frequent on banks', followed by numerous parish records. All squares except 68; 75; 78; 27; 50. *Illustrated page 493*

Plants with white and rose-coloured flowers at Burgh and Pin Mill.

Geranium rotundifolium L.   Round-leaved Cranesbill   Sir J. Cullum 1773

A denizen or colonist. Not very frequent, but increasing locally. This species was never abundant in Suffolk, but can still be found in several of the sites recorded in Hind's Flora. It usually occurs as single specimens, or small colonies, on wayside banks, roadsides, waste ground and fallow fields. In most seasons it is possible to find specimens near the inhabited parts of the villages of Belstead, Freston, Wherstead and Holbrook. It occurs in Ipswich, often in the most unlikely places, such as alongside paths and walls and also as a garden weed.

W: 77; 84; 86; 88; 93; 96; 97; 98.

77, Barton Mills, 1981; 78, Lakenheath, 1980; 97, Stanton, 1980.

E: 04; 06; 13; 14; 15; 17; 23; 24; 33; 39; 45; 46; 48; 49; 59; 50.

Geranium molle L.   Soft Cranesbill   J. Andrews 1754
Dove's-foot Cranesbill

Native. Cultivated and waste grounds, especially fallow fields on light or gravelly soils. Common.

All squares.

Var. **alba** — 'roadside Wantisden or Butley Aug. 9th 1787', Sutton and Kirby.

Geranium pusillum L.   Small-flowered Cranesbill   Sir J. Cullum 1773

Native or colonist. Pastures, fallow fields, waysides and old quarries. Frequent on gravelly soils. Often confused with *G. molle.*

W: All squares except 65; 68; 83; 85; 94; 96.

67, Freckenham, 1977; 76, Gazeley, 1981; 77, Barton Mills, 1977.

E: All squares except 27; 44.

13, Holbrook, 1979; 15, Henley, 1979; 23, Trimley Station, 1981; 34, Alderton, 1975.

Geranium columbinum L.   Long-stalked Cranesbill   Sir J. Cullum 1781

Native. Waysides, old pastures, margins of woods and quarries on dry calcareous soils or Red Crag sands. Rare or overlooked. No recent records, though it may still occur in the Butley/Chillesford area.

W: 75; 93.

E: 04; 25; 35; 36; 38; 46; 47.

Most of these records were made between 1950 and 1960.

Geranium dissectum L.   Cut-leaved Cranesbill   Sir J. Cullum 1773

Native. Waysides, fields, waste places, quarries and open clearings in woods. Common.

All squares.

Geranium lucidum L.   Shining Cranesbill   Sir J. Cullum 1773

Native or colonist. Shady hedgebanks and old walls. Locally frequent, but generally absent from coastal areas. This species persists in a number of parishes recorded in Hind's

Flora and can be found in most seasons on banks at Gt Bealings, Belstead, and Bromeswell.
W: 76; 84; 85; 86; 88; 93; 94; 96; 97.
86, Bury St Edmunds, 1980; 94, Lavenham, 1977.
E: 03; 04; 05; 07; 13; 14; 15; 16; 23; 24; 25; 35; 36; 38; 39.
03, East Bergholt Churchyard; Polstead; 13, Holbrook; Tattingstone, 1980; 24, Gt Bealings, 1981; 25, Bromeswell, 1980.

Geranium robertianum L.　　Herb Robert　　　　　Sir J. Cullum 1773
Ssp. **robertianum.** Native. Shady banks and woods. Common.
All squares.
White-flowered variety, Edwardstone, 1971.
Ssp. **maritimum** (Bab.) H. G. Baker. Native. On shingle beaches. Locally common.
Recorded from Landguard, Havergate Island and from shingle between Bawdsey and Aldeburgh, 1981.
Specimen in Hb. Ipswich Museum from Orford Beach, 1842.

Erodium maritimum (L.) L'Hérit.　　Sea Storksbill　　　　Hind 1876
Introduced. A rare casual on light soil. Native on dunes and sandy soils by the sea.
Recorded in Hind's Flora as accidentally introduced at Honington. There has been only one subsequent record, from the Lowestoft area, the date not recorded.

Erodium botrys (Cav.) Bertol.　　　　　　　　F. W. Simpson 1958
A casual, native in the Mediterranean region. Known in Suffolk from a single record from a waste heap at the Tannery, Combs, (sq. 05). Specimen determined at Kew.

Erodium cicutarium (L.) L'Hérit.　　Common Storksbill　　J. Andrews 1745
Native. Heaths, sandy open places, tracks, waysides and beaches. Very variable. Common. Both white and pale-flowered forms are frequent.
All squares except 65; 74; 75; 16.
No attempt has been made to ascribe the records to the subspecies, ssp. *cicutarium*, ssp. *dunense* Andreas and ssp. *bipinnatum* Tourlet.

Erodium moschatum (L.) L'Hérit.　　Musk Storksbill　　Dawson Turner 1805
Introduced. A rare casual of waste places. Native on dunes and sandy places near the sea.
W: 78, Lakenheath.
E: 05, waste heap at The Tannery, Combs, 1957 (F. W. Simpson).

LIMNANTHACEAE

MEADOW FOAM FAMILY

Limnanthes douglasii R. Brown　　Butter and Eggs　　F. W. Simpson 1967
　　　　　　　　　　　　　　　Meadow Foam
Alien. Introduced from California.
E: 14, Ipswich, 1967; 23, Chelmondiston Tip, 1974.

TROPAEOLACEAE

NASTURTIUM FAMILY

Tropaeolum majus L.   Garden Nasturtium   M. A. Hyde 1974

Introduction. Native of Peru. Rubbish tips and waste places, usually from garden refuse.
W: 66, Exning, 1977; 77, Barton Mills Tip, 1977; 94, Monks Eleigh, 1974.
E: 14, Ipswich, waste ground near the R. Gipping, also near Docks, 1981; 23,
Chelmondiston Tip, 1974-75; 57, Southwold, 1974; 40, Belton, 1975.

LINACEAE

FLAX FAMILY

Linum perenne L. ssp. **anglicum** (Mill.) Ockendon   Perennial Flax
                                                        Sir J. Cullum 1773

Native. On old chalky pastures, borders of fields and waysides. This species formerly
occurred at Bury St Edmunds, Stowlangtoft, Pakenham and Bardwell.
W: 78, Lakenheath Warren, 1980; 97, chalky roadside at Ixworth, 1974 (Dr F. Rose and
P. J. Lambley). Possibly the same site as that recorded in Hind's Flora by Davy and
Rickards early in the 19th century.

Linum bienne Mill.   Pale Flax   Sir J. Cullum 1775
(*L. angustifolium* Huds.)   Narrow-leaved Flax

Native. Dry, sunny hedgebanks, waysides and cliffs. Very rare and may become extinct.
Hind's Flora notes that it was already supposed extinct in 1889. There are, however,
recent records from between 1958 and 1980.
W: 87.
E: 13, Tattingstone By-pass, 1981; 46/47, Darsham; 58, Kessingland, 1974; 59, Pakefield
Cliffs.

Linum usitatissimum L.   Common Flax   Prof. Henslow 1859

Species of uncertain origin. Formerly extensively cultivated in the County, now only
occasionally. When in flower, fields of flax, especially on light soils, were a familiar and
attractive feature. It occurs as a casual in fields, waste places, gardens and rubbish tips, as
a relic of cultivation or from bird-seed. Few recent records.
W: 66, Exning, 1977; 77, Barton Mills Tip, 1977; 87, Elveden, 1977; 96, Ixworth.
E: 03; 13; 35; 37; 48; 49; 59.
03, Layham; 13, Harkstead; 37, Halesworth; 48, Brampton; 49, Beccles; 59, Corton.

Linum tenue Desf.   Mrs H. B. Miller 1978

Casual. Native of Iberian Peninsula.
E: 25, Dallinghoo, casual in garden of Mrs M. E. Daman, probably introduced with wild
bird food. Detd. E. J. Clement. First British record.

Linum catharticum L.   Purging Flax   Sir J. Cullum 1784
                            Fairy Flax

Native. Dry, grassy places on chalky soil, old pastures, railway banks and quarries.
Frequent over most of the County, but absent or rare in areas of the South-east.

W: All squares except 65; 93.
76, Dalham, 1981; 78, Lakenheath Warren, 1979; 98, Knettishall, 1981.
E: All squares except 03; 13; 23; 24; 26; 28; 33; 34; 35; 44; 45; 40.
05, Battisford, 1981; 15, Coddenham, 1980.

Linum grandiflorum Desf.   Mrs E. M. Hyde and M. A. Hyde 1977
Casual. Native of N. Africa. The red-flowered annual flax of gardens.
W: 78, edge of rubbish tip, Maidscross Hill, Lakenheath.

Radiola linoides Roth   Allseed   J. Andrews 1711
                             Flix-seed
Native. Moist, sandy, open paths and hollows. Now probably extinct.
Hind's Flora recorded it from Culford, Timworth, Tuddenham, Cavenham, Barton
Mills, Belton, Somerleyton, Lowestoft, Wortham and Westleton Heath.
There are specimens in Hb. Ipswich Museum from Cavenham and Icklingham, collected
by the Rev. G. R. Leathes, early 19th century, and also in Hb. Atkins from Worlingham,
1906.

EUPHORBIACEAE

SPURGE FAMILY

Mercurialis annua L.   Annual Mercury   Sir J. Cullum 1771
Colonist. Waste places, gardens and rubbish dumps. Common, especially in the Ipswich
area. The male plant is more frequent.
W: Recorded from squares 66; 67; 68; 77; 78; 84; 86; 87; 88; 94; 95; 96; 97.
E: All squares except 07; 26; 27; 35; 36; 37; 39.

Mercurialis perennis L.   Dog's Mercury   Sir J. Cullum 1771
Native. In woods, copses and old hedges. Nearly always on Clay, Chalk or loam. Very
frequent, often dominant, especially in the old Boulder Clay woods and copses, where it is
a relic of the ancient flora. The male plant is more frequent.
All squares.   *Illustrated page 448*

Euphorbia platyphyllos L.   Broad Spurge   Rev. G. R. Leathes 1812
                                 Broad-leaved Spurge
A colonist and rare weed of arable fields.
W: 86, Bury St Edmunds, 1952 (A. L. Bull).
The only record in Hind's Flora is from Cutthroat Lane, Hardwick in 1831. Rev. G. R.
Leathes' specimen from a field near Worlingworth is in Hb. Ipswich Museum, and there is
also a specimen in Hb. Atkins from near Bury in 1908.

Euphorbia helioscopia L.   Sun Spurge   Sir J. Cullum 1773
A colonist on cultivated ground, disturbed waysides and waste places near rubbish tips.
Common.
All squares.

Euphorbia lathyris L.   Caper Spurge   E. Skepper 1862

Introduced. Native in S. Europe. An established alien, usually an escape from gardens. It occurs as a weed of old gardens and waste places. The seed may remain dormant for many years. The fruits are poisonous and should not be eaten.
W: 64; 74; 77; 78; 84; 86; 87; 93; 96.
78, Brandon, 1978; 93, Polstead, 1979.
E: 05; 14; 16; 23; 24; 33; 35; 36; 37; 46; 47; 59.
23, Chelmondiston, 1975; 24, Bucklesham, 1974; Playford, 1981; 46, Westleton, 1978.

Illustrated page 516

Euphorbia exigua L.   Dwarf Spurge   Sir J. Cullum 1771

A colonist and a weed of cultivated fields and gardens. Formerly frequent on heavy and mixed soils. Now uncommon.
W: All squares except 65; 67; 68; 78; 87; 98.
77, Worlington, old chalk pit, 1980; 94, Brent Eleigh, same field, 1974-1981.
E: All squares except 34; 44; 49; 58; 40; 50.
04, Bramford, 1981; 15, Ashbocking, 1980.

Euphorbia peplus L.   Petty Spurge   Sir J. Cullum 1771

A colonist and a weed of cultivated ground, especially in gardens on light soils.
All squares except 68; 85; 98; 15.

Euphorbia portlandica L.   Portland Spurge   Dr G. Slater c. 1910

Native. Sandy beaches. In Hb. Ipswich Museum is an unnamed specimen of this species, collected by Dr G. Slater, when still a student. It probably came from Landguard Common with the other specimens in this small collection. The late S. J. Batchelder used to take parties of his students to Landguard Common in the years before the first World War. Frequently during conversation he would name former students, especially those who had succeeded in life, and Dr George Slater's name was often mentioned.

Euphorbia paralias L.   Sea Spurge   Johnson 1633

Native. Sea shore, on sand or shingle beaches. Local, often sporadic, appearing for a few years on disturbed ground and then dying out. A decreasing species.
E: 23, Landguard Common, 1980; 33, Bawdsey Ferry; 34, Shingle Street, Hollesley; 45, Aldeburgh, 1980; 46, Dunwich; Minsmere; Thorpeness, to Sizewell, 1981; 47, Walberswick; 58, Kessingland.   *Illustrated page 498*

Euphorbia esula L.   Leafy Spurge   Rev. E. F. Linton, pre-1928

A naturalised alien. Native of continental Europe. Waste places.
W: 77, Icklingham, 1953 (B. D. Jones); Eriswell, 1952; Barton Mills; Mildenhall; 78, Lakenheath, post-1970.
E: 03, East Bergholt, 1954; 14, Ipswich, 1934; 23, Nacton (Rev. E. F. Linton); 59, Oulton, c. 1930.

Euphorbia virgata Waldst. & Kit., non Desf.   Twiggy Spurge   R. D. English c. 1970
(*E. uralensis* Fisch. ex Link)

A casual, native in E. Europe and S. Russia. May be found in waste places. Rare.
E: 33, Felixstowe Ferry.

Euphorbia esula L. × **virgata** Waldst. & Kit., non Desf.   P. J. O. Trist 1971
(*E.* × *pseudovirgata* (Schur) Soó)

A rare hybrid, found on waste ground.
W: 77, near Barton Mills; 77/78, Eriswell, 1971. (Detd. by E. L. Swann).

Euphorbia cyparissias L.   Cypress Spurge   W. J. Cross 1888
                                Welcome-to-our-House

Introduced and naturalised. Sandy fields, roadsides and railway embankments.
W: 76, railway embankment, Barrow, 1980; Cavenham; 77, Barton Mills, 1981;
Tuddenham Gallops, Herringswell, 1981.
Recorded in Hind's Flora for Tuddenham St Mary.   *Illustrated page 490*

Euphorbia amygdaloides L.   Wood Spurge   Dr W. Turner 1562

Native. Mainly a species of old woods, hedge-banks and verges marking the boundaries of
former woodland. Frequent on the Boulder Clay.
W: 64; 66; 76; 84; 85; 93; 94; 95; 96; 97.
94, Groton Wood, 1981; 95, Monks' Park Wood, 1981.
E: 03; 04; 05; 06; 13; 14; 15; 23; 24; 25; 27; 35; 36; 46.
04, Hintlesham, 1981; 14, Bullen Lane, Bramford, 1981; 24, roadside at Gt Bealings,
1981.   *Illustrated page 450*

POLYGALACEAE

MILKWORT FAMILY

Polygala vulgaris L.   Common Milkwort   Sir J. Cullum 1773
(*P. oxyptera* Rchb.)

Native. On calcareous soils, old grassland, chalk quarries, open scrub and railway
embankments. Occasional. A variable species.
W: 64; 66; 68; 74; 76; 77; 78; 83; 84; 86; 88; 94; 96; 97; 98.
76, Cavenham and Risby, 1979; Hargrave, 1980; Dalham, 1981; 98, Knettishall, 1981.
E: 04; 07; 14; 15; 36; 59.
04, Hadleigh, 1981; 15, Coddenham, 1973.

Polygala serpyllifolia Hose   Heath Milkwort   Sir J. Cullum 1773
(*P. serpyllacea* Weihe)

Native. On grassy and open places, on heaths and in fens. Local or scarce, and decreasing;
usually on acid soils.
W: 77; 97.
E: 04; 07; 13; 23; 24; 45; 46; 47; 57; 58; 59; 40; 50.
07, Redgrave Fen; 13, Holbrook; 23, Chelmondiston, 1980; 46, Minsmere Heath;

Westleton; 47, Walberswick; Wenhaston; Blythburgh; 59, Lowestoft.
There is a specimen in Hb. Atkins from Bentley, 1909.

ANACARDIACEAE

SUMACH FAMILY

Rhus typhina L.   Stag's Horn Sumach   M. A. Hyde 1974

Introduced. Native of N. America. On sites of old gardens and shrubberies.
E: 14, Belstead and Woodbridge Roads, Ipswich, 1976; 33, former garden near Town Station, Felixstowe, 1974.

ACERACEAE

MAPLE FAMILY

Acer platanoides L.   Norway Maple   B.S.B.I. Records c. 1960

An alien, native in the mountainous regions of Europe and introduced into the forest plantations of Breckland during the present century. Natural regeneration occurs.
W: 86; 88; 95; 98.
98, Knettishall.
E: 05, Offton, seedling removed from hedge and planted in Castle Meadow, P. Chapman, 1973; 24, Gt Bealings, seedlings on a roadside bank, 1976-1981.

Acer campestre L.   Field Maple   Sir J. Cullum 1773
Common Maple

Native. Woods and copses, especially on the Boulder Clay, hedges, scrub and old quarries. Frequent. Formerly one of the coppice trees of the old Suffolk woods. Sometimes seen developed as a large tree. Ancient specimen, near Freston Tower.
All squares.

Acer pseudoplatanus L.   Sycamore   Sir J. Cullum 1773

Introduced from C. and S. Europe, but now completely naturalised. In woods, plantations and hedgerows. Very frequent and increasing rapidly by natural regeneration, replacing the native flora.
All squares.

HIPPOCASTANACEAE

HORSE CHESTNUT FAMILY

Aesculus hippocastanum L.   Horse Chestnut

An established alien. Introduced early in the 17th century. Native in S. Europe. Extensively planted in parks and plantations. Natural regeneration occurs on a small scale.
All squares.

Aesculus × carnea Hayne   Pink Horse Chestnut

A common ornamental tree frequently planted in parks and gardens, originating as a hybrid between *A. hippocastanum* and *A. pavia* L., a species from Eastern N. America. At one time included under *A. hippocastanum.*

BALSAMINACEAE

BALSAM FAMILY

Impatiens parviflora DC.   Small Balsam   Hind 1876

Introduced. Native of Siberia and Turkistan. Found on shady banks, woodland rides and in timber yards. Not very frequent. Persisting and naturalised in a few habitats. It is suggested that it has been introduced with imports of timber from Russia.

W: 76; 77; 84; 86; 87; 88; 96.

76, Dalham, 1981; 86, Abbey Gardens, Bury St Edmunds, 1977.

E: 05; 06; 13; 14; 17; 24; 46; 49; 59; 40.

05, Barking, timber yard, 1980; 06, Wetherden, 1981; 13, Holbrook, 1979; 14, Dock Street, Ipswich, 1979; 49, Beccles, 1976.   *Illustrated page 509*

Impatiens glandulifera Royle   Himalayan Balsam   E. R. Long 1943
(*I. roylei* Walp.)   Policeman's Helmet

A naturalised alien, native of the Himalayas. Often grown in gardens and may be found naturalised in waste places and beside rivers and streams. This species has been slow to spread in Suffolk, but is now increasing its distribution. In some counties it is now an abundant weed of river and canal banks.

W: 86, Bury St Edmunds; 94, Nayland, 1974; 95.

E: 07, Wortham, 1974; 13, Woolverstone, 1981; 14, Ipswich, Wherstead Rd, 1981; 16, Wetheringsett, 1979; 23, Chelmondiston, 1974; 37, Halesworth; 46, Dunwich; 49, Beccles; 59, Oulton Broad and Barnby Marshes.   *Illustrated page 510*

AQUIFOLIACEAE

HOLLY FAMILY

Ilex aquifolium L.   Holly   Dale 1696

Native. In woods, copses and hedges. Very frequent. Sometimes planted. Very old specimens in Staverton Thicks and in woods at Holbrook, Bentley, Polstead and Wherstead. A form with golden berries may be seen at Nacton, Stutton, Ufford, Woolverstone and East Bergholt. These are probably planted, as are those with variegated leaves.

All squares.

CELASTRACEAE

SPINDLE TREE FAMILY

Euonymus europaeus L.   Spindle Tree   Sir J. Cullum 1773
                            Prickwood
Native. Hedges, woods, copses and scrub. Very well distributed and frequent, especially on chalky soils.
W: All squares except 68; 88.
76, Cavenham, 1978; 78, Brandon, 1980; 86, Culford, 1980.
Variety with white capsules on roadside near Dalham (sq. 76), 1975-81 (Mrs E. M. Hyde).
E: All squares except 34; 44; 45; 49; 58; 59; 40; 50.
24, Newbourn, Playford, Gt Bealings, all 1981; 48, Wrentham, 1980.

BUXACEAE

BOX FAMILY

Buxus sempervirens L.   Box

Introduced. Frequent in coverts, shrubberies and plantations. Seedlings occasionally seen (F. W. Simpson).

RHAMNACEAE

BUCKTHORN FAMILY

Rhamnus catharticus L.   Buckthorn   J. Andrews 1745
                            Purging Buckthorn
Native. In hedges, thickets, chalk pits and margins of woods, usually on chalky soils. Very frequent in the parts of West Suffolk bordering Cambridgeshire and the Fens. Rare or almost extinct in East Suffolk.
W: All squares except 65; 83; 85.
66, Exning, very frequent, 1980; 76, Moulton, 1981; 78, Brandon, abundant, 1980.
E: Recorded only from squares 04; 05; 06; 07; 14; 15; 16; 38; 39.
04, Wolves Wood, 1981; 15, Barham, 1981.

Frangula alnus Mill.   Alder Buckthorn   Sir T. G. Cullum 1804
(*Rhamnus frangula* L.)   Black Dogwood
Native. Usually in carr type woods and fens. Scarce. More frequent in West Suffolk.
W: 68; 77; 78; 86; 95; 96; 97; 98.
95, Monks' Park Wood, 1980; 96, Pakenham Wood, 1978; 97/98, Hopton Fen, 1981.
E: 04; 05; 07; 14; 39; 49.
04, Hadleigh, Wolves Wood, 1980; 07, Wortham Ling, 1980; 49, North Cove, 1974.

VITACEAE

VINE FAMILY

Vitis vinifera L.   Grape Vine   F. W. Simpson 1975

Introduced. Native of the Mediterranean region. Seedlings appear on rubbish tips, waste places and gardens, where grapes and raisins, or their 'pips', have been deposited.
E: 14, Ipswich, good specimen in a 'well' below a pavement grating in Arcade Street, 1975. (Destroyed, 1976). Also waste ground, Bramford Road, 1981 (F. W. Simpson).

Parthenocissus quinquefolia (L.) Planch.   Virginia Creeper   Mrs E. M. Hyde 1965

Introduced ornamental creeper. Native of America. Occasionally self-seeding. Found on sites of former gardens and buildings.
E: 14, Ipswich, railway bank near Derby Road Station, 1981 (F. W. Simpson); Tuddenham, in an old quarry (1965-1977).
P. tricuspidata (Sieb. & Zucc.) Planch. is the common species, which is grown on walls for its red autumn foliage.

TILIACEAE

LIME TREE FAMILY

Tilia platyphyllos Scop.   Large-leaved Lime   Hind 1876
(*T. grandifolia* Ehrh. ex Hoffm.)

Introduced. Native of continental Europe, and possibly Britain. Found in plantations and parks.

Tilia cordata Mill.   Small-leaved Lime   Sir J. Cullum 1773
(*T. parvifolia* Ehrh. ex Hoffm.)

Native and introduced. Fairly frequent in the large woods of West Suffolk. Less frequent in East Suffolk. Although no doubt native in several old woods, it was extensively planted in medieval times, as its wood provided good charcoal.
W: 75; 76; 83; 84; 85; 86; 87; 93; 94; 95; 97.
76, Hargrave, 1980; 94, Groton Wood, plentiful, 1981.
E: 04; 05; 07; 13; 25; 34; 36; 46; 48.
04, Offton; Hintlesham, 1981; 13, Freston, 1981; 24, Playford, 1981.

Tilia cordata × platyphyllos   Common Lime   Mrs Dunlap 1846
(*T.* × *vulgaris* Hayne)   Linden

Introduced and naturalised. Much planted in parks, gardens, shrubberies, and roadsides. A very variable hybrid, reproducing by seed.

221

MALVACEAE

MALLOW FAMILY

Malva moschata L.   Musk Mallow   T. Martyn 1797

Native. Old pastures, waysides, lanes, churchyards and grassy quarries. Formerly frequent, now scarce and extinct in many areas, due to the destruction of habitats. This is one of our most attractive wild flowers and the building of the new Ipswich Southern By-Pass has destroyed several of its sites.

W: 64; 66; 67; 74; 76; 77; 85; 86; 88; 93; 95; 96; 98.

76, Gt Saxham, 1976; Gazeley, 1981; Kentford, 1980; 86, on A.45 verge at Westley and Rougham, 1981.

E: 03; 04; 05; 13; 14; 15; 16; 17; 23; 24; 25; 26; 27; 28; 34; 35; 39; 45; 46; 49; 59; 40.

04, Raydon, 1981; 14, Wherstead, 1981; 40, Belton, 1977.   *Illustrated page 491*

Variety with white flowers.

W: 85, Stanningfield; 96, Drinkstone Churchyard, 1980.

E: 13, Tattingstone, 1981 (N. Hunt); 14, Wherstead Churchyard, 1979, but the grass is usually cut and the plants prevented from flowering; 16, Wetheringsett, roadside, 1981; Rishangles, 1979 (Mrs E. M. Hyde); 26, roadside at Brandeston, 1975, (Miss M. Craig); 35, Tunstall Common, 1974; 47, Thorington, 1950.

Malva sylvestris L.   Common Mallow   Sir J. Cullum 1773

Native. Waysides, waste places and sea cliffs. Common and often abundant.

All squares.   *Illustrated page 489*

Var. **alba**: 15, Hemingstone, 1973 (Mrs H. B. Miller).

'Roadside between Wantisden and Butley, Aug. 9th 1787' Sutton and Kirby.

Malva parviflora L.   Least Mallow   F. W. Simpson 1936

A casual, native in the Mediterranean region. Only one record for Suffolk from Landguard Common, Felixstowe in 1936. Detd. at Kew.

Malva pusilla Sm.   Small Mallow   F. W. Simpson 1939

A casual, native in N. and C. Europe. Recorded only from a waste heap at the Maltings, Felixstowe. Detd. at Kew.

Malva neglecta Wallr.   Dwarf Mallow   Sir J. Cullum 1773
(*M. rotundifolia* auct.)

Probably not native, but a colonist. Roadsides and waste places, more especially about farmyards. Frequent.

W: All squares except 83; 85; 98.

67, Freckenham, 1977; 76, Moulton, 1981; 97, Hopton, 1981.

E: All squares except 27; 28; 38.

14, Ipswich, 1981; 23, Harkstead, 1981; 35, Snape, 1981; Butley, 1980.

Lavatera arborea L.   Tree Mallow   E. Skepper 1862

Introduced. Grown in gardens near the sea and sometimes escaping. Usually in small quantity.

E: 23, near the Manor House, adjacent to Landguard Common, 1976, several plants probably of garden origin; 34, Shingle Street, 1981; 35, Snape; Blaxhall; 57, Southwold, 1977.

Althaea hirsuta L.   Rough Mallow   Miss E. Jauncey 1940

Casual. Known in Suffolk only from a single record from Bramford Lane, Ipswich.

Althaea officinalis L.   Marsh Mallow   Rev. G. Crabbe 1783

Native. On the edges of salt marshes and beside brackish ditches. Locally frequent.
E: 03; 13; 23; 33; 34; 35; 45; 46; 47; 49; 58; 40.
13, Harkstead, 1981; 34, Sutton, 1979; 45, Snape, 1981; 58, Benacre, 1981; 40, Fritton, 1974; Burgh Castle, 1975.   *Illustrated page 491*

Alcea rosea L.   Garden Hollyhock   F. W. Simpson c. 1960
(*Althaea rosea* (L.) Cav.)

Origin uncertain, possibly China. Frequently naturalised in S. Europe. Sometimes found on rubbish tips, waste places and roadsides as a garden outcast.
W: 66, Exning, 1977; 77, Icklingham, 1976; Barton Mills Tip, 1980; 78, Lakenheath, 1980; 86, Bury St Edmunds, waste ground, 1980; Fornham St Martin, 1980.
E: 13, Holbrook, roadside, 1974; 14, The Strand, Wherstead, 1970-4 (site destroyed, 1975); 15, Barham, 1977; 23, edge of Landguard Common; 33, Felixstowe Ferry; 47, Southwold, near Harbour, 1974; Wenhaston, 1977.

Abutilon theophrasti Medic.   Chinese Jute   Miss M. M. Whiting 1957
                                    Indian Mallow

A casual. Probably introduced from the Mediterranean region.
E: 05, waste ground at Needham Market; 16, five plants in a field of Dwarf Beans at Brockford Hall, 1976 (P. R. Peecock); 47, a garden at Walberswick, 1957.

Hibiscus trionum L.   Flower-of-the-Hour   F. W. Simpson 1947
                            Bladder Ketmia

An alien, native in S.E. Europe and N. Africa. May be found in cultivated ground and waste places. Flowers are yellow or white with a purplish-brown centre. Attractive annual. Seed can be obtained from some merchants. Also found in bird-seed mixtures.
E: 05, Stowmarket garden, from waste bird-seed, 1976 (M. Taylor); 14, Ipswich garden, 1947; edge of car-park in Ipswich, 1974 (Mrs E. M. Hyde); 26, Kettleburgh, 1968 (W. M. Morfey).

THYMELAEACEAE

DAPHNE FAMILY

Daphne mezereum L.   Mezereon   Crowe 1777

Native. In plantations and an old chalk-pit. Occurs very occasionally on sites of old gardens where seeds, probably of garden origin, have been sown by birds. The only recent records are from sites near Mildenhall (sq. 77) and Helmingham (sq. 15).

223

Recorded by Hind from Stowlangtoft, Honington, Lt. Welnetham, Hawstead, Bungay, Laxfield and East Bergholt.

Daphne laureola L.   Spurge Laurel   Sir J. Cullum 1773

Native. Woods, copses, hedges and old quarries, chiefly on the Chalk and Boulder Clay. A decreasing species, formerly frequent.

W: 64; 66; 67; 74; 75; 76; 83; 84; 85; 86; 87; 93; 95; 96.

76, Moulton, 1980; 87, Culford.

E: 03; 04; 05; 06; 13; 14; 15; 16; 17; 24; 25; 26; 27; 28; 33; 35; 36; 38; 39; 48; 49; 58; 50.

04, Bramford, 1979; 05, Wattisham, 1980; 15, Coddenham, 1980; Stonham Aspal, 1981; 24, Grundisburgh, 1981; 38, Ilketshall St Margaret, 1973; South Elmham All Saints, 1974.

Illustrated page 451

ELEAGNACEAE

OLEASTER FAMILY

Hippophaë rhamnoides L.   Sea Buckthorn   Sir J. Cullum 1773

Possibly native, but usually planted. Found on the coast, cliffs, sandy soils, and in Crag pits. Locally common and spreading.

W: Edge of field at Gt Barton, 1964 (D. J. Mallett).

E: 03; 25; 33; 34; 45; 46; 58; 59.

25, Melton; 33, Bawdsey, 1980; 34, Shottisham; 45, Sudbourne; 46, Thorpeness, (thought to be native) 1978; 58, Kessingland, 1977; 59, Lowestoft; Corton; Gunton.

GUTTIFERAE *(HYPERICACEAE)*

ST JOHN'S WORT FAMILY

Hypericum calycinum L.   Rose of Sharon   Miss Bell 1835
Aaron's Beard

Introduced from S.E. Europe and sometimes well naturalised. Plantations, woods, and roadside banks, where it is frequently planted.

W: 66; 76; 77; 78; 83; 86; 87; 93; 94; 98.

76, Herringswell, 1980; Higham, 1980.

E: 14; 23; 24; 34; 39; 59.

34, Shingle Street, 1981; 39, Bungay, old station, 1981.

Hypericum hircinum L.   Stinking St John's Wort   J. Atkins 1908

Introduced. Native of Mediterranean region. Planted, and occasionally naturalised in woods.

E: Lt. Blakenham (Hb. Atkins).

Hypericum androsaemum L.   Tutsan   Sir J. Cullum 1779

Native. In old woods. Very rare and almost extinct in the County as a native. Usually a garden escape, or planted.

W: 86, Hardwick, near Bury St Edmunds, c. 1932; 87, Elveden; 93, Arger Fen, native, c. 1965.

E: 07, Rickinghall Inferior, c. 1940; 23, Trimley St Mary, outside garden, 1981; 33, Felixstowe, outside garden, 1981; 36, Bruisyard Wood (not seen recently); 37, Holton; 46, Theberton (now believed extinct); 59, Lowestoft.
Recorded in Hind's Flora from Brandon, Clare, Lidgate, Bungay and Weston. There is a specimen in Hb. Atkins from Sproughton (sq. 14) in 1909.

Hypericum hirsutum L.   Hairy St John's Wort   Rev. G. Crabbe 1805

Native. Rough waysides, hedges and woods, chiefly on the Boulder Clay. Frequent in West Suffolk, but distribution restricted in East Suffolk. Not recorded from coastal areas.
W: All squares except 66; 67; 68; 77; 78; 88; 98.
76, Barrow, 1980; 94, Brent Eleigh, 1981.
E: Recorded from squares 04; 05; 06; 07; 14; 15; 16; 25; 34; 36; 37; 48.
04, Hintlesham, 1980; Raydon, 1981; 16, Wetheringsett, 1980.   *Illustrated page 461*

Hypericum pulchrum L.   Slender St John's Wort   J. Andrews 1744
                              Beautiful St John's Wort

Native. Open glades in heathy woods, on sandy or gravelly soils, margins of fens and on heaths. Generally scarce.
W: 77; 83; 87; 93; 94; 95; 96; 97.
77, Tuddenham Fen, 1978; 93, Assington Thicks; 96, Woolpit, 1979.
E: 03; 07; 13; 14; 16; 23; 24; 35; 37; 39; 45; 46; 47; 48; 59; 40; 50.
13, Bentley, 1979; 14, Belstead Wood, 1978; 23, Harkstead, 1980; 35, Tunstall, 1974.
Hb. Ipswich Museum: 'Both sides of the Foxhall Road by the Mill, on the same bank with *H. humifusum*', c. 1810 (John Notcutt). A colony persisted in this area until the mid-1920's, when the banks and verges were destroyed (F. W. Simpson).

Hypericum elodes L.   Marsh St John's Wort   Sir J. Cullum 1775
                            Bog St John's Wort

Native. In wet heaths and bogs. Very scarce.
W: Not recorded recently. Hind recorded it for Tuddenham.
E: 46, Minsmere, 1981; 47, Walberswick, 1981; 59, Lowestoft.   *Illustrated page 488*

Hypericum humifusum L.   Trailing St John's Wort   J. Andrews 1745
                                Creeping St John's Wort

Native. Sandy and gravelly tracks and paths, heaths, commons and woodland glades. Frequent but overlooked.
W: 66; 74; 76; 77; 78; 87; 93; 95; 96; 97; 98.
76, Kentford, 1979.
E: 03; 04; 13; 14; 23; 24; 25; 34; 35; 45; 46; 47; 49; 58; 59; 40.
14, Belstead Wood, 1979; 35, Rendlesham, 1980; 47, Dunwich, 1980; Hinton, 1980.

Hypericum tetrapterum Fr.   Square-stalked St John's Wort   Sir J. Cullum 1773
(*H. quadrangulum* auct.)   St Peter's Wort

Native. In marshes, fens and damp woods, especially on the Boulder Clay. Also in ditches and beside rivers. Common.
W: All squares except 65; 66; 84.
67, Mildenhall, 1977; 94, Brent Eleigh, 1981; 96, Beyton, 1979.

E: All squares except 17; 33; 34; 50.

05, Barking, 1981; 15, Barham, 1979; 23, Chelmondiston, 1978; 39, Mettingham, 1976.

Hypericum undulatum Schousb. ex Willd.   Wavy St John's Wort   R. Burn 1933

Native in a few habitats in S.W. Britain, but probably introduced into Suffolk. In marshes and bogs near streams. Known only from a single record from Polstead.

Hypericum maculatum Crantz ssp. **obtusiusculum** (Tourlet) Hayek
(*H. dubium* Leers   Imperforate St John's Wort   Henslow & Skepper 1860
H. quadrangulum auct.)

Native. In damp places, ditches and open woods. Rare. Its distribution is imperfectly known. Some of the records may be incorrect.

W: 67; 77; 86; 87; 96; 97; 98.

67, Mildenhall, 1939; 86, Gt Livermere, 1980 (Mrs E. M. Hyde); 87, Troston, 1945.

E: 04; 35; 36; 37; 39; 45; 49; 59.

No recent records.

Hypericum perforatum L.   Common St John's Wort   Sir J. Cullum 1773

Native. Wood margins, rough pastures, scrub and hedgerows. Frequent.
All squares.

VIOLACEAE

VIOLET FAMILY

Viola odorata L.   Sweet Violet   Sir J. Cullum 1773

Native. In woods, copses, old pastures, orchards, churchyards and on hedge-banks. More common on light soils. Still very frequent, but has decreased considerably in recent years. The colour and size of the flowers vary considerably. They may be violet, purple, pink, apricot, cream or white. Sweet Violets found growing away from dwellings often have small flowers, more especially in old woods.

The variety with white flowers (var. **dumetorum** (Jord.) Rouy & Foucaud) is more vigorous, with larger flowers and a violet spur. Crosses are frequent between the two varieties and flowers of various colours can be found.

There is another variety of the Sweet Violet with very much larger flowers, up to an inch across, whose colour is best described as a shade of violet-purple. The scent of the flowers is stronger and somewhat different from the usual *V. odorata*. The plant is more vigorous and develops larger leaves. It may be of garden origin, but is not a throw-out in its woodland sites. It is most likely a cross between the wild species and cultivated violets.

All squares except 68; 58; 40; 50.   *Illustrated page 461*

Viola hirta L. ssp. **hirta**   Hairy Violet   Sir J. Cullum 1773

Native. Dry chalky banks, waysides, quarries and the edges of woods and copses on the Boulder Clay. Local and decreasing. Mainly in West Suffolk.

W: All squares except 65; 66; 67; 68; 77; 78; 83; 87; 88; 98.

76, Dalham, 1981; 94, Brent Eleigh, 1981.

E: Recorded from squares 04; 05; 06; 07; 14; 15; 16; 24; 25; 28; 34; 36.

04, Hadleigh, 1980; Hintlesham, 1981; 05, Barking, 1981.   *Illustrated page 492*

A white-flowered form has been recorded from Badley and Combs.

Ssp. **calcarea** (Bab.) E. F. Warb.   Chalk Violet   F. W. Simpson 1950

Native. In dry, chalky places. Rare. The only known records for Suffolk are from the edge of a chalk pit at Fornham St Martin, and from Gt Barton, both sq. 86. This may be only a very small form of *V. hirta* ssp. *hirta*.

Viola hirta × odorata   F. W. Simpson c. 1936
(*V. × permixta* Jord.)

Native. A hybrid with faintly scented flowers, usually having strong growth and runners. Found on banks, margins of woods, old quarries and chalky Boulder Clay scrub.
W: 76, Lt. Saxham; 85, Chadacre; 87, West Stow, 1979; 94, Bildeston; Semer; Lindsey; Chelsworth; 95, Hitcham; Bradfield St George; 96, Hessett.
Few recent records.
E: 04, Whatfield; Nedging; 07, Botesdale, 1976; 14, Bramford (site now destroyed).

VIOLA REICHENBACHIANA AND V. RIVINIANA   WOOD VIOLETS

When primary, or old secondary, woodland is felled or coppiced, a number of forms of Wood Violet usually appear, with flowers of various sizes and shades of blue and violet. Some often have very much larger flowers than normal, with very broad lips and pale, or slightly yellow, spurs. They appear to be hybrids. The majority are usually named as forms or subspecies of *V. riviniana*. These colonies usually only persist for a year or two in the open habitat created by felling and soon die out, owing to the stronger growth of other plants and shrubs.
In the older primary and secondary woodland, especially on the Boulder Clay, and associated with such indigenous plants as Wood Anemone, Primrose, Oxlip and Wood Sorrel, there is another Wood Violet, which blooms in May and early June. It is very regular in the size and growth of its leaves and flowers. The leaves are neat, smallish, usually cordate and when fully expanded, have long stalks. The colour of the flowers is an almost uniform bluish-violet, with violet spurs, having a slightly darker patch on the upper side of the upward-curved tip. The petals are not very wide, but are usually wider than those of the normal *V. reichenbachiana*. This Violet persists in these habitats and is fairly widespread in the County and might therefore be one of our truly native species. It may perhaps be forma *nemorosa* Neuman.

Viola reichenbachiana Jord. ex Bor.   Pale Wood Violet   Mrs Casborne 1830
(*V. sylvestris* Lam., p.p.)

Native. Occurs chiefly in rather open situations on clay soils. Hedge-banks, field margins, ditches, verges, open scrub, wood margins and copses and in areas of recent clearance. Frequent.
The first of the Wood Violets to flower, often commencing in early February. It has rather small flowers of a pale shade of violet.
W: 64; 74; 75; 76; 83; 85; 86; 88; 93; 94; 95; 96.
76, Gt Saxham, 1977; 95, Felshamhall Wood, 1978; Bull's Wood, Cockfield, 1979.
E: 03; 04; 05; 06; 07; 14; 15; 16; 25; 36; 38; 46; 47; 50.
04, Hintlesham, 1981; 24, Gt Bealings, 1981.   *Illustrated page 492*
A pure white-flowered form was found in a wood at Botesdale (sq. 07) in 1976.

Viola reichenbachiana × riviniana　　　　　　　　F. W. Simpson 1957
(*V. intermedia* Rchb., non Krock)

A very variable hybrid. Probably frequent and overlooked.
W: 85, Lawshall; 93, Assington; Stoke-by-Nayland; 94, Groton; Brent Eleigh; 95, Hitcham; Monks' Park Wood.
E: 04, Hintlesham and Ramsey Woods, 1981; Raydon Wood; 05, Gt Bricett; 06, Haughley; 16, Mickfield, 1981.

Viola riviniana Rchb. ssp. **riviniana**　　　Common Wood Violet　　　Sir J. Cullum 1773

Native. Woods, glades, copses, old hedge-banks and heaths, especially on the Boulder Clay, where it is sometimes abundant after a wood has been felled or coppiced. A variable species.
W: All squares except 66; 67; 68; 78.
95, Bradfield Woods, 1980; 96, Pakenham Wood, 1979.
E: All squares except 06; 35; 37; 44; 45.
04, Hintlesham, 1981; 05, Barking, 1981; 15, Gosbeck, 1980.　　　　*Illustrated page 492*

Viola canina L. ssp. **canina**　　　Heath Dog Violet　　　　　C. Rose 1832
　　　　　　　　　　　　　　　　　Heath Violet

Native. On heaths, in woods and in the drier parts of fens. Not very common. Probably often recorded in error for *V. riviniana,* the larger Wood Violet.
W: 67; 76; 77; 78; 83; 86; 87; 88; 95; 97; 98.
78, Wangford Warren, 1980; Lakenheath, 1980; 98, Knettishall, 1981.
E: 03; 04; 07; 13; 14; 24; 27; 35; 36; 37; 38; 39; 45; 46; 47; 58; 50.
07, Wortham, 1980; 14, Belstead; 24, Purdis Heath, 1977; Newbourn, 1981; Martlesham Heath, 1979.
Var. *ericetorum* Rchb. (Heath and Hill Dog Violet) recorded in Victoria County History 1911, as *V. ericetorum* Schrad., without details or location.

Viola stagnina Kit.　　　Fen Violet　　　M. Rutterford and Mrs M. Southwell 1951
(*V. persicifolia* Schreb.)　　Bog Violet

Native. In old, turfy fens. Now extinct, as the habitat has been changed. Recorded only from Lakenheath (sq. 78), where it existed for a few years. Last record, 1968.

Viola palustris L. ssp. **palustris**　　　Marsh Violet　　　　　　　Wigg 1802

Native. Fens, wet heaths, peaty ditches and carrs. Rare and decreasing. Extinct in most former habitats.
E: 47, Walberswick; Hinton, 1980; 49, Herringfleet Marshes; Worlingham; 58, Benacre; 59, Lound; 40, Fritton; Belton; 50.

Viola lutea Huds.　　Mountain Pansy

Recorded in Hind's Flora in 1889 from Barnham Heath and Santon Downham. His specimen was, however, not *V. lutea.* It was probably *V. tricolor* L. ssp. *curtisii.*
This species is usually confined to hilly districts and to sand dunes in a few localities.

VIOLACEAE

Viola tricolor L. ssp. **tricolor**   Wild Pansy   Sir J. Cullum 1773
                                            Heart's-ease
                                            Kiss-at-the-Garden-Gate (Suffolk)

Native. A weed of arable land. Now rare and difficult to find in the County. It has the
same habit of growth, leaf and stem as *V. arvensis,* but its flowers are three to four times
larger and are more attractive. They are carried on long pedicels and the petals usually
have more violet and orange in them. However, it is possible that forms of *V. arvensis*
have been recorded for this plant. It is suggested that its present-day disappearance may be
due to its having been hybridised almost out of existence by *V. arvensis.*
I have seen *V. tricolor* on the Continent as far north as Norway, where it is still common,
but occurs more as a weed of roadside and garden. Since *V. arvensis* is absent from the
area, no hybridisation has taken place.
W: 66; 75; 76; 77; 78; 83; 86; 87; 88; 93; 94; 96; 97.
E: 03; 04; 05; 14; 15; 23; 24; 25; 27; 34; 35; 36; 38; 39; 45; 46; 47; 58; 59.
14, Belstead, 1979; 24, Foxhall, 1977 (F. W. Simpson).
Some of these records may include ssp. *curtisii,* especially those from the Breckland
squares.

Viola tricolor L. ssp. **curtisii** (E. Forst.) Syme   Breckland Pansy F. W. Simpson 1933
                                                            Heath Pansy
                                                            Dune Pansy

Native. Sandy open heaths, disturbed ground and fallow fields, in the Sandlings and
Breckland. Formerly abundant in the Rendlesham/Tunstall/Iken area, now rare or local.
Much confusion and controversy surrounds the correct identification or status of the
plant. The flowers are most attractive, of many colours and shades. This plant appears to
be identical with the often abundant pansies found on sand dunes in many localities in
Britain, though not in such habitats in Suffolk itself. It is a weak perennial, biennial or
annual species. Those with pure yellow flowers are often mistaken for *V. lutea,* which has
not so far been correctly identified in the County. *V. lutea* has larger flowers than any
normal *V. tricolor.* It is probable that crosses between the subspecies are more frequent
than is generally supposed.
W: 77, Eriswell; Icklingham; 78, Lakenheath; 87, Barnham, 1980; 88, Barnham Cross
Common, 1978.
E: 24, Newbourn, 1981; 34, Sutton, 1980; Chillesford; 35, Rendlesham, 1980; Eyke;
Wantisden, 1980; 45, Sudbourne; Iken.   *Illustrated page 492*

Viola × wittrockiana Gams   Garden Pansy   M. A. Hyde 1974
(*V. tricolor* var. *hortensis* auct.)

Introduced. Commonly grown in gardens and found on rubbish tips and in waste places.
The origin of the Garden Pansy is not known with certainty.
W: 76, Moulton, 1981 (F. W. Simpson).
E: 14, Wherstead, 1975; Ipswich, waste ground, various sites, 1981; Gt Blakenham, 1980
(F. W. Simpson); 23, Chelmondiston Tip, 1974.

Viola arvensis Murr.   Field Pansy   Mrs French 1837

Colonist, probably not native. It is still a very common weed of arable fields and is often
abundant in stubble after the harvest. It has small flowers of a light yellow shade, the

upper petals usually tinged with violet or orange. *V. arvensis* exists in various forms and a large number of varieties or subspecies have been described.
All squares.

Viola arvensis × tricolor   F. W. Simpson 1974

In arable fields, especially during early autumn in unburnt stubble after the harvest. Probably overlooked and more frequent than is generally supposed.
W: 78, Brandon.
E: 24, Foxhall, 1974; Playford, 1977.

CISTACEAE

ROCKROSE FAMILY

Cistus laurifolius L.   Laurel-leaved Cistus   M. A. Hyde 1976

Introduced. Native of S.W. Europe.
E: 48, Barsham, two bushes in a roadside cutting. Perhaps planted. Conf. E. J. Clement.

Cistus ladanifer L.   Gum Cistus   E. C. Green c. 1921

Introduced. Native of the Mediterranean region.
E: 13, Martin's Hill Wood, Bentley, where it grew on the edge of the wood, which was cleared and planted with conifers after the Second World War. It survived until about 1952.
Legend says that this shrub was brought from France by the Dominican monks of Dodnash Priory, which was dissolved after the Reformation.

Helianthemum nummularium (L.) Mill.   Common Rockrose   Sir J. Cullum 1773
(*H. chamaecistus* Mill.)

Native. Dry, chalky heaths, banks, waysides and old quarries. Local and scarce. Decreasing. Extinct in many former habitats.
W: 64; 66; 67; 75; 76; 77; 84; 86; 87; 88; 95; 97; 98.
76, Dalham, 1981; Risby, 1980; 77, Worlington, 1981.
E: 14; 17; 24; 36.
Believed to be now extinct in East Suffolk.   *Illustrated page 474*

TAMARICACEAE

TAMARISK FAMILY

Tamarix gallica L.   Tamarisk   Sir T. G. Cullum 1804
(incl. *T. anglica* Webb)

A native of S. Europe and N. Africa. Introduced and planted near the sea and almost naturalised. Some of the Suffolk specimens are very old, such as those planted in the early 19th century at Landguard Fort. There is also another species, **T. africana** Poir., which is seen in gardens, usually near the sea. The attractive flower clusters appear on the woody branches before the leaves. The flowers are a deeper pink than *T. gallica* L.

TAMARICACEAE

E: 13; 14; 23; 24; 33; 34; 44; 45; 46; 47; 59.

13, Brantham, 1974; Stutton; 14, Wherstead Road, Ipswich, 1981; 23, Landguard Fort, 1981; Nacton, 1979; 24, Woodbridge; 33, Felixstowe; Bawdsey, 1981; 34, Ramsholt; Hollesley; 44, Havergate Island, 1979; 45, Aldeburgh; 46, Dunwich; Westleton; Minsmere, 1981; 47, Walberswick; 59, Lowestoft.

FRANKENIACEAE

SEA HEATH FAMILY

Frankenia laevis L.   Sea Heath   Ray 1696

Native. Dry, sandy areas of salt marshes. Very rare.

E: 34, beside R. Ore in salt marshes, Hollesley, 1979; 47, Blythburgh; Walberswick.

Hind records it for Felixstowe Ferry, Southwold and Thorpeness.

Hb. Ipswich Museum: 'Gathered near the Ferry at Southwold, Sept. 1798' (Rev. G. R. Leathes).   *Illustrated page 494*

CUCURBITACEAE

MELON FAMILY

Bryonia cretica L. ssp. **dioica** (Jacq.) Tutin   White Bryony   Sir J. Cullum 1773
(*B. dioica* Jacq.)   Mandrake

Native. Hedges, borders of woods, cliffs, quarries, especially on light soils such as the Red Crag sands. Frequent.

All squares except 68; 48; 57; 58.   *Illustrated page 474*

Citrullus lanatus (Thunb.) Mansfeld   Water Melon   M. A. Hyde 1977

W: 77, Barton Mills Tip, 1977. Detd. E. J. Clement.

Cucurbita pepo L.   Vegetable Marrow   Mrs E. M. Hyde 1971

Annual of garden origin. Native of America. May be found growing on rubbish tips.

E: 15, Coddenham Tip, several well-developed plants in 1971; 23, Chelmondiston Tip, 1971.

Ornamental Gourd

W: 77, Barton Mills Tip, 1977.

E: 23, Chelmondiston Tip, 1971 and 1975.

LYTHRACEAE

LOOSESTRIFE FAMILY

Lythrum salicaria L.   Purple Loosestrife   Sir J. Cullum 1773

Native. Marshes, banks of rivers and ditches. Sometimes clearings in woods. Very frequent.

All squares except 75; 76; 57.   *Illustrated page 487*

LYTHRACEAE

Lythrum junceum Banks & Solander   Greater Grass Poly   C. J. King 1969

Introduced. Native of S.W. Europe and Mediterranean region.
W: 85, casual in garden, Hollybush Green Stud, Chevington.
E: 48, bird-seed alien in garden, Frostenden, 1979 (P. G. Lawson).

Lythrum hyssopifolia L.   Grass Poly   Sir T. G. Cullum 1776

Native or casual. In damp hollows on bare ground, where water has stood. Very rare and uncertain to appear each season. It is a common species in parts of Europe, especially areas bordering the Mediterranean, where it can often be found growing and flowering in profusion on tracks of hard-baked ground which had been flooded during the previous autumn and winter. Although now probably extinct in Suffolk, there are records from Clare (Mr Bemrose, c. 1933), Barrow Bottom, Barton Mere, and Woodbridge (H. K. Airy Shaw, 1933).

Lythrum portula (L.) D. A. Webb   Water Purslane   J. Andrews 1745
(*Peplis portula* L.)

Native. On the edges of ponds and damp tracks in clay woods. Rare.
W: 77, Tuddenham St Mary; Mildenhall; 97, Fakenham Wood.
E: 03, Raydon Wood; 13, Bentley; 24, Foxhall; 47, Blythburgh; 49, Beccles.
Most of these records were made in the 1950's.
Hb. Atkins: specimen from Claydon, 1908.

ONAGRACEAE

WILLOWHERB FAMILY

Circaea lutetiana L.   Common Enchanter's Nightshade   Sir J. Cullum 1773

Native. In woods and copses, often abundant in damp woods on clay and mixed soils.
W: All squares except 66; 67; 68; 78; 88; 98.
76, Barrow, 1977; 94, Groton Wood, 1979; 95, Bull's Wood, Cockfield, 1979.
E: All squares except 33; 45.
13, Holbrook, 1981; 14, Tower Churchyard, Ipswich, 1981; 25, Bromeswell, 1980.

Oenothera biennis L.   Evening Primrose   Dawson Turner 1810

An established alien, native of continental Europe. In waste places, especially on sandy soils. Formerly frequent, but now much less common, and being replaced by *O. erythrosepala*.
W: 76; 77; 78; 86; 87; 88; 93; 96; 98.
E: 03; 04; 13; 14; 23; 24; 33; 36; 37; 39; 45; 46; 48; 49; 58; 59; 40; 50.
Many of the records may refer to *O. erythrosepala*.

Oenothera erythrosepala Borbás   Large-flowered Evening Primrose
(*O. lamarckiana* auct., non Sér.)   C. C. Babington, 1871

An established alien, native in N. America. Grown in gardens. Waste places, such as railway sidings. It has now become frequent.
Much confusion exists between *O. biennis* and *O. erythrosepala*. Hybrids occur between the two species.
W: 66; 67; 75; 77; 78; 88; 93.
66, Herringswell, 1981.

232

E: 04; 13; 14; 16; 23; 24; 25; 33; 35; 36; 45; 46; 47; 48; 49; 59; 40.
13, waste ground at Brantham, 1974; 14, Ipswich, 1981; 25, Bromeswell, 1980; 47, Southwold; Dunwich; 49, Beccles Station, 1980.

Oenothera stricta Ledeb. ex Link   Fragrant Evening Primrose   F. W. Simpson 1946
An introduction, native of Chile. Waste places and sea coast.
E: 23, Chelmondiston Tip, 1975-7; 24, Woodbridge, Broomhill railway cutting; 50, Gorleston, on beach, c. 1974.

Oenothera perangusta Gates var. **rubricalyx** Gates   M. A. Hyde 1975
E: 14, waste ground near Bourne Bridge, Ipswich, 1975-81. Detd. by Dr K. Rostański.

Epilobium angustifolium L.   Rosebay Willowherb   Sutton and Kirby 1787
(*Chamaenerion angustifolium* (L.) Scop.)   Fireweed
Native. Woodland clearings, especially on light soils, burnt heathland and waste places. Very frequent, often abundant and dominant. Formerly rare, and even planted as an ornamental species. About 1925, I observed it to be increasing rapidly in Brookhill Wood, Foxhall. During World War II it became abundant in all burnt and bombed sites, and it acquired the name of Fireweed.
All squares.
At the time of Hind's Flora in 1889, it was evidently a comparatively rare plant in Suffolk, and Hind has only a few recent records, from Mildenhall, Culford, Troston Heath, Belton, Wortham, Gosbeck and Felixstowe.
Sutton and Kirby mention it as being planted by Lord Hertford at Sudbourne Park to control wind erosion.
E. angustifolium and its beautiful white variety are recommended in 'The Garden' of September, 1885, for planting near the margins of lakes and running streams. Also frequently employed for backing mixed borders and shrubberies. A colony of the white variety was found at Exning (sq. 66) in 1977 (F.W.S.).   *Illustrated page 458*

Epilobium hirsutum L.   Great Hairy Willowherb   Sir J. Cullum 1773
                              Codlins and Cream
Native. Marshes, wet places beside rivers, streams and ditches. Sometimes also on dry waste ground. Very frequent.
All squares.   *Illustrated page 484*
White-flowered form at Shelley.
Var. **viride**   F. W. Simpson 1932
A well-marked variety, found on the banks of the Flowton Brook, Flowton (sq. 04), in September 1932, surviving for a number of years until the banks were cleared of their vegetation. Detd. at Kew.

Epilobium hirsutum × parviflorum   John Notcutt c. 1820
(*E. × intermedium* Ruhmer, non Mérat)

Ditches and wet meadows. Rare or overlooked.
The only recent record is from between Cotton and Finningham.
Herbarium specimen, Ipswich Museum, collected in the vicinity of the R. Gipping, c. 1820 (John Notcutt).

Epilobium parviflorum Schreb.   Hoary Willowherb   Rev. G. Crabbe 1798
Small-flowered Hairy Willowherb

Native. Wet places beside streams and rivers, also in marshes and fens. Common.
W: All squares except 64; 65; 67; 68.
77, Tuddenham Fen, 1979.
E: All squares except 07; 26; 27; 28; 35; 44; 40; 50.
14, Ipswich by R. Gipping, 1981; Bramford, 1979; 40, Belton, 1978.

Epilobium montanum L.   Broad-leaved Willowherb   Sir J. Cullum 1773

Native. In woods, pastures, and a frequent garden weed. Common.
All squares.

Epilobium montanum × parviflorum
(*E. × limosum* Schur)

This hybrid has been recorded for the County, but no further details are available.

Epilobium lanceolatum Seb. & Mauri   Spear-leaved Willowherb
Dr S. M. Walters 1955

Native. Dry waste places and waysides. Rare.
W: Lakenheath, 1955.
E: 28, gravel pit near West Lodge, Homersfield, 1961 (E. L. Swann).

Epilobium tetragonum L. ssp. **tetragonum**   Square-stemmed Willowherb
(*E. adnatum* Griseb.)   Sir J. Cullum 1773

Native. In damp woods and beside streams, sometimes a weed of cultivated and waste
ground. Locally frequent, but overlooked. Probably more common than the records
suggest.
W: 74; 76; 83; 85; 86; 87; 98.
E: 06; 14; 23; 34; 35; 36; 39; 46; 58; 59; 50.
14, Brazier's Wood, 1981 (M. A. Hyde).
Hind's Flora, with only eleven records for the County, suggests that it may have been a
rare or local species in the 19th century. There are, however, specimens collected c. 1815 at
Ipswich in Hb. Ipswich Museum (John Notcutt).

Ssp. **lamyi** (F. W. Schultz) Nyman
(*E. lamyi* F. W. Schultz)   Southern Square-stemmed Willowherb

Native. Probably occurs in the County and has been overlooked or confused with ssp.
tetragonum.

Epilobium obscurum Schreb.   Short-fruited Willowherb   Mrs Casborne 1833

Native. In damp woods and wet places. Apparently frequent, but there are few recent
records.
W: 75; 77; 83; 85; 86; 87; 93; 94; 95; 96.
E: 03; 05; 13; 14; 24; 25; 27; 33; 44; 45; 49; 58; 59; 40.

Epilobium roseum Schreb.   Pale Willowherb   First record c. 1950
Small-flowered Willowherb

Native. In damp places, sometimes a garden weed. Scarce. Although there are several records, it is possible that some of them may be errors.
W: 67, Freckenham, 1977; 76, Lt. Saxham; Gt Saxham; Barrow; 86, Chimney Mills, Culford; Ickworth; Fornham All Saints; Fornham St Martin; 88; 94; 98.
E: 05, Needham Market, near the R. Gipping; 25, Hasketon; 36, Yoxford; Gt Glemham; Badingham; 48, Beccles; 59, Lowestoft; 50.

Epilobium palustre L.   Marsh Willowherb   J. Andrews 1745

Native. Bogs, edges of ponds and dykes. Not very frequent and decreasing. It is probable that this species is often confused with small specimens of *E. hirsutum.*
W: 66; 77; 78; 86; 87; 88; 93; 94; 97; 98.
93, Nayland, 1974.
E: 03; 06; 07; 13; 16; 17; 23; 24; 25; 33; 34; 35; 37; 38; 39; 45; 46; 47; 49; 40.
23, Pin Mill, Chelmondiston, 1975; 37, Halesworth, 1976; 39, Bungay, 1980; 40, Belton, 1977.

Epilobium adenocaulon Hausskn.   American Willowherb   Finder not known c. 1952

A naturalised alien, introduced from N. America. Found in woods, waste places, sand and gravel pits, and on cultivated ground. Increasing in Suffolk and may, by now, probably be found in all squares.
W: 66; 74; 76; 77; 83; 86; 87; 88; 94; 95; 97; 98.
66, Herringswell, 1980; 76, Gazeley, 1980.
E: 03; 13; 14; 24; 25; 26; 38; 39; 47; 40.
14, Ipswich, frequent, 1981.

Clarkia unguiculata Lindl.   Annual Clarkia   M. A. Hyde 1974
(*C. elegans* Dougl., non Poir.)

Introduced. Native of California.
E: 14, Belstead Road, Ipswich, 1974; 23, Chelmondiston Tip, 1974.

HALORAGACEAE

WATER-MILFOIL FAMILY

Gunnera tinctoria (Molina) Mirb.   Prickly Rhubarb   F. W. Simpson 1934

Introduced. Native of Chile. Planted and naturalised by lake and in ornamental water-gardens at Fritton Lake.

Myriophyllum verticillatum L.   Whorled Water-milfoil   Ray 1696

Native. Chiefly in marshy dykes, slow-flowing rivers and deep ponds. Uncommon or overlooked.

W: 68; 78; 88.
88, near Euston.
E: 03; 34; 37; 39; 46; 47; 49; 58.
34, Bawdsey, 1970.
Hind's Flora does not record this species from the South-east of the County. There is a specimen in Hb. Ipswich Museum collected August, 1818 'In a broad deep ditch or rivulet near Boss Hall by the river (Gipping), with *Hottonia palustris* and *Hippuris vulgaris'* (John Notcutt).

Myriophyllum spicatum L.   Spiked Water-milfoil   J. Andrews 1745

Native. In ponds, slow-flowing rivers, marsh dykes. Frequent, especially in coastal areas northwards from Minsmere, and in Lothingland.
W: 74; 78; 84; 86; 87; 94; 97.
78, Lakenheath and Eriswell; 97, Ixworth, 1973.
E: 03; 07; 13; 23; 39; 44; 45; 46; 47; 57; 40; 50.
13, Holbrook, 1981 (F. W. Simpson); 23, Shotley, 1981 (Mrs E. M. Hyde); 39, Mettingham, 1976; 45, Thorpeness Mere, 1973; 57, Southwold, 1974.

Myriophyllum alterniflorum DC.   Alternate Water-milfoil   Hind 1876

Native, but uncommon in the East of England. Recorded in Hind's Flora from Market Weston Fen, Livermere and Ampton Lake. The only record in the present century comes from Stoke-by-Nayland (sq. 93) by R. Burn in 1930.

HIPPURIDACEAE

MARE'S TAIL FAMILY

Hippuris vulgaris L.   Mare's Tail   Sir J. Cullum 1775

Native. In rivers, streams, ponds and ditches. Formerly frequent, now decreasing.
W: All squares except 64; 65; 66; 68; 76; 87; 93; 95.
67, Freckenham, 1977; 96, Pakenham, 1979.
E: All squares except 05; 06; 15; 16; 24; 26; 27; 33; 35; 36; 44; 48; 58; 50.
14, in the R. Gipping at Ipswich, 1980; 25, in the R. Deben between Ufford and Wickham Market, 1981; 39, Bungay, 1981.   *Illustrated page 485*

CORNACEAE

DOGWOOD FAMILY

Aucuba japonica Thunb.   Japanese Laurel   F. W. Simpson 1978

Introduced. Native of Japan. Frequently planted, as this shrub can tolerate considerable atmospheric pollution from coal smoke. Berries are bright red. Self-sown or bird-sown seedlings occasionally observed.
14, St Lawrence Churchyard, Ipswich.

Cornus sanguinea L. ssp. **sanguinea**   Dogwood   Sir J. Cullum 1773
(*Thelycrania sanguinea* (L.) Fourr.)   Prickwood (Suffolk)

Native. Hedges, woods and copses, scrub. Very common on the Chalk and Boulder Clay. Less frequent on or absent from sandy soils.
All squares except 68; 77; 33; 34; 44; 57; 58; 59; 40; 50.

Cornus sericea L. F. W. Simpson 1950
(*C. stolonifera* Michx)

Introduced. Native of N. America. Planted and naturalised in damp shrubberies and carrs.
W: 86, Timworth; 98, Knettishall Heath.
E: 13, Woolverstone, 1980; Freston; 23, Nacton, 1981.

ARALIACEAE
IVY FAMILY

Hedera helix L.   Ivy   Sir J. Cullum 1773

Native. Woods, copses, hedges, old buildings. Climbing or creeping, often dominant. Very common. There is much variation in this species. A number of cultivated varieties have been described, some of which may become naturalised in shrubberies or on, or near, sites of former gardens.
All squares.
A variegated form was observed growing wild in Gosbeck Wood in 1973.

Hedera helix var. **hibernica** Kirchin   Irish Ivy   F. W. Simpson 1975
(*H. hibernica* hort.)

Introduced. Found wild in S.W. Ireland. Shrubberies, hedges and copses.
W: 67, Freckenham, 1977; 76, Lt. Saxham, 1976; Dalham, 1980; 77, Mildenhall, 1980; 86, Bury St Edmunds, 1978; 87, West Stow, 1978.
E: 04, Hadleigh; 13, Woolverstone; Harkstead; 14, grounds of Cauldwell Hall, Ipswich; Stoke, Ipswich; Bourne Park, Ipswich; Bramford; Rushmere; Wherstead; 15, Coddenham, 1980; 24, old garden and on ruins of Decoy Keeper's Cottage, Purdis Heath; Playford; Gt Bealings; Foxhall; Newbourn; Woodbridge; 33, abundant and spreading in the grounds of Bawdsey Manor, 1979; Old Felixstowe, 1980; Felixstowe, The Grove; 35, Blaxhall; Snape; 37, Halesworth; 46, Westleton, 1980; 48, Beccles, 1976; 59, Lowestoft, 1980.
All records, unless otherwise stated, 1981, made by Mrs E. M. Hyde and F. W. Simpson.

Hedera colchica (C. Koch) C. Koch   Persian Ivy   F. W. Simpson 1975

Introduced and cultivated in gardens. Native of the Caucasus. Frequently becomes naturalised.
W: 86, Bury St Edmunds, churchyard, 1979.
E: 33, abundant and spreading outside a large garden, Brook Lane, Felixstowe.

UMBELLIFERAE
UMBELLIFER FAMILY

Hydrocotyle vulgaris L.   Marsh Pennywort   Sir J. Cullum 1773

Native. In marshes, swampy woods and on wet heaths. Frequent. Chiefly in the damper parts of Breckland and along the coast.

W: 64; 68; 77; 78; 85; 87; 88; 97; 98.
77, Cavenham and Tuddenham Heaths, 1977; 78, Pashford Poor's Fen, 1980.
E: 03; 07; 13; 14; 24; 25; 35; 36; 38; 39; 45; 46; 47; 48; 49; 58; 59; 40; 50.
24, Purdis Heath, 1981; 45, Snape, 1981; 58, Benacre, 1981.　　*Illustrated page 487*

Sanicula europaea L.　　Wood Sanicle　　　　　　　　　　Sir J. Cullum 1773
Native. Woods and copses, chiefly on the Boulder Clay. Frequent, especially in ancient woods.
W: All squares except 66; 67; 68; 77; 78; 88; 98.
76, Dalham, 1981; Barrow, 1979; 95, Monks' Park Wood, 1980.
E: All squares except 13; 33; 44; 57; 40; 50.
04, Somersham, 1980; Hintlesham, 1981; 24, Hasketon, 1981.

Astrantia major L.　　Pink Masterwort　　　　　　　　　　E. W. Platten 1946
Introduced from S. and C. Europe and occasionally found as a relic of cultivation.
E: 05, Needham Market; 35, Farnham, 1953.

Eryngium maritimum L.　　Sea Holly　　　　　　　　　　　　Gerarde 1597
Native. On sand and shingle beaches. Local. Decreasing and now extinct in some former habitats.
E: 23, Landguard Common, 1980; Erwarton Ness, seedling, 1973; Trimley, 1977; 33, Bawdsey Ferry; Felixstowe Ferry, 1979; 34, Shingle Street; 45, Aldeburgh; 46, Sizewell Gap; Thorpeness; Minsmere, 1980; 47, Southwold; Dunwich; Walberswick; 58, Covehithe; Benacre; Kessingland; Pakefield; 59, Lowestoft; 50, Hopton.
　　　　　　　　　　　　　　　　　　　　　　　　　　　　　Illustrated page 497

Eryngium campestre L.　　Field Eryngo　　　　　　　　　　Buddle 1697
Native. Rough fields, heaths, banks and sea cliffs. Now extinct. Hind records it from the foot of Dunwich Cliffs in 1855/6, lost to erosion, and much earlier on the coast of Lothingland, in 1697. There is a specimen in Hb. Atkins from near Dunwich, 1902. In Hb. Ipswich Museum there is also a specimen, probably collected on Babergh Heath, c. 1820, and another from Hintlesham, 1856. Collectors unknown. Last record 1902.

Chaerophyllum temulentum L.　　Rough Chervil　　　　　　Sir J. Cullum 1773
Native. In hedgerows, banks and open woodland glades, on light soils. Frequent. This species is not as common as *Anthriscus sylvestris,* for which it is sometimes mistaken. It flowers later, is much smaller and can easily be identified by its solid hairy stems, which are purple or purple-spotted.
All squares.

Anthriscus sylvestris (L.) Hoffm.　　Cow Parsley　　　　　Sir J. Cullum 1773
(*Chaerophyllum sylvestre* L.)　　　　Queen Anne's Lace
Native or colonist. Waysides, pastures, woods and plantations. Very common everywhere. The most frequent and first to flower of the Hedge Parsleys.
All squares.

Anthriscus cerefolium (L.) Hoffm.   Garden Chervil   Dawson Turner 1797

Introduced. Native of C. and E. Europe. Usually an escape from cultivation. Formerly eaten as a vegetable. May be found in hedge-banks and waste places. Rare and not found recently. The only Suffolk record since Hind's Flora is from Stone Street, on the way to Peyton Hall, near Hadleigh, c. 1936 (R. Burn).

Hind's Flora contains a single record of the plant from between Halesworth and Wissett, where it was stated to have flourished in a wild state for over 90 years.

Anthriscus caucalis Bieb.   Bur Chervil   Sir T. G. Cullum 1800
(*A. neglecta* Boiss. & Reut.
Chaerophyllum anthriscus (L.) Crantz)

Native or colonist. On dry hedge-banks and waste places. Frequent, sometimes abundant on light soils, especially in Breckland and near the coast.

W: All squares except 64; 65; 66; 83; 84; 85; 95.
E: All squares except 07; 39; 48.

Scandix stellata Banks and Solander   Mrs F. Baker c. 1900
(*S. pinnatifida* Vent.)

A casual from the Mediterranean area recorded from Oulton Broad.

Scandix australis L.   Mrs F. Baker c. 1900

A casual, native of S. Europe. Recorded from Oulton Broad.

Scandix pecten-veneris L.   Shepherd's Needle   Sir J. Cullum 1773
                                   Venus's Comb

Native, or possibly only a colonist. In arable fields, usually on Chalk or Boulder Clay. A common weed up to about 1955. Now almost lost, due to spraying.

E: 05, Creeting St Peter, 1978; 06, Stowupland, 1974-8; 14, near Westerfield, 1981 (M. A. Hyde); 25, Boulge, 1981 (Mrs E. M. Hyde). (05 and 06 records by Mrs O. O. D. Sheppy.) During the period of recording found in all squares except:
W: 65; 66; 67; 76; 77; 87; 88; 96; 97; 98.
E: 03; 07; 17; 23; 26; 28; 33; 34; 35; 44; 46; 49; 40; 50.

Myrrhis odorata (L.) Scop.   Sweet Cicely   J. Atkins 1910

Casual or introduced. Frequent in the North of Britain.
E: 14, Sproughton (Hb. Atkins).

Coriandrum sativum L.   Coriander   Hudson 1762

A casual, native in the Eastern Mediterranean region. In waste places, docks and refuse tips. Introduced with imported birdseed and in sweepings from ships.
W: 93, Boxford.
E: 03, East Bergholt; 05, Stowmarket; Needham Market; 14, Ipswich Docks, 1980; 49, Beccles Tip, 1977; 58, Kessingland.

Bifora radians Bieb.   Mrs F. Baker c. 1890

Casual. Native in S. Europe. Recorded from Oulton Broad.

Smyrnium olusatrum L. Alexanders J. Andrews 1746

Alien, introduced, possibly by the Romans. Native of S. Europe. Naturalised in hedges and waste places, especially near the coast, where it is often abundant and dominant. Increasing. Less frequent inland. Cultivated as a garden vegetable up to the end of the 18th century.

W: 64; 74; 83; 86; 88; 93; 94; 96; 97.

74, Clare, Castle Mound, 1980 (P. G. Lawson); 86, Bury St Edmunds, 1981.

E: All squares.

Abundant in roadside sites inland at Hadleigh, Barham, Rushmere St Andrew and Mutford. *Illustrated page 496*

Conopodium majus (Gouan) Loret Earthnut Sir J. Cullum 1784
Pignut

Native. Parkland, pastures, heaths, woods and churchyards. Less common than formerly, but still fairly frequent.

W: All squares except 64; 65; 66; 67; 68; 74; 75; 78; 96; 98.

86, South Wood, Culford, 1979; 93, Bures, 1979.

E: All squares except 15; 17; 26; 27; 28; 33; 44; 49; 40; 50.

13, Woolverstone, 1981; 24, Rushmere Common, 1981; 46, Aldringham, 1981.

Pimpinella major (L.) Huds. Greater Burnet Saxifrage J. Andrews 1745
(*P. magna* L.)

Native. Old grassy places, marginal habitats around woods, and in wooded glades, especially on calcareous soils. Very local. It may have been more widely distributed in the past. This species is often mistaken for large examples of the variable *P. saxifraga*. In Suffolk, I do not believe that the two species of *Pimpinella* ever occur in the same habitats, although both favour the Chalk or Chalky Boulder Clay. *P. saxifraga* prefers dry, usually open grassy situations, such as commons and churchyards. *P. major*, although seen on some grassy banks and sides of ditches, is considered to be more of a woodland species and where it does occur in such open habitats, is thought to be possibly a relic plant of former woodland. Hind's Flora gives eleven records for the County, but his herbarium specimen from Burgh Castle is a large form of *P. saxifraga*.

W: 64; 65, Gt and Lt. Thurlow, 1976 (Mrs E. M. Hyde and F. W. Simpson); 75; 76, Lt. Saxham, c. 1955; Gt Saxham, 1980 (F.W.S.).

E: 05; 06, Old Newton, 1981 (Mrs J. Harris); 07, Botesdale, 1977 (F.W.S.).

Pimpinella saxifraga L. Lesser Burnet Saxifrage Sir J. Cullum 1774

Native. Waysides, chalk pits, churchyards and grassy places on Chalk and Chalky Boulder Clay. Frequent, but less so than formerly.

W: All squares.

66, Moulton Churchyard, 1981; 74, Clare Country Park, 1976; 76, Dalham Churchyard, 1981; 94, Brent Eleigh, 1981; 96, Pakenham Churchyard, 1981.

E: All squares except 13; 33; 34; 35; 44; 45; 49; 58; 59.

Recent records from Hadleigh, Wetheringsett, Gt Wenham and Mettingham, and churchyards at Aldham, Lt. Wenham, Sproughton, Bramford, Coddenham, Thorndon and Homersfield.

Aegopodium podagraria L. Ground Elder Sir J. Cullum 1773
Goutweed
Bishop's Weed

Probably introduced, and now naturalised. A very troublesome weed in some gardens. Waste places, waysides and plantations.
All squares.

Sium latifolium L. Greater Water Parsnip Sir J. Cullum 1773
Broad-leaved Water Parsnip

Native. In streams, ditches and fens. Now rare. Still occurs in Lothingland and in small quantity elsewhere. Extinct in some of the squares listed below.
W: 68; 77; 78; 88; 93.
E: 03; 05; 13; 17; 34; 35; 39; 47; 49; 40; 50.
17, Palgrave, 1980 (F. W. Simpson); 49, Carlton Colville, 1976.

Berula erecta (Huds.) Coville Lesser Water Parsnip Sir J. Cullum 1773
(*Sium erectum* Huds. Narrow-leaved Water Parsnip
S. angustifolium L.)

Native. In old ditches, fens and marshes. Locally common.
W: All squares except 64; 74; 75; 76.
68, Mildenhall, 1979.
E: All squares except 06; 15; 16; 25; 36; 44; 48; 58.
Frequent in ditches in the Waveney Valley and in the Sizewell area, 1980.

Crithmum maritimum L. Rock Samphire R. Wake 1839

Native. On old shingle beaches. Rare and local. Extinct in some of its former habitats, due to human activities.
E: 23, Landguard Common, (extinct); 33, Felixstowe Ferry, 1980; 34, Shingle Street, 1981; 47, Walberswick; 58, Kessingland; 59, Pakefield.
Former colonies on a shingle ridge at Dunwich and at Boyton are believed to be extinct. Hind's only record of this species is from the sands near Southwold Pier.

Illustrated page 496

Oenanthe fistulosa L. Tubular Water Dropwort J. Andrews 1739

Native. In old, wet pastures, fens, ditches and ponds. Formerly frequent, but now scarce in many areas, especially in West Suffolk. Common in Lothingland and in the Waveney Valley.
W: All squares except 64; 65; 66; 67; 74; 75; 76; 85; 93.
77, Icklingham, 1979.
E: All squares except 04; 05; 13; 15; 17; 24; 25; 28; 33; 44.
26, Framlingham, 1978; 39, Bungay, 1981; 40, Belton, 1977.

Oenanthe pimpinelloides L. Burnet Water Dropwort Mrs E. M. Hyde 1976
Corky-fruited Water Dropwort

Native. On banks and in dry pastures. Rare, though locally abundant. Records for this species in Hind's Flora from west of Bury, Tuddenham Bog, Lakenheath and marshes near Oulton Dyke are all now thought to refer to *O. lachenalii*. Certainly Davy's specimen from Leiston, in Hb. Ipswich Museum, is that species, as is Hind's from Tuddenham Bog (detd. C. E. Salmon). More recent records from Fritton, Belton and Carlton Colville are also believed to be *O. lachenalii*. The Ipswich site is the first confirmed record for the County.

In contrast with other British species of *Oenanthe*, *O. pimpinelloides* favours much drier habitats or those only wet or moist during the winter or early spring. It also flowers much earlier than *O. lachenalii*, in June and early July, several weeks before the other species.
E: 13, Brantham, 1979 (M. A. Hyde), conf. Professor T. G. Tutin; 14, Ipswich, near Bourne Bridge, 1976 (Mrs E. M. Hyde), detd. J. E. Lousley.

Since the Ipswich site will, regrettably, be destroyed through the construction of a new road and bridge, a few seedlings were removed in 1978 and re-planted in Woolverstone.

Illustrated page 482

Oenanthe silaifolia Bieb. Narrow-leaved Water Dropwort Hind's Flora 1889
Sulphurwort

Native. In marshes. Very rare. Probably now extinct, 1981.
W: 83, Shalford Meadows, Lt. Cornard (H. Dixon-Hewitt in 1912/13 and C. E. Ranson in 1974). Last record.

Oenanthe lachenalii C. C. Gmel. Parsley Water Dropwort Davy 1796

Native. Grassy salt marshes, sides of dykes and, rarely, in fens. Not uncommon in the coastal squares, although decreasing.
W: 77; 97.
E: 07, Redgrave Fen, 1977; 13; 23; 24; 34; 35, Blaxhall, 1975; 39; 45, Snape, 1981; 47, Blythburgh, 1980; 49; 57, Reydon and South Cove, 1974, 58, Benacre, 1980; 50.

Illustrated page 482

Oenanthe crocata L. Hemlock Water Dropwort Henslow and Skepper 1860

Native. In marshes and beside streams and rivers. Rare or overlooked. The site mentioned in Henslow and Skepper's Flora was West Stow.
W: 77, R. Lark at Icklingham; 83; 86, marshes of the R. Lark at Hengrave.
E: 23, Pin Mill, near Chelmondiston, since 1936 (R. Burn and F. W. Simpson); Trimley, 1972 (Mrs Curtis); 59, Camps Heath, Oulton, 1977 (A. Copping and P. G. Lawson).

Oenanthe fluviatilis (Bab.) Coleman River Water Dropwort Mrs French 1840

Native. Still occurs in our larger rivers, but has become scarce, as the rivers are often cleaned out too drastically and turned into canals or only drains.
W: 74; 83; 84; 88; 94; 97; 98.
88, in the Little Ouse.
E: 03; 04; 14; 23; 25; 35; 39; 48; 49.
14, in the R. Gipping, between Ipswich and Claydon, 1980; 25, in the R. Deben at Ufford, 1975; 39, Mettingham, 1980.

Oenanthe aquatica (L.) Poir. Fine-leaved Water Dropwort Sir J. Cullum 1773
(*O. phellandrium* Lam.)

Native. In ponds and ditches. Formerly frequent and generally distributed, now rare and disappearing, as its habitats have been rapidly destroyed in recent years.
W: 67; 68; 75; 77; 78; 83; 85; 86; 94; 96; 97.
67, Mildenhall, 1977; 95, Monks' Park Wood, 1980.

E: 05; 06; 14; 15; 17; 26; 27; 36; 38; 46; 47; 48; 49; 59.
06, Haughley, 1976; 15, Crowfield, c. 1960 (R. W. Butcher). See p. 865 in 'A New Illustrated British Flora, Vol. I'; 17, Stoke Ash, 1976; 27, Fressingfield, 1981.

Aethusa cynapium L. Fool's Parsley Sir J. Cullum 1773
Colonist. A common weed of cultivated fields, gardens, waste places and rubbish tips. All squares except 07; 17; 35.

Foeniculum vulgare Mill. Fennel Sir J. Cullum 1774
(*F. officinale* All.)

Colonist or native. Relic of cultivation. A weed of wayside, waste places and the coast, where it is often frequent. Less common inland.
W: 67; 77; 78; 86; 93; 94; 96.
67, Freckenham, 1977; 86, Bury St Edmunds, 1980.
E: All squares except 07; 16; 26; 27; 28.
13, Harkstead, 1981; 14, Ipswich, 1981; 23/33, Felixstowe, 1981; 24, Kesgrave, 1981; 35, Marlesford, 1981; 47, Holton, 1980.

Anethum graveolens L. Dill J. S. Wilkinson 1908
Cultivated. Native of Asia. Recorded as a casual in Ipswich.

Silaum silaus (L.) Schinz & Thell. Pepper Saxifrage John Notcutt c. 1820
(*S. flavescens* (Bernh.) Hayek) Sulphurwort

Native. Old pastures, wayside verges, railway embankments and open woodland. Chiefly confined to the Chalky Boulder Clay areas of the County.
W: 67; 74; 75; 76; 84; 85; 86; 87; 94; 95; 96; 97; 98.
76, Barrow, 1976; 87, Gt Livermere; 96, Elmswell, 1979; 98, Knettishall.
E: 04; 05; 06; 07; 14; 15; 16; 17; 23; 25; 27; 28; 34; 35; 36; 37; 38; 39; 46; 47; 48; 58; 59.
16, Mickfield, 1981; 25, Monewden, 1981. Frequent in parishes west of Halesworth, 1981.
Hb. Ipswich Museum: 'Meadows between the Locks & the lane leading from Handford Hall to New Place,' c. 1820 (John Notcutt).

Conium maculatum L. Hemlock Sir J. Cullum 1773
Native. Beside streams and ditches, in open woods on light soils and alluvium, quarries and waysides. Common.
All squares.

Bupleurum rotundifolium L. Hare's Ear Sir J. Cullum 1773
Thorow-wax

Native or introduced. At one time this was a common weed of cornfields on chalky soils. Now only a casual of waste places and field margins.
W: 87.
E: 23, Felixstowe Docks; 35, Farnham; 36, Badingham; 47, Reydon; 49, Carlton Colville; Worlingham; 59, Oulton Broad.
There are specimens in Hb. Atkins (1907) from 'near Bungay' and 'banks of the Orwell'.

Bupleurum subovatum Link ex Sprengel   Mrs M. Southwell 1950

An alien, native in the Mediterranean region. May be found on rubbish tips or as a garden weed, where cage-bird seed has been thrown away. It is probable that several records for *B. rotundifolium* are incorrect and refer to this species.
W: 78, Lakenheath (old poultry run), 1950; 84, Sudbury, 1966; 85, Chevington, 1969.
E: 14; 25; 26; 49; 59.
14, Ipswich, garden, 1981 (Mrs H. S. Thompson); 25, Wickham Market; Dallinghoo; 26, Brandeston, 1971; 49, Beccles (P. G. Lawson and A. Copping), 1970; 59, Lowestoft, 1976 (P. G. Lawson). Detd. by E. J. Clement.

Bupleurum tenuissimum L.   Slender Hare's Ear   Rev. G. Crabbe 1805

Native. In the drier parts of salt marshes and pastures and on clay embankments. Local.
E: 13, Seafield Bay, Brantham; 23, Shotley, 1980; Erwarton, 1978; Trimley St Mary, 1980; 33, Felixstowe Ferry, 1977; 34, Alderton; Shingle Street, 1980; 44, Orford; Havergate Island; 45, Sudbourne Marshes, beyond Slaughden; 46, Dunwich; 47, Southwold; Walberswick; 40, Bradwell; Breydon South Bank, 1975.

Apium graveolens L.   Wild Celery   Sir J. Cullum 1773
Smallage

Native. Drier parts of salt marshes, beside tidal rivers and ditches. Not very frequent and decreasing. Rare inland in marshes and beside rivers and streams.
W: Lackford; 86, Bury St Edmunds; Fornham St Genevieve; 96, Pakenham; 97, Ixworth; Hopton.
E: 03, East Bergholt; 04; 13, Harkstead; Holbrook, 1980; Woolverstone, 1980; Brantham; 14, R. Orwell banks, 1981; 23, Chelmondiston, 1981; 24, Woodbridge, 1981; 25, Wilford Bridge, Melton; 33, Felixstowe; 34, Shingle Street; 35, Snape, 1981; Wantisden; 45, Aldeburgh; 46, Dunwich; 47, Southwold; 49, Somerleyton; 58, Benacre; 40, Breydon Water; Belton, 1977.

Var. **dulce** (Mill.) DC.   Cultivated Celery   M. A. Hyde 1974
(*A. dulce* Mill.)

Derived from the Wild Celery by selection.
E: 14, Belstead Road, Ipswich, 1974.

Apium nodiflorum (L.) Lag.   Fool's Watercress   Sir J. Cullum 1773

Native. In ditches, streams and beside rivers. Very frequent.
All squares.

Apium inundatum (L.) Reichb. f.   Lesser Marshwort   J. Andrews 1745
Floating Smallage

Native. In ponds and slow moving rivers and streams. Always scarce, now rare or overlooked. There are 11 records in Hind's Flora. The only habitat in which I have observed this species in recent years was in the Black Bourn at Gt Fakenham.
W: 78; 87, Gt Fakenham, 1956.
E: 49, Beccles.

Petroselinum crispum (Mill.) A. W. Hill   Wild Parsley   Wilson 1835
(*P. sativum* Hoffm.)

A naturalised alien, introduced from S. Europe. Often a relic of cultivation. More frequent near the coast. The leaves of the naturalised plant are not curly, as in the cultivated plants.
W: No recent records. Hind gives Bury and Culford Heath.
E: 23, Chelmondiston, 1973-4; 23/33, on verge of new A 45 between Trimley St Martin and Felixstowe, 1980; 24; 33, Felixstowe Ferry, 1980; 34; 45, Aldeburgh, 1976; 47; 57, Southwold Cliffs, 1980.

Petroselinum segetum (L.) Koch   Corn Caraway   E. Skepper 1860
(*Carum segetum* (L.) Benth. ex Hook. f.)   Corn Parsley

Native or colonist. On dry chalky banks, fallow and arable fields. Rare and decreasing. Some of the East Suffolk records may be incorrect.
W: 83; 86; 94; 96.
86, Timworth; 94, roadside at Gt Waldingfield, 1974 (C. E. Ranson).
E: 06; 23; 24; 25; 36; 38; 39; 50.

Sison amomum L.   Stone Parsley   Sir J. Cullum 1773
              Stonewort

Native. On waysides, margins of woods, in old lanes and pastures, chiefly on heavy clay soils. Frequent, but decreasing. More frequent in central and High Suffolk.
W: 74; 75; 83; 84; 85; 86; 88; 93; 94; 95; 96; 97.
74, footpath at Barnardiston, 1976; 96, Pakenham, 1979; 97, Stanton, 1978.
E: 03; 04; 05; 06; 07; 14; 15; 16; 17; 23; 24; 25; 26; 27; 28; 36; 37; 38; 39; 47; 48; 49; 59; 40.
16, Bedingfield, Crowfield and Framsden, 1977; 25, Debach, Boulge and Burgh, 1981; 46, Darsham, 1981.

Cicuta virosa L.   Cowbane   Ray 1696

Native. Sides of ditches and rivers. Rare and decreasing. Now probably restricted to the Lothingland area of North-east Suffolk.
W: Recorded in Hind's Flora from Cavenham, Tuddenham, Brandon, Lakenheath, Wixoe and Kersey.
E: 49, Carlton Colville, 1978; St Olave's; Fritton, 1975; Barnby, 1979; 59, Flixton Run; 40, Fritton; Belton, c. 1952.
Recorded in Hind's Flora from the R. Gipping near Ipswich.

Ammi visnaga (L.) Lam.   P. G. Lawson 1976

Casual. Native of the Mediterranean region.
One specimen in a garden at Reydon. Detd. by E. J. Clement.

Ammi majus L.   False Bishop's Weed   Dr Babington 1876
              Bullwort

An alien. Native in the Mediterranean region. A casual of waste places and cultivated fields. Rare.
W: 96, Pakenham.

E: 14, Ipswich; 23, Landguard Common, c. 1952; Felixstowe Docks, c. 1939; 36, Badingham, in garden, Pound Corner, 1952 (Mrs Cook).

Falcaria vulgaris Bernh.　　Longleaf　　　　　　　Finder unknown 1973

Casual. Native of continental Europe and Asia. Waste places.
E: 04, near Wolves Wood, Hadleigh, 1973.

Carum carvi L.　　Caraway　　　　　　　　　　　Sir J. Cullum 1773

Introduced. Native of N. and C. Europe. The seeds are used as a flavouring and the plant was at one time cultivated in Suffolk. Most of the earlier records probably relate to escapes from cultivation. Hind recorded it from Westley Bottom, Hawstead, near Newmarket Racecourse, Framlingham and in pastures near Bergholt. There is only one recent record.
E: 59, Gunton, 1981 (Dr E. Beaumont, comm. P. G. Lawson). Four plants in rough grass, probably sown.
There is a specimen in Hb. Ipswich Museum from Westley, collected by the Rev. G. R. Leathes, not dated, probably early 19th century.

Angelica sylvestris L.　　Wild Angelica　　　　　Sir J. Cullum 1773

Native. In marshes, fens, and open swampy woods. Frequent.
All squares.　　　　　　　　　　　　　　　　　　*Illustrated page 481*

Angelica archangelica L.　　Garden Angelica　　　　　Merrett 1805
(*Archangelica officinalis* Hoffm.)

Introduced from N. and C. Europe. Formerly cultivated and sometimes naturalised. Rare and not seen recently. The last known record for Suffolk is from Beccles in 1932.

Peucedanum palustre (L.) Moench　　Hog's Fennel　　　　Wigg 1800
　　　　　　　　　　　　　　　　　Milk Parsley

Native. In old marshes and fens, usually among reeds or in open alder carrs, and sides of ditches. Very local or rare. Extinct in some former habitats.
W: 77, The Dolvers, Mildenhall; 78, Turf Fen, Lakenheath, 1976; 98.
E: 38; 47, Walberswick, 1981; 49, North Cove; Fritton; Worlingham; 59, Sprat's Water, Carlton Colville, 1981; 40, Fritton, 1975; Belton, 1978.

Pastinaca sativa L.　　Wild Parsnip　　　　　　Sir J. Cullum 1773
　　　　　　　　　　Common Parsnip

Native. Waysides, waste ground, quarries, scrub, former allotments and gardens. Very frequent. It is sometimes difficult to distinguish which colonies are native and which are relics of cultivation, (var. **edule** DC.) The true Wild Parsnip is more common on the Chalk and the very chalky Boulder Clay.
All squares.

Heracleum sphondylium L.　　Hogweed　　　　　　Sir J. Cullum 1773
　　　　　　　　　　　　　Cow Parsnip
　　　　　　　　　　　　　Cow Mumbles (Suffolk)

Native. Hedges, waysides, rough pastures, lanes and open glades in woods. Very common.

All squares.
Variety with purplish-red flowers and dark fruits recorded in 1981 from Harkstead, Sternfield and Knodishall (F. W. Simpson).

Heracleum mantegazzianum Somm. & Lev.　　　Giant Hogweed　　　F. W. Simpson 1946

An introduced and established alien. Native in the Caucasus. Plantations, roadside verges and by streams. Increasing.
W: 67, Worlington, 1980; 76, Risby; Gt Saxham; 77, Mildenhall, 1980; 86, Bury St Edmunds, 1976; 96, Ixworth; Pakenham, 1976.
E: 06, Stowupland; 13, Woolverstone; Holbrook, 1974; 14, Belstead, 1981; Sproughton Manor, 1975; 24, Playford, 1981; 35, Benhall, 1981; 36, Sternfield, 1981; 45, Aldeburgh, 1980; 46, Thorpeness, 1980; 47, Henham Park; 48, between Beccles and Barsham, 1980.
It is possible that the colony at Benhall Swales, which has been observed since 1946, may have originated from plants growing at Rosehill, Farnham, where it was said to have been introduced about 1890.　　　　　*Illustrated page 512*

Torilis nodosa (L.) Gaertn.　　　Knotted Hedge Parsley　　　Sir J. Cullum 1773
(*Caucalis nodosa* (L.) Scop.)

Native. In dry, open sites. Rather scarce inland, more frequent near the coast, especially on the sea embankments.
W: 76; 77; 78; 83; 86; 87; 96.
76, Risby; 77, Barton Mills; Icklingham.
E: 04; 14; 16; 23; 26; 33; 34; 36; 39; 44; 45; 46; 47; 49; 57; 40; 50.
33, Felixstowe Ferry, 1977; 34, Boyton, 1979; Shingle Street, 1981; 57, Southwold, 1971; 40, Belton, 1977.

Torilis arvensis (Huds.) Link　　　Spreading Hedge Parsley　　　Rev. G. Crabbe 1798
(*Caucalis arvensis* Huds.)　　　Corn Hen's-foot

A colonist of arable fields and waste places. Rare and decreasing. Not seen recently.
W: 77; 87; 88; 97.
77, Mildenhall; Eriswell; 87, Elveden; 97, Ixworth.
E: 03; 04; 06; 14; 36; 39; 58; 59.
14, Ipswich, 1956.
Hb. Ipswich Museum; 'Corn Fields, common. On the site of the towing path between the Locks and Handford Bridge', c. 1820 (John Notcutt).

Torilis japonica (Houtt.) DC.　　　Upright Hedge Parsley　　　Sir J. Cullum 1774
(*Caucalis anthriscus* (L.) Huds.)

Native. In hedges and on the edges of heaths and margins of woods. Frequent and common.
All squares.

Torilis leptophylla (L.) Rchb. f.　　　　　　　　　Mrs F. Baker 1900
(*Caucalis leptophylla* L.)

A casual from S. Europe. The original record was for Oulton Broad.
W: 78, Lakenheath, 1950. Collected by W. Farren from M. G. Rutterford's chicken run. Specimen in Cambridge University Herbarium.

Caucalis platycarpos L. Small Bur Parsley Sir J. Cullum 1773
(*C. daucoides* L.) Small Hen's-foot

A casual. Native in continental Europe. A colonist of fields and waste places, chiefly on dry, chalky soils. Very local.
W: 67, Mildenhall; 77, Mildenhall, near the Mill; 86, Bury St Edmunds; 97, Stanton Chair.
E: 23, Felixstowe Docks, c. 1936 (F. W. Simpson).

Turgenia latifolia (L.) Hoffm. Great Bur Parsley Sir J. Cullum 1771
(*Caucalis latifolia* L.) Broad-leaved Hen's-foot

Casual. Native in C. and S. Europe. Occurs in waste places and arable fields. Rare.
W: 77, Mildenhall, near the Mill; 78, Lakenheath.
E: 03, East Bergholt, in a chicken run.
Recorded in Hind's Flora only from Lt. Saxham and Newmarket.
Hb. Ipswich Museum: specimen from Newmarket, collected by Dawson Turner, c. 1800.

Daucus carota L. ssp. **carota** Wild Carrot Sir J. Cullum 1773

Native. Old grassland, waysides, especially on Chalk and the Boulder Clay. On sea coast cliffs and clay banks. Common. In some habitats a relic of cultivation.
All squares.
Variety without petals, Holbrook Creek, 1978-81 (F. W. Simpson).
Ssp. **sativus** (Hoffm.) Hayek is the cultivated carrot.
Ssp. **gummifer** Hook. f. (*D. gingidium* auct.) recorded from Old Felixstowe Cliffs, c. 1938.

PYROLACEAE

WINTERGREEN FAMILY

Pyrola rotundifolia L. Round-leaved Wintergreen Wigg 1800

Native. Wet heaths. Now probably extinct in Suffolk. Hind recorded it for Bradwell Common, Gorleston, Ashen Spring at Theberton and Middleton, and there is a specimen in Hb. Atkins from Middleton in 1906. This was probably the last record.
Although *P. rotundifolia* has not been recorded in the County since 1906, it may still survive or re-appear in a suitable habitat on a light, sandy, damp and mossy site among Heathers or Dwarf Willows, in the coastal belt of the County. A few such habitats still exist in its old haunts between Leiston and Dunwich and it may also be worth searching the Fritton and Ashby areas.

Monotropa hypopitys L. sensu lato Yellow Bird's Nest D. Stock 1835
(*Hypopitys multiflora* Scop.)

Native. Found in coniferous woods and plantations. Rare. There are two segregates, but it is not known to which segregate our plants belong.
W: 87, Wordwell, 1974 (Z. Gathercole).
There is a specimen in Hb. Atkins from near Bungay, 1907.
Hind records from Ickworth Park, Barnham, Lidgate, Bungay and Redgrave Park.

ERICACEAE

HEAT FAMILY

Erica tetralix L.   Cross-leaved Heath   Sir J. Cullum 1773
                          Bog Heather

Native. Moist heaths and bogs. Very local. Extinct in some former habitats. It is still common on areas of Westleton Heath which are usually dry, especially during the summer months. The plants grow in a thin layer of peaty soil resting on the pebbly Westleton Beds. **W:** 77; 78.
77, Tuddenham and Cavenham Heaths, 1979.
E: 07; 24; 34; 35; 36; 45; 46; 47; 48; 49; 59; 40; 50.
07, Redgrave Fen, 1980; 46, Westleton, 1980; 47, Walberswick, 1979.
Hb. Ipswich Museum: Pakefield, c. 1830 and Westleton Common, August, 1832.

Illustrated page 471

Erica cinerea L.   Bell Heather   Wilson 1833
                         Fine-leaved Heath

Native. Sandy, dry heaths and edges of tracks over former heathland. Locally still abundant, but decreasing. Rare in the west of the County.
W: 77; 86; 96.
77, Icklingham.
E: 07; 14; 24; 25; 34; 35; 37; 38; 39; 45; 46; 47; 48; 49; 57; 58; 59; 40; 50.
24, Rushmere Common, 1981; Purdis Heath, 1981; 34, Hollesley Heath, 1981; 45, Snape Warren, 1981; Iken, 1981; 46, Westleton, 1981; 47, Blythburgh, 1981.

Illustrated page 475

A pale pink-flowered form has been recorded from Snape on a tumulus near the Lodge Gate of Snape Priory, and one with white flowers from Westleton.

Erica erigena R. Ross   Irish Heath
(*E. mediterranea* auct., non L.
E. hibernica (Hook. & Arn.) Syme)

Introduced. Native of W. Ireland, S.W. France and the Iberian Peninsula. Planted in the 1930's on a bank beside the A12 at Marlesford, near Wickham Market. Originated from Notcutt's Nursery, Woodbridge. A frequent garden shrub. Still there, 1980.

Erica erigena × herbacea
(*E. × darleyensis* Bean)

Introduced. Planted in the 1930's on a bank beside the A12 between Martlesham and Woodbridge. Originated from Notcutt's Nursery, Woodbridge. Frequently thought to be one of our uncommon wild flowers, with amateur botanists, and others, collecting specimens for identification as a 'rare find'! Still there, 1981.

Calluna vulgaris (L.) Hull   Ling   Sir J. Cullum 1773
                                   Heather

Native. Heaths, open parts of heathy woods, railway banks. Sometimes dominant. The area of heath and common land forming the habitat for this species has very much decreased in recent years, due to afforestation and cultivation. It is now extinct in former habitats in S.W. Suffolk.

W: 67; 76; 77; 78; 84; 86; 87; 88; 93; 96; 97; 98.

E: 03; 07; 13; 14; 17; 24; 25; 34; 35; 37; 39; 45; 46; 47; 49; 58; 59; 40; 50.

A white-flowered variety has been recorded from Fritton c. 1950, Rushmere Common 1973, and Westleton (Mrs D. Jay), 1953.

Rhododendron ponticum L.   Rhododendron   F. W. Simpson 1921

Introduced and naturalised. A native of S. Europe. Frequently planted in woods and becoming dominant, as in areas around Ashby and Fritton. Widespread and increasing.

Daboecia cantabrica (Huds.) C. Koch   St Dabeoc's Heath   E. R. Long c. 1930
(*D. polifolia* D. Don)

Native in the British Isles, but mainly on heaths and rocky ground in Mayo and West Galway in Ireland. There is one record of the species in Suffolk, from Corton Wood (sq. 59) by E. R. Long; this may well have been a relic of cultivation.

Arbutus unedo L.   Strawberry Tree
                         Arbutus

Native of Mediterranean regions and Ireland. Frequently planted in gardens and shrubberies. Bird-sown specimens are a possibility.

Vaccinium oxycoccos L.   Common Cranberry   T. J. Woodward 1805
(*Oxycoccus palustris* Pers.)

Native. In bogs, but now extinct in Suffolk. Formerly found at Wangford, and Worlingham Common, near Beccles. Extensive quaking bogs once existed at Worlingham, North Cove and Barnby. Last record c. 1810.

Vaccinium uliginosum L.   Great Bilberry
                               Bog Whortleberry

There is a single record for Suffolk by E. R. Long from Barnby (sq. 49), but its occurrence in the County must be considered very doubtful. Although Mr Long was an excellent botanist, it is felt that he may have found the Common Bilberry, *V. myrtillus,* which could very well have occurred in the Barnby area.

Vaccinium myrtillus L.   Common Bilberry

Doubtfully native. There are no authentic records of this species for the County. However, it is possible that small colonies do exist. The most likely districts in which it may occur are Lothingland, on heaths and open dunes in the parishes of Ashby, Barnby, Fritton and Lound, and further south between Dunwich and Westleton.

In Suffolk, the Dewberry (*Rubus caesius*) is sometimes known as the Bilberry. One can understand the reason when comparing the colour of the fruits of both species. They both have a similar bluish or mauve bloom.

PRIMULACEAE

PRIMROSE FAMILY

Primula vulgaris L.   Common Primrose   Sir J. Cullum 1773

Native. In woods, copses, hedgebanks, sides of ditches and on railway banks, chiefly on clays. Frequent, except in Breckland, sometimes abundant in clearings in woods. However it has much decreased in recent years due to destruction of habitats, sprays and removal of plants to gardens. Here soils and conditions are often unsuitable and plants soon die.

P. vulgaris is a colonist of new territory, such as scrub, plantations and orchards, whereas *P. elatior* rarely extends its range and is confined to ancient habitats.

Variations of *P. vulgaris* include var. **caulescens** (Koch) Schinz & Thell., having umbels on a longer raised stalk, instead of their being sessile and radical. This form is uncommon and is sometimes confused with both the Oxlip (*P. elatior*) and the hybrids *P. elatior* × *vulgaris* and *P. veris* × *vulgaris*.

White-flowered forms with a pale yellow 'eye' have been recorded from Brent Eleigh, Bruisyard Wood, Shelland, Polstead, Woolpit, Hintlesham, Harkstead and Chillesford. Plants with pink flowers have been found in woods at Gt Bealings, Hasketon and Hintlesham and one with rose-red flowers at Brent Eleigh. Hybrids with the garden Polyanthus have been observed at Hessett, c. 1954 and Playford, 1981. (All the records made by F. W. Simpson).

All squares except 65; 67; 68; 77.   *Illustrated page 443*

COLOURED PRIMROSES AND HYBRIDS

Coloured Primroses, usually pink shades, can often be seen naturalised among ordinary Primroses in orchards, churchyards and the semi-wild areas surrounding gardens. The flowers of the coloured plants are usually about the same size as those of the wild ones. Coloured plants occasionally occur in woods, copses, ditches and hedgebanks away from gardens, but they usually have much smaller flowers and the pinks are of a rather washed-out shade, and the plants weaker. However, there is another variety with white or cream flowers with a light yellow eye, which frequently grows in woodland glades, which is indigenous and has nothing to do with garden Primroses.

Very rarely, one also finds Oxlips with pink flowers and Cowslips varying from deep pink, almost red, to dark orange and pale yellow, which are obviously hybrids with the garden Primrose or Polyanthus. The caulescent form of the Primrose must not be confused with any of the various hybrids which bear their flowers on stalks.

OXLIP

Distribution of the Oxlip in Suffolk and its Hybrids with the Primrose and Cowslip.

The Oxlip has a very well-defined distribution, occurring mainly in the ancient woods and copses on the higher parts of the Boulder Clay. It can, however, be found in old, wet pastures, alder carrs, willow swamps and borders of streams and rivers which flow from its main area and drain the Boulder Clay.

In 1922 Miller Christy published an article on Primulaceae and its distribution in Britain in 'The Journal of Ecology, Vol. X, No. 2, November, 1922'. The map shows its distribution over the whole of its then known area in Britain. Since then a number of new sites have been discovered, which have considerably extended its range. It is likely that the Oxlip extended over more eastern areas of High Suffolk, before the ancient woodland was cleared and specimens may be found in out-of-the-way places and possibly on the banks of streams. Some of the outlying localities may once have been contained within the main area of distribution, as, for example, the sites at Gipping Woods. These ancient woods obviously formed part of the main Oxlip area, although seemingly separated by the Gipping Valley.

Plants can be found in the meadows, swamps and old osier plantations north of Stowmarket at Haughley and Old Newton. Miller Christy's map shows the main northern boundary to be just south of the A45; this is incorrect, as I have been able to trace the Oxlip in a large area north of the A45 and the Bury Railway line.

The line of the Oxlip can be traced through Wetherden, Elmswell and Stowlangtoft to Livermere. It has, however, disappeared from a number of sites in recent years, as woods have been destroyed. At one time it was probably abundant in woods at Stowlangtoft. Very little is left of the once extensive East Wood, Elmswell, where the Oxlip was common, as also in Dairy Grove. The site at Livermere Thicks has been destroyed.

It is likely that its range extended northwards on the Boulder Clay to Honington and there are a number of records from Sapiston, Ixworth Thorpe, and Walsham. The habitats where some specimens were found were probably valley sites. Hind records it from Fakenham Wood, where he reported it as 'tolerably abundant' and where 'occasionally hybrids with *Primula vulgaris* and *P. veris* occur'. I have searched this fine, extensive wood several times and have so far been unable to find a single specimen of the Oxlip, or any of its hybrids with the Primrose. It could be possible that they have died out, although I think it unlikely. The woods are on elevated ground and the soil is suitable chalky Boulder Clay. The Oxlip has died out in a number of woods in recent years, as at Pakenham and Beyton.

It is not uncommon in the valley of the River Lark and its tributaries, north and north-west of Bury, at Fornham, Culford, Timworth and Cavenham and a number of sites near Mildenhall. Up to about 1940 in the Rat Valley, between Onehouse and Combs, the old pastures were often yellow with thousands of Oxlips. It is possible that its range once extended down the Gipping Valley, perhaps almost as far as Baylham.

It did occur, and still may do so, at Badley. East of Needham Market it occurs at Gosbeck in an ancient wood and I have seen specimens further east at Great Bealings, again in a small ancient wood on the Boulder Clay. Its range extends further south than shown on Miller Christy's map, through Elmsett, where it was abundant in the former Lucy Wood. Westward it grows at Whatfield and across the Brett Valley in Milden Thicks and Little Waldingfield.

Miller Christy states that the Oxlip has been found at Botesdale and Rickinghall, although these are unconfirmed records. I have searched the parishes several times without success, as also did the late Arthur Mayfield. However, it could still be found in the area, if a thorough search were made, as there are a number of suitable sites. Botesdale is, of course, only a few miles from its station at Dickleburgh, Norfolk, on the north side of the Waveney. It is, therefore, probable that the Oxlip area once extended as far north as the Waveney and its original distribution in the County was probably almost twice the area as shown on Miller Christy's map.

Although the Oxlip prefers chalky Boulder Clay, I have never found it growing actually on chalk deposits. It is to be found at Dalham and Gazeley, which are in areas not shown by Miller Christy, right to the point where the chalk comes to the surface.

In the Breckland area of West Suffolk, the Oxlip occurs only in the valleys, growing where the soil is peaty alluvium, which contains a calcareous material derived from the streams which flow from the Boulder Clay. The habitats are boggy meadows or swampy woods, or on the banks of streams and rivers. Miller Christy records it at Westley, — a batch of plants that was found in Old Warren Wood in 1911. The soil of the wood is mainly light, as it is on the edge of the Breckland area. However, there must be traces of Boulder Clay. For a number of years I frequently searched the wood without success, until it was clear-felled in the early 1960's. The Oxlip does occur on quite light Boulder Clay at Barrow and Denham. The Tostock site mentioned by Miller Christy was a boggy meadow near the railway line, and the Oxlip grew there until the site was drained and ploughed up in about 1950.

At one time the Oxlip grew in the greatest abundance in a large number of woodland habitats, and with Dog's Mercury was almost the dominant plant of the ground flora. In favourable seasons, when the flower buds were not attacked by birds, the flowers presented a sight of unparalleled beauty and filled the whole atmosphere with a scent like apricots. Very few woods and copses exist today where such a profusion of flowers can be seen. The growth and flowering of the Oxlip was encouraged by the management and coppicing of the woods, although there are some instances where the Oxlip has occurred in similar profusion in woods where coppicing has not taken place for many years.

At one time, in the main Oxlip area, there was a large number of pure Oxlip woods and copses; that is, woods where no Primroses occurred and in all parishes where the Oxlip occurred, the Primrose was absent. There are still quite a number of woods and copses today where the Oxlip is dominant, but the Primrose seems to have invaded the majority of its habitats. Where both Primrose and Oxlip occur, hybrids are frequent. Miller Christy asserted the belief that the Primrose was hybridising the Oxlip out of existence. There seems to me to be some positive truth in this statement, as I have observed woods and copses, where once only Oxlips occurred, invaded by Primroses, which hybridised with the Oxlip. The true Oxlip became rare and eventually disappeared.

Oxlip-Primrose hybrids are exceedingly variable and almost every conceivable form can be found between the species. There are some which might be mistaken for Primroses, or even pure Oxlips. The hybrids are most attractive and strongly-scented. The Oxlip does vary in the size and colour of its flowers and sometimes one can observe pure Oxlips, which can easily be mistaken for hybrid forms, near to the Primrose. These Oxlips produce single flowers early in the season. It is also possible to mistake caulescent Primroses for hybrids. Although the flowers are borne in umbels, this form of the Primrose must not be confused with the False Oxlip.

On the edges of woods and copses, and in damp pastures within the Oxlip district, where the Cowslip also occurs, hybrids with the Cowslip can occasionally be found, but they are now distinctly rare or local.

Oxlip hybrids are not sterile and occasionally I have observed specimens which I have considered to be tertiary hybrids — that is, hybrids between the three species, Oxlip, Primrose and Cowslip. They bear characteristics of the three species and some experiments which I conducted by hybridising Oxlip and Primrose hybrids with pollen from Cowslips, produced plants which were almost identical with those observed in the field.

Coloured Oxlip hybrids are very rare; they are evidently produced by pollen brought by the bees from Garden Primroses. Occasionally one can also find hybrids which appear to have Garden Polyanthus strains.

Many naturalists frequently confuse the False Oxlip (*P. veris* × *vulgaris*), that is, the hybrid between the Cowslip and the Primrose. It occurs fairly frequently where Cowslips and Primroses grow in association; it is also a very variable hybrid and almost every conceivable form can be found between the species. The flowers are usually Cowslip-coloured rather than Primrose-coloured, although I have found pale forms. Occasionally hybrids occur with pink or even dark rose-coloured flowers. These obviously have some connection with the garden Primrose or Polyanthus. At one time, when the Suffolk meadows and pastures had abundant Cowslips, the various hybrids were quite common and were called 'Five Fingers'. However, I consider that this name can be best referred to the true Oxlip.

Primula elatior (L.) Hill   Oxlip   Ray 1960
                                Five Fingers
                                Paigle

Native. Old woods, copses, sides of streams and ditches, ancient wet pastures, marshes and alder carrs. Almost confined to the Chalky Boulder Clay, where it is sometimes abundant and dominant.
W: All squares except 66; 67; 68; 78; 88; 93; 98.
95, Bull's Woods, Cockfield, 1981; Bradfield Woods, 1981.
E: Recorded from squares 04; 05; 06; 15; 24.
05, Combs; Gt Finborough; Onehouse, 1981.   *Illustrated pages 444 and 445*

Primula elatior × vulgaris   Hybrid Oxlip   F. W. Simpson 1929
(*P.* × *digenea* A. Kerner)   Hybrid Paigle

Found in woods, copses and very old wet pastures, where the two species occur together, or near to one another. A common hybrid, but very variable, and every form or intermediate can be found between the two species. Some of the hybrids are most attractive and rival the cultivated garden Polyanthus. Very rarely, pink or orange-flowered forms can be found, which are obviously crosses with garden flowers. These hybrids should not be confused with the False Oxlip, *P. veris* × *vulgaris.*
W: 76, Saxham; 84, Stanstead; 85, Lawshall; Gt Welnetham; Shimpling; 86, Ickworth; 94, Lavenham; Gt Waldingfield; Brent Eleigh; Kettlebaston; 95, Cockfield Rectory; Bradfield St George; Buxhall; Gedding; 96, Beyton; Woolpit; Drinkstone; Tostock; Hessett.
E: 04, Willisham; Bricett; 05, Gt Finborough; Shelland; Badley; Combs; Barking; 06, Gt Ashfield; 15, Gosbeck; 24, Gt Bealings, 1979.   *Illustrated page 444*

Primula elatior × veris   R. Burn c. 1932
(*P.* × *media* Petermann)

A rare hybrid, found on the margins of woods and copses and small wet pastures in the Oxlip (*P. elatior*) area and where the parents occur together. The hybrids vary considerably, some being more like one parent. All possess a strong and pleasant scent resembling Cowslips, or even apricots.
W: 75, Chevington; 94, Kettlebaston; 95, Bradfield St George; Rattlesden; 96, Drinkstone; Hessett.
E: 04, Elmsett; Gt Bricett; 05, Gt Finborough; Badley; Ringshall; 06, Gipping.

Primula elatior × veris × vulgaris   Oxlip-Cowslip-Primrose Hybrid
(*P.* × *murbeckii* Lindquist)   F. W. Simpson 1935

Margins of woods, copses and pastures within the Oxlip area. Very rare or overlooked. For a number of years this tertiary hybrid was thought to occur occasionally with the colonies of the hybrid *P. elatior* × *vulgaris.* Some hybrids I found seemed to exhibit the characteristics of the three parents. Plants of *P. elatior* × *vulgaris* were grown in pots and the flowers fertilised with the pollen of *P. veris.* Some seed was collected and germinated and the resulting plants matched the wild hybrids in their habit of growth and the colour and shape of their flowers. Some of the hybrids could easily have been mistaken for *P. veris* × *vulgaris* crosses.
W: 84, Long Melford; 95, Bradfield St George.

Primula veris L.   Cowslip   Sir J. Cullum 1773
Paigle

Native. Old grasslands, waysides, hedge-banks, railway embankments and cuttings, lanes, marginal land and scrub. Rare in woods, except in very open glades. Chiefly on the Boulder Clay and Chalk. Found occasionally on the Red and Coralline Crags. Rare in, or absent from, some of the coastal areas, especially the Shotley Peninsula and also from Breckland. A colony occurs in a small valley wood at Cavenham with *P. elatior.*
Formerly abundant, now rapidly decreasing, due to intensive farming, and likely to become far more local and restricted. The Cowslip can become almost a weed of neglected farmland in the Boulder Clay area. Pink, rose, and other coloured flowers are rare and these are probably crossings with garden Polyanthus. Recorded from Theberton (sq. 46), Tattingstone (sq. 13), on the Red Crag, and in 1981 from Stonham Aspal (sq. 15).
All squares except 67; 68; 23; 33; 50.   *Illustrated page 444*

Primula veris × vulgaris   Ladies' Fingers   Collector unknown 1842
(*P.* × *variabilis* Goupil, non Bast.)   False Oxlip

A frequent hybrid where Cowslips and Primroses grow together. Coloured hybrids occur occasionally; these are the result of crosses with the garden Primrose or Polyanthus. Much confused with the Oxlip.
W: 84; 85; 87; 93; 94; 95; 96; 97.
96, Hessett, 1979.
E: 04; 05; 06; 07; 15; 16; 24; 25; 26; 28; 36; 38; 59.
04, Hintlesham, 1981; 05, Barking Churchyard, 1981 (R. Mabey); 24, Culpho, 1981.
Hb. Ipswich Museum; a specimen from near Needham, 1842.   *Illustrated page 444*

Primula farinosa L.   Bird's-eye Primrose   Henslow & Skepper 1860

Native. In damp, grassy, old pastures and wet heaths. Recorded in Henslow & Skepper's Flora as having been found at East Bergholt and Cavenham Severals. Although no herbarium specimens have been found and the species is now confined to Northern counties, there is a possibility that this attractive little *Primula* did occur in Suffolk. Both the authors of this Flora were excellent botanists of the period. Great changes were taking place in the County, especially in the drainage of poorer land and old marshes and fens. Loss of habitats even then was having its effect on several rare species, which were becoming, or were already, almost extinct. There are several species with a generally Northern distribution occurring in East Anglia and the southern counties. *Trientalis*

PRIMULACEAE

europaea L., is an example which has been found in the North of our County and is probably indigenous. Others no doubt occurred at one time and were unrecorded. The chances of finding other relic species are now very slender.

Hottonia palustris L.   Water Violet   Sir J. Cullum 1773

Native. In ponds, ditches and slow-flowing rivers. Frequent in Lothingland, but now scarce over most of the County where formerly common, due to pollution, drainage and destruction of habitats. Up to 1940 this beautiful aquatic was to be found in almost every ditch and pond bordering the R. Gipping, even in the river at Handford Bridge, Ipswich.
W: 68, Lakenheath; 77, Mildenhall; Barton Mills; 78, Lakenheath; 84, Rodbridge, near Long Melford; 87, Fakenham; 96, Tostock and Norton.
E: 06; 07, Thelnetham; 14, Bramford; Ipswich; 25, Letheringham; Hoo; 35, Farnham; 36; 37, Halesworth; 38, South Elmham; 39, Barsham; Mettingham, 1980; Bungay, 1980; 45; 46, Darsham; Leiston; 47, Blythburgh, 1980; 48; 49, Oulton; Beccles; Carlton Colville; Worlingham; 59, Lowestoft; Gunton; 40, Fritton.
Hb. Ipswich Museum: 'Ditches by Boss Hall plentifully', c. 1810 (John Notcutt).

Illustrated page 488

Cyclamen hederifolium Ait.   Cyclamen   Davy 1799
(*C. neapolitanum* Ten.)   Sowbread

Introduced from C. and S. Europe. Naturalised in old gardens, plantations and woods. Very rare.
W: 94 (introduced).
E: 36, Rosehill gardens, Benhall (introduced); 59, Oulton Broad.
Specimens of leaves in Hb. Ipswich Museum from Bramfield, collected by Rev. G. R. Leathes c. 1800. This was probably the habitat recorded in Hind's Flora, which also noted that it grew in Henham Park and Abbey Wood, Sibton.

Lysimachia nemorum L.   Yellow Pimpernel   Sir J. Cullum 1773

Native. In shady woodland glades and tracks, especially in the old Boulder Clay woods, where it is locally common. Scarce elsewhere.
W: 75; 76; 86; 87; 93; 94; 95; 96; 97.
94, Brent Eleigh, 1981; 95, Monks' Park and Felshamhall Wood, 1980;
E: 03; 04; 05; 06; 07; 13; 14; 15; 17; 23; 24; 25; 27; 34; 35; 36; 37; 39; 46; 47; 48; 57; 58; 59; 40.
Woodland paths at Belstead, Bentley, Freston and Holbrook in 1981.

Illustrated page 453

Lysimachia vulgaris L.   Yellow Loosestrife   J. Andrews 1744

Native. In marshes, fens, and beside rivers and dykes. Not very frequent and decreasing.
W: 67; 68; 76; 77; 78; 83; 85; 87; 88; 93; 94; 96; 98.
67, Mildenhall, 1980; 77, Tuddenham Fen, 1980; 83, Cornard Mere, 1981.
E: 03; 07; 14; 16; 24; 25; 26; 27; 34; 35; 36; 38; 44; 45; 47; 48; 49; 58; 59; 40.
35, Blaxhall, 1980 (Mrs I. M. Vaughan); 59, Oulton, 1976 (P. G. Lawson). It is probably now extinct in some of the East Suffolk squares.   *Illustrated page 487*

Lysimachia nummularia L.   Creeping Jenny   Sir J. Cullum 1773
                                 Moneywort

Native. Old damp pastures, sides of ditches, woodland tracks and margins of pools. Was

256

fairly frequent, but has decreased in recent years, and is now scarce and perhaps extinct in many districts.

W: All squares except 66; 67; 68; 77.

94, Brent Eleigh, 1981; 95, Monks' Park and Felshamhall Wood, 1980; 96 Pakenham Wood, 1978.

E: All squares except 03; 23; 28; 33; 37; 44; 45; 47; 58; 50.

04, Raydon Wood, 1981; Somersham, 1980; Hintlesham, 1981; 05, Barking, 1981.

Illustrated page 454

Lysimachia punctata L.　　Dotted Loosestrife　　　　　F. W. Simpson 1952

A garden introduction. Native of Austria, the Caucasus and Asia Minor. Sometimes escaping and spreading, becoming naturalised in damp places and beside ponds and rivers.

W: 86, waste ground, Bury St Edmunds, 1980.

E: 06, Bacton; 14, waste ground, Neale Street, Ipswich, 1976; 23, Landguard Common, 1973; 24, Foxhall, 1975; Purdis Heath, 1977; 35, Snape; 45, Aldeburgh; 46, Thorpeness.

Trientalis europaea L.　　Chickweed Wintergreen　　　　　Dr F. Rose 1955

Native. Typically found in mossy places, in pine woods. Locally common in Scotland, scarce in the North of England. The first record for Suffolk was in an area of sphagnum moss on Ashby Warren, near Somerleyton (sq. 40). It was further recorded in the same area in 1962 and 1973.

Glaux maritima L.　　Sea Milkwort　　　　　Sir J. Cullum 1773

Native. Salt marshes, usually the drier areas. Also on damp, sandy and shingle beaches, especially those of estuaries just above the high tide mark. Common in all suitable habitats.

E: 03; 13; 14; 23; 24; 25; 33; 34; 35; 44; 45; 46; 47; 49; 57; 58; 59; 40; 50.

13, Harkstead, 1981; 23, Pin Mill, 1981; 45, Snape, 1981.　　*Illustrated page 504*

Anagallis minima (L.) E. H. L. Krause　　Chaffweed　　　　　Wigg 1805
(*Centunculus minimus* L.)

Native. On damp, sandy tracks on heaths and open places. Very rare and not seen recently, but perhaps overlooked. Last record 1955.

W: 77, Tuddenham Heath; West Stow, 1955; 78, Wangford.

E: 13; 23; 25; 47; 49; 59; 40.

13, East Bergholt; 23, Levington; 49, Herringfleet, c. 1800 (specimen in Hb. Ipswich Museum, Rev. G. R. Leathes); 59, Oulton Broad; 40, Belton.

Anagallis tenella (L.) L.　　Bog Pimpernel　　　　　Sir J. Cullum 1773

Native. In bogs, fens and old wet heathy pastures. Rare and decreasing.

W: 77; 78; 98.

77, Tuddenham Heath, 1978.

E: 07; 17; 24; 25; 27; 35; 38; 46; 47; 49; 58; 59; 40; 50.

46, Sizewell, c. 1970; 47, Blythburgh, 1979.

Hb. Ipswich Museum, specimen from Burstall, 1833. Hb. Atkins: 24, Bixley, 1908.

Illustrated page 487

Anagallis arvensis L.   Scarlet Pimpernel   Sir J. Cullum 1733
Poor Man's Weather-glass
Shepherd's Sundial (Suffolk)

Probably native on the sea coast, on sand dunes and sandy cliffs. Elsewhere a colonist of arable land, gardens, waste places. Very frequent. Various colour forms occur.
All squares.
A form with lilac flowers was recorded from Snape in 1975, and one with intense blue flowers from Tunstall in 1981.

Anagallis foemina Mill.   Blue Pimpernel   J. Andrews 1738
(*A. caerulea* Schreb., non L.
A. arvensis ssp. *foemina* (Mill.) Schinz & Thell.)

An uncommon casual or garden escape. This may be mistaken for colour variations of *A. arvensis*.
W: 78, Lakenheath, 1957 (M. G. Rutterford); 93, Newton Green, 1941 (B. M. Warner).
E: 16, Mendlesham, 1902 (A. Mayfield).

Samolus valerandi L.   Brookweed   Sir J. Cullum 1773

Native. Fens, marshes and sides of ditches, often near the sea. Formerly frequent, now scarce and absent from many areas.
W: 67; 77; 78; 83; 88; 96.
67, Mildenhall, 1977.
E: 03; 07; 13; 23; 24; 33; 34; 35; 39; 45; 46; 47; 49; 58; 59; 40; 50.
34, Ramsholt, 1976; 46, East Bridge, 1980; 58, Benacre, 1977; 59, Oulton, 1978 (P. G. Lawson).
Hb. Ipswich Museum: 'Corner of a meadow between Stoke Bridge and the Locks, close to the second Flood gate within the flux of the Salt river', c. 1810 (John Notcutt).

PLUMBAGINACEAE

SEA LAVENDER FAMILY

Armeria maritima (Mill.) Willd.   Thrift   Sir J. Cullum 1773
(*Statice armeria* L.)   Sea Pink

Native. Frequent, especially in salt marshes and on the drier, grassy ridges and old shingle beaches of the Orford area, where it is sometimes abundant and dominant. There is considerable variation in the colour of the flowers from very pale pink to dark pink. White-flowered specimens were recorded from Boyton and Sudbourne.
E: 13; 14; 23; 24; 25; 33; 34; 35; 44; 45; 46; 47; 57; 59.
13, Holbrook Creek, 1981; 14, Wherstead, 1981; Nacton, 1981; 45, Snape, 1981.

Illustrated page 495

Limonium vulgare Mill.   Common Sea Lavender   Sutton & Kirby 1787
Native. Found in salt marshes, where it is often abundant and dominant.
Variable; those forms found growing on the older and drier zones are much larger and have been named forma *pyramidale* C. E. Salmon (*Statice pyramidalis* Syme). Flowering stems more lax.

E: 03; 13; 14; 23; 24; 25; 33; 34; 35; 44; 45; 46; 47; 57; 58; 40.

Common up the coast from the Stour Estuary to the Blyth Estuary. Rare north of Southwold. *Illustrated page 497*

Limonium humile Mill.　　Lax-flowered Sea Lavender　　　　Woodward 1807
(*Statice bahusiensis* Fries)

Native. Found in salt marshes, now scarce and decreasing, as many of its habitats have been invaded by *Spartina* grass.

E: 13, Holbrook, 1981; Cattawade; Stutton; Brantham; Harkstead, 1981; 14, Wherstead, 1981; 23, Chelmondiston; 34, Sutton Marshes; 44, Lantern Marshes, Orford.

Hb. Ipswich Museum: 'On the east side of the wall between the Ostrich and Freston Brook. On the shore between Hog Island and Downham Reach' c. 1820 (John Notcutt).

Illustrated page 497

Limonium humile × vulgare　　Hybrid Sea Lavender　　　　F. W. Simpson c. 1937
(*L. × neumanii* C. E. Salmon)

In salt marshes. Rare.

E: 13, Holbrook Creek; Harkstead, 1981; 23, Chelmondiston; 34, Sutton; 44, Orford.

Limonium bellidifolium (Gouan) Dum.　　Matted Sea Lavender
(*Statice bellidifolia* (Gouan) DC.)

Native. May occur on margins of salt marshes. Although it is said to have been found in Suffolk, I have not so far been able to trace any authentic specimens. I have searched all suitable habitats in the County. It is possible that it did occur at one time, but is now extinct. The species is still frequent in parts of Norfolk.

It is named as *S. caspia* in Hind's Flora, quoting three authorities, but giving no localities. Hind concluded that the records were errors.

Limonium binervosum (G. E. Sm.) C. E. Salmon　　Rock Sea Lavender
(*Statice binervosa* G. E. Sm.)　　　　　　　　　　　　F. W. Simpson 1960

Native. Dry salt marshes, with sand and shingle. Very rare.

E: 34, Boyton, 1960, still there, 1979; 44, Havergate Island, 1979.

Possibly occurs elsewhere, overlooked.

OLEACEAE

OLIVE FAMILY

Jasminum officinale L.　　Jasmine　　　　　　　　　F. W. Simpson 1967

Introduced. Native of S.W. Asia. Grown in gardens and occasionally naturalised, usually on sites of former gardens.

E: 14, site of garden, Commercial Road, Ipswich, 1967; Wolsey Street, Ipswich, 1981 (Mrs E. M. Hyde).

Fraxinus excelsior L.　　Ash　　　　　　　　　　　Sir J. Cullum 1773

Native. Woods, copses, plantations and hedges. Common, especially on clay soils. Natural regeneration is very frequent.

All squares.

Var. **pendula** Ait., the weeping form, is frequently planted in parks and gardens.

Syringa vulgaris L.　　Lilac　　　　　　　　　　　　F. W. Simpson 1922

Introduced from S.E. Europe. Found planted in hedges and shrubberies or on the sites of former gardens. Frequent, especially in Breckland.

W: 66; 67; 76; 77; 78; 86; 87; 88; 93; 96; 97; 98.

76, Gazeley, 1981; 86, Culford, 1981.

E: 03; 06; 07; 13; 14; 16; 23; 24; 35; 45; 46; 47.

14, railway embankment, Derby Road, Ipswich, 1981; 24, Foxhall, 1981.

Ligustrum vulgare L.　　Wild Privet　　　　　　　　　　Sir J. Cullum 1773

Native. In woods, copses, hedges, chalk-pits and a few carrs. Planted or introduced, though probably wild on the Chalk. Many of the records probably refer to *L. ovalifolium*.

W: All squares.

76, Herringswell, Moulton, Dalham, all 1981; 84, Acton, 1980.

E: All squares except 59.

14, Lt. Blakenham, 1976; 15, Barham, 1977; Coddenham, 1980; 27, Syleham, 1980.

Ligustrum ovalifolium Hassk.　　Garden Privet

An alien, introduced from Japan and now naturalised in many areas. Bird-sown specimens may be found in a few places. This is the species which is usually planted for garden hedges. It has much larger leaves than the Wild Privet, and they do not fall so much during the autumn and winter months.

Many of the records for *L. vulgare* probably refer to this species.

GENTIANACEAE

GENTIAN FAMILY

Blackstonia perfoliata (L.) Huds.　　Yellow-wort　　　　J. Andrews 1744
(*Chlora perfoliata* (L.) L.)

Native. On chalky soils in open grassy places, scrub, quarries and on railway embankments. Not very frequent and decreasing.

W: 64; 76; 77; 84; 85; 86; 94; 95.

84, Acton, 1979.

E: 04; 05; 06; 14; 17; 25; 33; 35; 36; 37; 46; 47; 59.

36, Saxmundham, on railway bank, 1974; 46, Darsham, 1980.

Specimen in Hb. Ipswich Museum from the once extensive Babergh Heath, near Gt Waldingfield, in 1824.　　　　　　　　　　　　　　*Illustrated page 475*

Centaurium erythraea Rafn　　Common Centaury　　　　Sir J. Cullum 1773
(*C. minus* auct.)

Native. Dry, grassy banks, open places and clearings in woods. Also coastal sites, cliffs and beaches. Common.

W: All squares except 64; 65; 68; 93.

78, Lakenheath, 1980; 77, Cavenham Heath, 1979; Icklingham, 1980; 96, Woolpit, 1980.

E: All squares except 26; 38; 39; 44; 49; 50.
04, Hadleigh, old railway track, 1981; 14, Belstead, 1978; 35, Bromeswell, 1981; Rendlesham, 1980; 47, Hinton, 1980.   *Illustrated page 471*
A white-flowered form was seen at Westleton in 1962.

Centaurium littorale (D. Turner) Gilmour   Seaside Centaury   E. Skepper 1860
(*C. vulgare* Rafn
Erythraea compressa Kunth)

Native. Sandy places near the sea and in Breckland. Although there are several old records, there is some doubt that this species actually occurs in Suffolk, and it is likely that dwarf or narrow-leaved forms of *C. erythraea* were observed.

Centaurium pulchellum (Sw.) Druce   Lesser Centaury   Davy 1828
(Erythraea pulchella (Sw.) Fr.)

Native. Damp, open places on heaths, old pastures and tracks near the coast. Very rare, possibly extinct.
E: 13, Stutton, c. 1960; 34, Sutton, 1972; 45, Snape, saltings by the Alde river, c. 1958. All records by F. W. Simpson.

Gentiana pneumonanthe L.   Marsh Gentian   Sir J. Cullum 1777

Native. Formerly found on moist, turfy heaths, but now extinct. The species was recorded in Hind's Flora as occurring in Lothingland, Belton, Carlton Colville and on Corton and Hopton heaths, near Lowestoft. These heaths no longer exist. There are no known records of the plant since 1860.

Gentianella campestris (L.) Börner   Field Gentian   Sir J. Cullum 1773
(*Gentiana campestris* L.)

Native. Dry, chalky grassland and heaths. Extinct.
Recorded by Hind from Thurston Heath, Cavenham Severals, Deadman's Green, near Hardwick, Bury St Edmunds, Icklingham Heath, Rougham, Melford Wood, and Hartest. Some of the records may refer to *G. amarella*. Last record, mid-19th century.
G. campestris still occurs, or did until recently, in Norfolk.
There is a specimen collected by Rev. G. R. Leathes from near Bury in Hb. Ipswich Museum in the early 19th century.

Gentianella amarella (L.) Börner ssp. **amarella**   Felwort   J. Andrews 1746
(*Gentiana amarella* L.)   Autumn Gentian

Native. Old chalky grassland, heaths, chalk quarries, verges, and open scrub on chalky Boulder Clay. Scarce. Formerly frequent in several habitats, but suitable sites have been much changed in recent years by ploughing and other use.
W: 64; 66; 76; 77; 78; 88; 94.
64, Haverhill; 66, Newmarket Heath, 1981 (Mrs E. M. Hyde); 76, Cavenham; Risby; 77, Eriswell; Icklingham; 78, Lakenheath; 88, Santon Downham; 94, Lavenham, 1970 (F. W. Simpson); Acton, 1981 (E. Milne-Redhead).
E: 05, Needham Market; 07, Redgrave Fen; 14, Lt. Blakenham; Bramford.
The majority of these records are pre-1960.

MENYANTHACEAE

BOGBEAN FAMILY

Menyanthes trifoliata L.　　Bogbean　　　　　　　　　　Sir J. Cullum 1773
　　　　　　　　　　　　　　　　Buckbean

Native. Bogs, fens, edges of ponds, and in ditches. Not very frequent and decreasing. Now extinct in some former habitats.
W: 76; 77; 78; 83; 84; 86; 96; 98.
78, Pashford Poor's Fen; 83, Cornard Mere, 1981.
E: 07; 14; 24; 34; 35; 36; 39; 45; 46; 47; 49; 58; 59; 40.
35, Gromford, 1979; 36, Benhall, 1981; 45, Snape, 1980; 59, Carlton Colville, 1981.
Specimen Hb. Ipswich Museum, collected May 1818, near Boss Hall. A number of local habitats are given, suggesting that this plant, then named as Water Trefoil, Marsh Clover and Trefoil Buckbean, must have been extremely frequent around Ipswich, especially in the Gipping valley. Last seen in a ditch by the towing path near Boss Hall, in 1952. The ditches have now (1980) been destroyed between Ipswich and Sproughton (F. W. Simpson).

Nymphoides peltata (S. G. Gmel.) O. Kuntze　　Fringed Water Lily　Sir J. Cullum 1773
(*Limnanthemum peltatum* S. G. Gmel.)

Native and introduced. In sluggish rivers, ponds and lakes. Very local and rare.
W: 68/78, Lakenheath in the Lode (site now destroyed); 83, Lt. Cornard, roadside pond, 1978 (E. Milne-Redhead).
E: 14, R. Gipping, Ipswich, 1974-1981 (Mrs E. M. Hyde); 15, farm pond at Coddenham, 1974; 48, Beccles.

APOCYNACEAE

PERIWINKLE FAMILY

Vinca minor L.　　Lesser Periwinkle　　　　　　　　　　Sir J. Cullum 1773

Probably not native. Usually occurring as a naturalised garden escape, on sites of former gardens and in shrubberies and hedges. Frequent, and sometimes found to be increasing rapidly. A white-flowered form recorded from Lt. Saxham (sq. 76) and Pakenham (sq. 96), 1981. A variegated form recorded from Gt Bealings (sq. 24) in 1976.
W: All squares except 64; 65; 66; 67; 68; 74; 77; 87; 88; 97; 98.
94, Polstead, 1975.
E: All squares except 07; 17; 28; 33; 35; 44; 45; 46; 47; 48; 49; 58; 59; 40; 50.
03, Capel St Mary, 1981; 13, Brantham, 1980; 15, Coddenham; Stonham Aspal, 1981.

Vinca major L.　　Greater Periwinkle　　　　　　　　　　Sir J. Cullum 1773

Introduced from C. and S. Europe and N. Africa. Found as a naturalised garden escape. In hedges, and on the sites of former gardens and shrubberies. Fairly frequent.
W: All squares except 64; 68; 74; 75; 84; 98.
66, Moulton, 1978; 88, Santon Downham, 1980; 94, Edwardstone, 1979.

E: All squares except 36; 48.
07, Wortham, 1980; 13, Freston, 1980; 14, Westerfield, 1980; 23, Harkstead, 1981; 34, Shingle Street, 1981.

RUBIACEAE

BEDSTRAW FAMILY

Sherardia arvensis L.   Field Madder   Sir J. Cullum 1773

Native or colonist. A weed of arable fields, grassland, chalk quarries and waste ground. Frequent.
W: All squares except 65; 67; 68.
76, Dalham, 1981; Kentford, 1980.
E: All squares except 07; 33; 44; 58; 40.
23, Chelmondiston, 1981; 35, Tunstall, 1981.

Phuopsis stylosa (Trin.) B. D. Jackson   Finder not recorded 1965
(*Crucianella stylosa* Trin.)

Introduced. Native of Iran. Usually found in Britain as a garden escape. The only record for Suffolk is from Stonham Aspal. Determined at the British Museum.

Asperula cynanchica L.   Squinancy Wort   Dillenius 1724

Native. On old chalky grassland and heaths in West Suffolk. Now scarce and decreasing.
W: 76, Risby Poor's Heath; Dalham, 1981; Cavenham, 1980; 78, Lakenheath Warren, 1974; Wangford; 87, Elveden, near Iveagh Obelisk; 88, Santon Downham.

Asperula arvensis L.   Blue Field Woodruff   Mrs F. Baker 1899

Alien. Native of S. and C. Europe. Waste places and gardens as a bird-seed alien.
Recorded in 1899 from a ballast heap at Lowestoft and in the vicinity of Oulton Broad. Specimen in Hb. Atkins from the banks of the Orwell, 1909.
Both white and the more normal blue-flowered forms with other bird-seed aliens in a garden at Lowestoft, 1976 (P. G. Lawson). Detd. E. J. Clement.

Galium odoratum (L.) Scop.   Sweet Woodruff   Sir J. Cullum 1773
(*Asperula odorata* L.)

Native. Woods and copses, chiefly on the Chalky Boulder Clay. Local. Frequently introduced into gardens and shrubberies, from where it spreads into ditches and on to waysides.
W: 64; 75; 76; 83; 84; 85; 87; 93; 94; 96; 98.
75, Hundon Churchyard, 1974; 94, Groton Wood, 1981.
E: 03; 04; 05; 13; 15; 16; 26; 35; 59; 40.
03, Polstead, 1976; 05, Barking, 1981.   *Illustrated page 450*

Galium uliginosum L.   Fen Bedstraw   J. Andrews 1746
                             Rough Marsh Bedstraw

Native. In fens and marshes. Infrequent.
W: 68; 77; 78; 83; 86; 87; 88; 93; 94; 95; 97; 98.
83, Cornard Mere, 1975.

E: 04; 05; 07; 15; 16; 17; 23; 24; 25; 27; 28; 35; 36; 39; 46; 47; 49; 58; 59; 40.
07, Redgrave, 1977; 25, Bromeswell, 1980.
Many records for this species are probably incorrect and refer to *G. palustre.*

Galium palustre L. ssp. **palustre**   Marsh Bedstraw   Sir J. Cullum 1773
(incl. var. *witheringii* Sm.)

Native. In ditches, beside ponds and in damp glades in Boulder Clay woods. Frequent.
All squares except 65; 66; 84; 44.

Galium elongatum C. Presl   F. W. Simpson c. 1952
(*G. palustre* L. ssp. *elongatum* (C. Presl) Lange)

Native. In fens, dykes, reed swamps and open carrs in Lothingland. Distribution outside
this area is not known.

Galium verum L.   Lady's Bedstraw   Sir J. Cullum 1773

Native. Dry pastures, heaths, waysides and the sea coast on old dunes of sand and fixed
shingle. Frequent.
All squares.   *Illustrated page 516*
Var. **maritima** has been recorded from Benacre and Dunwich.

G. mollugo L. ssp. **mollugo**   Great Hedge Bedstraw   Sir J. Cullum 1773

Native. Hedges, marshes, edges of woods and copses, old quarries. Frequent.
W: All squares except 67; 68; 98.
76, Dalham, 1981; 94, Brent Eleigh, 1981.
E: All squares except 44; 40; 50.
04, Hadleigh, disused railway line, 1981; 17, Eye, 1980; 23, Harkstead, 1981; 39, Bungay,
1980.

Galium album Mill. ssp. **album**   Upright Bedstraw   Lady Blake 1840
(*G. mollugo* L. ssp. *erectum* Syme)

Native. Rare or overlooked. Dry, chalky soils and old Red Crag quarries.
W: 76, Cavenham, 1978 (F. W. Simpson).
E: 34, Sutton, Red Crag Pit, 1977 (F. W. Simpson); 35, Marlesford, 1954; 38, Barsham,
1956.

Galium mollugo × verum
(*G. × pomeranicum* Retz.)

A very rare hybrid, in grassy places, on waysides and sandy heaths, where the parents
occur. It is surprising that this hybrid has not been recorded in the County, as both parent
species still grow in some abundance. It may well be overlooked.

Galium saxatile L.   Heath Bedstraw   Sir J. Cullum 1773
(*G. hercynicum* auct.)

Native. Dry soils, sandy heaths, poor pastures, waysides and open glades in woods and
plantations on former heathland. Frequent. Commonest in Breckland and on the heaths
of East Suffolk. Apparently absent from quite a large area of Central Suffolk.

W: All squares except 64; 65; 66; 68; 74; 75; 83; 84; 85; 95.
77, West Stow and Icklingham, 1981.
E: All squares except 04; 05; 15; 16; 26; 27; 28; 33; 36; 37; 38.
24, Rushmere Common, 1981; 35, Tunstall Common, 1981; 45, Snape, 1981.

Galium aparine L.   Goosegrass   Sir J. Cullum 1773
                        Cleavers
                        Gentlemen's Tormentors (Suffolk)

Native. Hedges, fields, open woods and on the sea coast on old shingle beaches.
Common.
All squares.

Galium tricornutum Dandy   Corn Cleavers   Sir J. Cullum 1775
(G. tricorne Stokes, pro parte)   Rough Corn Bedstraw

A colonist, doubtfully native. Widespread in continental Europe. In cornfields on chalky
soils. Now very rare or extinct. Hind gives fifteen parishes. Last record c. 1960.
W: 77, Barton Mills, 1939.
E: 16; 25, Dallinghoo, c. 1960.

Galium parisiense ssp. **anglicum** (Huds.) Clapham   Wall Bedstraw   Sir J. Cullum 1776
(G. anglicum Huds.)   English Bedstraw

Native. Old walls, dry sand and chalk pits. Very rare, or overlooked. Recorded in Hind's
Flora from Mildenhall, Icklingham, Brandon, Wangford, Barton Mills, Bury St
Edmunds, Great Barton, Cavenham and the Thetford area.
W: 67, Mildenhall; 77, Eriswell; Tuddenham and Icklingham; 78, Lakenheath Warren;
88, Thetford, 1964 (J. M. Schofield).
Most of these records date from the 1950's.

Cruciata laevipes Opiz   Crosswort   Sir J. Cullum 1773
(Galium cruciata (L.) Scop.)   Mugwort

Native. Damp, grassy waysides, old pastures and woodland glades. Frequent.
W: All squares except 64; 65; 68; 74; 75; 85; 87; 93; 98.
76, Dalham, 1981; 94, Brent Eleigh, 1981.
E: All squares except 07; 28; 33; 44; 40; 50.
05, The Causeway, Barking, 1981; 13, roadsides at Tattingstone and Holbrook, 1981; 14,
by the R. Gipping at Ipswich and Sproughton, 1981; Washbrook, 1979; 48, Sotterley,
1980.   *Illustrated page 485*

POLEMONIACEAE

PHLOX FAMILY

Polemonium caeruleum L.   Jacob's Ladder   Mrs Parker 1889

Though a native of Britain, this plant is not indigenous in Suffolk. There is a single record
in Hind's Flora from Woolpit, where it was probably a garden stray.

POLEMONIACEAE

Collomia grandiflora Douglas ex Lindley   Miss E. S. Rowling 1956

A native of Western N. America, probably introduced into Britain in consignments of grain. The only record for Suffolk is from Wingfield, determined at Kew.

Gilia capitata Sims   W. A. Dutt c. 1890

Casual. Native in Columbia. Recorded from Oulton Broad about 1890.

CONVOLVULACEAE

CONVOLVULUS FAMILY

Cuscuta campestris Yuncker   P. J. O. Trist 1969

A casual, native of N. America, parasitic on various plants. Recorded on China Asters at West Row, Mildenhall (sq. 67) and on carrots at Lakenheath, both in 1969.

Cuscuta europaea L.   Large Dodder   Sir J. Cullum 1773
                            Great Dodder

Probably native. Parasitic on hops, nettles and other plants. Now very rare, and uncertain in its appearance. I have only seen it on wild hops and nettles, in hedges at Whatfield and Semer, before crop sprays came into use.
W: 94, Semer.
E: 04, Whatfield; 14, allotment in London Road, Ipswich, 1973 (L. Maxim).
Hind's Flora records the plant from near the gaol at Bury St Edmunds, Semer, Lavenham, Haverhill, Hadleigh, Whatfield, Hemingstone and Barking.
Hb. Ipswich Museum: specimen on Creeping Thistle, collected by J. L. Fison c. 1859, from Nacton.

Cuscuta epilinum Weihe   Flax Dodder   Henslow and Skepper 1860

An alien, probably introduced with foreign flax seed. Parasitic on cultivated flax. Very little flax is now grown in Suffolk. The last known record is from Hoxne in 1935.

Cuscuta epithymum (L.) L. ssp. **epithymum**   Common Dodder   Sir J. Cullum 1773
(includes Hind's *C. trifolii* Bab.)   Heath Dodder

Native. Parasitic on heather (*Calluna*), gorse, and other plants. Local and not appearing every year. Usually on dry, sandy heaths.
W: 67; 68; 77; 78; 95; 98.
77, Tuddenham Heath, 1980; 98, Knettishall Heath.
E: 16; 17; 24; 25; 34; 46; 47; 59; 40.
47, Walberswick, 1974; Westleton, 1981.
Hb. Ipswich Museum: 'Attached to *Euphrasia officinalis,* 1816. On the Race Ground' (John Notcutt).

Calystegia soldanella (L.) R. Br.   Sea Convolvulus   Sir J. Cullum 1773
(*Convolvulus soldanella* L.)   Sea Bindweed

Native. Sandy beaches and dunes. Not very common, and decreasing. A number of former habitats have now been destroyed, due to development and erosion.

266

CONVOLVULACEAE

E: 23; 33; 34; 45; 46; 47; 57; 58; 59; 50.
23, Landguard Common, 1979; 46, Sizewell and Minsmere, 1980.   *Illustrated page 498*

Calystegia sepium (L.) R. Br. ssp. **sepium**   Convolvulus   Sir J. Cullum 1773
(*Convolvulus sepium* L.)   Bellbine

Native. In old marshes, fens, alder carrs and open glades in damp woods and margins of rivers and dykes. Common.
All squares.

Calystegia silvatica (Kit.) Griseb.   Large Bindweed   F. W. Simpson 1924
(*C. sylvestris* (Waldst. & Kit. ex Willd.) Roem. & Schult.)

A colonist, native in S. Europe. A frequent weed in hedges, gardens and waste places. It is likely that hybrids with *C. sepium* are very frequent, but overlooked. They are fertile.
W: 66; 67; 75; 76; 77; 83; 84; 86; 94; 95; 96.
E: 03; 04; 05; 06; 07; 14; 16; 17; 26; 33; 36; 38; 39; 47; 48; 49; 59; 40; 50.

Calystegia pulchra Brummitt & Heywood   Pink-flowered Bindweed
(*C. sepium* (L.) R. Br. ssp. *pulchra*   Mrs Marriott c. 1889
(Brummitt & Heywood) Tutin)

Introduced. In hedges and old gardens, near habitations or the sites of cottages. Usually a relic of cultivation. Not very frequent.
W: 68, Lakenheath, 1980; 76, Kentford, 1969; 78, Lakenheath; 86, Flempton, 1941.
E: 14; 33; 35; 36; 38; 45; 47.
14, Ipswich; Tuddenham; Rushmere Common; Sproughton; 33, Felixstowe; 35, Bromeswell and Campsey Ash; 36, Saxmundham; 38, Barsham; 45, Aldeburgh; 47, Blythburgh.

Convolvulus arvensis L.   Bindweed   Sir J. Cullum 1773
Field Bindweed

Native or colonist. A weed of cultivated ground and waste places, probably native on shingle beaches. Ripe fruits are rare. The colour of the corolla and its markings can vary considerably. Uusually the colours are a very pale pink with light rose stripes. Occasionally the stripes are bright rose, almost red or lilac. White flowers with faint cream stripes were found on a roadside bank at Harkstead in 1976.
A form was observed on Dunwich Beach from 1937 to 1939, with much larger flowers than usual, very similar to *Calystegia soldanella*.
All squares.

BORAGINACEAE

BORAGE FAMILY

Lithospermum officinale L.   Common Gromwell   Sir J. Cullum 1773

Native. Old hedgerows, scrub and wood margins, edges of quarries and copses on Chalk and Chalky Boulder Clay, and on the margins of fens. Formerly frequent, now becoming scarce. Not usually in any quantity.

267

W: All squares except 68; 75; 83; 88; 93; 98.
94, Brent Eleigh, 1981; 97, Hopton Fen, 1980.
E: All squares except 03; 06; 13; 17; 23; 27; 33; 34; 35; 37; 39; 45; 47; 48; 58; 59; 40; 50.
04, Raydon, 1980; 07, Hinderclay Fen, 1978; 14, Bramford, 1978; 15, Coddenham, 1980.

Buglossoides purpurocaerula (L.) I. M. Johnston   D. J. Carpenter 1939
(*Lithospermum purpurocaeruleum* L.)   Purple Gromwell
          Blue Gromwell
Native or introduced. In rough, bushy marginal habitats and neglected fields. Rare.
W: 78, Lakenheath; 84, Long Melford.
E: 04, Bushy Coopers Wood, before the wood was destroyed (Mr Read); 24, Martlesham
(L. W. Howard).

Buglossoides arvensis (L.) I. M. Johnston   Corn Gromwell   Sir J. Cullum 1773
(*Lithospermum arvense* L.)
Native. In cultivated fields, chiefly on the Boulder Clay or Chalk. Formerly fairly
frequent, but now usually in small numbers, due to spraying.
W: All squares except 65; 68; 84; 87; 88; 98.
67, Mildenhall, 1977; 75, Hundon, 1974; 77, Barton Mills, 1980; 94, Brent Eleigh, 1981.
E: All squares except 07; 15; 23; 26; 28; 34; 38; 44; 45; 47; 48; 49; 58; 40; 50.
04, Hintlesham, 1975; 16, Wetheringsett, 1976.

Echium vulgare L.   Viper's Bugloss   Sir J. Cullum 1773
Native. On dry, light soils, fallow fields, road verges and sea cliffs. Frequent.
W: All squares except 65; 68; 74; 75; 83; 85.
Very common in the Breckland, 1981.
E: All squares except 03; 06; 17; 37; 48; 50.
04, Hadleigh, 1981; 15, Barham, 1981; 34, Shingle Street, 1981.   *Illustrated page 469*

Echium plantagineum L.   Purple Viper's Bugloss   J. S. Wilkinson 1908
(*E. lycopsis* L., pro parte
E. violaceum L.)
A rare casual. Native in the South-west of England and Jersey. Very common in the
Mediterranean region.
E: 14, Ipswich, 1908; Crane Hill, Ipswich, 1956 (Miss E. S. Rowling).

Pulmonaria officinalis L.   Common Lungwort   C. J. Ashfield 1862
          Soldiers-and-Sailors (Suffolk)
Status doubtful. It looks almost native in its Suffolk habitats, where it is local and
decreasing. Suffolk woodland plants have unspotted or, rarely, faintly spotted leaves. In
the 1930's the Common Lungwort was still quite abundant in both Burgate Wood and
Stubbing's Grove. When the sites were visited in the 1950's, it could only be found in
limited quantity in one area of Burgate Wood. In 1976, a search of both sites revealed a
small colony in Burgate Wood and a single plant in Stubbing's Grove. A colony was also
found in 1948 in Millfield Wood, Polstead. Unfortunately, this habitat was destroyed,
when electricity pylons were erected.
W: 93, Polstead.

BORAGINACEAE

E: 07, Burgate Wood; Stubbing's Grove, Botesdale.
There is a specimen in Hb. Atkins from Layham in 1910, incorrectly identified as *P. angustifolia.* It has unspotted leaves.
The plant which is commonly grown in gardens has larger, prominently spotted radical leaves. It is sometimes planted on banks and rockeries outside gardens, where it may persist for a few years. In some counties it has been introduced in woods, where it has become naturalised. There is a specimen in Hb. Atkins from Sproughton, 1910.

Symphytum officinale L.   Common Comfrey   Sir J. Cullum 1773

Native. Beside streams, rivers, margins of fens and in wet places. The records suggest that this is a very frequent species in Suffolk. However, my observations seem to prove that this is far from the case, and it is, indeed, now local. What is usually thought to be *S. officinale* is probably the hybrid *S.* × *uplandicum,* an introduction or a relic of cultivation. Its flowers are various shades of pink, purple, mauve and violet and it grows in damp places by roadsides, in ditches and frequently about farmyards.
S. officinale occurs by rivers and streams and in open carrs. The flowers are a cream colour and are usually larger than the coloured hybrids; also, the plants have slightly larger basal leaves. It must not be confused with *S. orientale,* which is often incorrectly identified as Common Comfrey.
W: 67, Mildenhall, 1977; 68, Lakenheath, frequent, 1980; 77, West Stow to Mildenhall by the R. Lark; 78, Brandon, 1979; 84, Sudbury.
E: 03, Stratford St Mary; 07, near the Little Ouse, Thelnetham; 14, Bramford, 1980; 24, Bucklesham and Newbourn, 1981.
In my copy of William Withering's 'British Plants' there is the coloured engraving of a drawing by James Sowerby, 1800, of *S. officinale,* described as having blossoms yellowish-white and 'the valves of the mouth . . . toothed down to the base'. This illustration and description are of the correct species, whereas a later illustration of a plant in 'English Botany', with bluish flowers, looks more like *S.* × *uplandicum.* This illustration appears in the third edition, edited by Boswell-Syme.   *Illustrated page 489*

Symphytum asperum × officinale   Russian Comfrey   (?) Hind's Flora 1889
(*S.* × *uplandicum* Nyman)

An established alien. Naturalised in N. and C. Europe. Damp waysides, waste places, marshes and margins of woods. Frequent. A very variable plant; the corolla is usually purplish-blue. Often confused with *S. officinale.*
W: 64; 65; 66; 67; 74; 75; 76; 77; 86; 87; 88; 94; 95.
66, Exning, 1980; 78, Brandon, 1980; 86, Bury St Edmunds, 1981; 87, West Stow, 1980.
E: 03; 05; 13; 14; 15; 16; 17; 23; 24; 26; 27; 33; 34; 39; 45; 49; 50.
14, Paper Mill Lane, Bramford, 1981; 24, Lt. Sutton Hoo, 1981; Playford, 1981; 34, Boyton, 1979; 45, Aldeburgh, 1980; 46, Knodishall, 1980.
This plant was first introduced into Britain c. 1827 and grown as a green fodder plant. Many of the colonies seen today are probably relics of cultivation. Earlier confusion with *S. officinale* prevents us being able to give the exact date of the first Suffolk record, although it was very likely grown or established in the County when Hind's Flora was published in 1889.   *Illustrated page 489*

Symphytum tuberosum L.   Tuberous Comfrey   E. R. Long c. 1935

Native or introduced. In woods and hedgebanks. Rare or overlooked.

Recorded by E. R. Long from Beccles, Halesworth, Carlton Colville and Lowestoft. Since then recorded from:
E: 13, Holbrook, damp woodland, 1977-81; 14, Washbrook, 1980 (both records Mrs E. M. Hyde); 47, Henham Park, 1954 (Lowestoft Field Club).

Symphytum ibiricum Steven   Creeping Comfrey   Miss E. V. C. Easto 1959
(*S. grandiflorum* auct., non DC.)
Introduced from the Caucasus. Sometimes naturalised in hedges and woods in S. England. The only record for Suffolk is from Walberswick (sq. 47), where it was found in 1959 on a hedge-bank. Specimen determined at the British Museum.

Symphytum tauricum Willd.   Hind's Flora 1889

An alien species with white flowers, native of Asia Minor, sometimes found in Britain as a garden escape. Hind's Flora records it as established in a copse between Bury St Edmunds and Barton, also in a plantation at Bradfield Manger. There have been no records of the species during the present century.

Symphytum orientale L.   White Comfrey   Hind's Flora 1889

A naturalised alien, introduced from Turkey. Found as a garden escape, in churchyards, on hedge-banks, waysides, waste places and in copses, generally around villages. Widespread and increasing, but more frequent in the South of the County.
W: 76, Gazeley, 1981; Kentford, 1980; Higham, 1981; 78, Wangford; 84, Sudbury, 1976; 86, Abbey Gardens, Bury St Edmunds, 1981; 96, Thurston Station, 1981; Woolpit, 1978; 84, Sudbury, 1976.
E: 03; 04; 05; 07; 13; 14; 15; 23; 24; 25; 27; 33; 34; 35; 36; 37; 50.
13, Holbrook, 1979; 24, Rushmere, Playford, Gt Bealings, all 1981; 37, Halesworth, 1981.
This species is recorded by Hind as established in a grove at Tendring Park, Stoke-by-Nayland, and also near Ipswich. There is a specimen in Hb. Atkins from Wherstead in 1908, where it is still plentiful.   *Illustrated page 489*

Symphytum caucasicum Bieb.   F. W. Simpson c. 1952

Introduced. Native of the Caucasus.
E: 15, a well established colony in a ditch and hedge was observed for a number of years at Claydon, before it was destroyed by housing development, c. 1967. A few plants were removed to the safety of a garden; 25, one plant on a roadside bank at Ufford growing with *S. orientale,* 1972-6 (Mrs E. Dickson and L. W. Lewis).

Brunnera macrophylla (Adams) I. M. Johnston   Mrs E. M. Hyde 1979

Introduced, sometimes thrown out from gardens and persisting.
W: 96, Thurston, one plant flowering in roadside ditch, 1979.

Anchusa officinalis L.   Alkanet   Rev. E. J. Moore 1840

Introduced. A relic or escape from cultivation, sometimes a casual. Scarce.
W: 78, Lakenheath, c. 1940-80 (M. G. Rutterford).
E: 14, Ipswich, waste ground, 1980 (J. R. Palmer); 35, Staverton Thicks, Butley, c. 1932 (T. G. Powell); 47, Wenhaston; 58, Kessingland; 59, Pakefield; Oulton Broad.

BORAGINACEAE

Anchusa azurea Mill.   F. W. Simpson 1969
(*A. italica* Retz.)
An alien from S. Europe. Known in Suffolk only from Bawdsey Cliffs (sq. 33).

Anchusa arvensis (L.) Bieb.   Field Bugloss   Sir J. Cullum 1773
(*Lycopsis arvensis* L.)
Colonist. A weed of arable land and waste places. Common. More frequent on light soils.
All squares except 65; 68; 85; 16.

Pentaglottis sempervirens (L.) Tausch   Green Alkanet   Sir J. Cullum 1773
(*Anchusa sempervirens* L.)   Evergreen Alkanet
Alien. Introduced from W. Europe. Found as a naturalised garden escape, sometimes
spreading freely along waysides, as at Barham and Bentley.
W: 66; 74; 76; 83; 86; 87; 94; 96; 97.
76, Moulton, 1979; 86, Bury St Edmunds, 1979; 96, Rougham, 1980.
E: 03; 04; 05; 13; 14; 15; 16; 23; 24; 33; 35; 36; 37; 38; 39; 44; 45; 46; 47; 49; 58; 59; 40.
13, Bentley, 1981; 15, Barham, 1981; 23, Chelmondiston, 1981; 24, Rushmere, 1981;
Martlesham, 1981; Sutton Hoo, 1981; 49, Beccles, 1980; 59, Lowestoft, 1980.

Borago officinalis L.   Borage   Sir J. Cullum 1773
An introduction or garden escape. Native in C. Europe and the Mediterranean. Found on
hedge-banks and waste places. Formerly cultivated by bee-keepers. Not very common.
W: 86; 93; 94; 97.
94, Monks Eleigh, 1975.
E: 03; 04; 05; 06; 13; 14; 23; 24; 25; 35; 36; 38; 45; 59; 40.
06, Wickham Skeith, 1972; 15, Otley, 1978; 23, Chelmondiston, 1974.
Illustrated page 508

Trachystemon orientalis (L.) G. Don f.   Abraham, Isaac and Jacob
                                                             F. W. Simpson 1953
A native of the E. Mediterranean region. Introduced and naturalised in Britain.
E: 13, Woolverstone, naturalised. Increased greatly in the period 1950-81. 23, Erwarton,
1978.

Amsinckia lycopsoides Lehmann   Mrs F. Baker c. 1900
A casual from N. America. First recorded at Oulton Broad.
There may be some confusion between records of this species and of *A. intermedia*.
E: 14, entrance to farm, Dales Hall Lane, Ipswich, 1974 (R. B. Warren); 37,
Heveningham, 1968; 46, Dunwich, 1957; 47, Walberswick, 1957.

Amsinckia intermedia Fisch. & Mey.   Tarweed   Mrs J. Foljambe 1939
                                            Californian Borage
An established alien, increasing on light, sandy, arable fields and waste places. Said to
have been introduced with American carrot seed during World War II. Up to 1939 it was a
rare casual. Although most records refer to this species, the genus is under revision and it
is possible that other species may be identified. Now (1981) a very abundant weed of
arable fields at Brightwell, Bucklesham, Foxhall, Hemley, Newbourn and Waldringfield
and in the Walberswick and Westleton areas. Once established it is difficult to eradicate.

W: 77, Eriswell, 1980; Barton Mills, 1980; 78, Brandon, 1980.
E: 04, Elmsett, 1974; 13, Freston; Harkstead, 1981; Woolverstone; 14, Bramford; Ipswich, 1981; Kesgrave; Rushmere; Sproughton; Tuddenham, 1975; Wherstead; 23, Chelmondiston; Felixstowe Docks; Kirton; 24, Brightwell; Bucklesham; Foxhall; Hemley; Kirton; Kesgrave; Levington; Martlesham; Newbourn, 1981; Purdis Farm; Stratton Hall; Waldringfield; Woodbridge; 25, Bromeswell; 33, Felixstowe Ferry; 34, Ramsholt; 35, Blaxhall; Bromeswell; Eyke; Farnham; Snape Maltings; Tunstall; Wantisden; 38, Flixton; 45, Aldeburgh, 1981; Sudbourne; 46, Aldringham; Minsmere; Sizewell; Westleton; Yoxford; 47, Blythburgh; Dunwich; Henham Park; Walberswick; Wangford; Westleton; 49, Carlton Colville, 1974; Beccles, 1974; 58, Benacre, 1974; Covehithe; South Cove.
The above distribution of this species in the County was assisted by the records collated by M. A. Hyde. *Illustrated page 514*

Asperugo procumbens L.   Madwort   Dillenius 1724

A rare casual, native of Europe, West Asia and North Africa. Sometimes found on waste ground, especially near ports.
E: 15; 33, Felixstowe Docks; 45, Sudbourne, four plants in sugar-beet field, 1980 (M. A. Hyde); 59, Lowestoft.
Hb. Atkins, specimen from banks of R. Orwell, 1908-9.

Myosotis arvensis (L.) Hill   Field Forget-me-not   J. Andrews 1743
Common Forget-me-not

Native. Open places in woods and a weed of waste places and arable land. Common. Some varieties growing in woods have larger flowers and may be mistaken for *M. sylvatica*.
All squares.

Myosotis ramosissima Rochel   Early Forget-me-not   D. Stock 1835
(*M. collina* auct.)

Native. On dry, sandy heaths, open poor fallow fields and marginal land. Locally common, especially in Breckland and on the Sandlings.
W: All squares except 65; 68; 74; 75; 83; 85; 95; 97.
76, Kentford, Herringswell and Higham, 1981.
E: All squares except 05; 13; 15; 16; 17; 26; 27; 37; 38; 48; 59; 50.
24, Brightwell, 1981; 34, Sutton, 1981.

Myosotis discolor Pers.   Yellow and Blue Forget-me-not   Rev. G. Crabbe 1798
(*M. versicolor* Sm.)   Changing Forget-me-not

Native. In dry open places, on heaths, fallow fields, banks and poor marginal land. Common, especially in Breckland, where it is sometimes abundant.
W: 66; 67; 76; 77; 78; 87; 88; 93; 94; 97; 98.
77, Cavenham, 1980; 78, Lakenheath, 1980.
E: 03; 04; 07; 13; 23; 24; 25; 33; 34; 35; 36; 39; 44; 45; 46; 47; 49; 58; 59; 40; 50.
13, Holbrook and Tattingstone, 1976; 24, Brightwell and Newbourn, 1981.

Myosotis sylvatica Hoffm.   Wood Forget-me-not   Mrs French 1831
Native. In old woods and copses, chiefly on the Boulder Clay. Sometimes abundant.

Frequently observed in other habitats, such as waysides, ditches and plantations. These colonies are usually of garden origin and the colour of the flowers a much darker blue.

W: 64; 65; 75; 76; 77; 84; 85; 86; 87; 93; 94; 95; 96.

76, Herringswell, 1980; 94, Brent Eleigh, 1976.

E: 04; 05; 13; 14; 24; 36.

04, Hintlesham, 1981; 05, Barking, 1981; 36, Bruisyard, 1976.

Varieties with white or pink flowers are not uncommon.

Myosotis secunda A. Murray   Creeping Water Forget-me-not

(*M. repens* D. Don)   Rev. F. W. Galpin c. 1880

Native. In bogs, beside streams and in Alder carrs. It is doubtful whether this species occurs in the County. It may have been wrongly identified. Hind also expresses doubts as to whether it is native in East Anglia.

E: 38, Barsham; 46, Dunwich.

Hind records it from St Margaret South Elmham.

Myosotis laxa Lehm. ssp. **caespitosa** (C. F. Schultz) Hyl. ex Nordh.   Paget 1834

(*M. caespitosa* C. F. Schultz)   Tufted Forget-me-not

Native. In wet places, by rivers, streams and ponds. Occasional.

W: 74; 75; 76; 77; 86; 87; 88; 93; 97; 98.

77, Cavenham, 1979; 97, Coney Weston, 1981.

E: 03; 04; 13; 14; 23; 27; 33; 38; 39; 46; 47; 48; 49; 58; 40; 50.

39, Bungay, 1981; 58, Benacre, 1981; 40, Belton, 1977.

Myosotis scorpioides L.   Water Forget-me-not   Sir J. Cullum 1773

(*M. palustris* (L.) Hill)   Water Scorpion-grass

Native. In and beside streams, ditches and ponds. Common. Plentiful by the Gipping, Stour and other rivers.

All squares.

Lappula squarrosa (Retz.) Dum. ssp. **squarrosa**   Rev. E. A. Holmes 1839

(*Echinospermum lappula* (L.) Lehm.)

Casual. An annual species widespread in Europe.

Recorded in Hind's Flora as occurring between Southwold and the Pier, from 1839-48. Also found c. 1890 by Mrs F. Baker at Oulton Broad, and on waste land near Woodbridge Station, 1934 (H. K. Airy Shaw).

Omphalodes verna Moench   Blue-eyed Mary   C. J. Palmer 1918

Introduced. Native in S.E. Europe. Cultivated in Britain, and sometimes found naturalised in woods and plantations. Known in Suffolk from a plantation at Coddenham (sq. 15) in 1918.

Cynoglossum officinale L.   Hound's-tongue   J. Andrews 1748

Native. Dry, sandy or chalky soils, heaths, open places in woods, quarries and on the sea coast on cliffs and dunes. Frequent.

BORAGINACEAE

W: All squares except 64; 65; 83; 93.
Very frequent in Breckland, 1981.
E: All squares except 07; 17; 27; 28; 38; 50.
34, Shingle Street, 1981; 35, Tunstall, 1980.
Very common on the coastal strip between Bawdsey and Orford, 1981.

Cynoglossum germanicum Jacq.   Green Hound's-tongue   W. A. Dutt 1899
(*C. montanum* auct., non L.)
A casual in Suffolk. First recorded by W. A. Dutt from Carlton Colville.
E: Darsham Common, 1952 (Miss E. S. Rowling).

VERBENACEAE

VERBENA FAMILY

Verbena officinalis L.   Vervain   Sir J. Cullum 1773
Native or colonist. Waysides, old quarries and waste places. Not very frequent.
W: All squares except 65; 74; 83; 85; 93; 95; 96.
66/76, Moulton, roadside, 1981; 68, Lakenheath, 1980; 78, Brandon, 1980.
E: All squares except 03; 07; 13; 17; 26; 28; 33; 37.
14, Ipswich, several sites, 1981; 15, Coddenham, 1980.

Verbena bracteata Lag. & Rodr.   Prostrate Vervain   Mr & Mrs E. C. Green 1953
A casual, native in Mexico. Known in Suffolk from Barham Crossing (sq. 15) in July
1953. Specimen determined at Kew.

CALLITRICHACEAE

STARWORT FAMILY

CALLITRICHE   WATER STARWORTS
A very neglected genus; often difficult to identify, because of the absence of mature fruits,
which may not always be found when the plants are growing in deep water. Variations of
the same species occur according to conditions and the type of habitat, such as whether
the plant is growing on dry, damp, or wet mud of ponds or ditches, in an open situation or
in shade, or in shallow or deep water, which may be stagnant or running.

Callitriche stagnalis Scop..   Common Water Starwort   Sir J. Cullum 1773
Native. Chiefly found on wet mud, in shallow ponds and ditches. Common, but variable;
some forms are very small, especially when growing on mud.
W: All squares except 64; 65; 74; 78; 87; 96.
E: All squares except 25; 45; 48; 58.

Callitriche obtusangula Le Gall   Blunt-fruited Water Starwort   Hind 1883
Native. In ponds, muddy ditches, pools and dykes. Probably fairly frequent. Under-
recorded.

274

W: 67; 77; 84; 88; 94; 97; 98.
67, Mildenhall, 1978 (Mrs E. M. Hyde).
E: 05; 46; 47.
There are only two records in Hind's Flora, West Row, Mildenhall and Burgh Castle.

Callitriche platycarpa Kütz.   Long-styled Water Starwort   Hind 1881
(*C. polymorpha* auct.)

Native. In muddy pools or wet mud of drying ponds, streams and rivers. Probably not uncommon, but overlooked. Much confusion exists over this species, and the Suffolk records in Hind's Flora are somewhat misleading.
W: Recorded from squares 86 and 88 (Trist, 1979).

Callitriche verna L.   Vernal Water Starwort   Sir J. Cullum 1773
(*C. vernalis* Koch)

Recorded in Hind's Flora as common in all districts in ditches and ponds. As there is no known herbarium specimen, it is difficult to be certain which species he was recording.

Callitriche hamulata Kütz. ex Koch   Hooked Water Starwort   J. Andrews 1745

Native. In stagnant ponds, ditches and streams. Fairly frequent. The fruits of this species are dark olive and its leaves shaped like bicycle spanners.
W: 74; 75; 77; 78; 84; 86; 93.
77, Mildenhall; 78, near Brandon.
E: 03; 06; 13; 25; 35; 39; 46; 48; 49; 50.
35, in the Deben at Ufford, 1974; 39, Bungay, 1981.

Callitriche brutia Petagna   Henslow & Skepper 1860
(*C. pedunculata* DC.)

Native. In rivers, streams and broads.
Recorded in Hind's Flora under *C. hamulata,* for Thetford Warren and Ipswich.

LABIATAE

MINT FAMILY

Ajuga reptans L.   Bugle   Sir J. Cullum 1773

Native. Damp glades in woods, especially on the Boulder Clay; also wet pastures and waysides. Frequent. A number of varieties may be found, the colour of the flowers varying from blue and pale blue-white to mauve, purplish-rose and pink.
All squares except 67; 68; 33; 49; 50.   *Illustrated page 448*

Ajuga chamaepitys (L.) Schreb.   Ground-pine   A. L. Bull 1948

Native. Very rare. First recorded in Suffolk on the edge of a dry field at West Stow (sq. 77). Still occurred there in 1979.

Teucrium scorodonia L.   Wood Sage   Sir J. Cullum 1773

Native. On dry heaths, banks and open woods on sandy and gravelly soils. Frequent.
W: All squares except 65; 66; 67; 68; 74; 75; 76; 84; 95.
78, Wangford; 87, West Stow, 1980; 98, Knettishall, 1980.
E: All squares except 06; 15; 16; 17; 26; 27; 28; 33; 36.
23, Nacton Cliffs, 1981; 25, Bromeswell, 1980; 58, Benacre, 1981.

Teucrium scordium L.   Water Germander   F. K. Eagle 1810

Native. Wet places, sides of rivers and ditches. Very rare. Recorded in Hind's Flora for
Lakenheath. Hind questioned the occurrence of this species in the County, but in 1976 M.
G. Rutterford and S. Rutterford refound it in this parish. There is a record for
Gedgrave in 1957 by Miss C. J. Blake, but the ditches where it was found have since
been cleaned out.

Scutellaria galericulata L.   Common Skull-cap   Sir J. Cullum 1773

Native. Beside rivers, ponds and in marshes and fens. Fairly frequent.
W: 74; 77; 78; 83; 84; 86; 88; 93; 94; 96; 98.
77, Cavenham, 1979; 83, Cornard Mere, 1975; 96, Norton Wood, 1979.
E: 03; 04; 07; 13; 14; 15; 16; 23; 25; 26; 27; 28; 36; 38; 39; 45; 46; 47; 48; 49; 58; 40.
03, by the R. Stour at East Bergholt, 1979; 13, banks of the R. Orwell at Woolverstone,
1981; 23, Chelmondiston (tolerant of salt spray), 1981; 58, Benacre, 1981; 40, Belton,
1977.   *Illustrated page 501*

Scutellaria minor Huds.   Lesser Skull-cap   J. Andrews 1745

Native. On damp heaths. Very rare. Last authenticated record in 1905.
W: Not recorded recently.
E: 04, Flowton, 1950 (doubtful record).
There is a specimen in Hb. Atkins from 'near Saxmundham' in 1905. Hind listed
Tuddenham (West Suffolk) and Friston.

Marrubium alysson L.   Mrs F. Baker 1899

A casual. Native of Spain and S. E. Europe. Known in Suffolk only from the record from
Everett's Wharf, near Carlton Colville.

Marrubium vulgare L.   White Horehound   J. Andrews 1755

Native. Also introduced. Dry waysides, heaths and waste places. Rare and decreasing.
Formerly cultivated, but it was also doubtless a native of the County. Its distribution is
mainly confined to Breckland and the coastal areas.
W: 67; 76; 77; 78; 86; 87; 88; 98.
78, Lakenheath, 1974.
E: 03; 14; 15; 23; 33; 34; 45; 46; 47; 59.
15, Barham, 1979; 23, Landguard Common, 1977; 33, Felixstowe Ferry, 1977; 34, Shingle
Street, 1981.

Sideritis montana L.   Mrs F. Baker c. 1900

Casual. Native of S. Europe. Known in the County from a single record from Oulton
Broad.

Galeopsis segetum Neck.   Cream-coloured Hemp-nettle   Hind's Flora 1862
(*G. dubia* Leers   Downy Hemp-nettle
G. ochroleuca Lam.)

Possibly native or a colonist. A very rare or overlooked weed or casual of arable land. Not recorded in Suffolk during the present century, and the only known record is that in Hind's Flora from St Olave's in 1862.

Galeopsis ladanum L.   Red Hemp-nettle   Sutton & Kirby 1787

An alien, introduced from continental Europe. A colonist of arable land, gardens and waste places. Probably uncommon. Much confusion exists concerning its status as a British species. The numerous records in Hind's Flora for this species are probably incorrect and no doubt refer to *G. angustifolia*.
There is a record from Mildenhall in 1921 and a specimen in Hb. Atkins from Claydon, 1908.

Galeopsis angustifolia Ehrh. ex Hoffm.   Narrow-leaved Hemp-nettle
(*G. ladanum* ssp. *angustifolia* Gaudin)   Sir J. Cullum 1773

Probably a colonist. Native of Europe. A rare weed of arable fields and waste places, chiefly on chalky soils. Distribution not properly known. Decreasing.
The records in Hind's Flora for the genus *Galeopsis* are confusing.
W: 64; 75; 76; 77; 78; 86; 87; 93; 96.
76, Herringswell; 87, West Stow.
E: 13; 14; 23; 46.
23, Erwarton, 1974.
Hb. Ipswich Museum: 'Cornfields frequent. Border of cornfields by the side of the path between Rivers's Farm and Rushmere Heath. Septr. 1817' (John Notcutt).
Hb. Atkins: Sproughton, 1908.

Galeopsis speciosa Mill.   Bee Hemp-nettle   Rev. G. Crabbe 1798
(*G. versicolor* Curt.)

Native and a colonist. A weed of arable land and waysides, especially of fen land west of Mildenhall, where it is sometimes abundant. Rare elsewhere or a casual.
W: 67; 68; 77; 78; 86; 87; 88; 98.
68/78, Lakenheath, 1980; 78, Brandon, 1980.
E: 03; 14; 16; 17; 59.
These East Suffolk records are doubtful.   *Illustrated page 512*

Galeopsis tetrahit L.   Common Hemp-nettle   Sir J. Cullum 1773
Native. Arable land, waysides, wood margins and clearings, fenny places and waste ground. Frequent and sometimes abundant.
W: All squares except 64; 66.
76, Gazeley, 1978 (white flowers with cream markings); 94, Groton, 1974, (white-flowered).
E: All squares except 33; 37; 44; 58; 40; 50.
13, Woolverstone, 1974 (white-flowered); 24, Rushmere, 1981; 46, Westleton, 1979.
The last two records are for plants with white flowers with cream markings (F.W.S.).

Galeopsis bifida Boenn.   Sir J. Cullum 1773
(*G. tetrahit* ssp. *bifida* (Boenn.) Lej. & Court.)

Introduced. Native in N. and C. Europe. Fens and damp woodland glades. Probably not infrequent, but overlooked.
Recorded in Hind's Flora under *G. tetrahit*.
W: 78, Pashford Poor's Fen, 1979; Wangford; 98, Knettishall Heath.
E: 13, Tattingstone, 1977 (Mrs E. M. Hyde); 35, Eyke, woodland glade, 1969 (F. W. Simpson).

Lamium maculatum L.   Spotted Dead-nettle   Rev. S. Rickards 1840

Introduced. Native of parts of Europe. Cultivated in gardens and often found planted on roadside banks outside gardens, and occasionally as an outcast on waste ground and in ditches. Sometimes established in churchyards.
W: 65; 76; 77; 84; 86; 87; 96.
76, Moulton, 1975; 77, Icklingham, 1981.
E: 14, Tuddenham; 16, Thorndon; 25, Dallinghoo; 33, Felixstowe, 1979.

Lamium album L.   White Dead-nettle   Sir J. Cullum 1773

A native or colonist of waysides and waste places. Very common.
All squares.
A rare pinkish-flowered form has been recorded from East Bergholt (sq. 03) and Harkstead (sq. 13).

Lamium purpureum L.   Red Dead-nettle   Sir J. Cullum 1773

A native or colonist of cultivated and waste ground, waysides and banks. Very frequent and often abundant.
Recorded from all squares.
Albino forms have been recorded from the sites listed below.
W: 76, Barrow, edge of arable field, 1980; Kentford, 1978; 86, Bury St Edmunds; 93, Polstead, 1977; 96, Gt Barton, 1978-81.
E: 03, Capel St Mary, 1980; 13, Harkstead, 1978; Woolverstone, 1980; Tattingstone, 1976; 14, Ipswich, 1978; Bramford; Sproughton; 23, Chelmondiston; 47, Walberswick, 1977; 58, Benacre.
All above records by Mrs E. M. Hyde or F. W. Simpson.

Lamium hybridum Vill.   Cut-leaved Dead-nettle   Wigg 1802
(*L. incisum* Willd.)

A colonist and weed of arable ground, waste places and waysides. Not very common and decreasing. Two plants of the species were found at Blundeston in 1933 by Dr E. A. Ellis, which possessed cleistogamous flowers producing their full quantum of seeds.
W: 67; 68; 76; 77; 86; 87; 93; 94; 95; 96.
67, Freckenham, 1977; 76, Barrow, 1980; 96, Beyton, 1979.
E: 03; 13; 16; 23; 24; 25; 26; 33; 34; 35; 36; 39; 45; 47; 59; 40; 50.
23, Harkstead, 1981; 24, Gt Bealings, 1981; 47, Westleton, 1980.
Hb. Ipswich Museum: 'On a bank, east side and near the entrance of the lane leading from the Nacton Road by the Race Ground to Pond Hall', c. 1820 (John Notcutt).

Lamium molucellifolium Fr. Intermediate Dead-nettle R. Burn c. 1936
(*L. intermedium* Fr.) Northern Dead-nettle

Native. In arable fields. The only known Suffolk record is of a cleistogamous form from Cavenham. There is some doubt about this record, though it is thought to have been made by R. Burn.

Lamium amplexicaule L. Henbit J. Andrews 1746

A colonist and weed of cultivated ground, disturbed waysides and waste places. Usually on sandy or gravelly soils. Frequent.
W: All squares except 65; 67; 68; 85; 93; 98.
66, Moulton; 76, Dalham, 1981; 77, Worlington, chalk-pit, 1980; 96, Rougham, 1980.
E: All squares except 07; 17; 37; 49.
13, Harkstead, 1981; 24, Gt Bealings, 1981; 35, Blaxhall, 1980. *Illustrated page 514*

Lamiastrum galeobdolon (L.) Ehrend. & Polatsch. Yellow Archangel
(*Galeobdolon luteum* Huds. Sir J. Cullum 1773
Lamium galeobdolon (L.) L.)

Native. In woods, copses and shady lanes. Frequent on clay and loamy soils. Absent or uncommon in Breckland.
W: All squares except 65; 66; 67; 68; 74; 76; 77; 78; 87; 88; 97; 98.
95, Buxhall, 1978; Bradfield Woods, 1980.
E: All squares except 17; 33; 34; 35; 44; 46; 49; 58; 59; 40; 50.
04, Hintlesham, 1981; 13, Freston, lane by Monkey Lodge, 1981; 23, abundant on cliffs between Pin Mill and Clamp House, 1981.
Hb. Ipswich Museum; 'Freston Wood; Dunham Reach Woods', c. 1815 (John Notcutt).
Still occurs in these habitats in 1981. *Illustrated page 452 and page 463*
Form with variegated leaves at Shotley, 1974, Burgate, 1976, and Hadleigh, 1981.

Leonurus cardiaca L. Motherwort Sir J. Cullum 1773

Introduced. A native of continental Europe, found on waysides, hedge-banks and waste places. Occasional.
W: Not recorded recently, although Hind lists Bury St Edmunds, Pakenham and Stowlangtoft.
E: 26, Cretingham; 35, Snape; 38, Bungay (Hb. Atkins, 1907); 44, Orford, 1956 (Miss C. J. Blake); 46, Leiston.

Ballota nigra L. ssp. **foetida** Hayek Black Horehound Sir J. Cullum 1773
(*B. foetida* Lam.)

Native. Roadsides and waste places. Common. White-flowered forms are uncommon.
All squares.
White-flowered forms from Chelmondiston 1974-80 and Levington (Mrs E. M. Hyde).

Stachys officinalis (L.) Trev. Betony Sir J. Cullum 1773
(*Betonica officinalis* L.)

Native. In woodland glades, old rough pastures and lanes. Now scarce or extinct in most of its former habitats.

W: 64; 76; 83; 84; 86; 87; 88; 93; 95; 96; 97.
76, Barrow, 1980; 95, Monks' Park Wood, 1980; 97, Fakenham Parva.
E: 03; 04; 07; 13; 14; 16; 24; 25; 26; 27; 34; 36; 37; 38; 45; 47; 49; 59.
04, Hintlesham, 1981; 13, Bentley, 1975.
Betony must have been very frequent, even common, in the early 19th century, judging by
the number of herbarium specimens. *Illustrated page 455*

Stachys byzantina C. Koch Lamb's Ear M. A. Hyde 1974
(*S. lanata* Jacq., non Crantz)

Native of E. Europe and Asia. Common in gardens.
E: 23, Chelmondiston Tip.

Stachys sylvatica L. Hedge Woundwort J. Andrews 1754

Native. Hedges, wood margins and waysides. Frequent.
All squares.

Stachys palustris L. Marsh Woundwort Parkinson 1640

Native. In marshes, fens, beside rivers and ditches. Also a weed of wet arable land.
Frequent.
W: All squares except 64; 65; 66; 67; 75; 98.
93, by the Stour at Nayland, 1975; 97, Hopton Fen, 1981.
E: All squares except 28; 44; 47; 40; 50.
07, Thelnetham Fen, 1981; 13, Woolverstone, by the Orwell, 1981; 14, by the Gipping at
Ipswich, 1981; 24, Grundisburgh, 1981; 33, Felixstowe, 1980.

Stachys palustris × sylvatica Hybrid Woundwort Hind 1882
(*S. × ambigua* Sm.)

A native hybrid, found in damp fields and wet places. Rare or possibly overlooked.
E: 14, Bramford, 1935 (F. W. Simpson); 59, Mobb's Field, Oulton, 1959 (a member of
the Lowestoft Field Club).
There is a specimen in Hb. Atkins from the Gipping Valley, 1908, and Hind lists Sapiston,
Lakenheath and Belton.

Stachys annua (L.) L. Annual Woundwort Mrs F. Baker 1907

A casual, introduced from C. and S. Europe. Found in waste places. Rare.
E: 24, Woodbridge, 1934 (E. Milne-Redhead and H. K. Airy Shaw). Specimen in Kew.
59, Lowestoft, 1907.

Stachys arvensis (L.) L. Field Woundwort Sir J. Cullum 1773

A colonist and a weed of cultivated fields and gardens. Formerly common, now becoming
scarce.
W: All squares except 64; 65; 66; 67; 68; 74; 84; 85; 88; 96; 98.
94, Monks Eleigh, 1974.
E: All squares except 04; 17; 24; 26; 27; 44; 49; 58; 50.
13, Tattingstone, 1975; 16, Wetheringsett, 1979; 23, Harkstead, 1981; 59, Lowestoft,
same field, 1974-80.

Nepeta cataria L.   Catmint   J. Andrews 1749

Native or introduced. Roadside banks and margins. Generally rare. More frequent in West Suffolk.

W: 66; 67; 76; 77; 78; 84; 86; 93; 94; 96; 97; 98.

76, Dalham, 1979; 78, Brandon, 1980; 86, Bury St Edmunds, 1978. (All three, F. W. Simpson).

E: 04; 13; 14; 23; 28; 33; 35; 36; 45; 46; 47; 49.

14, Ipswich, 1980 (M. A. Hyde); 46, Wenhaston, c. 1970 (R. V. Ellis).

Catmint must have been common early in the 19th century around Ipswich. Specimen in Hb. Ipswich Museum, c. 1820. 'In the hedges between Handford Hall and Crane Hall. Hedges north side of the Bramford Road. Wherstead Road between the Ostrich and the Brick Kiln, west side of the road' (John Notcutt).   *Illustrated page 477*

Glechoma hederacea L.   Ground Ivy   Sir J. Cullum 1773
(*Nepeta hederacea* (L.) Trev.)

Native. In woods, copses, hedge-banks, etc. Very common. Prefers light, loamy soils, where it is sometimes abundant and dominant in clearings of old woodland. Flowers of various shades occur, from pale to dark violet and a form with pink flowers has been recorded from Arger Fen, Bures (sq. 93) and Dalham (sq. 76).

All squares.

Prunella laciniata (L.) L.   Cut-leaved Self-heal   Dr J. R. Ellis 1950

Introduced. Native in C. and S. Europe. Found in grassy old pastures and heaths. Rare or possibly overlooked. It was first found in Suffolk on a heath at Sotterley (sq. 48) in 1950, and was reported by members of Lowestoft Field Club to have increased in this locality over the following three years. In 1953 all flowers were cream-coloured, but in 1952 50% were pale blue. Some of the colour variations may well be hybrids with *P. vulgaris.*

Prunella vulgaris L.   Self-heal   Sir J. Cullum 1773

Native. Woods and damp grassland. Frequent. A form with white-coloured flowers has been reported from Sotterley and a rose-coloured form from Polstead.

All squares.

Melissa officinalis L.   Balm   Victoria County History of Suffolk, 1911

Introduced. Native of C. and S. Europe. Its occurrence in Suffolk is recorded in the Victoria County History of Suffolk, 1911, but no localities are given.

W: 96, Thurston, in wood, 1979 (Mrs E. M. Hyde).

E: 13, Woolverstone, 1971-81, thought to be a garden escape (Mrs E. M. Hyde); Brantham, waste ground near Bexford's car park, 1974; 14, Ipswich, Tower Ramparts, 1981; St Nicholas Churchyard, 1981; 48, Sotterley, 1978; 59, Lowestoft, 1978 (last two records, P. G. Lawson).

Acinos arvensis (Lam.) Dandy   Basil Thyme   Sir J. Cullum 1773
(*Calamintha acinos* (L.) Clairv.)

Native. Dry chalky and sandy heaths, old quarries and banks. Mainly concentrated in Breckland, but also found in the South and East of the County, where it is now decreasing.

W: 66; 67; 68; 76; 78; 86; 87; 94; 95; 96; 97; 98.
78, Lakenheath Warren, 1974; 87, West Stow, 1977; 98, Knettishall, 1981.
Still frequent in Breckland, 1981.
Pale-flowered forms, West Stow, 1977.
E: 04; 05; 14; 15; 45; 46; 47; 49; 59; 40.
05, roadside bank, A45, at Barking, 1973; 15, Barham, 1980; 47, Westleton, 1978; 49, Beccles, 1975.

Acinos rotundifolius Pers. Mrs F. Baker c. 1890
(*Calamintha graveolens* (Bieb.) Bentham)

An alien from the Mediterranean region. Known in Suffolk only from Oulton Broad, c. 1890.

CALAMINTHA CALAMINTS

The identification of the two species of Calamint, *C. sylvatica* ssp. *ascendens* and *C. nepeta* appears to have been as difficult for botanists in the 19th century as it is today. The distribution of the species as given in Hind's Flora is obviously incorrect. It gives the impression that *C. nepeta* only occurs in a few sites in West Suffolk and not at all in East Suffolk. *C. sylvatica* ssp. *ascendens* is, however, given for many parishes in both West and East Suffolk.
Recent investigations have shown that *C. nepeta* occurs in both West and East Suffolk, with its main concentrations in the valleys of the R. Stour and its tributaries, the Box and the Brett. *C. sylvatica* ssp. *ascendens* has a more scattered distribution, occurring in both West and East Suffolk. It is generally less common and the colonies smaller.
Both species occur on dry roadside banks and in and around churchyards. *C. nepeta* is abundant on at least three stretches of railway bank, at Brantham, Hadleigh and Westley. With the present practice of constantly machine-cutting the verges, plants now have less chance of growing and flowering naturally and the botanists less chance of finding well developed specimens. *C. sylvatica* ssp. *ascendens* can be distinguished from *C. nepeta* by the long cilia on the calyx teeth. In *C. nepeta* these are much shorter, fewer or absent. *C. nepeta,* moreover, has hairs protruding from the mouth of the calyx after flowering.

Calamintha sylvatica ssp. **ascendens** (Jordan) P. W. Ball   Common Calamint
Sir J. Cullum 1773

Native. On dry hedge-banks. Locally common, but decreasing.
W: 77; 86; 87; 88; 96; 97.
77, Icklingham, 1981; 86, Bury St Edmunds, 1980; 97, Sapiston, 1981; Lt. Fakenham, 1980.
E: 04; 05; 13; 15; 23; 25; 26; 28; 35; 46; 47; 49; 58; 59.
05, Creeting St Mary, 1981; 13, Freston, 1981; 23, Erwarton, 1980; 26, Framlingham, 1980; 59, Carlton Colville, 1980.
All parish records, Mrs E. M. Hyde.

Calamintha nepeta (L.) Savi   Lesser Calamint   J. Andrews 1744

Native. Dry hedge-banks, churchyards and railway banks. Local. Sometimes in great quantity.

W: 66; 74; 76; 84; 86; 93; 94.
66/76, roadside at Moulton, 1981; 93, Polstead, 1980.
E: 03; 04; 07; 13; 14.
03, East Bergholt, 1980; Higham, abundant, 1980; 13, churchyard and roadside at Brantham, 1980; 14, Chattisham, 1980.

Clinopodium vulgare L.   Wild Basil   Sir J. Cullum 1773
(*Calamintha clinopodium* Benth.)

Native. Hedge-banks, chalk-pits, railway embankments, open scrub, usually on Chalk or chalky Boulder Clay. Frequent.
W: All squares except 67; 83; 85.
76, Dalham, 1981; Gt Saxham, 1980; 86, Gt Livermere, 1980; 94, Brent Eleigh, 1981.
E: All squares except 03; 13; 24; 28; 33; 34; 36; 37; 44; 48; 49; 59; 40; 50.
04, Hadleigh, disused railway line, 1981; 15, Coddenham, 1981; 17, Braiseworth, 1980; 46, Westleton, 1980.   *Illustrated page 473*

Origanum vulgare L.   Marjoram   Sir J. Cullum 1781
Native. Old grassy waysides, railway cuttings, banks, chalk-pits. Now scarce and decreasing.
W: 76; 78; 83; 86; 96.
78, Wangford, 1973; 86, Bury St Edmunds, railway cutting, 1981. Variety with white flowers also seen here.
E: 04; 06; 13; 14; 15; 16; 25; 34; 38; 46; 59.
13, Woolverstone, 1977; 15, Coddenham, 1978.
There is a specimen in Hb. Atkins from Burstall, 1908. A colony was observed on a roadside bank between Burstall and Sproughton until 1940 (F. W. Simpson).
                                                                       Illustrated page 475

Thymus praecox Opiz ssp. **britannicus** (Ronn.) Holub   Common Wild Thyme
(*T. drucei* Ronn.)   Sir J. Cullum 1773

Native. On dry grassland and heaths. Mainly occurs in Breckland, but may be found on dunes and other heathy places. Local.
W: 67; 76; 77; 78; 86; 87; 88; 96; 97.
67, Mildenhall; Freckenham; 76, Herringswell; Risby; 77, Barton Mills; Cavenham; 78, Lakenheath Warren; 87, Elveden; Wordwell; 88, Thetford Heath; 97, Euston.
E: 07; 13; 17; 35; 45; 46.
07, Hinderclay; Wortham Common; 13, Holbrook; 17, Stuston Common; 35, Tunstall, 1980; 45, Friston; 46, Thorpeness; Dunwich; Westleton.

Thymus pulegioides L.   Larger Wild Thyme   Sir J. Cullum 1773
(*T. chamaedrys* Fr.
T. ovatus Mill.
T. glaber Mill.)

Native. On dry chalky banks, old quarries, grassland, commons and heaths. Also occurs on the Red and Coralline Crags and some sands. This species is often found flourishing on old ant-hills on the margins of fens, and elsewhere. Formerly frequent, now much rarer, and extinct in many areas, due to loss of habitats.
W: 67, Worlington; 76, Risby; Cavenham; 77, Cavenham; Eriswell; 78, Lakenheath Warren; 84, Long Melford; 87; 88, Thetford Heath; 95; 98, Knettishall, 1981.

E: 04, Somersham; 07, Redgrave; 14, Lt. Blakenham; Bramford; 15, Coddenham, 1974; 17; 23, Nacton Heath; 24; 35, Snape Warren; 38, Bungay; 39; 45, Sudbourne Park; Knodishall Whin.
A rare white-flowered form has been recorded from Sudbourne Park.

Thymus serpyllum L.   Breckland Wild Thyme   C. C. Babington 1852
Native . On dry, open sandy heaths and banks, only in the Breckland area. Rare.
W: 66, Herringswell, 1980; 67, Mildenhall; 76, Risby; 77, Icklingham, 1980; West Stow, 1980; Mildenhall, 1980; Eriswell, 1980; Cavenham; Barton Mills; 78, Lakenheath Warren, 1980; 87, West Stow Heath; Barnham; Elveden, 1980; 88, Thetford Heath; Barnham Cross Common, 1976; 98, Knettishall, 1981.

Lycopus europaeus L.   Gipsy-wort   J. Andrews 1744
Native. Sides of ponds, rivers and in marshes. Frequent. Can be found beside all the main rivers and their tributaries.
All squares.

MENTHA   **MINTS**

A difficult genus with identification of species often complicated, due to their hybrid origin. It is now thought that there are four species native in Britain, *Mentha pulegium* L. Penny Royal; *M. aquatica* L. Water Mint; *M. arvensis* L. Corn Mint; *M. suaveolens* Ehrh. (*M. rotundifolia* auct.) Apple-scented Mint. There are at least two introduced species, *M. spicata* L. Spearmint, a native of Europe, cultivated and well naturalised, and *M. requienii* Benth., from Corsica and Sardinia, which I have not yet seen in Suffolk.
M. longifolia (L.) Huds., Horse Mint, a native of Europe, N. Africa and Asia, is now said to be absent from Britain and N.W. Europe, although many of our records have been identified as this species. Some may perhaps be hairy-leaved forms or hybrids, involving *M. spicata* and *M. suaveolens* and *M. aquatica*. The issue is very confusing, as there are many hairy or glabrous hybrids and intermediates. However, *M. longifolia* or its hybrids, may well be in cultivation in the County or occur as escapes or throw-outs. Some hybrids are sterile, but they survive and increase in many habitats, because of the vigorous nature of their root system. It is, therefore, a complicated and difficult situation and remains, at present, unresolved.

Mentha pulegium L.   Penny Royal   Sir J. Cullum 1773
Native. In damp places and margins of ponds. Formerly not uncommon, but now very rare, perhaps extinct. The reason for its disappearance is unknown. At one time this species was much used medicinally. In the Mediterranean countries and islands, *M. pulegium* can often be found growing and flowering profusely in early summer, on rather bare, hard ground in hollows which have been wet during the winter. It may be that our English summers are not so hot as formerly and are unsuitable for this species. Its disappearance is general in Britain. Hind gives 10 parishes.
W: 77, Tuddenham St Mary, 1946; 84, Acton and Sudbury, 1939. All three records by Mrs M. Southwell.
E: No recent records. There is a specimen in Hb. Atkins from Bungay, 1907.

Mentha arvensis L.   Corn Mint   J. Andrews 1743

Native and a colonist. By ponds and in woodland glades, where it is probably native. A weed of arable fields. Common.
W: All squares except 65; 67.
68, Lakenheath, 1980; 94, Brent Eleigh, 1981; 95, Felshamhall Wood, 1980.
E: All squares except 15; 17; 33; 44; 49; 50.
04, Bramford, 1981; 23, Harkstead, 1981; 47, Bramfield, 1980.

Mentha aquatica × arvensis   Whorled Mint   Sir J. Cullum 1773
(*M. × verticillata* L.)

In ditches, beside ponds and damp fields. Occasional, but overlooked.
W: 75; 77, Herringswell; 88; 95, Felshamhall Wood, 1980.
E: 16; 34; 35; 37; 47; 50.
16, Mickfield, c. 1955; 34, Sutton; 35, Snape; 37, Wenhaston; 47, Southwold.

Mentha arvensis × spicata   Cardiac Mint   J. Andrews 1745
(*M. × gentilis* L.
M. cardiaca (S. F. Gray) Baker)

Grown in gardens. Often thrown out and becoming naturalised. A very variable plant.
W: 66, Herringswell, Red Lodge Warren, 1979 (Mrs E. M. Hyde), conf. Dr R. M. Harley.
E: 13, Woolverstone, 1979, conf. Dr R. M. Harley; 49, Beccles Tip, 1975 (P. G. Lawson).

Mentha aquatica × arvensis × spicata   Glabrous Red Mint   Paget 1834
(*M. × smithiana* R. A. Graham   Black Peppermint
M. rubra Sm., non Mill.)

Probably a hybrid of garden origin. Damp waysides, ditches, waste ground. Rare.
W: 86, Bury St Edmunds, waste ground near Railway Station, 1979 (M. A. Hyde), conf. Dr R. M. Harley; 94, Newton.
E: 46, Dunwich.

Mentha aquatica L.   Water Mint   J. Andrews 1743

Native. In marshes, bogs and beside ponds, rivers and streams. Very frequent.
All squares.
Beside all rivers and their tributaries, 1981.   *Illustrated page 478*

Mentha aquatica × spicata   Peppermint   Sir T. G. Cullum 1804
(*M. × piperita* L.)

A very variable hybrid, much cultivated at one time. Now rare. Found in damp places.
W: No recent records. Hind recorded it for Honington, Bury and Ousden.
E: 13, marsh at Brantham, 1975 (Mrs E. M. Hyde). Identified by Dr R. M. Harley. A spontaneously produced wild hybrid, hairy form; 36, Gt Glemham Park; 46, East Bridge.

Mentha aquatica × longifolia   Downy Mint   Hind 1886
(*M. × dumetorum* Schultes
M. pubescens auct.)

In wet places, marshes and wayside ditches. Rare. Recorded in Hind's Flora from

Redgrave Fen, Mellis and Lakenheath. The only recent record is from Black Hill, Icklingham, in 1967 by A. W. Punter.

Mentha suaveolens Ehrh.   Apple-scented Mint   J. Andrews 1744
(*M. rotundifolia* auct., non (L.) Huds.)   Round-leaved Mint

Doubtfully native and probably introduced. On damp waysides and in ditches. Uncommon. It is suggested that some of the records may refer to hybrids.
W: 86, Bury St Edmunds; 88, Thetford Nunnery; 97.
E: 04; 06; 07; 14; 35; 36; 45; 46; 59.
04, Hadleigh; 06, Bacton; 14, Ipswich; Bramford; 35, Snape; 36, Benhall; Badingham; 45, Aldeburgh; 46, Dunwich; 59, Oulton.

Mentha spicata × suaveolens   Lamb Mint   W. Jordan 1883
(*M. × villosa* Huds. nm. *alopecuroides* (Hull) Briq.   Velvet Mint
M. × niliaca Juss. ex Jacq.)

Found in waysides and ditches, often as an escape from cultivation or thrown out with garden rubbish.
W: 66; 67; 75; 77; 78; 83; 84; 86; 87; 88; 93; 94; 97.
66, Herringswell, 1980; 78, Brandon, 1978; 86, Shaker's Lane, Bury St Edmunds, 1976.
E: 06; 13; 14; 23; 25; 27; 36; 37; 46; 47; 49; 58; 59; 40.
13, Brantham, 1979; 14, by the R. Gipping at Ipswich, 1974; 37, Walpole, 1981; 58, Covehithe, 1981; 59, Lowestoft, 1980.

Mentha longifolia (L.) Huds.   Horse Mint   Jackson 1685
(*M. sylvestris* L.)   Long-leaved Mint

Doubtfully native. Probably introduced and cultivated, escaping or thrown out of gardens and naturalised in damp places and on waysides. Confused with forms of *M. spicata* and hybrids, to which most of the records below probably refer. True *M. longifolia* probably does not occur in Britain at all.
W: 86; 87; 94; 95; 97.
E: 05; 06; 13; 16; 36; 46; 47.

Mentha spicata L.   Spearmint   Sir J. Cullum 1773
(*M. viridis* (L.) L.
M. longifolia auct., non (L.) Huds.)

Introduced from C. Europe and grown in gardens. Often escaping or thrown out. Near sites of former cultivation, in ditches and waste places. More frequent than the records suggest. May be overlooked or mistaken for other species. The origin of this species is not known and it may have been derived in cultivation.
W: 66; 67; 74; 77; 78; 86; 97.
67, Mildenhall, 1980; 97, Lt. Fakenham, 1980.
E: 14; 15; 23; 24; 44; 46; 48; 49; 57; 59; 40.
14, Ipswich, 1981; 24, Woodbridge, 1981; 46, Middleton, 1979 (hairy form).

Lavandula angustifolia Mill.   Lavender   M. A. Hyde 1976

Introduced. Native of the Mediterranean region. Commonly grown in gardens. Sometimes thrown out and persisting.
E: 23, Chelmondiston Tip, 1976-7.

Salvia triloba L. f.   Three-lobed Sage   M. Taylor 1976

Introduced. Native of the Mediterranean region. A very variable species. Aromatic. The leaves are used for making a beverage in some areas. One plant appeared in a garden at Stowmarket with other casuals from bird-seed.

Salvia glutinosa L.   Jupiter's Distaff   Mrs J. Willis 1974

Casual. Native of C. and S.E. Europe, where it is found in mountain woods.
E: 04, Hadleigh. One plant on bank near the old railway arch, Hook Lane, 1974.

Salvia pratensis L.   Meadow Clary   Henslow & Skepper 1860
                           Meadow Sage

Recorded doubtfully in Hind's Flora from Pakenham, Hadleigh and Woodbridge. No authentic records. It could occur on chalk grassland or in old pits in the Breckland.

Salvia verbenaca L.   Wild Clary   J. Andrews 1745
(*S. horminoides* Pourr.)

Possibly native. Introduced into some areas for the reputed medicinal properties of its seeds. Dry banks, waysides, quarries and especially churchyards. The flowers are usually small, cleistogamous, and shorter than the calyx. (Rarely colonies can be found with more open and larger flowers, hermaphrodite, and the plant may then be mistaken for *S. pratensis*. This plant grows at Burgh and Clopton, and formerly grew at Rushmere.) Some Suffolk colonies have persisted for very many years. One, on the roadside bank by Newbourn Church, has been observed since 1926.
W: All squares except 65; 83; 85; 93; 95; 98.
86, by railway, Bury St Edmunds, 1981; 97, Sapiston, 1981.
E: All squares except 26; 27; 58; 59.
14, Derby Road Station, Ipswich, 1981; St Peter's Churchyard, 1980; 23, Erwarton Churchyard, 1978; 57, Southwold, 1980.

Salvia verticillata L.   Whorled Clary   Hind 1884

Introduced. Native in the mountains of S. Europe. Found in quarries and on waysides. Prefers chalky soil. The last known record was from a chalk pit at Gt Cornard (sq. 93) in 1936.
W: 93, Gt Cornard.
E: 14, Bramford, c. 1935.
Hind's Flora records the plant from two sites, at Higham Railway Station in 1884, and at Long Melford in 1888.

SOLANACEAE

NIGHTSHADE FAMILY

Nicandra physalodes (L.) Gaertn.   Apple of Peru   M. L. Boldero 1882
                                        Shoo-fly Plant

Native of Peru. A casual of cultivated ground.
W: No recent records. Hind recorded it for Somerton, 1882 and Honington, 1894.

E: 14, garden of the Convent of Jesus and Mary, Ipswich, 1954; among a crop of potatoes in a garden at Claydon, 1971 (C. A. Watchman); 23, Chelmondiston Tip, 1978 (Mrs E. M. Hyde); 49, Beccles Tip, 1977 (P. G. Lawson); 59, Lowestoft, 1974.

| **Lycium barbarum** L. | Duke of Argyll's Tea Tree | Hind's Flora 1889 |
| (*L. halimifolium* Mill. | Box Thorn | |

including *L. chinense* Mill.)

Introduced. A native of S.E. Europe and W. Asia. Now a frequent and naturalised alien in hedges and waste places, especially near the coast, and on the sites of former cottages. This species has variable types of growth. Specimens in sheltered habitats on good soil produce larger leaves and stems, with few or small thorns, compared with those naturalised on poor soil especially near the coast on sand and shingle. In the latter habitat, bushes are generally very thorny, although there are sometimes a few branches with few, or no thorns.

All squares except 64; 68; 98; 06; 25; 27; 48.

| **Atropa bella-donna** L. | Deadly Nightshade | Parkinson 1640 |
| | Dwale | |

Perhaps formerly native in woods on chalky soils. A casual or relic of cultivation in waste places, quarries, and sites of old gardens and shrubberies. *Solanum dulcamara* L. is often mistaken for this species. Contains a very poisonous narcotic due to the presence of the alkaloids atropine and hyoscyamine.

It has been observed at Felixstowe for approximately the past 50 years. Plants have been found on six sites; four of the sites are in the vicinity of Old Felixstowe. It is suggested that they may be survivals of introduction by the Romans, as there was quite an extensive garrison at Old Felixstowe. All the Felixstowe plants have very pale lilac-coloured flowers compared with those found in other areas. However, the berries are just as bright and shiny as in the more normal coloured flowers. They are, of course, poisonous and on no account must be eaten. There is a danger that one day these plants and their berries may be found by some over-zealous person and destroyed, as frequently occurs with this species. When it is possible I visit the sites and remove the berries, in order to protect the plants. Some of the berries have been planted at Woolverstone near a site where a colony has existed for a number of years.

W: 78; 84; 85; 86; 88.

85, Stanningfield, c. 1960.

E: 13; 14; 23; 33; 36; 59.

13, Woolverstone, 1981; 14, Ipswich, two sites, 1981; 33, Felixstowe, 1980.

Illustrated page 511

| **Hyoscyamus niger** L. | Henbane | Sir J. Cullum 1773 |

Possibly native on the sea coast in sandy places. Elsewhere a weed or casual of waste places and fields, sometimes appearing in large numbers. In 1975 hundreds of plants were observed in a pig enclosure at Harkstead, together with a large number of the Great Mullein. The pigs cleared the field of other vegetation, leaving the Henbane and Mullein untouched (Mrs E. M. Hyde).

W: 66; 76; 77; 78; 87; 94; 96.

76, Cavenham; 78, Lakenheath, 1975; 87, Elveden, very large colony, 1979, in field crossed by cattle, remained untouched (F. W. Simpson).

E: 03; 05; 13; 14; 16; 23; 25; 33; 34; 36; 44; 45; 48; 49; 59.
14, Ipswich, 1981; 23, Landguard Common, 1980; 33, Bawdsey, 1979; 35, Chillesford, 1981. *Illustrated page 511*

Hyoscyamus albus L.   White Henbane   F. W. Simpson 1932
An alien, native in the Mediterranean region. A single plant was found on waste ground on the edge of Bixley Heath, Ipswich (sq. 14). Detd. at Kew.

Physalis alkekengi L.   Chinese Lantern   Miss E. S. Rowling 1956
Introduced. A native of C. and S. Europe. A casual or garden escape.
W: 68/78, Lakenheath; 86, Fornham St Genevieve, 1957.
E: 13, Stutton, 1976; 14, Ipswich; Lt. Blakenham; 49, Beccles, 1978 (P. G. Lawson).

Salpichroa origanifolia (Lam.) Baillon   Mrs C. H. Jones 1970
Alien, native in the temperate areas of Eastern S. America, but known to be naturalised in the Channel Islands and along the South Coast of England. There are two records for Suffolk. One is that of Mrs Jones, who found a plant growing at the base of the cliffs at Lowestoft (identified by Dr E. A. Ellis), the other is from Pakefield in 1974. Still at Lowestoft, 1980.

Solanum nigrum L.   Black Nightshade   Sir J. Cullum 1773
Colonist. A weed of gardens, fields and waste places. Common and sometimes abundant. All squares.

Solanum nigrum × nitidibaccatum   Dr A. C. Leslie 1980
(*S. × procurrens* Leslie)
W: 77, Eriswell, three plants in a market garden. Both parents were present in abundance.

Solanum sarrachoides Sendtn.   Green Nightshade   F. W. Simpson 1953
Alien. Native of Brazil. An increasing weed of fields, gardens and waste places.
W: 66, roadside at Moulton; Exning, 1977; 77, Barton Mills Tip, 1977; Icklingham, 1981; Eriswell, 1980; 78, Lakenheath.
E: 13, Freston, 1981; Brantham; 14, waste ground, Belstead Road, Ipswich, 1974; Woodbridge Road, Ipswich, 1981; 23, Landguard Common; Chelmondiston Tip, 1975; 24, Foxhall, 1953 and in same site, 1976; Martlesham, 1978; 33, Felixstowe, 1980; 35, Snape Maltings, 1977; 47, Blythburgh; Southwold; Wenhaston, 1978; 58, Benacre, 1977; 59, North Denes, Lowestoft, 1976.
Some of these records may refer to *S. nitidibaccatum* Bitter.

Solanum nitidibaccatum Bitter
Alien. Native of S. America. A weed of fields, gardens and waste places.
W: 77, Eriswell, 1980 (Dr A. C. Leslie); 78, Lakenheath, three sites. Conf. Dr A. C. Leslie.

Solanum triflorum Nutt.   Mrs M. Southwell 1948

An alien. Native in N. America and probably introduced with American seed during the
Second World War. In fields and waste places, usually on sandy soils, where it may persist
and become naturalised.
W: 77, Icklingham, 1948 to 1975.
E: 45, Iken, 1975 (Mrs M. Stephenson; P. G. Lawson).

Solanum dulcamara L.   Bittersweet   Sir J. Cullum 1773
                           Woody Nightshade

Native. In hedges and damp places, beside ponds and ditches, and on the coast. Frequent.
All squares.
White-flowered form rare: 14, Felixstowe Road, Ipswich, c. 1930 (F. W. Simpson); 49,
North Cove, 1975 (M. A. Hyde).

Solanum tuberosum L.   Potato

Cultivated. Native of S. America. May be found in waste and cultivated fields and on
rubbish tips.

Solanum sisymbrifolium Lam.   Mrs E. M. Hyde 1974

Alien. Native of temperate S. America.
E: 14, car park, Turret Lane, Ipswich, 1974-75. Detd. at the British Museum.

Solanum cornutum Lam.   Buffalo Bur   J. R. Egerton 1940
(*S. rostratum* Dunal)

An alien, introduced from Mexico. Probably introduced with animal feed. A common
weed in N. America.
E: 05, Tarston Farm, near Darmsden, 1972 (J. Vane); 14, Bramford Tye, 1940; Crane
Hill, Ipswich; 48, North Cove, 1975; 49, Beccles, 1979 (P. G. Lawson).

Lycopersicon esculentum Mill.   Tomato   F. W. Simpson c. 1947

A native of S. America. May be found on rubbish tips, waste places, beaches, picnic sites
and about septic tanks and sewerage works.
W: 66, Newmarket, 1980; 67; 68; 77, Barton Mills Tip, 1977; 94, Brent Eleigh; 96,
Woolpit Tip, 1975.
E: 04; 13; 14; 15; 23; 33; 45.
04, Raydon; 13, Woolverstone (septic tank); 14, Ipswich, several sites, 1981; 15,
Coddenham; 23, Chelmondiston Tip, 1974; Erwarton; Shotley; 33, Felixstowe Ferry; 45,
Aldeburgh.
Several years ago a seedling appeared on the beach at Felixstowe Ferry and flourished and
I was able to gather about two pounds of ripe and green fruit of fair quality.

Datura stramonium L.   Thorn Apple   Rev. G. Crabbe 1798

An alien, introduced and naturalised. Native in many temperate and sub-tropical parts of
the Northern Hemisphere. Found in cultivated and waste places. Very widespread, though
apparently more common in East than in West Suffolk. Sporadic in appearance. Seeds
may remain dormant for a number of years. Sometimes plants occur in large numbers in

favourable years. Formerly cultivated for its medicinal properties, as it contains the alkaloids hyoscyamine, hyocine and scopolamine. Flowers are usually white, more rarely mauve or violet.

W: 67; 68; 76; 77; 78; 87; 94; 96.

77, Mildenhall, 1976; 87, West Stow, 1979.

E: 03; 04; 05; 07; 13; 14; 15; 16; 23; 24; 25; 26; 27; 33; 34; 35; 37; 38; 45; 46; 47; 48; 57; 58.

14, Ipswich, 1980; 34, Ramsholt, 1981 (Miss L. E. Neal). *Illustrated page 511*

An unarmed variety with purple flowers was found in an Ipswich garden by Miss Denniss, 1973.

Var. **tatula** (L.) Torr. — a mauve form, was seen at Chelmondiston in 1971 and 1975, Felixstowe in 1974, and at Gazeley in 1975.

Nicotiana rustica L. Small Tobacco Plant G. L. Ransome 1975

Introduced. Native of N. America. Casual. Occasionally cultivated. Nicotine, used as an insecticide, is obtained from this plant.

E: 34, two plants on the edge of an excavation for a reservoir at Hollesley, September 1975.

Nicotiana alata Link & Otto Tobacco Plant M. A. Hyde 1974

Casual. Native of Argentina and Brazil. Cultivated in gardens and naturalised in parts of Europe.

E: 14, Belstead Road, waste ground, Ipswich, 1974.

Petunia × hybrida Hort. Vilm.-Andr. Petunia M. A. Hyde 1974

Introduced. Native of S. America. Commonly grown in gardens.

W: 77, Barton Mills Tip, 1977.

E: 14, Ipswich, waste ground, 1974; 23, Chelmondiston Tip, 1974.

BUDDLEJACEAE

BUDDLEIA FAMILY

Buddleja davidii Franch. Buddleia G. M. French 1944
Butterfly Bush

An established alien or colonist. Native of China. Found about towns and waste places, especially derelict housing sites; on walls and buildings, even high up on roofs and chimney stacks. Frequent. This plant increased rapidly during the Second World War on bomb sites. It is abundant about Ipswich. Its flower panicles attract butterflies. ('Buddleia' so named in honour of the botanist Adam Buddle d. 1715, one time Rector of Henley in Suffolk.)

W: 66; 77; 78; 86; 88; 94.

78, Brandon, 1980.

E: 05; 13; 14; 23; 24; 25; 33; 35; 37; 45; 46; 49.

14, Ipswich, abundant, 1981; 35, Campsey Ash, 1980; 46, Leiston, 1979.

A specimen with white flowers was noted from Halesworth, near the Station, in 1973.

SCROPHULARIACEAE

FIGWORT FAMILY

Limosella aquatica L.   Mudwort   Borrer 1808

Native. On wet mud on the edges of pools, ponds and muddy places. Probably extinct. Has not been seen in Suffolk since c. 1860.

Hind records the plant from Barton Mills on low wet ground, and from Lowestoft 'near the fish houses' in 1808.

Mimulus guttatus DC.   Monkey Flower   Miss E. S. Rowling 1902
(*M. luteus* auct., non L.)

Introduced. Native of N. America. Naturalised on the sides of streams and ditches. Frequent from c. 1925 to 1940 and at that time increasing. Now scarce. Extinct in some of the parishes listed below.

E: 13, Wherstead; Woolverstone; 23, Chelmondiston, 1974; 24, Purdis Farm; 34, Capel St Andrew; 35, Lt. Glemham; Blaxhall, 1980 (Mrs I. M. Vaughan); 44, Orford; 59, Lowestoft Denes.

Mimulus moschatus Dougl. ex Lindl.   Mrs E. M. Hyde 1973

Introduced. Native of N. America. Cultivated and escaping.

E: 13, Woolverstone Churchyard, 1973-81; 35, Ufford, appeared in a vegetable garden, 1975 (W. E. Lewis).

Verbascum blattaria L.   Moth Mullein   Wigg 1805

Introduced into gardens. Occurs as a casual on waysides and waste places. Native of continental Europe.

W: 87, Elveden.

E: 06, Ash Farm, Mendlesham; 23, Felixstowe Maltings, c. 1936; 25, Bredfield; Dallinghoo; 45, Friston; 49, Beccles.

Verbascum virgatum Stokes   Twiggy Mullein   Davy 1828
                                   Large-flowered Mullein

An introduced plant in Suffolk, though native in Cornwall and South Devon. On waysides and waste places. Rare.

W: 87, West Stow.

E: 04, Hadleigh; 24, Martlesham; Foxhall, 1975-1981 (F. W. Simpson). Detd. Dr I. K. Ferguson. 35, Tunstall, by a rubbish dump, 1974; Iken, 1974.

Verbascum phoeniceum L.   Purple Mullein   Hind 1880

An alien, native in E. Europe and W. Asia. Known in Suffolk only from the original record by Hind from a gravelly bank near the tail-race of Nayland Mill (sq. 93).

Verbascum phlomoides L.   Woolly Mullein   P. G. Lawson 1977

Introduced. Native of continental Europe. Frequently grown in gardens. Increasingly occurring on roadsides, waste places and tips. Probably overlooked or confused with *V. thapsus,* with which it hybridises.

E: 03, Stratford St Mary, 1980 (N. Hunt); 14, Ipswich and Sproughton, waste ground, on industrial estate and beside the railway line, c. 200 plants, 1981 (F. W. Simpson); Bramford, 1980 (E. Milne-Redhead); 25, Bromeswell, 1981, two specimens in the colony with white flowers (F.W.S.); 35, Blaxhall, 1980; 57, Walberswick, 1980, detd. E. J. Clement; 59, Oulton, 1977 (P. G. Lawson).

Verbascum densiflorum Bertol. H. Boreham 1952
(*V. thapsiforme* Schrad.)

An alien, native in continental Europe and N. Africa. Found as a casual in a sand pit at Mildenhall Road, Bury St Edmunds (sq. 86). The habitat was destroyed in 1953.

Verbascum thapsus L. Great Mullein Sir J. Cullum 1773
  Aaron's Rod

Native. Heaths, clearings in woods, quarries, cliffs and waste places. Frequent.
All squares except 75; 17; 48; 50.
W: 77, Cavenham Heath; 76, Dalham; Barrow, 1981.
E: 14, Ipswich, 1981; 13, Stutton, 1980; 23, Harkstead, 1981; 24, Foxhall, 1981; 33, Bawdsey, 1980.

Verbascum speciosum Schrad. F. W. Simpson 1930

Alien. Native of S. E. Europe. Small colony naturalised on railway bank at Gt Blakenham (sq. 15), 1930-81. Detd. Dr I. K. Ferguson.

Verbascum pulverulentum Vill. Hoary Mullein Dillenius 1724

Native. On banks, waysides, verges and marginal land. Generally uncommon, though locally abundant. Mainly restricted to two districts.
W: 76, Higham, 1980; Barrow Bottom, 1981; Kentford; 86, Bury St Edmunds, 1981; Lt. Saxham; Fornham All Saints; Westley; Rushbrooke; 88, clearing near Elveden.
E: 48, Sotterley; 49, St Olave's; Herringfleet; Beccles Station, 1980; 59, Oulton Broad.

Illustrated page 476

Verbascum lychnitis L. White Mullein Sir J. Cullum 1773

Doubtfully native. Waysides, waste places and quarries. Rare. Recorded from squares 88, 96 and 46 (Westleton) in the 1950's. Hind's Flora has several records.

Verbascum nigrum L. Dark Mullein J. Andrews 1746

Native. Dry chalky banks, waysides, quarries and in grassy places. More frequent in Breckland.
W: All squares except 64; 65; 74; 75; 83; 85.
66/76, Moulton, 1981; 87, West Stow, 1981.
E: All squares except 06; 07; 13; 16; 17; 26; 27; 33; 34; 36; 38; 44; 48; 49; 58; 59; 40; 50.
14, Belstead, 1980; Ipswich, railway bank, 1978; 15, Creeting St Mary, 1981; 47, Blythburgh, 1981; Walberswick, 1977.
Hb. Ipswich Museum: 'Corner of corn field S.E. of Brook's Hall adjoining the lane at the back of the King's Barracks', c. 1810 (John Notcutt). *Illustrated page 477*

Verbascum nigrum × pulverulentum
(*V. × wirtgenii* Franch.)
W: 76, Barrow, 1980 (F. W. Simpson); 88, south of Thetford, date and finder not known.

Verbascum nigrum × thapsus   P. D. Sell 1966
(*V. × semialbum* Chaub.)
W: 77, between Tuddenham and Temple Bridge, 1969; 87, north of Culford, 1966. Both records by P. D. Sell.

Scrophularia vernalis L.   Yellow Figwort   Sir J. Cullum 1774
Introduced. Native of C. and S. Europe. Naturalised in shady plantations, shrubberies and waste places. This species was first recorded at Fornham St Genevieve in 1774 and was still there in 1979.
W: 86, Bury St Edmunds; Fornham St Genevieve; Hardwick Heath; 94, Gt Waldingfield, 1978 (E. Milne-Redhead); 96, Beyton; Gt Barton; Thurston.
E: 03; 24, Nacton.

Scrophularia nodosa L.   Common Figwort   Sir J. Cullum 1773
                                              Knotted Figwort
Native. In damp and wet woods and copses. Common.
W: All squares except 67; 68; 98.
95, Monks' Park Wood, 1980.
E: All squares except 27; 33; 37; 45; 58; 40; 50.
24, Playford, 1981; 39, Bungay, 1981.

Scrophularia auriculata L.   Water Figwort   Sir J. Cullum 1773
(*S. aquatica* auct., non L.)   Water Betony
Native. Beside streams and rivers, in wet woodland glades, old meadows and ditches. Common.
All squares.
W: 86, Bury St Edmunds, by R. Lark; 97, Sapiston, by the Black Bourn, 1980.
E: 13, Holbrook, mill-stream, 1981; 14, Ipswich, by R. Gipping, 1981; 23, Erwarton, 1980.

Scrophularia umbrosa Dum.   Green Figwort   Hind 1882
(*S. alata* auct.)   Shady Figwort
Native. In damp, shady woods and beside rivers. Very rare, but possibly local and overlooked. It probably occurs beside the Little Ouse in North-west Suffolk and elsewhere in the valleys bordering the Fens.
W: 78, Brandon; 95, Felshamhall and Monks' Park Woods.
E: Not recorded recently.
Hind's Flora records the species only from Hinderclay Wood (sq. 07), but there is some doubt concerning the correct identification of his specimen.

Antirrhinum majus L.   Greater Snapdragon   Sir J. Cullum 1773
An alien introduced from the Mediterranean region, sometimes established on old walls,

railway embankments and waste places, and on rubbish tips as a garden throw-out or escape. Usually red-flowered.

W: 66; 67; 74; 76; 77; 83; 86; 88; 93.

77, Barton Mills, 1980; 86, Bury St Edmunds, near Station, 1980.

E: 13; 14; 15; 16; 17; 23; 24; 27; 39; 48.

14, Ipswich, several sites, 1981; 24, near Woodbridge Station, 1979.

Misopates orontium (L.) Raf.　　Weasel's Snout　　　　　　J. Andrews 1745
(*Antirrhinum orontium* L.)　　Lesser Snapdragon

A colonist and weed of light arable land, formerly common, especially on the eastern side of the County, now only occasional.

W: 86; 93; 94; 96.

E: 03; 04; 06; 13; 14; 15; 16; 23; 24; 25; 27; 34; 35; 36; 38; 39; 45; 46; 47; 48; 49; 57; 59; 40; 50.

13, Harkstead, 1978; 23, fields at Chelmondiston and Erwarton, 1979; 35, Blaxhall, 1981; 47, Dunwich, 1980 (P. G. Lawson); 48, Beccles, 1974.

Chaenorhinum minus (L.) Lange　　Small Toadflax　　　　　Sir J. Cullum 1773
(*Linaria minor* (L.) Desf.)　　Lesser Toadflax

A colonist of waste places, especially railway embankments, tracks and fields. Not very frequent and decreasing. Formerly a common weed of farmland on the Chalk and Boulder Clay, now reduced by spraying.

W: All squares except 65; 67; 83; 85; 88.

76, Moulton, 1981; Gazeley, 1980; 87, Barnham, 1980.

E: All squares except 07; 17; 25; 34; 35; 38; 39; 44; 46; 47; 48; 58; 59; 50.

15, Coddenham, 1977.

Very large specimens were observed in 1970 growing on the railway track at Felixstowe Town Station (sq. 33), despite the heavy pollution by diesel oil. Seedlings appeared annually until 1977.

Linaria triphylla (L.) Mill.　　　　　　　　　　　J. S. Wilkinson 1908

Casual. Native of the Mediterranean region. Known in Suffolk only from the one record in 1908, at Ipswich.

Linaria chalepensis (L.) Mill.　　White Toadflax　　　　F. W. Simpson 1936

Casual. Native in the Mediterranean region. Recorded from Ipswich (sq. 14) in 1936.

Linaria purpurea (L.) Mill.　　Purple Toadflax　　　　　Miss Woods 1933

Introduced from S. and C. Italy. Grown in gardens, especially on rockeries and banks. Sometimes seeding and becoming naturalised. Not uncommon.

W: 66, Newmarket, 1977; 76, Dalham, 1981; 77, Barton Mills, 1977; 86, Bury St Edmunds; 88; 96, Ixworth.

E: 13, Freston; 14, Ipswich, 1981; Sproughton; 16, Brockford, 1981; 23, Trimley, 1977; 24; 25, Melton; 33, Felixstowe Ferry, 1977; 39, Bungay, 1980; 40, Belton, 1975.

A variety with pale pink flowers has been found by P. F. Sheppy at Station Yard, Hadleigh (1975) and in a roadside habitat at West Stow. Probably of garden origin, as this variety breeds true from seed and is sold under the name of 'Canon J. Went'.

Linaria repens (L.) Mill.   Pale Toadflax   Miss E. S. Rowling 1957

Introduced and sometimes semi-naturalised. Sometimes grown in gardens and found in waste places near gardens or on the sites of former gardens.
W: 77, Eriswell, rough grassland.
E: 13; 23; 35; 39; 45; 40.
13, Tattingstone, 1957; 35, Farnham; 45, between Aldeburgh and Thorpeness, 1970.

Linaria repens × vulgaris   B. D. Jones 1956
(*L.* × *sepium* Allman)

A hybrid, known in Suffolk only from a single record from Hartest (sq. 85) in 1956.

Linaria pelisseriana (L.) Mill.   Jersey Toadflax   N. S. P. Mitchell 1956

Casual. Native in the Mediterranean region. Recorded only from Combs (sq. 05) in 1956.

Linaria vulgaris Mill.   Common Toadflax   Sir J. Cullum 1773

Native. Waysides, edges of heaths and on old sand and shingle beaches. Frequent.
All squares.   *Illustrated page 516*
A peloric form was recorded at Worlingworth in 1968 (sq. 26).

Linaria maroccana Hook. f.   Annual Garden Toadflax   M. A. Hyde 1975

Introduced. Native of Morocco.
E: 23, Chelmondiston Tip.

Cymbalaria muralis Gaertn., Mey. & Scherb.   Ivy-leaved Toadflax   Wilson 1831
(*Linaria cymbalaria* (L.) Mill.)

Introduced. Native in S. Europe. Found on walls and old buildings. Formerly rare, now very frequent and increasing.
W: All squares except 68; 85.
67, Freckenham, 1981; 87, West Stow, 1981.
E: All squares except 28; 34; 45; 58.
14, Ipswich, common on walls, 1981; 24, Westerfield, 1981; 39, Bungay, 1981.

Kickxia elatine (L.) Dum.   Sharp-leaved Fluellen   Sir J. Cullum 1773
(*Linaria elatine* (L.) Mill.)

A colonist, and a weed of arable fields. Frequent.
W: All squares except 67; 68; 84; 88; 93; 98.
66, Exning, 1977; 94, Brent Eleigh, 1981.
E: All squares except 07; 26; 28; 33; 34; 37; 38; 44; 47; 49; 40; 50.
06, Haughley, 1976; 23, Harkstead, 1981; 24, Bucklesham, 1974.

Kickxia spuria (L.) Dum.   Round-leaved Fluellen   Sir J. Cullum 1773
(*Linaria spuria* (L.) Mill.)

Colonist. A frequent weed of arable fields, which prefers lighter soils than *K. elatine,* but both species can often be found growing together in mixed soils and on the Chalky Boulder Clay. More frequent than *K. elatine.*
W: 64; 66; 74; 75; 76; 83; 85; 87; 94; 95; 97.
76, Dalham, 1981; 94, Brent Eleigh, 1981.   *Illustrated page 511*

E: 03; 04; 05; 06; 14; 15; 16; 23; 25; 26; 27; 35; 36; 38; 39; 45; 46.
04, Bramford, 1981; 06, Haughley, 1976; 23, Harkstead, 1981; 25, field near the Rectory, Clopton, 1974, (Rev. F. Rowell).
It is thought that some seeds of these two species germinate late in the summer and are therefore not affected by spraying.

Digitalis purpurea L.   Foxglove   Davy c. 1800
Native, or a naturalised escape from cultivation. Woods, copses, plantations and hedges, chiefly on light or heathy soils. The true native Wild Foxglove is now found chiefly in the South-east of the County in the valleys of the Orwell and the Stour on sands, gravels and London Clay. Elsewhere its occurrence often appears to be connected with former cultivation; it is variable in the colour and markings of the flowers. Variations are uncommon in the true native colonies.
W: Recorded from squares 64; 66; 76; 83; 84; 85; 86; 87; 88; 93; 94; 95; 96; 98.
Most of these West Suffolk records refer to plants of garden origin.
E: All squares except 05; 06; 17; 27; 28; 37; 38; 57; 50.
Very frequent on the Shotley Peninsula, 1981.   *Illustrated page 458*

Veronica serpyllifolia L. ssp. **serpyllifolia**   Thyme-leaved Speedwell
                                                              Sir J. Cullum 1773
Native. Wet pastures, woodland glades and damp arable soils. Widespread and often common.
W: All squares except 65; 68; 84; 85.
77, Tuddenham Heath, 1979; 96, Pakenham Wood, in ride, 1980.
E: All squares except 15; 17; 33; 34; 44; 45; 49; 50.
13, Stutton Churchyard, 1980; 16, Mickfield Meadow, 1981; 35, Rendlesham, 1980.

Veronica officinalis L.   Heath Speedwell   Sir J. Cullum 1773
                               Common Speedwell
Native. In dry habitats, grassy heaths, old pastures, clearings and rides in woods, particularly on sandy and gravelly soils. Generally distributed and frequent in parts of Breckland in plantation rides.
W: All squares except 65; 66; 68; 85.
67, Freckenham, 1980; Tuddenham Heath, 1979.
E: All squares except 05; 06; 15; 25; 26; 27; 28; 33; 36; 45; 59; 50.
03, Bentley and Capel St Mary, 1980; 46, Westleton, 1980; 47, Hinton, 1980.

Veronica chamaedrys L.   Germander Speedwell   Sir J. Cullum 1774
                              Bird's Eye ˙
Native. On hedge-banks, old grassland and clearings in woods. Common.
All squares.

Veronica montana L.   Wood Speedwell   Sir J. Cullum 1773
Native. Glades and rides in damp woods, especially on the Boulder Clay. Common.
W: All squares except 65; 66; 67; 68; 77; 78; 84; 87; 97.
76, Barrow, 1977; 94, Brent Eleigh, 1981.

E: All squares except 06; 07; 16; 17; 26; 27; 33; 34; 35; 37; 58; 40; 50.
13, Holbrook, 1979; 23, near Pin Mill, Chelmondiston, 1981; Nacton, 1981; 24, in Alder Carr at Playford, 1981.
Hb. Ipswich Museum: specimens from Freston Wood, c. 1820 (John Notcutt). Still there, 1981.

Veronica scutellata L.   Marsh Speedwell   Sir J. Cullum 1773
Native. By margins of old ponds and ditches, in bogs and marshes. Now rare and decreasing, as habitats are destroyed.
W: 77; 78; 87; 97; 98.
78, Wangford.
E: 04; 07; 14; 15; 16; 17; 27; 36; 38; 39; 49; 58; 59; 40.
39, Bungay, 1981; 58, Benacre, 1974.
Hb. Ipswich Museum: 'On the N.E. side of a Bog in the second meadow west of Mr Alexander's Cottage, south side of the Bramford Road,' c. 1820 (John Notcutt).
Var. **villosa** Schum. The hairy variety. Hb. Ipswich Museum: 'In the boggy part of a field between the Bramford Road and the River, between Handford Bridge and Boss Hall', c. 1820 (John Notcutt).

Veronica beccabunga L.   Brooklime   Sir J. Cullum 1773
Native. On the margins of ponds and ditches, and beside streams and rivers. Very frequent.
All squares.

Veronica anagallis-aquatica L.   Blue Water Speedwell   Sir J. Cullum 1773
Native. In ditches, ponds and streams. Frequent, sometimes dominant.
W: All squares except 64; 68.
67, Mildenhall, 1980; 86, Bury St Edmunds, 1979.
E: All squares except 05; 33; 59; 50.
04, Hadleigh, by R. Brett, 1981; 14, Ipswich, by the R. Gipping, 1981; 39, Bungay, 1981.

Veronica catenata Pennell   Pink Water Speedwell   R. Burn c. 1931
(*V. aquatica* Bernh., non S. F. Gray)
Native. In ditches, ponds and streams. Less frequent than formerly. Few recent records.
W: All squares except 64; 65; 66; 75; 76; 78; 88.
83, Cornard Mere.
E: All squares except 05; 13; 23; 24; 25; 33; 34; 35; 44; 45; 48; 58; 59; 50.
46, East Bridge, 1977.
Hind included this species under *V. anagallis-aquatica.*

Veronica praecox All.   Breck Speedwell   J. E. Lousley 1933
Possibly a native, or an introduction from C. and S. Europe. In dry, fallow fields and sandy places in Breckland. This species was not recorded in the British Isles until 1933, when it was found at Barton Mills (sq. 77). Perhaps it has been a Breckland plant for many years, overlooked by the earlier botanists.
W: 77, Barton Mills, 1980; Herringswell, 1980; Icklingham; Eriswell, 1980; 78, Lakenheath, 1980; 88, Brandon.

SCROPHULARIACEAE

At a private site in Herringswell, known as Tuddenham Gallops, and managed by the Suffolk Trust, the three rare species of Speedwell, *Veronica praecox, V. triphyllos* and *V. verna*, are preserved. This site, a strip of sandy Breckland, bordering a plantation and arable, was set up by Dr A. S. Watt in 1967, and seeds of the three species were sown in short rows.

Veronica triphyllos L.   Fingered Speedwell   Willisell 1724
Native. In fallow fields and sandy places in Breckland and occasionally on the East Suffolk heaths. Rare or overlooked.
W: 77, Cavenham; Icklingham; Herringswell, introduced; 78, Lakenheath, 1980; 87, Barnham.
E: 34, Shottisham; 35, Snape; 45, Aldeburgh.
Hind's Flora gives sixteen Breckland parishes and also records it for Lt. Thurlow, Bungay and Barham Heath.

Veronica arvensis L.   Wall Speedwell   Sir J. Cullum 1773
                             Field Speedwell
Native. Dry, open places on grassy heaths, fallow fields, tracks and walls. Common. The very small forms growing in Breckland and the sandy fields of East Suffolk are often mistaken for other species.
All squares.

Veronica verna L.   Spring Speedwell   Sir J. Cullum 1771
Native. In dry, fallow fields and sandy places in Breckland, especially where rabbits have been burrowing. Local or rare, but probably overlooked. Can be confused with *V. arvensis*.
W: 77, Barton Mills; Foxhole Heath, Eriswell; Tuddenham; Icklingham, 1981; Cavenham, 1980; Herringswell, introduced; 78, Lakenheath; Wangford Warren; 87/88, Thetford Heath, Barnham (introduced on an earlier site).
Locally abundant at sites in Eriswell and Icklingham.
E: Not recorded recently. Hind gives Thorpe and Cookley.

Veronica grisebachii Walters   Mrs F. Baker c. 1890
(*V. chamaepitys* Griseb., non Pers.)
Casual. Native of Balkan Peninsula. The only record for the County is from Oulton Broad.

Veronica agrestis L.   Green Field Speedwell   Sir J. Cullum 1773
Native and a colonist. A weed of cultivation in fields and gardens. Formerly common, now rare.
W: 74; 77; 86; 94.
E: 03; 04; 06; 13; 15; 16; 24; 36; 38; 39; 46; 47.
06, Haughley, 1981 (Mrs J. Harris); 15, Witnesham, 1973.

Veronica polita Fries   Grey Field Speedwell   D. Stock 1835
(*V. didyma* auct., vix Ten.)
Native or a colonist. On dry banks and cultivated ground. Now infrequent or overlooked.

299

W: 76; 77; 78; 83; 85; 86; 87; 88; 93; 94; 95; 96; 97.
E: 04; 06; 14; 16; 24; 25; 36; 38; 39; 58.
24, between Rushmere and Playford, 1981.
It is possible that some of these records are incorrect.

Veronica persica Poir.	Common Field Speedwell	F. K. Eagle 1852
(*V. buxbaumii* Ten., non Schmidt)	Buxbaum's Speedwell	

A colonist, introduced from C. and S. Europe. Now a very common weed of cultivated land and waste places.
All squares.

Veronica filiformis Sm.	Slender Speedwell	F. W. Simpson 1953

Introduced. Native of Asia Minor, and now a naturalised escape from cultivation. A weed of lawns and gardens, which is increasing its range and frequency in Suffolk.
W: 65; 66; 75; 76; 83; 86; 88; 93.
76, Hargrave, 1980; 86, Gt Barton, 1979.
E: 03; 04; 05; 13; 14; 15; 24; 25; 26; 28; 36; 39; 46; 49.
05, Needham Market, 1981; 14, Westerfield, 1980; 15, Gosbeck, 1980; Stonham Aspal, 1981; 25, Otley, 1978; 36, Saxmundham, 1981. (All records F. W. Simpson).

Illustrated page 517

Veronica hederifolia L.	Ivy-leaved Speedwell	Sir J. Cullum 1773
	Winter-weed (Suffolk)	

Native and a colonist. A weed of arable fields, gardens, waste places, hedge-banks, and open, sandy copses. Common.
All squares except 65; 67; 68; 85; 07; 27; 48; 58.

Veronica longifolia L.	Mrs E. M. Hyde 1971

An alien, native on the continent of Europe. May be found as a casual or garden escape.
E: 14, Ipswich Docks.

Veronica paniculata L.	D. J. Allen 1962
(*V. spuria* auct., non L.)	

Introduced. Native of C. and E. Europe. Frequently grown in gardens on rockeries. Sometimes escaping or seeding on banks outside gardens.
W: 77, Eriswell, near Foxhole Heath, 1962; 86, on a bank in Horsecroft Road, Bury St Edmunds, 1974 (Mrs G. Townsend).

Veronica spicata L. ssp. **spicata**	Spiked Speedwell	Ray 1660

Native. On chalky heaths, old banks and earthworks in Breckland. Now very rare. Extinct in some of its former sites. Growth and flowering may be restricted by rabbits.
W: 77, Cavenham; 78, Brandon (M. G. Rutterford); 87, Culford Heath; 87/88, Thetford Heath, Barnham (introduced)
Hind's Flora records it for Bury, Icklingham, Risby, Tuddenham, Newmarket Heath, Herringswell, Culford and Thetford Heaths, and between Barnham and Euston. It may possibly still survive in small quantities in any of these parishes, especially on Newmarket Heath, where it was first recorded.

Hebe lewisii (Armstrong) Cockayne & Allan   Shrubby Veronica

F. W. Simpson 1972

Introduced, native of New Zealand. Probably of hybrid origin. Cultivated and occasionally naturalised.

E: 33, Felixstowe and Bawdsey Cliffs.

Sibthorpia europaea L.   Cornish Moneywort   E. R. Long c. 1910

Native in the Western part of the British Isles, but probably introduced in Suffolk. Known from a single record from Lowestoft. Probably a garden escape.

Melampyrum cristatum L.   Crested Cow-wheat   Sir J. Cullum 1773

Native. On the edges of old woods and copses on the Boulder Clay. Very local and scarce. Extinct in many former habitats.

W: 64, Haverhill; 74, Kedington; 75, Ousden; 76, Dalham; Denham; Hargrave, 1980; 97, Hepworth, c. 1933.

E: Elmswell, c. 1954 (B. D. Jones).

There are records in Hind's Flora from at least 19 West Suffolk parishes and two in East Suffolk, Burgate and Bramford.   *Illustrated page 477*

Melampyrum arvense L.   Field Cow-wheat   Sir J. Cullum 1773

Purple Cow-wheat

Probably native. Cornfields. Now extinct. It has always been very local and rare. No Suffolk records during the present century.

A specimen was collected by Sir J. Cullum in 1773. Parish not known, but probably near Bury St Edmunds. Recorded in Hind's Flora from Hitcham in 1860, by Prof. Henslow, its last authentic record. There is an unconfirmed record from Red House Park, Ipswich in 1894 by Miss E. S. Rowling.

Melampyrum sylvaticum L.   Small Cow-wheat   Wilson 1833

Wood Cow-wheat

Normally a native of mountain woods. Very doubtful if this species has ever occurred in Suffolk. Hind's Flora records it for Monk's Wood, Hessett, in 1833. This wood has now been destroyed. The only other known record for Suffolk is by Mrs J. Gray at Farnham (sq. 35) in 1941. It is possible that in both these cases the plant was confused with *M. pratense*.

There is a specimen in Hb. Ipswich Museum from Burstall, collected about 1835, identified at the time as *M. sylvaticum*, but obviously only a variety of *M. pratense*.

Melampyrum pratense L.   Common Cow-wheat   Sir J. Cullum 1773

Native. In clearings and glades in old woods, copses and woody lanes. Not very common and decreasing. In some habitats its appearance every season is uncertain. A very variable species.

W: 83; 93; 94; 95; 96.

95, Felshamhall Wood, 1980.

E: 03; 04; 05; 13; 14; 15; 24; 25; 26; 36; 38; 46; 47; 48; 59.

03, Polstead, 1976.

Hb. Ipswich Museum: 'In a meadow, under some lofty oaks, north of Mr Fonnereau's Grove', c. 1820 (John Notcutt).

Euphrasia officinalis agg.   Eyebright   Sir J. Cullum 1773

Native. Heaths, pastures, old quarries and open woodland tracks. Formerly frequent, now local or rare. This genus has a number of species and numerous varieties and hybrids, which are difficult to identify. Identification is best carried out in the field, when plants are fresh. They are very variable in growth, depending upon the season and habitat, and it is best to select specimens in which some capsules are present. Dried or herbarium specimens are usually of little value for identification.

Un-determined Eyebrights have been found in the following localities and parishes.

W: 77, Cavenham; 87, Barnham; 95, Buxhall.

E: 03, East Bergholt; 04, Raydon Great Wood; 07, Thelnetham Fen; 35, Chillesford: 36, Benhall; 45, Sudbourne; 47, Hinton; 59, Lowestoft. Unrecorded squares: Beccles, Ilketshall St Lawrence; Barnby; Oulton; Corton.

Euphrasia anglica Pugsl.   E. K. Horwood 1950

Native. On wet heaths and commons, usually on a peaty soil. Rare or overlooked.

W: 77, The Dolvers, Mildenhall.

E: 48, Wrentham.

Euphrasia nemorosa (Pers.) Wallr.   Sir J. Cullum 1773

Native. On heaths, old grassland, chalk pits and pastures. Very variable. Formerly frequent, now much reduced owing to loss of habitats.

W: 66; 67; 75; 76; 77; 87; 88; 94; 96; 97; 98.

66, Newmarket Heath, 1981; 76, Cavenham, 1975; 77, Icklingham; 94, Nedging.

E: 04; 06; 07; 14; 27; 47; 48; 49; 40.

04, Somersham; 14, Bramford; Lt. Blakenham; 15, Coddenham, 1979.

Euphrasia pseudokerneri Pugsl.   A. Shrubbs 1885

Native. In calcareous grassland and chalk pits. Uncommon. Likely to be confused with *E. nemorosa.*

W: 76, Risby Poor's Heath.

Euphrasia confusa Pugsl.   Dr P. F. Yeo 1954

Native. On heaths and commons. Overlooked. This species is probably common on Breckland heaths.

W: 76, Risby Poor's Heath; 77, Foxhole Heath; 78, Lakenheath Warren; 87, West Stow, 1980; 98, Knettishall Heath.

Euphrasia micrantha Rchb.   R. Burn 1930
(*E. gracilis* (Fr.) Drej.)

Native. On heaths and commons and in bogs. Recorded by R. Burn from Groton, Semer and Aldham.

Odontites verna (Bell.) Dum.   Red Bartsia   Sir J. Cullum 1773
(*Bartsia odontites* (L.) Huds.)

Native. Old, poor pastures, marginal and arable land, waysides, quarries and woodland rides. This is a variable plant. There are two subspecies. Colonies of both are sometimes

found growing together and identification is very difficult, as their characteristics are not always distinctive. Plants found growing in old pastures, chalk pits and open woodland glades appear to have larger and usually darker-coloured flowers than those in cultivated and uncultivated fields. The records have not been separated.
Ssp. **verna** is considered to be less frequent and is a smaller plant.
Ssp. **serotina** (Dum.) Corb. is a larger and taller plant.
W: All squares except 67; 68.
87, Gt Livermere, 1980; 94, Brent Eleigh, 1981.
E: All squares except 13; 33.
04, Hadleigh, disused railway track, 1981; 14, Bramford, 1981; 39, Bungay, 1981.

Parentucellia viscosa (L.) Caruel   Yellow Bartsia   F. W. Simpson 1952
(*Bartsia viscosa* L.)

Introduced or casual. In damp, grassy places. Also introduced in grass seed. Rare. Native near the South and West Coasts of Britain and in Ireland.
W: 86, Bury St Edmunds.
E: 13, Bentley, 1975 (Mrs E. M. Hyde, one plant); 33, Bawdsey, 1952; 47, Wenhaston.

Pedicularis palustris L.   Red Rattle   Sir J. Cullum 1773
Marsh Lousewort

Native. In fens and very old wet pastures. Rare and decreasing. Extinct in many former habitats.
W: 78; 83; 84; 93; 97; 98.
78, Brandon, c. 1965.
E: 07; 23; 34; 36; 46; 49; 59; 40.
07, Redgrave Fen, 1978; 46, East Bridge, 1977.

Pedicularis sylvatica L.   Heath Lousewort   Sir J. Cullum 1773

Native. In wet, acid pastures and heaths. Rare and decreasing. Extinct in many of its former habitats.
W: 77; 78; 93; 95; 97; 98.
E: 03; 07; 13; 14; 24; 34; 38; 45; 46; 47; 48; 58; 59; 50.
07, Redgrave Fen, 1979; Hinderclay Fen, 1974. Belstead and Bixley Heath in the early 1960's.
Hb. Ipswich Museum: 'In a boggy meadow between Bolton Mill and Dale Hall', c. 1820 (John Notcutt).

Rhinanthus minor L.   Yellow Rattle   Sir J. Cullum 1773
Native. The species comprises four subspecies, two of which are found in Suffolk.
Ssp. **minor.** In old pastures, meadows, and grassy dunes. Formerly frequent, now greatly decreased.
Ssp. **stenophyllus** (Schur) O. Schwarz. In fens and old damp pastures. Distribution not properly known. It has been recorded at Redgrave, Palgrave, Thelnetham and Leiston. The following records have not been divided into the subspecies.
W: Recorded from squares 64; 77; 78; 84; 86; 87; 88; 93; 94; 95; 96.
87, West Stow, 1981.

E: All squares except 05; 06; 13; 14; 15; 23; 44; 47; 58.
39, Bungay, 1981; 45, Aldringham, 1979; 46, East Bridge, 1978; 40, Belton, 1978.

Illustrated page 478

Lathraea squamária L.   Toothwort   Mrs A. Hart 1968

Native. Parasitic on the roots of *Corylus avellana, Acer campestre*, and *Ulmus* species. Very rare. There is a record for Monks' Park Wood in the Parish of Bradfield St George (sq. 95) by Mrs Hart in 1968. This area of the wood has now been destroyed. It was also reported from Bucklesham (sq. 24) by Miss J. C. N. Willis.

With the abundance of suitable hosts and sites in the County, especially the old woods on the chalky Boulder Clay, its absence is surprising. It occurs very sparingly in Essex and Cambridgeshire, but has not been found in Norfolk. I have observed it in several counties, growing in many old woods which are similar in many ways to our Suffolk woods, both in the North and South of England.

ACANTHACEAE

ACANTHUS FAMILY

Acanthus mollis L.   Bear's Breech   S. J. Batchelder 1949

Introduced from S. Europe.
E: 14, Ipswich, allotments near Bank Road, and Convent in Woodbridge Road, believed to be escapes from a nearby nursery, 1949; 33, Spa Gardens, Felixstowe, almost naturalised, 1981.

OROBANCHACEAE

BROOMRAPE FAMILY

Orobanche ramosa L.   Hemp Broomrape   J. Sherard 1724
                            Branched Broomrape

Introduced. Native of C. and S. Europe. Parasitic on Hemp *(Cannabis)*, and also on Tobacco, Potatoes and Tomatoes. Now extinct in Suffolk.
Recorded in Hind's Flora from near Beccles, Mettingham, Bungay and Brome.

Orobanche purpurea Jacq.   Yarrow Broomrape   Davy 1828
(O. caerulea Vill.)   Purple Broomrape

Native. Parasitic on Yarrow *(Achillea millefolium)* and other Compositae. Very rare. The only recent record is by Miss Cracknell from the Woodbridge area (sq. 24) c. 1933. Recorded by Hind from Cockfield and Pettistree.

Orobanche alba Steph. ex Willd.   Thyme Broomrape   H. J. Boreham 1953
(O. epithymum DC.   Red Broomrape
O. rubra Sm.)

Native. Usually parasitic on *Thymus* and other Labiatae. Recorded for Bury St Edmunds from 1953-55, where it was parasitic on Ground Ivy *(Glechoma hederacea)*. There is some doubt attached to this record.

Orobanche loricata Reichenb.   Ox-tongue Broomrape   E. Skepper 1862
(*O. picridis* F. Schultz ex Koch)   Picris Broomrape

Native. A parasite on *Picris* and other Compositae, in grassland and on wayside banks. Very rare. Can be confused with *O. minor*.
W: 86, Sicklesmere, 1952; 94, Semer, c. 1933.
E: 04, Whatfield, 1931; 38, Barsham, 1956.
Hind records it for Great Welnetham (Hb. Skepper).

Orobanche minor Sm.   Common Broomrape   Rev. G. Crabbe 1805
                            Lesser Broomrape

Native. Parasitic, chiefly on wild and cultivated Clovers, and on *Crepis capillaris* and other Composites. Common.
W: All squares except 65; 68; 83; 84; 87; 95; 97; 98.
66, Herringswell, 1979; 77, Worlington, 1980.
E: All squares except 28; 37; 44.
13, Woolverstone; Erwarton, 1974; 15, Baylham, 1977; 23, Harkstead and Chelmondiston, 1977; 39, Bungay, 1981.   *Illustrated page 509*
Var. **lutea** Tourlet, with attractive yellow stems and flowers, 17 specimens on a bank at Sudbourne, 1974 (Misses B. & R. Copinger Hill). Also seen at Sizewell.

Orobanche maritima Pugsl.   Carrot Broomrape   Botanical Exchange Club 1912

Native. Usually on *Daucus carota* or *Ononis repens*. A coastal species. Perhaps only a variety of *O. minor*.
E: 45, Aldeburgh.

Orobanche hederae Duby   Ivy Broomrape   J. Atkins 1909

Native. Parasitic on Ivy *(Hedera helix)*. Very rare. The first Suffolk record was for Felixstowe in 1909 (Hb. Atkins). It was also seen in the Spa gardens by F.W. Simpson about 1950. There is one further record for the County, that of J. Goddard from the Rectory garden at Gisleham in 1939.

Orobanche caryophyllacea Sm.   Bedstraw Broomrape   Henslow and Skepper 1860
(*O. vulgaris* Poir.)   Clove-scented Broomrape

Native. Usually parasitic on *Galium mollugo*. Very rare. The only recent record is c. 1940 from Clare (sq. 74) by C.C.T. Giles, where it was parasitic on Lady's Bedstraw *(G. verum)*. Recorded in Hind's Flora from Hawstead, Semer, and near Sudbury.

Orobanche elatior Sutt.   Knapweed Broomrape   Sir T. G. Cullum 1804
                                Tall Broomrape

Native. A parasite on *Centaurea scabiosa*. Scarce.
W: 56, Exning, 1974; 66; 75, Stansfield, 1981 (Dr L. Harrison Matthews); 76, Dalham, 1981; 77; 78; 84; 86, Bury St Edmunds; 87, Duke's Ride, Barnham; West Stow; 95.
E: 14, Lt. Blakenham; 15, Barham; Coddenham; 34, Alderton; Hollesley; 36, Benhall; 45, Sudbourne.
In Hb. Ipswich Museum there is a specimen dated 1856, from Sudbourne.

OROBANCHACEAE

Orobanche rapum-genistae Thuill.   Greater Broomrape   Sir J. Cullum 1773

Native. A parasite on Broom *(Cytisus scoparius)*. Rare.
W: 64, Haverhill; 93, Polstead; Bures.
E: 24, Sutton, The Tips; 35, Snape; 49, Herringfleet.
Probably now extinct in all the sites, except Bures.

LENTIBULARIACEAE

BUTTERWORT FAMILY

Pinguicula lusitanica L.   Pale Butterwort   Sir J. Cullum 1773

Native. In bogs and on wet heaths. A note in Hind's Flora under *P. vulgaris* suggests that
Sir J. Cullum found both *P. lusitanica* and *P. vulgaris* in the bogs near Lackford Bridge,
seven miles from Bury St Edmunds. The habitat was much changed, and various plants
became extinct, when the River Lark was converted to a canal. Any records made by such
a competent botanist as Sir John Cullum must be respected, although no authentic
herbarium specimen has been traced. The record comes from a manuscript note in a copy
of Dill. Ray in the library of the Oxford Botanical Garden, attributed to Mr Pitchford,
1780.
In 1954 I observed a small colony of *P. lusitanica* at Alderbury Common in Wiltshire,
growing in very much the same type of wet heath as is found in Suffolk.

Pinguicula vulgaris L.   Common Butterwort   J. Andrews 1746

Native. In fens and bogs. Now almost extinct. The habitats have become too dry and
invaded by scrub. Too many specimens have also been removed by collectors, especially
students of insectivorous plants.
W: 97, Hopton and Weston Fens.
E: 07, Redgrave and Thelnetham Fens; 36, Benhall Green, c. 1940.
Hind also records it from Coney Weston, Hinderclay, Lackford, Pakenham,
Stowlangtoft, Mildenhall, Tuddenham and Langham. There is a record for Wingfield
made by Miss E. S. Rowling, 1898-1906.

Utricularia minor L.   Lesser Bladderwort   Sir J. Cullum 1775

Native. In fens and dykes. Rare and decreasing. Seldom flowering.
W: Not recorded recently. Hind gives Lackford Bog, bogs at Cavenham, Icklingham,
Tuddenham and Cockfield.
E: 07, Thelnetham and Redgrave Fens; 27, Wingfield; 46, Leiston; Sizewell, 1958; 49,
Herringfleet; Carlton Colville.

Utricularia intermedia Hayne   Intermediate Bladderwort
                                                  Atlas of the British Flora, post-1930.
Native. In old dykes. The only known Suffolk record is from sq. 49.

Utricularia vulgaris L.   Common Bladderwort   Sir J. Cullum 1773

Native. In fen pools, old dykes and ponds. Rare. Not flowering every year.
W: 78, Lakenheath; 97, Hopton Fen, 1981.

LENTIBULARIACEAE

E: 07; 17; 39; 46; 49; 58; 59; 50.
07, Redgrave Fen, 1980; Thelnetham Fen; 39, Mettingham, 1980; 46, Sizewell Belts; 49, Carlton Colville Marshes; Beccles; Barnby; North Cove, 1976; 59, Oulton.
There is a specimen in Hb. Atkins from Bungay in 1907.   *Illustrated page 487*

Utricularia australis R. Br.   J. Grubbe 1882
(*U. neglecta* Lehm.)
Native. In old dykes and fen pools. No authentic specimens. The original record is from Southwold. Hind's Flora includes further records from Lakenheath, Kessingland, and Belton. However, his specimens from Kessingland and Belton are *U. vulgaris*.

PLANTAGINACEAE

PLANTAIN FAMILY

Plantago major L.   Greater Plaintain   Sir J. Cullum 1773
                          Broad-leaved Plantain
Probably a colonist, found in waste places, especially on farm tracks, disturbed grassland and lawns. Common.
All squares.

Plantago coronopus L.   Buck's-horn Plantain   Sir J. Cullum 1773
Native. In dry places, especially tracks, sea cliffs, and the edges of shingle or sandy beaches. Often abundant and dominant.
W: All squares except 64; 65; 74; 75; 83; 84; 85; 94; 95.
Very frequent in Breckland, 1981.
E: All squares except 26; 36; 37; 38.
Frequent on the coast and on the East Suffolk heaths, 1981.

Plantago maritima L.   Sea Plantain   Sir J. Cullum 1773
Native. In salt marshes, usually in the drier areas, among grass and near sea embankments. Frequent.
E: 03; 13; 14; 23; 24; 25; 33; 34; 35; 44; 45; 46; 47; 49; 58; 59; 40; 50.
Frequent all up the coast in suitable habitats, 1981.

Plantago media L.   Hoary Plantain   Sir J. Cullum 1773
                          Lamb's Tongue
Native. Old grassy waysides, pastures, churchyards, railway embankments and quarries, chiefly on the Chalk or Chalky Boulder Clay. Frequent.
W: All squares.
76, Higham, 1981; 94, Brent Eleigh, 1981; 96, Pakenham, 1981.
E: All squares except 13; 23; 33; 35; 44; 45; 49.
04, Hadleigh, 1981; Flowton, 1981; 07, Wortham Ling, 1981.

Plantago lanceolata L.   Ribwort Plantain   Sir J. Cullum 1773
(including *P. timbali* Jord.)   Fighting Cocks (Suffolk)

Native. A weed of grassland, waysides and waste places. Very frequent and sometimes abundant. A variable species, often exhibiting forms with compound heads, proliferous heads and leaves with heads.
All squares.   *Illustrated page 516*

Plantago lagopus L.   Hare's-foot Plantain   W. A. Dutt 1899
A casual from the Mediterranean region. Recorded from Oulton Broad.

Plantago indica L.   Branched Plantain   J. S. Wilkinson 1908
(*P. psyllium* L., nom. ambig.
P. arenaria Waldst. & Kit.)

Casual. Native of S. and C. Europe. Recorded at Ipswich in 1908, and at Eriswell by J. E. Lousley in 1957, where it was abundant in an arable field.

Littorella uniflora (L.) Aschers.   Shore-weed   Sir J. Cullum 1773
(*L. lacustris* L.)

Native. On the margins of lakes and broads, often submerged. Very rare, possibly now extinct. Recorded in Hind's Flora from Great Livermere, Ampton Lake, Tuddenham St Mary, Cavenham, Mildenhall, Oulton Broad, Belton Common, Benacre and Easton Broad. There is a specimen in Hb. Atkins, 1909, from Felixstowe Ferry (sq. 33), possibly collected from the ponds on the Golf Course, to the left of the road before you reach the Ferry.
The last known records are from Easton Broad in 1931 and from Cavenham, c. 1950.

CAPRIFOLIACEAE

HONEYSUCKLE FAMILY

Sambucus ebulus L.   Danewort   Sir J. Cullum 1773
                              Dwarf Elder

Introduced. Possibly native. Hedges and waste ground near dwellings. Rare and decreasing.
W: 84, Long Melford, 1980; 94, Semer (A. L. Bull).
E: 13, Stutton; 14, Whitton; Witnesham, 1979 (E. Milne-Redhead); 46, Sizewell; 47, Minsmere; 48, Brampton; 59, Carlton Colville.
Danewort is an old country name for the Dwarf Elder. Its berries are called Dane's Blood, as it was considered to grow where there had been a battle with the Danes, as on the Bartlow Hill, N.W. Essex, just across the Suffolk border.
The Pasque Flower *(Pulsatilla vulgaris)* is also known as Dane's Blood, and it is another species that is said to grow only where blood has flowed.

Sambucus nigra L.   Elderberry   Sir J. Cullum 1773
Native. Woods, copses, hedges and waste places, especially on the Chalk and Red Crag sands. Very frequent.
All squares.

Var. **laciniata** L.
67, Freckenham, 1977 (Mrs E. M. Hyde); 78, Brandon, 1980 (F. W. Simpson); Lakenheath, 1979 (M. G. Rutterford).

Sambucus racemosa L.   Red-berried Elder   Miss J. C. N. Willis 1956
An introduced species, native of Europe and West Asia. Recorded from Chimney Mills, near Culford.

Viburnum opulus L.   Guelder Rose   Sir J. Cullum 1773
Native. Woods and hedges, especially on moist clays. Alder carrs, fens and damp scrub. Frequent, except on the light, sandy soils of the coastal region.
W: All squares except 67.
94, Brent Eleigh and Lavenham, 1981; 96, Norton Wood, 1981; 97, Sapiston, 1981.
E: All squares except 33; 44; 50.
04, Raydon, 1981; 07, Thelnetham Fen, 1981; 24, Playford, 1981.   *Illustrated page 455*

Viburnum lantana L.   Wayfaring Tree   J. Andrews 1759
                          Mealy Guelder Rose
Native. Found in hedgerows, woods, edges of old quarries, on Chalk or very chalky Boulder Clay. Locally frequent; distribution mainly confined to South-west Suffolk, where it is a conspicuous tree or shrub of old hedgerows.
W: 64; 65; 66; 74; 75; 76; 77; 83; 84; 86; 93; 94; 95; 96.
76, Moulton; Barrow; Gt Saxham, 1981; 86, Shaker's Lane, Bury St Edmunds, 1980.
E: 05; 14; 27.
05, Onehouse, c. 1952 (F. W. Simpson).   *Illustrated page 473*

Symphoricarpos rivularis Suksdorf   Snowberry   Rev. J. D. Gray 1881
(*S. racemosus* auct.)
Introduced from Western N. America and now established and spreading. Frequently planted in woods and coverts. Common, particularly in West Suffolk.
W: All squares.
E: Recorded from squares 04; 06; 13; 14; 16; 17; 23; 24; 25; 26; 28; 33; 34; 35; 38; 39; 45; 46; 40; 50.
This plant has spread considerably since Hind's time, as he recorded it only from Pakenham, Hinderclay, Nayland, Worlingham and Hollesley.

Lonicera tatarica L.   Mrs E. M. Hyde 1977
Introduced. Native of W. and C. Asia. Grown in gardens and occasionally naturalised.
E: 23, Chelmondiston Tip, a garden outcast.

Lonicera xylosteum L.   Fly Honeysuckle   Mrs French c. 1840
Introduced into Suffolk, though native in some other parts of Britain. Found in hedges and shrubberies, where it has been planted.
Recorded only from squares 93 and 03.
Hind records it from Walks, Little Thurlow.

Lonicera caprifolium L.   Perfoliate Honeysuckle   Prof. Henslow 1856
Introduced from C. and S. Europe. Possibly native in one Suffolk habitat. Found in

hedges and old garden sites. This species was found in 1936 in a small ancient wood at Acton, growing in the same natural way as I have observed it in many European woods, thickets and scrub. It appeared to be genuinely native in this habitat.

W: 76, Tuddenham St Mary; 77, Barton Mills; 84, Acton; 86, Bury St Edmunds, railway embankment, 1980.

E: 15, Gt Blakenham, site of former garden, 1980; 34, Shingle Street, c. 1950.

Lonicera periclymenum L.   Honeysuckle   Sir J. Cullum 1773
                                   Woodbine

Native. In woods, copses, hedges, heaths and sea coast on old dunes. Common. The colours of the flowers vary considerably, from creamy white, yellow and pink, to rose and purple shades.

All squares.

Lonicera nitida Wils.   Hedging Honeysuckle   B.S.B.I. Mapping Scheme c. 1960

Introduced from China. Commonly planted.

E: 05; 23, Chelmondiston Tip, 1974; 24, Culpho, spreading in wood, 1981 (F. W. Simpson).

ADOXACEAE

MOSCHATEL FAMILY

Adoxa moschatellina L.   Moschatel   Sir J. Cullum 1773
                                 Townhall Clock

Native. In woods, copses and hedge-banks on light, sandy or alluvial soils, especially Alder carr or valley woods. Frequent and often abundant.

W: Recorded from squares 64; 75; 83; 84; 86; 93; 94; 95; 96.
93, Bures, 1975.

E: All squares except 26; 33; 40; 50.
04, Hadleigh, wood by the R. Brett, 1981; 14, frequent in the Ipswich area; 24, Sutton, 1981; Alder Carr, Playford, 1981.   *Illustrated page 458*

VALERIANACEAE

VALERIAN FAMILY

Valerianella locusta (L.) Laterrade   Lamb's Lettuce   Sir J. Cullum 1774
(*V. olitoria* (L.) Poll.)   Corn Salad

Native, and a colonist of warm sunny banks, cultivated fields and the sea coast. Generally distributed, but less frequent in West Suffolk.

W: 76; 77; 78; 86; 87; 88.
87, Barnham, 1977.

E: 04; 05; 06; 13; 14; 15; 16; 23; 24; 25; 28; 33; 34; 36; 37; 38; 39; 44; 45; 46; 47; 48; 59; 40; 50.
23, Landguard Common, 1980; 24, hedge-banks at Playford, 1979; 33, Felixstowe Ferry, 1980; 47, Walberswick roadside, 1976.

VALERIANACEAE

Valerianella carinata Loisel.   Keeled Corn Salad   Rev. T. Hedley 1882

A colonist on dry, sunny banks and in fields. Rare. It is possible that some of the records are incorrect.
W: 87, Barnham Cross Common, 1966 (E. J. Clement); 93, Polstead, c. 1930 (R. Burn).
E: 13, Cattawade; 23, Landguard Common; 24, Woodbridge; 25, Melton Lodge.

Valerianella dentata (L.) Poll.   Narrow-fruited Corn Salad   Wigg 1816
                                       Toothed Corn Salad

Colonist. Arable fields chiefly on the Chalk and Chalky Boulder Clay. Rare and decreasing.
W: 76, Dalham, 1980 (F. W. Simpson), conf. E. J. Clement; 78, Lakenheath; Wangford; 93, Polstead, c. 1930 (R. Burn).
E: 06, Bacton; 15, Witnesham, 1958 (F. W. Simpson).
There are specimens in Hb. Ipswich Museum collected by the Rev. G. R. Leathes from cornfields at Saxham and around Bury, in the early 19th century.
Var. **eriosperma** (Wallr.) Janch.   Hairy-fruited Corn Salad   Sir J. E. Smith 1824
(var. *mixta* (Vahl) Dufr.)
W: 77, Tuddenham, 1952 (E. L. Swann).
E: No recent records. Hind gives Halesworth and Felixstowe.

Valerianella rimosa Bast.   Broad-fruited Corn Salad   W. A. Dutt 1901
(*V. auricula* DC.)

Native. Found in cornfields, but of local distribution. Recorded from Kirkley (sq. 59).

Valeriana officinalis L.   Common Valerian   Sir J. Cullum 1773

Native. Marshes, carrs, swamps, fens and beside rivers. Frequent.
W: All squares except 65; 66; 67; 68; 74.
84, Acton, 1979; 98, Knettishall, 1981.
E: All squares except 15; 26; 27; 44; 45; 50.
13, Holbrook, 1981; 14, by the Gipping at Ipswich, 1980; 24, Alder Carr at Playford, 1980; 39, Bungay, 1981.   *Illustrated page 484*

Valeriana pyrenaica L.   Pyrenean Valerian   Victoria County History 1911

Introduced, and sometimes found naturalised in woods in Britain. Its occurrence in Suffolk is recorded in the Victoria County History of Suffolk. No site is named.

Valeriana dioica L.   Marsh Valerian   Sir J. Cullum 1773

Native. Old, wet pastures, marshes and fens. Not very frequent and decreasing, due to drainage and cultivation of its former habitats.
W: 68; 76; 77; 78; 84; 87; 88; 93; 96; 97; 98.
77, Worlington, 1981; 78, Pashford Poor's Fen, 1975; 97, Hopton and Thelnetham Fens, 1981.
E: 03; 05; 06; 07; 14; 15; 24; 34; 35; 36; 38; 39; 46; 47; 49; 59; 40; 50.
24, Newbourn, 1981; 35, Gromford, 1975.   *Illustrated page 484*

Centranthus ruber (L.) DC.　　Red Valerian　　　　　　Unknown collector 1836
(*Kentranthus ruber* (L.) DC.)

An introduced and established alien, native in C. and S. Europe. Naturalised on old walls, ruins, railway cuttings and shingle beaches. Frequent and spreading. The colour of the flowers is variable. White-flowered forms at Shingle Street and Brantham.
W: 66; 74; 78; 85; 86; 87; 88; 93; 94; 96; 97.
66, Newmarket, 1975; 86, Bury St Edmunds, 1981.
E: 04; 05; 13; 14; 17; 23; 24; 25; 33; 34; 38; 44; 45; 46; 47; 48; 49; 57; 59.
24, Woodbridge, 1981; 33, Felixstowe Ferry, 1980; 34, Shingle Street, 1981.
There is a specimen in Hb. Ipswich Museum from 'Walls of Leiston Abbey' in 1836, by an unknown collector　　　　　　　　　　　　　　　　　　　　*Illustrated page 501*

DIPSACACEAE

SCABIOUS FAMILY

Cephalaria syriaca Schrad.　　　　　　　　　　　　Mrs F. Baker c. 1890

Casual. Native in the Mediterranean region. Recorded from Oulton Broad.

Cephalaria gigantea (Ledeb.) Bobrov　　Giant Scabious　　F. W. Simpson c. 1930

Introduced and grown in gardens. Native of Siberia and West Asia. It is very hardy and, when cultivated, persists for many years. It was observed in a garden at Combs Ford (sq. 05) in the early thirties. Still there, 1981. A plant was found growing on waste ground almost opposite this site by Mrs E. M. Hyde in 1974.

Dipsacus fullonum L. ssp. **fullonum**　　Teasel　　　　　Sir J. Cullum 1773
(*D. sylvestris* Huds.)

Native. Clearings in woods, waysides, quarries, river banks. Common.
All squares except 87; 88; 98; 59.　　　　　　　　　　*Illustrated page 506*
Ssp. **sativus** (L.) Thell. (Fullers' Teasel) was formerly cultivated in the County, but there are no recent records.

Dipsacus pilosus L.　　Small Teasel　　　　　　　　Sir J. Cullum 1773
　　　　　　　　　　　Shepherd's Rod

Native. Damp valley woods and shady hedge-banks. Scarce.
W: 74; 86; 87; 93; 94; 95; 97.
87, Elveden; 97, Ixworth Thorpe, c. 1972.
E: 04; 05; 06; 07; 14; 15; 16; 25; 26; 27; 35; 36; 37; 38; 39; 47; 48; 49; 59.
04, Hadleigh, 1979; 05, Bosmere, 1979; Stowupland, 1975; 14, Washbrook, 1980; 15, Shrubland Park, 1979: 35, Lt. Glemham, 1980.　　　　　　*Illustrated page 505*

Succisa pratensis Moench　　Devil's-bit Scabious　　　Sir J. Cullum 1773
(*Scabiosa succisa* L.)

Native. Damp old pastures, marshes, heaths, and woodland glades. Frequent, sometimes abundant.
W: All squares except 65; 66; 67; 74; 75; 85.
78, Lakenheath, 1976; 95, Monks' Park Wood, 1980.

DIPSACACEAE

E: All squares except 03; 06; 13; 14; 15; 17; 28; 34; 39; 44; 58.
07, Redgrave Fen, 1980; 35, Gromford, 1975; Snape, 1981; 59, Oulton, 1978; 40, Belton, 1977.

Knautia arvensis (L.) Coult.   Field Scabious   Sir J. Cullum 1773
(*Scabiosa arvensis* L.)
Native. Waysides, rough fields and quarries. Frequent, especially on chalky soils.
All squares.   *Illustrated page 490*

Scabiosa columbaria L.   Small Scabious   Sir J. Cullum 1773
Native. Old chalk grassland, churchyards and quarries. Scarce, except in parts of Breckland and the Newmarket area. Now rare, where formerly locally frequent, on the Chalk of the Gipping Valley.
W: All squares except 64; 65; 83; 85; 93; 94; 95.
76, Dalham, 1981; Moulton, 1980; 77, Icklingham, 1981; Barton Mills, 1981.
E: Recorded from squares 03; 04; 05; 14; 15; 17; 25; 35; 45; 48; 58; 40.
14, Bramford, 1979; 15, Coddenham, 1980.   *Illustrated page 490*

CAMPANULACEAE

BELLFLOWER FAMILY

Campanula rapunculus L.   Rampion Bellflower   Mrs Casborne 1832
Introduced. Native in N. and C. Italy. In field borders and hedge-banks. Recorded in Hind's Flora from Rougham and from near Beccles.
The species has also been recorded from Mildenhall, Bury St Edmunds and Orford, but the records are considered doubtful. The species may have been confused with *C. rapunculoides*.

Campanula persicifolia L.   Narrow-leaved Bellflower   Finder not known, c. 1950
Introduced. Native of Europe and Asia. Commonly grown in gardens. Sometimes naturalised in woods and waste places.
W: 86, recorded from the Bury area, possibly the Abbey Gardens, c. 1950.
E: 23, Levington Creek, 1980; 24, Playford, one seedling in small sand-pit with garden rubbish, 1976; 39, Bungay, 1981.

Campanula medium L.   Canterbury Bell   Mrs E. M. Hyde 1974
Introduced. Native of Italy. A common garden flower.
E: 17, Eye, waste ground on site of former garden, 1974; 34, Shingle Street, 1981.

Campanula glomerata L.   Clustered Bellflower   Sir J. Cullum 1773
Native. Old chalky grassland, heaths, banks and earthworks. Now very scarce.
W: 66, Moulton, 1979 (F. W. Simpson); 75, Chevington; 76, Risby Poor's Heath, 1956; Barrow; Dalham, 1981 (F. W. Simpson); 77, Barton Mills; Lackford; 86, Bury St Edmunds, on wall, 1979 (garden form).
E: 14, Ipswich; 25, Burgh; Debach; Hoo.   *Illustrated page 490*

The East Suffolk records probably all refer to the garden form, which has larger and earlier flowers.

Campanula latifolia L.   Giant Bellflower   Woodward 1805
                        Throatwort

Native. In woods and thickets. Rare. Also occasionally in old gardens, where it has been introduced.
W: 67, West Row (P. J. O. Trist); 77, Mildenhall, 1965 (Mrs R. Clarke); 86, Bury St Edmunds, Abbey Gardens (C. Grange).
E: Hind records it in the Waveney Valley at Shipmeadow and Mettingham and also at Chediston and Linstead Parva. There have been a few reports of the plant still existing in this area and a specimen was collected by the late E. R. Long by the R. Waveney at Dunburgh (Norfolk), near Beccles, and it is also recorded in the 'Flora of Norfolk' for Ditchingham. It is considered that it may yet survive in the district, although a number of so-called *C. latifolia* may well be *C. trachelium*. In 1976 a search of some of its former parishes was unsuccessful.

Campanula trachelium L.   Nettle-leaved Bellflower   Sir J. Cullum 1773
                        Bats-in-the-Belfry

Native. Woods, thickets and hedges, especially on the Chalky Boulder Clay of West Suffolk, where it is locally frequent.
W: 75; 76; 83; 84; 85; 86; 93; 94; 95; 96; 98.
94, Brent Eleigh, 1981; 95, Monks' Park Wood, 1980; 98, Knettishall, 1981.
E: 03; 04; 05; 14; 15; 16; 36; 39; 47.
03, Capel St Mary, 1981 (N. Hunt); 05, Barking, 1981; 15, Baylham, 1981.
Hb. Ipswich Museum: 'In a Lane leading from the Sproughton Road and beyond Boss Hall', also 'In a Lane between Bramford and Whitton', c. 1820 (John Notcutt).
Illustrated page 491

Campanula rapunculoides L.   Creeping Bellflower   L. N. Rickards 1841
                        Creeping Campanula

Introduced. Native of continental Europe. Usually of garden origin. Waysides, hedges, waste places and embankments. Well distributed and increasing.
W: 67; 76; 77; 78; 85; 86; 96.
77, Icklingham, 1978; Mildenhall, 1980; 86, Shaker's Lane, Bury St Edmunds, 1979, in abundance (M. A. Hyde); 96, Stowlangtoft (Hb. specimen collected by L. N. Rickards, 1841). Still there, 1979.
E: 03; 07; 13; 14; 15; 17; 23; 24; 26; 27; 33; 35; 36; 38; 39; 45; 48; 49; 58; 59; 40.
07, Thelnetham, 1981; 24, Gt Bealings, roadside, 1981; 39, Bungay, 1980; 45, Aldeburgh, 1979.   *Illustrated page 491*

Campanula rotundifolia L.   Harebell   Sir J. Cullum 1773

Native. Grassy heaths, old chalk quarries, banks, waysides and dunes. Well distributed, but has become scarce or rare in some areas in recent years.
W: All squares except 64; 65; 74; 75; 83.
Common in Breckland, 1981.
E: All squares except 05; 06; 16; 23; 26; 27; 33.

It has been observed in the same area of Purdis Heath and Rushmere Common for over sixty years, 1918-81 (F.W.S.).
A colony with white flowers at Snape Common (Mrs M. Harrison), 1960, and also in Westleton Churchyard, 1981.

Legousia hybrida (L.) Delarb.   Venus's Looking-glass   Sir J. Cullum 1773
(*Specularia hybrida* (L.) A. DC.)
A colonist of cultivated fields, chiefly on sandy and chalky soils. Generally uncommon, but locally frequent.
W: 56; 64; 67; 75; 76; 77; 78; 84; 86; 87; 88; 94; 96; 97.
76, Dalham, 1981; Barrow, 1979; 86, Shaker's Lane, Bury St Edmunds, 1978.
E: 03; 04; 06; 13; 14; 15; 16; 23; 24; 35; 37; 38; 39; 45; 46; 47.
13, Harkstead, 1980; 24, Levington, 1974; 37, Cookley, 1979; 47, Walberswick, 1975.

Legousia speculum-veneris (L.) Chaix   Mrs F. Baker c. 1900
(*Specularia speculum-veneris* (L.) A. DC.)
A casual from S. Europe, recorded from Oulton Broad.

Jasione montana L.   Sheep's Bit   Sir J. Cullum 1773
                          Sheep's Scabious

Native. On dry, open sandy heaths, banks and dunes. Locally common. Distribution mainly confined to Breckland and the Sandlings.
W: 77; 78; 87; 88; 97; 98.
78, Lakenheath, 1979; 88, Barnham, 1980.
E: 04; 14; 23; 24; 33; 34; 35; 36; 37; 45; 46; 47; 49; 58; 40; 50.
04, Hadleigh, 1980; 45, Aldringham, 1979; Snape Common, 1979; 46, Sizewell, very frequent, 1979; 58, Benacre, 1980.
Hb. Ipswich Museum: 'On the west side of a stony field adjoining the Locks by Boss Hall. In an enclosure nearly opposite the Mill in the Foxhall Road', c. 1820 (John Notcutt).
A white-flowered variety has been recorded from Sizewell.

Lobelia erinus L.   Blue Lobelia   M. A. Hyde 1978

Casual. Native of S. Africa. Frequently grown in gardens.
E: 14, Ipswich, pavement weed, 1981 (F. W. Simpson); 23, Chelmondiston Tip, introduced with garden rubbish.

COMPOSITAE

DAISY FAMILY

Eupatorium cannabinum L.   Hemp Agrimony   Sir J. Cullum 1773
Native. Beside rivers and ditches and in marshes and fens. Frequent.
W: All squares except 65.
67, Mildenhall, 1981; 83, Cornard Mere, 1981.
E: All squares except 50.
13, Holbrook, 1981; 14, by the R. Gipping at Ipswich, 1981; 24, Foxhall, 1981; Alder Carr, Playford, 1981; 46, Leiston and Sizewell, 1980.   *Illustrated page 480*
Variety with white flowers at Theberton (sq. 46), 1975.

315

Solidago virgaurea L.   Golden Rod   Sir J. Cullum 1773

Native. Heaths, waysides and railway banks on gravelly soils. Locally frequent. Extinct in some habitats and decreasing in others.
W: 77; 78; 85; 87; 88; 96.
77, Herringswell; 78, Brandon Park.
E: 04; 07; 13; 14; 15; 16; 17; 28; 36; 37; 38; 45; 46; 47; 48; 49; 59; 40; 50.
07, Wortham Ling, 1980; 14, railway embankment between Ipswich and Wherstead, 1981; 47, Blythburgh, 1970; Wenhaston, 1980.
Hb. Ipswich Museum: 'In the first lane leading from the Bucklesham Road to Foxhall and in the small plantation east of the lane, plentiful. Sept. 1819, a very dry summer' (John Notcutt).   *Illustrated page 508*

Solidago canadensis L.   Garden Golden Rod   F. W. Simpson 1950

An alien, introduced from N. America. It is commonly grown in gardens, whence it escapes and is found on waste ground and the margins of rubbish tips. It may become naturalised.
W: 66, Newmarket, waste ground near railway station; 67, Freckenham; Mildenhall, 1977; 68, Lakenheath, 1980; 76, Herringswell, 1980; 77, Cavenham; 78, Brandon Waterworks; 86, Westley, 1980; Bury St Edmunds, 1981; 88, Barnham, 1980; 94, Edwardstone.
E: 05, Stowmarket, 1981; 07, Mellis; 14, Ipswich, waste ground and railway embankments, 1981; 16, Wetheringsett, 1979; 23, Chelmondiston, 1980; 24, Rushmere Common and Purdis Heath, 1981; 33, Felixstowe station, 1980; 35, Snape; Marlesford, 1980; 37, Halesworth, 1976; 46, Dunwich; 59, Lowestoft Cliff, 1974.

Solidago gigantea Ait.   Giant Golden Rod   F. W. Simpson 1966
(*S. serotina* Ait.)

An alien, native of N. America. Sometimes cultivated and appearing as a self-sown weed in gardens. First recorded in 1966 in gardens on the east side of Ipswich and then in Tower Churchyard in 1974. Still there, 1980. Also, Bramford, 1981.

Bellis perennis L.   Common Daisy   Sir J. Cullum 1773
Lawn Daisy

Native. Short turf, pastures and waysides. Very frequent and variable.
All squares.
Double-flowered forms occur, some of which may possibly be hybrids with garden forms.

ASTER   MICHAELMAS DAISIES

A number of species and hybrids have been introduced and grown in gardens. They are natives of North America and frequently become naturalised. They can often be seen in waste places and on tips where garden rubbish has been thrown, on sites of former gardens and on railway embankments. The plant increases rapidly once it becomes established.
Although more than one species and several subspecies and hybrids are involved, the seedlings usually have small flowers and appear to be reversions to *A. novi-belgii*.

Aster novi-belgii L.   Michaelmas Daisy   Hind's Flora 1889

Introduced. Found on rubbish tips, waste places and waysides where garden refuse has been deposited. Frequent, sometimes naturalised. Records may refer to one of several species.

W: 66; 74; 77; 78; 86; 87; 88; 96.

77, Mildenhall, 1980; 87, Barnham, 1980.

E: 03; 04; 05; 06; 07; 13; 14; 15; 16; 23; 24; 33; 35; 45; 57; 59.

07, Thelnetham, 1981; 14, frequent on waste ground and sites of former gardens in Ipswich, 1981; 24, Woodbridge, 1981; 33, Felixstowe Station, 1977.

Aster lanceolatus × novi-belgii   C. J. Ashfield 1846

(*A. × salignus* Willd.)

Introduced. Native of N. America. Recorded in Hind's Flora under *A. novi-belgii* as occurring on a dry patch of Redgrave Fen (sq. 07) in 1846. Still there in 1884. Determined by C. E. Salmon and recorded in the Victoria County History of Suffolk, 1911.

Aster tripolium L.   Sea Aster   Sutton & Kirby 1787

Native. Saltings, muddy creeks and beside brackish ditches. Very frequent.

All coastal and estuarine squares, 1981.   *Illustrated page 499*

Var. **discoideus** Reichb. f. This variety is frequent in very wet and muddy salt marshes, especially in the South of the County along the estuaries of the Deben, Orwell and Stour. Intermediate forms, with a few ray florets, occur frequently.

Erigeron karvinskianus DC.   Mexican Fleabane   Mrs E. M. Hyde 1964

(*E. mucronatus* DC.)

Introduced. Native of Mexico. Naturalised on walls.

E: 03, Layham, 1975; 14, Ipswich, at the foot of wall, 1972 (F. W. Simpson); 26, Earl Soham Church, 1964-75. Detd. 1975 by C. Jeffrey.

Erigeron acer L.   Blue Fleabane   J. Andrews 1744

Native. Heaths, dry sandy banks, quarries and sea cliffs. Frequent, especially in the Breckland and on the Sandlings.

W: All squares except 64; 65; 68; 75; 83; 85; 93.

77, Cavenham, 1978; 78, Lakenheath, 1980; 87, West Stow, 1980.

E: All squares except 17; 27; 38; 44; 48.

14, Bramford, 1980; 15, Gt Blakenham, 1981; 35, Tunstall, 1981; Campsey Ash, 1981. Hb. Ipswich Museum: 'Amongst some furze bushes at the N.W. corner of a dry stony field adjoining the Locks by Boss Hall. The dry summer of 1818' (John Notcutt).

Conyza canadensis (L.) Cronq.   Canadian Fleabane   E. Skepper 1862

(*Erigeron canadensis* L.)

An established and well-naturalised alien, native of N. America. A weed on sandy soils, near old buildings and ruins, and on the sea coast.

All squares except 65; 68; 83; 25.

COMPOSITAE

Filago vulgaris Lam.　　Common Cudweed　　　　　　Sir J. Cullum 1773
(*F. germanica* (L.) L.)
Native. On heaths, cliffs and fallow fields. On light acid soils. Frequent.
W: All squares except 64; 65; 66; 67; 68; 75; 83; 85; 93.
76, Kentford, 1980; 77, Worlington, 1980; 97, Coney Weston, 1981.
E: All squares except 06; 07
33, Bawdsey, 1979; 35, Blaxhall, 1980; Tunstall, 1981; 45, Snape, 1981.

Filago lutescens Jord.　　Red-tipped Cudweed　　　　　J. W. Salter 1849
(*F. apiculata* G. E. Sm. ex Bab.)
Native. On dry, sandy heaths, and arable land. Rare or overlooked. Often associated with
F. vulgaris, but flowers later.
W: 87; 97, Honington, 1942.
E: 45, Snape, 1975-1981 (Mrs E. M. Hyde); 46, Westleton, 1981.
Hind records the plant from Troston Heath, Rushbrooke, Redneck Heath, Elveden,
Cavenham, Westleton Heath and Sutton Ferry.

Filago pyramidata L.　　Broad-leaved Cudweed　　　　　Lathbury 1856
(*F. spathulata* C. Presl)
Native. In sandy fields, and on heaths. Rare or possibly extinct. The latest known record
is from Bury St Edmunds in 1953/55.
W: 86, Bury St Edmunds; 93, Wiston; Bures; Newton; 94, Edwardstone.
E: 58, Covehithe.
Recorded in Hind's Flora from Wangford, Elveden, Icklingham, Lackford, Bury St
Edmunds and Fornham. Herbarium specimen from Saxham, Dr G. C. Druce, 1883.

Filago minima (Sm.) Pers.　　Small Cudweed　　　　　　J. Andrews 1745
　　　　　　　　　　　　　　　Slender Cudweed
Native. Sandy heaths, tracks and fallow fields, especially in Breckland. Locally common.
W: Recorded from squares 67; 76; 77; 78; 86; 87; 88; 93; 95; 96; 97; 98.
76, Gazeley, 1981; 78, Lakenheath, 1980; 87, Barnham, 1980.
E: All squares except 06; 16; 26; 27; 38; 44; 50.
13, Holbrook Churchyard, 1974-1981; 35, Tunstall Common, 1981; 46/47, Dunwich and
Westleton, 1980.

Filago gallica L.　　Narrow-leaved Cudweed　　　　　　J. Andrews 1745
An introduced alien, native in S. Europe. Found in dry, sandy and gravelly places. Rare,
or possibly extinct.
Hind's record in 1883 was from Sutton. The only known records since then are from
Wherstead, in 1909 (Hb. Atkins) and from Henstead and Frostenden by E. R. Long, c.
1930.

Gnaphalium sylvaticum L.　　Heath Cudweed　　　　　Sir J. Cullum 1773
　　　　　　　　　　　　　　Wood Cudweed
Native. Rare and decreasing and now extinct in several former habitats. Open glades, in
heathy woods and beside old tracks.

318

W: 77; 86; 93; 96; 98.
86, Fornham St Genevieve.
E: 05; 13; 23; 33; 35; 36; 39; 46; 47; 58; 59.
13, Stutton, 1974; 46, Dunwich Forest, 1972-80. *Illustrated page 472*

Gnaphalium uliginosum L.   Marsh Cudweed   Sir J. Cullum 1773

Native. Found in damp waste places, margins of arable land, waysides and woodland tracks. Frequent.
W: All squares except 64; 65; 66; 67; 68; 74; 75; 83; 84; 85.
78, Brandon, 1979; 95, Monks' Park Wood, 1980.
E: All squares except 05; 06; 44; 48.
17, Redlingfield, 1979; 23, Harkstead, 1981; 35, Tunstall Common, 1981; 47, Dunwich Forest track, 1980.

Gnaphalium luteo-album L.   Jersey Cudweed   J. Denson 1836

A native of the Channel Islands and probably also of sandy fields in Breckland and old chalk quarries. Extinct.
W: 77, Eriswell; 78, Lakenheath, in chalk pit. Last record, 1956 (M. G. Rutterford).

Helichrysum bracteatum (Vent.) Andr.   Everlasting Flower   M. A. Hyde 1974

Grown in gardens. Native of Australia.
E: 23, Chelmondiston Tip, 1974. Detd. R. H. S. Wisley.

Antennaria dioica (L.) Gaertn.   Cat's Foot   Sir J. Cullum 1773
                                     Mountain Everlasting

Native. On calcareous heaths. Recorded in Hind from Cavenham, Culford and Newmarket Heaths. Last recorded c. 1935 by Miss E. Rawlins from Cavenham.
Hb. Atkins: 'specimen collected in 1906 from near Bury'.

Anaphalis margaritacea (L.) Benth.   Pearly Everlasting   Lady Blake 1850
(*Antennaria margaritacea* (L.) S. F. Gray)

Introduced. Native in N. America. Cultivated in gardens and sometimes escaping and becoming naturalised in moist meadows. There are two records in Hind's Flora, from Bentley and Eriswell. Specimen in Hb. Atkins from Bentley, 1909.

Inula helenium L.   Elecampane   Sir J. Cullum 1775

Introduced or a garden escape. In ditches and waste places. Rare. It was formerly grown for its medicinal properties, and also the roots were used in wine making and flavouring.
W: 85, Shimpling; Stanstead, 1980 (Dr K. T. Brown).
E: 06; 15; 16; 25; 26; 48; 58.
06, Bacton; 15, Hemingstone; Barham; 16, Mendlesham; 25, Ufford Thicks; 26, Framlingham; Saxtead, 1976 (G. H. Ransome); 48, Stoven; 58, Gisleham.

Inula conyza DC.   Ploughman's Spikenard   J. Andrews 1749
(*Conyza squarrosa* L.)

Native. Found on dry banks, quarries, railway cuttings and wood margins, usually on Chalk and Chalky Boulder Clay. Not very frequent and decreasing. Extinct in several former habitats.

W: 67; 76; 77; 78; 83; 84; 86; 88; 94; 96; 98.
78, Lakenheath Warren, 1973; Brandon, in plenty, 1979.
E: 03; 04; 05; 06; 07; 14; 15; 16; 23; 25; 28; 33; 34; 36; 39.
14, Lt. Blakenham, 1976; Westerfield Station, 1981; 15, Coddenham, 1980; 33, cliffs at Old Felixstowe, 1979, on Red Crag Sands.
Hb. Ipswich Museum: 'In the London Road, on the north hedge bank between Handford Hall and Crane Hall', c. 1810 (John Notcutt). *Illustrated page 473*

Inula crithmoides L. Golden Samphire E. Forster 1789

Native. Found in salt marshes. Rare in Suffolk, but still frequent in North Essex.
E: 23, Shotley, 1977; Erwarton, 1980; Trimley Marshes, 1980 (F. W. Simpson); 47, Walberswick, c. 1960 (H. E. Chipperfield). *Illustrated page 495*

Pulicaria dysenterica (L.) Bernh. Fleabane Sir J. Cullum 1773

Native. Old wet pastures, marshes, banks of rivers and ditches. Frequent.
All squares except 65; 66. *Illustrated page 481*

Pulicaria vulgaris Gaertn. Small Fleabane Rev. G. Crabbe 1798
(*Inula pulicaria* L.)

Native. Found in old damp pastures. Now very rare, or extinct. The plant was recorded in Hind's Flora from only two places, from Framlingham 'in places where water stood in the winter' and from Bramford 'on a bank by the side of a wet ditch'. The last known record for Suffolk was by D. J. Martin in 1963 from Lackford Heath.
W: 67, Mildenhall; 76, Lackford Heath.
E: 35, Snape; 48, between Wrentham and Sotterley.

Guizotia abyssinica (L.f.) Cass. P. G. Lawson & A. Copping 1971

An alien, native in East Africa. May occasionally be found as a casual on rubbish tips and in waste places. Cultivated in some countries for an edible oil produced from the achenes. It can also be used for fuel and in the manufacture of soap.
W: 77, Barton Mills Tip, 1977 (M. A. Hyde).
E: 14, Ipswich, 1978, in potato patch; 49, Beccles.

Bidens tripartita L. Trifid Bur Marigold J. Andrews 1743

Native. Beside ponds, ditches and rivers. Rather local and decreasing.
W: 75; 77; 78; 83; 84; 86; 87; 88; 93; 94; 96; 97.
96, Pakenham, 1974.
E: 03; 06; 08; 13; 14; 16; 17; 23; 24; 26; 34; 38; 39; 46; 47; 48; 49.
08, Hopton, Little Ouse, 1974; 23, edge of Trimley Lake, 1980; 24, Rushmere, 1977; 46, East Bridge, 1977.

Bidens cernua L. Nodding Bur Marigold J. Andrews 1743

Native. Moist and muddy places beside ponds, ditches, rivers and streams. Local, more common in East Suffolk. Occurs more frequently than *B. tripartita*.
W: 77; 78; 83; 84; 86; 87; 88; 93.
78, Mildenhall, 1980.

E: 03; 07; 13; 15; 17; 23; 24; 27; 28; 33; 34; 35; 37; 38; 39; 45; 46; 47; 48; 49; 59.
13, Holbrook, 1981; 23, Falkenham, 1974; 24, Bixley, 1979; 46, Leiston and Sizewell, 1979; 47, Walberswick, 1976; Blyth Valley, 1976.
In 1980 abundant at edge of Alton Water, Tattingstone and Holbrook (N. Hunt).

Bidens pilosa L.   E. Q. Bitton 1957

An alien. Native of S. America. Found on waste heaps at the Tannery, Combs (sq. 05), 1957-8.

Rudbeckia laciniata L.   Cone-flower   F. W. Simpson 1980

Introduced. Native of N. America. A garden throw-out.
W: 77, Mildenhall, on waste ground. Detd. M. A. Hyde.
The double-flowered variety, 'Golden Glow', also found on the edge of a ditch by a Poplar plantation.

Helianthus annuus L.   Common Sunflower   Mrs E. M. Hyde 1974

Introduced and cultivated. Probably native in Mexico. May be found as a casual in fields and waste places, particularly near the coast.
W: 77, Barton Mills Tip, 1977; 96, Woolpit Tip, 1974.
E: 13, Freston; 14, Ipswich; 15, Coddenham Tip, 1974; 23, Chelmondiston Tip, 1974; Harkstead, relic of cultivation, 1981; 34, Boyton; 58, Kessingland Beach, 1980.

Helianthus tuberosus L.   Jerusalem Artichoke   F. W. Simpson 1954

Introduction. Native of America. Garden throw-out of waste places and rubbish-tips.
W: 66, Exning, waste ground, 1977; 77, Mildenhall, 1980.
E: 13, Chelmondiston, 1974 (M. A. Hyde); 14, Rushmere Common, 1954; 23, Chelmondiston Tip; Trimley, 1981; 24, Woodbridge, 1976.

Helianthus petiolaris Nutt.   F. W. Simpson 1952

Casual. Native of N. America. Found on waste ground at Felixstowe Docks. Detd. at Kew.

Helianthus rigidus (Cass.) Desf.   Perennial Sunflower   N. S. P. Mitchell 1959
(*H. scaberrimus* Ell.)

Introduced from Eastern N. America and cultivated as a garden plant, often escaping or thrown out and becoming naturalised. Waste places and rubbish tips.
E: 05, Stowmarket; 13, Wherstead; 14, Ipswich, 1978; 23, Chelmondiston Tip, 1973-5; 33, Felixstowe; 45, Aldeburgh; 59, Lowestoft.

Iva xanthifolia Nutt.   Prairie Ragweed   Mrs C. Bull 1938

Alien. Native in N. America. The plant is said to be an important cause of hay fever.
E: 14, by the R. Gipping near Riverside Road, Ipswich, 1975-1981 (Mrs E. M. Hyde); 23, Felixstowe Docks, 1938 and 1957, detd. British Museum.

Ambrosia maritima L.   Mrs F. Baker c. 1890

A casual from continental Europe. Recorded from Oulton Broad.

Ambrosia artemisiifolia L. Roman Wormwood F. W. Simpson 1951
An alien introduced from N. America. Found as a rare casual of waste places. Said to be a cause of hay fever.
E: 14, Rutters Farm, Bramford; Ipswich; 57, Reydon, 1974.

Ambrosia trifida L. Great Ragweed Mrs F. Baker c. 1890
Casual. Native of N. America. First recorded from Oulton Broad about 1890.
W: 77, Barton Mills Tip, 1977 (M. A. Hyde). Detd. E. J. Clement.
E: 03, East Bergholt, 1963.

Ambrosia psilostachya DC. Ragweed Finder not recorded, 1975
Casual. Native of N. America.
E: 24, Woodbridge. Comm. N. R. Kerr.

Xanthium strumarium L. Rough Cocklebur Mrs Parker c. 1880
A casual, probably native in America. There is a single record in Hind's Flora from Drinkstone (sq. 96). More recently it has been recorded from Falkenham (sq. 23) by Mrs E. Stephenson in 1957. Also as a casual on a waste heap at the Tannery, Combs (sq. 05) by F. W. Simpson in 1958, detd. at Kew.

Xanthium spinosum L. Spiny Cocklebur F. W. Simpson 1939
Introduced from S. America. A casual of waste places, especially where waste from imported wool and skins has been deposited.
E: 05, The Tannery, Combs, 1957; 13, Harkstead; 23, Felixstowe Docks, 1939; Erwarton, c. 1974.
All records by F. W. Simpson.

Galinsoga parviflora Cav. Gallant Soldier Lowestoft Field Club 1950
Kew Weed
Introduced from S. America and now an established alien, which is increasing in Suffolk. Found in waste places, gardens and arable fields. Not recorded in Hind's Flora.
E: 04, Hintlesham, 1976; 05, Wattisham; 13, Woolverstone, 1979; 14, East side of Ipswich, 1981; 23, Chelmondiston, 1981; Levington, 1974; 35, Tunstall and Snape; 46, Dunwich; 49, Somerleyton; 59, Oulton; Blundeston; Lowestoft; 40, Burgh Castle; Belton, 1978; 50, South Town.

Galinsoga ciliata (Raf.) Blake Shaggy Soldier Dr G. Griffith 1953
An established alien, native in America from Mexico to Chile. Found on cultivated ground and in waste places. Spreading, but less frequent than *G. parviflora*.
W: 83, Gt Cornard, 1953; 97, Ixworth.
E: 03; 14, Ipswich, several sites, 1980; 57, South Green, Southwold, 1958; 59, Lowestoft; Oulton Broad; 50.

Schkuhria pinnata (Lam.) Thell. E. Q. Bitton 1957
A casual, native in Mexico. First recorded from a waste heap at the Tannery, Combs (sq. 05) by E. Q. Bitton in 1957. Its presence at the same place was confirmed in the following year by F. W. Simpson. Specimen determined at Kew.

COMPOSITAE

Schkuhria isopappa Benth. Miss B. Schafer 1952

A casual, found on waste ground at Brantham (sq. 13) and determined at the British Museum.

Gaillardia aristata Pursh Blanket Flower Mrs E. M. Hyde 1975

Introduced. Native of N. America. Cultivated in gardens and sometimes escaping.
E: 23, Felixstowe, near Coastguard Station, 1975.

Tagetes minuta L. Mexican Marigold F. W. Simpson 1952

An alien, native in N. America. Found in Britain on rubbish tips and waste places. The seed is possibly introduced with poultry food.
E: 05, The Tannery at Combs, 1952; 14, Sproughton; 23, Chelmondiston; 46, Dunwich.

Anthemis punctata Vahl ssp. **cupaniana** (Tod. ex Nyman) R. Fernandes
F. W. Simpson 1948

Alien. Native of Sicily. Grown in gardens.
E: 13, Brantham (Mrs E. M. Hyde), 1974; 23, Landguard Common, 1948-1980. Detd E. J. Clement.

Anthemis arvensis L. ssp. **arvensis** Corn Chamomile Sir J. Cullum 1773

Colonist. A weed of cultivated fields and waste ground. Locally frequent.
W: 64; 66; 74; 75; 76; 77; 78; 83; 86; 87; 88; 93; 94; 97; 98.
77, Icklingham, 1980; Barton Mills, 1981; 94, Brent Eleigh, 1981.
E: 03; 13; 14; 16; 23; 24; 25; 33; 34; 47.
24, Foxhall and Brightwell, 1980.
A glabrous variety was found on the edge of a cornfield at Foxhall, 1974.

Anthemis cotula L. Stinking Mayweed Sir J. Cullum 1775

Colonist. A weed of cultivated land and waste places, usually on the margins of farm tracks and stackyards. Sometimes abundant, but generally not frequent.
W: All squares except 65; 67; 68.
86, Bury St Edmunds, 1976.
E: All squares except 05; 14; 15; 49; 40; 50.
23, Harkstead, 1977.

Anthemis tinctoria L. Yellow Chamomile Rev. E. N. Bloomfield 1862

Introduced from S. and C. Europe. Occurs as a casual on waste ground and is sometimes found as a garden escape. Recorded by Hind only from Lowestoft in 1862, where he considered it to have been introduced with ballast.
W: 87, West Stow, 1979.
E: 23, Felixstowe Docks, 1933; 46, Westleton, 1957.

Achillea ptarmica L. Sneezewort J. Andrews 1744

Native. Old wet pastures, heaths and fens. Not very frequent.
W: 68; 77; 78; 83; 94; 97.
78, Lakenheath, Pashford Poor's Fen, 1979.

E: 14; 36; 37; 38; 39; 46; 47; 48; 49; 58; 59.
47, Walberswick, 1979. *Illustrated page 479*
A form with double flowers is frequent in cottage gardens and is known as Bachelors' Buttons. It often persists on the sites of former gardens long after the other garden plants have died out. This has been noted at Pettistree, Crowfield, Felixstowe, Iken and Gt Finborough. Also on a wayside verge, Wherstead, 1978 (F. W. Simpson).

Achillea millefolium L.   Yarrow   Sir J. Cullum 1773
Milfoil

Native. Waysides, pastures and waste places. Very common. The colour of the flowers varies from white to rose.
All squares.

Achillea decolorans Schrad.   Serrated Yarrow   Mrs French c. 1850
(*A. serrata* Sm.)

There is a single record of this species in Hind's Flora from a roadside by the brook near Drinkstone Rectory.

Chamaemelum nobile (L.) All.   Chamomile   Sir J. Cullum 1773
(*Anthemis nobilis* L.)

Native. On dry, sandy and gravelly commons and pastures. Now uncommon as a native and possibly extinct. Chamomile has been used as a lawn plant from at least Tudor times, especially on dry soils; some of our wild specimens may therefore be relics of cultivation. One often sees it used for this purpose in Mediterranean countries. The plant gives off a pleasant scent. Seed can still be obtained from merchants. Formerly used for medicinal purposes.
W: 77, Icklingham.
E: 14, Rushmere Common; 23, Nacton; Landguard Common; 33, Felixstowe.
Recorded in Hind's Flora from Santon Downham, Lidgate, Bungay, Blundeston and Bradwell Commons, Flixton and Lowestoft.

Chamaemelum mixtum (L.) All.   Mrs F. Baker c. 1890
(*Anthemis mixta* L.)

A casual, native of the Mediterranean region. Recorded only from Oulton Broad.

Matricaria maritima L. ssp. **maritima**   Sea Mayweed   Sir J. Cullum 1773
(*Tripleurospermum maritimum* (L.) Koch ssp. *maritimum*)

Native. Usually perennial. Found on the sea coast on shingle beaches and cliffs. Rare, though possibly overlooked.
This species is distinct from the common Scentless Mayweed of arable fields and waste places. The flowers are fewer and are usually much larger, the stems more woody and prostrate with fewer branches. Some specimens I have observed, for instance on the Wexford Coast of Ireland, have branches with only one or two flowers, which have very long stalks and the flowers are almost as large as an Ox-eye or Moon Daisy. They may measure 2¼" across and have a disc, when developed, ¾" across and ½" high.
E: 23, Trimley St Mary, 1981; 33, Bawdsey, 1976; 34, Hollesley, 1981; 44, Havergate Island, 1979.

Matricaria perforata Mérat   Scentless Mayweed   J. Andrews 1745
(*M. inodora* L.
Tripleurospermum inodorum Schultz Bip.)
An annual or biennial colonist. A very common weed of cultivated ground, waste places and coastal cliffs and beaches.
All squares.

Chamomilla recutita (L.) Rauschert   Scented Mayweed   Sir J. Cullum 1773
(*Matricaria recutita* L.   Wild Chamomile
M. chamomilla auct.)
Probably introduced into Suffolk and formerly cultivated. Waste places and arable fields. Frequent.
W: All squares except 65; 66; 67; 68.
E: All squares except 15; 17; 28; 37; 38; 45; 46; 48; 49; 50.
13, Holbrook, 1978; 14, Ipswich by R. Gipping, 1980; 16, Wetheringsett, 1979.
Flore-pleno form, Honington, 1883, Hind.

Chamomilla suaveolens (Pursh) Rydb.   Pineapple Weed
(*Matricaria matricarioides* (Less.) Porter pro parte   Rayless Mayweed
M. discoidea DC.)   H. Dixon Hewitt c. 1907
Alien, now completely naturalised. Probably native in N.E. Asia, but established in N. America, Europe, Chile and New Zealand. A common, often abundant, weed of farmland, tracks, waste places and woodlands. The seeds are transported on the mud carried by vehicles, boots and shoes. In Suffolk it was almost unknown, except as a casual, in the 1920's, but by the 30's it had increased considerably and could be found in almost half the parishes. By the late 40's, it had spread over the entire County. It still seems to be increasing. Plants with fasciated flowers like 'coxcombs' were frequent by the borders of fields at Chelmondiston and Harkstead in 1974.
All squares.   *Illustrated page 512*

Otanthus maritimus (L.) Hoffmanns. & Link   Sea Cottonweed   Sir J. E. Smith 1800
(*Diotis maritima* (L.) Desf. ex Cass.)
Native. On sandy and old shingly beaches, which are wild and undisturbed. Believed to be extinct in Suffolk. Formerly occurring in a number of localities and recorded by Hind for Lowestoft, Pakefield, Southwold, Benacre, Dunwich, Aldeburgh, Orford and Landguard Fort. There is a specimen in Hb. Ipswich Museum collected from one mile north of Landguard Fort by Rev. G. R. Leathes. It is believed that the last specimens were collected at Southwold about 1880. The species is unlikely to occur again in Suffolk, since the coast is now too developed and overrun for it to grow and survive.

Chrysanthemum carinatum Schousboe   J. M. Schofield c. 1965
A casual with white and purple flowers, native on the N. African coast. Known in Suffolk from a single record near Elveden (sq. 88).

Chrysanthemum segetum L.   Corn Marigold   J. Andrews 1744
                                  Dunwich Buddle
A colonist from the Mediterranean and West Asia. A weed of light arable fields,

sometimes very abundant. More widely distributed in East than in West Suffolk. It grows in great abundance around Dunwich and is known locally as the 'Dunwich Buddle'.
W: 66; 76; 78; 83; 85; 96; 98.
76, Kentford Heath, 1979 (F. E. Wrighton).
E: 03; 04; 13; 14; 23; 24; 25; 33; 34; 35; 36; 39; 45; 46; 47; 49; 59; 40; 50.
Very common on the Shotley Peninsula, 1981; 46/47, very frequent; 24, fields at Rushmere, Bixley and Foxhall. *Illustrated page 514 and page 515*

Chrysanthemum coronarium L.   Crown Daisy   Mrs F. Baker c. 1890

A yellow-flowered casual, native in the Mediterranean. Known in Suffolk from a single record from Oulton Broad in 1890. Possibly a garden escape.

Tanacetum vulgare L.   Tansy   Sir J. Cullum 1773
(*Chrysanthemum vulgare* (L.) Bernh.)

Introduced. Formerly cultivated as a medicinal and pot herb, found on roadsides, in hedges, waste places and sites of old gardens. Tansy used to be abundant in the Shotley Peninsula in the 20's and 30's and as a young botanist I used to refer to the area as 'tansy country'. Nowadays it is still quite frequent, but with the removal of the hedgebanks, ploughing up of verges and too much cutting, it is becoming less common. Tansy is also to be seen in the Capel St Mary and Holton and Wenham areas, and in the coastal belt east of Halesworth, and in parts of Lothingland.
All squares except 65; 66; 75; 76; 85; 44. *Illustrated page 508*

Tanacetum parthenium (L.) Schultz Bip.   Feverfew   Sir J. Cullum 1773
(*Chrysanthemum parthenium* (L.) Bernh.)

An established alien, introduced from S. E. Europe. Frequent garden escape, found by walls, beside dry ditches and on waste ground.
W: All squares except 68; 75; 84.
86, Bury St Edmunds, near Station, 1981; 96, Pakenham, on walls, 1978.
E: All squares except 28; 35; 37; 39; 40.
14, Ipswich, frequent, 1981; 33, Felixstowe Ferry, 1978; Bawdsey, 1975.
Illustrated page 507
Double-flowered or semi-double flowered forms are frequent, and are cultivated for ornamental beds and borders.
W: 66, Exning, 1977.
E: 13, near Holbrook Creek, 1981; 14, Ipswich, 1981; Wherstead; 15, Barham Pits, 1981 (N. Hunt); 23, Chelmondiston Tip, 1974 (M. A. Hyde).

Tanacetum macrophyllum (Waldst. & Kit.) Schultz Bip.   Mrs B. A. Curtis 1963
(*Chrysanthemum macrophyllum* Waldst. & Kit.)

Introduced. Sometimes a garden escape. Native in S. E. Europe. Recorded from the side of the River Finn at Playford Hall (sq. 24) in 1963. (Detd. D. McClintock). Also, Little Wenham, 1976, (Mrs E. M. Hyde).

Pyrethrum decipiens Fisch. & Mey.   Mrs F. Baker c. 1900

Casual. Possibly a garden escape. Recorded from Oulton Broad.

Leucanthemum vulgare Lam. Marguerite   Sir J. Cullum 1773
(*Chrysanthemum leucanthemum* L.) Moon Daisy
          Ox-eye Daisy
          Bull Daisy

Native. Old pastures, railway banks and waste places. Common, especially on heavy soils. All squares.   *Illustrated page 516*

Leucanthemum maximum (Ramond) DC. Shasta Daisy F. W. Simpson 1950
(*Chrysanthemum maximum* Ramond) Garden Marguerite

An alien, native in the Pyrenees. May occur as a garden escape, and is occasionally naturalised on sea cliffs and in waste places.
E: 23, Chelmondiston Tip, 1974; 24, Kesgrave; Purdis Heath; 33, Cobbold's Point, 1977; Felixstowe Ferry, 1974; 58, Kessingland Cliffs, 1977; 59, Lowestoft, 1974, cliffs and waste ground.

Artemisia vulgaris L. Common Mugwort   Sir J. Cullum 1774

Native or naturalised. Hedges, waysides and waste places. Very common. All squares.

Artemisia verlotiorum Lamotte Verlots' Mugwort Mrs E. M. Hyde 1975
           Chinese Mugwort

Introduced. Native of China. Increasing.
W: 96, Beyton, 1981 (Mrs E. M. Hyde).
E: 14, waste ground at Wherstead Strand, 1975; Ipswich, near Lattice Barn, 1981, detd E. J. Clement. Also several colonies in the Landseer Rd area, 1981.

Artemisia absinthium L. Common Wormwood   Sir J. Cullum 1773

Possibly introduced. Waste places, waysides and rough pastures. Occasional. The plant has many uses medicinally and in the preparation of liqueurs and aperitifs, and also insecticides.
W: 66; 68; 77; 78; 84; 86; 96.
78, Lakenheath, 1979; 86, Bury St Edmunds, 1980.
E: 14; 23; 25; 35; 44; 45; 46; 47; 57; 58.
45, Aldeburgh, 1975; 47, Walberswick, 1976; Wangford, 1979.

Artemisia maritima L. Sea Wormwood   T. Martyn 1763

Native. Drier parts of salt marshes and sea embankments. Fairly frequent, but rarely very abundant. Var. **subgallica** Rouy has been recorded from Felixstowe, Brantham, Stutton, Holbrook, Harkstead, Sutton, Shingle Street and Hollesley.
E: 03, East Bergholt; 13, Brantham, Seafield Bay; Harkstead, 1981; Holbrook; 23, Trimley, 1980, formerly at Landguard Common; 24, Hemley, 1980; 33, Bawdsey; Felixstowe; 34, Butley; Shingle Street; Sutton; Hollesley; 35, Chillesford; 44, Havergate Island; Orford; Gedgrave; 45, Aldeburgh; 47/57, Walberswick; Reydon; Southwold; 40, Burgh Castle; Breydon Water; 50, Hopton.
Abundant on Havergate Island in 1980 at the base of the sea embankment (F. W. Simpson).   *Illustrated page 495*

Artemisia campestris L. ssp. **campestris**   Field Wormwood   Willisell 1724
Field Southernwood

Native. Restricted to sandy heaths in Norfolk and Suffolk. Very rare.
W: 78, Lakenheath, 1980; Brandon, 1980; Wangford, 1980; 87/88, introduced on to earlier sites on Thetford Heath, Barnham and Barnham Cross Common, Thetford; 88, Elveden.
Recorded in Hind's Flora from Brandon, Thetford Heath, Barnham Heath, Lakenheath, Eriswell, Barton Mills, Elveden, Icklingham, Mildenhall, Wangford and the Nunnery Wall at Thetford.   *Illustrated page 468*

Tussilago farfara L.   Coltsfoot   Sir J. Cullum 1773

Native and a colonist. A weed of farmland and waste places, especially on clay soils. Probably native in some old woods. Very common. Although a troublesome weed to the farmer, the flowers are attractive in the early spring. Coltsfoot is one of the few plants which can withstand pollution of the atmosphere and soil and it thrives on old coal tips and slag heaps in industrial areas.
All squares.

Petasites hybridus (L.) Gaertn., Mey. & Scherb.   Butterbur   Sir J. Cullum 1773
Wild Rhubarb

Native. By streams and rivers, in damp, neglected old pastures, on wet banks and sides of ditches. Fairly frequent. It is thought that all the Suffolk colonies are of the male plant only.
W: All squares except 65; 66; 75; 84; 98.
77, Mildenhall, 1980; 86, Timworth, 1981.
E: All squares except 06; 07; 16; 26; 33; 44; 48; 49; 58; 59; 50.
04, Hadleigh, 1981; 14, by the R. Gipping at Sproughton, 1980; 24, Gt Bealings, 1981; 34, roadside, Shottisham, 1981; 39, Mettingham, 1980.   *Illustrated page 488*

Petasites fragrans (Vill.) C. Presl   Winter Heliotrope   E. Skepper 1862
Fragrant Butterbur

Introduced from W. Mediterranean. Planted in shrubberies, wild gardens and near streams. Naturalised. This species has spread rapidly in some habitats and has become dominant, as in the grounds of the Convalescent Hospital at Felixstowe. Flowers from late autumn until the spring. Only the male plant is known.
W: 64; 74; 75; 76; 85; 86; 88; 93; 94; 96.
93, Polstead, 1977; 96, Elmswell, near Church, 1977.
E: 03; 04; 05; 13; 14; 15; 16; 17; 24; 25; 26; 27; 33; 34; 35; 36; 37; 38; 39; 45; 47; 48; 49; 57; 40; 50.
13, Stutton, 1981; 24, Playford, 1981; 35, roadside at Tunstall, 1981.
    Illustrated page 482

Petasites japonicus (Sieb. & Zucc.) Maxim.   Miss R. Brownhill 1966

Introduced. Native in Japan and Sakhalin. Sometimes found naturalised in Britain. The only Suffolk record is from the riverside at Layham, near Hadleigh.

Doronicum plantagineum L.   Plantain-leaved Leopard's Bane
    Rev. E. N. Bloomfield 1855

An introduced and naturalised alien from S. W. Europe. Sometimes a garden throw-out.

In plantations and on banks and in ditches. This species is frequently confused with *D. pardalianches*. It is usually a taller plant with larger flowers and is often grown in gardens for its early flowers.
W: 76, Higham; 86, Abbey Gardens, Bury St Edmunds.
E: 36, Gt Glemham.

Var. **excelsum** N. E. Brown
E: 06, Wyverstone, roadside, 1977 (Dr A. C. Leslie); 36, old Chantry Garden, Saxmundham, 1981; 37, Huntingfield, in woodland, 1981. Both records by F. W. Simpson and determined by Dr A. C. Leslie.

Var. **willdenowii** (Rouy) A. B. Jackson
W: 77, Mildenhall, 1916 (W. C. Barton). Comm. Dr A. C. Leslie.

Doronicum pardalianches L.   Great Leopard's Bane   Rev. T. Brown 1860
An introduced and established alien, native in W. Europe. Sometimes a garden escape. May be found in open plantations and copses, on banks of streams and outside gardens. Prefers a light, sandy, moist soil. In a number of stations it has been known for several years.
W: 74, Clare, 1974; 78; 85, Lawshall; 86, Ickworth Park; 94; 95, Hitcham; 96, Pakenham, 1981, detd Dr A. C. Leslie.
E: 05, Battisford, 1981, detd Dr A. C. Leslie; 13, Bentley; 14, Lt. Blakenham; 15, Witnesham; 25, Glevering, near the Deben; 38/39, Barsham, 1973; 46, Dunwich.
Specimen in Hb. Atkins, from Washbrook, 1909.

Senecio bicolor (Willd.) Tod. ssp. **cineraria** (DC.) Chater   J. Atkins 1908
(*S. cineraria* DC.)   Silver Ragwort

Introduced from the Mediterranean region. Frequently found naturalised on sea cliffs in S. England. Also on waste ground, of garden origin.
W: 86, waste ground, Bury St Edmunds, 1976.
E: 15, Gt Blakenham, 1980; 33, Felixstowe Ferry, 1977; Bawdsey, 1981, where it has been naturalised on the cliffs for many years.
The Hb. Atkins specimen, 1908, was from the 'beach at Felixstowe'.

Illustrated page 502

Senecio bicolor ssp. **cineraria** × **S. jacobaea**   F. W. Simpson 1969
(*S.* × *albescens* Burbidge & Colgan)
A sterile hybrid recorded from the cliffs at Bawdsey (sq. 33) in both 1969 and 1976.

Senecio fluviatilis Wallr.   Broad-leaved Ragwort   E. R. Long c. 1940
Introduced from C. and S. Europe. Recorded from the banks of the R. Waveney, opposite Dunburgh.

Senecio paludosus L.   Great Fen Ragwort   F. K. Eagle 1798
Formerly native and occurring in fen ditches in East Anglia. Recorded in Hind's Flora from Lakenheath Fen, near Wangford. There are no records of the species during the present century, and it is almost certainly extinct in Suffolk. Last record c. 1850.

329

Senecio integrifolius (L.) Clairv.   Field Fleawort   Sir J. Cullum 1774
(*S. campestris* (Retz.) DC.)

Native, inhabiting chalk and limestone areas. Hind's herbarium specimen was collected by
W. Jordan in 1876 on Newmarket Heath (sq. 66), which is its last record for the County.
It has been recorded from the Devil's Dyke, just in Cambridgeshire.

Senecio congestus (R. Br.) DC.   Marsh Fleawort   Sherard 1724
(*S. palustris* (L.) Hook.)

Native. In fen ditches and beside dykes. Probably extinct. Formerly found at Brandon,
Wangford, Lackford, Worlingham Common and Belton. The only recent record for the
County is from Minsmere (sq. 46) in 1947, but this must be regarded as very doubtful and
may have been *Sonchus palustris*. Last authentic record, mid-19th century.

Senecio jacobaea L.   Common Ragwort   J. Andrews 1743

Native. Poor grassland, breck, heaths, waysides and the sea coast. Very frequent.
All squares.
Var. **flosculosus** DC. The rayless variety. 67, Mildenhall, 1979 (Mrs E. M. Hyde).
Some botanists find it difficult to distinguish between *S. jacobaea* and *S. erucifolius*.
There is one simple method I have discovered. Both species are common, so no harm can
be done in picking them. The stems of *S. jacobaea* are very tough and difficult to break
off, but the stems of *S. erucifolius* break quite easily. *S. jacobaea* is more favoured by the
caterpillars of the Cinnabar moth and it is rare to find any caterpillars of this moth on *S.
erucifolius.*

Senecio aquaticus Hill   Marsh Ragwort   J. Andrews 1744
                               Water Ragwort

Native. In marshes, wet pastures, sides of ditches, streams, rivers and in fens. Decreasing,
becoming scarce.
W: All squares except 64; 65; 66; 67; 68; 76; 85; 87; 94; 95; 97.
68, Lakenheath, 1980; 77, Tuddenham; Mildenhall, 1980; 78, Brandon, 1979.
E: All squares except 03; 05; 06;'07; 13; 15; 16; 23; 24; 28; 58.
26, Framlingham, 1978; 37, Halesworth, 1976; 45, Friston, 1977.

Senecio aquaticus × jacobaea   F. W. Simpson 1978
(*S. × ostenfeldii* Druce)

W: 78, Brandon, one plant near the river.
E: 26, Framlingham, 1978 (Mrs E. M. Hyde).

Senecio erucifolius L.   Hoary Ragwort   Woodward c. 1790

Native. Waysides, clay banks, waste places near the sea, and railway embankments,
especially on the Chalky Boulder Clay. Frequent.
W: All squares except 67; 78; 88.
68, Lakenheath, 1980; 87, Gt Livermere, 1980; 94, Brent Eleigh, 1981.
E: All squares.
14, Bramford, 1981; 45, Snape, 1981; 58, Kessingland Cliffs, 1980.

Senecio squalidus L.   Oxford Ragwort   Rev. P. Lathbury 1849

An attractive and colourful alien. Native in Sicily and S. Italy. Found on waste ground, old buildings, railway embankments and cleared housing sites. Very frequent and still spreading. Formerly rare, but greatly increased since the Second World War. It is said that this species has spread via the railways from Oxford, where it has been known since 1794 on old walls. Especially abundant about Ipswich.
W: All squares except 64; 65; 68; 74; 75; 97; 98.
66, Exning, 1980; 86, Bury St Edmunds, 1981; 96, Elmswell Station, 1981.
E: All squares except 07; 27; 28; 36; 38; 44; 48.
23, on the shingle beach at Trimley, 1978.
Hind's Flora contains only one record of this species, namely from Northgate Street, Bury St Edmunds.

Senecio squalidus × viscosus   H. J. Killick 1973
(*S.* × *londinensis* Lousley)

E: 14, Ipswich, behind Suffolk College, one plant, 1981 (F. W. Simpson); 33, Felixstowe Town Station, 1975-7, three specimens with parents (F. W. Simpson); 59, Lowestoft, specimen shown at B.S.B.I. Meeting, 1973.

Senecio squalidus × vulgaris   Mrs E. M. Hyde 1977
(*S.* × *baxteri* Druce)

A very variable hybrid. Probably overlooked. It is considered that what are thought to be rayed forms of the Common Groundsel may be this hybrid.
E: 04, Hadleigh, railway yard.

Senecio crassifolius Willd.   Hind 1885

A casual found on ballast, Ipswich Docks. Specimen in Hind's herbarium.

Senecio vernalis Waldst. & Kit.   Spring Groundsel   W. C. Barton 1913

Introduced. Native of S. E. Europe. Specimen from Mildenhall, in the Herbarium of Oxford University, collected by W. C. Barton in 1913.

Senecio sylvaticus L.   Heath Groundsel   Sir J. Cullum 1773
                             Wood Groundsel

Native. On commons, heaths and in open woods on light, sandy, or gravelly soils. Locally frequent. In West Suffolk it is more or less confined to the Breckland.
W: Recorded from squares 64; 67; 76; 77; 78; 86; 87; 88; 96; 97; 98.
67, Freckenham, 1980; 78, Brandon, 1980; 87, West Stow, 1980.
E: All squares except 05; 06; 16; 26; 27; 37.
14/24, Rushmere Common, 1981; 35, Tunstall, 1981; 47, Hinton, 1981.

Senecio sylvaticus × viscosus   F. W. Simpson 1965
(*S.* × *viscidulus* Scheele)

One plant of this rare hybrid was found growing at the back of the shingle beach at Bawdsey (sq. 34) with both parents in 1965. The shingle at this point was later removed by the farmer of the adjacent land and the habitat destroyed.

Senecio viscosus L.   Sticky Groundsel   J. Andrews 1749
Stinking Groundsel

Probably a native of the coast, a colonist elsewhere. A weed of waste places, especially railway tracks, shingle and sandy beaches. Common, sometimes abundant. It has increased since 1945.
W: All squares except 64; 67; 74; 75; 83; 85.
78, Lakenheath, 1980; 86, Bury St Edmunds, 1981; 96, Thurston Station, 1979.
E: All squares except 26; 38; 48; 49; 40; 50.
04, Hadleigh, 1981; 23, Landguard Common; 33, Felixstowe, 1981; 34, Shingle Street, 1981.   *Illustrated page 500*

Senecio vulgaris L.   Groundsel   Sir J. Cullum 1773

Native or colonist. A common weed of cultivated ground, waste places and the sea coast. It is probably native on the coast on fixed dunes and in sandy open places on heaths.
All squares.
Var. **radiatus** Koch: 04, Hadleigh, 1980 (F. W. Simpson); 14, Belstead, 1978; 23, Chelmondiston Tip, 1973 (M. A. Hyde).

Senecio tanguticus Maxim.   F. W. Simpson 1958

Introduced, native in W. China. Sometimes found naturalised as a garden escape. Recorded from Ipswich in September 1958. Specimen determined at the British Museum.

Calendula officinalis L.   Pot Marigold   F. W. Simpson 1939
Garden Marigold

Introduced from C. Europe and the Mediterranean. Usually found as a garden escape on rubbish tips and waste places, but not persisting.
W: 76, Dalham, 1981; 77, Barton Mills Tip, 1977; 78, Lakenheath, 1974; 94, Monks Eleigh; 97, Hopton, 1981.
E: 13; 14; 15; 23; 25; 33; 34; 44; 45; 49; 58.
14, waste ground, Wherstead Road, Ipswich, 1981; 23, Chelmondiston Tip, 1977; 25, Debach, 1981; 33, Old Felixstowe, Felixstowe Ferry and Town Station, 1975; 34, Shingle Street, 1980.

Carlina vulgaris L.   Carline Thistle   J. Andrews 1739

Native. Dry chalky and sandy heaths, rough pastures, quarries, sea cliffs and dunes. Formerly fairly frequent, now scarce or extinct in many areas.
W: 76; 77; 78; 84; 86; 87; 88; 94; 96; 97; 98.
77, Barton Mills, 1977; 78, Lakenheath, 1979; 87, Barnham, 1980; West Stow, 1979; 98, Knettishall, 1981.
E: 05; 14; 15; 23; 24; 25; 33; 45; 46; 47; 48; 58; 59.
14, Bramford, 1979; 15, Creeting St Mary, 1979; 24, Newbourn, 1981; 47, Hinton, 1980.
Illustrated page 472

Echinops sphaerocephalus L.   Pale Globe Thistle   R. Burn 1931

An alien, native of C. and S. Europe and W. Asia. A casual of garden origin, sometimes found on roadsides and naturalised.
W: 94, Brent Eleigh, on site of former cottage, 1974 (M. A. Hyde). Detd. at Kew. Still there, 1981.

COMPOSITAE

E: 04, Whatfield, 1931-40; 34, between Virtues Farm, Hollesley and Alderton, 1948-52; 35, Tunstall, 1980. Detd. E. J. Clement.

Echinops exaltatus Schrader   Globe Thistle   Mrs E. M. Hyde 1975
Casual of garden origin. Native of C. Europe.
E: 45, roadside, Friston. Detd. E. J. Clement. Still there, 1981.

ARCTIUM SPECIES   BURDOCKS

It is probable that there are really only two native species of *Arctium* in the County, *A. lappa* and *A. minus,* plus a whole range of hybrids and intermediates (= *A. intermedium* Lange).
A. minus has been divided into two subspecies: *A. minus* ssp. *minus* and *A. minus* ssp. *nemorosum* (Lej.) Syme. The latter subspecies has a more northern distribution in Britain and possibly does not occur in Suffolk.
A minus ssp. *minus* varies according to habitat and general growing conditions, whether in open sites or woodland glades, on dry or moist soils. *A. lappa* usually occurs in open habitats on waysides, besides rivers and ditches, in farmyards and woods. It is now much less frequent than it was some 50 years ago, and is quite absent from many areas. It has always been uncommon compared with *A. minus.*
Intermediates are quite common and it is suggested that *A. lappa* as a species has now become rare, due to hybridisation.
Recorders have confused the distribution of *Arctium* in Suffolk. Plants with small heads, usually ovoid in shape and about ¾ " in diameter may be considered as *A. minus.* Plants with large globular heads, about 1½ " in diameter are *A. lappa.*

Arctium tomentosum Mill.   Woolly Burdock   A. W. Punter 1966
A rare casual, native in continental Europe. Recorded at Higham Heath (sq. 76) in 1966.

Arctium lappa L.   Great Burdock   Sir J. Cullum 1773
(*A. majus* Bernh.)
Native or a colonist. On waysides, sides of ditches and river banks, especially on rich peaty soils. Formerly locally frequent, even common, now much reduced and scarce in many areas.
W: All squares except 78.
66, Moulton, banks of the R. Kennett, 1981; 68, Lakenheath, 1980; 74, Clare Country Park, 1976; 76, Gazeley, 1981.
E: All squares except 06; 07; 23; 28; 33; 44; 45; 40; 50.
24, Playford, 1980; 39, Mettingham, 1980; 46, Westleton, 1980.   *Illustrated page 517*

Arctium lappa × minus   Hybrid Burdock   Hind 1878
(*?A. intermedium* Lange)
Native. Waysides, farmyards, wood margins and waste places. Frequent, but usually overlooked. The few records do not give a true indication of its distribution.
W: 66, Exning; 67, Freckenham, 1977; 74, Clare, 1976; 76, Moulton, 1975; 77, Mildenhall, 1980; 78, Brandon, 1980; 84, Lineage Wood, Long Melford; 97, Fakenham Wood.

333

E: 04, Hintlesham, 1974; 06, Old Newton, 1975; 17, Hoxne; 23, Harkstead, 1974; 24, Playford, 1981; 33, Alderton; 34, Hollesley; 47, Westleton, 1980.
Hind's records for *A. nemorosum* Lej. are probably this hybrid.

Arctium minus Bernh.   Lesser Burdock   Sir J. Cullum 1773
                            Common Burdock

Native. Waysides, field margins, woods, waste places. Common.
All squares.

Carduus nutans L.   Musk Thistle   J. Andrews 1747
                         Nodding Thistle

Native. Dry pastures, waysides, quarries and cliffs, especially on chalky or sandy soils.
Frequent.
W: All squares except 64; 65; 74; 85.
Common in Breckland, 1981.
E: All squares except 06; 17; 26; 27; 37.
13, Woolverstone, 1981; 45, Iken Heath, 1981; 47, Blythburgh, 1981.
                                                        Illustrated page 509
A white-flowered form has been recorded from **W:** Barnham, 1973. **E:** 24, Martlesham
Heath, 1979; 33, Bawdsey, 1979.

Carduus acanthoides L.   Welted Thistle   Sir J. Cullum 1773
(*C. crispus* auct.)

Native. Damp waysides, beside streams and rivers, and in open woodland. Frequent.
W: All squares.
76, Barrow, 1980; Dalham and Moulton, 1981; 97, Hopton Fen, 1981.
E: All squares except 16; 17; 27; 33; 34; 37; 44; 45.
04, Hadleigh, 1981; 07, Thelnetham Fen, 1981; 13, Tattingstone, 1981; 24, Rushmere,
1981.
White-flowered form at Bury St Edmunds, 1979 (F. W. Simpson).

Carduus acanthoides × nutans   F. W. Simpson 1962
(*C. × orthocephalus* Wallr.)

An uncommon hybrid, first found on waste ground on the margin of an arable field at
Bawdsey.
W: 66, Moulton, 1977; 76, Barrow, 1980; 94, Semer.
E: 04, Hadleigh; 14, Wherstead and Belstead Road, Ipswich, 1975; 15, Gt Blakenham; 33,
Bawdsey.

Carduus tenuiflorus Curt.   Slender Thistle   Wigg 1805

Native. Waste places, sea cliffs and the edges of salt marshes. Locally common.
E: 13; 14; 23; 24; 33; 34; 35; 37; 38; 39; 44; 45; 46; 47; 57; 58; 59; 40; 50.
14, Ipswich, 1981; 23/44, between Felixstowe and Orford, common, 1981; 45, Snape,
1981; 58, Benacre, 1980.   *Illustrated page 499*

Cirsium eriophorum (L.) Scop. ssp. **britannicum** Petrak   J. Andrews 1743
(*Carduus eriophorus* L.)   Woolly Thistle
                             Woolly-headed Thistle

Native. Open scrub on Chalk and Boulder Clay. Very rare. Some of the records are probably errors.
W: 76; 77; 78; 84; 86; 87; 96.
76, Dalham, 1978 (F. W. Simpson); 77, Eriswell; 84, Acton, 1935-74 (F. W. Simpson).

Cirsium vulgare (Savi) Ten. Spear Thistle Sir J. Cullum 1773
(*Carduus lanceolatus* L.)

Native. In waste places, waysides and cultivated ground. Very common.
All squares.

Cirsium dissectum (L.) Hill Meadow Thistle J. Andrews 1752
(*Carduus dissectus* L. Marsh Plume Thistle
C. pratensis Huds.)

Native. In fens and very old wet pastures. Very rare and decreasing, due to land drainage. Probably now reduced to one or two sites.
W: 68; 77; 78; 88; 97.
77, Eriswell; 78, Turf Fen, Lakenheath (P. J. O. Trist).
E: 07; 17; 39; 46; 49; 58; 59; 40.
07, Redgrave Fen, 1977.

Cirsium acaule Scop. ssp. **acaule** Dwarf Thistle J. Andrews 1739
(*Carduus acaulos* L.) Stemless Thistle

Native. Old pastures, quarries, railway banks, cuttings and earthworks on chalky soils or Coralline Crag. Formerly frequent and widespread, now less so.
W: All squares except 65; 67; 68.
76, Dalham, 1981; Risby and Cavenham, 1979; 77, Icklingham, roadside, 1981; 78, Lakenheath, 1980.
E: All squares except 13; 23; 25; 26; 27; 28; 33; 34; 39; 46; 47; 48; 49; 58; 59; 40; 50.
07, Mellis; Wortham, 1979; 38, Ilketshall St Andrew, 1976; 45, Sudbourne, 1978.
Illustrated page 472

Cirsium palustre (L.) Scop. Marsh Thistle Sir J. Cullum 1773
(*Carduus palustris* L.)

Native. In marshes, wet places, open glades in woods. Common.
All squares except 66; 67.
A white-flowered form has been reported from **E:** 04, Gt Wenham; 13, Belstead; Freston; Bentley; Holbrook; 24, Purdis Heath, 1981; 25, Bromeswell Green, 1980; 35, Gromford; 47, Bramfield; Dunwich; Walberswick; 57, South Cove, 1974.

Cirsium arvense (L.) Scop. Creeping Thistle Sir J. Cullum 1772
(*Carduus arvensis* (L.) Hill)

Native or a colonist. A weed of arable fields, pastures, waste places and open glades in woods. Very common or abundant.
All squares.
A white-flowered form has been recorded from **W:** 87, Livermere.
E: 13, Holbrook; Woolverstone; 14, Lt. Blakenham; Wherstead; 23, Shotley; 35, Blaxhall; 45, Snape, 1981; 47, Dunwich; Walberswick.

Onopordum acanthium L. Scotch Thistle Sir J. Cullum 1773
Cotton Thistle

Perhaps native or an established alien. Frequent on light soils. Roadside verges, arable field edges, waste places and sand pits.
W: All squares except 65; 75; 84; 85; 93; 95.
77, Cavenham, 1981; 78, Brandon, 1980; 97, Euston, 1980.
E: All squares except 07; 16; 17; 26; 27; 28; 38; 49; 50.
24, Gt Bealings, 1981; 44, Gedgrave, 1980; 45, Iken, 1981.

Cynara cardunculus L. Cardoon F. W. Simpson 1947

Introduced. Native of the Mediterranean region. Cultivated in gardens. Occasionally specimens become naturalised.
E: 33, Bawdsey, 1947-1978.

Silybum marianum (L.) Gaertn. Milk Thistle Sir J. Cullum 1773
(*Carduus marianus* L.) Holy Thistle

A naturalised alien. Native of S. Europe. In waste places, on roadside banks and cliffs. More frequent near the coast.
W: 93, Nayland; Thorington Street, near Stoke-by-Nayland, 1974; 94.
E: 03, Stratford St Mary; Higham; 04, Hintlesham; 05, Stowmarket; 13, Brantham; Cattawade; Stutton, 1978; 14, Bramford; 23, Landguard Common; Chelmondiston; 25, Burgh, 1981; 28, Weybread, near Shelford Bridge; 33, Bawdsey Cliff; 34, Hollesley; 35, Marlesford Hall; 36, Gt Glemham; 45, Aldeburgh; 46, Middleton; 47, Henham; Thorington; Blyford; Bulcamp, near Blythburgh; 48, Brampton; North Cove; 49, Somerleyton; Worlingham. *Illustrated page 499*

Serratula tinctoria L. Saw-wort Gerarde 1597

Native. In thickets, copses, old hedges and wayside verges. Very rare and probably now extinct in Suffolk. Formerly to be found in a few habitats where it was obviously a relic of the ancient Suffolk flora. It was chiefly confined to an area in the North-west of the County, growing on gravelly or light glacial drift. Now a decreasing species everywhere in Britain, as old habitats are destroyed.
Its last known site in Suffolk was at Livermere Thicks, where a very fine colony was bulldozed in 1969. This action is much regretted, as the site was one of great scientific importance. It was also recorded for Pakenham Wood (sq. 96), but this habitat has also been destroyed. It was also reported by D. J. Martin as occurring in a colony near the moat in Thornham Park (sq. 07) in 1972, but it was not found when the site was thoroughly searched. Part of the thicket was being removed. An old estate worker informed us that he could recall a plant similar to *S. tinctoria,* as we described it, growing in the vicinity. It had been introduced with some shrubs brought from France many years previously.
It was recorded in Hind's Flora from Coney Weston, Barton Park, Bury St Edmunds, Icklingham and Hemingstone. Other old records come from Coddenham (Hb. Atkins, 1908), Gt Glemham and Theberton.

Mantisalca salmantica (L.) Briq. & Cav. J. S. Wilkinson 1908
(*Centaurea salmantica* L.)

Casual. Native in S. Europe. Recorded from Ipswich in 1908.

Centaurea scabiosa L.   Greater Knapweed   J. Andrews 1746

Native. Waysides, old grassy places, quarries and cliffs. More frequent on chalky soils and Red or Coralline Crag sands.
W: All squares.
Common in Breckland, 1981.
E: All squares except 07; 17; 27; 28; 33; 44.
14, Claydon, 1981; Lt. Blakenham, 1980; 15, Coddenham, 1980.
Variety with white flowers at Cavenham, 1975; Dalham, 1980; Barrow, 1980; and at Iken, 1980.   *Illustrated page 474*

Centaurea calcitrapa L.   Red Star Thistle   Sir J. Cullum 1773

A casual, native of C. Europe. Waste places. Rare.
W: 78, Lakenheath, in old poultry run (M. G. Rutterford).
E: 15, Witnesham, c. 1960; 23, Felixstowe Docks, 1948 (F. W. Simpson); 46, Minsmere. Hb. Atkins: specimen from Lowestoft, 1906.
July 3rd 1797, Rev. William Kirby: 'by the way from Newmarket to the Stands, plentiful'.

Centaurea solstitialis L.   St Barnaby's Thistle   Sir T. G. Cullum 1804
Yellow Star Thistle

Casual. Native of S. Europe. Found near docks and in waste places. Usually on light, sandy soils. Rare.
W: 67, Mildenhall; 78, Lakenheath.
E: 03, Capel St Mary; 14, Ipswich; 23, Landguard Common; Felixstowe Docks (both c. 1948); 34, Capel St Andrew; 36, Yoxford, 1979; 48, South Cove; 59, Pakefield.
Most of these records were made between 1945 and 1955.

Centaurea diluta Ait.   M. G. Rutterford 1962

A casual. Native in S.W. Spain and N. Africa. Probably introduced with bird-seed. Recorded by M. G. Rutterford from sq. 78 and by Mrs E. M. Hyde from Tuddenham Quarry (sq. 14) in 1964. There is a third record from an Ipswich garden.

Centaurea jacea L.   Brown-rayed Knapweed   Sir J. Cullum 1775

A casual from continental Europe. Probably introduced with imported grass or other seed. Recorded from Hardwick in 1775.

Centaurea jacea × nemoralis   F. W. Simpson 1947
(*C. × drucei* Britton)

Old, damp neglected pasture adjacent to Easton Wood, near Southwold, sq. 57. Probably the site of the keeper's old cottage garden.

Centaurea nemoralis Jord.   Slender Knapweed   Marsden-Jones 1926
Meadow Knapweed

Native. Damp grassland, fens, waysides and woodland rides. Infrequent or overlooked. The majority of colonies examined contained specimens with *C. nigra* characteristics, probably hybrids or intermediates.
W: 74, Barnardiston, 1976 (F. W. Simpson); 77, Cavenham Heath; 86, Bury St Edmunds;

95, Hitcham; Monks' Park Wood, 1973 (F. W. Simpson), detd. E. L. Swann; 97.
E: 05, Barking; 13, Harkstead, 1981; 17, Stoke Ash; 24, Foxhall, 1974; 25; 47, Wangford; 48, Wrentham; Sotterley; 57, Easton Bavents.

Centaurea nigra L.   Common Knapweed   J. Andrews 1749
                          Hardheads
Native. Pastures, grassy places, old quarries, waysides and sea cliffs. Common. Frequently abundant and dominant on clay soils. Variable. Some forms are probably hybrids with *C. nemoralis*.
All squares.
A form with white flowers was seen at Westley in 1962.

Centaurea nigra × scabiosa   F. W. Simpson c. 1960
E: 34, with both parents at Alderton.

Centaurea montana L.   Mountain Cornflower   M. A. Hyde 1974
Native of C. Europe. A garden outcast.
E: 23, Chelmondiston Tip.

Centaurea depressa Bieb.   Mrs F. Baker c. 1890
Casual. Native of the Caucasus. Found at Oulton Broad.

Centaurea cyanus L.   Cornflower   Sir J. Cullum 1773
                          Corn Bluebottle
Colonist. Cornfields. Also a garden escape or on sites of former gardens. Once frequent, but now very rare in cornfields, due to improved farming methods, as sprays and stubble burning destroy the seeds. Almost extinct as an arable weed, persisting only as a casual on rubbish tips and waste places.
W: 78; 83; 86; 88; 93; 94; 96; 98.
93, Bures, abundant in cornfields until the mid-1950's. Persisted until about 1965. 94, cornfield in Potash Lane, Polstead Heath, 1971 (Mrs K. Riddleston).
E: 03; 06; 13; 14; 16; 33; 34; 35; 45; 46; 49; 59.
06, cornfield at Haughley, 1971-80 (Mrs J. Harris). The plants appeared after gas pipes were laid. This is the only recent record for the plant as a cornfield weed. 14, Wherstead Road and other sites in Ipswich on waste ground, 1981; 34, Shingle Street, 1981.
There is a specimen in Hb. Atkins from Holbrook, 1909.

Centaurea pullata L.   Finder not recorded c. 1950
Casual. Native of Spain and Portugal.
E: 14, waste ground at Ipswich.

Carthamus tinctorius L.   Safflower   N. R. Kerr 1963
                              False Saffron
Introduced into Britain from Egypt in 1551. Formerly grown in gardens and used for dyeing and for its oil. Found on rubbish tips and in gardens, where it is probably a relic of cultivation.

W: 77, Barton Mills Tip, 1977.
E: 15, Coddenham Tip, 1974 (M. A. Hyde); 47, Southwold, appeared in garden in 1963.

Carthamus lanatus L. F. W. Simpson 1958

A casual from S.E. Europe and the Mediterranean. Recorded from a waste heap at the Tannery, Combs (sq. 05). Detd. at Kew.

Cichorium intybus L. Chicory J. Andrews 1746
Wild Succory
Bunks (Suffolk)

Possibly native. Also an introduced and established alien, occasionally cultivated. Found on waysides, field borders and in rought pastures. Still fairly frequent.
W: All squares except 64; 65; 67; 85.
68, Mildenhall, 1977; 76, Barrow, 1980.
E: All squares except 50.
13, Harkstead, 1981; 14, Bramford, 1981; Ipswich, 1981; 46, Darsham, 1980.
Such an attractive flower can hardly be missed and it has therefore been recorded by and received more attention from, wild flower lovers than many inconspicuous and more abundant species. *Illustrated page 508*

Arnoseris minima (L.) Schweigg. & Koerte Lamb's Succory Sir J. Cullum 1774
(*Hyoseris minima* L.) Swine's Succory

Doubtfully native on sandy, arable and fallow fields, formerly chiefly in Breckland and the Sandlings. Very rare. Last record, 1955.
W: 86, Bury St Edmunds, 1955.
E: 44; 45; 46; 47.
Hb. Ipswich Museum: 'In a stony field adjoining the Locks a little beyond Boss Hall', 2nd July 1819 (John Notcutt).

Rhagadiolus stellatus (L.) Gaertn. Starry Hawkbit J. S. Wilkinson 1908

Casual. Waste places. Native of the Mediterranean region.
E: 14, Ipswich, 1908; 59, Lowestoft, 1976 (P. G. Lawson). Detd. E. J. Clement.

Hypochoeris maculata L. Spotted Cat's Ear Sir T. G. Cullum 1804

Native. Ancient chalky pastures, heaths and earthworks. Very rare. Still in Risby (sq. 76) in 1980.
Recorded in Hind's Flora from Cavenham, Risby, Icklingham, Newmarket.

Hypochoeris glabra L. Smooth Cat's Ear Sir J. Cullum 1773

Native. On dry heaths and commons. Mainly in the Breckland area, where it is frequent in fallow fields. Overlooked elsewhere.
W: 67; 76; 77; 78; 86; 87; 88; 98.
77, Mildenhall, 1980 (M. A. Hyde).
E: 03; 04; 14; 15; 23; 24; 25; 33; 34; 35; 39; 45; 46; 47; 58; 40.
24, Foxhall, 1975 (F. W. Simpson); Martlesham, 1980 (J. R. Palmer).
Many of the above records were made in the 1950's.

Hypochoeris radicata L.   Common Cat's Ear   Sir J. Cullum 1773
                               Long-rooted Cat's Ear

Native. Waysides, pastures and grassy places. Common.
All squares.

Leontodon autumnalis L.   Autumnal Hawkbit   Sir J. Cullum 1773

Native. On old pastures, commons, waysides and grassy places near the sea. Frequent.
All squares.

Leontodon hispidus L.   Rough Hawkbit   Sir J. Cullum 1773

Native. Old pastures, grassy waysides and banks, quarries, railway cuttings and the drier
parts of fens. Usually on calcareous soils. Formerly common, now scarce in some areas,
due to loss of habitat.
W: All squares except 65; 68; 93.
66, Moulton, 1981; 76, Dalham, 1981; Hargrave, 1980; 94, Brent Eleigh, 1981.
E: All squares except 13; 14; 28; 33; 34; 44; 49; 40; 50.
04, roadside bank between Whatfield and Elmsett, 1980; Hadleigh, disused railway line,
1981; 07, Thelnetham, 1981.

Leontodon taraxacoides (Vill.) Mérat   Lesser Hawkbit   John Notcutt c. 1820
(*L. leysseri* Beck)

Native. On dry grassy heaths, old pastures, waysides, coastal dunes, and fixed shingle.
Formerly fairly frequent, now rather local and scarce.
W: 66; 68; 77; 86; 87; 93; 94; 96; 97.
87, West Stow, 1980.
E: 03; 05; 06; 07; 13; 14; 16; 23; 25; 33; 34; 35; 36; 37; 38; 45; 46; 47; 48; 49; 58; 59; 40.
13, Woolverstone, 1981; 46/47, Dunwich to Sizewell, 1979; 58, Benacre, 1980; 59,
Lowestoft, 1980.
Hb. Ipswich Museum: 'In a hilly pasture (with *Leontodon hispidus*) between Dale Hall
and the Whitton Road', c. 1820 (John Notcutt).

Picris echioides L.   Bristly Ox-tongue   Sir J. Cullum 1773

Native or colonist. Rough pastures, quarries, a weed of the Boulder Clay. Frequent near
the coast on cliffs and embankments. Common.
All squares.

Picris hieracioides L.   Hawkweed Ox-tongue   J. Andrews 1745

Native. Old, dry banks, chalk pits, open scrub and railway cuttings, especially on the
Chalky Boulder Clay. Locally frequent.
W: All squares except 65; 66; 67; 68; 74; 87; 88; 97; 98.
76, Hargrave, 1979; 77, Barton Mills; 94, Brent Eleigh, 1981.
E: All squares except 13; 17; 24; 28; 33; 34; 48.
14, Bramford, 1977; 39, Bungay, 1981; 46, Middleton, 1980; 58, Kessingland, 1977.

Tragopogon porrifolius L.   Salsify   Sir J. Cullum 1781

Introduced. A native of the Mediterranean region. Usually a relic of cultivation or a
casual. Rare.

W: Not recorded recently. Hind lists it for Honington and between Hawstead and Great Welnetham.

E: 23, Walton Ferry; 35, Marlesford; 45; 48, Mutford; 49, Beccles; 59, Lowestoft, 1980; 50.

Tragopogon pratensis L. ssp. **minor** (Mill.) Wahlenb.   Sir J. Cullum 1773

Goat's Beard

John-go-to-bed-at-noon

Native. Waysides, pastures and grassy waste places. Frequent.

All squares.   *Illustrated page 517*

There are unconfirmed records for the County for ssp. **pratensis.** Ssp. **orientalis** (L.) Čelak. was recorded from Polstead (sq. 93) in 1980 (J. C. Williams). Conf. E. Milne-Redhead.

Sonchus asper (L.) Hill   Prickly Sow-thistle   Sir J. Cullum 1773

Spiny Sow-thistle

Native and a colonist. Probably native on the sea coast. Elsewhere a weed of fields and waste places. Common. All squares.

At one time recorded as a form of *S. oleraceus* L.

Sonchus oleraceus L.   Smooth Sow-thistle   Sir J. Cullum 1773

Native and a colonist. Probably native near the coast and on heaths. A weed of waste places and fields. Frequent.

All squares.

Sonchus palustris L.   Marsh Sow-thistle   Sherard 1724

Native. In old marshes, beside dykes and rivers. Formerly confined to Lothingland, where it is still frequent and often abundant, usually growing among the reed-beds. It is probably as common there today as it was over two centuries ago. It has now spread south to the marshes at Blythburgh, Minsmere, East Bridge, Snape, Tunstall and Iken.

E: 17; 35; 36; 45; 46; 47; 49; 59; 40.

17, Palgrave; 35, Snape; Blaxhall; Tunstall; 36, Farnham; 45, Friston; Snape; Iken; 46, Dunwich; Minsmere; East Bridge, 1980; 47, Blythburgh, 1981; 49, Herringfleet; St Olave's; Oulton; Barnby; Carlton Colville; Worlingham; Somerleyton; North Cove; Beccles, 1981; 59, Lowestoft; Oulton Broad; 40, Fritton; Burgh Castle, 1980; Belton, 1977.   *Illustrated page 486*

Sonchus arvensis L.   Corn Sow-thistle   Sir J. Cullum 1775

Native and a colonist. Probably native near the coast in the drier parts of salt marshes and on dunes. A weed of cultivation and waste places. Common.

All squares.   *Illustrated page 500*

Lactuca tatarica (L.) C. A. Meyer   Hind 1884

(*Mulgedium tataricum* (L.) DC.)

Introduced. Native of E. Europe. First found on a marshy bank of the Stour at Stoke-by-Nayland and probably introduced with foreign grain brought to Nayland Mill. No subsequent records.

Lactuca serriola L.   Prickly Lettuce   Sir J. Cullum 1773
(*L. scariola* L.)

Status doubtful. Possibly native, in some habitats near the coast on dunes, elsewhere a colonist, alien or casual of waste places and quarries. Not frequent. Much confused with *L. virosa,* which is a larger and more frequent species, growing in similar habitats. It is likely that many of the records for *L. serriola* are incorrect and recorders have been tempted by its English name only, without making a proper check. Although *L. virosa* is sometimes known as Acrid Lettuce, it is better to give it the name of Greater Prickly Lettuce.
W: All squares except 65; 67; 68; 77; 83; 87; 93; 97.
66, Exning, 1977; 68, Lakenheath, 1980; 97, Knettishall.
E: All squares except 06; 07; 15; 16; 17; 26; 44; 47; 40; 50.
35, Tunstall, 1981.

Lactuca sativa L.   Garden Lettuce   Mrs E. M. Hyde 1975

Introduced and cultivated. Occasionally found on waste ground and on rubbish rips.
W: 66, Exning, 1977; 78, Lakenheath Tip, 1977.
E: 14, Ipswich, waste ground near R. Orwell, 1975; 24, Martlesham Heath, 1980.

Lactuca saligna L.   Least Lettuce   Henslow & Skepper 1860

Native. In grassy places near the sea and on the edges of saltings. Very rare, possibly now extinct. It was last seen in 1958 at Easton Broad (sq. 58). The original record was from Aldeburgh.

Lactuca virosa L.   Greater Prickly Lettuce   J. Andrews 1739

A colonist or perhaps native on the coast. A weed of waste places, waysides and quarries. Frequent. Common near the sea on sand and shingle beaches and embankments.
W: 66; 67; 68; 83; 84; 86; 87; 88; 94; 97.
67, Freckenham, 1977; 68, Mildenhall, 1980; 78, Lakenheath, 1977.
E: 03; 04; 05; 13; 14; 15; 16; 17; 23; 24; 25; 28; 33; 34; 37; 44; 46; 49; 59.
04, Hadleigh, 1981; 14, Sproughton, 1981; 23, Landguard Common, 1977.

Cicerbita macrophylla (Willd.) Wallr.   Blue Sow-thistle   Miss J. D. Denniss 1973

Introduced. Now established in several parts of Britain. Native of the Caucasus. The only record is from an overgrown garden in Berners Street, Ipswich.

Mycelis muralis (L.) Dum.   Wall Lettuce   J. Andrews 1744
(*Lactuca muralis* (L.) Gaertn.)

Native. Shady banks, lanes and old walls. Not very frequent.
W: 64; 67; 77; 78; 84; 86; 95.
77, Mildenhall, 1981; 86, Bury St Edmunds, 1955; 78, Brandon, 1980.
E: 03; 14; 23; 24; 28; 38; 45; 48.
24, Foxhall, 1950.

TARAXACUM   DANDELIONS

Some 132 British species, or micro-species, of *Taraxacum* have been described in Dr A. J.

Richard's publication 'The Taraxacum Flora of the British Isles' (in Watsonia as a Supplement to Vol. 9, 1972) I am indebted to Dr Richards and to P. D. Sell for much of the information which follows.

The distribution of *Taraxacum* species and micro-species in Suffolk is still largely unknown and the information given represents the sum total of present available knowledge.

Taraxacum officinale Weber sensu lato   Common Dandelion   Sir J. Cullum 1773
Pittlebed (Suffolk)

Native. Pastures, waysides, open woodland and waste places. Very frequent and variable. All squares.

SECTION: ERYTHROSPERMA

Taraxacum brachyglossum (Dahlst.) Dahlst.

Native. In dry places in Breckland, sandy heaths, sand dunes and walls.
Recorded for both East and West Suffolk.
W: 77, Icklingham Plains (P. D. Sell); 78, Lakenheath Warren (E. L. Swann); 97, Honington (Dr A. J. Richards).

Taraxacum argutum Dahlst.   A. Fitter 1968

Endemic in the British Isles. Dry calcareous places and sandy roadsides under light shade.
W: Icklingham.

Taraxacum lacistophyllum (Dahlst.) Raunk.   Lesser Dandelion
Mrs M. Southwell 1950

Native. In dry places, in Breckland, on sandy heaths, walls and paths. Widespread and locally common.
W: 66; 67; 68; 75; 76; 77; 78; 86; 87; 88; 93; 94; 97; 98.
77, Eriswell; Tuddenham; Icklingham (P. D. Sell and Dr A. J. Richards); 78, Lakenheath.
E: 05; 07; 17; 25; 35; 44; 45; 47; 50.

Taraxacum rubicundum (Dahlst.) Dahlst.   P. D. Sell 1967

Native. In dry places in Breckland. Locally common.
W: 77, Foxhole Heath; Icklingham Plains; Eriswell; Codson Hill Heath; Dead Man's Grave, Icklingham and Icklingham Heath.

Taraxacum commixtum Hagl.   P. D. Sell 1967

Probably native. On sandy heaths.
E: 46, Minsmere.

Taraxacum fulvum Raunk.   W. Phillips 1931

Native. In dry grassland in Breckland.
W: 77, Icklingham.

Taraxacum fulviforme Dahlst.
W: 88, Warren Lodge, Thetford (R. P. Libbey and E. L. Swann).

Taraxacum oxoniense Dahlst.   Mrs M. Southwell 1953
Native. On dry, neutral or calcareous ground and sand dunes.
W: 76, Risby; 77, Eriswell; Icklingham (Mrs G. Crompton); 78, Lakenheath (P. D. Sell).
E: Recorded without locality.

Taraxacum retzii Van Soest
W: 77, Icklingham (P. D. Sell).

Taraxacum proximum (Dahlst.) Dahlst.   P. D. Sell 1967
Native. In dry grassland in Breckland.
W: 77, between Icklingham and Tuddenham St Mary; 88, Santon Downham.

SECTION: PALUSTRIA

Taraxacum palustre (Lyons) Symons   Marsh Dandelion   R. A. Graham 1952
                                           Narrow-leaved Marsh Dandelion
Native in marshes and fens. Very rare or nearly extinct. 'Probably less than 500 plants left
in the British Isles' (Dr A. J. Richards).
W: 78, Lakenheath.
E: 07, Redgrave; Thelnetham, c. 1956.

SECTION: SPECTABILIA

Taraxacum unguilobum Dahlst.
On wet paths and roadsides. Likely to have been introduced.
W: 77, Icklingham (Dr A. J. Richards).

Taraxacum spectabile Dahlst.   Red-veined Dandelion   F. J. Bingley 1954
                                      Broad-leaved Marsh Dandelion
Native. Wet pastures, marshes and the sides of streams.
E: 07; 35, Padley Water, Chillesford.

Taraxacum nordstedtii Dahlst.
Native. In wet meadows.
W: 88, Santon Downham (P. D. Sell).
E: Recorded without locality.

Taraxacum litorale Raunk.
W: 77, Icklingham (P. D. Sell).

SECTION: VULGARIA

Taraxacum subcyanolepis M. P. Chr.   P. D. Sell 1967

Native. Grassland and grassy roadside banks.
W: 77, Icklingham.
E: 25, Grundisburgh.

Taraxacum pallescens Dahlst.

Native. In old rich pastures.
Recorded for East Suffolk, without locality.

Taraxacum pannucium Dahlst.   P. D. Sell 1967

Native. In meadows.
W: 77, Icklingham.

Taraxacum tenebricans (Dahlst.) Dahlst.

W: 88, Santon Downham (P. D. Sell).

Taraxacum porrectidens Dahlst.

Endemic in the British Isles. Waste places and roadsides.
Recorded for West Suffolk without details.

Taraxacum xanthostigma H. Lindb. f.   P. D. Sell 1968

Possibly introduced. Roadsides and grassy places.
W: 77, Icklingham.

Taraxacum dilatatum H. Lindb. f.   P. D. Sell 1967

Native. Roadsides and grassy places. Recorded only from East Suffolk.

Taraxacum adsimile Dahlst.   P. D. Sell 1967

Endemic in Suffolk. Waste places, gardens and paths.
W: 77, Icklingham.

Taraxacum longisquameum H. Lindb. f.

W: 77, Icklingham Plains (P. D. Sell).

Taraxacum dahlstedtii H. Lindb. f.   P. D. Sell 1968

Native. Grassy places and roadsides.
W: 77, Icklingham.

Taraxacum duplidens H. Lindb. f.   P. D. Sell 1967

Probably native. Waste places, gardens, walls and paths.
E: 47, between Walberswick and Dunwich.

Taraxacum hamatiforme Dahlst.   P. D. Sell 1967

Native. Grassy places, roadsides and hedge-banks.
W: 77, Lt. Eriswell.

345

Taraxacum marklundii Palmgr.   P. D. Sell 1967

Native. Grassy places, especially roadsides, and poor pastures.
W: 77, Icklingham.

Taraxacum duplidentifrons Dahlst.   P. D. Sell 1967

Native. In grassy places and on well-drained, base-rich soils.
W: 77, by the R. Lark.

Taraxacum reflexilobum H. Lindb. f.   F. G. Bell 1967

Native. Grassy places and roadsides.
W: 78, Lakenheath.
E: Recorded for East Suffolk, but without locality.

Taraxacum canoviride H. Lindb. f. ex Puolanne   P. D. Sell 1967

Native. Wet pastures.
W: 77, Icklingham.

Lapsana communis L.   Nipplewort   Sir J. Cullum 1773

Native or colonist. Clearings in woods and plantations, hedges and roadsides, and on
cultivated and waste ground. Common.
All squares.

Crepis biennis L.   Rough Hawksbeard   Sir J. Cullum 1773

Probably originally native, but also a colonist. Old pastures and waysides. Native in its old
stations on the Chalk around Bury St Edmunds. Very rare and possibly now extinct in
former sites.
W: 76; 77; 78; 86; 87.
76, Barrow Bottom; 77, Eriswell; 78, Wangford; Lakenheath, 1969; 87, Ampton.
E: 04; 24; 25; 38. All doubtful records.

Crepis pulchra L.   R. Burn c. 1938

A casual, found by the railway at Hadleigh. Native of S. Europe.

Crepis foetida L.   Stinking Hawksbeard   Sir T. G. Cullum & Rev. G. Crabbe 1804

Probably native, occurring on chalky banks and rough grassland. Now extinct in Suffolk,
but Hind's Flora contains records from the 19th century from Gt Saxham, Brandon,
Claydon and Coddenham.
Last record c. 1880.

Crepis nicaeensis Balb.   French Hawksbeard   Mrs R. Clark 1965

A casual. Native of the Mediterranean region. Recorded from sq. 87, S.E. of West
Calthorpe Heath.

Crepis capillaris (L.) Wallr.   Smooth Hawksbeard   Sir J. Cullum 1773
(*C. virens* L.)

Native. Waysides, commons and sea coast. A weed of poor arable land. Very frequent. All squares.

Crepis vesicaria L. ssp. **haenseleri** (Boiss. ex DC.) P. D. Sell   Beaked Hawksbeard
(*C. taraxacifolia* Thuill.)   Rev. E. N. Bloomfield 1860

A colonist, introduced from W. and S. Europe. On disturbed banks, especially gravel and chalk, and in quarries. Very frequent. There has been a marked increase in recent years. All squares except 68; 27.

Crepis setosa Haller f.   Bristly Hawksbeard   Dr Babington and W. Jordan 1879

A casual, sometimes naturalised, in fields, gardens and waste places. Native in S. Europe. Hind's Herbarium contains two specimens:
(a) Cockfield, garden specimen, collected by Dr Babington and W. Jordan.
(b) Rougham, J. Rasor, 1884. Detd. C. E. Salmon.
E: 13, Tattingstone By-pass, 1978 (M. A. Hyde and Mrs E. M. Hyde). Conf. E. J. Clement.

HIERACIUM   HAWKWEEDS

A very large number of British species have been described in this difficult genus. The majority are to be found in small colonies on ancient rocks in hilly or mountainous regions. Only a few species are known to occur in Eastern England.
The occurrence and distribution of some species in the County are at present uncertain and have therefore had to be omitted from this Flora.

Hieracium pilosella L.   Mouse-ear Hawkweed   Sir J. Cullum 1773
(*Pilosella officinarum* F. W. Schultz & Schultz Bip.)

Native. On dry heaths, sunny banks, fixed dunes and shingle beaches. Frequent, especially on chalky soils.
All squares except 85; 27.
This is a variable plant and a number of subspecies occur.

Hieracium aurantiacum L.   Fox and Cubs   W. J. Cross 1883
                          Orange Hawkweed

A garden escape, which may be found in dry, grassy, places and on waysides. Sometimes naturalised.
There are two subspecies, and intermediates. These are ssp. **aurantiacum** and ssp. **carpathicola** Naegeli & Peter (*H. brunneocroceum* Pugsl.) It is not known to which subspecies the records refer.
W: 83; 84; 88.
E: 03, East Bergholt, 1958 (F. J. Bingley); 13, Woolverstone; 14, Grove Lane, Ipswich, 1971; 16; 49, Beccles, 1974; 58; 59.

Hieracium exotericum Jord. ex Bor.   P. D. Sell 1978

E: 48, near Beccles, margin of railway track, with *H. zygophorum*.

Hieracium zygophorum Hyl. J. O. Mountford 1977

E: 48; near Beccles. Colonies on calcareous railway bank and on the margin of the track, growing in loose cinders.
New to the British Isles. Detd. by P. D. Sell and C. West (Watsonia 13, 27-29, 1980).

Hieracium murorum L. Wall Hawkweed Sir J. Cullum 1773

This name is not referable to any definite species as now understood. Recorded in Hind's Flora from sites about Bury St Edmunds and lanes near Framlingham. The Bury record may refer to *H. pellucidum.*

Hieracium pellucidum Laest. Hind's Flora 1889

A specimen in Hind's Herbarium from near Bury St Edmunds was determined by C. E. Salmon as var. *lucidulum* Ley. Hind named it as *H. murorum.*

Hieracium vulgatum Fr. Common Hawkweed E. Skepper 1862

Five doubtful records in Hind's Flora. This Hawkweed possibly occurs as a casual in woods, on banks and walls. Hind's Herbarium specimen from Sapiston Grove was named by C. E. Salmon as *H. sciaphilum* (Uechtr.) F. J. Hanb.

Hieracium maculatum Sm. Spotted Hawkweed Rev. J. S. Henslow 1840

Introduced. Walls and gardens. The status of this plant in Britain is usually described as an established alien.
The first record for the County was by Rev. J. S. Henslow at Hitcham. Hind's Flora records it as collected by Dr White at Sudbury, ?1862 (Hb. Skepper).
In 1935 R. Burn and I found a colony on an old wall at Ballingdon, Sudbury (sq. 84). The wall was being repaired, so some plants in danger of being destroyed were removed and transferred to my Ipswich garden. They survived and seeded and still exist in 1981. A. E. V. Betteridge recorded it at Sudbury and Ballingdon in 1972. I have also observed it growing in a wild part of the gardens of Shrubland Park (sq. 15) between 1956 and 1959, where it was no doubt introduced.

Hieracium acuminatum Jord. Hind's Flora 1889
(*H. strumosum* (W. R. Linton) A. Ley
H. lachenalii auct.)

Native. Woodland, railway and roadside banks. Rare or overlooked.
W: 97, Sapiston Grove (Hind).
E: 59, Oulton Broad, 1977 (P. G. Lawson). Detd. E. L. Swann.

Hieracium perpropinquum (Zahn) Druce Broad-leaved Hawkweed
(*H. boreale* auct.) Wood Hawkweed Sir J. Cullum 1777

This species is included in the *H. sabaudum* group.
Native. In dry, open and shady woodland, banks, heathy places and railway embankments. Locally frequent.
W: 77, Eriswell; 93, Polstead Dollops; Wiston Woods; 94, Edwardstone; Newton; 95, Monks' Park Wood; 96, Pakenham Wood; Hessett.

E: 03, East Bergholt, 1981; Bentley; Shelley; Raydon; 13, Wherstead; Bentley; Holbrook; Tattingstone; 14, Foxhall; Belstead; 25, Melton; 35, Rendlesham; 37, Heveningham; Huntingfield.

Hieracium umbellatum L.   Narrow-leaved Hawkweed   Sir J. Cullum 1773

Native. On the margins of heathy woods, hedge-banks, roadside verges and railway embankments. Locally frequent.
W: 77; 87; 93; 95.
95, Monks' Park Wood, c. 1973.
E: 07; 13; 14; 28; 37; 45; 46; 47; 48; 49; 58; 59; 40; 50.
14, Ipswich, railway embankment, 1981; 45, Chillesford, 1976; 46, Westleton, 1980; 59, Corton, 1973; Lowestoft Denes, 1980.

Cosmos bipinnatus Cav.   Cosmos   F. W. Simpson 1950

A casual, native of Mexico. Recorded from sq. 33 in 1950 and naturalised on a wayside near Leiston (sq. 46) in 1956. Also on the Stowmarket By-pass in 1977 (sq. 05).

Callistephus chinensis (L.) Nees   China Aster   M. A. Hyde 1974

Introduction. Native of China. Common annual of gardens, sometimes found on rubbish tips and waste places.
E: 23, Chelmondiston Tip, 1974.

Dahlia spp.   Mrs E. M. Hyde 1974

Introduced. Native of Mexico. Grown in gardens. Although tender, the tubers will survive some winters.
E: 14, Ipswich outskirts, near Akenham; 23, Chelmondiston Tip; 33, Felixstowe Ferry, 1977.

Hemizonia pungens Torr. & Gray   Spike-weed   F. W. Simpson 1935

A casual. Native of N. America. Found at Felixstowe Docks (sq. 23) in 1935. Detd. at Kew.

Hemizonia kelloggii Greene   F. W. Simpson 1952

A casual. Native of N. America. Known in Suffolk from waste ground at Felixstowe Docks (sq. 23) in 1952. Detd. at Kew.

MONOCOTYLEDONES

ALISMATACEAE

WATER PLANTAIN FAMILY

Baldellia ranunculoides (L.) Parl.   Lesser Water Plantain   Sir J. Cullum 1773
(*Alisma ranunculoides* L.)

Native. Edges of shallow ponds, fens and ditches. Very scarce and decreasing.
W: 67, West Row; 78, Lakenheath; 96, Pakenham.

E: 07, Redgrave Fen; 27, Wingfield; 38, Bungay; 46, East Bridge, 1981; 49, Beccles; Carlton Colville; 58, Kessingland; 59, Oulton; Pakefield; 50, Hopton (Lound Waterworks).
Most of these records date from the 1950's.
There is a specimen in Hb. Atkins from the Gipping Valley in 1909.

Alisma plantago-aquatica L.   Common Water Plantain   Sir J. Cullum 1773
Native. In ponds, ditches, and beside rivers, sometimes growing in deep water. Common. All squares.

Alisma lanceolatum With.   Narrow-leaved Water Plaintain   Hind's Flora 1889
Native. In ponds, ditches and beside rivers. Distribution imperfectly known, but it appears to be now rare or extinct in former habitats. Included in Hind's Flora under *A. plantago-aquatica,* with which there is possibly some confusion in the records below.
W: 67; 78; 86; 94; 95.
E: 03; 04; 49.
Hind gives Honington, Ixworth Thorpe, Sapiston, Thelnetham, Cavenham, Santon Downham, Mildenhall, Hawstead, Nayland, Acton, Beccles, Bungay, Belton and Oulton.

Damasonium alisma Mill.   Starfruit   Rev. G. Crabbe 1798
(*Actinocarpus damasonium* R. Br.)   Thrumwort
Native. In ditches and ponds, usually on mud. Very rare and may now be extinct in Suffolk. The plant is similar in appearance to a very small Water Plantain. The last known record is from Sizewell (sq. 46) by F. W. Simpson in 1957/8. The only record of the plant in Hind's Flora is from Framlingham, where it was believed by Hind to be extinct.

Sagittaria sagittifolia L.   Arrowhead   Sir J. Cullum 1773
Native. In larger rivers and dykes. Frequent.
W: All squares except 65; 66; 67; 75; 76; 95.
68, Mildenhall, 1980; 97, Lt. Fakenham, 1980.
E: All squares except 06; 07; 13; 16; 24; 33; 37; 45; 46; 50.
14, in the R. Gipping between Ipswich and Bramford, 1981; 35, Wickham Market, 1973; 39, Mettingham, 1980.   *Illustrated page 482*

BUTOMACEAE
FLOWERING RUSH FAMILY

Butomus umbellatus L.   Flowering Rush   Sir J. Cullum 1773
Native. Sides of rivers, streams and ditches. Formerly frequent, now local or rare. This very beautiful waterside plant has become rare since the end of the Second World War, mainly due to the activities of the River Authorities in cutting back the vegetation. In the 1930's it was still very frequent along the banks of the R. Gipping between Ipswich and Gt Blakenham. Very little now survives. A fine colony grew for many years beside the weir near the Seven Arches Bridge, London Road, Ipswich. This was destroyed in the late 1960's, when the weir was reconstructed. The species survives in small quantities beside the R. Stour, R. Brett and R. Deben, in a few sites. It has disappeared from many parishes recorded in Hind's Flora.

W: 77; 78; 93; 96; 97.
78, Lakenheath, 1976 (M. G. Rutterford); 93, Nayland, 1981.
E: All squares except 06; 07; 13; 16; 17; 23; 24; 33; 34; 44; 45; 47; 58; 40; 50.
03, Layham, 1980; 04, Hadleigh, R. Brett, 1979; 14, by the R. Gipping at Ipswich, 1980;
15, Barham Pits, 1981 (N. Hunt); 26, by the R. Deben, Brandeston, 1975 (Miss M. Craig);
39, Shipmeadow; 49, Beccles, 1975. *Illustrated page 485*

HYDROCHARITACEAE
FROG-BIT FAMILY

Hydrocharis morsus-ranae L.   Frog-bit   Sir J. Cullum 1773
Native. In ponds and ditches. Mainly restricted to the East of the County in coastal areas,
where it is often abundant, especially in Lothingland.
W: Not recorded recently. Hind lists a number of parishes chiefly in the North-west.
E: 03; 07; 28; 35; 37; 38; 39; 45; 46; 47; 48; 49; 58; 59; 40; 50.
46, East Bridge, 1980; 49, North Cove, 1975; 40, Belton, 1977.
Hb. Ipswich Museum: 'in the Delphs & Bogs between Handford Bridge and the Bramford
Road', c. 1820 (John Notcutt).

Stratiotes aloides L.   Water Soldier   Rev. G. Crabbe 1798
Native. In dykes and ponds. Rare or local. Chiefly confined to the Lothingland area,
where it can sometimes be abundant and dominant.
W: 84, Long Melford.
E: 14, pond near Westerfield Road, Ipswich (site destroyed); 39; 49, Herringfleet; Barnby;
North Cove; 59, Blundeston; Flixton; Carlton Colville, 1980; 50.

Elodea canadensis Michx   Canadian Pondweed   Prof. Henslow 1855
(*Anacharis canadensis* Planch.)   Canadian Waterweed
A naturalised alien, introduced from N. America. Found in ponds, rivers, streams and
ditches. At one time very abundant. It is now decreasing in all areas and may become rare.
W: All squares except 64; 65; 66; 75; 76; 85; 86; 87; 93.
97, Ixworth.
E: All squares except 06; 13; 16; 23; 27; 34; 44.
14, R. Gipping at Sproughton, 1974, and Ipswich, 1980; 24, Purdis Heath, 1981; 39,
Bungay, 1981; 45, Thorpeness Mere, 1973; 49, Mettingham, 1980.

Elodea nuttallii (Planch.) St John   A. C. Jermy 1980
Introduced. In ponds and ditches. An American species grown in aquaria and becoming
naturalised.
E: 50, Lound, detd. Dr E. A. Ellis. Comm. D. Simpson.

JUNCAGINACEAE
ARROW-GRASS FAMILY

Triglochin palustris L.   Marsh Arrow-grass   J. Andrews 1746
Native: Wet pastures, marshes, beside ditches, even in slightly brackish habitats.

Occasional. Probably no longer in all the squares listed below.
W: 68; 77; 78; 86; 87; 96.
87, West Stow.
E: 07; 13; 14; 23; 24; 33; 34; 35; 36; 39; 44; 45; 46; 47; 48; 49; 59; 40.
23, Levington, 1980; Woolverstone, 1981; 24, marshes between Woodbridge and Melton, near the R. Deben, 1974; 39, Mettingham, 1976.

Triglochin maritima L. Sea Arrow-grass Sir J. Cullum 1773
Native. Salt marshes, estuaries and brackish ditches. Very frequent.
E: 03; 13; 14; 23; 24; 25; 33; 34; 35; 44; 45; 46; 47; 48; 49; 58; 59; 40; 50.
Frequent in estuaries between the Stour and the Blyth, 1981.
Hb. Ipswich Museum: 'By the sides of Delphs between St Peter's Dockyard & Nova Scotia', c. 1815 (John Notcutt).

ZOSTERACEAE

EEL-GRASS FAMILY

Zostera marina L. Common Eel-grass Mrs Casborne 1819
Broad-leaved Grass-wrack

Native. An aquatic herb usually growing in the sea between high and low tide marks. Occasionally in estuaries. Now scarce and has completely disappeared from much of the Suffolk coast, possibly due to disease. It was recorded from Breydon Water by the Lowestoft Field Club in 1947, where it was then said to be increasing. Also Dunwich, 1948-1952 (F.W.S.).
Hind recorded it for Gorleston, Kessingland, Lowestoft, Dunwich, Stutton, Felixstowe, Walton and Aldeburgh. W. A. Dutt recorded it for Lake Lothing in 1898.

Zostera angustifolia (Hornem.) Rchb. Narrow-leaved Eel-grass Mrs Casborne 1819
(*Z. hornemanniana* Tutin)

Native. Found on muddy seashores and estuaries below the high water mark.
E: 13, Holbrook; Cattawade; Harkstead, 1981; Woolverstone, 1977, detd. T. G. Tutin; 23, Trimley; Nacton; Chelmondiston, 1980; Erwarton, 1977; Shotley; 24, Martlesham Creek; 34, Bromeswell; Sutton; Shingle Street; 44, Orford; 45, Sudbourne; 46, Dunwich; 47, Walberswick; Southwold, 1974.

Zostera noltii Hornem. Dwarf Eel-grass B.S.B.I. Record c. 1955
(*Z. nana* Roth pro parte)

Native. On mud banks, in coastal creeks and estuaries, between high and low water marks.

E: 13, Stour Estuary, Holbrook and Harkstead, 1973 (F. W. Simpson); Woolverstone, 1974; 14, Wherstead, 1974; 23, Shotley; Chelmondiston; Trimley; Nacton, 1974. (All 1974 records by D. W. Wyer.)

POTAMOGETONACEAE

POTAMOGETONACEAE

PONDWEED FAMILY

POTAMOGETON   PONDWEEDS

Several species have not been seen in the County for a number of years. Many habitats have disappeared, the ponds and ditches having been filled in. Conditions in water habitats vary considerably from season to season and in some years a species may become abundant in a site where it had not previously been noticed. It may then completely disappear, not to be seen again.
The author acknowledges help from Sir George Taylor and the late J. E. Dandy.

Potamogeton natans L.   Broad-leaved Pondweed   J. Andrews 1728
Native. In ponds, rivers and dykes. Frequent. This is the most frequent species of *Potamogeton* occurring in the County.
W: All squares except 64; 66; 77.
68, Mildenhall, 1980; 88, Santon Downham, 1980; 97, Hopton Fen, 1981.
E: All squares except 23; 28; 33; 34; 44; 45.
24, Brightwell, 1981; 35, Blaxhall, in static water tank in forest, 1980; 39, Mettingham, 1980.

Potamogeton polygonifolius Pourr.   Bog Pondweed   Hind 1879
(*P. oblongus* Viv.)
Native. In pools, streams and bogs. Very local or overlooked.
W: 77, Cavenham Heath, 1938 (T. G. Tutin).
E: 47, Blythburgh Reserve and Walberswick, 1973; 50.

Potamogeton coloratus Hornem.   Fen Pondweed   E. Skepper 1860
(*P. plantagineus* Du Croz ex Roem. & Schult.)
Native. In fen pools and ditches. Very local. A rare form with cuspidate leaves has been recorded from Tuddenham Fen.
W: 77, Tuddenham Fen; 97, Hopton Fen, 1981 (F. W. Simpson), detd. R. C. L. Howitt.
E: 07, Redgrave, 1979; Hinderclay and Thelnetham Fens, c. 1960.

Potamogeton lucens L.   Shining Pondweed   J. Andrews 1748
Native. In rivers and dykes. Not very common. Usually found in deep water.
W: 67; 77; 78; 84; 86; 87; 88; 93; 96; 97; 98.
67, Worlington, in the R. Lark, 1977; 78, Brandon, 1978; 88, Santon Downham, 1977.
E: 03; 05; 07; 14; 23; 39; 48; 49; 59.
14, Ipswich, in the R. Gipping, 1976; 39, Bungay, 1980; 49, Beccles in the R. Waveney, 1974.

Potamogeton lucens × natans   F. W. Simpson 1931
(*P. × fluitans* Roth)
A rare hybrid, probably now extinct. Formerly found in the R. Brett between Whatfield and Semer (sq. 04). Detd. by W. H. Pearsall.

Potamogeton gramineus L.   Various-leaved Pondweed   J. Andrews 1739
(*P. heterophyllus* Schreb.)

Native. In ponds and ditches. Rare or overlooked. A variable species, depending on habitat and depth of water.
W: Not recorded recently, but listed in Hind for Mildenhall and Lakenheath.
E: 33, Felixstowe Ferry; 35, Snape; Chillesford; 46, Leiston; Sizewell; 57, Easton Bavents. Most of these records date from the 1960's.

Potamogeton gramineus × lucens   Zizi's Pondweed   Hind 1886
(*P. × zizii* Koch ex Roth)

In ditches and ponds. Recorded in Hind's Flora from Mildenhall, Barsham, Beccles, Worlingham, Carlton Colville. Some of his records are thought to be incorrect. No recent records.

Potamogeton gramineus × perfoliatus   G. Fitt 1843
(*P. × nitens* Weber)

Known in Suffolk only from the Bungay area in 1843.

Potamogeton alpinus Balb.   Reddish Pondweed   Dawson Turner 1804
(*P. rufescens* Schrad.)

Native. In ponds and rivers. Rare.
E: 25, Wickham Market; 35, Blaxhall, 1970 (Miss D. A. Cadbury); 47, Blythburgh; Wangford, 1951 (G. H. Rocke).
Recorded in Hind for Bardwell, Ixworth Thorpe, Sapiston, Santon Downham, Beccles and the Waveney, near Scole.

Potamogeton praelongus Wulf.   Long-stalked Pondweed   C. C. Babington 1840

Native. In lakes and rivers. Very rare or extinct. Not seen recently.
W: 86, Ickworth Park.
E: 49, Beccles, 1931. (Last record).
Hind records it for several places in the Waveney Valley.

Potamogeton perfoliatus L.   Perfoliate Pondweed   Sir J. Cullum 1773

Native. In rivers, streams and ditches. Not seen recently, though possibly overlooked. It probably occurs in the Waveney and Little Ouse.
W: 78; 88; 98.
78, Brandon; 88, Euston.
E: 59; 40.
Hind records it from a number of localities, where it now appears to be absent.

Potamogeton friesii Rupr.   Flat-stalked Pondweed   Dr G. C. Druce 1883
(*P. mucronatus* Schrad. ex Sond.)

Native. In rivers, ditches and lakes. Rare or overlooked. Occurs in some of the dykes in the marshes of Lothingland.
W: 78, New Fen, Brandon.
E: 49, Worlingham, 1956; 59, Oulton, 1977; Carlton Colville, 1979.

Potamogeton pusillus L.   Lesser Pondweed   Rev. G. Crabbe 1798

Native. In ditches. Rare. Dandy considers that most of the records in Hind's Flora of this species were, in fact, *P. berchtoldii*.
W: 78, The Delph, Lakenheath, 1971; 95, Bradfield St Clare.
E: 03; 15, Barham, 1970 (Miss D. A. Cadbury); 34, Butley; 45, Aldeburgh Marshes; 46, Westleton; Thorpeness Mere, 1970 (Miss D. A. Cadbury); 47, Blythburgh; 49, Beccles; Worlingham; 58, Benacre Broad, 1917 (A. R. Horwood).

Potamogeton obtusifolius Mert. & Koch   Blunt-leaved Pondweed   J. Andrews 1745
Grassy Pondweed

Native. In streams, ditches and ponds. Rare or overlooked.
E: 46, Sizewell, c. 1960 (F. W. Simpson); 47, Walberswick, 1938 (J. Walton); 48, Stoven Common, 1920 (A. W. Graveson); 49, Somerleyton.

Potamogeton berchtoldii Fieb.   Small Pondweed   Hind 1881
(*P. pusillus* auct. mult., non L.)

Native. In rivers and ditches. Rare, or confused with *P. pusillus*. Distribution uncertain.
W: 78, The Delph, Lakenheath, 1971; 94, Semer.
E: 03, R. Stour at Flatford Mill, 1952 (Sir George Taylor); 25, Melton; 35, R. Deben at Eyke, 1970 (Miss D. A. Cadbury); Butley, 1974 (F. W. Simpson).

Potamogeton trichoides Cham. & Schlecht.   Hair-like Pondweed   E. Skepper 1864

Native. In rivers, ponds and ditches. Rare. Recorded in the R. Gipping at Barham (sq. 15) in 1970 (Miss D. A. Cadbury).
Recorded by Hind from Tuddenham, Barton Mere, and Wortham Long Green.

Potamogeton compressus L.   Grass-wrack Pondweed
(*P. zosterifolius* Schumach.)   Canon G. R. Bullock-Webster 1897

Native. In ponds and ditches. Rare or overlooked. The only recent record is from Mildenhall (sq. 77) in c. 1950. The first record was also made in Mildenhall.

Potamogeton acutifolius Link   Sharp-leaved Pondweed   E. R. Long c. 1910
(*P. cuspidatus* Schrad.)

Native. In dykes. Recorded from Oulton (sq. 59). No specimen seen.

Potamogeton crispus L.   Curled Pondweed   Sir J. Cullum 1773

Native. In ponds, ditches and rivers. Sometimes abundant, although far less frequent than formerly, due to loss of habitats.
W: All squares except 64; 66; 68; 85; 87; 88; 96; 97.
67, Freckenham, 1977; 78, Lakenheath.
E: All squares except 04; 15; 25; 27; 33; 36; 45.
23, Harkstead, 1981; 24, Purdis Heath, 1981; Brightwell, 1981; 39, Bungay, 1981.

Potamogeton pectinatus L.   Fennel-leaved Pondweed   Sir J. Cullum 1773
(*P. interruptus* Kit.)

Native. In pools and dykes, and brackish ditches. Often abundant. Mainly confined to the coastal and estuarine areas of East Suffolk. Less frequent inland. Some of the records may be errors for other species.

W: 77; 86; 87; 93; 97.
77, R. Lark, Icklingham in the 1960's.
E: 03; 13; 23; 25; 33; 34; 35; 44; 45; 46; 47; 49; 57; 58; 40; 50.
13, Holbrook, 1981; 23, Shotley, 1978; Trimley St Mary, 1977; 49, Beccles and North Cove, 1974; 57, Southwold, 1971.

Groenlandia densa (L.) Fourr.   Opposite-leaved Pondweed   J. Andrews 1746
(*Potamogeton densus* L.)

Native. In rivers, streams, ditches and ponds. Probably locally frequent, but the present distribution is not clearly known.
W: 67, Worlington, 1977; 77, Barton Mills; 78, Brandon Waterworks.
E: 03; 05; 07, Redgrave Fen; 37, Halesworth, marsh dyke, 1979; 38, Barsham; 49; 57, Southwold (D. H. Marlow); 40.

RUPPIACEAE

TASSEL-PONDWEED FAMILY

Ruppia spiralis L. ex Dum.   Spiral Tassel-pondweed   Woodward 1805
(*R. maritima* auct., non L.)

Native. In brackish ditches near the sea. Very rare or overlooked.
E: 34, Shingle Street; 35, Snape; 46, Dunwich; 47, Walberswick. All records by F. W. Simpson.
Some confusion exists in Hind's Flora over the two species of *Ruppia*.

Ruppia maritima L.   Beaked Tassel-pondweed   Davy 1796
(*R. rostellata* Koch)
Native. In brackish ditches and pools near the sea. Locally frequent, but decreasing.
E: 13; 24; 33; 44; 45; 46; 47; 58; 50.
44, Havergate Island, 1972; 45, Sudbourne, c. 1960; 58, Benacre, 1974. These are the only fairly recent records.
Specimen in Hb. Davy from 'ditches at Dunwich, 1796'.

ZANNICHELLIACEAE

HORNED PONDWEED FAMILY

Zannichellia palustris L.   Horned Pondweed   J. Andrews 1743
Native. In ponds, rivers, streams, ditches and pools. Formerly frequent, but now decreasing. A variable species.
W: 64; 67; 74; 76; 83; 84; 85; 86; 94; 95; 96.
67, Freckenham and Mildenhall, 1977; 94, Brent Eleigh, 1981.
E: 03; 04; 06; 07; 13; 14; 15; 16; 23; 24; 37; 38; 39; 44; 46; 47; 49.
13, Holbrook, 1981.
Var. **pedicellata** (Fr.) Wahlenb. & Rosen, occurs in brackish habitats, as at Walberswick (sq. 47). Other varieties may well occur.

LILIACEAE

LILY FAMILY

Narthecium ossifragum (L.) Huds.   Bog Asphodel

Native. In old bogs. Although not recorded for Suffolk, I feel sure that it once occurred in the County, in habitats similar to those in which it still occurs in West Norfolk, such as the fens and bogs of the Little Ouse Valley and in Lothingland.

Hemerocallis fulva (L.) L.   Day Lily   F. W. Simpson 1939

Introduced. Native in temperate Asia. Frequently grown in gardens and sometimes found naturalised, or thrown out with garden waste.

E: 13, Holbrook, in wood, 1974; 16, Mickfield in a ditch, probably from garden waste, 1956; 23, Harkstead, 1976; 24, Foxhall, by a pond in 1939, and still there in 1977.

Ipheion uniflorum (R. C. Graham) Rafin.   Spring Star-flower   P. G. Lawson 1980

Introduced. Native of N. America.

E: 57, Southwold, on cliffs in town. Garden outcast.

Convallaria majalis L.   Lily-of-the-Valley   Sir J. Cullum 1773
Woolpit Lily (Suffolk)

Native. Usually in old, dry woods. More frequent on gravelly soils with a layer of leaf mould. Local or rare. Not so abundant in some habitats as formerly, due to the felling of deciduous woods and planting of conifers. Perhaps introduced in some habitats or bird-sown.

W: 77, Mildenhall, 1975; 95, Free Wood, Bradfield St George; 96, Woolpit.

E: 03/13; Bentley; Capel St Mary, 1981; 04, Aldham, 1980; 05, Ringshall; 06, Shelland; 24, Foxhall, 1980; 38, Ilketshall St Lawrence; 46, Leiston, 1980; 59, Oulton.

Some of these records, including Mildenhall, Aldham and Foxhall, refer to the larger garden variety.   *Illustrated page 447*

Polygonatum multiflorum (L.) All.   Common Solomon's Seal   Wigg 1800

Native. Occasionally found in woods and copses. Sometimes introduced or bird-sown.

W: 93, Assington Thicks.

E: 23, Levington; Chelmondiston; 34, Red Crag pit, Ramsholt, 1930-1970; 40, Burgh Castle.

Maianthemum bifolium (L.) Schmidt   May Lily   G. H. Burdon 1973

Introduced? Probably native in a few woods in Britain.

E: 46, Dunwich, a small colony in a mixed wood near Dunwich Common, mainly growing round the base of a sawn-down tree. The wood is not ancient, but of Victorian age, with introduced trees, such as Sycamore, conifers and Holm Oak. This colony may perhaps be a relic of a former semi-wild garden. A number of other naturalised 'garden' plants have been found in this area. Still there, 1978.

Asparagus officinalis L. ssp. **officinalis**   Wild Asparagus   Sir J. Cullum 1773

Introduced. Much cultivated and found in waste places, on waysides and on the sea coast; the seed is probably bird-sown. Frequent. The native ssp. **prostratus** (Dum.) E. F. Warburg, of sea cliffs and dunes, has not been observed in Suffolk.
W: 66; 67; 68; 77; 78; 86; 87; 96; 97.
66, Moulton, 1978; 78, Lakenheath, 1980; 87, West Stow, 1980.
E: 04; 13; 14; 23; 24; 25; 33; 34; 35; 37; 45; 47; 57; 58; 59.
14, Ipswich, near Bourne Bridge, 1981; 33, Bawdsey Ferry, 1979; 34, Shingle Street, 1981; 59, Lowestoft Denes, 1980.

Ruscus aculeatus L.   Butcher's Broom   Sir J. Cullum 1773
                              Knee Holly

Native. In woods, copses and old hedges and on cliffs and verges of estuaries. Introduced into shrubberies and hedges surrounding gardens. Frequent in the South-east of the County, usually found growing on stony soils, as at Stutton Ness and Bentley. Some of the colonies must be very old and have not extended during the past 50 years (1930-80). No seedling or any colony of recent origin has been observed during this period. It is considered that several colonies have survived for more than a thousand years. Butcher's Broom is known locally as the 'Prehistoric Plant'. The old hedges in which it is sometimes found are obviously relics of former woodland or the extensive forest which once covered much of the County.
W: 67; 77; 86; 87; 93; 94; 96.
67, Worlington, 1980 (probably introduced); 93/94, Polstead; 96, Gt Barton, 1980 (probably introduced).
E: 03; 04; 07; 13; 14; 16; 23; 24; 25; 33; 34; 35; 36; 37; 38; 45; 46; 47; 48; 49; 59.
07, Thelnetham Churchyard, 1975; 13, Bentley; Brantham; Freston; Holbrook; Stutton; Woolverstone; Tattingstone; all 1981; 14, Alnesbourn Priory, near R. Orwell, 1979; 23, Chelmondiston and Harkstead, 1981; 24, Purdis Farm, 1979; Foxhall and Rushmere, (introduced); Nacton and Levington, 1981; 35, Butley, 1980; Chillesford; Wantisden; 48, South Cove (probably native), 1972.   *Illustrated page 449*

Lilium martagon L.   Martagon Lily   Rev. F. W. Galpin 1884
                              Turk's Cap Lily

Introduced. Native in continental Europe. Sometimes found naturalised in woods in Britain.
The only record is from a small plantation at Flixton.

Fritillaria meleagris L.   Fritillary   Crowe 1776
                                  Snake's Head
                                  Chequered Lily

Native. Found in old damp pastures, meadows and the marshes of river valleys. Introduced into orchards and parks. Formerly frequent in several areas, now very local, due to the reclamation of sites. This is one of our most attractive wild flowers.
W: 75, Stradishall; Wickhambrook; 85, Whepstead, in the Rectory grounds; 96, Tostock. The Whepstead plants have smaller, darker flowers than those in East Suffolk.
E: 05, Stowmarket; 07, Walsham-le-Willows; 14, Bramford; Westerfield; 15, Ashbocking; Henley Rectory, 1974 (bulbs originally from Framsden); 16, Mickfield;

Debenham; Framsden; Wetheringsett; 17, Stuston; 24, Martlesham; 25, Monewden; Charsfield; 28, St Cross South Elmham.
Several of these sites have been lost since 1950.   *Illustrated page 478 and page 479*

Fritillaria imperialis L.   Crown Imperial   F. W. Simpson 1966
A native of the Orient. Commonly cultivated in gardens, and sometimes seen in old shrubberies and plantations, where it has obviously been introduced. Recorded at Hemingstone (sq. 15) in 1966.

Tulipa sylvestris L.   Wild Tulip   Sir T. G. Cullum 1800
Introduced. Native of S. Europe. In copses, paddocks, old gardens and pastures. Rare. The colonies usually produce many leaves, but few flowers. The leaves are narrow, linear or lanceolate, and of a particular glaucous-green shade and may be mistaken for those of the various Garden Tulips, which occur frequently as throw-outs.
W: 86, Bury St Edmunds, at Southgate on the site of Petronella's Hospital for Leprous Maidens; Gt Barton, former garden and parkland, 1979.
E: 04, Nettlestead; 14, Sproughton (site destroyed by development); 17, Stuston (site ploughed-up in 1957); Hoxne; Eye; 35, paddock at 'Chestnuts', Hacheston, 1980; 37, Heveningham, 1981.
A few bulbs from the Sproughton site were transferred in 1954 into the garden of Park House, Saxmundham, where they have survived and increased (Misses B. and R. Copinger Hill). Two small colonies were discovered in old Chantry garden, Saxmundham, 1980.
The Wild Tulip may have been introduced into Britain by the Romans. A former site at Hacheston was beside an old Roman road and there are reports that it occurred on Romano-British sites at Ashbocking and Helmingham (last observed c. 1960).
Illustrated page 479

Tulipa gesnerana L.   Garden Tulip

Introduced. A relic of cultivation. Tulip bulbs of various species are fairly frequently thrown out from gardens into ditches, waste places and on tips, but do not usually survive for many years.

Gagea lutea (L.) Ker—Gawl.   Yellow Star-of-Bethlehem   Dawson Turner 1805
Native. In old woods, copses and pastures. Very rare. This is a decreasing species, which only flowers with any regularity at its Gt Glemham site and in the old Chantry garden at Saxmundham. There may be other sites in the County, but as the plant does not often flower, it may be overlooked. A small colony I have been observing at Playford since 1930 has produced flowers in only two seasons, the last flowering being in 1937.
Gagea lutea was well-known around Ipswich to botanists in the early 19th century and a number of specimens in the herbarium at Ipswich Museum are from Waller's Grove, including one collected in 1817 by John Notcutt. This once important botanical habitat adjoins Gippeswyk Park and the Chantry housing estate. It is now managed as part of the Park and, although the area still contains many of the original oak trees, the ground flora has disappeared, due to constant cutting of the under-cover and suppression by trampling. Its flora, known to Georgian and Victorian botanists, also included Wood Anemone, Goldilocks, Wood Sanicle, Pendulous Sedge, Moschatel and Earthnut.
A further herbarium specimen came from a 'wood by the canal, at Bramford', (C.

Gower), c. 1859, which was probably Hazel Wood. The 'canal' being the R. Gipping, which was, in those days, used extensively by canal traffic.
Also in Hb. Atkins at Ipswich Museum: Shipmeadow, 1907. First recorded at this site in 1834, in Low Road, near the Church.
Hind also recorded the species from Sproughton Wood by the R. Gipping, now the site of the Sugar-beet Factory, from a pasture near Woodbridge and from Nayland.

Illustrated page 451

Ornithogalum umbellatum L.   Common Star-of-Bethlehem   Sir J. Cullum 1772

Probably native on the margins of sandy fields in Breckland. Elsewhere a naturalised plant of waysides and old pastures, of garden origin.
W: All squares except 64; 65; 68; 75; 98.
77, Cavenham, growing with *Muscari atlanticum,* 1981; Icklingham, 1981; 78, Lakenheath, 1980; Brandon, 1977; 87, Culford, 1980.
E: All squares except 03; 06; 26; 27; 38; 44; 58.
15, Barham, 1979; 24, Gt Bealings and Playford, 1981; 33, Felixstowe, the Grove, 1981.

Illustrated page 470

Ornithogalum nutans L.   Drooping Star-of-Bethlehem   Sir J. Cullum 1776
                              Nodding Star-of-Bethlehem

Introduced. Native in Mediterranean Europe. Naturalised in old orchards and shrubberies, on waysides and sites of former gardens. Mainly confined to East Suffolk, where it is quite frequent in many parishes.
W: 76, Barrow.
E: 14, Gt Blakenham, 1976; Bramford, 1980; 15, Coddenham; Hemingstone, 1980; 24, Woodbridge; Gt Bealings Churchyard, 1981; 25, Melton, 1981; Easton; 27; 35, Tunstall; Campsey Ash; 36, Gt Glemham, Swefling and Saxmundham, all 1981; 37, Bramfield; Wenhaston; 38, Barsham; 39; 47, Dunwich; 49, Beccles; 57, Easton Bavents; 58, Gisleham; 59, Sparrow's Nest, Lowestoft; 40, Burgh Castle.
Specimen in Hb. Atkins from Woolpit, 1910.

Scilla siberica Andr.   Siberian Squill   M. A. Hyde 1976

Native of Siberia. Grown in gardens and sometimes seen as a throw-out on roadside banks and outside gardens.
W: 87, West Stow, 1979.
E: 25, Ufford, 1976.

Chionodoxa luciliae Boiss.   Glory of the Snow   M. A. Hyde 1976

Native in Crete and the mountains of W. Turkey. Grown in gardens.
E: 24, Foxhall, edge of pit, with other garden throw-outs, 1976; Martlesham, in a plantation, 1979 (F. W. Simpson).

Endymion non-scriptus (L.) Garcke   Bluebell   Sir J. Cullum 1773
(Scilla nutans Sm.)   Wild Hyacinth

Native. Old woods, copses and ancient hedges, especially on light soils. Often dominant and very abundant. Rare or absent in most of Breckland and scarce on the heavy clay soils, except on the edges of woods, banks and well drained slopes. Varieties are frequently found, including white, pink and purple flowered forms. Some of the ancient Bluebell woods still existing in the South and South-east of the County are very fine, and should be preserved. Several, however, have already been felled and replanted, mainly with conifers, which do not provide a suitable habitat for the Bluebell. Suffolk Bluebell woods are as fine as any in the British Isles.

All squares except 67; 68; 78; 98; 17; 26; 50.

Var. **bracteata** Druce This is a fairly frequent variety with enlarged and elongated bracts.
W: 05, Stowupland (Miss J. B. Cobbold).

E: 23, Shotley, 1975 (Mrs E. M. Hyde). *Illustrated page 444 and page 446*

Endymion hispanicus × non-scriptus   Garden Bluebell   F. W. Simpson c. 1960

Hybrids are more frequent than is generally supposed, and can be found naturalised among colonies of Common Bluebells, especially near the edges of woods and copses, on banks and in old gardens and shrubberies, where the Spanish Bluebell has become naturalised. Having grown both species in a small garden for a number of years, I have found that the hybrids are very variable indeed, especially in the shape and arrangement of the bells, and the colour of the anthers. The flowers are often white or pink.

Endymion hispanicus (Mill.) Chouard   Spanish Bluebell   F. W. Simpson c. 1924
(*Scilla hispanica* Mill.)

Introduced. Native of S.W. Europe. Frequently grown in gardens and becoming naturalised in shrubberies, on sites of former gardens, in hedges and in waste places, where garden rubbish has been deposited. Often mistaken for more robust forms of the Common Bluebell or the hybrid.
W: 66, Moulton; 75, Wickhambrook; 76, Herringswell; 77, Barton Mills; 86, Gt Barton, 1976; 87, Fakenham Magna; 94, Brent Eleigh.
E: 04, Hintlesham; 14, Ipswich; 23, Erwarton; 24, Rushmere; Kesgrave; Brightwell, 1981; 33, Felixstowe, 1980; 34, Sutton, 1981; 35, Stratford St Andrew; 47, Southwold; Reydon; 58, Kessingland Denes. *Illustrated page 448*

Muscari atlanticum Boiss. & Reut.   Grape Hyacinth   Sir J. Cullum 1776
(*M. racemosum* auct.)

Native. Open plantations, field verges, dry chalky and sandy banks, mainly in Breckland. Locally not uncommon, although not always flowering. Also found as a relic of cultivation and naturalised on banks and verges. This species is now rarely grown in gardens.
The thriving colony on a roadside bank at Swefling is probably on the site where it was recorded in Hind's Flora.
W: 67, Freckenham; Worlington, 1981; 76, Lt. Saxhan; 77, Cavenham, 1981; Icklingham, 1963; Herringswell, 1981; Tuddenham, 1980; Eriswell; 78, Lakenheath, 1980, several sites; Eriswell; 86, Fornham All Saints/Bury boundary hedge on Golf Course (F. A. Basham), still there, 1981; 87, Culford, 1981; 97, Bardwell, 1932; Sapiston, 1970.
Also recorded by Dixon Hewitt for Gt Cornard in 1912.
E: 03, East Bergholt, 1980; 04, Burstall, 1935; 05, Lt. Finborough, c. 1950; 14, Lt. Blakenham, 1981; Bramford, 1940; Claydon, 1980; Washbrook, 1981; 15, Coddenham, 1981; 36, Swefling, 1981; 44, Orford Castle, 1951; 48, Reydon; Rushmere (E. R. Long, c. 1930), no specimen. *Illustrated page 469*

Muscari comosum (L.) Mill.   Tassel Hyacinth   Miss Egerton 1930
(*Hyacinthus comosus* L.)   Feathered Hyacinth

Introduced. Relic of cultivation or garden throw-out. Native of the Mediterranean region and S.E. Europe. Recorded from Bramford (sq. 14) in 1930 and again in 1949 by Miss E. S. Rowling. Also from Offton (sq. 04) by F. W. Simpson.

Muscari armeniacum Leichtlin ex Baker   Garden Grape Hyacinth   M. A. Hyde 1975

Introduced. Native of Asia Minor and the Caucasus. It is considered that this is the species most frequently grown in gardens. When thrown out with garden rubbish, it can become naturalised. Other garden species may also occur. Further investigation is needed.
W: 76, Moulton, 1980; 77, Eriswell, 1977; Icklingham, about ½ mile from village, 1977; Mildenhall, 1981; Barton Mills, 1980; Cavenham, 1980, near site of *M. atlanticum*; 78, Lakenheath, with *M. atlanticum*, 1980; 86, Timworth, 1981; 96, Elmswell, 1980.
E: 03, Gt Wenham, Gypsy Row, 1979; 13, Holbrook, 1981; 14, Lt. Blakenham, 1979; edge of Rushmere Common, Playford Road, 1981; 23, Felixstowe, nr Coastguard Station, 1977; Shotley Cliffs, 1979; 24, Purdis Farm, 2 sites, 1981; 25, Pettistree, 1976; Ufford, 1976; 33, The Grove, Felixstowe, 1980.

Colchicum autumnale L.   Meadow Saffron   Sir J. Cullum 1773
                              Autumn Crocus

Native or introduced. Old meadows, pastures, woods and copses. Formerly frequent and often abundant, as at Ashbocking. Now very local or rare, due to the destruction of habitats.
W: 86; 93; 94; 95; 96.
94, Kersey; 95, Buxhall; Hitcham; Brettenham Park, pre-1950.
Now thought to be extinct in West Suffolk.
E: 06, Stowupland; 07, Botesdale; Rickinghall; 15, Ashbocking (now extinct); 16, Mendlesham; 24, Gt Bealings; 25, Grundisburgh; Monewden; Charsfield; Debach; Boulge; Otley; 26, Cretingham; Framlingham; 36, Parham.
It is thought to be extinct in most of these parishes. Corms were introduced on to the Mickfield Reserve, when the Ashbocking meadow was ploughed.
Normal and white-flowered forms on Suffolk Trust Reserve at Monewden, 1981.

Illustrated page 479

Paris quadrifolia L.   Herb Paris   Sir J. Cullum 1773

Native. This most attractive plant is far more frequent in Suffolk than is generally supposed by botanists. There are probably more colonies in this County than in any other area of Britain. It is to be found in the majority of the ancient or primary woods and copses on the Boulder Clay, and also in a few areas of secondary woodland, which are adjacent to primary woodland. In some woods as many as fifty separate colonies have been found. It is rare on the Chillesford Clay. Formerly very frequent over a wide area, but much reduced by the destruction of its habitats.
W: 64, Gt Wratting; 65, Gt Bradley; 74, Cavendish; 75, Ousden; 84, Long Melford; 85, Shimpling; Bradfield Combust; Chadacre; 86, Rushbrooke; 94, Lavenham Wood; Bull's Cross Wood; Groton Wood; 95, Rattlesden; Felshamhall and Monks' Park Woods; Bradfield St George; Cockfield; Buxhall; 96, Hessett; Gt Ashfield; Stowlangtoft; 97, Bardwell; Ixworth.
E: 04, Elmsett; Hintlesham; Offton; Hadleigh; 05, Onehouse; Barking; Gt Finborough; Wattisfield; Ringshall; Badley; 06, Haughley; 07, Burgate; Botesdale; 15, Gosbeck; Coddenham; 24, Culpho; 25, Dallinghoo; 26, Dennington; 34, Butley; 35, Chillesford; Lt. Glemham; 36, Bruisyard; 45, Friston.   *Illustrated page 449*

JUNCACEAE

JUNCACEAE

RUSH FAMILY

Juncus squarrosus L.   Heath Rush   Paget 1834

Native. Damp, acid heaths, usually on tracks. Not very common. It has decreased in recent years.
W: 67; 68; 77; 78; 87; 98.
77, Cavenham, 1978; 78, Wangford Warren, 1979; 98, Knettishall Heath.
E: 07; 14; 24; 25; 34; 35; 39; 45; 46; 47; 48; 49; 58; 40.
14, Ipswich, 1981 (M. A. Hyde); 45, Snape Common, 1981; 47, Walberswick, 1979; Westleton, 1980.

Juncus tenuis Willd.   Slender Rush   M. A. Hyde 1980

An alien, native of N. and S. America. Cart tracks and waste places. It is common and spreading in many areas of the British Isles.
14, Ipswich, two colonies on waste ground, 1980. Conf. Dr C. A. Stace.

Juncus compressus Jacq.   Round-fruited Rush   Prof. Henslow 1853

Native. In damp pastures and besides ponds. Very rare. It may be confused with *J. gerardii,* to which some of the coastal records may refer.
W: 86; 87; 88; 97.
86, Fornham All Saints; 97, Euston.
E: 04; 07; 17; 23; 34; 46; 47; 49; 40.
34, Sutton, 1970.

Juncus gerardii Lois.   Mud Rush   Mrs Casborne 1829
                             Salt Marsh Rush

Native. Salt marshes and beside brackish ponds and ditches. Very frequent.
E: 03; 13; 14; 23; 24; 25; 34; 35; 44; 45; 46; 47; 49; 57; 58; 40; 50.
Salt marshes, from the Stour estuary to Kessingland, 1981.

Juncus bufonius L.   Toad Rush   J. Andrews 1749

Native. Damp, open places beside ponds, marshes, cart tracks and woodland paths. Very frequent. Growth varies considerably with habitat.
W: All squares except 68.
76, Dalham, 1981; 95, Bradfield Woods, 1980.
E: All squares except 36; 44; 59.
04, Raydon, 1981; 23, Harkstead, 1981; 35, Tunstall, 1981.

Juncus ambiguus Guss.
(*J. ranarius* Song. & Perr.)
Recorded at Stowlangtoft (sq. 96) and Flatford Mill (sq. 03). No further details are available.

Juncus inflexus L.   Hard Rush   Paget 1834
(*J. glaucus* Sibth.)
Native. Poor pastures, wet heaths and the sides of ditches. Common.
All squares.

Juncus effusus L.   Soft Rush   J. Andrews 1746
(*J. communis* E. Mey. var. *effusus* (L.) E. Mey.)

Native. In marshes, wet woods, bogs and fens. Common. Often confused with *J. conglomeratus.*
All squares except 66; 68.

Juncus effusus × inflexus   Diffuse Rush   Prof. Henslow 1860
(*J.* × *diffusus* Hoppe)

Native. Wet pastures, ditches, damp woods and bogs. Probably not uncommon, but overlooked.
W: 77, Tuddenham; 78, Wangford; 87, near Barnham.
E: 34, Sutton.

Juncus conglomeratus L.   Compact Rush   Paget 1834
(*J. communis* E. Mey. var. *conglomeratus* (L.) E. Mey.   Common Rush
J. subuliflorus Drejer)

Native. Wet, old pastures, heaths, and open fen carrs. Not very frequent and confused with *J. effusus,* a common species, to which some of the records may refer.
W: All squares except 66; 67; 78; 83; 84; 87; 88; 96.
95, Bradfield Woods, 1980.
E: All squares except 05; 06; 15; 17; 23; 24; 26; 27; 33; 34; 35; 38; 39; 44; 45; 59; 40; 50.
07, Wortham Ling, 1980; 47, Walberswick, 1979.

Juncus conglomeratus × inflexus
(*J.* × *ruhmeri* Aschers. & Graebn.)

E: 25, Bromeswell, c. 1976. No further details available.

Juncus maritimus Lam.   Sea Rush   Davy 1796
(*J. spinosus* Forsk.)

Native. Drier areas of salt marshes. Frequent.
E: 03; 13; 14; 23; 24; 25; 33; 34; 35; 45; 46; 47; 57; 58; 40; 50.
13, Harkstead, 1981; 23, Landguard Common, 1980; 58, Benacre, 1980.

Juncus acutus L.   Sharp Rush   Davy 1805

Native. On the sea coast. Although *J. acutus* has from time to time been recorded for Suffolk, I have been unable to find any authentic specimens. They have usually turned out to be stronger-than-usual clumps of *J. maritimus. J. acutus* is still found in Norfolk, but it is very rare and diminishing.
Hind expressed doubts about the record from Aldeburgh attributed to Davy and suggests that *J. maritimus* was more likely.

Juncus subnodulosus Schrank   Blunt-flowered Rush   Paget 1834
(*J. obtusiflorus* Ehrh. ex Hoffm.)

Native. Grassy, open fens, old wet pastures and ditches, even those which may be slightly brackish. Frequent.

W: 67; 68; 74; 77; 78; 83; 87; 88; 94; 95; 97; 98.
67, Mildenhall, 1977; 74, Clare, 1976; 97, Coney Weston, 1981.
E: 04; 05; 07; 13; 14; 23; 25; 34; 35; 39; 45; 46; 47; 49; 58; 59; 40; 50.
07, Thelnetham Fen, 1981; 24, Foxhall, 1981; Purdis Heath, 1979; 34, Bromeswell, 1981; 40, Belton, 1978.

Juncus acutiflorus Ehrh. ex Hoffm.   Sharp-flowered Rush   J. Andrews 1739
(*J. sylvaticus* auct.)

Native. Marshes, wet woods, and often dominant in bogs. Common.
W: 75; 76; 77; 78; 86; 88; 93; 95; 96; 97.
78, Pashford Poor's Fen, 1980; 95, Bradfield Woods, 1980.
E: 03; 04; 05; 07; 13; 14; 16; 24; 25; 35; 39; 45; 46; 47; 49; 58; 59; 40.
13, Holbrook, 1981; 24, Foxhall, 1976; 46, Westleton, 1979.

Juncus articulatus L.   Jointed Rush   Davy 1796
(*J. lampocarpus* Ehrh. ex Hoffm.)

Native. In ditches, ponds and wet places. Frequent.
W: All squares except 64; 65; 66; 83.
67, Mildenhall, in ditch, 1977; 95, Bradfield Woods, 1980.
E: All squares except 15; 59.
13, Woolverstone, 1981; 40, Belton, marsh, 1978.
Viviparous forms are frequent; Davy's 1796 record was for this form.

Juncus bulbosus L.   Bulbous Rush   J. Andrews 1746
(*J. supinus* Moench)

Native. Wet heaths and damp, acid pastures. Now very rare and almost extinct.
W: 93, Polstead, c. 1950.
E: 34, Butley; 46, Westleton, 1979 (Mrs E. M. Hyde); 47, Walberswick, 1979; 40, Fritton Decoy; Lound; Belton, 1977.

Juncus kochii F. W. Schultz

Native. In bogs, marshes and streams, usually in heathy habitats. Very similar to *J. bulbosus* L. Although there are no definite records for the County, it probably occurs in a few sites where it has been overlooked, such as Redgrave Fen. It is found only a few yards over the border in Lopham Fen, Norfolk.

Luzula pilosa (L.) Willd.   Hairy Woodrush   Sir J. Cullum 1773

Native. Woods and copses, chiefly on the Boulder and London Clays. Very frequent, especially in clearings.
W: 64; 74; 75; 76; 83; 85; 87; 93; 94; 95; 96; 97.
94, Groton Wood, 1980; 95, Monks' Park Wood, 1980; 96, Pakenham Wood, 1979.
E: 03; 04; 05; 07; 13; 16; 23; 36; 37; 39; 46; 48; 59.
04, Raydon Wood, 1981; Wolves Wood, 1981; 13, Bentley Woods, 1980.

Luzula forsteri (Sm.) DC.   Narrow-leaved Hairy Woodrush   Hind 1882
Forster's Woodrush

Native. In woods, old shady hedge-banks and sides of ditches. Very rare.
W: 94, Polstead.
E: 03/04, Polstead; 13, Bentley, 1979 (Mrs E. M. Hyde).
Recorded in Hind's Flora only from Polstead Wood. A small colony was observed in 1965 at Hadleigh Heath. The site was a roadside ditch bank. Another habitat at Hadleigh Heath, where *L. forsteri* was often abundant, was a shady roadside bank, with a hedge and oak trees. Reference to the 1838 Survey Map shows that this bank was then the boundary of a wood, known as Polts Wood. After the hedge and trees were removed, c. 1950, the plant rapidly disappeared.
There is a specimen in Hb. Atkins, collected at Bentley in 1910.

Luzula forsteri × **pilosa**   Hind 1889
(*L.* × *borreri* Bromf. ex Bab.)

Native. Old shady banks and the edges of woods. Very rare. Recorded in Hind's Flora for Wiston (sq. 93).
W: 93, Polstead, c. 1965 (F. W. Simpson).

Luzula sylvatica (Huds.) Gaud.   Great Woodrush   Hind's Flora 1889
(*L. maxima* (Reich.) DC.)

Native. Old heathy woods. Very local. It was plentiful for many years in much of Woolpit Wood, when the wood consisted mainly of Oak. The wood was virtually clear felled, reduced in area, and replanted with conifers, which destroyed its original flora. It has also been further desecrated by the new A45.
At one time, when woodland in the area was more extensive, it probably had a much wider range. Many years ago I found it in the small remaining section of the once large East Wood at Elmswell. A little occurs in Shelland Wood and Haughley Thicks. Hind's Flora gives Rede as a possible parish. It is possible that it survives in this area, overlooked. I found it in Lopham's Wood, at Carlton, Cambridgeshire, near Little Thurlow, in 1966. Large specimens of *L. pilosa* are frequently mistaken for this species.
W: 87, Ampton; 95, Monks' Park Wood, 1969 (Dr O. Rackham); 96, Woolpit Wood, 1972.
E: 06, Shelland, 1972; Haughley Thicks, 1972; East Wood, Elmswell, 1938.

Luzula campestris (L.) DC.   Field Woodrush   Sir J. Cullum 1773
Sweep's Brush
Good Friday Grass

Native. Heaths, old pastures, waysides and open parts of woods. More frequent on sandy soils. Common.
All squares except 64; 65; 68; 85; 05; 33; 59.

Luzula multiflora (Retz.) Lej.   Heath Woodrush   Prof. Henslow 1853
Many-headed Woodrush

Native. Damp heaths, bogs and open glades in woods, usually on acid soils. Frequent.
W: All squares except 65; 66; 68; 74; 75; 83; 84; 85.
78, Brandon, 1977; 96, Woolpit Wood, 1975; 97, Hopton Fen, 1981.

E: All squares except 03; 06; 15; 16; 17; 25; 26; 27; 28; 33; 34; 37; 38; 39; 44; 58.
04, Raydon, 1981; 13, Holbrook; Bentley; Belstead, 1979.
Var. **congesta** (DC.) Lej. is common, but this may only be an ecological form, occurring where conditions are unfavourable for normal growth. It has been recorded from Felshamhall Wood, Bentley, Belstead, Blythburgh and Theberton.

Luzula pallescens Sw.   Fen Woodrush

This is recorded in Hind's Flora under *L. multiflora* for Hinderclay Wood, a record made by a Dr Bird of Wattisfield, which is an adjacent parish to Hinderclay. It is probably an error, as this species is restricted to open grassy fen.

AMARYLLIDACEAE

DAFFODIL FAMILY

Some authorities place the genus *Allium* in the Liliaceae. It was decided to follow the classification of J. E. Dandy and to retain it in the Amaryllidaceae.

Allium scorodoprasum L.   Sand Leek   F. W. Simpson 1940

A rare casual.
W: 86, near Barracks, Bury St Edmunds, 1942 (J. L. Gilbert).
E: 04, Hintlesham, 1940.

Allium vineale L.   Crow Garlic   J. Andrews 1739
                          Wild Onion

Native. Dry sandy pastures, waysides and sandy places. Local, sometimes common, especially near the coast. Probably increasing.
W: 65; 66; 67; 74; 76; 77; 86; 87; 88; 93; 96; 97.
66, roadside at Moulton, 1976; 77, Barton Mills, 1981; Icklingham, roadside verge, 1981, abundant; 87, Barnham, 1980; 96, Pakenham, 1980.
E: 04; 13; 14; 15; 23; 24; 25; 33; 37; 38; 45; 47; 57; 40; 50.
23, Landguard Common, 1980; 33, Felixstowe Ferry; Bawdsey, 1977; 34, Shingle Street, 1981; 45, Iken, 1981; 57, Southwold Cliffs, 1975.
Hb. Ipswich Museum: 'In the Marshes and on the Marsh Wall between St Peter's Dock and Nova Scotia', c. 1820 (John Notcutt).

Allium oleraceum L.   Field Garlic   Rev. G. R. Leathes 1830

Native. On the edges of fields and dry grassy places. Rare or casual. It is possible that some records may refer to other species of *Allium*. Hind's Flora records it as common in fields at Hadleigh and Lakenheath (1830).
W: 85, Whepstead; 86, Shaker's Lane, Bury St Edmunds, 1921.
E: 36, Gt Glemham, 1953.

Allium schoenoprasum L.   Chives   J. L. Gilbert 1942
(*A. sibiricum* L.)

Introduced from N. Europe or Asia and cultivated, sometimes escaping and becoming naturalised.

W: 86, old roadway near Blenheim Barracks, Bury St Edmunds, 1942.
E: 14, Tuddenham, 1964 (Mrs E. M. Hyde). Since died out.

Allium cepa L.   Onion   F. W. Simpson 1972

Introduced and commonly cultivated, probably a native of Asia. Onions frequently survive for a few years on abandoned gardens and allotments, and on rubbish tips. They occasionally wash up on the beaches along our estuaries, derived from rubbish thrown from boats, especially boats using Felixstowe, Harwich and Parkeston Harbours. Occasionally, as in 1972, specimens take root on the foreshore, above the high tide-mark, as at Erwarton in 1972/3 when specimens survived through one year, flowering the next.

Allium roseum ssp. **bulbiferum** (DC.) E. F. Warburg   Rosy Garlic   W. Borrer 1840
(*A. ambiguum* Sm., non DC.)

Introduced. Native of the Mediterranean region.
E: 17, Eye Castle Hill, 1840, specimen in Cambridge University Herbarium; 25, Framsden, 1980; 47, Blyford, 1965 (R. D. English). Still there, 1980.

Allium triquetrum L.   Triquetrous Garlic

Native of the Iberian Peninsula and the Mediterranean. Introduced into Britain and now quite naturalised in some Western counties of England and Wales. In S.W. Ireland it has spread rapidly in suitable habitats. Some bulbs brought back from West Cork in 1938 and planted in my Ipswich garden have survived in dry and unsuitable conditions, and are now slowly spreading. There seems to be no reason why it should not occur in Suffolk, but the several records received so far have proved incorrect. *A. paradoxum* is usually the species mistaken for *A. triquetrum*.

Allium paradoxum (Bieb.) G. Don   Few-flowered Leek   Mrs C. Bull 1938

An introduced and established alien from the Caucasus. Sometimes abundant, as at one time in the Abbey Gardens at Bury St Edmunds. Occurs in churchyards and on roadside banks.
W: 66, roadside verge, Newmarket, 1981; 77, West Stow; Eriswell; 86, Bury St Edmunds; Fornham All Saints, 1960; Gt Barton, 1979 (Mrs E. M. Hyde); 97, Ixworth Churchyard.
E: 03, Layham; 14, Ipswich; 24, roadside bank at Gt Bealings; 49, Beccles; 57, South Cove, 1978 (P. G. Lawson).
Although this species is attractive during spring with its fresh green stems and white pendulous flowers, it is unwise to introduce specimens into the garden. If conditions are favourable, it can spread very rapidly by means of its round bulbils and soon dominates beds, borders and shrubberies. Introduced into my small garden at Ipswich about 1950 from specimens brought from Bury, it has become a great nuisance, and has also spread to neighbouring gardens. When established it is difficult or almost impossible to eradicate completely.

Allium ursinum L.   Ramsons   Rev. G. Crabbe 1798
Wild Garlic

Native. In wet woods, beside streams and rivers. Often abundant and dominant.
W: 64; 75; 76; 83; 85; 87; 93; 94; 95; 96; 97.
94, Brent Eleigh, 1980; 95, Monks' Park Wood, 1980.

E: 03; 04; 05; 06; 07; 13; 14; 15; 23; 24; 25; 27; 28; 33; 34; 35; 36; 37; 45; 47; 48; 57; 59; 40. 03, Bentley and Capel St Mary; 04, Hintlesham; 05, Barking; 13, Freston Wood; 14, Piper's Vale, Ipswich. All records, 1981. *Illustrated page 447*

Leucojum vernum L.   Spring Snowflake   E. R. Long c. 1900

Introduced in Suffolk. Sometimes cultivated in gardens. The only record for Suffolk is from Thorington Churchyard (sq. 47), date unknown, but probably about the beginning of the century.

Leucojum aestivum L.   Summer Snowflake   Mrs Cobbold 1800

Introduced, though perhaps formerly native. By streams and in wet pastures. Planted in shrubberies and gardens and sometimes found on banks and sides of ditches, where it may be a throw-out or a relic of cultivation. Hind records this species as being a troublesome weed in pastures at Little Stonham, and it still grows in the churchyard there.
W: 75, Stradishall.
E: 05, Bosmere, 1975; 13, Woolverstone, 1981; Harkstead, 1980 (Mrs E. M. Hyde); 16, Little Stonham; 27, Fressingfield; 33, Felixstowe, 1977; 46, Dunwich.

GALANTHUS   SNOWDROPS

Snowdrops, both single and double, are very variable and a large number of varieties have been introduced; several have become naturalised. In a small wood at Polstead there are colonies of single *Galanthus nivalis* with green tips on the outer perianth segments, which I think can be named *G. nivalis* 'viridapicis'. This variety has larger flowers than the normal *G. nivalis* and the spathe is also much larger and unsplit. There are also numbers of the variety *G. nivalis* 'Scharlokii', originating in Germany. This is a small-flowered variety, which usually has split spathes and more drooping flowers, tinged with green, on long pedicels. There is also in this wood the double Snowdrop, *G. nivalis,* 'Pusey Green Tips'. The date of the introduction of the Snowdrops into this wood is unknown. A dwelling existed at the entrance early in the 19th century.
Snowdrops increase quite rapidly by the division of the bulbs. In many colonies, although seed pods are produced, seedlings are infrequent. It is considered that the seeds are infertile because the colonies of Snowdrops which have been introduced are usually from one stock. If, however, another species of *Galanthus* or even a variety of *G. nivalis,* is introduced into the colonies, the flowers are cross-fertilized and seedlings become frequent. The single leaves of seedling Snowdrops are bright green, very similar in colour and appearance to those of seedling Bluebells, for which they could very easily be mistaken. It is not until the bulbs are large enough to produce the normal pair of leaves that they assume their characteristic grey-green colour.

Galanthus nivalis L.   Snowdrop   Davy & Dawson Turner 1805

Doubtfully native in Suffolk. Frequent. Naturalised in woods, copses, orchards, churchyards and on hedge-banks and the sites of former gardens. The majority of colonies suggest that the bulbs have been deliberately introduced or thrown out from gardens. Double-flowered forms are fairly common, and are recorded from Cavenham, Nacton, Playford, Polstead, Wetheringsett and elsewhere.
W: 64; 67; 76; 77; 78; 86; 87; 93; 94; 96.
E: 03; 04; 13; 14; 15; 16; 17; 24; 26; 27; 33; 35; 36; 37; 38; 46; 48; 49; 58; 59; 40.
Illustrated page 457

Galanthus plicatus M. Bieb. Crimean Snowdrop F. W. Simpson 1947

Introduced. Native to the Crimea.

W: 77, Barton Mills, 1980 (Mrs E. M. Hyde); 86, on the site of an old garden, Barton Park, 1969 (D. McClintock). Detd. R. H. S., Wisley. This is the same area where *Crocus biflorus* and *C. flavus* have been recorded. 87, Culford, 1979.

E: 24, in plantations, copses and hedges at Gt and Lt. Bealings. Growing with *G. nivalis* and hybridising freely, 1947-1981 (F. W. Simpson).

Galanthus nivalis × plicatus F. W. Simpson 1947

E: 24, copses at Gt and Lt. Bealings, occurring where both species are found growing in close proximity. The hybrids are very variable, and a whole range of forms between the species have been found.

NARCISSUS SINGLE DAFFODILS

It is sometimes difficult to distinguish between the wild species and some small varieties of cultivated single Trumpet Daffodils, such as 'Golden Spur', when found in woodland habitats and grassy parks. The wild plant is much smaller, with narrower leaves and more nodding flowers. The six outer perianth segments surrounding the trumpet are about equal to its length. They are usually a paler shade of yellow (rarely cream or white) than the trumpet, and are always more pointed forward than in cultivated or introduced varieties, and at an angle rarely exceeding 45° with the trumpet.

Narcissus pseudonarcissus L. Wild Daffodil Sir J. Cullum 1775
Lent Lily

Native, but probably introduced and naturalised in some habitats. Woods, old pastures, and banks of streams, where it is almost certainly native. Not very frequent, yet abundant in some habitats, as at Water Wood, Butley. Here it was perhaps originally introduced. Formerly in several old pastures, where it appeared to be genuinely wild, but these have been ploughed up in recent years.

W: 86, Bury St Edmunds; 87, Fakenham Wood; 94, Kettlebaston; 95, Hitcham.

E: 03, East Bergholt; 13, Woolverstone; 14, Westerfield; Bixley; 23, Harkstead; 25, Monewden; 33, Felixstowe, The Grove; 34, Butley; 36, Benhall; Gt Glemham; Bruisyard Wood; 38, Ilketshall St Lawrence; 48, South Cove; Wrentham; Henstead, 1974; Frostenden; 49, Herringfleet; 58, South Cove; Covehithe, 1974. *Illustrated page 459* Growing among the Wild Daffodils in the Butley Woods is a small colony of a double-flowered form. This is distinct, the trumpet being fully double. The plants are small and of the same dimensions as the single Daffodils. This double form is the true Wild Daffodil and must not be confused with any garden variety.

Narcissus hispanicus Gouan Common Daffodil 'Golden Spur'
(*N. major* Curt.)

Introduced. Native of S.W. France and the Northern parts of Spain and Portugal. Grown in gardens and often naturalised in parkland, plantations, old orchards, the sites of former gardens and hedge-banks. This Daffodil is often mistaken for *N. pseudonarcissus*.

Narcissus 'Telamonius Plenus' Common Double Daffodil F. W. Simpson 1920

A number of forms of Double Daffodils occur. They are semi-wild, or naturalised and usually yellow. They are found in hedges and copses where garden rubbish has been dumped, or often on the sites of former gardens, old orchards and meadows. The most frequent Double Daffodil, which increases rapidly by division of the bulbs, is a rather open, untidy form with no really distinct trumpet. There is a more refined form, in which the outer perianth segments are distinct from the double flowering trumpet. Although the origin of the Common Double Daffodil is unknown, it may have originated from the single variety, known as 'Golden Spur', which flowers at the same time.

W: 86, Ampton; 87, Gt Fakenham.

E: 13, Stutton; Freston; Woolverstone; 14, Bixley; 23, Chelmondiston; 24, Purdis Heath; Playford; Kesgrave; 34, Boyton; 36, silted-up pond, Gt Glemham.

Narcissus 'van Sion' has been planted at Rookery Farm, Monewden on the Suffolk Trust Reserve.

NARCISSUS   HYBRIDS

Garden hybrids are often found semi-naturalised or thrown out of gardens into ditches, waysides and hedge-banks. These include *N.* × *incomparabilis* Mill., *N.* × *medioluteus* Mill. and others.

Narcissus majalis Curt.   Pheasant's Eye Narcissus   Sir J. Cullum 1773
(*N. poeticus* auct.)

Introduced. Naturalised as a garden relic or throw-out. Recorded in Hind's Flora as occurring at Bury St Edmunds, Cove and Hemley.

Narcissus poeticus agg. × **tazetta**   'Primrose Peerless'   Sir C. J. F. Bunbury 1824
(*N.* × *medioluteus* Mill.   Jonquil
N. × *biflorus* Curt.)

Introduced. Planted in gardens, open shrubberies, lawns and parks, sometimes escaping and becoming naturalised. The only recent records are from Little Welnetham (sq. 86), and Woolverstone (sq. 13), 1976-1980.

Recorded by Hind from Bury St Edmunds, Mildenhall, Rattlesden, Hengrave, Hitcham, St Margaret's, Oulton and Barking Wood.

IRIDACEAE

IRIS FAMILY

Sisyrinchium bermudiana L.   Blue-eyed Grass   Miss J. C. N. Willis 1957
(*S. angustifolium* Mill.)

Introduced. Native of N. America, now naturalised in many counties in Gt Britain, as well as on the Continent. In marshy places and on the sides of ponds. Recorded from Felixstowe in 1957, where it was regarded as a garden escape.

Sisyrinchium striatum Smith   M. A. Hyde 1978

Introduced. Native of Chile.

E: 13, Brantham, several plants persisting for a number of years. Conf. E. J. Clement.

Iris foetidissima L. Stinking Iris Sir T. G. Cullum 1804
Gladdon
Roast-beef Plant

Native. In old woods and copses, on hedge-banks and in churchyards, usually on chalky or clay soils. Sometimes introduced into plantations, where it may become naturalised. Locally frequent. Its occurrence in churchyards is due to the use of its attractive capsules, with their orange-red seeds, as church decoration or for placing on graves. The seeds of discarded specimens germinate in the undisturbed areas of the churchyards. The colour of the seeds gives this plant the name of 'Roast-beef Plant'.
W: 74; 75; 76; 77; 84; 85; 86; 94; 95.
76, Higham, 1980; Dalham Churchyard, 1981; 86, Rougham, 1980; 94, Groton Wood, 1976.
E: 04; 05; 06; 07; 13; 14; 15; 16; 17; 23; 24; 25; 26; 33; 35; 36; 37; 38; 39; 46; 47; 48; 49; 59.
04, Chattisham, 1980; 14, St Nicholas Churchyard, Ipswich, 1978; 15, Coddenham, 1980; Gosbeck Churchyard, 1980; 17, Eye, 1980; 37, Linstead Parva.   *Illustrated page 449*
Plants with yellow flowers at Rickinghall Superior, c. 1970 (P. R. Peecock), and at Saxtead (S. A. Notcutt).

Iris pseudacorus L. Yellow Flag Sir J. Cullum 1773
Yellow Iris

Native. Marshes, swamps, alder carr, streams, ditches, ponds and the sides of rivers. Very frequent.
All squares except 65; 76.   *Illustrated page 482*

Iris germanica L. Flag Iris H. E. Boreham 1956

Introduced from the Mediterranean region. Widely cultivated. A garden throw-out. Occasionally found naturalised on waste ground, rubbish tips, roadsides and sites of former gardens.
W: 76, Lt. Saxham, 1976; 77, Barton Mills, 1957-1978 (F. W. Simpson); West Stow, 1956; Eriswell, 1977; Mildenhall; 78, Lakenheath, 1974; 86, Bury St Edmunds, 1976; 88, Euston; 94, Groton, 1973; 96, Pakenham, 1978.
W: 13, Brantham; Bentley; 14, Wherstead; New Cut, Ipswich, 1974-1981 (M. A. Hyde); 23, Chelmondiston, 1977; 24, Kesgrave and Playford, 1974 (F. W. Simpson).

Hermodactylus tuberosus (L.) Mill. Snake's-head Iris Mrs Jordan 1974
(*Iris tuberosa* L.)

Growing for several years at Manor Farm, Burgh (sq. 25). The pigs usually eat the plant before it flowers.

Crocus nudiflorus Sm. Autumn Crocus Atlas of the British Flora 1962
Naked-flowered Crocus

Introduced. Native of S.W. France and the Iberian Peninsula. Only two Suffolk records.
W: 78, parish unknown, believed to be Lakenheath (post-1930, Atlas of the British Flora).
E: 36, on a gravelly bank among old trees at Saxmundham, 1974 (Misses B. & R. Copinger Hill).

Crocus purpureus Weston   Purple Crocus   Rev. G. Crabbe 1805
(*C. vernus* auct.)   Spring Crocus

Introduced. Native of C. and S. Europe. Naturalised in old pastures. Very rare or even extinct.
This species was thought to be extinct in the County until 1965, when it was reported by R. R. Rolfe of Palgrave as occurring in some profusion in grassland at Wortham Manor (sq. 07). It was still to be found there in 1972, though very much reduced by spraying.
Hind recorded it from Barton and Beccles. The Rev. G. Crabbe (in letters) described this species as being abundant in meadows at Swefling.

Crocus biflorus Mill.   Silvery Crocus   Sir C. J. F. Bunbury c. 1830

Introduced. Native of S. Europe. Naturalised in old pastures and on the sites of old gardens. Now very rare or extinct. Formerly growing in some profusion in two old pastures, one at Grundisburgh, the other at Clopton. It flowered during late February or early March. Both habitats were ploughed up c. 1950. A few corms were saved from the Grundisburgh site at Whitehouse Farm, and planted by Mrs Harris in the garden of her cottage opposite. In 1972 three corms were taken from the garden and replanted on the margin of the original field. One flowered in February, 1973. There was no trace of these plants the following year and it was considered that crop spraying had destroyed them, although some protection had been afforded. Due to the illness of Mrs Harris, the remaining corms in her garden were removed in 1975 and planted in one of the old pastures at Rookery Farm, Monewden, managed by the Suffolk Trust for Nature Conservation. A few corms were also taken in 1971 by Mrs E. Dickson and planted in her garden at Westerfield.
There is a record in Hind's Flora by Sir C. J. F. Bunbury 'on the site of an old garden at Barton Park'. Relics of this garden still exist, but the species does not appear to have survived.   *Illustrated page 40*

GARDEN CROCUSES

A number of species and varieties of *Crocus* are grown in gardens. Many have originated from growers in Holland. Flowers are various shades of purple, mauve, white, cream, yellow and orange, plain or striped. Frequently the corms get thrown out with rubbish and become naturalised in waste places or on verges. Some species are fertile and increase by seeding in favourable sites. Others are sterile and increase more slowly by division of the corms.

Crocus tommasinianus Herbert   ?Hind's Flora 1889

Introduced. A native of S.E. Europe. This species has small lavender flowers which can easily be confused with *C. purpureus*. It flowers usually in late February and early March at the same time as *C. biflorus* and before *C. purpureus*.
W: 86, Barton Park, 1969 (D. McClintock and C. Grange). Derelict kitchen garden.
E: 25, Grundisburgh, c. 1976, detd. D. McClintock. The habitat was formerly a meadow. A house was built on the site, c. 1934; however, the *Crocus* survived in the grassy area in front of the house, which had not been cultivated.

IRIDACEAE

Crocus flavus Weston   Golden Crocus   Sir C. J. F. Bunbury 1930
(*C. aureus* Sibth. & Sm.)

Grown in gardens. Recorded in Hind's Flora from the site of an old garden at Barton Park, near Bury St Edmunds, where it was re-found by D. McClintock and C. Grange in 1969.

Crocus speciosus Bieb.   D. Smee 1975

Introduced. Native of E. Europe and Asia Minor. An autumn-flowering species.
E: 13, roadside at Tattingstone, 1975. Several specimens, probably growing from garden waste. Identified by R. H. S. Wisley.

Crocosmia aurea × pottsii   Montbretia   F. W. Simpson 1946
(*C. × crocosmiflora* (Lemoine) N. E. Br.)

An artificial hybrid, originally raised in France from parents originating in S. Africa. Commonly grown in gardens, and often naturalised in damp places, on the sites of former gardens and where garden rubbish has been dumped.
E: 13, Holbrook, 1974; 23, Chelmondiston Tip, 1974; 24, Foxhall, 1977; 46, Dunwich; 57, Easton Wood, 1946.

Gladiolus byzantinus Mill.   Eastern Gladiolus   F. W. Simpson 1973

Introduced. Probably a native of N. Africa.
A few plants on a tip and in a former garden beside a small stream at Martlesham (sq. 24). This is an early-flowering species with rosy purple flowers, frequently seen in gardens.

DIOSCOREACEAE

YAM FAMILY

Tamus communis L.   Black Bryony   Sir J. Cullum 1773
                         Snake-berry (Suffolk)

Native. Common and widespread. It has increased considerably in Suffolk since the 1930's. At one time it appeared to be restricted to the clay soils of the County, but can now be found on sandy and gravelly soils and in waste places, as well as in its more usual habitats of hedges, woods and copses.
All squares except 67; 44; 49.
Hind stated that it was 'absent from the Breck Country'.

ORCHIDACEAE

ORCHID FAMILY

Cephalanthera damasonium (Mill.) Druce   White Helleborine   A. Mayfield 1902
(*C. latifolia* Janchen
C. grandiflora S. F. Gray)

Native. Calcareous woods.
A. Mayfield of Mendlesham recorded this species for the County in 1902. No accurate

details of the exact site are known, although I was once informed that a specimen was found in Shrubland Park (sq. 15), an area where there are certainly favourable habitats.

Cephalanthera longifolia (L.) Fritsch   Sir T. G. Cullum c. 1804
Narrow-leaved Helleborine
Long-leaved Helleborine

Native. Woods and shady places on calcareous soils. Hind recorded the species from near Bury St Edmunds from an old record in the Botanist's Guide.

Epipactis palustris (L.) Crantz   Marsh Helleborine   J. Andrews 1745

Native. In fens and marshes. Scarce and decreasing. Extinct in many of its former habitats.
W: 77; 78; 83; 93; 97.
77, Icklingham.
E: 07; 17; 35; 37; 46; 49; 59; 40.
07, Redgrave Fen, 1977.
Recorded from Chillesford in 1787 by Sutton and Kirby. Re-found by N. Kerr c. 1960 in the same parish. The site has since been destroyed.   *Illustrated page 521*

Epipactis helleborine (L.) Crantz   Broad-leaved Helleborine   Dr W. Turner 1562
(*E. latifolia* (L.) All.)

Native. Usually in old deciduous woods and copses. Local or rare. Also decreasing. Usually in small numbers.
Formerly frequent in the South-west of the County in Oak woods with Hazel and Hornbeam coppice. The growth, size and colour of the flowers is very variable.
W: 78, Brandon, 1979, in coniferous plantations; 93, Polstead, c. 1960; 94, Edwardstone; Milden, c. 1950; Groton; 95, Hitcham; Monks' Park Wood, c. 1970.
E: 04, Hintlesham, 1976; Offton, pre-1950; 05, Gt Finborough, c. 1970; Abbot's Hall, Stowmarket, 1974 (J. Shackles); Barking, pre-1950; 23, Chelmondiston, 1978 (Mrs E. M. Hyde); 24, Martlesham, 1979 (M. A. Hyde); 33, Felixstowe, 1946-1977; 48, Weston; 59, Corton, pre-1950.   *Illustrated page 521*

Epipactis purpurata Sm.   Violet Helleborine   B. T. Lowne 1912
(*E. sessilifolia* Peterm.
E. violacea (Dur. Duq.) Bor.)

Native. In old Oak woods with Hornbeam and Hazel coppice. Rare.
W: 93, Grays Wood, Cornard, 1912; re-found, 1956 (Dr D. P. Young); Assington, 1934-65 (F. W. Simpson); 94, Groton Wood, 1980; Milden.
E: 04, Aldham, 1980; Hadleigh, 1980; Hintlesham, c. 1978. (All records, F. W. Simpson).

Illustrated page 521

Epipactis helleborine × purpurata   F. W. Simpson 1930
(*E. × schulzei* P. Fourn.)

This hybrid is probably more frequent in the County than is generally realised, more especially in woods in the South-west. By searching a number of woods one can find specimens showing various intermediate characters of both species. The flowers are visited by several species of wasps and cross-fertilisation must be common.

W: 93, Assington; 94, Milden; 95, Monks' Park Wood.
E: 04, Elmsett, 1930, in Lucy Wood, before the wood was destroyed.

Epipactis phyllanthes G. E. Sm.   Green-flowered Helleborine
(*E. vectensis* (T. & T. A. Stephenson) Brooke and Rose)   Dr E. F. Warburg 1952
Native. In woods and copses. Very rare.
E: 25, Melton Hall. Detd. Dr D. P. Young.

Spiranthes spiralis (L.) Chevall.   Autumn Lady's Tresses   Gerarde 1597
(*S. autumnalis* L. C. M. Rich.)
Native. Old pastures, heaths and lawns. Very rare. Last record, Ilketshall St Lawrence, in 1957.
W: No recent records. Recorded in Hind's Flora from sixteen parishes.
E: 04, in lawn at the old Whatfield Rectory (R. Burn); 36, Benhall; Gt Glemham; 38, Ilketshall St Lawrence; 48, Sotterley; 59, Lound; 40, Belton Heath; 50, meadow at Hopton.
Most of these records date from the 1950's.

Listera ovata (L.) R. Br.   Common Twayblade   J. Andrews 1748
Native. Woods, copses, old pastures and chalk-pits, chiefly on clays, loams and chalky soils. Frequent, but steadily decreasing.
W: All squares except 66; 68; 93; 98.
77, Mildenhall, 1981; 78, Brandon, 1977; 95, Monks' Park Wood, 1980; 97, Hopton Fen, 1981.
E: All squares except 03; 13; 14; 23; 33; 38; 45.
04, Hadleigh, 1981; Hintlesham, 1981.   *Illustrated page 522*

Neottia nidus-avis (L.) L. C. M. Rich.   Bird's-nest Orchid   J. Andrews 1728
Native. In old woods and copses, chiefly on the Boulder Clay. Not very frequent, though sometimes appearing in large numbers in favourable seasons. In 1969 sixty spikes were observed in a small wood near Woodbridge.
W: 64; 93; 94; 95; 96; 97.
94, Groton, 1976.
E: 03; 04; 05; 13; 14; 17; 24; 28; 35; 36; 46; 48.
04, Raydon, 1977 (D. Smee); 14, Ipswich, 1980 (L. J. Hyde); 24, Hasketon, 1981.
There is a specimen in Hb. Ipswich Museum collected by the Rev. C. Davy in 1787 at Onehouse (probably Northfield Wood).   *Illustrated page 522*

Goodyera repens (L.) R. Br.   Creeping Lady's Tresses   A. Mayfield c. 1935
Native. Usually found in coniferous woods. Recorded only from Stuston (sq. 17).

Hammarbya paludosa (L.) O. Kuntze   Bog Orchid   Rev. G. R. Leathes 1834
(*Malaxis paludosa* (L.) Sw.)
Native. This little Orchid is probably extinct in Suffolk and no specimen has, to my knowledge, been found for nearly 100 years. It required bogs and damp hollows on heaths, where there is sphagnum moss. In the early part of the 19th century it was reported

as being abundant on Ashby Warren and also on Belton Common. Recorded by Hind from Belton Common, Ashby Warren, Herringfleet and Redgrave Fen.

Liparis loeselii (L.) L. C. M. Rich.   Fen Orchid   Sir T. G. Cullum 1804

Native. In wet calcareous fens. Possibly now extinct. Formerly found in fair numbers in a few habitats. Collectors and more especially the drainage of sites, have caused its disappearance. The only recent records are from Thelnetham in 1970 and 1974, and Hinderclay Fen in 1967.
Recorded in Hind's Flora also from Tuddenham St Mary, Lakenheath and Redgrave Fen.

Illustrated page 68

Herminium monorchis (L.) R. Br.   Musk Orchid   Sir T. G. Cullum 1779

Native. Grassy places on chalky soils, and on the edges of fens. Almost certainly extinct. Last record c. 1936, from Redgrave Fen (R. Burn).
Recorded in Hind's Flora from a chalk-pit near Sicklesmere and at Lt. Saxham and Bury St Edmunds.

Coeloglossum viride (L.) Hartm.   Frog Orchid   J. Andrews 1744
(*Habenaria viridis* (L.) R. Br.)

Native. In old pastures and rough semi-scrub areas. This orchid must now be very rare in the County. I have not seen a specimen for 30 years. At one time it was fairly frequent, although overlooked by many botanists, because of its small size and insignificant appearance, blending with grasses and other vegetation. Its habitats in Suffolk were the old horse pastures which existed on most farms before the introduction of tractors.
W: 86, Bury St Edmunds; 95, Thorpe Morieux; Hitcham.
E: 04, Naughton; 05, Barking; 16, Debenham, 1960; 34; 48, Sotterley.
Hb. Ipswich Museum: 'In the boggy uncultivated part of a field N.W. of Boss Hall, between the Bramford and the Sproughton Roads,' c. 1810 (John Notcutt).

Gymnadenia conopsea (L.) R. Br. ssp. **conopsea**   Fragrant Orchid   Sir J. Cullum 1773
(*Habenaria conopsea* (L.) Benth.)

Native. Old calcareous pastures, chalk grassland and old earthworks and quarries. Very rare, possibly now extinct.
Hind's Flora records *G. conopsea* as occurring in all the districts, in moist meadows and fens. Ssp. *conopsea* is a plant of much drier habitats than ssp. *densiflora*. I consider Hind to have been incorrect and that this Orchid was already local or scarce in the 19th century. There are certainly no examples in the majority of the Suffolk herbaria and it has been completely absent from large areas of the County during my explorations. Specimens of ssp. *conopsea* have only been observed on the edge of Newmarket Heath in Cambridgeshire. A. L. Bull found it in two old pastures at Hitcham, but these were ploughed up about 1950. M. Bendix records it at Coddenham in 1960 and there are also unverified records for the Stour Valley.
W: 95, Hitcham.
E: 15, Coddenham.

Ssp. **densiflora** (Wahlenb.) Lindl.   Marsh Fragrant Orchid   F. W. Simpson 1930

Native. Calcareous grassy fens. Rare and decreasing.
This subspecies is usually a very much larger plant with long tapering dense spikes which

are very fragrant. Formerly to be found in a few habitats in considerable numbers. It is possible that ssp. *densiflora* is a habitat form.

W: 97, Market Weston.

E: 07, Redgrave and Thelnetham Fens, 1981; 46, Theberton, now extinct; 58, Kessingland.

White and pink-flowered forms at Redgrave Fen.   *Illustrated page 519*

PLATANTHERA   BUTTERFLY ORCHIDS

Hind's Flora lists a number of sites for both species. He calls the greater Butterfly Orchid the 'Wood Butterfly Orchis', indicating its preference for this type of habitat; and the Lesser Butterfly Orchid the 'Field Butterfly Orchis', stating that its grows in pastures and on heaths. Although I have searched all possible Suffolk habitats over a number of years, and examined many old herbaria, I have yet to discover an authentic specimen of the Lesser Butterfly Orchid, and no botanist has yet been able to produce a specimen.

Although the Greater Butterfly Orchid prefers woodland glades, it also grows in rough pastures and neglected fields, especially on the Boulder Clay, with other species of Orchid. The type of habitat that the Lesser Butterfly Orchid requires is damp, heathy pasture or marginal fen, and one would expect to find it on the edge of Redgrave Fen, or similar habitats which occur in the County. It occurs in Norfolk on such sites.

However, I have observed both species of the Butterfly Orchid growing together in hilly pastures on various sites in Northern England, Scotland and Ireland, and on the Continent. They occur together in open habitats. Other plants which occur in such sites are typical of acid soils, such as *Calluna vulgaris* and *Pedicularis sylvatica*.

Platanthera chlorantha (Cust.) Rchb.   John Notcutt c. 1820
(*Habenaria chlorantha* (Cust.) Bab., non Spreng.)   Greater Butterfly Orchid
                                                       Wood Butterfly Orchid

Native. In woods, copses, old scrub and pastures on chalky soil. The number of flowering spikes of this most attractive Orchid varies from year to year. Now scarce and decreasing, due to the changes in the management of the old Oak woods which this species favours. Coppicing, which encouraged growth, has now almost ceased, and coniferous trees have replaced the native deciduous species in many former habitats.

W: 64; 75; 84; 86; 87; 95; 96; 97.

84, Acton, 1979; 96, Hessett, 1977.

E: 04; 05; 06; 07; 15; 17; 24; 25; 26; 27; 28; 38; 46; 47; 48; 58.

04, Raydon, 1981; 05/06, Onehouse, 1979; 07, Botesdale, 1977.

Hb. Ipswich Museum: 'Plentifully under the trees, S.W. of Bourne Bridge', c. 1820 (John Notcutt). This site was probably destroyed when the railway was constructed.

Illustrated page 519

Platanthera bifolia (L.) L. C. M. Rich.   Lesser Butterfly Orchid   Sir J. Cullum 1773
(*Habenaria bifolia* (L.) R. Br.)   Field Butterfly Orchid

Native. Wet heaths, old pastures and margins of fens. No recent records. The earliest record by Sir J. Cullum may well refer to *P. chlorantha*. At this period only one species, *P. bifolia,* was recognised. Hind, in his Flora, states that older localities for *P. bifolia* have been omitted as possibly referring to *P. chlorantha*. Even so, I believe that his records for *P. bifolia* are incorrect, with the possible exceptions of those for Troston, near Barton

Mere, Weybread and Mendham. This species rarely occurs in woods and could be mistaken for small specimens of *P. chlorantha*.

Ophrys apifera Huds.   Bee Orchid   Dale 1690

Native. Rough pastures, embankments, quarries and verges. Usually on chalky soils, especially the Boulder Clay. Very rarely on sands and gravels. Less frequent than formerly. It was sometimes abundant on derelict farmland between 1930 and 1940 and on airfields between 1950 and 1960.
W: All squares except 65; 66; 68; 74; 75; 87; 88; 93; 97; 98.
84, Chilton, 1981; 94, Lavenham, 1976.
E: All squares except 13; 23; 33; 34; 44; 47; 40; 50.
04, Hadleigh, 1981; 14, Bramford, 1981; 25, Burgh and Boulge, 1981.
Illustrated page 521
Var. **trollii** (Heg.) Druce, Wasp Orchid, recorded from Whatfield and Monk Soham.
Var. **chlorantha** Godf. at Gt Blakenham and formerly at Grundisburgh.
Varieties with white, greenish-white or pale yellow flowers are not uncommon.
Hb. Ipswich Museum: white Bee Orchid from Burstall, 1835.   *Illustrated page 521*

Ophrys fuciflora (Crantz) Moench   Late Spider Orchid   H. C. Watson 1800
(*O. arachnites* (L.) Reichard)

This species is recorded in Hind's Flora from near Bury St Edmunds, but was believed by him to have been a mistake. There have been no other records, but it is possible that it may have occurred in Suffolk.

Ophrys sphegodes Mill.   Early Spider Orchid   Ray c. 1670
(*O. aranifera* Huds.)

Native in S. and E. England. Local or rare in grassy places on Chalk or Limestone. Recorded in Henslow & Skepper for a chalk-pit at Dallinghoo. This is thought to be a mistake for Ballingdon, where the species was recorded by Ray in c. 1670 and by J. Andrews in 1745. Hind repeated Henslow & Skepper's records for Westley Bottom, Gt and Lt. Saxham, Sicklesmere, Ickworth and Chevington.
There is a herbarium specimen in Ipswich Museum from a chalk-pit near Bury, 1793, possibly collected by Rev. G. R. Leathes. There are no known records for the present century. Last record, 1793.

Ophrys insectifera L.   Fly Orchid   Dale 1690
(*O. muscifera* Huds.)

Native. Woods, copses and scrub usually on Chalk and Chalky Boulder Clay. Rare and decreasing.
In 1929, in a small wood in East Suffolk, I found about 50 flowering plants. The exact site has so far remained a closely guarded secret, so as to safeguard the species from the many orchid vandals. At present the habitat is still reasonably safe and the orchid survives, but certain dangers have arisen which may affect it in the future. The number of flowering spikes varies from year to year. In 1981 I counted 37. It is hoped that if the site is discovered in the future by other naturalists, the same code of secrecy will be followed.
W: 64; 84; 95.
E: 04; 05; 06; 24.

Recorded since 1930 from Acton, Hessett, Nedging, Elmsett, Whatfield, Ringshall, Gt Finborough, Barking, Offton, Raydon and Bacton, but now extinct in the majority of these sites. *Illustrated page 521*

Himantoglossum hircinum (L.) Spreng.   Lizard Orchid   Finder unknown 1812
(*Orchis hircina* (L.) Crantz)   Goat Orchid

Native. Grassy banks, old pastures, scrub, road verges and quarries on chalky soils and on Red and Coralline Crags. Rare and uncertain in appearance from year to year. Most of the following records represent single occurrences.
W: 78, Lakenheath, two sites, 1980; 88, roadside between Brandon and Santon Downham.
E: 05, Stowmarket, site now reclaimed (F. W. Simpson); 13, Tattingstone, on Red Crag, pre-1950; 15, Coddenham, pre-1940; 23, Landguard Common, pre-1940; 35, Campsey Ash; 36, Saxmundham; 45, Sudbourne, on Coralline Crag, 1935 (F. W. Simpson).
There is only one record in Hind's Flora, namely from Great Glemham by Rev. E. N. Bloomfield in 1847. The original record is from Marlesford Hall on July 13th, 1812.
Illustrated page 522

Orchis militaris L.   Military Orchid   Mrs M. Southwell 1955
Soldier Orchid

Native. The discovery of a fine colony of this rare orchid in Mildenhall, West Suffolk (sq. 77) by Mrs M. Southwell in 1955, ranks as one of the most interesting records made in the area during the B.S.B.I. Mapping Scheme. The habitat is a small and deep disused chalk-pit on Forestry Commission land, now surrounded by coniferous plantations. In the 1930's, the area was fairly open Breckland with various grasses and Sand Sedge, and one would hardly have expected to find this orchid in the area. It probably derived from windborne seed, perhaps at the beginning of this century. The date of the pit, or when it was last worked, is unknown. The number of flowering spikes fluctuates from year to year, up to a maximum of about 200.
As it is fairly close to a main road and a picnic area, it has been necessary to enclose the site to protect it from collectors, vandals and photographers, who would otherwise damage the seedlings by trampling. It is under the management of the Suffolk Trust and the Forestry Commission. *Illustrated page 519*

Orchis ustulata L.   Burnt Orchid   Sir J. Cullum 1773
Dark-winged Orchid

Native. On chalky banks and heaths. The only two records this century are from Shelland, 1921 (F. Woolnough) 'Nature Notes' in East Anglian Daily Times and Hadleigh, 1961 (Sir C. Morris). Probably now extinct in Suffolk. Recorded in Hind's Flora from Cavenham, Risby Heath, Dalham and Newmarket Heath.

Orchis morio L.   Green-winged Orchid   Sir J. Cullum 1773
Green-veined Orchid

Native. In old pastures and semi-scrub. Formerly frequent, now rare, and exterminated in many localities. The colour of the flowers is very variable, from dark reddish purple to paler shades of pink, rose, cream and white.
W: 67; 76; 77; 78; 83; 84; 87; 93; 94; 95.
77, Mildenhall, 1976.

ORCHIDACEAE

E: 03; 04; 05; 06; 07; 13; 15; 16; 24; 25; 27; 34; 36; 37; 38; 39; 46; 47; 48; 49; 59; 40.
06, Haughley, 1981 (Mrs J. Harris); 25, Monewden, plentiful in an old pasture, Rookery Farm, 1981; 27, Fressingfield, 1981; 36, Cransford.
Now extinct in most of the above squares.   *Illustrated page 518*

Orchis mascula (L.) L.   Early Purple Orchid   Sir J. Cullum 1773
                               Cuckoo Flower

Native. Woods, copses, old pastures and woody lanes, chiefly on clay soils. Frequent, but decreasing. The number of flowering specimens varies each season. This is an Orchid especially of coppiced deciduous woodland. Formerly also common in pastures, but suitable old untreated pastures have now almost all disappeared from the County. It is absent from many parishes, especially in Breckland.
W: All squares except 65; 66; 67; 68; 77; 78; 88; 98.
94, Groton Wood, 1981; 95, Monks' Park Wood, 1980; Cockfield, 1980.
E: All squares except 44; 49; 50.
25, Monewden, 1981, growing with *O. morio*; 36, Cransford, 1979. *Illustrated page 518*
Peliorate forms recorded from: 94, Milden; 95, Cockfield; 24, Falkenham.
An attractive variety with white flowers and unspotted leaves occurs very occasionally.
                                                               Illustrated page 522

Orchis mascula × morio   F. W. Simpson 1926
One specimen of this rare hybrid was found in a small damp pasture at Waldringfield. Both parent species were growing abundantly. The soil was alluvium, mixed with Red Crag sand and broken shells. The site has since been ploughed up.

DACTYLORHIZA FUCHSII AND D. MACULATA

COMMON AND HEATH SPOTTED ORCHIDS

D. fuchsii in Suffolk is usually associated with damp, woodland glades and rough pastures on the Boulder Clay. It is sometimes also found in much wetter habitats, such as marshes and fens. *D. maculata* is usually found on wet heaths and pastures where the soil is decidedly acid. Sometimes this species occurs in considerable profusion and hybrids can be found between this species and the Common Spotted Orchid and the Marsh Orchids. Occasionally both species of the Spotted Orchids can be found sharing the same habitat and it is not always easy to decide which is the correct species or hybrid.
The Heath Spotted Orchid has a very attractive spike of flowers, the lips of which are often very strongly marked with lines or dots. The lips are much wider than those of the Common Spotted Orchid. However, in Suffolk there do appear to be some differences in the Heath Spotted Orchid found in wet pastures and those of heaths growing among Heather and other plants.

Dactylorhiza fuchsii (Druce) Soó ssp. **fuchsii**   Common Spotted Orchid
(*Dactylorchis fuchsii* (Druce) Vermeul.)   Wood Spotted Orchid
                                                       Sir J. Cullum 1773
Native. Woods, copses, scrub, wet pastures, marshes and quarries, chiefly on the Chalky Boulder Clay. Frequent, and occasionally abundant, but decreasing as its habitats are destroyed. Very variable in the colour and markings of its flowers.

381

W: All squares except 66; 67; 68; 78; 86.
76, Dalham, 1980; 95, Bradfield Woods, 1980; 97, Coney Weston, 1981.
E: All squares except 03; 44; 45; 49.
04, Raydon, 1981; 17, Redlingfield, 1977; 24, Hasketon, 1981; 47, Bramfield, 1979.
Illustrated page 462 and page 520

Dactylorhiza fuchsii × praetermissa   Leopard Spotted Marsh Orchid
(*D.* × *grandis* (Druce) P. F. Hunt   F. W. Simpson 1937
Orchis pardalina Pugsl.)

In marshes and old wet pits. Occasionally in quantity and more robust than either of the parents. An attractive hybrid which is very variable, with forms intermediate between the parents.
W: 77; 94; 97; 98.
97, Coney Weston, 1981.
E: 05; 07; 14; 15; 24; 34; 35; 49; 40.
07, Redgrave, 1937; 23/24, Nacton, 1981; 24, Foxhall, 1977; 34, Sutton.
All parish records, F. W. Simpson.

Dactylorhiza fuchsii × incarnata   F. W. Simpson 1937
(*D.* × *kernerorum* (Soó) Soó)

In fens and marshes. Very rare.
E: 07, Redgrave Fen.

Dactylorhiza maculata (L.) Soó ssp. **ericetorum** (Linton) P. F. Hunt & Summerhayes
(*Dactylorchis maculata* ssp. *ericetorum* (Linton) Vermeul.)   Sir J. Cullum 1773
        Heath Spotted Orchid

Native. Moist, heathy pastures and marshes. Locally frequent, sometimes abundant in a few habitats, but generally decreasing due to drainage and ploughing. Extinct in many of the squares listed below.
W: 93; 94.
E: 03; 04; 13; 14; 15; 23; 24; 25; 33; 34; 35; 36; 39; 45; 46; 47; 58; 40.
03, Capel St Mary, 1981 (N. V. Hunt); 24, Martlesham, 1975; Hemley, 1980; 45, Snape, 1977; 46, Sizewell, 1977.   *Illustrated page 520*

Dactylorhiza fuchsii × maculata   R. Burn 1937
(*D.* × *transiens* (Druce) Soó)

Old pastures. Rare, perhaps overlooked.
E: 04, Whatfield, 1937, site ploughed up in 1940; 36, Cransford, 1972; 46, Sizewell, 1967 (F. W. Simpson).

Dactylorhiza maculata × praetermissa   Hybrid Marsh Orchid   F. W. Simpson 1938
(*D.* × *hallii* (Druce) Soó)

In marshes, usually where the two species occur. The hybrids are often very fine and vigorous, and much larger than the parents. Although *D. maculata* prefers acid habitats, and *D. praetermissa* alkaline or basic soils, both species show considerable tolerance in many sites.
E: 14, Belstead, 1976; 24, Lt. Bealings and Martlesham, 1975; Foxhall, 1977; 34, Sutton,

1979; 45, Snape, 1976; 46, Sizewell, 1975; 40, Belton, 1977. All these records, F. W. Simpson.

One habitat at Sizewell has been destroyed in preparation for a second Nuclear Power Station. *Illustrated page 520*

Dactylorhiza incarnata (L.) Soó   Early Marsh Orchid   Dr White 1860

Native. In fens, marshes and wet pastures. Rare and decreasing. Flowers usually pale pink or creamy white. Leaves light green, narrow and unspotted. The subspecies have not been separated in the records below.

W: 77, Tuddenham; Icklingham; 83, Cornard Mere; 86; 88; 93, Arger Fen, Bures; 96, Tostock; 97, Hopton Fen.

E: 04, Whatfield, c. 1932 (R. Burn); 05; 07, Redgrave and Thelnetham Fens; 13, Bentley; 25, Melton, 1980 (E. Milne-Redhead); 34, Butley; 35, Snape; Chillesford; 36, Gt Glemham; Benhall; Sternfield; 38; 46, Dunwich; 47, Walberswick; Blythburgh; 49, Beccles; 58, Benacre; 59, Lowestoft; 40, Belton.

This species is probably now extinct in many of these sites due to draining and ploughing. *Illustrated page 520*

Ssp. **incarnata**   F. W. Simpson c. 1930

Native. In fens and marshes. Rare and decreasing.

W: 67, Mildenhall; 77, Cavenham Heath; 78, Wangford; Lakenheath; 86, Fornham St Genevieve.

E: 07, Redgrave Fen; Thelnetham Fen; 46, East Bridge; Theberton; 47, between Wenhaston and Blythburgh Common.

Ssp. **pulchella** (Druce) Soó   F. W. Simpson 1930

Native. In fens and marshes. Very rare. Possibly overlooked. A bright-flowered form.
E: 07, Redgrave Fen.

Ssp. **ochroleuca** (Boll) P. F. Hunt & Summerh.   F. W. Simpson 1930

Native. In fens and marshes. Rare and decreasing.
W: 97, Coney Weston, 1981.
E: 07, Redgrave Fen, 1930-1980.

Dactylorhiza praetermissa (Druce) Soó   Common Marsh Orchid   Sir J. Cullum 1773
                                              Southern Marsh Orchid

Native. In wet cattle and hay pastures, marshes, alkaline fens, ditches, chalk-pits and quarries. Locally frequent and sometimes abundant. Extinct in many of its former sites. Leaves clear, mid-green and unspotted. It usually has much larger spikes than *D. incarnata,* which commences to flower first. However, specimens of *D. praetermissa* are often small when growing in sites which may be dry in summer.

W: 77; 83; 84; 86; 93; 94; 95; 96; 97; 98.
86, Timworth; Culford, 1981; 97, Coney Weston, 1981.
E: 04; 05; 07; 13; 14; 24; 25; 34; 35; 36; 38; 45; 46; 47; 48; 58; 59; 40; 50.
14, Bramford; 23/24, Nacton, 1981; Hemley, 1980; 25, Bromeswell, 1980; 36, Parham, 1981; 59, Carlton Colville. *Illustrated page 520*

Dactylorhiza traunsteineri (Saut.) Soó   Narrow-leaved Marsh Orchid
E. L. Swann c. 1958

Native. In marshes and fens. Rare.
W: 97, Weston Fen; Coney Weston, 1981 (F. W. Simpson).
E: 07, Redgrave, Hinderclay and Thelnetham Fens.   *Illustrated page 520*

Aceras anthropophorum (L.) Ait. f.   Green-man Orchid   J. Andrews 1744
Man Orchid

Native. On dry chalky banks and in old grassy quarries. Now very rare, due to the destruction of habitats. Botanists sometimes confuse this species with the Common Twayblade, *Listera ovata,* which also has spikes of green flowers. The Common Twayblade however has two large ovate leaves at the base of the flowering stems.
W: 94, Semer, roadside verge, last seen 1945.
E: 04, Nedging, formerly in chalk-pit and on verge of grassy drive, last seen c. 1975. The private verge is now frequently mown preventing the growth of this Orchid. 05, Wattisham, road verge, 1940-81; 14, Bramford, 1980; Lt. Blakenham; 15, Gt Blakenham.
In the 1930's there was a colony on the bank of a grassy lane at Nedging Tye, and in a small chalk-pit, near Sproughton, now part of an Industrial Estate. Hind's Flora gives 27 records.   *Illustrated page 519*

Anacamptis pyramidalis (L.) L. C. M. Rich.   Pyramidal Orchid   Sir J. Cullum 1775
(*Orchis pyramidalis* L.)

Native. Grassy waysides, banks, quarries and churchyards on Boulder Clay and Chalk. Very occasionally on Red and Coralline Crags. Well distributed.
W: All squares except 65; 68; 74; 75; 83; 88.
76, Dalham, 1981; Hargrave, 1980.
E: All squares except 03; 23; 33; 44; 45; 47; 57; 58; 59; 40; 50.
04, Hadleigh, 1981; 14, Bramford, 1981; 15, Gt Blakenham, 1980.   *Illustrated page 519*
White-flowered variety recorded from Bramford and Needham Market.

ARACEAE

ARUM FAMILY

Acorus calamus L.   Sweet Flag   T. Martyn 1797
Sweet Sedge

Introduced. Native in S. and E. Asia, N. and W. America. Found on the edges of ponds, ornamental lakes and rivers. Not frequent.
W: 67; 77, Mildenhall; 78, Brandon; 86, Ickworth, 1956; 95, Cockfield Rectory moat, introduced by Dr Babington, and still there in c. 1950.
E: 13, Holbrook, 1974 (M. A. Hyde); 38, Darsham; 39, Mettingham, 1976; 49, Beccles; Fritton, 1975; 40, Burgh Castle.
Hb. Atkins: specimen from Bungay, 1907.

ARUM

The Wild Arum (*Arum maculatum*) is a very variable species. In Suffolk, the form with unspotted leaves is more frequent. The shape of the leaves of both forms vary considerably. Some have rounded lobes at their bases, others have pointed lobes and are generally more arrow-shaped. The veining also varies, some plants having conspicuous white veins, whilst in others the veins are scarcely noticeable. Examples with arrow-shaped, unspotted leaves with conspicuous white veins can easily be mistaken for the Italian Arum (*A. italicum* ssp. *italicum*).

In the unspotted form the hood (or spathe) can also be deceptive, often being greenish-white or light yellow. The spike (or spadix) is pale yellow, almost identical to the Italian Arum. The latter usually has much larger leaves with wavy margins. These appear during late October, much earlier than those of the Wild Arum. Spotted-leaved forms of the Wild Arum have darker green and purple hoods and chocolate-coloured spikes.

Arum maculatum L.   Wild Arum   Sir J. Cullum 1773
Lords-and-Ladies
Cuckoo Pint

Native. Woods, hedges, thickets and old quarries, in shady habitats. Very frequent. The form with unspotted leaves (var. **immaculatum** Mutel) is by far the commoner form in Suffolk.
All squares.   *Illustrated page 456*

Arum italicum Mill. ssp. **italicum**   Italian Arum   F. W. Simpson 1970

Introduced. Native of S. and W. England and S. Europe. The plant was probably introduced into Suffolk in the middle of the 19th century, when it became popular with gardeners. It is also spread by bird-sown seeds.
E: 13, Woolverstone, 1970-79 (F. W. Simpson, detd. by Dr C. T. Prime), growing with other introductions; 14, Bramford, old shrubbery, 1975; Gt Bealings, 1971-76, in two old plantations with other introductions (F. W. Simpson); 34, Boyton, 1972 (L. W. Howard).

LEMNACEAE

DUCKWEED FAMILY

Lemna polyrhiza L.   Greater Duckweed   Rev. G. Crabbe 1798

Native. In ponds, lakes, dykes and rivers. Local, but often overlooked.
W: 77; 78; 83; 84; 86; 94; 95; 96; 97.
83, in the R. Stour at Bures.
E: 03; 04; 05; 06; 14; 23; 34; 45; 46; 48; 49; 59; 40.
14, in the R. Gipping between Ipswich and Bramford, 1981 (M. A. Hyde); 59, Blundeston Marshes, 1975 (Mrs E. M. Hyde); 40, Belton, 1977.

Lemna trisulca L.   Ivy-leaved Duckweed   Sir J. Cullum 1773

Native. In ponds, dykes, rivers and fens. Common.
W: All squares except 66; 93.
67, Mildenhall, 1977; 94, Brent Eleigh, 1981.

E: All squares except 15; 17; 27; 58.
24, Purdis Heath, 1979; 39, Mettingham, 1980; 44, Gedgrave, 1976.

Lemna minor L.   Common Duckweed   Rev. G. Crabbe 1798
    Lesser Duckweed

Native. In ponds, rivers and ditches. Very common. Increases rapidly, but not always found with flowers.
All squares.

Lemna gibba L.   Fat Duckweed   D. Stock 1835
    Gibbous Duckweed

Native. In rivers, ponds and dykes, fairly frequent but often overlooked, as it associates with *L. minor*. It is common in East Suffolk along the coastal belt, but rarer in West Suffolk.
W: 68; 74; 83; 84; 88; 94; 95; 97.
E: 03; 14; 15; 17; 23; 33; 39; 44; 46; 47; 49; 59; 40.
14, in the R. Gipping, Ipswich to Bramford, 1978; 23, Walton, 1980; 39, in the R. Waveney, Mettingham, 1976; 40, Belton, 1977.

SPARGANIACEAE

BUR-REED FAMILY

Sparganium erectum L. ssp. **erectum**   Branched Bur-reed   Sir J. Cullum 1773
(*S. ramosum* Huds.)   Great Bur-reed

Native. In ponds and ditches and beside streams and rivers. Common.
W: All squares except 66; 76.
78, Brandon, in the Lt. Ouse, 1980; 86, Bury St Edmunds, in ditch, 1979; 95, Bradfield Woods, 1980; 93, in the R. Stour at Lt. Cornard, 1979.
E: All squares.
14, in the R. Gipping, Ipswich to Bramford, 1981; 24, Brightwell, in pond, 1981; 25, Bromeswell, 1980; 35, Ufford in the R. Deben, 1981; 47, Henham.
Ssp. **microcarpum** (Neum.) Domin.
E: 48, Frostenden; 49, Beccles Marshes.
Ssp. **neglectum** (Beeby) Schinz & Thell.
W: 77, Icklingham; 95.
E: 04, Kersey.
Further work is required on this species in Suffolk.

Sparganium emersum Rehm.   Unbranched Bur-reed   Sir J. Cullum 1773
(*S. simplex* Huds., pro parte)   Floating Bur-reed

Native. In ditches, ponds and slow-flowing rivers. Formerly not uncommon, now scarce.
W: 77; 78; 86; 87; 88; 94; 96; 97.
E: 03; 04; 07; 14; 15; 17; 24; 25; 34; 36; 37; 38; 39; 45; 46; 47; 48; 49; 58; 59.
17, Palgrave, 1980; 39, Mettingham, 1976; 49, North Cove, 1975.
Hb. Ipswich Museum: 'In ditches with *S. ramosum,* but not quite so common. On the east side of the Locks near the foot bridge with *Butomus umbellatus* and *Samolus valerandi',* c. 1820 (John Notcutt).

SPARGANIACEAE

Sparganium minimum Wallr. Small Bur-reed J. Andrews 1746

Native. In ponds, ditches and pools, in bogs and fens. Rare. No recent records.
W: 78, Lakenheath; Wangford.
E: 07, Redgrave Fen, c. 1950; 49, Carlton Colville.
Hind recorded it from Mildenhall, Eriswell, Gedding, Wangford, Lavenham, Bricett Wood, and a ditch near the Gipping at Ipswich.

TYPHACEAE

REEDMACE FAMILY

Typha latifolia L. Great Reedmace Sir J. Cullum 1773
  Bulrush

Native. In ponds, dykes, marshes and the margins of rivers. Frequent.
All squares except 65; 76. *Illustrated page 480*

Typha angustifolia L. Lesser Reedmace Rev. G. Crabbe 1798
  Lesser Bulrush

Native. In ponds, dykes and on the margins of rivers. Not very frequent and decreasing. Now extinct in a number of the recorded sites.
W: All squares except 64; 65; 66; 67; 74; 75; 76; 85; 88; 93; 98.
78, Lakenheath.
E: All squares except 04; 06; 17; 26; 27; 37; 46; 48; 58; 50.
13, Woolverstone, 1981; 33, Bawdsey, 1978; King's Fleet, 1979; 36, Benhall Green, 1981; 59, Sprat's Water, Carlton Colville, 1980.

Typha angustifolia × latifolia F. W. Simpson 1934
(*T. × glauca* Godr.)

This hybrid is not uncommon and is usually intermediate in size between the two parent species. Marshes, dykes and ponds. Possibly confused with *T. angustifolia*.
E: 03, Flatford; 13, Holbrook; Brantham; 15, Gt Blakenham, 1972; 23, Trimley Marshes; 33, King's Fleet, 1977; 45, Sudbourne Park.

CYPERACEAE

SEDGE FAMILY

Eriophorum angustifolium Honck. Common Cotton-grass Sir J. Cullum 1773
(*E. polystachion* L., nom. ambig.)

Native. In fens, wet heaths and bogs. Formerly frequent, now very scarce, due to drainage and ploughing up of habitats and to afforestation.
W: 68; 77; 78; 87; 98.
77, Cavenham, c. 1970.
E: 07; 24; 25; 35; 37; 45; 46; 47; 49; 58; 59; 40; 50.
07, Redgrave Fen; 45, Snape, 1978; 46, Aldringham, 1978; 47, Walberswick, 1979.

Eriophorum gracile Roth   Slender Cotton-grass   Sir J. Cullum 1773
Native. In bogs and fens.
Records in Hind's Flora of *E. minus* Koch (?*E. gracile* Roth) for Hopton Fen, Thelnetham, Brandon and Lavenham were probably small forms of *E. angustifolium.*

Eriophorum latifolium Hoppe   Broad-leaved Cotton-grass   ?E. Skepper 1860
(*E. paniculatum* Druce)
Native. In bogs and wet ditches. Probably extinct. This species does not occur in acid bogs.
W: 84, Acton, 1936-52; 94, Brent Eleigh, 1936-40. Both records by F. W. Simpson.
Recorded in Hind's Flora for Tuddenham, Mildenhall, Somerleyton, Belton and Worlingham. These seem unlikely sites.   *Illustrated page 62*

Scirpus caespitosus L.   Deer-grass   J. Andrews 1729
(*Trichophorum caespitosum* (L.) Hartm.)
Native. On wet heaths and in fens. Very local, rare and decreasing.
W: Not recorded recently. Hind listed Market Weston Fen and Cavenham.
E: 07; 46, Westleton, 1978 (Mrs E. M. Hyde).

Scirpus maritimus L.   Sea Club-rush   Paget 1834
Native. In salt marshes, beside tidal rivers and ditches. Very frequent, often abundant and dominant. Sometimes inland, as in a Bramford quarry.
E: 03; 13; 14; 23; 24; 25; 33; 34; 35; 44; 45; 46; 47; 49; 57; 58; 59; 40; 50.
    Illustrated page 498

Scirpus sylvaticus L.   Wood Club-rush   J. Andrews 1744
Native. Beside ponds and in wet woods. Now very scarce. Probably extinct in the majority of squares listed below.
W: 75; 85; 93; 96; 98.
E: 13; 14; 16; 24; 34; 35; 37; 46; 47.
13, Holbrook, 1974 (M. A. Hyde); Bentley, 1980 (Mrs E. M. Hyde); 47, Yoxford, 1974 (J. Shackles), possibly in the same habitat as found by Davy in 1794.
There is a specimen in Hb. Ipswich Museum from Burstall in 1856.

Scirpus lacustris L.   Common Bulrush   J. Andrews 1739
(*Schoenoplectus lacustris* (L.) Palla)
Native. In rivers, ponds, lakes and dykes. Frequent.
W: 67; 74; 83; 84; 87; 88; 93; 94; 96; 97; 98.
67, Freckenham, 1977; 83, Lt. Cornard, 1979; 97, Sapiston and Lt. Fakenham, 1980.
E: 03; 04, in the R. Brett, Hadleigh, 1981; 05; 13; 14, in the R. Gipping between Sproughton and Bramford, 1980; 15; 16; 23; 25; 28; 33; 36; 39; 45; 46; 47; 49; 59; 50.

Scirpus tabernaemontani C. C. Gmel.   Glaucous Bulrush   Mrs Casborne 1833
(*Schoenoplectus tabernaemontani* (C. C. Gmel.) Palla)
Native. In ditches, pools and brackish wet places, usually near the sea. Frequent, but decreasing, as many habitats have recently been destroyed. This is usually a coastal species, frequently associated with *S. maritimus.* It is very similar to *S. lacustris.*

W: Not recorded recently, possibly overlooked. Hind lists Lesser Ouse at Knettishall and Pakenham Fen.
E: 03; 13; 23; 24; 33; 34; 36; 44; 45; 46; 47; 48; 49; 58; 40; 50.
23, ditches at Erwarton and Shotley, 1981; Trimley St Mary, 1981; 24, Woodbridge, 1976; 33, near Felixstowe Ferry, 1977; 34, Boyton, 1979.

Scirpus setaceus L.   Bristle Scirpus   J. Andrews 1728
(*Isolepis setacea* (L.) R. Br.)   Bristle Club-rush

Native. On wet heaths, usually where there is sand or gravel. Also on old, wet pastures. Rare and decreasing.
W: 96; 97; 98.
96, Woolpit, 1979; 97, Fakenham Wood.
E: 03; 13; 14; 23; 46; 47; 49; 59; 40.
49, North Cove, 1976; 40, Fritton, 1976; Belton, 1977.

Scirpus cernuus Vahl   Nodding Scirpus   Rev. E. N. Bloomfield 1854
(*S. savii* Seb. & Mauri   Savi's Club-rush
Isolepis cernua (Vahl) Roem. & Schult.)

Native. In fens and bogs, where there are patches of sand and gravel. Very rare and possibly now extinct. The last record for Suffolk is from Lowestoft (sq. 59) in 1934 (E. R. Long).

Scirpus fluitans L.   Floating Scirpus   J. Andrews 1745
(*Eleogiton fluitans* (L.) Link)   Floating Club-rush

Native. In boggy pools, fens and ditches. Very rare. There are few recent records. It is, however, possible that the species still survives in Lothingland. There is one post-1930 record from sq. 46 given in the Atlas of the British Flora, and in 1971 it was recorded from Hopton (Lound Waterworks) by P. G. Lawson and A. Copping. Recorded by Hind from Mildenhall, Market Weston Fen, Lound, Benacre, Belton, Lowestoft, Fritton, and Walton.

Eleocharis acicularis (L.) Roem. & Schult.   Needle Spike-rush   Dawson Turner 1805
(*Scirpus acicularis* L.)   Needle Club-rush

Native. Found on damp heaths. The latest records are from sq. 59 and sq. 50, about 1950, but the plant has not been seen since and may now be extinct in Suffolk.
E: 59, Carlton Colville; 50.

Eleocharis quinqueflora (F. X. Hartmann) Schwarz   Few-flowered Spike-rush
(*Scirpus pauciflorus* Lightf.)   Few-flowered Club-rush
                                                Davy 1796

Native. In marshes and bogs. Extinct. Last record, c. 1860. Hind records the species under the name *Scirpus pauciflorus* Lightf. from Mildenhall, Tuddenham, Bungay, Belton, Bradwell, Lound, Worlingham, Snape.
There is a specimen in Hb. Ipswich Museum, Davy Collection, from Brome Fen in 1796.

Eleocharis multicaulis (Sm.) Sm.   Many-stemmed Spike-rush   Wigg 1805
(*Scirpus multicaulis* Sm.)

Native. In bogs on acid heaths. Very rare, possibly now extinct, though still frequent in Norfolk. Recorded prior to 1930 from squares 03; 07; 28; 38; 50. Since then there have been only three records, one from Dunwich, another from Sizewell (both in sq. 46), and another from Ipswich (sq. 14). There is a specimen from the Gipping Valley in Hb. Atkins, 1901. Last record c. 1950.

Eleocharis palustris (L.) Roem. & Schult.   Common Spike-rush   Sir J. Cullum 1773
(*Scirpus palustris* L.)   Marsh Club-rush

Native. In marshes, the sides of rivers, ponds and ditches. Less common than formerly. There are two recognised subs7ecies, ssp. **palustris** which is probably the commoner, and ssp. **microcarpa** S. M. Walters, the distribution of which is not known; it is probably more a coastal plant and the only two records of it are from Southwold (sq. 47) and Bradwell (sq. 50). No distinction has been made in the records below.
W: All squares except 64; 74; 76; 84; 94.
E: All squares except 04; 24; 25; 28; 39; 44; 48.

Eleocharis uniglumis (Link) Schult.   Slender Spike-rush
(*Scirpus uniglumis* Link)   One-glumed Bog-rush
Victoria County History of Suffolk 1911

Native. In marshes near the coast. Very rare and decreasing.
E: 46, Minsmere; Dunwich; Leiston; Westleton, 1976; 47, Dunwich; 49, Carlton Colville; 58, Benacre; 59, Oulton Marshes; Camps Heath.

Blysmus compressus (L.) Panz. ex Link   Flat Sedge   Davy 1796
(*Scirpus planifolius* Grimm   Broad Blysmus
S. compressus (L.) Pers., non Moench)

Native. Fens, damp pastures and, near the coast, on damp sand and shingle. Rare and decreasing and likely to become extinct.
W: 77, Tuddenham Fen; 83, Cornard, pre-1950; 93; 97, Weston Fen, 1960.
E: 34, Shingle Street, c. 1950; 39; 46, Dunwich, c. 1950; 47, Walberswick Marshes.
Hb. specimen, Davy Collection, from marshes at Middleton, 1796.

Blysmus rufus (Huds.) Link   Salt Marsh Flat Sedge   Sir C. J. F. Bunbury 1832
(*Scirpus rufus* (Huds.) Schrad.)   Narrow Blysmus

Native. In salt marshes. Probably extinct in Suffolk. The only record is from the edge of Thorpe Mere, near Aldeburgh, in 1832, but this habitat changed when the mere was drained in 1911-1912.
Specimen in Lady Blake's Herbarium in Ipswich Museum, from Thorpe Mere.

Cyperus longus L.   Galingale   L. W. Howard 1972

Native or introduced. Rare. First found in a marsh near the R. Deben, between Ufford and Eyke (sq. 25) in 1972. Introduced at Witnesham Horticultural Gardens.

Schoenus nigricans L.   Black Bog-rush   J. Andrews 1746

Native. Calcareous fens and wet heaths. Local and decreasing. This plant is often associated with a rich and interesting flora.

W: 77; 97; 98.
97, Hopton, 1980.
E: 07, Redgrave Fen, 1980; Thelnetham Fen, 1981; 17; 24, Bromeswell (habitat destroyed); 37; 49; 40.
There is a specimen in Hb. Davy from Brome Fen, 1796. *Illustrated page 486*

Rhynchospora alba (L.) Vahl   White Beak-sedge   Wigg 1805
Native. In ancient bogs. Now extinct in Suffolk. It was formerly to be found at Lound and Belton Bog, where it was recorded as plentiful in the early 19th century. It is still locally abundant in some Norfolk bogs. Last record, early 19th century.

Cladium mariscus (L.) Pohl   Great Fen Sedge   Wigg 1805
                             Twig-rush
Native. In fens, where it is sometimes abundant, although it has decreased in recent years.
W: 68, Lakenheath Poor's Fen; 77, Tuddenham Fen; Eriswell; 78, Pashford Poor's Fen; 97, Hopton Fen, 1981; Weston Fen, 1970.
E: 07, Thelnetham Fen, 1981; Hinderclay and Redgrave Fens; 59, Flixton; Carlton Colville. *Illustrated page 488*

Carex laevigata Sm.   Smooth-stalked Sedge   Dr G. C. Druce 1911
Native. By ponds and pools, usually in shady woods on clay soils. Rare.
W: 93, Nayland.
E: 07, Rickinghall Inferior; 58, Benacre, 1911; 59, Lowestoft.

Carex distans L.   Distant Sedge   Sir J. Cullum 1774
Native. Salt pastures, edges of sea dykes and pools. Occasional. Rare inland in fens and marshes.
W: 97, Weston Fen; Stanton Chare.
E: 23, Landguard Common, (habitat now destroyed); 33, Bawdsey; Falkenham, 1978; 34, Shingle Street, Hollesley; 35, Snape, 1981; 38, Barsham; 45, Aldeburgh, 1978; 46, Dunwich; 47, Walberswick; Blythburgh, 1980; Buss Creek, Southwold; 57, Easton Bavents; 59, Lowestoft.

Carex punctata Gaud.   Dotted Sedge   Hind 1879
The occurrence of this species in Suffolk is very doubtful, although it was recorded by Hind on gravelly banks close to the sea at Dunwich. It is very similar in growth and appearance to *C. distans* and Hind's specimen is almost certainly *C. distans.* I have searched the area many times and been unable to find any trace of this species. R. Burn's record for Blythburgh is also doubtful. *C. punctata* is a very local species.

Carex hostiana DC.   Tawny Sedge   Davy 1805
Native. In marshes, bogs and fens. Rare or overlooked.
W: 77, Mildenhall, 1956 (Mrs M. Southwell); 78, Wangford, 1974; 97.
E: 07; 45; 47.

CYPERACEAE

Carex binervis Sm. Green-ribbed Sedge Dawson Turner 1805

Native. Heaths and rough, acid pastures. Rare. This Sedge can be mistaken for *C. distans,* which grows in maritime habitats.
W: 77, Barton Mills, 1957; Tuddenham.
E: 46, Dunwich, 1966; 47, Blythburgh; 40, Ashby Warren; Fritton.

Carex flava L. Large Yellow Sedge Paget 1834

Native. In marshes and fens. Although there are several records for this species, there is some doubt that it occurs in Suffolk. The species is known to be rare and decreasing in Britain. These records may refer to *C. demissa* or *C. lepidocarpa.*
W: 95, Bradfield St Clare.
E: 07, Hinderclay Fen; 35, Wantisden; 49, Carlton Colville; 58, Benacre; 40, Belton, 1977.

Carex lepidocarpa Tausch Long-stalked Yellow Sedge Mrs M. Southwell 1955

Native. In wet, alkaline fens and marshes. Rare.
W: 77, the Dolvers, Mildenhall, 1955; 97, Weston Fen; 98.
E: 07, Redgrave Fen; Thelnetham Fen, 1981; Hinderclay Fen; 34, Hollesley, pre-1960; 35, Wantisden, (site destroyed, c. 1948); 40.

Carex demissa Hornem. Common Yellow Sedge F. W. Simpson 1924

Native. Wet heaths and heathy parts of fens. Rare and confused with other members of the *Carex flava* group. Probably extinct in most of the sites below.
W: 87, Barnham.
E: 07, Redgrave Fen; 24, Woodbridge; Bromeswell (habitat now destroyed); 35, Butley; 46, Sizewell; 49, Worlingham.

Carex serotina Mérat Small-fruited Yellow Sedge Dawson Turner 1805
(*C. oederi* auct.)

Native. In open fens and marshes. Recorded in Hind's Flora from Tuddenham St Mary, Mildenhall, Bradwell, Belton, Lound, Lowestoft, Bungay, Dunwich, Brome and Framlingham. There are records for Lakenheath Poor's Fen in 1951 and for Minsmere Level in 1964. Some confusion existed in the past over the correct naming of this species.

Carex extensa Gooden. Long-bracted Sedge Rev. G. Crabbe 1798

Native. Salt marshes and beside brackish ditches and pools. Scarce.
E: 23, Landguard Common (habitat now destroyed); 33, Felixstowe Ferry; 34, Hollesley, Shingle Street, 1981; 45, Snape; 47, Dunwich area: 58, Benacre.
All records, F. W. Simpson. *Illustrated page 502*

Carex sylvatica Huds. Wood Sedge J. Andrews 1739

Native. In woods, copses and shady places, chiefly on clay soils. Common.
W: All squares except 66; 67; 68; 77; 78; 88; 98.
94, Brent Eleigh, 1981; 95, Bradfield Woods, 1980; 97, Sapiston, 1981.
E: All squares except 33; 34; 44; 45; 49; 50.
04, Raydon, 1981; 14, Ipswich, Fishpond Covert, 1981; 24, Hasketon and Gt Bealings, 1981.
Hb. Ipswich Museum: 'Waller's Grove. May, 1819' (John Notcutt).

Carex pseudocyperus L.   Cyperus Sedge   J. Andrews 1746
                              Hop Sedge

Native. Sides of ponds and ditches and wet shady places. Locally frequent.
W: All squares except 64; 65; 66; 67; 68; 74; 76; 85; 87; 96.
78, Lakenheath (P. J. O. Trist); 97, Hopton Fen, 1981.
E: All squares except 15; 17; 25; 26; 28; 33; 36; 38; 44; 48; 59; 50.
04, Wolves Wood, 1979; Raydon Gt Wood, 1980; 07, Thelnetham, 1981; 24, Purdis
Heath, 1979; 49, North Cove, 1976; 40, Belton, 1979.   *Illustrated page 485*

Carex rostrata Stokes   Bottle Sedge   J. Andrews 1746
(*C. ampullacea* Gooden.)

Native. In bogs, fens, carrs and the margins of ponds. Rare. May be confused with *C. vesicaria.*
W: 77; 78; 84; 88; 97; 98.
E: 07; 14; 24; 35; 39; 45; 46; 48; 49; 59; 40; 50.
07, Redgrave Fen, c. 1950 (F. W. Simpson); 45, Snape, 1976-1980; 46, Aldringham, 1978
(both Mrs E. M. Hyde).
Hb. Ipswich Museum: 'With *C. acuta* in a Delph in a meadow near the Town between the
Bramford Road and the River. 28th May 1819' (John Notcutt).

Carex vesicaria L.   Bladder Sedge   Prof. Henslow 1853

Native. In bogs, fens, carrs and woodland pools. Rare.
W: 77, Barton Mills; Eriswell; 78, Lakenheath; 97, Barningham.
E: 35, Snape; 47, Wangford; 40, Belton.

Carex riparia Curt.   Greater Pond Sedge   John Notcutt c. 1820

Native. In marshes, ditches, wet woods and by rivers, streams and dykes. Also in brackish
water. Common.
W: All squares except 64; 65; 75; 76.
77, Cavenham, 1980; Icklingham, 1980; Mildenhall, 1980; 78, Brandon, 1980; 83, Lt.
Cornard, 1980.
E: All squares except 06; 16; 26; 27; 36; 37; 44.
04, Hadleigh, R. Brett, 1981; 14, Ipswich, R. Gipping, 1981; 24, Playford, R. Finn, 1981;
45, Snape, 1981.

Carex acutiformis Ehrhart   Lesser Pond Sedge   Mrs Casborne 1833
(*C. paludosa* Gooden.)

Native. Beside ponds, ditches, rivers and in swamps and wet woods. Very common and
frequently dominant. Sometimes confused with small forms of *C. riparia.*
W: All squares except 64; 65; 66; 75; 85.
Beside the R. Stour and its tributaries and adjacent marshes, 1980.
E: All squares except 28; 37; 44; 48.
04, Hadleigh, R. Brett, 1981; 13, Holbrook and Bentley, 1981; 14, Ipswich, R. Gipping,
1981; 24, Rushmere and Playford, 1981; 35, Eyke, R. Deben, 1980; 58, Benacre, 1981.
                                                          Illustrated page 486

Carex pendula Huds.   Pendulous Sedge   Sir J. Cullum 1775

Native. In ditches and damp woods, chiefly on the Chalky Boulder Clay of West Suffolk, where it is very frequent and sometimes abundant. This is one of our most attractive and largest Sedges.

W: 64; 65; 74; 75; 76; 83; 84; 85; 86; 88; 93; 94; 95; 97.

64, Withersfield; 84, Acton, 1980; 85, Whepstead, 1979; 95, Bradfield Woods, 1980.

E: 04; 05: 13; 16; 24; 26; 33; 46; 49.

24, Culpho, 1979; Foxhall, 1981; 33, Felixstowe, 1981.   *Illustrated page 455*

Carex strigosa Huds.   Thin-spiked Wood Sedge   Henslow & Skepper 1860
                                   Loose Pendulous Sedge

Native. Damp glades in old woods and shady lanes. Rare.

W: 93, Polstead; Arger Fen; 95, Cockfield, now extinct.

E: 03; 04, Offton; 13, Bentley; 14, Ipswich, Stoke Park, 1979-1981 (Mrs E. M. Hyde). Conf. E. C. Wallace.

All but the Ipswich record were made in the 1950's.

Carex pallescens L.   Pale Sedge   Mrs Casborne 1833

Native. Damp glades and clearings in woods, especially on Boulder Clay. Formerly frequent, now scarce. This is probably due to changes in management of the woods, the end of coppicing and the planting of conifers.

W: 64; 76; 77; 85; 94; 95; 96; 97.

95, Felshamhall Wood, 1978; 96, Beyton, 1972; Pakenham Wood, abundant, 1978; Woolpit, 1979; 97, Fakenham Wood.

E: 04; 05; 06; 07; 24; 25; 36; 39; 44; 46; 48; 59.

48, Sotterley Woods (Lowestoft Field Club).

Carex panicea L.   Carnation Sedge   Sir J. Cullum 1774

Native. In marshes and fens. Formerly frequent, now scarce, due to drainage and ploughing up of the ancient habitats. This Sedge is usually associated with other interesting and attractive native flora.

W: 68; 76; 77; 78; 83; 87; 93; 94; 97; 98.

78, Pashford Poor's Fen, Lakenheath; 93, Polstead, 1974; 97, Coney Weston, 1981.

E: 04; 05; 06; 07; 13; 14; 15; 16; 24; 34; 35; 36; 39; 45; 46; 48; 49; 58; 59; 40; 50.

24, Nacton, 1981; 35, Gromford, 1975; 45, Snape, 1980.

Carex limosa L.   Mud Sedge   Paget 1834
                             Bog Sedge

Native. Edges of pools in bogs. It is possible that it is now extinct in Suffolk, the only record being the original one from Belton Bog.

Carex flacca Schreb.   Glaucous Sedge   John Notcutt c. 1820
(*C. glauca* Scop.)

Native. Rough pastures, open scrub, woodland glades, road verges, quarries and railway banks. Very frequent, especially on Chalk and Chalky Boulder Clay.

W: All squares except 65; 93.

76, Hargrave, 1981; 78, Brandon, 1980; 84, Acton, 1980; 96, Pakenham Wood, 1979.

E: All squares except 13; 17; 33; 34; 44; 58.

04, Hintlesham and Raydon, 1981; 15, Barham Pits, 1980; 46, Darsham, 1981.

Hb. Ipswich Museum: 'Corner of a field between Mr Fonnereau's Grove and the Sparrow's Nest Farm. *Spiraea filipendula* is found under some trees in the same field,' c. 1820 (John Notcutt).

Carex hirta L.　　Hammer Sedge　　　　　　　　　John Notcutt 1819
　　　　　　　　　　Hairy Sedge

Native. Damp pastures, grassy waysides and heaths. Widespread and fairly common.
W: All squares.
77, Cavenham and Icklingham roadsides, 1981; 87, West Stow, 1980.
E: All squares except 27.
07, Wortham Ling, 1980; 14, Ipswich, by the R. Gipping, 1981; 24, Foxhall and Playford, 1981.
Hb. Ipswich Museum: 'By the River's side and in meadows. Near the Locks, plentiful. May 1819' (John Notcutt).

Carex lasiocarpa Ehrhart　　Slender Sedge　　　　　　Dawson Turner 1805
(*C. filiformis* auct.)　　　　　Downy-fruited Sedge

Native. In reed swamps and fens. The distribution of this Sedge in Suffolk is unknown. It is probably now extinct. Last record 1938, in a bog between Eriswell and Mildenhall (E. Nelmes). Hind's records: Lakenheath, Brandon, Mildenhall, Lound and Worlingham.

Carex pilulifera L.　　Pill Sedge　　　　　　　　　Sir J. Cullum 1774

Native. Heaths and open, heathy woods. Not uncommon.
W: 77; 86; 88.
77, Mildenhall, Butt Plantation, 1979 (Mrs E. M. Hyde).
E: 05; 06; 07; 13; 23; 24; 34; 35; 45; 46; 47; 48; 58; 59; 40; 50.
23, Harkstead, 1981; 24, Newbourn, 1981; 35, Tunstall, 1981; Butley, 1979; 46, Dunwich, 1980.

Carex caryophyllea Latourr.　　Spring Sedge　　　　　Prof. Henslow 1836
(*C. verna* Chaix)

Native. Pastures, heaths, and dry grassy places. Occasional. Certainly not as common as formerly, due to destruction of habitats, especially in East Suffolk.
W: 76; 77; 78; 83; 86; 87; 88; 97; 98.
77, Cavenham and Icklingham, 1980; Eriswell, 1980; 87, Barnham, 1980.
E: 03; 16; 17; 23; 24; 33; 35; 36; 39; 47.
24, Playford, 1981 (F. W. Simpson).

Carex ericetorum Poll.　　Silvery Heath Sedge　　　Sir W. C. Trevelyan 1829

Native. In dry, calcareous, grassy areas of Breckland. Rare.
W: 76, Risby Black Ditches, 1980; 77, Foxhole Heath, Eriswell, 1980; Icklingham, 1981; 78, Lakenheath Warren; 98, Knettishall, 1981.

Carex acuta L.　　Slender Tufted Sedge　　　　　　J. Andrews 1739

Native. Ponds, dykes, and sides of streams and rivers, and in marshes. Rare or overlooked and possibly confused with *C. acutiformis*. Very few recent records.
W: 77, Cavenham; Tuddenham Fen; 88; 93; 94, Preston and Kettlebaston, pre-1940.

E: 04, Elmsett and Hadleigh, pre-1940; 16, Mickfield, up to 1960 (F. W. Simpson); 49, North Cove; 58, Kessingland; Covehithe.

Hb. Ipswich Museum: 'With *C. riparia* by the river's side between Handford Bridge and Boss Hall. With *C. ampullacea* in a meadow near the town between Bramford and the river. May 1819' (John Notcutt).

Carex nigra (L.) Reichard   Common Sedge   Sir J. Cullum 1773
(*C. vulgaris* Fr.)

Native. In marshes and damp places, chiefly on poor, acid soils. Not as frequent as formerly. Very variable.
W: 68; 76; 77; 84; 86; 87; 88; 94; 97; 98.
84, Stanstead, c. 1960; 88, Thetford Warren.
E: 05; 07; 13; 15; 16; 23; 26; 36; 38; 39; 45; 46; 47; 49; 58; 59; 40; 50.
24, Nacton, 1981; Hemley, 1980; 25, Bromeswell Green, 1980; 39, Bungay, 1981; 45, Aldringham, 1981; 46, Westleton, 1978.

Carex elata All.   Tufted Sedge   J. Andrews 1729
(*C. hudsonii* A. Benn.)

Native. In fens, marshes and ditches. Local. Often with *C. acutiformis, C. riparia* and *Phragmites.*
W: 67; 68; 77; 78; 83; 84; 88; 96; 97; 98.
77, Cavenham, 1977; Tuddenham Fen, 1979; 78, Pashford Poor's Fen; 83, Cornard Mere.
E: 05; 07; 14; 25; 36; 46; 49; 59; 40.
25, Bromeswell Green, 1975.
Hb. Ipswich Museum: specimen collected in 1819 from between Bramford Road and the R. Gipping, Ipswich (John Notcutt).

Carex pulicaris L.   Flea Sedge   Woodward 1812

Native. Bogs, fens and wet heaths. Now very rare and decreasing.
W: 78, Wangford; Pashford Poor's Fen, 1970 (M. G. Rutterford); 97, Weston Fen.
E: 07, Thelnetham, 1981; Redgrave and Hinderclay Fens; 24, Bixley Decoy (habitat now changed); 25, Bromeswell (habitat now destroyed); 40.

Carex dioica L.   Dioecious Sedge   Sir J. Cullum 1774

Native. In bogs and fens. Rare or possibly now extinct. Last record c. 1958.
W: 97, Hopton Fen.
E: 07, Redgrave Fen, c. 1958; 46, East Bridge, 1950.

Carex paniculata L.   Great Tussock Sedge   J. Andrews 1744
                  Panicled Sedge

Native. Alder carr woods and swamps on heaths. Frequent, but decreasing.
W: All squares except 64; 65; 66; 74; 75; 76; 85.
68, Lakenheath, 1980; 77, Cavenham, 1980; 97, Hopton Fen, 1981.
E: All squares except 03; 04; 06; 15; 17; 23; 25; 26; 27; 28; 33; 37; 44; 47.
24, Foxhall, 1981; Alder Carr at Playford, 1981; 35, Eyke, 1980; 46, Westleton, 1981.

Carex appropinquata Schumacher   Fibrous Tussock Sedge   Rev. J. D. Gray 1884
(*C. paradoxa* Willd.)

Native. In fens and bogs. Rare or overlooked and confused with *C. paniculata*. It still occurs, or did until recently, in the same habitats as recorded in Hind's Flora.
W: 77, Bombay Fen, Mildenhall, 1955; Icklingham Poor's Fen; 97, Weston Fen, 1960. Hind records it for Market Weston in 1884 and between Icklingham and Mildenhall in 1887.
E: Not recorded.

Carex diandra Schrank   Lesser Tussock Sedge   Crowe 1804
(*C. teretiuscula* Gooden.)   Lesser Panicled Sedge

Native. In bogs and fens. Rare and decreasing.
W: 78, Palmer's Heath; 94, Kersey, pre-1940 (R. Burn); 97, Weston Fen.
E: 04, Semer, pre-1950 (R. Burn); 07, Hinderclay and Thelnetham Fens in the 1960's; 47, Blythburgh Reserve, 1972, detd. A. Copping.

Carex otrubae Podp.   False Fox Sedge   Paget 1834
(*C. vulpina* auct.)

Native. Edges of salt marshes, ponds, ditches and damp glades in clay woods. Widespread and common. This Sedge is sometimes mistaken for *C. vulpina* L. (Fox Sedge), which is at present unrecorded for Suffolk. Hind's records for *C. vulpina* are probably this species.
W: All squares except 66; 67; 68; 77; 88.
76, Hargrave, 1979; 94, Brent Eleigh, 1981; 87, Barnham, 1979; 95, Bradfield Woods, 1980.
E: All squares.
04, Raydon, 1981; 14, Ipswich by the R. Gipping, 1981; 23, edge of salt marsh, near Pin Mill, 1981; 26, Framlingham, near Castle, 1980.

Carex otrubae × remota   D. Stock 1832
(*C. × pseudoaxillaris* K. Richt.)

Margins of ponds and ditches on clay soil, usually growing with the parents. Formerly not uncommon, now very scarce.
W: 75, Chedburgh; 93, Newton; 94, Milden; Edwardstone; Brent Eleigh; 95, Brettenham; Felshamhall Wood, 1980.
E: 04, Offton; Elmsett; 05, Gt Bricett; Ringshall, 1980.
All these records, except those for Felshamhall Wood and Ringshall, are pre-1960.

Carex disticha Huds.   Soft Brown Sedge   John Notcutt c. 1820

Native. In wet pastures and marshes. Also beside rivers and dykes. Not very frequent, though occasionally abundant.
W: 68; 76; 77; 78; 83; 84; 86; 87; 93; 94; 95; 97; 98.
97, Coney Weston, 1981.
E: 03; 04; 07; 13; 14; 23; 24; 33; 34; 35; 45; 47; 59; 40; 50.
03, Capel St Mary, 1980; 04, Hadleigh, 1981; 24, Hemley, 1980.
Hb. Ipswich Museum: 'With *Stellaria glauca* in the wet uncultivated part of a field between Bramford Road and the River,' June, c. 1820 (John Notcutt).

Carex arenaria L.   Sand Sedge   Sir J. Cullum 1775

Native. Sandy heaths in Breckland and on sandy heaths and dunes near the sea coast. Locally abundant.
W: 67; 77; 78; 87; 88; 96; 97; 98.
Abundant in Breckland, 1981.
E: 23; 24; 33; 34; 35; 44; 45; 46; 47; 57; 58; 59; 40; 50.
Very frequent on the dunes and heaths of East Suffolk, 1981.

Carex divisa Huds.   Divided Sedge   Rev. E. A. Holmes 1850

Native. In pastures and on the sides of fresh or slightly brackish ditches near the sea. Not in very salt pastures or saltings. Rare, though locally frequent.
E: 14, Wherstead, 1975; 23, Felixstowe; Landguard Common; Trimley, 1981; Erwarton, 1981; Shotley, 1981; 24, Woodbridge; 33, Felixstowe; 34, Ramsholt, 1978; Shingle Street, Hollesley; 46, Dunwich; 47, Walberswick; Reydon; 40, near Breydon Water.

CAREX MURICATA L. Agg.

Difficulty is experienced by very many botanists in identifying the species and subspecies of the British taxa. In Suffolk we have *C. spicata*, *C. muricata* ssp. *lamprocarpa*, *C. divulsa* ssp. *divulsa* and ssp. *leersii*. *C. muricata* ssp. *muricata* is very rare in Britain and has not been found in Suffolk. *C. divulsa* is very variable and intermediates between the two subspecies are frequent. Perhaps some are only habitat variations.
R. W. David, who has made a study of the aggregate, has given considerable help, confirming and determining many of our recent finds.

Carex spicata Huds.   Spiked Sedge
(*C. contigua* Hoppe)

Native. Grassy places, hedge-banks and open woodland rides. Not very frequent, or overlooked. Prefers Chalk and Chalky Boulder Clay soils. Date of first record uncertain.
Records confirmed or determined by R. W. David:
W: 76, Barrow Bottom, 1980; 77, Cavenham ('An Ecological Flora of Breckland').
E: 04, Raydon Gt Wood, 1981; 05, Bildeston, 1980; Needham Market, 1981; 13, Woolverstone, 1980; 48, Wrentham, 1980 (P. G. Lawson).
Unconfirmed record:
E: 24, Gt Bealings, 1981.
The above records, except those for squares 77 and 48, were made by Mrs E. M. Hyde or F. W. Simpson.

Carex muricata L. ssp. **lamprocarpa** Čelak.   Prickly Sedge
(*C. pairaei* F. W. Schultz)

Native. Dry grassy banks, verges, heaths and scrub. Chiefly on sandy and gravelly soils. Frequent in Breckland and on the Sandlings.
Earlier confusion with *C. spicata* prevents our giving an accurate first record.
Records confirmed or determined by R. W. David:
W: 76, Gazeley, 1980; 87, Barnham, 1980; 98, Knettishall Heath, 1981.
E: 04, Hadleigh, 1980; 13, Tattingstone, 1980; Woolverstone, 1981; 14, Sproughton, 1980; Ipswich, 1981; 15, Barham Pits, 1979; 24, Martlesham; Kesgrave; Sutton;

Bromeswell, all 1981; 35, Blaxhall, 1980; 45, Aldeburgh, 1981.
Unconfirmed records:
W: 67, Freckenham; 76, Kentford; 77, Icklingham, 1979; West Stow, 1980; 78, Brandon; Lakenheath, 1974; 97, Coney Weston, 1981; Bardwell, 1981.
E: 13, Stutton, 1975; Holbrook Churchyard; Tattingstone, 1978; 14, Belstead, 1979; Wherstead, 1978; 23, Erwarton, 1978; Shotley, 1981; 24, Newbourn, 1981; Rushmere, 1979; Brightwell, 1981; 34, Hollesley; 35, Rendlesham; 46, Hinton, 1980; 46/47, Westleton.
All the above records were made by Mrs E. M. Hyde or F. W. Simpson.

Carex divulsa Stokes ssp. **divulsa**   Grey Sedge   J. Andrews 1746
Native. Hedge-banks, open woodland, churchyards and scrub. Frequent, especially on Chalk and Chalky Boulder Clay.
Records confirmed or determined by R. W. David:
W: 97, Sapiston ('An Ecological Flora of Breckland').
E: 03, East Bergholt, 1978; 04, Raydon Gt Wood, 1981; 05, Bildeston, 1980; 16, Wetheringsett, 1981; 23, Chelmondiston, Clamp House; 24, Hasketon, 1981; 35, Marlesford, 1981.
Unconfirmed records:
W: 65, Gt Thurlow, 1977; Lt. Thurlow, 1976; 76, Dalham, 1981; 77, Tuddenham Churchyard, 1975; 94, Brent Eleigh, 1981; 96, Pakenham, 1980.
E: 04, Hintlesham, 1976; 05, Wattisham; 07, Hinderclay Fen; Burgate, Little Green, 1977; 13, Woolverstone; 14, Bramford Churchyard, 1974; 15, Baylham, 1981; 17, Braiseworth, 1976; Redlingfield, 1977; 25, Hacheston, 1976; 33, Felixstowe, 1981; 46, Darsham, 1981; 47, Reydon, 1979; 48, Sotterley, 1980.
All the above records, except that for square 97, were made by Mrs E. M. Hyde or F. W. Simpson.

Ssp. **leersii** (Kneucker) W. Koch
(*C. polyphylla* Kar. & Kir.)

W: Recorded for seven sites in the Suffolk Breckland in 'An Ecological Flora of Breckland'.
E: 07, Redgrave Fen, 1977 (F. W. Simpson), detd. Dr C. P. Petch and E. L. Swann.

Intermediates between ssp. **divulsa** and ssp. **leersii.**

Records determined by R. W. David:
W: 76, Moulton, 1981; 86, Bury St Edmunds, 1978; 96, Elmswell, 1979.
E: 24, Playford, 1981; 48, Wrentham, 1980 (P. G. Lawson).
Records of Mrs E. M. Hyde or F. W. Simpson, apart from that for Wrentham.

Carex elongata L.   Elongated Sedge   A. R. Horwood 1917
Native. Beside ditches, in boggy meadows, and open, wet woodland. Very rare or overlooked.
E: 47, Reydon Wood, 1917. Hb. British Museum, utricles only, (comm. by R. W. David, 1977); also wet, grassy lane near a pond, possibly Sotherton, 1958 (Miss M. M. Whiting), detd. E. Nelmes; 58, Benacre, Holly Grove, 1917, but no specimen traced.

CYPERACEAE

Carex echinata Murr. Star Sedge Paget 1834
(C. stellulata Gooden.) Little Prickly Sedge
Native. In bogs and marshes. Scarce and decreasing.
W: 86; 95; 97; 98.
E: 07; 14; 16; 23; 24; 36; 39; 45; 47; 49; 58; 40; 50.
45, Snape, 1981; 46, Aldringham, 1978; 47, Walberswick, 1981; Hinton Bog, 1979.

Carex remota L. Remote Sedge Dawson Turner 1805
Native. Damp woods, sides of ditches and ponds. Common.
W: All squares except 66; 67; 68; 77; 78.
84, Acton, 1980; 94, Edwardstone, 1979; 95, Bradfield Woods, 1980; 96, Tostock, 1980.
E: All squares except 33; 44; 45; 50.
04, Raydon, 1981; 14, Ipswich, Fishpond Covert, 1981; 25, Bromeswell Green, 1980; 27, Fressingfield, 1981.

Carex curta Gooden. White Sedge Rev. G. Crabbe 1798
(C. canescens auct.)
Native. Marshes, bogs and wet heaths. Rare or overlooked. Now extinct in most of the sites listed below.
W: 84, Sudbury; 86, Rushbrooke; 93, Assington; 95, Thorpe Morieux; Felsham Wood.
E: 07, Burgate Wood; 24, Newbourn; 45, Snape, 1978; 46, Theberton; 47, Blythburgh Reserve, 1973; 59, Flixton; Lound; 40.

Carex ovalis Gooden. Oval Sedge Paget 1834
Native. In heathy pastures, marshes and woodland rides. Fairly frequent. Often associated with the Heath Spotted Orchid (*Dactylorhiza maculata* ssp. *ericetorum*).
W: 64; 77; 87; 94; 96; 97; 98.
96, Pakenham Wood, 1978; 98, Knettishall Heath.
E: 03; 04; 07; 13; 14; 15; 16; 23; 24; 25; 33; 34; 35; 39; 45; 46; 47; 48; 49; 40; 50.
04, Raydon Wood, 1981; 13, Woolverstone, 1981; Bentley, 1980; 25, Bromeswell, 1980; Bungay Common, 1981; 45, Snape, abundant, 1981.

GRAMINEAE

GRASS FAMILY

Bromus sterilis L. Barren Brome Sir J. Cullum 1773
(Anisantha sterilis (L.) Nevski)
Native or colonist. On cultivated and waste ground, especially sunny hedge-banks. Very common.
All squares.

Bromus tectorum L. Drooping Brome Rev. E. F. Linton 1886
(Anisantha tectorum (L.) Nevski)
Naturalised alien. Native of the Mediterranean Region. Locally frequent in Breckland on the edges of fields, sandy banks and heaths. First found near Thetford. Also occurs occasionally on waste ground and rubbish tips.

W: 77, Eriswell; Cavenham Heath, 1980; Mildenhall, 1978; 78, Lakenheath, 1978; 87, Elveden.
E: 04, Hadleigh, old Railway Station Yard (J. Digby).

Bromus madritensis L.   Compact Brome   Hind 1879
(*Anisantha madritensis* (L.) Nevski)

Native. Found in dry, open, sandy places. Rare. Recorded by Hind from Rede and Westleton Heath.
E: 23, Felixstowe Maltings, 1936 (F. W. Simpson).

Bromus diandrus Roth   Great Brome   F. W. Simpson 1936
(*B. maximus* auct. angl., pro parte
Anisantha diandra (Roth) Tutin)

An established alien from the Mediterranean region. Waste places, field margins, rubbish tips and waysides. Formerly only a casual, now very frequent, even dominant, especially on the light soils of Breckland. Increasing generally.
W: 67; 68; 76; 77; 78; 87; 95; 96; 97; 98.
77, Cherry Hill, Barton Mills, 1981; Cavenham Heath, 1979; 87, Culford (P. J. O. Trist); 96, Thurston, 1979; 97, Knettishall, 1981.
E: 04; 06; 07; 15; 23; 25; 26; 33; 35; 45; 58.
04, Hadleigh, old Railway Station Yard, 1980 (M. A. Hyde); 13, roadside, Holbrook, 1981; 23, Felixstowe Docks, 1936; near Coastguard Station, 1980; Shotley, 1978; 24, Kesgrave to Martlesham, along the A12, 1980; 35, Campsey Ash, 1980; 45, Knodishall, 1980.

Bromus rigidus Roth   Ripgut Grass   Hind 1883
(*B. maximus* Desf.
Anisantha rigida (Roth) Hyl.)

An established alien from S. and W. Europe. Disturbed ground on light, sandy soils. Very similar to *B. diandrus*. First recorded by Hind (as *B. maximus* Desf.) from Fakenham, West Suffolk in 1883. The identity of the specimen in Hind's herbarium at Ipswich Museum was confirmed by Dr P. M. Smith in 1979.
W: 76, Risby, edge of barley field, 1980 (E. Milne-Redhead), detd. at Kew; 77, arable land opposite Foxhole Heath, 1974 (R. P. Libbey and E. L. Swann), also in 1975 (P. J. O. Trist); 98, Euston, 1981.
E: 23, Landguard Common, 1978 (M. A. Hyde), detd. Dr P. M. Smith.

Bromus ramosus Huds.   Hairy Brome   John Notcutt c. 1820
(*B. asper* Murr.   Wood Brome
Zerna ramosa (Huds.) Lindm.)

Native. Old hedgerows, edges of woods and clearings, copses and thickets. Very frequent on the Chalk and Chalky Boulder Clay, less so on other soils. Absent from some areas of Breckland and the Sandlings.
W: All squares except 67; 68; 78.
76, Dalham, 1981; Hargrave, 1979; 95, Bradfield Woods, 1980.
E: All squares except 28; 44; 45; 58; 40; 50.
04, between Hadleigh and Raydon, 1981; 33, Felixstowe, 1980; 46, Middleton, 1979; 48, Westhall, 1979.

Bromus unioloides Kunth   Rescue Grass   F. W. Simpson 1958
(*Ceratochloa unioloides* (Willd.) Beauv.)

A casual, native of S. America. Found in waste places.
E: 05, The Tannery, Combs. Detd. by Dr J. G. Dony.

Bromus carinatus Hook. & Arn.   California Brome   Mrs E. M. Hyde 1978
(*Ceratochloa carinata* (Hook. & Arn.) Tutin)

Introduced. Native of N. America.
E: 13, Woolverstone. Conf. E. J. Clement. Spreading on to roadside verge from adjacent field, where it had been sown for silage. Still spreading, 1981.

Bromus laciniatus Beal   F. W. Simpson 1958

A casual, found in waste places. The only record is from sq. 23, Felixstowe Docks, in 1958, detd. at Kew.

Bromus erectus Huds.   Upright Brome   ·   J. Townsend 1841
(*Zerna erecta* (Huds.) Gray)

Native. Calcareous heaths, pastures, scrub and railway embankments. Not frequent, though occasionally abundant.
W: 66; 67; 75; 76; 78; 87; 88; 98.
66, Newmarket and Moulton, 1981 (Mrs E. M. Hyde); 76, Dalham, 1981 (F. W. Simpson); Barrow Bottom, 1980; 78, Lakenheath.
E: 05; 14; 36; 37; 58; 59.
05, Combs, c. 1952 (N. S. P. Mitchell); 14, Tuddenham, 1975 (F. W. Simpson).

Bromus inermis Leyss.   Hungarian Brome   P. J. O. Trist 1961
(*Zerna inermis* (Leyss.) Lindm.)

Native in C. Europe. Introduced and now a naturalised alien on light sandy soils. First recorded in Suffolk from Lakenheath on a re-seeded playing field in 1961.
W: 66, Newmarket, 1980; 76, Higham; Barrow Bottom, 1980; 77, Herringswell; 78, Lakenheath, 1961; 86, Bury St Edmunds Railway Station, 1979 (M. A. Hyde).
E: 45, Thorpeness, 1978; 49, Somerleyton, planted in pheasant covert, 1968.

Bromus lanceolatus Roth var. **lanuginosus** (Poir.) Coss. & Dur.   J. Digby 1968
(*B. macrostachys* Desf.
Serrafalcus macrostachys (Desf.) Parl.)

Casual. Native of Europe.
E: 15, Sycamore Farm, Swilland, 1968, detd. Dr C. E. Hubbard; 33, Felixstowe Ferry, on beach, 1978 (M. A. Hyde), detd. E. J. Clement.

Bromus arvensis L.   Field Brome   E. Skepper 1862
(*Serrafalcus arvensis* (L.) Godr.)

Casual. Native in S. Europe. Waste places near docks and sometimes as a weed of cultivation.
W: 67, Mildenhall, 1948 (Mrs M. Southwell).
E: 23, Landguard Common, 1936; Felixstowe Docks, 1958 (both records, F. W. Simpson); 47, Southwold, 1978 (E. T. Daniels); 58, Kessingland.

Bromus japonicus Thunb.   Spreading Field Brome   Hind 1889
(*B. patulus* Mert. & Koch
Serrafalcus patulus (Mert. & Koch) Parl.)

Casual. Native in C. and E. Europe. Rubbish tips and waste places. Recorded in Hind's Flora from Market Weston and Fakenham.

Bromus hordeaceus L. ssp. **hordeaceus**   Soft Brome   Sir J. Cullum 1773
(*B. mollis* L.)

Native. Pastures, verges, sea coast and waste places. Common. A very variable species. All squares.

Ssp. **thominii** (Hard.) Maire & Weiller   Lesser Soft Brome   Sir J. Cullum 1773
(*B. thominii* Hard.)

Native or perhaps introduced. Hay-fields, roadsides, coastal sands and waste places. Fairly frequent, but confused with ssp. *hordeaceus*.
W: 64; 76; 77; 78; 87; 95; 97.
76, Herringswell; 77, Tuddenham Gallops; Icklingham; 78, Lakenheath.
E: 03; 04; 05; 13; 14; 15; 16; 25; 33; 34; 46; 47; 48; 50.

Bromus lepidus Holmb.   Slender Brome   W. B. Turrill 1936
Introduced or doubtfully native. On light, cultivated soils and grassland. Possibly frequent and under-recorded. Perhaps confused with small forms of *B. hordeaceus*.
W: 74; 77; 78; 83; 84; 87; 93; 95.
78, Lakenheath, 1975.
E: 03; 04; 13; 14; 23; 25; 34; 35; 44; 45; 47; 48; 49.
14, Freston, 1980 (Mrs E. M. Hyde); 45, Thorpeness, 1974.

Bromus hordeaceus × lepidus
(*B. × pseudothominii* Philip Smith)

Native. Widespread in the Suffolk Breckland on roadside verges and sandy places ('An Ecological Flora of Breckland').

Bromus interruptus (Hack.) Druce   Interrupted Brome   E. Armitage 1902
Probably native. First recorded in Gt Britain in 1849. Formerly common in fields of Sainfoin, Rye-grass and Clover. Last record, 1957.
W: 67, Mildenhall, roadside, in 1916 (W. C. Barton), Kew record; and in 1957 (E. Q. Bitton); 86, Bury St Edmunds, 1907 (J. Rasor), Kew record.

Bromus racemosus L.   Smooth Brome   Rev. G. R. Leathes c. 1800
(*Serrafalcus racemosus* (L.) Parl.)

Native. Arable and waste land. Rare or overlooked.
W: Recorded in Hind's Flora for Ixworth Thorpe, Honington, Fakenham, Bury, Stoke and Cockfield.
E: 07; 16; 24; 44; 49, Carlton Colville, 1907 (W. A. Dutt).
No recent East Suffolk specimens seen. Recorded in Hind's Flora for Bungay, Corton, Lowestoft, St Margaret's and Cattawade.
Rev. G. R. Leathes's specimen from Lowestoft is in Hb. Ipswich Museum.

Bromus commutatus Schrad.   Meadow Brome   E. Skepper 1862
(*Serrafalcus commutatus* (Schrad.) Bab.)

Native or a naturalised alien. Arable fields, meadows and hedgerows. Not very frequent,
or overlooked.
W: 75; 85.
E: 15; 16; 28; 37; 38; 39; 44; 46; 58; 59.
39, Bungay Common, 1981; 44, Orford, c. 1950; 46, Dunwich, c. 1950 (two preceding
records, F. W. Simpson).
Var. **pubens** Wats., a form with softly hairy spikelets, was recorded from Framsden (sq.
16) in 1960 and 1968 (P. J. O. Trist), detd. Dr C. E. Hubbard, and from Walpole (sq. 37)
in 1979 (M. A. Hyde), detd. Dr P. M. Smith.

Bromus secalinus L.   Rye Brome   Rev. G. Crabbe 1798
(*Serrafalcus secalinus* (L.) Bab.)

Casual. Native in S. Europe. Found in waste places, especially near docks and on field
borders.
W: 66, Newmarket, sidings, 1978 (G. M. S. Easy), conf. P. J. O. Trist.
Var. **hirtus** (F. Schultz) Aschers. & Graebn. With hairy spikelets.
W: 97, Stanton, 1952 (J. Marshall).
E: 23, Landguard Common, 1936; Felixstowe Maltings, 1939 and 1958, detd. at Kew.
Both records, F. W. Simpson.

Brachypodium sylvaticum (Huds.) Beauv.   Wood False Brome   John Notcutt c. 1820

Native. Woods, copses, railway banks, rough pastures, scrub and chalk-pits. Very
frequent, especially on the chalky Boulder Clay. Often dominant.
All squares except 68.

Brachypodium pinnatum (L.) Beauv.   Chalk False Brome   T. J. Woodward 1805
                                          Tor Grass

Native. Old grassland and open woodland glades on calcareous soils. Rare or local.
The first record in Hind's Flora for Bungay in 1805 may be incorrect, as a specimen in Hb.
Ipswich Museum collected by T. J. Woodward in 1805 is from the Bath Hills in Norfolk,
on the opposite side of the river from Bungay.
W: 76, Barrow, 1980 (Mrs E. M. Hyde), detd. as var. **pubescens** S. F. Gray by Dr A.
Melderis; 87, Ampton, The Holmes, 1966.
E: 07, Thornham Parva, 1972 (J. Digby and F. W. Simpson), edge of an old plantation,
with *B. sylvaticum*; 59, Lowestoft, 1950 (E. R. Long).

Agropyron caninum (L.) Beauv.   Bearded Couch   Prof. Henslow 1853
(*Triticum caninum* L.)

Native. Margins of woods and shady hedges on Chalk and Boulder Clay. Uncommon.
Probably extinct in many of its former habitats. Possibly confused with long-awned forms
of *A. repens,* as few of the records have been supported by specimens.
W: 74; 75; 76; 77; 85; 86; 87; 94; 95; 96; 97; 98.
76, Dalham and Moulton, 1980.
E: 04; 05.

GRAMINEAE

Agropyron repens (L.) Beauv. Common Couch Sutton & Kirby 1787
(*Triticum repens* L.)   Twitch
           Scutch

Native. A very common weed of cultivated land, waysides and waste places. Many varieties occur, with or without awns, glabrous or hairy.
All squares.
Var. **aristatum** Baumg., with long awns, is frequent.

Agropyron pungens (Pers.) Roem. & Schult. Sea Couch John Notcutt c. 1820
(*Triticum pungens* Pers.)

Native. Very common. An often abundant and dominant species of the coast. Drier areas of salt marshes, sea banks and brackish ditches. Variable. Awned forms frequent.
All coastal and estuarine squares, 1981.
Viviparous form at Shotley, 1974-6 (Mrs E. M. Hyde).
Hb. Ipswich Museum: 'By the River's side, between Stoke Bridge and the Locks', c. 1820 (John Notcutt). Still there in 1981, but much reduced, due to the paving of the banks of the tidal river and the consequent loss of the former more natural habitat.

Agropyron pungens × repens   F. W. Simpson 1962
(*A. × oliveri* Druce)

A not uncommon, very variable hybrid, found on the sea coast.
E: 13, Harkstead, 1981; 23, Erwarton, 1976; Trimley St Mary, 1981; 33, Bawdsey, 1962; 45, Aldeburgh, 1979; 58, Benacre, 1981; Kessingland, 1980. All records, F. W. Simpson.

Agropyron junceiforme (A. & D. Löve) Á. & D. Löve Sand Couch Buddle 1724
(*Triticum junceum* L.)

Native. Sandy seashores. Frequent.
E: 23; 24; 33; 34; 45; 46; 47; 57; 58; 59; 50.
23, Shotley, 1979; Landguard Common, 1979; 46, Sizewell, 1980; Minsmere, 1981; 58, Kessingland, 1980; Benacre, 1979.

Agropyron junceiforme × pungens Hybrid Sea Couch F. W. Simpson 1962
(*A. × obtusiusculum* Lange)

A hybrid found on the coastal sands.
E: 13, Harkstead, 1979; 23, Landguard Common; Trimley; Walton, all 1979; 33, Bawdsey, 1975; 46, Leiston, 1979; 47, Southwold; 58, Benacre and Kessingland, 1977. All records, F. W. Simpson.

Agropyron junceiforme × repens Hybrid Sea Couch F. W. Simpson 1958
(*A. × laxum* (Fries) Almq.)

A rare hybrid occasionally found in coastal areas.
E: 13, Harkstead, 1979; 23, Landguard Common, 1958; 33, Felixstowe Ferry. All records, F. W. Simpson.

Triticum aestivum L. Wheat

Cultivated. Frequently found growing wild around farmyards and docks and on rubbish tips and roadsides.

Secale cereale L.　　Rye

A cultivated crop, usually on poorer light soils. Occasionally found growing wild around docks and in waste places. Persists for a year or two on the verges of new roads cut through former arable land.

Echinaria capitata (L.) Desf.　　Prickle Grass　　　　　　Mrs F. Baker 1897

Casual. Native in S. Europe and the Mediterranean region.
Recorded from Oulton Broad.

Elymus arenarius L.　　Sea Lyme-grass　　　　　　　　Gerarde 1597

Native. Sea coast, usually on sandy beaches. Local.
E: 23, Felixstowe (probably now extinct); 33, Bawdsey; 45, Aldeburgh; Thorpeness; 46, Sizewell; Minsmere; Dunwich; 47, Southwold; Walberswick; 57, Easton, 1980; Southwold, 1981; 58, Kessingland, 1980; 59, Lowestoft; Pakefield, 1980.

Hordelymus europaeus (L.) Harz　　Wood Barley　　　F. W. Simpson 1936
(*Hordeum sylvaticum* Huds.)

Native. In woods and copses, on Chalk or Chalky Boulder Clay. Very rare.
First recorded from a small copse at Witnesham in 1936. This habitat changed after the oak trees were felled, c. 1950 and no specimens were observed until 1973, when one plant was found.
W: 86, Fornham All Saints, 1963 (Lady Tollemache); 95, Bull's Wood, Cockfield, 1973 (Dr O. Rackham).
E: 04, Offton, 1976 (Dr O. Rackham); 15, Witnesham, 1936-1973.

Hordeum murinum L.　　Wall Barley　　　　　　John Notcutt c. 1820
　　　　　　　　　　　　Jack-go-up-your-arm (Suffolk)

A colonist. Waste places and waysides, especially in towns and villages. Frequent, sometimes abundant.
All squares.

Hordeum marinum Huds.　　Sea Barley　　　　　Rev. G. Crabbe 1805
(*H. maritimum* Stokes ex With.)

Native. Sea embankments, commons by the sea, salt pastures and marshes. Not as frequent as formerly and thought to be extinct in some of the squares below.
E: 03; 23; 33; 34; 35; 44; 46; 47; 49; 58; 40.
44, Havergate Island, 1979; 47, Reydon, 1978 (P. G. Lawson).

Hordeum secalinum Schreb.　　Meadow Barley　　　John Notcutt c. 1820
(*H. pratense* Huds.)

Native. In pastures and grassy places, especially near the sea. Frequent.
W: 75; 85; 86; 87; 93; 94; 95; 96; 97.
93, Nayland; 97, Stanton.
E: 03; 04; 05; 06; 13; 14; 16; 23; 24; 25; 33; 34; 35; 36; 38; 39; 44; 46; 47; 57; 58; 59; 40.
14, Wherstead, 1980; 23, Shotley, 1981 (Mrs E. M. Hyde); Walton and Trimley, 1981; 39, Bungay, 1981; 47, Blythburgh, 1974.

Hb. Ipswich Museum: 'In the meadows by the Locks and above Handford Bridge', c. 1820 (John Notcutt).

Hordeum jubatum L.   Fox-tail Barley   M. G. Rutterford 1958

An alien from N. America, occasionally occurring as a casual. The first record was from a carrot field in Lakenheath Fen in 1958.
W: 78, Lakenheath, on a re-seeded playing field, 1961 (P. J. O. Trist).
E: 14, Belstead Road, Ipswich, and near the church at Belstead, 1974 (M. A. Hyde).

Hordeum vulgare L.   Six-rowed Barley

Escape from cultivation. Found in waste places and on rubbish tips.

Hordeum distichon L.   Two-rowed Barley   Mrs E. M. Hyde 1974

A relic of cultivation, arable fields and waste places. Probably fairly frequent, but under-recorded.
W: 66, Exning, 1977; 86, Bury By-pass, 1976.
E: 14, Ipswich Docks, 1974-1980; Freston Hill, in lay-by, 1977; 24, Bucklesham, several specimens among a crop of carrots.

Glyceria declinata Bréb.   Glaucous Sweet-grass   F. W. Simpson c. 1936

Native. On the margins of woodland ponds, ditches and watery places. Scarce or overlooked. Perhaps confused with *G. plicata* or *G. fluitans*.
W: 75; 76; 87; 93; 95; 97.
95, Felsham, pre-1960 (F. W. Simpson).
E: 03; 04; 05; 39; 46.
04, Offton; Hintlesham, 1980; 05, Barking; 46, Leiston, pre-1960 (F. W. Simpson).

Glyceria fluitans (L.) R. Br.   Flote-grass   John Notcutt c. 1820
                                       Floating Sweet-grass

Native. In shallow ponds, streams, rivers and ditches. Common.
W: All squares except 66; 67; 78.
65, Lt. Thurlow, 1977; 95, Felshamhall Wood, 1980.
E: All squares.
13, Freston, Wherstead and Bentley, 1980; 23, Shotley, 1981; 24, Hemley, 1980.

Glyceria fluitans × plicata   Hybrid Sweet-grass   Dr E. F. Warburg 1954
(*G. × pedicellata* Towns.)

Native. In ponds, ditches and swampy old pastures, usually found together with the parents. Rare or overlooked. A male-sterile hybrid.
W: 93.
E: 14; 25; 26; 58; 59.
14, Westerfield, 1981 (M. A. Hyde); 59, Carlton Colville, 1978 (P. G. Lawson).

Glyceria plicata Fries   Plicate Sweet-grass   E. Skepper 1862
                                Plicate Flote-grass

Native. In ponds, ditches, streams and wet woods. Occasional, but overlooked, with a more restricted distribution than *G. fluitans*.

W: 64; 65; 66; 74; 77; 85; 86; 93; 94; 95; 96; 97.
96, Ixworth, 1974; 95, Bradfield Woods, 1980.
E: 03; 05; 06; 13; 14; 16; 17; 23; 25; 26; 28; 33; 38; 39; 47; 49.
04, Hadleigh, 1981; 14, by the R. Gipping at Ipswich, 1976; 23, Chelmondiston, in The Grindle, 1979 (M. A. Hyde).

Glyceria maxima (Hartm.) Holmb.   Reed Sweet-grass   Sir J. Cullum 1773
(*G. aquatica* (L.) Wahl.)   Reed Meadow-grass

Native. Beside rivers and ponds, in ditches, marshes and fens. Fairly frequent, sometimes abundant.
W: All squares except 64; 65; 75; 85; 94; 95.
67, Mildenhall, 1980; 74, Clare Country Park, 1976; 78, Wangford, 1980; 88, Barnham, 1980.
E: All squares except 05; 06; 07; 16; 33; 34; 44; 45; 50.
04, Hadleigh, 1981; 23, Trimley Lakes, 1981; 37, Walpole, 1979; 39, Bungay Common, 1981; 47, Wenhaston, 1974 (mentioned by Davy for this parish in 1796).

Festuca tenuifolia Sibth.   Fine-leaved Sheep's Fescue   Rev. J. D. Gray 1893
(*F. ovina* L. ssp. *tenuifolia* (Sibth.) Peterm.)

Native. Heath, open plantations and margins of woods on light, sandy soils. Not very frequent, but perhaps overlooked. Various forms and varieties have been described.
W: 77; 78; 97.
77, Foxhole Heath; West Stow; Icklingham.
E: 07; 24; 35; 39; 45; 46; 58; 59; 50.
24, Foxhall, near Stadium, 1980 (Mrs E. M. Hyde); 39, Bungay Common, 1980 (F. W. Simpson).

Festuca ovina L.   Sheep's Fescue   Sir J. Cullum 1773

Native. Heaths, commons, old grasslands, on Sand and Chalk, especially in Breckland. Frequent, sometimes almost dominant.
W: All squares except 64; 65; 68; 74; 75; 85.
E: All squares except 15; 26; 27; 36; 37; 48; 49.
24, Purdis Heath, 1979; 46/47, Westleton, 1980.
Var. **hispidula** (Hack.), Hack., plants with lemmas with short hairs, frequently occur with normal plants in the Breckland.

Festuca longifolia Thuill.   Hard Fescue   R. Burn 1934
(*F. duriuscula* auct., non L.)

An introduced and naturalised alien. Planted on banks, golf courses and roadsides. Naturalised in waste places, on heaths, and on the sea coast. Frequent in Breckland.
W: 76, Risby; Lt. Saxham; 77, Eriswell; 78, Wangford, roadside, A1065; 87, Barnham Heath; 96, Beyton.
E: 24, Martlesham, roadside, A12, 1980 (J. R. Palmer); 34, Shingle Street, 1981 (F. W. Simpson).
Var. **villosa** (Schrad.) Howarth
Recorded from Honington, Barton, Mildenhall and Euston ('An Ecological Flora of Breckland').

Festuca caesia Sm.   Blue Fescue   Sir C. J. F. Bunbury c. 1840
                            Grey Fescue

Native. Rare. Sandy heaths, tracks and roadsides in the Breckland.
W: 77, Eriswell, several sites, 1980; Barton Mills, 1981; West Stow, 1980; Cavenham, 1981; 87, West Stow, 1980.
Recorded from a number of E. Suffolk coastal sites, probably in error for *F. rubra* var. *pruinosa*.

Festuca rubra L. ssp. **rubra**   Red Fescue   Paget 1834
                                        Creeping Fescue

Native. Heaths, commons, grasslands, open woodland, sand dunes and the drier parts of salt marshes. Common, sometimes abundant. A very variable species.
All squares.
Var. **barbata** (Schrank) Richt. Said to be common. Has hairy spikelets.
Var. **glaucescens** (Heget. & Heer) Richt. A salt marsh variety. Common.
Var. **arenaria** Fries (*F. oraria* Dum.) Sand Fescue. On sand dunes. Frequent. Confused with *F. juncifolia*.
Var. **pruinosa** (Hack.) Howarth Coastal. Landguard Common; Shingle Street; Sudbourne; Dunwich; Walberswick.

Ssp. **commutata** Gaud.   Chewings Fescue   P. J. O. Trist 1968

An introduced and naturalised alien. Seed included in grass seed mixtures. Found on roadsides and in waste places. Its distribution in the County has not been fully recorded.
E: 14, banks of R. Gipping, Ipswich, 1980 (Mrs E. M. Hyde). Conf. S. M. Cunningham.

Festuca rubra ssp. **rubra** × **Vulpia bromoides**   P. J. O. Trist 1969

A rare hybrid, first found in thin sand covering shingle, about 150 yards from the sea at Shingle Street, Hollesley, in 1969, and determined by Dr C. E. Hubbard. Refound in 1973.

Festuca juncifolia St-Amans   Creeping Dune Fescue   F. W. Simpson 1958
                                    Rush-leaved Fescue

Native. On the sea coast, on sand dunes. Rare.
E: 33, Felixstowe Ferry, 1958; 46, Sizewell, 1974; 58, Benacre, 1980; 59, Lowestoft.

Festuca pratensis Huds.   Meadow Fescue   Paget 1834
Native. Meadows, pastures, waysides and grassy places. Common.
All squares.

Festuca arundinacea Schreb.   Tall Fescue   Prof. Henslow 1856
(*F. elatior* L.)

Native. Meadows, waysides, rough pastures, edges of salt marshes and cliffs. Very frequent, especially near the coast. Favours heavy, damp soils. A variable species, according to habitat.
W: All squares except 65; 66; 84; 97; 98.
68, Mildenhall, 1980; 76, Dalham, 1981; Barrow Bottom, 1980.

E: All squares except 14; 17; 26; 35; 44.
06, Battisford, 1980; 13, Holbrook, 1981; 25, Burgh, 1981; 37, Cookley, 1981.

Festuca gigantea (L.) Vill. Giant Fescue Paget 1834
(*Bromus giganteus* L.)

Native. In woods, copses and old hedges, chiefly on Chalk and Boulder Clay. Frequent in West Suffolk, rare or absent in many areas of East Suffolk.
W: All squares except 64; 66; 67; 68; 78; 96.
76, Cavenham; Dalham, 1981; 87, Gt Livermere, 1980.
E: All squares except 28; 34; 36; 38; 39; 44; 45; 46; 47; 49; 58; 40; 50.
04, Hadleigh, 1981; 26, Framlingham Castle Mound, 1979; 48, Westhall Churchyard, 1979. (The two preceding records, M. A. Hyde.)
Var. **triflora** (L.) Hook.
E: 23, Trimley St Mary, 1981; 24, Playford, 1976-81, conf. Dr C. E. Hubbard; 33, The Grove, Felixstowe, 1977. All records made by F. W. Simpson.

Festuca pratensis × **Lolium perenne** Paget 1834
(× *Festulolium loliaceum* (Huds.) P. Fourn.)

Native. In meadows and grassland where one or both parents occur. Occasional, but probably overlooked. A sterile intergeneric hybrid.
W: 68; 77; 78; 87; 93; 94; 96.
96, Pakenham Fen, 1955 (Dr J. G. Dony).
E: 03; 04; 15; 17; 25; 26; 28; 38; 39; 49; 59.
04, Hadleigh, pre-1940 (R. Burn); 39, Shipmeadow, 1975 (A. Copping); 49, Beccles, 1976; 59, Oulton, 1977.

Festuca pratensis × **Lolium multiflorum** P. J. O. Trist 1968
(× *Festulolium braunii* (K. Richt.) A. Camus)

A rare hybrid, recorded from Higham Hill, Stratford St Mary.

Lolium perenne L. Perennial Rye-grass Sir J. Cullum 1775

Native. Waysides, pastures and waste places. Very common. A variable species, often cultivated.
All squares.
Proliferous forms occur frequently.

Lolium multiflorum Lam. Italian Rye-grass Henslow & Skepper 1860
(*L. italicum* A. Br.)

Introduced from W. and S. Europe in about 1830. Cultivated and naturalised. Also found as a weed of waste places and rubbish dumps. Frequent.
W: All squares except 64; 68; 74; 83; 84; 85; 98.
77, Barton Mills, 1981; 96, Beyton, by A45, 1979.
E: All squares except 07; 28; 37; 38; 45; 59; 50.
14, Ipswich Docks, 1981; 24, Gt Bealings, 1981.
Var. **compositum** Thuill.
E: 23, Felixstowe Docks, 1937 (F. W. Simpson). Detd. at Kew.

Lolium multiflorum × perenne   P. J. O. Trist 1966
(*L. × hybridum* Hausskn.)

This fertile hybrid is sown as a crop and is probably frequent as an escape from cultivation, but overlooked. The only Suffolk record is from Hall Farm, Fornham St Martin (sq. 86) in 1966.

Lolium temulentum L.   Darnel   Rev. G. Crabbe 1798
                               Bearded Rye-grass

Alien. Native of S. Europe and N. Africa. Formerly a common weed of cultivation. Now a rare casual of waste places and rubbish dumps.
W: No recent records.
E: 23, Landguard Common, 1936; Felixstowe Maltings, 1958 (both records, F. W. Simpson); 36, Gt Glemham; 39; 47, Blythburgh; 49, Beccles; 58, Kessingland.
Var. **arvense** Lilj. (without awns):
W: 78, Lakenheath, old rubbish tip, 1972 (M. G. Rutterford).
E: 13, Woolverstone, probably from bird-seed, 1975-6 (Mrs E. M. Hyde); 46, Dunwich, c. 1950 (F. W. Simpson).

Vulpia bromoides (L.) S. F. Gray   Squirrel-tail Fescue   Sir J. Cullum 1773
(*Festuca sciuroides* Roth)

Native. Dry hedge-banks, waysides, walls, river and sea banks, in quarries and open sandy places, especially in the Breckland. Frequent, sometimes abundant.
W: All squares except 65; 83; 85.
66, Herringswell, 1981; 76, Kentford and Gazeley, 1981; 96, Elmswell, 1978.
E: All squares except 26; 27; 38; 44; 49; 59.
14, Ipswich, several sites, 1981; 15, Barham Pits, 1980; 45, Snape, 1981; 46, Aldeburgh, 1981.

Vulpia myuros (L.) C. C. Gmel.   Rat's-tail Fescue   Rev. G. R. Leathes 1793
(*Festuca myuros* L.)   Wall Fescue

Native. In dry sandy and gravelly places and on waste ground, especially in the Breckland and near the coast. Frequent.
W: 64; 66; 74; 76; 77; 78; 86; 87; 88; 93; 96; 97.
76, Herringswell, 1980; 86, Bury St Edmunds Station, 1980; 96, Thurston Station, 1981; 97, Knettishall, 1981.
E: 03; 04; 06; 13; 14; 15; 16; 23; 24; 26; 27; 33; 34; 35; 39; 45; 46; 47; 59; 40.
14, Ipswich, abundant, 1981; 23, Felixstowe, 1981; 39, Bungay, old Station Yard, 1981; 45, Snape, 1981.
Hb. Ipswich Museum: 'Caston's Garden Wall towards Friar's Bridges. The moistened seeds, if bruised, will stain linen or paper a purple colour, June 1820' (John Notcutt).

Vulpia ambigua (Le Gall) A. G. More   Bearded Fescue   J. Townsend 1846
(*Festuca ambigua* Le Gall)

Native. On dry sandy tracks in Breckland, where it is locally abundant, and on open heaths and coastal sands.
W: 66, Herringswell, 1980; 67, Mildenhall; 76, Kentford, 1979; Gazeley, 1980; Higham, 1979; Herringswell, 1979; 77, Barton Mills; Tuddenham; Icklingham; Eriswell; West

Stow; Worlington, 1979; Cavenham; 78, Wangford; Lakenheath; 87, Elveden; 88, Thetford; 97, Coney Weston, 1981, conf. Dr C. A. Stace.
E: 15, Barham, 1979, (Mrs E. M. Hyde), conf. Dr C. A. Stace; 23, Landguard Common, 1980; 33, Bawdsey, 1976; 34, Sutton Heath; Shingle Street, 1978; 35, Bromeswell; 45, Thorpeness, 1974.

Vulpia fasciculata (Forsk.) Samp.   Dune Fescue   Dr Goodenough 1777
(*V. membranacea* auct.)   One-glumed Fescue Grass
Native. In dry, sandy places near the sea. Rare or very local.
E: 23, Landguard Common, still there in 1977 after two centuries; Felixstowe, near Coastguard Station, 1981; 33, Felixstowe Ferry, c. 1948 and Bawdsey, 1976 (F. W. Simpson); 45, Aldeburgh, 1978; Thorpeness, 1978; 58, Kessingland, 1980 (F. W. Simpson).

Poa annua L.   Annual Meadow-grass   Sir J. Cullum 1773
Native or colonist. In all types of habitat, especially a weed of gardens and paths. Very common everywhere.
All squares.

Poa bulbosa L.   Bulbous Meadow-grass   Sir J. E. Smith 1804
    Bulbous Poa
Native. On sandy soil and dunes by the sea. Local. This species still survives on loose sand amongst the beach huts at the south end of Felixstowe and also near the Ferry, despite being very much disturbed and trampled. At one time much of the spring grass on the Lowestoft Denes consisted of *P. bulbosa*; it is still there, but in much smaller quantity and decreasing, as the Denes become more developed.
E: 23, Landguard Common; Felixstowe, 1980; 33, Felixstowe Ferry, 1980; 34, Shingle Street, 1980; 39, Bungay, Outney Common, 1974; 45, Aldeburgh; Iken; 46, Sizewell Car Park; 47, Southwold Common, 1980; 49, Beccles Common; 59, Lowestoft Denes.

Poa nemoralis L.   Wood Meadow-grass   Dr White 1860
    Wood Poa
Native. On old shady banks, edges of woods and plantations. Usually on light, well-drained soils. Not uncommon. More frequent in East Suffolk.
W: All squares except 64; 65; 67; 68; 75; 85; 94; 95; 98.
76, Lt. Saxham, 1980; Dalham, 1981; 77, Cavenham; 78, Brandon, 1981.
E: All squares except 33; 35; 38; 44; 46; 49; 58; 50.
13, Freston, 1981; 14, Ipswich Cemetery, 1981; Spring Road, Ipswich, 1981; 23, Trimley St Mary, 1981; 46, Yoxford, 1981.

Poa palustris L.   Swamp Meadow-grass   Finder not known c. 1950
(*P. serotina* Ehrh.)
Introduced. Native of N. America. Known in Suffolk only from a single record from sq. 07, without locality.

GRAMINEAE

Poa trivialis L.   Rough Meadow-grass   J. Andrews 1728
Native. In woods, copses and shady places. Very frequent.
All squares.

Poa angustifolia L.   Narrow-leaved Meadow-grass   Hind 1888
(*P. pratensis* ssp. *angustifolia* (L.) Gaud.)
Native. Dry, grassy commons, heaths and banks. Scarce, possibly overlooked.
W: 66; 74; 76; 77; 84; 87; 88; 97.
66, Moulton, 1963; 74, Clare, 1976 (F. W. Simpson); 76, Gazeley, 1963; 87, Culford (P. J. O. Trist); 88, Brandon; Euston.
E: 05; 23; 35; 47; 58; 50.
23, Landguard Common, 1939 (J. E. Lousley); 35, Bromeswell Common, 1955.

Poa pratensis L.   Smooth Meadow-grass   Sir J. Cullum 1773
Native. Pastures, waysides and open woods. Very common.
All squares.

Poa subcaerulea Sm.   Spreading Meadow-grass   Lady Blake c. 1840
Native. Usually in damp, sandy places, but also in plantation rides and fens. Much overlooked, or included under *P. pratensis*.
W: 66, Herringswell, 1979 (Mrs E. M. Hyde), conf. Professor T. G. Tutin; 77, Icklingham; Eriswell; Mildenhall; Cavenham; 78, Brandon; Pashford Poor's Fen (P. J. O. Trist); Lakenheath, Maidscross Hill; 87, Elveden, West Gouch Plantation.
E: 15, Barham Pits, 1979; 46, Thorpeness; 47, Blythburgh; 50, Yarmouth, South Town.

Poa compressa L.   Flattened Meadow-grass   Davy 1790
Native. On dry banks, commons, waysides and walls. Not frequent. Some of the records may be incorrect.
W: 64; 68; 75; 76; 77; 78; 87; 93; 94; 95.
76, Hargrave, 1980 (E. Milne-Redhead); 78, Wangford; 87, Barnham Railway Station, 1960 (P. J. O. Trist).
E: 04; 07; 13; 14; 16; 17; 23; 25; 33; 34; 35; 36; 38; 39; 44; 45; 46; 48; 49; 59; 50.
13, Brantham, 1980 (M. A. Hyde); 25, Boulge and Burgh, 1981 (Mrs E. M. Hyde); 34, Shingle Street, 1979 (F. W. Simpson); 49, Beccles, 1976.
There are specimens in Hb. Davy from Ubbeston, 1790, the Hoxne Pound, 1799 and walls at Beccles, 1801.

Puccinellia fasciculata (Torr.) Bicknell   Borrer's Salt Marsh Grass   Newbould 1869
(*Glyceria borreri* (Bab.) Bab.)
Native. In salt marshes, especially on tracks beside dykes. Frequently in association with *P. distans*. Uncommon.
E: 03, East Bergholt; 23, Trimley, 1980; Erwarton, 1980; 24, Woodbridge; 33, Felixstowe; 34; 44, Orford; Havergate Island, 1972; 45, Aldeburgh, 1977; 46, Dunwich; 47, Walberswick Beach; Blythburgh, 1980.

Puccinellia distans (L.) Parl.   Reflexed Salt Marsh Grass   John Notcutt c. 1820
(*Glyceria distans* (L.) Wahlenb.)

413

Native. On the edges of salt marshes and on damp shingle. Found in nearly all coastal parishes between Felixstowe and Lowestoft. Formerly quite frequent, now scarce.
W: Hind recorded this grass for Culford Heath, as a casual.
E: 03; 13; 14; 23; 24; 25; 33; 34; 35; 44; 46; 47; 57; 58; 59; 40; 50.
23, Trimley, 1981; 33, Felixstowe Ferry, 1979; 35, Blaxhall; Iken, 1981 (F. W. Simpson).
Hb. Ipswich Museum: 'With *Arenaria marina* between Greenwich Farm and Hog Island, above high water mark, but within the flux of lofty spring tides, August' c. 1820 (John Notcutt).

Puccinellia distans × maritima
(*P.* × *hybrida* Holmb.)
Between Dunwich and Walberswick in 1937 (F. W. Simpson).

Puccinellia pseudodistans (Crép.) Jans. & Wacht.   Greater Salt Marsh Grass
Atlas of the British Flora 1962
Native. The higher parts of salt marshes. Rare or overlooked.
E: 57, Southwold.

Puccinellia maritima (Huds.) Parl.   Common Salt Marsh Grass   Paget 1834
(*Glyceria maritima* (Huds.) Wahlb.)
Native. In salt marshes and pastures near the sea and on the edges of sea dykes and muddy channels. Very frequent, sometimes dominant.
E: All coastal and estuarine squares.

Puccinellia rupestris (With.) Fern. & Weath.   Stiff Salt Marsh Grass   Paget 1834
(*Glyceria procumbens* (Curt.) Dum.)
Native. In salt marshes and muddy estuaries. Rare.
E: 23, Trimley, 1980 (F. W. Simpson); 24, Woodbridge; 33, Felixstowe; 44, Orford; 45, Aldeburgh; Sudbourne (F. W. Simpson).

Catapodium rigidum (L.) C. E. Hubbard   Fern-grass   J. Andrews 1752
(*Desmazeria rigida* (L.) Tutin   Hard Fescue
Festuca rigida (L.) Rasp.)
Native. On sandy soils, heaths, sea embankments, walls and paths. Common, but frequently overlooked and confused with *C. marinum*.
W: All squares except 65; 68; 75; 85; 86; 93.
66, Herringswell, 1981; 76, Gazeley, 1981; 87, West Stow, 1980; 97, Hopton, 1981.
E: All squares except 03; 06; 07; 13; 17; 27; 28; 35; 36; 37; 48.
15, Barham Pits, 1980; 34, Shingle Street, 1981; 39, Bungay, old Station, 1981; 44, Orford, 1981.
Hb. Ipswich Museum: 'On the old stone wall by Caston's Garden, near his house, part of the ruins of the Convent of Grey Friars, June 1819' (John Notcutt).

Catapodium marinum (L.) C. E. Hubbard   Sea Fern-grass   Davy 1795
(*Desmazeria marina* (L.) Druce   Darnel Poa
Festuca marina L.)
Native. On coastal sands and shingle. Locally frequent and common.

E: 23; 24; 33; 34; 44; 45; 46; 47; 58; 59; 50.
33, Felixstowe, 1978; Bawdsey, 1979; 34, Shingle Street, Hollesley, 1981; 58, Kessingland, 1980.
There is a specimen in Hb. Davy from 'beach at Aldbrough, 1795'.

Briza minor L.   Lesser Quaking-grass   Mrs E. M. Hyde 1971
Introduced. A native of the Mediterranean region.
E: 13, Harkstead, in arable field. Still there, 1981.

Briza maxima L.   Large Quaking-grass   F. W. Simpson c. 1954
Introduced. Very common in dry places in Mediterranean countries. In Suffolk usually a casual of garden origin, on rubbish tips and waste places. Frequently cultivated for its attractive spikelets.
E: 05; 13, Freston Hill, 1963; 15, Gosbeck; 33, Felixstowe, 1974, and Felixstowe Ferry, 1975-1978; 45, Aldeburgh; 58.

Briza media L.   Common Quaking-grass   John Notcutt c. 1815
                        Totter-grass
                        Maidenhair-grass
Native. On old chalky grassland, meadows, churchyards, fens, railway banks. Formerly very frequent, now scarce or extinct in many areas.
W: All squares except 65; 68; 83.
67, Freckenham, 1977; 76, Dalham, 1981; Risby and Cavenham, 1980; 78, Lakenheath, 1979; 94, Lavenham, 1980.
E: All squares except 23; 28; 33; 34.
04, Hadleigh, disused railway line, 1981; 16, Rishangles, 1977; 39, Bungay, 1980; 58, Kessingland Cliffs, 1977.

Dactylis glomerata L.   Cock's-foot   Willisell 1724
Native. Also cultivated. Waysides, grassland, waste places, open woods and copses. Very common.
All squares.
Proliferous forms, which usually occur late in the season, recorded from:
W: 68, Lakenheath, 1980; 94, Brent Eleigh, 1974.
E: 04, Hintlesham, 1974; 13, Woolverstone, 1974; Harkstead, 1977; 14, by the R. Gipping between Ipswich and Sproughton, 1974; 23, Chelmondiston, 1974; 34, Hollesley, 1976; 46, Sizewell, 1975; 47, Wangford; 49, North Cove, 1975.

Cynosurus echinatus L.   Rough Dog's-tail   E. Skepper c. 1860
Introduced. Native in S. Europe and the Mediterranean. Found in waste places, especially near the sea coast. Rare. It has been observed on Landguard Common, Felixstowe, for a number of years.
E: 23, Landguard Common, 1980; Felixstowe Maltings; 34, Shingle Street, Hollesley; 46, Thorpeness, 1978; 49, St Olave's; 59, Lowestoft.

Cynosurus cristatus L.   Crested Dog's-tail   Sir J. Cullum 1773
Native. Pastures, waysides, and grassy places. Common.
All squares.

Catabrosa aquatica (L.) Beauv.   Water Whorl-grass   J. Andrews 1728

Native. Beside rivers, streams and in ditches. Not very frequent.
W: 77, Barton Mills; 83, Gt Cornard; 86, Bury St Edmunds; 88, Barnham (P. J. O. Trist); 96, Norton; 97, Honington; Sapiston; Stanton.
E: 07, Hinderclay Fen; Thelnetham Fen, 1981; 08, Hopton, Little Ouse, 1974; 13, Woolverstone; Harkstead, 1980; Freston; Wherstead; 23, Erwarton, 1980; 24, Hemley, 1979; Martlesham, 1973; 37, Halesworth, 1980; 47, Southwold; 49, Worlingham; Beccles, 1977; 59, Oulton, Camps Heath.

Eragrostis multicaulis Steud.   A. Copping 1975

Casual. Native of E. Asia and Malaysia. Waste places.
E: 59, Lowestoft, 1975. Detd. Dr C. E. Hubbard.

Eragrostis cilianensis (All.) F. T. Hubbard   P. G. Lawson 1976
(*E. major* Host)

Casual. Native of S. Europe. Waste places, rubbish tips.
E: 59, Commercial Road, Lowestoft. Detd. Dr C. E. Hubbard.

Melica nutans L.   Mountain Melick
Nodding Melick

Recorded in Hind's Flora by the Rev. G. Crabbe, c. 1800, from Cransford, Swefling, and Glemham and elsewhere in the County. These records are very doubtful, as is also a later record by A. Mayfield for Mendlesham, 1902-09.
M. uniflora was no doubt the species found. *M. nutans* was at once time included under *M. uniflora. M. nutans* is a larger species, found mainly in limestone woods.

Melica uniflora Retz.   Wood Melick   Rev. G. Crabbe 1798

Native. Margins of woods, shady banks and lanes. Frequent in some areas, especially in old woods on the Boulder Clay.
W: 65; 75; 76; 83; 85; 87; 93; 94; 95; 96.
93, Polstead, 1978; 95, Bradfield Woods, 1980; 96, Pakenham Wood, 1978.
E: 03; 04; 05; 06; 07; 13; 14; 15; 16; 23; 24; 25; 28; 33; 36; 37; 39; 47; 48; 49; 59.
03, Stoke-by-Nayland, 1979; 04, Raydon, Cocksedge Wood, 1981; 13, Bentley and Wherstead, 1980; 24, Playford, 1981; 47, Reydon Wood, 1979.

Helictotrichon pubescens (Huds.) Pilger   Hairy Oat-grass   Sir J. Cullum 1773
(*Avena pubescens* Huds.)   Downy Oat-grass

Native. On dry, chalky heaths, old grassland, waysides and railway banks on Chalk and Chalky Boulder Clay. Frequent in Breckland. Rare elsewhere in the County.
W: 64; 66; 67; 74; 75; 76; 77; 78; 86; 87; 88; 94; 95; 97; 98.
76, Dalham, 1981; 77, Cavenham Heath, 1977; Worlington, 1980; 78, Lakenheath and Brandon, 1981.
E: 05; 07; 14; 39.
14, Tuddenham, 1975 (F. W. Simpson).

Helictotrichon pratense (L.) Pilger   Meadow Oat-grass   Ray 1696
(*Avena pratensis* L.)

Native. Old dry, chalky grassland, heaths, waysides and quarries. Still fairly frequent in Breckland, but rare outside this area. Occasionally on railway banks.
W: 66; 75; 76; 77; 78; 84; 86; 87; 88; 97; 98.
66, Exning, 1977; 76, Cavenham, 1975; 98, Knettishall, 1981.
E: 14; 15; 39;
14, Bramford and Lt. Blakenham, c. 1955; 15, Coddenham, 1970. All East Suffolk parish records, F. W. Simpson.

Arrhenatherum elatius (L.) Beauv. ex J. & C. Presl   Tall Oat-grass   Sir J. Cullum 1773
(*A. avenaceum* Beauv.)   False Oat

Native. Pastures, waysides, lanes, waste places and old shingle beaches. Abundant. A very variable plant.
All squares.

Avena strigosa Schreb.   Bristle Oat   E. Skepper 1860
                             Black Oat

Alien. Found in cornfields, and near docks. Native on the continent of Europe. Not very common.
E: 04, Naughton, pre-1940; 14, Ipswich; 23, Felixstowe Docks, c. 1936 (F. W. Simpson).

Avena fatua L.   Common Wild Oat   Dawson Turner 1805
                     Spring Wild Oat

A naturalised alien, widespread in Europe and elsewhere. Frequent and common weed of cultivated and waste land. Very variable.
Var. **fatua** (*A. pilosissima* Gray) with very hairy lemmas, which become brownish-red when ripe. Common.
Var. **pilosa** Syme, with only slightly hairy lemmas, which become greyish. Common.
Var. **glabrata** Peterm. with hairless lemmas, which become yellowish. Apparently rare.

Avena ludoviciana Durieu   Winter Wild Oat

Introduced. Native in Europe and Asia. A weed on heavy soils.
There have been a few records, but these have proved to be *A. fatua*.

Avena sterilis L.   Animated Oat   Mrs E. M. Hyde 1977

Casual. Native of the Mediterranean, where it is cultivated.
E: 13, Freston, 1977-8. Detd. Dr C. E. Hubbard.

Avena sativa L.   Cultivated Oat

Casual. A relic of cultivation found on roadsides, around farms and stockyards, and on waste ground.

Koeleria cristata (L.) Pers.   Crested Hair-grass   Davy 1796
(*K. gracilis* Pers.)

Native. On open sandy and chalky heaths, especially in Breckland, where it is very frequent. More rarely on coastal dunes and old grassy shingle beaches.

417

W: 66; 67; 75; 76; 77; 78; 86; 87; 88; 93; 96; 97; 98.

66, Herringswell, 1980; 67, Freckenham, 1980; 76, Risby, 1980; 77, Barton Mills and Tuddenham, 1981.

E: 07; 17; 25; 33; 34; 35; 39; 44; 45; 46; 47.

33, Felixstowe Ferry, 1979; 34, Shingle Street, 1981; 45, Aldeburgh, 1976; 46, Minsmere, 1981.

Trisetum flavescens (L.) Beauv. Yellow Oat-grass Sir J. Cullum 1773

Native. Dry, grassy places, heaths and waysides. Frequent.

W: All squares except 65; 67; 68; 83.

76, Herringswell and Kentford, 1979; 94, Brent Eleigh, 1981.

E: All squares except 44.

13, Harkstead, Tattingstone and Woolverstone, 1981; 24, Gt Bealings, 1981; 39, Bungay, 1980.

Deschampsia flexuosa (L.) Trin. Wavy Hair-grass Sir J. Cullum 1773
(*Aira flexuosa* L.)

Native. Dry heaths and banks. Locally abundant and dominant. Now extinct in some former habitats. Recorded by Hind as being comparatively rare in Suffolk.

W: 76; 77; 78; 83; 87; 88; 93; 97; 98.

76, Herringswell, 1978; 87, Icklingham, 1977; 98, Knettishall Heath, abundant, 1981.

E: 23; 24; 25; 35; 39; 45; 46; 47; 58; 59; 40; 50.

23, Felixstowe, railway bank, 1980; 24, Purdis Heath and Rushmere Common, 1981; 35, Tunstall Common, 1980; 46/47, Blythburgh, Dunwich and Walberswick, 1981.

Deschampsia caespitosa (L.) Beauv. Tufted Hair-grass J. Andrews 1743
(*Aira caespitosa* L.) Tussock-grass

Native. Wet pastures, fens and open woods. Common. More frequent on the Boulder Clay.

W: All squares.

68, Lakenheath, 1980; 87, Gt Livermere, 1980; 95, Bradfield Woods, 1980.

E: All squares except 33; 44.

14, Ipswich, Bourne Park, 1981; 16, Mickfield Reserve, 1981; 25, Bromeswell Green, 1981; 39, Bungay Common, 1981.

Corynephorus canescens (L.) Beauv. Grey Hair-grass Sir J. E. Smith 1800

Native. On sandy beaches and Breckland warrens. Locally common, though generally rare. Introduced by planting at Dunwich, Walberswick and Minsmere after the 1953 floods, from Norfolk stock.

W: 78, Lakenheath, 1980 (Mrs G. Crompton); Wangford Warren, 1980.

Two of the very rare inland sites.

E: 46, Dunwich, 1980; Minsmere; 47, Walberswick; 58, Benacre; Kessingland; Covehithe, 1980.

Hind records the species from between Lakenheath and Wangford, and from Lackford Heath. *Illustrated page 501*

Aira caryophyllea L. Silvery Hair-grass Sir J. Cullum 1775

Native. On dry, sandy and gravelly heaths and banks, especially in Breckland and near the coast. Frequent.

W: 67; 76; 77; 78; 87; 88; 98.
67, Mildenhall, 1977; 76, Kentford, 1979; 77, West Stow, 1980.
E: 03; 13; 14; 16; 17; 23; 24; 34; 35; 36; 39; 44; 45; 46; 47; 58; 59; 40; 50.
14, Belstead, 1979; 39, Bungay Common, 1981; 45, Knodishall, 1981; Snape, 1980; 46, Aldringham, 1981.

Aira praecox L. Early Hair-grass Sir J. Cullum 1773
Native. Dry, sunny banks, waysides, heaths and coastal areas. Frequent.
W: All squares except 64; 65; 68; 74; 75; 84; 85; 86; 94.
67, Mildenhall, 1977; Freckenham, 1979; 78, Wangford Warren, 1980.
E: All squares except 06; 16; 26; 27; 38.
13, Woolverstone, 1981; Stutton, 1981; 23, Erwarton and Shotley, 1981; 40, Belton, Howard's Common, 1979.

Holcus lanatus L. Yorkshire Fog Sir J. Cullum 1775
Common Soft-grass
Native. Waysides, waste places, pastures, heaths, fallow and arable land. Very common and abundant.
All squares.

Holcus mollis L. Creeping Soft-grass John Notcutt c. 1820
Native. Dry, sandy heaths and woods. Locally plentiful.
W: All squares except 64; 65; 66; 68; 75; 84; 94.
67, Freckenham, 1979; 95, Bradfield Woods, 1980; 98, Knettishall, 1981.
E: All squares except 26; 27; 28; 36; 37.
23, Harkstead, 1981; 47, Hinton, 1980; 58, Benacre, 1981.

Anthoxanthum puelii Lecoq & Lamotte Annual Vernal-grass Hind 1884
A colonist, probably introduced from France in the latter half of the 19th century. A weed or casual of light arable fields.
W: 67, Mildenhall, pre-1950.
E: 04, Broomhill, Hadleigh, pre-1940 (R. Burn); 58, Covehithe, 1969-70 (Lowestoft Field Club). Now extinct.

Anthoxanthum odoratum L. Sweet Vernal-grass Sir J. Cullum 1773
Native. Pastures, heaths, open woodland and coastal sands. Very frequent.
W: All squares except 65; 68; 75.
E: All squares except 27.
Viviparous forms at Woolverstone in 1977.

Phalaris aquatica L.
(*P. tuberosa* L.)
Introduced. Native of S. Europe.
W: 76, planted at Higham, 1981 (Mrs E. M. Hyde).
E: 24, Gt Bealings, 1981, planted on a very poor sandy field (F. W. Simpson). Also at Somerleyton, 1968, planted for pheasant cover (Lowestoft Field Club).

Phalaris canariensis L.   Common Canary-grass   Lady Blake 1840

Casual. Native of N. Africa and the Canary Islands. Rubbish dumps, waste places and gardens. Not infrequent. Usually arising from waste cage-bird seed.
W; 66; 75; 77; 78; 84; 86; 87; 88; 94; 96.
66, Exning, waste ground, 1977; 78, Lakenheath Tip (P. J. O. Trist); 86, Bury St Edmunds, waste ground, 1979.
E: 03; 04; 13; 14; 15; 23; 33; 35; 45; 46; 47; 48; 49; 59.
03, Stratford St Mary, 1980 (N. V. Hunt); 14, Sproughton Tip, 1977; 59, Lowestoft, 1980.

Phalaris minor Retz.   Lesser Canary-grass   F. W. Simpson 1936

A casual from the Mediterranean region. Occasionally found in waste places.
E: 06, Haughley, from bird-seed, 1981 (Mrs J. Harris); 23, Felixstowe Docks, 1936. Detd. at Kew.

Phalaris paradoxa L. var. **praemorsa** Coss. & Dur.   Mrs F. Baker 1899

A casual. Native in the Mediterranean. Waste places and ballast heaps. Rare. First found at Lowestoft and Oulton in 1899.
E: 23, Felixstowe Docks, 1936 (F. W. Simpson). Detd. at Kew.

Phalaris arundinacea L.   Reed-grass   Sir J. Cullum 1773

Native. Rivers, streams and marshes. Very frequent.
W: All squares.
66, Moulton, 1981; 76, Hargrave, 1979; 83, Lt. Cornard, by R. Stour, 1980.
E: All squares except 44.
04, Hadleigh, by the R. Brett, 1981; 13, Holbrook Millstream, 1981; 14, by the R. Gipping, between Ipswich and Bramford, 1981; 39, Bungay, 1981.   *Illustrated page 479*
Var. **picta** L.
Form with variegated leaves, known as 'Ribbon Grass' or 'Gardener's Garters', is occasionally found as a garden throw-out on tips and in waste places.
E: 13, Brantham, 1974; 23, Chelmondiston, 1974. Both records, M. A. Hyde.

Milium effusum L.   Wood Millet   Davy 1794

Native. Edges of woods, glades and copses. Frequent on the Boulder Clay. Formerly sown by gamekeepers.
W: All squares except 66; 67; 68; 77; 78; 87; 98.
76, Barrow, 1980; Herringswell, 1979; 94, Brent Eleigh, 1981; 95, Bradfield Woods, 1980.
E: All squares except 16; 26; 28; 34; 35; 44; 45; 46; 47; 49; 58; 40; 50.
04, Hintlesham, 1981; 05, Barking, 1981; 14, Bramford, Bullen Lane, 1981; 17, Eye, 1980; 24, Gt Bealings and Hasketon, 1981.
Hb. Ipswich Museum: Davy's specimen, 1794, from Yoxford Wood.

Calamagrostis stricta (Timm) Koel.   Narrow Small-reed   Mrs M. Southwell 1951
(*C. neglecta* auct., non (Ehrh.) Beauv.)

Native. Old grassy fens and carrs. Rare.
W: 68, Lakenheath Fen; 77, Mildenhall, S.E. of Bombay Fen, 1951; 78, Turf Fen, Lakenheath, 1972.

Calamagrostis canescens (Weber) Roth   Purple Small-reed   Prof. Henslow 1852
(*C. lanceolata* Roth)

Native. In damp woods and marshes. Scarce.
W: 68; 76; 77; 78; 86; 87; 88; 95; 97; 98.
78, Pashford Poor's Fen, 1979; 95, Felshamhall Wood, 1980; 97, Hopton Fen, 1981.
E: 03; 07; 48; 49; 58; 59; 40; 50.
49, North Cove, 1976; 58, Benacre, 1981; 40, Belton, 1977.

Calamagrostis epigejos (L.) Roth   Wood Small-reed   D. Stock 1835
Bush Grass

Native. Damp woods, thickets and waysides, especially on the Boulder Clay. Also in open, drier habitats in Breckland. Frequent, sometimes abundant.
W: All squares except 65; 66; 83; 84.
68, Lakenheath, 1980; 77, Mildenhall, 1981; West Stow, 1981; 96, Pakenham Wood, 1978.
E: Recorded for squares 03; 04; 05; 06; 07; 15; 16; 17; 27; 34; 36; 47.
04, Raydon Gt Wood, 1981; 07, Wortham Ling, 1980; Redgrave Fen, 1980; 47, Blythburgh, 1980.

Ammophila arenaria × **Calamagrostis epigejos**   F. W. Simpson 1953
(× *Ammocalamagrostis baltica* (Fluegge ex Schrad.) P. Fourn.)   Hybrid Marram
Purple Marram

Native and introduced. Found on coastal dunes. Plants from the Norfolk coast were introduced at Minsmere, Dunwich and Walberswick after the 1953 floods.
E: 46, Sizewell to Minsmere, 1981; 47, Dunwich; Walberswick, now much reduced, probably becoming extinct due to erosion, 1981; 58, Kessingland, 1977; 59, Gunton, probably now extinct, due to the construction of the sea wall; 50, Gorleston, 1974.

Ammophila arenaria (L.) Link   Marram   Gerarde 1597

Native. Sea coast, especially on sand dunes. Decreasing, due to erosion.
E: 23; 33; 34; 45; 46; 47; 57; 58; 59; 50.
23, Trimley, 1981, now almost extinct; Landguard Common, 1980; 33, Bawdsey, 1981; 46, between Thorpeness and Dunwich, 1981; 58, Benacre, 1981.   *Illustrated page 504*

Apera spica-venti (L.) Beauv.   Loose Silky Bent   Rev. R. Relhan 1785

Native or colonist. Frequent in Breckland, as a weed of cultivation. Also on the light sandy soils of East Suffolk, in fields, waste places and sand-pits.
W: 76; 77, Eriswell; Cavenham; 78, Lakenheath, 1980; 83; 96; 97, Hopton, 1981; Knettishall, 1981; 98, Euston, 1981.
E: 13, Freston, 1981; 14, Ipswich, 1981; Bramford, 1981; 23, Erwarton, 1976; Chelmondiston, 1978; 24, Bucklesham and Foxhall, 1975.

Apera interrupta (L.) Beauv.   Dense Silky Bent   Rev. W. W. Newbould 1848

Native. Frequent in Breckland on disturbed ground, especially in fire breaks and fallow fields. Rare on the sandy heaths of East Suffolk.
W: 66, Newmarket, 1979 (G. M. S. Easy); 76, Risby Poors Heath, 1977; Kentford Heath, 1980; 77, Cavenham and Icklingham; Eriswell; Barton Mills; West Stow; 78, between

Brandon and Lakenheath; Lakenheath and Wangford Warrens; 87, Barnham; Culford; 88, Thetford; 97, Euston.
E: 45, Iken; Thorpeness, 1981 (P. G. Lawson), conf. A. Copping.

Agrostis canina L. ssp. **canina**   Velvet Bent   Paget 1834
Native. On damp heaths. Probably frequent, but overlooked. Recent confirmed records include:
E: 47, Blythburgh Reserve, 1973; 48, Stoven, 1973, detd. A. Copping.
Ssp. **montana** (Hartm.) Hartm. Brown Bent. On heaths, more especially in Breckland. Locally frequent. This grass may be mistaken for *A. tenuis,* as both grow in association. The records below have not been divided into the subspecies.
W: All squares except 64; 65; 66; 68; 74; 75; 84; 93; 94.
E: All squares except 04; 05; 06; 15; 17; 25; 26; 27; 33; 36; 37; 44; 59; 50.

Agrostis tenuis Sibth.   Common Bent   Sir J. Cullum 1773
(*A. vulgaris* With.)
Native. On dry heaths, old grassland, poor arable, roadsides and in open woods and plantations. Very common and frequently dominant.
All squares.

Agrostis gigantea Roth   Black Bent   F. W. Simpson 1936
(*A. nigra* With.)
Native. A weed of cultivated and waste land, roadsides and margins of streams. Common.
W: All squares except 64; 65; 67; 68; 85; 93; 95.
Frequent in Breckland, 1981.
E: All squares except 06; 07; 16; 26; 27; 36; 44; 48.
23, Landguard Common, 1980; Chelmondiston, 1978; 35, Tunstall, 1979.

Agrostis stolonifera L.   Creeping Bent   Paget 1834
(*A. alba* auct.)   White Bent
                     Fiorin
Native. A very variable grass, occurring in many and varied habitats.
Var. **stolonifera** Chiefly poor, wet pastures, salt marshes, waste and cultivated ground, open woods and tracks. Very common.
Var. **palustris** (Huds.) Farw. In damp places, shallow or dried-up ponds and ditches. Very frequent. This form is possibly only a habitat variation.
All squares.

Polypogon monspeliensis (L.) Desf.   Annual Beard-grass   F. W. Simpson 1936
Native. Found in salt marshes and occasionally as a casual in waste places. Near a brackish ditch near the former Felixstowe Pier Station (sq. 23).

Gastridium ventricosum (Gouan) Schinz & Thell.   Nit-grass   J. Andrews 1739
(*G. lendigerum* (L.) Desv.)
A rare weed of cultivated fields and waste places.
W: 93, Polstead, pre-1940 (F. W. Simpson).
E: 03, Flatford, 1961; 23, Landguard Common, pre-1940 (F. W. Simpson).

Lagurus ovatus L. Hare's-tail Grass W. A. Dutt 1899

Introduced. Native of the Mediterranean region. Frequently grown in gardens. The first record for Suffolk was from a rubbish heap at Oulton in 1899.
W: 86, Bury By-pass, 1976 (Mrs E. M. Hyde).
E: 24, Dobb's Lane, Kesgrave, 1974 (Mrs B. A. Curtis); 33, Felixstowe Ferry, 1978 (M. A. Hyde); 38, Bungay Churchyard, 1972 (J. Digby).

Phleum arenarium L. Sand Cat's-tail Sir J. Cullum 1773

Native. On dry, fairly open, sandy coastal sites and in Breckland. Locally frequent.
W: 77, Icklingham; Tuddenham Gallops, 1981; 78, Lakenheath, 1974; 87; 96.
E: 23, Landguard Common, 1978; 33, Felixstowe Ferry and Bawdsey, 1979; 34, Shingle Street, 1981; 45, Thorpeness, 1980; 46, Sizewell, 1980; 57, Southwold; 58, Benacre, 1981; Pakefield, 1974; 59, Lowestoft, North Denes, 1976; 50, Gorleston, 1974.

Phleum phleoides (L.) Karst. Purple-stem Cat's-tail Sir C. J. F. Bunbury 1850
(*P. boehmeri* Wibel)

Native. A Breckland grass, preferring chalky soils. Locally frequent.
W: 67, Mildenhall; Freckenham; 68, Lakenheath, 1979; 76, Herringswell; Risby; Cavenham; 77, Icklingham, 1980; Eriswell, 1980; Barton Mills; Herringswell, 1979; Mildenhall; 78, Brandon; Lakenheath Warren; Eriswell, 1980; 87, Wordwell; Culford; West Stow; 88, Barnham Cross Common; 97, Euston.

Phleum bertolonii DC. Smaller Cat's-tail J. Andrews 1745
(P. nodosum auct., non L.)

Native. In dry habitats. Grassland, heaths and waysides. Frequent. A much smaller grass than *P. pratense,* although often difficult to distinguish from depauperate forms of the latter species.
W: All squares except 64; 68; 93.
Frequent in Breckland, 1981.
E: All squares except 23; 27; 28; 33; 36; 37; 50.
Common on the Sandlings, 1981.

Phleum pratense L. Timothy Sir J. Cullum 1775
  Cat's-tail

Native. Also cultivated. Pastures, roadsides and field margins. Very frequent.
All squares.

Alopecurus myosuroides Huds. Slender Foxtail Rev. G. Crabbe 1798
(*A. agrestis* L.) Black Twitch

Colonist. A weed of cultivated ground and waste places, especially on the Boulder Clay, where it is often abundant.
W: All squares except 66; 67; 88; 98.
94, Brent Eleigh, 1981; 96, Beyton, 1980.
E: All squares except 34; 35; 44; 58; 40; 50.
04, Bramford, 1981; 13, Harkstead and Holbrook, 1981; 14, Washbrook, 1980.

Alopecurus aequalis Sobol.   Orange Foxtail   Henslow & Skepper 1860
(*A. fulvus* Sm.)   Short-awn Foxtail

Native. In pools, ditches and damp pastures. Rare, perhaps overlooked. No recent records.
W: 77, Tuddenham, c. 1950 (F. W. Simpson); 94, Groton.
E: 04, Hintlesham; 07, Redgrave, c. 1950; 39, Bungay; 45, Sudbourne, c. 1948 (F. W. Simpson).

Alopecurus bulbosus Gouan   Tuberous Foxtail   Woodward 1797
                                Bulbous Foxtail

Native. Salt marshes and brackish pastures. Rare.
E: 03, East Bergholt, old site re-discovered, 1979; 24, Martlesham, pre-1940; 46, Sizewell and Dunwich, both pre-1940 (F. W. Simpson); 40, Burgh Castle, 1978; 50, South Town, marshes, 1978.
Recorded for the area south of Breydon Water in Hind's Flora. Re-found there in 1962 (F. W. Simpson) and 1978 (P. J. O. Trist).

Alopecurus geniculatus L.   Marsh Foxtail   John Notcutt c. 1820
                          Floating Foxtail

Native. Margins of shallow pools, ditches, streams and damp meadows. Less frequent than formerly.
W: All squares except 64; 66; 67; 68; 74; 75; 76.
65, Lt. Thurlow, 1977; 97, Coney Weston, 1981.
E: All squares except 05; 06; 07; 15; 17; 25; 26; 37; 59.
13, Holbrook Creek, 1980; 23, Trimley, 1981; 33, Felixstowe Golf Course, 1977; 39, Bungay, 1981.
Hb. Ipswich Museum; 'Common in meadows that are flooded in the winter and in shallow ditches and ponds,' c. 1820 (John Notcutt).

Alopecurus pratensis L.   Meadow Foxtail   Sir J. Cullum 1773
                        Common Foxtail

Native. Damp meadows and waysides. Common.
All squares.

Mibora minima (L.) Desv.   Early Sand-grass   Miss E. Jauncey 1936
(*M. verna* Beauv.)   Sand Bent

Naturalised alien. Native of S. Europe. The only record for Suffolk is from Notcutt's Nurseries at Woodbridge (sq. 24), where it was abundant.

Parapholis strigosa (Dum.) C. E. Hubbard   Sea Hard-grass   Woodward 1812
(*Lepturus filiformis* auct., non (Roth) Trin.)

Native. Near the sea, along the margins of salt marshes and in damp grassy hollows. Frequent, sometimes abundant, but overlooked.
E: 03; 13; 14; 23; 33; 34; 44; 45; 46; 47; 57.
14, Wherstead, in quantity, 1976 (Mrs E. M. Hyde); 23, Shotley, 1977; Trimley, 1981; Chelmondiston, 1975; 33, Felixstowe Ferry, 1978; 34, Shingle Street, 1981 (F. W. Simpson); 47, Walberswick; Blythburgh, 1979; 57, Southwold.

Parapholis incurva (L.) C. E. Hubbard   Curved Hard-grass   Davy 1796
(*Lepturus incurvus* (L.) Druce)

Native. Margins of grassy salt marshes, and on embankments by the sea. Frequent, but often overlooked and mistaken for *P. strigosa*.
E: 03, Brantham; 13, Woolverstone, 1975; Harkstead, 1978; 14, Wherstead, 1975; 33, Felixstowe Ferry; 34, Bawdsey; Boyton, 1979; 35, Iken; 44, Orford; Havergate Island, 1973; 45, Sudbourne; 46, Dunwich, 1979; 47, Walberswick; 59, Lowestoft.
Hind's Flora records it only for Dunwich.
There is a specimen in Hb. Davy, 'On the beach at Dunwich, 1796'.
Hb. Ipswich Museum: 'On the Shore between St Peter's Dock and Nova Scotia. By Bourne Bridge', c. 1820 (John Notcutt). Mrs E. M. Hyde found it in the salt pastures near Bourne Bridge in 1975.

Nardus stricta L.   Mat-grass   Sir J. Cullum 1773

Native. On dry heaths. Locally frequent, but generally rare. It has decreased in recent years.
W: 77, Icklingham; 87, West Stow; 98, Knettishall.
E: 07, Wortham Ling, 1980; 14/24, Rushmere Heath, 1981; 39, Bungay, 1981; 45, Snape Warren, 1981; 46, Westleton, 1980; 47, Blythburgh, 1981; Walberswick, 1979; 49, Beccles Common; 40, Belton.
Hb. Ipswich Museum: 'South side of Rushmere Heath towards the Foxhall Road', c. 1820 (John Notcutt). Still there, 1981 (F. W. Simpson).

Phragmites australis (Cav.) Trin. ex Steud.   Common Reed   Sir J. Cullum 1773
(*P. communis* Trin.)

Native. Marshes, fens, wet woods, ditches and ponds. Very common and sometimes abundant and dominant.
All squares except 65.

Cortaderia selloana (J. A. & J. H. Schult.) Aschers. & Graebn.   Pampas Grass
(*C. argentea* (Nees) Stapf)   F. W. Simpson 1958

Introduced. Native of S. America. Occasionally planted on waysides and railway embankments.
E: 14, railway embankment, Spring Road, Ipswich, several well-established plants.

Molinia caerulea (L.) Moench   Purple Moor-grass   J. Andrews 1745

Native. On heaths, in bogs, fens and woodland rides. Locally common, sometimes abundant and dominant. A very variable grass. A number of varieties, which may only be habitat forms, have been described.
W: 68; 77; 78; 87; 96; 97; 98.
77, Tuddenham Fen, 1980; 78, Lakenheath, Pashford Poor's Fen, 1981; 98, Knettishall, 1981.
E: 07; 17; 24; 35; 45; 46; 47; 49; 58; 59; 40.
07, Redgrave Fen and Wortham Ling, 1980; 35, Tunstall Forest, 1981; 46, Westleton, 1980; 47, Walberswick, 1979; Wenhaston, 1977; 58, Benacre, 1981.

Sieglingia decumbens (L.) Bernh.   Heath Grass   Rev. G. R. Leathes 1810
(*Triodia decumbens* (L.) Beauv.)

Native. On heaths and old pastures. Formerly not uncommon, now very scarce.
W: 77; 78; 87; 94; 96; 97; 98.
78, Lakenheath Warren, 1973; 87, Gt Livermere; 98, Knettishall, 1981.
E: 03; 07; 13; 14; 16; 24; 35; 38; 39; 45; 46; 47; 48; 49; 40; 50.
13, Woolverstone, 1981; 24, Rushmere Common, 1976; 39, Bungay Common, 1980.

Spartina maritima (Curt.) Fernald   Small Cord-grass   Rev. G. R. Leathes 1796
(*S. stricta* (Ait.) Roth)

Native. In salt marshes. At one time fairly frequent, now rare or extinct in many of its
former habitats.
E: 13, Stutton; Holbrook, 1981; Woolverstone; 23, Trimley, 1981; 24, Hemley, 1980; 25,
Melton; 33, Felixstowe Ferry; Bawdsey; 34, Hollesley; Boyton, 1979; 44, Havergate
Island; 45, Aldeburgh; Snape, 1981. All records, F. W. Simpson.
Hb. Ipswich Museum contains specimens collected by **Rev. G. R. Leathes** from
'Landguard Fort, August 1796' and by Davy from 'River Alde, Aldeburgh, 1802'.

Spartina alterniflora × maritima   Townsend's Cord-grass
(*S. × townsendii* H. & J. Groves)

Said to have been introduced with *S. anglica* to mud-flats at Brantham. A male-sterile
hybrid. Its present distribution in the County is uncertain, due to confusion with *S.
anglica.* This plant is much smaller than *S. anglica,* with narrower leaves and shorter
spikelets.
Recorded since 1950 from the following sites:
E: 13, Stour Estuary at Stutton, Holbrook Creek and Brantham; 23, Orwell Estuary at
Pin Mill; 24, Waldringfield; 45, Slaughden Saltings, Aldeburgh; 47, Bulcamp Marshes,
Blythburgh.

Spartina anglica C. E. Hubbard   Cord-grass   Professor F. W. Oliver 1923
                                       Rice-grass

Introduced. Now naturalised, frequently dominant and spreading rapidly in tidal estuaries
and on mud-flats, especially since about 1950. It can now be found in considerable
abundance, colonising the mud-flats of the estuaries, often to the detriment of the native
flora.
This grass was first recorded from Lymington, Hampshire in 1892 and quickly spread,
colonising large areas of mud-flats on the South Coast. Its great potential was soon
realised in assisting reclamation. In 1923 Professor Oliver of University College, London,
introduced cuttings on the Suffolk side of the Stour Estuary at Seafield Bay, Brantham.
This experiment was very successful and the grass soon spread and appeared on the
opposite side of the Estuary at Mistley, Essex. About 1930, John H. Keeble of Brantham
Hall was able to supply cuttings for various sites in Britain and also for projects overseas.
E: 03, Brantham; 13, Stutton; Holbrook; Harkstead; 14, Nacton; Wherstead; 23,
estuaries of the Stour and Orwell; 24, R. Deben, abundant in areas on both sides; 33,
Felixstowe Ferry; Bawdsey; 34, Hollesley; Boyton; 44, Orford; Havergate Island; Butley
River; 45, R. Alde from Snape to Aldeburgh; 47, Blythe Estuary, Dunwich to
Walberswick; 57, Reydon and Southwold.   *Illustrated page 501*

Cynodon dactylon (L.) Pers.   Bermuda-grass   F. W. Simpson 1958

Casual. Native of continental Europe.
W: 77, Barton Mills Tip, 1977 (Mrs E. M. Hyde).
E: 05, The Tannery, Combs, 1958.

Echinochloa crus-galli (L.) Beauv.   Cockspur Grass   Hind 1880
                                       Barnyard Millet

An alien, native of N. America. Although recorded in Hind's Flora from Honington, Nayland and Gorleston, there was probably a re-introduction with carrot seed from America during the Second World War, and it is still a weed in carrot fields. Also a casual of rubbish tips and waste places.
W: 67, Mildenhall; 77, Herringswell; 87, Barnham; Euston.
E: 05, The Tannery, Combs, 1958-9 (E. Q. Bitton); 06, Old Newton; 14, Ipswich, several records between 1950 and 1981; 15, Coddenham Tip, 1974; 23, Felixstowe Docks; 35, Butley; 59, Lowestoft, 1976.
Var. **breviseta** (Doell) Neilr.
W: 77, Herringswell, in carrot crop, 1971 (P. J. O. Trist).

Echinochloa utilis Ohwi & Yabano   Japanese Millet   Mrs E. M. Hyde 1977
(*E. frumentacea* auct., non Link)

Casual. Usually from bird seed.
W: 66, Exning, waste ground, 1977, detd. E. J. Clement; 77, Barton Mills Tip, 1977.

Setaria viridis (L.) Beauv.   Green Bristle-grass   Rev. G. Crabbe 1805
(*Panicum viride* L.)

Casual. Native of C. and S. Europe and N. Africa. Waste places.
W: 77, Barton Mills Tip, 1977 (Mrs E. M. Hyde); 97, Euston.
E: 14, Bath Street, Ipswich, 1974; Strand, Wherstead, 1976; 15, Coddenham Tip, 1974; (these three records by Mrs E. M. Hyde); 23, Stratton Hall; 49, Beccles; 59, Lowestoft, 1980 (P. G. Lawson).

Setaria verticillata (L.) Beauv.   Rough Bristle-grass   P. J. O. Trist 1960
(*Panicum verticillatum* L.)

Casual. Native of S. Europe. Waste places.
W: 86, Bury St Edmunds, 1960.
E: 59, Lowestoft, 1975 (A. Copping). Still there, 1980.

Setaria italica (L.) Beauv.   Foxtail Millet   B. W. Smith 1953
                                     Italian Millet

Casual. Native of S. Europe. Usually a bird-seed alien of waste places and tips.
W: 66, Exning, 1977; 77, Barton Mills Tip, 1977. (Both records, M. A. Hyde).
E: 23, Chelmondiston Tip, 1971 and 1975; 36, Swefling, 1953; 59, Lowestoft, North Denes, 1960.

Setaria faberi Herrm.   G. M. S. Easy 1979

Casual. Native of China. Waste places.
W: 66, Newmarket, rail sidings to corn silo.

Setaria glauca (L.) Beauv.   Yellow Bristle-grass   Hind 1880
(*S. lutescens* (Weigel) F. T. Hubbard)
Casual. Native of S. Europe. Found in waste places.
W: 67, Mildenhall.
E: 14, Nelson Road, Ipswich, c. 1950 (F. W. Simpson); 49, Beccles, rubbish tip; 59, Lowestoft, 1980 (P. G. Lawson).
Recorded in Hind's Flora from Honington, Nayland and Stoke.

Digitaria ischaemum (Schreb.) Muhl.   Smooth Finger-grass   Sir J. E. Smith 1800
(*Panicum glabrum* Gaud.)   Red Millet
Casual. Native of C. and S. Europe. Sandy fallow fields and waste places.
Recorded by Hind from Bury St Edmunds, Bungay, Ipswich and Shottisham.
W: 66, Newmarket, sidings, near corn silo, 1979 (G. M. S. Easy).

Digitaria sanguinalis (L.) Scop.   Crab-grass   Dickson 1780
(*Panicum sanguinale* L.)   Bloody Finger-grass
    Hairy Finger-grass
Casual. Native of S. Europe. Usually derived from cage-bird seed or waste from grain silos.
W: 66, Newmarket, near corn silo, 1979 (G. M. S. Easy).
E: 45, Snape, 1960; 57, Southwold, 1979 (P. G. Lawson); 59, Lowestoft, 1975 (A. Copping) by grain silo. Still there, 1980.

Panicum miliaceum L.   Common Millet   F. W. Simpson 1958
    Broom-corn Millet
An introduced alien or casual. Native of Asia, cultivated in S. Europe. On rubbish dumps, waste places, and in gardens, especially where bird seed has been thrown out.
W: 77, Barton Mills Tip, 1977; 96, Woolpit Tip, 1974 (Mrs E. M. Hyde).
E: 05, Combs Ford, 1958; 14, Ipswich, several records, 1976-81; 15, Coddenham Tip, 1974; 23, Chelmondiston Tip, 1975; 24, Bucklesham, 1976; 33, Felixstowe Ferry, on dumped soil; 49, Beccles; 59, Lowestoft, 1980 (P. G. Lawson).

Panicum capillare L.   Witch Grass   P. G. Lawson 1976
Casual. Native of N. America. Waste places, rubbish tips. Probably from bird seed waste.
E: 59, Commercial Road, Lowestoft, detd. by Dr C. E. Hubbard.

Zea mays L.   Maize   Mrs E. M. Hyde 1971
    Indian Corn
Introduced. Native of S. America. Frequently cultivated as a folder crop and sweetcorn. Occasionally found on waste ground, rubbish tips, and near docks, or as a relic of cultivation.
W: 77, Barton Mills Tip, 1977 (M. A. Hyde).
E: 14, Ipswich Docks, 1971; 23, Harkstead, 1976-81 (F. W. Simpson); 47, Bramfield, dumped soil, 1976 (Mrs E. M. Hyde).

Sorghum halepense (L.) Pers.   Johnson Grass   Mrs E. M. Hyde 1974

Casual. Waste places. Native of N. Africa and S.W. Asia, but widely naturalised in the Mediterranean region.
E: 14, Ipswich Docks, 1974-5; Ipswich, Bath St, 1978, detd. E. J. Clement. (Both records, Mrs E. M. Hyde); 59, Lowestoft, 1978 (P. G. Lawson), detd. R. P. Libbey.

BAMBOOS

These species are mainly natives of Western Asia. Some twenty species are grown in gardens, but only three or four can be said to have become naturalised and to have spread. This usually occurs in damp habitats bordering streams and rivers. Flowering occurs at irregular intervals.

Arundinaria anceps Mitf.   Bamboo   F. W. Simpson 1930

Introduced. Native of N.W. Himalayas.
E: 13, Woolverstone, planted, flowering 1979-81 (M. A. Hyde); 24, Nacton.

Pseudosasa japonica (Sieb. & Zucc. ex Steud.) Mak.   Bamboo   F. W. Simpson c. 1930
(*Arundinaria japonica* Sieb. & Zucc. ex Steud.)   Metake

Introduced. Native of Japan. This is the most frequently grown species in this country and becomes naturalised, forming dense thickets.
W: 86, Timworth.
E: 13, Woolverstone Park, planted, flowering, 1980 and 1981 (M. A. Hyde); 14, Chantry, Christchurch and Holywells Parks, Ipswich; 24, Nacton; Levington; Falkenham; Foxhall; 25, Bromeswell; Ufford; 49, Fritton.

ADDENDA

The following hybrids are recorded in C. A. Stace's, 'Hybridization and the Flora of the British Isles, 1975', on a vice-county basis. A list was supplied by R. J. Pankhurst.

Ulmus coritana × plotii v.c. 26.

Ulmus coritana × glabra × plotii
(*U.* × *diversifolia* Melville) v.c. 25 and 26.

Rumex hydrolapathum × obtusifolius
(*R.* × *weberi* Fisch.-Benz.) v.c. 26.

Rumex crispus × hydrolapathum
(*R.* × *schreberi* Hausskn.) v.c. 25.

Rumex conglomeratus × crispus
(*R.* × *schulzei* Hausskn.) v.c. 25.

Salicornia pusilla × ramosissima v.c. 25.

Ranunculus circinatus × trichopyllus
(R. × *glueckii* A. Félix)
v.c. 26. (Mildenhall). The only British record.

Viola canina × riviniana
(*V.* × *berkleyi* Druce, nom. nud.)
v.c. 26.

Verbascum lychnitis × thapsus
(*V.* × *thapsi* L.) v.c. 26.

Verbascum nigrum × thapsus
(*V.* × *semialbum* Chaub.) v.c. 25.

Conyza canadensis × Erigeron acer
(*E.* × *huelsenii* Vatke) v.c. 26.

Hypochoeris glabra × radicata v.c. 26.

Holcus lanatus × mollis
(*H.* × *hybridus* K. Wein.)
v.c. 26, sandy heath near Brandon.

Avena fatua × sativa
(*A.* × *marquandii* Druce) v.c. 25/26.

OTHER RECORDS NOT INCLUDED IN THE CATALOGUE

Polystichum aculeatum × setiferum   A. W. Punter 1970

W: 94, Parliament Heath, Groton. Detd. J. W. Dyce. Comm. Mrs G. Crompton. This hybrid may be frequent but overlooked.

Azolla filiculoides Lam.

W: 76, Barrow, 1981 (Dr. G. D. Heathcote).

Lepidium densiflorum Schrad.   G. M. S. Easy 1978

Casual. Native of N. America. Widely naturalised in W. and C. Europe.
W: 66, Newmarket, railway sidings, near corn silo.

Philadelphus coronarius L.   Mock Orange   M. A. Hyde 1974
                                       Syringa

Introduced. Native of continental Europe. Planted in hedges and shrubberies. Persisting on sites of former gardens.
E: 03, Lt. Wenham, two bushes in hedge of disused railway, 1982 (F. W. Simpson); 13, Woolverstone, several bushes near the river. Still there, 1980.

Forsythia europaea Degen & Bald.   Forsythia   F. W. Simpson 1952

Introduced. Native of Albania and Yugoslavia. Commonly grown in gardens and occasionally found in hedges and on the sites of former gardens.
W: 86, Bury St Edmunds, formerly in a hedge and copse between the town and Fornham Priory, 1952-1970. Destroyed by housing development.
E: 03, Lt. Wenham, in hedge of disused railway, 1982.

Rubus armipotens Barton ex A. Newton   A. L. Bull 1981
(*R. pseudo-bifrons* sensu W. C. R. Wats.)

E: 35, Eyke, in roadside spinney. Conf. A. Newton.

Rubus leptothyrsus G. Braun   A. L. Bull 1979
(*R. danicus* sensu W. C. R. Wats.)

E: 35, Campsey Ash, Frequent in Long Grove. Conf. A. Newton.

Oenothera biennis × erythrosepala   J. E. Lousley & P. D. Sell 1961
(*O.* × *albivelutina* Renner)

W: Mayday Farm, between Elveden and Brandon. Still there, 1970 (D. McClintock).

Oenothera cambrica Rostański   C. M. Lemann 1834
(*O. parviflora* auct. brit., non L.)

Introduced. Native of Canada. Waste places, railway banks and sandy sea coast. Distribution uncertain. Possibly frequent and overlooked. Various strains of this species are grown in gardens.
The original record was for Sizewell.

Lathraea clandestina L.   Purple Toothwort   J. W. Hale 1978

Introduced. On roots of Poplar and Willow. Native of Spain, Italy, France and Belgium.
E: 25, Letheringham Mill.

BIBLIOGRAPHY

Books consulted during the compilation of the Flora.

ALLEN, G. O.: British Stoneworts, 1950.

BENTHAM, G. & HOOKER, Sir J. D.: Handbook of the British Flora, 1947.

BOTANICAL SOCIETY OF THE BRITISH ISLES: Journal and Proceedings, 'Watsonia'.

BUTCHER, R. W.: Illustrated British Flora, 1961.

CLAPHAM, A. R., TUTIN, T. G. & WARBURG, E. F.: Flora of the British Isles, 2nd Edn, 1962.

CLARKE, W. G.: In Breckland Wilds (revised by R. Rainbird-Clarke, 1937).

DANDY, J. E.: List of British Vascular Plants, 1958.

DRUCE, G. C.: Hayward's Botanist's Pocket Guide Book, 19th Edn, 1930.

FLORA EUROPAEA. Vols I, II, III, IV, 1964-76.

GALPIN, F. W.: An Account of the Flowering Plants of Harleston, 1888.

GIBSON, G. S.: Flora of Essex, 1862.

GROSE, D.: The Flora of Wiltshire, 1957.

HENSLOW, Rev. J. S. & SKEPPER, E.: Flora of Suffolk, 1860.

HEREMAN, S.: Paxton's Botanical Dictionary, 2nd Edn, 1868.

HIND, Rev. W. M.: The Flora of Suffolk, 1889.

HUBBARD, C. E.: Grasses, 2nd Edn, 1968.

JERMY, A. C., ARNOLD, H. R., FARRELL, L. & PERRING, F. H.: Atlas of Ferns of the British Isles, 1978.

JERMY, A. C. & TUTIN, T. G.: British Sedges, 1968.

KENT, D. H. & LOUSLEY, J. E.: A Hand List of the Plants of the London Area ('The London Naturalist', 1951-57).

LINNAEAN SOCIETY. The Journal of the,

LONDON CATALOGUE OF BRITISH PLANTS, 10th Edn, 1908.

MARTIN, Rev. W. Keble: The Concise British Flora in Colour, 1965.

McCLINTOCK, D. & FITTER, R. S. R.: A Pocket Guide to Wild Flowers, 1956.

PERRING, F. H. & WALTERS, S. M.: Atlas of the British Flora, 1962.

PERRING, F. H. & SELL, P. D.: Critical Supplement to the Atlas of the British Flora, 1968.

PERRING, F. H., SELL, P. D., WALTERS, S. M. & WHITEHOUSE, H. L. K.: A Flora of Cambridgeshire, 1964.

PETCH, C. P. & SWANN, E. L.: Flora of Norfolk, 1968, and Supplement, 1975, by E. L. Swann.

PETERKEN, G. F.: Development of Vegetation in Staverton Park, Suffolk. ('Field Studies' Vol. 3, No. 1-1969).

POLUNIN, O.: Flowers of Europe, a Field Guide, 1969.

POLUNIN, O. & HUXLEY, A.: Flowers of the Mediterranean, 1965.

RICHARDS, A. J.: The Taraxacum Flora of the British Isles (Supplement to 'Watsonia' Vol. 9, 1972.)

SALISBURY, E. J.: The East Anglian Flora (Trans. of the Norfolk and Norwich Naturalists Society. Vol. XIII Pt 3, 1931-32).

SAVIDGE, J. P., HEYWOOD, V. H. & GORDON, V.: Travis' Flora of South Lancashire, 1963.

SIMPSON, N. D.: A Bibliographical Index to the British Flora, 1960, pages 228-231.
SMITH, J. E.: The English Flora, 1825.
SOWERBY, J. E.: English Botany, 1863.
STACE, C. A.: Hybridization and the Flora of the British Isles, 1975.
TRANSACTIONS OF THE SUFFOLK NATURALISTS' SOCIETY, 1929-1981.
TRANSACTIONS OF THE LOWESTOFT FIELD CLUB.
TRIST, P. J. O.: An Ecological Flora of Breckland, 1979.
VICTORIA COUNTY HISTORY OF SUFFOLK, 1911.
WATSON, W. C. R.: Handbook of the Rubi of Great Britain and Ireland, 1958.
ZINCKE, Rev. F. Barham: Some Materials for the History of Wherstead, 2nd Edn, 1893.

Suggestions for further reading:

HEPBURN, I.: Flowers of the Coast, 1952.
JERMYN, S. T.: Flora of Essex, 1974.
LOUSLEY, J. E.: Wild Flowers of Chalk and Limestone, 1950.
MITCHELL, A.: Field Guide to the Trees of Britain and Northern Europe, 1974.
SALISBURY, Sir E. J.: Weeds and Aliens, 1961.
SUMMERHAYES, V. S.: Wild Orchids of Britain, 1951.
TANSLEY, A. G.: The British Isles and their Vegetation, 1939.
TURRILL, W. B.: British Plant Life, 1948.

RECORDERS 1950 – 1981

Ackeroyd, J.
Adams, F. W.
Airy Shaw, H. K.
Aldred, Mrs A. E.
Allen, D. E.
Armitage, Miss P. R. K.
Ashdown, Miss
Aston, A.
Aves, Miss A.

Backhouse, Miss E. M.
Barker, Rev. P. R. P.
Barker, Miss R.
Barlee, Miss P.
Barrington, The Hon. W. B. L.
Barton, Mrs A.
Basham, F. A.
Beaufoy, Miss A.
Beaufoy, S.
Beaumont, Dr E.
Bell, F. G.

Bendix, M.
Bernard, Miss E. H.
Bettridge, A. E. V.
Bingley, F. J.
Bitton, E. Q.
Blake, Miss C. J.
Blowers, K. E.
Boatfield, Mrs J.
Boreham, H. J.
Botanical Society of the British Isles
Bowtell, Miss E.
Bramford Junior School
Brebner, Miss K. M. R.
Brewins, Mrs
Briggs, R. S.
Bristow, A.
Brown, Mrs E. K.
Brown, Dr K. T.
Brownhill, Miss R.
Brownlow, Lt.-Col. H. G.
Bull, A. L.

Recorders (1950-1981) — *continued*

Bull, Mrs C.
Burdon, G. H.
Burgess, Miss C.
Burton, R. M.
Bury St Edmunds & District Naturalists' Society
Butcher, Dr R. W.

Cadbury, C. J.
Cadbury, Miss D. A.
Carpenter, D. J.
Carter, Mrs J.
Cautley, Mrs H. Munro
Chapman, P.
Chenery, Miss C. M.
Chipperfield, Mrs F. J. W.
Chipperfield, H. E.
Churchman, Miss N.
Churley, Miss G.
Clark, Mrs R.
Clement, E. J.
Clements, G. A.
Clodd, Mrs E.
Cobbold, Miss J. B.
Convent of St Louis
Cook, Mrs
Coombe, Dr D. E.
Copinger-Hill, The Misses B. & R.
Copithorne, Dr R. E. C.
Copping, A.
Coxon, Mrs. E.
Crackles, Miss F. E.
Craig, Mrs A. H.
Craig, Miss M. E. C.
Cramp, K. V.
Cranbrook, The Earl of
Cranbrook, The Dowager Countess of
Crompton, Mrs G.
Cross, Lady J.
Cross, J. S.
Culford School
Curtis, Mrs B. A.

Daman, Mrs M.
Dandy, J. E.
Daniels, E. T.
David, R. W.

Day, F. M.
Debenham, Miss E.
Denniss, Miss J. D.
Dickinson, P. G. M.
Dickinson, Mrs G. E.
Dickson, Mrs E. M. L.
Digby, J.
Dodd, Mrs E.
Donald, D. R.
Dony, Dr J. G.
Downing, Miss P.
Ducker, B.

East Anglian Girls' School
Easto, Miss E. V. C.
Eastwood, Dr N. B.
Easy, G. M. S.
Edwardstone School
Ellis, Dr E. A.
Ellis, J. H.
Ellis, Dr J. R.
Ellis, R. V.
Elwell, Miss G.
Emms, R. E.
Engleheart, F. H.
English, R. D.

Fiddian, W. E. H.
Fitter, A.
Forrest, Miss C.
Forrest, J. D.
Foster, J. A.
Framlingham College

Garrett, Miss D.
Garrett, Dr D. G.
Gathorne-Hardy, Mrs R.
Gathercole, Z.
Geater, Mrs D.
Gilbert, J. L.
Goddard, Mrs L.
Goldsworthy, H. H.
Goodman, Miss
Goodway, K. M.
Graham, R. A.
Grange, C.
Gray, Mrs J.

Recorders (1950-1981) — *continued*

Green, E. C.
Green, Mrs M.
Griffith, Dr G.

Halesworth Modern School
Hall, C.
Hall, Mrs J.
Hall, P. C.
Hallam, Miss A. R.
Harkness, R.
Harley, Dr R. M.
Harris, Mrs J.
Harrison, Mrs M.
Harrison, Mrs R. A.
Hart, Mrs A.
Hartley, Rev. P. H. T.
Hawes, C. J.
Haworth, Miss M.
Hayter, Miss E. E.
Holdsworth, G.
Holdsworth, Mrs M.
Holloway, Mrs W. D.
Horne, Mrs W. J.
Horrill, Miss M.
Horwood, E. K.
Horwood, Mrs I.
Hovells, Mrs M.
Howard, L. W.
Howarth, J.
Howarth, M. M.
Hubbard, A.
Hubbard, Dr C. E.
Hughes, Mrs J.
Hull, D. C. H.
Hunt, N. V.
Hurrell, A. B.
Hyde, Mrs E. M.
Hyde, L. J.
Hyde, M. A.

Ipswich & District Natural History Society

Jackson, Miss P.
Jauncey, Miss E.
Jay, Mrs D.
Jermy, A. C.
Jermyn, S. T.

Johnson, C.
Johnson, I. G.
Jolly, Miss M.
Jones, B. D.
Jones, C. H.
Jones, R.
Judge, Miss K.

Keeble, J.
Keer, Miss D.
Kefford, R. W. J.
Kerr, M.
Kerr, N. R.
Kershaw, Mrs M.
Kiddall, Miss F.
Killick, H. J.
King, C. J.

Lambley, P. J.
Larter, Miss
Lawson, P. G.
Lee, H. J.
Lee, Miss P. E.
Leslie, Dr A. C.
Levy, Dr B. G.
Lewis, W. E.
Libbey, R. P.
Lingwood, Mrs H. R.
Linnch, Mrs L.
Little, A. C.
Llewellyn Jones, J. E.
Lousley, J. E.
Lovett, Mrs W. V. J.
Lowestoft Field Club
Lynn-Allen, Miss M. L.

Mabey, R.
Mallett, D. J.
Marlow, D. H.
Marsden, P. T.
Marsh, N. A.
Marson, J. E.
Martin, Miss C. M.
Martin, D. J.
Matthews, Dr L. Harrison
Mayhew, Mrs R. M.
McClintock, D.

Recorders (1950-1981) — *continued*

McCosh, Miss A.
McVean, D. N.
Mead, G.
Mead, Dr J. C.
Mead, J. N.
Miles, B. A.
Miller, Mrs H. B.
Mills, Mrs M.
Milne-Redhead, E.
Mitchell, N. S. P.
Morfey, W. M.
Morgan, Miss B. M. C.
Morris, Sir C.
Morse, Miss C. B.
Morton, Mrs A. M.
Mountford, J. O.

Nash, Mrs J.
Nash, J. R. A.
Neal, Miss L. E.
Norman, E. C.
Northeast, P.
Notcutt, S. A.

Oliver, Miss J. M.
Oostveen, Miss M. S. van
Orford, A. E.
Ovey, Miss M.

Pagan, Dr A. T.
Palmer, J. R.
Pankhurst, R. J.
Paternoster, Mrs J. O.
Paul, Mrs W. S. H.
Payn, Major W. H.
Payne, R. M.
Peecock, P. R.
Pemberton, J. E. L.
Perkins, Mrs G.
Perring, Dr F. H.
Peterken, Dr J. H. G.
Phillips, W.
Pickard, Dr O. G.
Pierce, C. W.
Prime, Dr C. T.
Punter, A. W.
Pyman, G. A.

Rackham, Mrs G. E.
Rackham, Dr O.
Ransome, G. H.
Ransome, G. L.
Ranson, C.
Ranwell, Dr D. S.
Reed, Mr
Reid, Mrs E.
Reid, Mrs J.
Richards, Dr A. J.
Richardson, Dr D. W. Ryder-
Riches, Miss L.
Riddleston, Mrs K.
Robinson, Miss M.
Robinson, Mrs R.
Rolfe, R. R.
Rope, Miss M. H.
Rose, Dr F.
Rowell, R. W. F.
Rowley, Lady
Rowling, Miss E. S.
Royal Botanic Gardens, Kew
Royal Horticultural Society, Wisley
Rudolf, Miss L. de M.
Ruffles, C.
Rutterford, M. G.

Saunders, Miss M.
Savidge, Dr J. P.
St John, Mrs G.
Schafer, Miss B.
Schofield, J. M.
Sell, P. D.
Seward, Miss A.
Shackles, C. J. D.
Shaw, Miss A. Y.
Shawcross, Mrs
Shelley, Mrs D. E.
Shelley, R.
Sheppey, Mrs O.
Sheppey, P.
Sherwood, Miss I.
Shiell, Miss D. M.
Simpson, F. W.
Small, Miss E.
Smee, D.
Smith, B. W.

Recorders (1950-1981) — *continued*

Smith, Miss D.
Smith, Mrs V. L.
Southwell, Mrs M.
Standing, S. G.
Starr, Miss E.
Stearn, P.
Steggall, Miss M.
Stephenson, Mrs M.
Stradbroke, The Earl of
Strapps, Miss J.
Streather, Miss M.
Suffolk Naturalists' Society
Swann, E. L.

Taylor, Sir George
Taylor, Miss J.
Taylor, J. C.
Taylor, M.
Temple, H.
Thomson, Mrs H.
Thurlow, W. G.
Tollemache, Lady D.
Townsend, Mrs G.
Townsend, T. P.
Trist, P. J. O.
Tuck, Mrs G.
Turner, C.

Vane, J.
Vaughan, Mrs I. M.
Vulliamy, Miss L.

Walker, Miss J.
Walker, Mrs M.
Waller, Mrs T.
Walters, Dr S. M.
Warburg, Dr E. F.
Ward, B. T.
Warren, R. B.
Watchman, C. A.
Watson, Hon. Mrs J.
Watson, S. F.
Welch, Mrs B.
Whiting, Miss M. M.
Wiard, H. D.
Widgery, J. P.
Wigginton, M. J.
Wightman, H. L. C.
Wille, Mrs A.
Williams, Mrs G.
Williams, J. C.
Willis, Mrs J.
Willis, Miss J. C. N.
Wood, J. R. Ironside-
Woodward, Miss G.
Worland, A. J.
Wright, Miss M.
Wurr, S. F.
Wyer, D. W.

Yeo, Dr P. F.
Young, Dr D. P.

ALPHABETICAL LIST OF THE PARISHES AND OTHER IMPORTANT SITES OF SUFFOLK WITH REFERENCES TO THE 10 km SQUARES IN WHICH THEY LIE.

Name of Parish and site	Map square/s
Acton	TL 84/94
Akenham	TM 14/15
Aldeburgh	TM 45
Alderton	TM 33/34
Aldham	TM 04
Aldringham-with-Thorpe	TM 45/46
All Saints & St Nicholas South Elmham	TM 38
Alpheton	TL 84/85
Ampton	TL 86/87
Arger Fen	TL 93
Ashbocking	TM 15
Ashby	TM 49/TG 40
Ashfield-cum-Thorpe	TN 16/26
Aspall	TM 16
Assington	TL 93/94
Athelington	TM 17/26/27
Bacton	TM 06
Badingham	TM 26/36/37
Badley	TM 05
Badwell Ash	TL 96/97/TM 06/07
Ballingdon-with-Brundon	TL 83/84
Bardwell	TL 96/97
Barham	TM 15
Barking	TM 05/15
Barnardiston	TL 64/65/74/75
Barnby	TM 48/49
Barnham	TL 87/88
Barningham	TL 97
Barrow	TL 76
Barsham	TM 38/39/48/49
Barton Mills	TL 77
Battisford	TM 05
Bawdsey	TM 33/34
Baylham	TM 05/15
Beccles	TM 48/49
Bedfield	TM 26
Bedingfield	TM 16/17/26
Belstead	TM 13/14
Belton	TG 40/50
Benacre	TM 58
Benhall	TM 35/36
Bentley	TM 03/13/14
Beyton	TL 96
Bildeston	TL 94/95/TM 04/05
Bixley	TM 24

Name of Parish and site	Map square/s
Blaxhall	TM 35
Blundeston	TM 49/59
Blyford	TM 47
Blythburgh	TM 47
Bosmere	TM 05
Botesdale	TM 07
Boulge	TM 25
Boxford	TL 93/94
Boxted	TL 75/84/85
Boyton	TM 34
Bradfield Combust	TL 85/95
Bradfield St Clare	TL 85/95
Bradfield St George	TL 85/86/95/96
Bradwell	TG 40/50
Braiseworth	TM 17
Bramfield	TM 37/47
Bramford	TM 04/14
Brampton	TM 47/48
Brandeston	TM 25/26
Brandon	TL 78/88
Brantham	TM 03/13
Bredfield	TM 25
Brent Eleigh	TL 94
Brettenham	TL 95
Breydon Water	TG 40/50
Brightwell	TM 24
Brockford	TM 16
Brockley	TL 85
Brome	TM 17
Bromeswell	TM 24/25/34/35
Bruisyard	TM 36
Brundish	TM 26/27
Bucklesham	TM 24
Bungay	TM 38/39
Bures St Mary	TL 83/93
Burgate	TM 07/17
Burgh	TM 25
Burgh Castle	TG 40
Burstall	TM 04/14
Bury St Edmunds	TL 86
Butley	TM 34/35
Buxhall	TL 95/TM 05
Campsey Ash	TM 35
Capel St Andrew	TM 34
Capel St Mary	TM 03/13
Carlton	TM 36/46

437

Name of Parish and site	Map square/s	Name of Parish and site	Map square/s
Carlton Colville	TM 48/49/58/59	Earl Stonham	TM 05/06/15/16
Cattawade	TM 13	East Bergholt	TM 03/13
Cavendish	TL 74/75/84/85	East Bridge	TM 46
Cavenham	TL 76/77	Easton	TM 25/26
Chadacre	TL 85	Easton Bavents	TM 57
Charsfield	TM 25	Edwardstone	TL 94
Chattisham	TM 04/14	Ellough	TM 48
Chedburgh	TL 75/85	Elmsett	TM 04
Chediston	TM 37/38	Elmswell	TL 96/TM 06
Chelmondiston	TM 13/23	Elveden	TL 77/78/87/88
Chelsworth	TL 94	Eriswell	TL 77/78
Chevington	TL 75/76/85/86	Erwarton	TM 23
Chillesford	TM 35/45	Euston	TL 87/88/97/98
Chilton	TL 84/94	Exning	TL 56/66
Clare	TL 74	Eye	TM 17
Claydon	TM 14/15	Eyke	TM 34/35
Clopton	TM 25		
Cockfield	TL 85/95	Fakenham Magna	TL 87/97
Coddenham	TM 15	Falkenham	TM 23/24/33/34
Combs	TM 05	Farnham	TM 35/36
Coney Weston	TL 97/98	Felixstowe	TM 23/33
Cookley	TM 37	Felsham	TL 95
Copdock	TM 03/04/13/14	Finningham	TM 06/07
Cornard Mere	TL 83	Flatford Mill	TM 03
Corton	TG 50/TM 59	Flempton	TL 76/86/87
Cotton	TM 06	Flixton, near Lowestoft	TM 59
Covehithe	TM 57/58	Flixton, near Bungay	TM 28/38
Cowlinge	TL 65/75	Flowton	TM 04
Cransford	TM 36	Fornham All Saints	TL 86
Cratfield	TM 27/37	Fornham St Genevieve	TL 86
Creeting St Mary	TM 05/15	Fornham St Martin	TL 86
Creeting St Peter	TM 05	Foxhall	TM 24
Cretingham	TM 25/26	Framlingham	TM 26/36
Crowfield	TM 15	Framsden	TM 15/16/25/26
Culford	TL 86/87	Freckenham	TL 66/67/76/77
Culpho	TM 24/25	Freston	TM 13/14
		Fressingfield	TM 27/37
Dagworth	TM 06	Friston	TM 36/45/46
Dalham	TL 75/76	Fritton	TG 40/TM 49
Dallinghoo	TM 25	Frostenden	TM 48
Darmsden	TM 05/15		
Darsham	TM 46/47	Gazeley	TL 76
Debach	TM 25	Gedding	TL 95
Debenham	TM 16/26	Gedgrave	TM 34/35/44/45
Denham (W. Suffolk)	TL 76	Gipping	TM 06
Denham (E. Suffolk)	TM 17	Gisleham	TM 58/59
Dennington	TM 26/27/36	Gislingham	TM 07
Denston	TL 75	Glemsford	TL 84
Depden	TL 75	Glevering	TM 25/35
Drinkstone	TL 95/96	Gorleston	TG 50
Dunwich	TM 46/47/57	Gosbeck	TM 15
Earl Soham	TM 26	Great Ashfield	TL 96/TM 06

Name of Parish and site	Map square/s	Name of Parish and site	Map square/s
Great Barton	TL 86/96	Holbrook	TM 13
Great Bealings	TM 24/25	Hollesley	TM 34
Great Blakenham	TM 14/15	Holton, near Halesworth	TM 37/38/47/48
Great Bradley	TL 65	Holton St Mary, near	
Great Bricett	TM 04/05	East Bergholt	TM 03
Great Cornard	TL 83/84/93/94	Homersfield	TM 28/38
Great Finborough	TL 95/TM 05	Honington	TL 87/97
Great Glemham	TM 36	Hoo	TM 25
Great Livermere	TL 86/87/96/97	Hopton (W. Suffolk)	TL 97/98/TM 07/08
Great Saxham	TL 76	Hopton (E. Suffolk)	TG 50/TM 59
Great Thurlow	TL 64/65/75	Horham	TM 17/27
Great Waldingfield	TL 84/94	Horringer	TL 85/86
Great Welnetham	TL 85/86	Hoxne	TM 17/27
Great Wenham	TM 03/04	Hundon	TL 74/75
Great Wratting	TL 64/74	Hunston	TL 96
Gromford	TM 35	Huntingfield	TM 37
Groton	TL 94		
Grundisburgh	TM 15/24/25	Icklingham	TL 77/87
Gunton	TM 59	Ickworth	TL 85/86
		Iken	TM 35/45
Hacheston	TM 25/35	Ilketshall St Andrew	TM 38
Hadleigh	TL 94/TM 04	Ilketshall St Lawrence	TM 38
Halesworth	TM 37	Ilketshall St John	TM 38
Hardwick	TL 86	Ilketshall St Margaret	TM 38
Hargrave	TL 75/76	Ingham	TL 86/87
Harkstead	TM 13/23	Ipswich	TM 14/24
Harleston	TM 05/06	Ixworth	TL 96/97
Hartest	TL 85	Ixworth Thorpe	TL 97
Hasketon	TM 24/25		
Haughley	TM 05/06	Kedington	TL 64/74
Havergate Island	TM 34/44	Kelsale	TM 36/46
Haverhill	TL 64	Kentford	TL 76
Hawkedon	TL 75/85	Kenton	TM 16/26
Hawstead	TL 85/86	Kersey	TL 94/TM 04
Helmingham	TM 15/25	Kesgrave	TM 24
Hemingstone	TM 15	Kessingland	TM 58
Hemley	TM 24	Kettlebaston	TL 94/95
Hengrave	TL 86	Kettleburgh	TM 25/26
Henham	TM 47	Kirkley	TM 59
Henley	TM 15	Kirton	TM 23/24/34
Henstead	TM 48/58	Knettishall	TL 97/98
Hepworth	TL 97	Knodishall	TM 45/46
Herringfleet	TM 49		
Herringswell	TL 66/76/77	Lackford	TL 76/77/86/87
Hessett	TL 95/96	Lakenheath	TL 68/77/78
Heveningham	TM 37	Landguard Common	TM 23
Higham, near		Langham	TL 96/97
Newmarket	TL 76	Lavenham	TL 84/85/94/95
Higham, near Hadleigh	TM 03	Lawshall	TL 85
Hinderclay	TM 07	Laxfield	TM 26/27/36/37
Hintlesham	TM 04/14	Layham	TL 94/TM 03/04
Hinton	TM 47	Leavenheath	TL 93
Hitcham	TL 94/95/TM 05	Leiston	TM 46

Name of Parish and site	Map square/s	Name of Parish and site	Map square/s
Letheringham	TM 25	Needham Market	TM 05
Levington	TM 23/24	Nettlestead	TM 04/05/14/15
Lidgate	TL 75/76	Newbourn	TM 24
Lindsey	TL 94	Newmarket	TL 66
Linstead Magna	TM 37	Newton	TL 93/94
Linstead Parva	TM 37	North Cove	TM 48/49
Little Bealings	TM 24	Norton	TL 96
Little Blakenham	TM 04/14/15	Nowton	TL 85/86
Little Bradley	TL 65/75		
Little Bricett	TM 04/05	Oakley	TM 17
Little Cornard	TL 83/93	Occold	TM 16/17
Little Fakenham	TL 97	Offton	TM 04/05
Little Finborough	TM 05	Old Newton	TM 06
Little Glemham	TM 35/36	Onehouse	TM 05/06
Little Livermere	TL 87	Orford	TM 34/44/45
Little Saxham	TL 76/86	Otley	TM 15/25
Little Stonham	TM 15/16	Oulton	TM 49/59
Little Thurlow	TL 64/65/75	Ousden	TL 75/76
Little Waldingfield	TL 94	Outney Common	TM 39
Little Welnetham	TL 85/86/95		
Little Wenham	TM 03/04	Pakefield	TM 59
Little Wratting	TL 64/74	Pakenham	TL 86/96/97
Long Melford	TL 84/85	Palgrave	TM 07/17
Loudham	TM 35	Parham	TM 25/26/35/36
Lound	TG 40/50/	Peasenhall	TM 36/37
	TM 49/59	Pettaugh	TM 15/16
Lowestoft	TM 58/59	Pettistree	TM 25/35
		Playford	TM 24
Market Weston	TL 97	Poslingford	TL 74/75
Marlesford	TM 35/36	Polstead	TL 93/94/TM 03/04
Martlesham	TM 24	Preston	TL 94/95
Mellis	TM 07/17	Purdis Farm	TM 14/24
Melton	TM 24/25		
Mendham	TM 27/28	Ramsholt	TM 24/33/34
Mendlesham	TM 06/16	Rattlesden	TL 95/96
Metfield	TM 27/28/37/38	Raydon	TM 03/04
Mettingham	TM 38/39	Rede	TL 75/85
Mickfield	TM 16	Redgrave	TM 07
Middleton	TM 36/46	Redisham	TM 38/48
Milden	TL 94	Redlingfield	TM 16/17/27
Mildenhall	TL 67/68/77/78	Rendham	TM 36
Minsmere	TM 46	Rendlesham	TM 35
Monewden	TM 25/26	Reydon	TM 47/48/57
Monk Soham	TM 26	Rickinghall Inferior	TM 07
Monks Eleigh	TL 94	Rickinghall Superior	TM 07
Monks' Park Wood	TL 95	Ringsfield	TM 38/48
Monks Risbridge	TL 75	Ringshall	TM 05
Moulton	TL 66/76	Risby	TL 76/86
Mutford	TM 48	Rishangles	TM 16
		Rougham	TL 86/96
Nacton	TM 13/14/23/24	Rumburgh	TM 37/38
Nayland-with-Wissington	TL 93	Rushbrooke	TL 86/96
Nedging-with-Naughton	TL 94/TM 04/05		

Name of Parish and site	Map square/s
Rushmere, near	
Lowestoft	TM 48/58
Rushmere St Andrew	TM 14/24
St Cross South Elmham	TM 28/38
St James South Elmham	TM 37/38
St Margaret South	
Elmham	TM 38
St Mary South Elmham	TM 28/38
St Michael South	
Elmham	TM 38
St Peter South Elmham	TM 38
St Olave's	TM 49
Santon Downham	TL 78/88
Sapiston	TL 97
Saxmundham	TM 36/46
Saxtead	TM 26
Semer	TL 94/TM 04
Shadingfield	TM 48
Shelland	TL 95/96/TM 05/06
Shelley	TM 03
Shimpling	TL 84/85
Shingle Street	TM 34
Shipmeadow	TM 38/39
Shotley	TM 23
Shottisham	TM 34
Shrubland Park	TM 15
Sibton	TM 36/37
Sicklesmere	TL 86
Sizewell	TM 46
Slaughden	TM 45
Snape	TM 35/36/45/46
Somerleyton	TM 49/59
Somersham	TM 04
Somerton	TL 85
Sotherton	TM 47
Sotterley	TM 48
South Cove	TM 47/48/57/58
Southolt	TM 16/17/26/27
Southwold	TM 47/57
Spexhall	TM 37/38
Sproughton	TM 14
Stanningfield	TL 85
Stansfield	TL 75
Stanstead	TL 84/85
Stanton	TL 97
Staverton	TM 35
Sternfield	TM 35/36/46
Stoke Ash	TM 16/17
Stoke-by-Clare	TL 74
Stoke-by-Nayland	TL 93/TM 03
Stonham Aspal	TM 15/16
Stoven	TM 48

Name of Parish and site	Map square/s
Stowlangtoft	TL 96/97
Stowmarket	TM 05/06
Stowupland	TM 05/06
Stradbroke	TM 27
Stradishall	TL 75
Stratford St Andrew	TM 35/36
Stratford St Mary	TM 03
Stratton Hall	TM 23
Stuston	TM 17
Stutton	TM 13
Sudbourne	TM 45
Sudbury	TL 83/84
Sutton	TM 24/34
Swefling	TM 36
Swilland	TM 15/25
Syleham	TM 17/27
Tannington	TM 26
Tattingstone	TM 13
Theberton	TM 46
Thelnetham	TL 97/TM 07
Thetford	TL 87/88
Thorington	TM 47
Thorington Street	TM 03
Thorndon	TM 16/17
Thornham Magna	TM 06/07/16/17
Thornham Parva	TM 07/17
Thorpe Morieux	TM 95
Thorpeness	TM 45/46
Thrandeston	TM 07/17
Thurston	TL 96
Thwaite	TM 16
Timworth	TL 86/87
Tostock	TL 96
Trimley St Martin	TM 23/24/33
Trimley St Mary	TM 23
Troston	TL 87/97
Tuddenham St Martin	TM 14/15/24/25
Tuddenham St Mary	TL 76/77
Tunstall	TM 35/45
Ubbeston	TM 37
Ufford	TM 25/35
Uggeshall	TM 47/48
Walberswick	TM 47/57
Waldringfield	TM 24
Walpole	TM 37
Walsham-le-Willows	TL 97/TM 06/07
Walton	TM 33
Wangford (Breckland)	TL 78
Wangford, near	
Lowestoft	TM 47/48

Name of Parish and site	Map square/s	Name of Parish and site	Map square/s
Wantisden	TM 34/35	Wickham Skeith	TM 06/07/16
Washbrook	TM 03/04/14	Wilby	TM 26/27
Wattisfield	TL 97/TM 07	Willingham	TM 48
Wattisham	TL 95/TM 05	Willisham	TM 04/05
Wenhaston-with-Mells		Wingfield	TM 27
Hamlet	TM 37/47	Winston	TM 16/26
Westerfield	TM 14	Wissett	TM 37/38
Westhall	TM 38/47/48	Wiston	TL 93
Westhorpe	TM 06/07	Withersfield	TL 64
Westleton	TM 46/47	Witnesham	TM 14/15/25
Westley	TL 86	Wixoe	TL 74
Weston	TM 48	Woodbridge	TM 24/25
West Row	TL 67	Woolpit	TL 95/96/TM 06
West Stow	TL 77/87	Woolverstone	TM 13/23
Wetherden	TL 96/TM 06	Wordwell	TL 87
Wetheringsett-cum-		Worlingham	TM 48/49
Brockford	TM 16	Worlington	TL 67/77
Weybread	TM 27/28	Worlingworth	TM 26/27
Whatfield	TM 04	Wortham	TM 07/08/17
Whepstead	TL 85	Wrentham	TM 48/58
Wherstead	TM 13/14	Wyverstone	TM 06
Whitton	TM 14		
Wickhambrook	TL 75	Yaxley	TM 17
Wickham Market	TM 25/35	Yoxford	TM 36/37/46/47

Primula vulgaris   Primrose

Primula elatior　Oxlip　　　　　*Primula veris*　Cowslip

Primula veris × *vulgaris* *Primula elatior* × *vulgaris*　Hybrid Oxlip
Ladies' Fingers

444

Endymion non-scriptus　Bluebell — Pink *Endymion non-scriptus*　Bluebell — White

Primula elatior   Oxlip

445

Anemone nemorosa   Wood Anemone

Endymion non-scriptus Bluebell

Convallaria majalis Lily-of-the-Valley

Allium ursinum Ramsons

447

Vicia sepium
Bush Vetch

Carpinus betulus Hornbeam

Endymion hispanicus Spanish Bluebell

Mercurialis perennis Dog's Mercury

448

Ajuga reptans Bugle

Paris quadrifolia Herb Paris

Iris foetidissima Stinking Iris

Helleborus viridis
Green Hellebore

Ruscus aculeatus Butcher's Broom (inset) Fruit

Euphorbia amygdaloides   Wood Spurge

450

Galium odoratum   Sweet Woodruff

Helleborus foetidus Stinking Hellebore

Daphne laureola Spurge Laurel

Oxalis acetosella Wood Sorrel

451

Gagea lutea Yellow Star-of-Bethlehem

Aconitum napellus Monkshood

Prunus padus Bird Cherry

452

Lamiastrum galeobdolon Yellow Archangel

Lysimachia nemorum   Yellow Pimpernel

453

Stellaria holostea   Greater Stitchwort

Geum rivale   Water Avens

Lysimachia nummularia   Creeping Jenny   *Silene dioica*   Red Campion

Geum urbanum Herb Bennet

Stachys officinalis Betony

455

Viburnum opulus
Guelder Rose berries

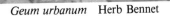

Carex pendula Pendulous Sedge

Salix caprea   Great Sallow, male

Salix caprea   Great Sallow, male

456

Arum maculatum   Wild Arum

Arum maculatum
Wild Arum berries

Eranthis hyemalis   Winter Aconite

457

Galanthus nivalis   Snowdrop

Adoxa moschatellina   Moschatel

458   *Digitalis purpurea*   Foxglove
Epilobium angustifolium   Rosebay Willowherb

Narcissus pseudonarcissus   Wild Daffodil, Butley

Staverton Park, Wantisden

Populus nigra   Black Poplar

Hypericum hirsutum   Hairy St John's Wort   *Ranunculus auricomus*   Goldilocks

461

Viola odorata   Sweet Violet

Dactylorhiza fuchsii   Common Spotted Orchid

462

Castanea sativa
Sweet Chestnut at Erwarton

Sedum telephium   Orpine

Lamiastrum galeobdolon Yellow Archangel
Endymion non-scriptus Bluebell

463

Blechnum spicant Hard Fern

Asplenium ruta-muraria   Wall-rue

464

Gymnocarpium robertianum   Limestone Fern

Dryopteris pseudomas
Golden-scaled Male Fern

Polypodium interjectum   Intermediate Polypody

465

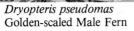

Adiantum capillus-veneris   Maidenhair Fern   *Phyllitis scolopendrium*   Hart's-tongue Fern

Ophioglossum vulgatum   Adder's Tongue

466   *Equisetum telmateia*
Great Horsetail

Equisetum telmateia   Great Horsetail

Scleranthus perennis Perennial Knawel

467

Wangford Warren

Silene otites
Spanish Catchfly

Dianthus deltoides   Maiden Pink

468

Cerastium arvense
Field Mouse-ear Chickweed

Artemisia campestris   Field Wormwood

Echium vulgare   Viper's Bugloss

Muscari atlanticum   Grape Hyacinth

Muscari atlanticum
Grape Hyacinth

Silene conica   Sand Catchfly

Sedum acre Wall-pepper

Saxifraga granulata Meadow Saxifrage

Reseda lutea Wild Mignonette

Medicago arabica Spotted Medic

470

Cytisus scoparius Broom

Ornithogalum umbellatum
Common Star-of-Bethlehem

Tinker's Walks, Walberswick

Vicia angustifolia
Narrow-leaved Vetch

Centaurium erythraea
Common Centaury

Erica tetralix Cross-leaved Heath

Ulex gallii Western Gorse

Carlina vulgaris Carline Thistle

Gnaphalium sylvaticum
Wood Cudweed

472

Astragalus danicus
Purple Milk Vetch

Cirsium acaule Dwarf Thistle

Astragalus glycyphyllos Milk Vetch

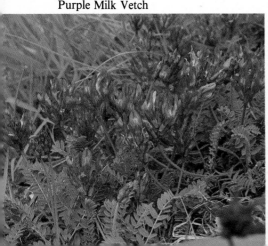

Agrimonia eupatoria
Common Agrimony

Clinopodium vulgare   Wild Basil

Viburnum lantana   Wayfaring Tree, berries

Inula conyza
Ploughman's Spikenard

Silene vulgaris ssp. *vulgaris*   Bladder Campion

Helianthemum nummularium
Common Rockrose

Bryonia cretica ssp. *dioica*
White Bryony

Centaurea scabiosa   Greater Knapweed

Erica cinerea Bell Heather

Hippocrepis comosa
Horseshoe Vetch

Blackstonia perfoliata
Yellow Wort

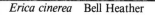

Origanum vulgare Marjoram

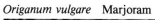

Verbascum pulverulentum   Hoary Mullein

Filipendula vulgaris Dropwort

Rubus ulmifolius Bramble

477

Verbascum nigrum
Dark Mullein

Melampyrum cristatum
Crested Cow-wheat

Nepeta cataria Catmint

Rhinanthus minor Fritillary Reserve
Yellow Rattle

Lychnis flos-cuculi Ragged Robin

Mentha aquatica Water Mint

Fritillaria meleagris White variety

Ranunculus lingua Greater Spearwort

Colchicum autumnale Meadow Saffron

Achillea ptarmica Sneezewort

479

Fritillaria meleagris Fritillary

Tulipa sylvestris Wild Tulip

Polygonum bistorta
Common Bistort

BOTTOM LEFT:
Eupatorium cannabinu
Hemp Agrimony

Typha latifolia
Great Reedmace

Pulicaria dysenterica Fleabane

Phalaris arundinacea
Reed-grass

481

Filipendula ulmaria Meadow Sweet

Angelica sylvestris Wild Angelica

Oenanthe lachenalii
Parsley Water Dropwort

Caltha palustris Kingcup

482

Oenanthe pimpinelloides
Corky-fruited Water Dropwort

Iris pseudacorus Yellow Flag

Petasites fragrans Winter Heliotrope

Sagittaria sagittifolia Arrowhead

Sanguisorba officinalis Great Burnet

483

Chrysosplenium oppositifolium Opposite-leaved Golden Saxifrage

Valeriana officinalis
Common Valerian

ABOVE LEFT:
Valeriana dioica
Marsh Valerian

Filipendula ulmaria
Meadow Sweet and
Epilobium hirsutum
Great Hairy Willowherb
at Holbrook

Cruciata laevipes Crosswort

Carex pseudocyperus Cyperus Sedge

485

Butomus umbellatus
Flowering Rush

Hippuris vulgaris Mare's-tail

Sonchus palustris   Marsh Sow-thistle

Carex acutiformis
Lesser Pond Sedge

Schoenus nigricans
Black Bog-rush

Lepidium latifolium   Dittander

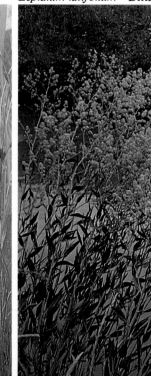

Anagallis tenella
Bog Pimpernel
Hydrocotyle vulgaris
Marsh Pennywort

Lythrum salicaria   Purple Loosestrife

Nuphar lutea   Yellow Water Lily

Utricularia vulgaris
Common Bladderwort   **487**

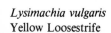
Lysimachia vulgaris
Yellow Loosestrife

Ranunculus peltatus   Water Crowfoot

Petasites hybridus Butterbur

Cardamine amara Large Bitter Cress

Hypericum elodes
Marsh St John's Wort

Redgrave Fen

488

Cladium mariscus
Great Fen Sedge

Potentilla palustris
Marsh Cinquefoil

Hottonia palustris Water Violet

Symphytum × uplandicum
Russian Comfrey

Symphytum officinale   Common Comfrey

489

Symphytum orientale   White Comfrey

Malva sylvestris   Common Mallow

Campanula glomerata   *Knautia arvensis*   Field Scabious
Clustered Bellflower

490

Scabiosa columbaria   Small Scabious   *Euphorbia cyparissias*   Cypress Spurge

Malva moschata Musk Mallow

Althaea officinalis Marsh Mallow

Campanula trachelium
Nettle-leaved Bellflower

Campanula rapunculoides
Creeping Bellflower

Viola reichenbachiana Pale Wood Violet   *Viola hirta* Hairy Violet

Viola tricolor ssp. *curtisii* Breckland Pansy   *Viola riviniana* Common Wood Violet

492

Geranium sanguineum Bloody Cranesbill

Geranium pyrenaicum Mountain Cranesbill

Geranium pratense
Meadow Cranesbill

493

Benacre Broad

Lathyrus japonicus Sea Pea

Frankenia laevis Sea Heath

Glaucium flavum Yellow Horned Poppy

Armeria maritima Thrift

Inula crithmoides Golden Samphire

Artemisia maritima
Sea Wormwood

Vicia lutea Yellow Vetch

Smyrnium olusatrum Alexanders

Crithmum maritimum Rock Samphire

Eryngium maritimum   Sea Holly

Limonium humile   Lax-flowered Sea Lavender   *Limonium vulgare*   Sea Lavender

Calystegia soldanella Sea Convolvulus

Euphorbia paralias Sea Spurge

Scirpus maritimus Sea Clubrush

Salsola kali Prickly Saltwort

498

Arthrocnemum perenne
Perennial Glasswort

Aster tripolium Sea Aster

Lathyrus nissolia
Grass Vetchling

Silybum marianum Milk Thistle

Carduus tenuiflorus Slender Thistle

Beta vulgaris Sea Beet
ssp. *maritima*

Crambe maritima Sea Kale

Senecio viscosus Sticky Groundsel

Sonchus arvensis
Corn Sow-thistle

Corynephorus canescens Grey Hair-grass

Honkenya peploides Sea Sandwort

Centranthus ruber Red Valerian

Spartina anglica Cord-grass

501

Suaeda vera Shrubby Sea Blite

Scutellaria galericulata Skullcap

Senecio bicolor Silver Ragwort ssp. *cineraria*	*Carex extensa* Long-bracted Sedge

502

Lupinus arboreus Tree Lupin	*Salicornia europaea* Marsh Samphire

Silene vulgaris ssp. *maritima*   Sea Campion

Cochlearia anglica   Long-leaved Scurvy Grass

Rumex acetosella   Sheep's Sorrel

504

Ammophila arenaria   Marram

Glaux maritima   Sea Milkwort

Lotus corniculatus   Common Bird's-foot Trefoil

505

Trifolium squamosum   Sea Clover

Dipsacus pilosus   Small Teasel

Trifolium fragiferum　Strawberry Clover

Trifolium ochroleucon
Sulphur Clover

Trifolium medium　Zigzag Clover

Dipsacus fullonum　Teasel

Lathyrus aphaca Yellow Vetchling

Tanacetum vulgare Tansy

507

Rosa arvensis Field Rose

Ononis spinosa Spiny Restharrow

Saponaria officinalis Soapwort

Cichorium intybus Chicory

Borago officinalis Borage

Tanacetum parthenium Feverfew

508

Solidago virgaurea Golden Rod

Orobanche minor　　　Carduus nutans　Musk Thistle
Common Broomrape

Chenopodium bonus-henricus
Good King Henry

Impatiens glandulifera　Himalayan Balsam

509

Corydalis claviculata   *Corydalis bulbosa* Tuberous Corydalis
White Climbing Fumitory

510

Montia perfoliata Spring Beauty   *Impatiens parviflora* Small Balsam

Atropa bella-donna   Deadly Nightshade

Hyoscyamus niger   Henbane

Datura stramonium   Thorn Apple

Kickxia spuria   Round-leaved Fluellen

Chamomilla suaveolens Pineapple Weed

Galeopsis speciosa Bee Hemp-nettle

512

Heracleum mantegazzianum
Giant Hogweed

RIGHT: *Papaver rhoeas* Common Poppy, Moulto

Polygonum persicaria Redshank

Chrysanthemum segetum
Corn Marigold

BOTTOM LEFT:
Lamium amplexicaule
Henbit

Amsinckia intermedia
Tarweed

Lathyrus latifolius
Everlasting Pea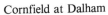

Chrysanthemum segetum Corn Marigold

Papaver argemone
Prickly Poppy

Cornfield at Dalham

Euphorbia lathyris Caper Spurge

Plantago lanceolata Ribwort Plantain

Galium verum Lady's Bedstraw

516

Viscum album Mistletoe on Limes at Haughley

Linaria vulgaris Common Toadflax

Leucanthemum vulgare Marguerite

Veronica filiformis Slender Speedwell

Tragopogon pratensis ssp. *minor* Goat's Beard

517

Arctium lappa Great Burdock

Trifolium arvense Hare's-foot Clover

Orchis mascula Early Purple Orchid

Orchis mascula
Early Purple Orchid

518

Orchis morio
Green-winged Orchid

Orchis morio Green-winged Orchid

Anacamptis pyramidalis Pyramidal Orchid   *Orchis militaris* Military Orchid

Platanthera chlorantha
Greater Butterfly Orchid

Gymnadenia conopsea ssp.
densiflora Marsh Fragrant Orchid

Aceras anthropophorum
Green-man Orchid

Dactylorhiza praetermissa
Common Marsh Orchid

Dactylorhiza fuchsii
Common Spotted Orchid

Dactylorhiza maculata ×
praetermissa Hybrid Marsh Orch

520

Dactylorhiza traunsteineri
Narrow-leaved Marsh Orchid

Dactylorhiza maculata
Heath Spotted Orchid

Dactylorhiza incarnata
Early Marsh Orchid

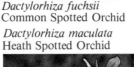

Epipactis purpurata
Violet Helleborine

Epipactis helleborine
Broad-leaved Helleborine

Epipactis palustris
Marsh Helleborine

521

Ophrys apifera Bee Orchid *Ophrys apifera* Bee Orchid variety *Ophrys insectifera* Fly Orchid

Neottia nidus-avis
Bird's-nest Orchid

*Himantoglossum
hircinum* Lizard Orchid

Orchis mascula Early
Purple Orchid white variety

Listera ovata Common Twayblade

Listera ovata
Common Twayblade

Index to Illustrations

LATIN NAMES

523

Index to Illustrations
ENGLISH NAMES

Index to Catalogue

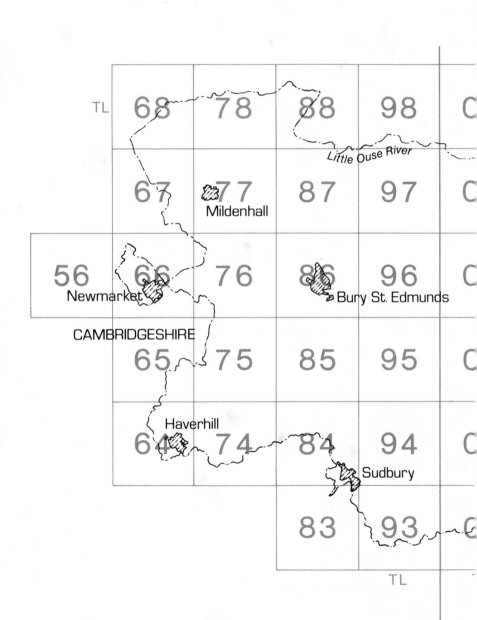

TL 68 78 88 98 0

Little Ouse River

67 77 87 97 0

Mildenhall

56 66 76 86 96 0

Newmarket Bury St. Edmunds

CAMBRIDGESHIRE

65 75 85 95 0

64 74 84 94 0

Haverhill

Sudbury

83 93 0

TL